THE PARLIAMENTARY DIARY
OF SIR RICHARD COCKS, 1698–1702

Sir Richard Cocks. Painter unknown.
(Reproduced by kind permission of Mr J. F. S. Hervey-Bathurst.)

The Parliamentary Diary
of Sir Richard Cocks,
1698–1702

Edited by
D. W. HAYTON

CLARENDON PRESS · OXFORD
1996

Oxford University Press, Walton Street, Oxford OX2 6DP
Oxford New York
Athens Auckland Bangkok Bombay
Calcutta Cape Town Dar es Salaam Delhi
Florence Hong Kong Istanbul Karachi
Kuala Lumpur Madras Madrid Melbourne
Mexico City Nairobi Paris Singapore
Taipei Tokyo Toronto
and associated companies in
Berlin Ibadan

Oxford is a trade mark of Oxford University Press

Published in the United States
by Oxford University Press Inc., New York

British Library Cataloguing in Publication Data
Data available

Library of Congress Cataloging in Publication Data
Cocks, Richard, Sir, ca. 1658–1726.
The parliamentary diary of Sir Richard Cocks, 1698–1702 / edited
by D.W. Hayton.
p.   cm.
1. Great Britain—Politics and government—1698–1702—Sources.
2. Cocks, Richard, Sir, ca. 1658–1726—Diaries. 3. Legislators—
Great Britain—Diaries. I. Hayton, David, 1949– . II. Title.
DA460.C63 1996
328.41'092—dc20   95–49947
ISBN 0–19–822370–6

1 3 5 7 9 10 8 6 4 2

Typeset by J&L Composition Ltd, Filey, North Yorkshire

Printed in Great Britain
on acid-free paper by
Bookcraft Ltd., Midsomer-Norton Nr. Bath, Avon

In memory of
Geoffrey Holmes

'O quantum eruditorum aut modestia ipsorum aut quies operit ac subtrahit famae.' (What a number of scholars are hidden and lost to fame through their own modesty or retiring habits!)

Pliny the Younger, *Letters*, 7. 15. 1

Acknowledgements

Pride of place in this litany of thanks must go to Miss Betty Kemp, who, having completed much of the groundwork for an edition of the Cocks diary, not only graciously made way for me to bring the project to a conclusion, but also turned over to me her transcripts and preparatory notes on problems of annotation. I hope the appearance of this volume will be some repayment for many instances of kindness, and for keeping faith that our labours would eventually come to a conclusion. Another very considerable debt is owed to Professor Henry Horwitz, for making available his supplementary suggestions on the many problematical passages in the text, for allowing me to draw freely on his encyclopaedic knowledge of the period, and, not least, for reading a draft of the Introduction.

The diary forms part of Bodleian Library manuscripts Eng. hist. b. 209–10, and I thank the Keeper of Western Manuscripts at the library, Mrs Mary Clapinson, for permission to publish it. She and her staff, in particular my old undergraduate friend Steven Tomlinson, have been unstinting in their help and advice whenever called upon.

This edition would not have been possible without the expert assistance of librarians and archivists in many other places, especially Clyve Jones, Robert Lyons, and Donald Munro, at the University of London Institute of Historical Research; Frances Harris, and Christopher Wright, in the Department of Manuscripts at the British Library; David Brown, at the Scottish Record Office; Jane Anderson, at Glamis Castle; another friend from Manchester student days, Peter Durrant, at the Berkshire Record Office; and staff at the Centre for Kentish Studies at Maidstone, the Henry E. Huntington Library at San Marino, California, the House of Lords Record Office, Lambeth Palace Library, Liverpool Record Office, the National Archives of Ireland, the Public Record Office of Northern Ireland, the Society of Friends Library, the library of Trinity College, Dublin, the Beinecke Library at Yale University, the Yorkshire Archaeological Society, and the county record offices of Cumbria (at Carlisle), Hertfordshire, Northamptonshire, Somerset, Suffolk (at Ipswich), and Surrey (at Kingston upon Thames). I must also thank the Duke of Beaufort, the Marquess of Bath, the Earl of Strathmore, Sir John Carew Pole, Bt., and Sir David Ogilvy for allowing me to consult and to cite documents in their possession.

The portrait of Sir Richard Cocks, from Eastnor Castle, is reproduced by kind permission of the owner, Mr J. F. S. Hervey-Bathurst. The family historian, John Somers Cocks, not only directed my attention to the picture collection at Eastnor, but also put at my disposal his unrivalled knowledge of the Cocks family in all its ramifications. I owe him a tremendous debt.

Most of the work on this edition was undertaken while I enjoyed the good fortune to serve on the research staff of the *History of Parliament*. I must thank the Editorial Board for permission to make use of the draft articles and transcripts of original documents prepared for the 1690–1715 section, and the former colleagues (so many of them, I regret to say, no longer on the staff of the *History*), whose knowledge and expertise, freely given, made my task much lighter: Linda Clark, Eveline Cruickshanks, John Ferris, Perry Gauci, Stuart Handley, Andrew Hanham, Sarah Jones, Frances Kelly, Mark Knights, Peter Le Fevre, Virginia Moseley, Carole Rawcliffe, Roland Thorne, and George Yerby.

For help with particular points, or for drawing my attention to unsuspected sources, I am also indebted to Mrs Elizabeth Boardman, Dr Justin Champion, Dr Kathryn Ellis, Mr Graham Gibbs, Dr Paul Hopkins, Mr Tim Keirn, Professor Joseph Levine, Dr Albert Lovett, Dr Patricia Murrell, Mrs Julia Page, Dr Craig Rose, Professor Bill Speck, Dr Stephen Taylor, and Professor Peter Thomas. At a crucial stage Bob Owens gave me vital practical assistance, as well as sharing his considerable experience in the editing of texts. A number of friends provided hospitality and sustenance on my travels, notably Robin and Joy Kempster, Bruce Campbell, Anthony Malcomson, John Milner, and Allen Warren. Special thanks are due to my sister- and brother-in-law, Ella and Neil Barclay, for keeping open the best free restaurant in Oxford to a very persistent customer.

My wife and children have endured for far too many years the intrusion into our household of a long-dead Gloucestershire squire. Their occasional valiant attempts to feign interest in Sir Richard and his writings would more than warrant my dedicating this book to them, were it not for a surpassing professional obligation to the memory of the greatest of modern scholars of late-Stuart politics, whose example I have tried to follow, and whose encouragement was for so long an inspiration.

                                                                    D.W.H.

Contents

Abbreviations

Add.	Additional
Archs.	Archives
BL	British Library
Bodl.	Bodleian Library
Cal. Treas. Bks.	*Calendar of Treasury Books*
Cal. Treas. Pprs.	*Calendar of Treasury Papers*
CJ	*Commons' Journals*
CP	G. E. C[okayne], *The Complete Peerage*, ed. Vicary Gibbs *et al.* (13 vols.; London, 1910–40)
CSP Colonial	*Calendar of State Papers, Colonial*
CSP Dom.	*Calendar of State Papers, Domestic*
'Debates 1697–9'	D. W. Hayton (ed.), 'Debates in the House of Commons, 1697–1699', *Camden Miscellany XXIX* (Camden 4th ser., xxxiv; London, 1987), pp. 343–407
DNB	*Dictionary of National Biography*
DZA	Deutsches Zentralarchiv, Merseburg
EHR	*English Historical Review*
HC 1660–90	B. D. Henning (ed.), *The House of Commons 1660–1690* (3 vols.; London, 1983)
HC 1715–54	R. R. Sedgwick (ed.), *The House of Commons 1715–1754* (2 vols.; London, 1970)
Hervey Letterbooks	S. H. A. Hervey (ed.), *Letter-Books of John Hervey, First Earl of Bristol . . . 1651 to 1750* (Suffolk Green Books 1, 3 vols.; Wells, 1894)
HMC	Historical Manuscripts Commission
Horwitz, *Parliament, Policy and Politics*	Henry Horwitz, *Parliament, Policy and Politics in the Reign of William III* (Manchester, 1977)
James (ed.), *Letters Illustrative . . .*	G. P. R. James (ed.), *Letters Illustrative of the Reign of William III from 1696 to 1708* (3 vols.; London, 1841)
LJ	*Lords' Journals*

Luttrell, *Brief Relation*	Narcissus Luttrell, *A Brief Historical Relation of State Affairs* (6 vols.; Oxford, 1857)
MS(S)	Manuscript(s)
PRO	Public Record Office
RO	Record Office
ser.	series
Somers's Tracts	Sir Walter Scott (ed.), *A Collection of Scarce and Valuable Tracts* . . . (2nd edn., 13 vols.; London, 1809–15)
William III State Tracts	*A Collection of State Tracts, Publish'd during the Reign of King William III* (3 vols.; London, 1705–7)

Note

Since this edition was prepared, the Portland papers in the British Library (cited here as Loan 29) have been furnished with Add. MSS numbers; and the Deutsches Zentralarchiv, Merseburg, has been renamed as the Geheimes Staatsarchiv Preussische Kulturbesitz Abteilung Merseburg.

Introduction

SIR RICHARD COCKS

I

Unlike David Copperfield, Sir Richard Cocks had firmly decided long before taking up his pen that he was to be the hero of his own story, and in this account of the Parliaments of 1698–1702, written largely in the form of a diary of Commons proceedings, he automatically cast himself in the leading role. He thus differed from the handful of competing parliamentary diarists of the late seventeenth and early eighteenth centuries, all of whom tended towards self-effacement rather than self-promotion. While Narcissus Luttrell, without doubt the most conscientious chronicler of his times, revealed nothing of his own opinions even when reporting parliamentary debates in the 1691–3 sessions in which he may have taken part, Cocks was an insistent presence in his own writings. In some respects the document printed below is not so much a 'parliamentary diary' as a parliamentary autobiography. Cocks's personality runs through the events he describes, ubiquitous and ubiquitously important.

It was an importance which, to be frank, those of his contemporaries who were not privy to this account would probably have failed to recognize.[1] The reputation under which he laboured was that of a self-opinionated eccentric; derided as 'Cockbrain', 'a whimsical crazed man', and once, in a sly reference to his diminutive stature, a 'peevish elf'.[2] In his prime, as a knight of the shire, he was generally regarded as at best a singular character, at worst a crank. Even in a House of Commons which contained an example of clinical insanity

---

[1] In this account of Cocks's life, character, and ideas, I have drawn upon my earlier essay, 'Sir Richard Cocks: The Political Anatomy of a Country Whig', *Albion*, 20 (1988), 221–46. I am grateful to the North American Conference on British Studies for permission to reproduce parts of that paper here.

[2] Charles Davenant, *Tom Double Returned out of the Country* (London, 1702), 13; C. E. Doble *et al.* (edd.), *Remarks and Collections of Thomas Hearne* . . . , (11 vols., Oxford Historical Society; Oxford, 1885–1921), vii. 372; Bodl. MS Ballard 47, fo. 18, 'On Sir Dicky Wimble, i.e. Sir Richard Cocks . . . by Wm. Somerville Esq.'; ibid. 48, fo. 212, 'Epitaph on Sir Richard Cox of Dumbleton by Wm. Somervile Esq.'

in the volcanic personality of the Lincolnshire squire Sir John Bolles, Cocks's peculiarities were striking enough to give the impression of a man with a swarm of bees in his bonnet. He was renowned for the obsessive animosity he harboured towards his rival in county politics, Jack Howe, and towards the Master of the Rolls and disgraced ex-Speaker, Sir John Trevor; his penchant for long and meandering speeches, spiced with anecdotes of ancient Rome; the slips of the tongue and unconsciously humorous effects which could sometimes dissolve an audience into laughter. His own somewhat ungracious verdict on his closest parliamentary comrade, Sir Edward Hussey, may serve as a fair self-assessment: 'very honest but has no great judgment and a great opinion of his own abilities that he thinks nobody able to advise him'. On such occasions Cocks can sound every bit like some seventeenth-century Squire Pooter.

In the sublimity of his self-regard Cocks was carrying to an extreme what sometimes appears as the cardinal indulgence of his caste. The idealization of the country gentleman as the prime agent of prosperity and harmony in society, the regulator of morals, and the guardian of the subject's liberties, was not peculiar to the Augustans, but was carried by them almost to a fetish. Cocks himself once wrote that he would much rather be a plain country gentleman, content with his lot and with a modest opportunity of 'doing good in his generation', than a soldier or statesman of the calibre of Alexander the Great, restless and angry with God for failing to provide unlimited opportunities for conquest. In common with many of his fellow squires he was conscious of peculiar responsibilities, as landowner, justice of the peace and Member of Parliament: a 'father to his tenants and patron to his neighbours';[3] a godly magistrate, 'doing service to his country' by 'correcting ill manners and punishing ill practices'; a disinterested and incorrupt representative of his locality in 'the grand inquest of the nation'.[4]

This was an ideal which blended the qualities of pastoral innocence, classical virtue, and Puritan sobriety. Taken separately, each element was a common feature in the intellectual environment of young gentlemen of Cocks's generation, fostered by parental example, education, and private study. Combined, they induced a particular view of the world and of the right conduct of politics, contrasting civic responsibility with governmental corruption, and emphasizing the duty of the man of property to uphold virtue and resist tyranny: a version of Whiggism to which contemporaries attached

---

[3] This phrase comes from D. F. Bond (ed.), *The Tatler* (3 vols.; Oxford, 1987), ii. 432–3.

[4] [Bodl.] MS Eng. hist. b. 209, fos. 1–4, 28–9; Gloucestershire RO, Gloucester consistory court wills 1737/105, Cocks's will, 29 Nov. 1724 (a reference I owe to the kindness of Mr J. V. Somers Cocks).

various adjectives — 'old', 'real', or 'true' — and which modern historians have often preferred to call 'Country' Whiggism. Over-exposure in his formative years to godly piety and to the culture of civic humanism helped to produce in Cocks a character deeply coloured by such notions and dedicated to their public expression; almost a perfect specimen, or a 'true picture', of the Country Whig.

II

Ironically, for one who was to be throughout his political life a determined advocate of 'Revolution principles', there was in Cocks's genetic inheritance a strong Cavalier element. Tradition located the origin of the family in Kent, but Sir Richard's pedigree went back little more than a century, to a Thomas Cocks of Castleditch in Herefordshire.[5] The baronetcy had been granted in 1662 to a younger son of a younger son of this Thomas Cocks, another Richard, who was said to have been 'a great sufferer for his love to the royal family and for his zeal for the laws and established religion of his country', although no evidence has surfaced to substantiate claims of active Civil War service in the Royalist cause. The necessary support for the title was a newly acquired country seat, the house and lands of Dumbleton in the north-east of Gloucestershire, not far from Evesham. This desirable property had come into the family through the marriage of an aunt of the first baronet. She, outliving her husband, had taken over the estate and, obligingly for her nephew, died without a direct heir. The first Sir Richard Cocks of Dumbleton had several sons, the eldest of whom, yet another Richard, died in early middle age, leaving his own children, including the future parliamentary diarist, in their grandfather's care.

Cocks, the eldest of three boys, was born about 1659. We know little about his early life. His grandfather, head of the household until his death in 1684, remains a shadowy figure; as does his grandmother, who survived for another six years in possession of the estate. Their Royalist sympathies left no discernible impression. Instead, the dominant ethos seems to have been the moderate Puritanism inherited through Cocks's mother Mary, a daughter of

---

[5] My principal source for the following paragraphs is J. V. Somers Cocks, *A History of the Cocks Family* (4 parts, privately printed; Teignmouth, 1966–7), esp. pt. 3, pp. 38–56, 76, 97–104. I am very grateful to Mr Somers Cocks for lending me a copy of this work, and for much useful advice besides on the history of the Cocks family.

the Parliamentarian Sir Robert Cooke, of Highnam in Gloucestershire;[6] and, after her decease, nurtured by her daughter Dorothy, for whose monument in the parish church Cocks composed a heartfelt tribute.[7]

She was of a middle stature, endowed with great ornaments of body, and with far greater of the mind. She was a woman of a very good and compassionate nature, of a great understanding, and made very good use of it; she chose rather to be a mother to her younger sisters, than to be engaged in another family; and by her care and good instructions, she helped to breed them up in piety and religion, and other necessary knowledge . . . She was a woman of great piety, patience and humanity; she spent great part of her life in her devotions and prayers, for herself, her friends, and her country . . .

This atmosphere of intense spirituality evidently affected Dorothy's brothers: the two younger, Charles and Robert, took holy orders, while Sir Richard himself maintained throughout his life a strong sense of religion and a marked interest in matters ecclesiastical. Of Charles nothing has been discovered beyond the mere fact of his education and ordination: his nepotistic preferment to the rectory of Dumbleton argues no great distinction of scholarship or ministry, and indeed Sir Richard on one occasion made him the butt of his own pungent anticlericalism. 'My parson is not inspired', he wrote, 'I was bred up with him, and I had then as much learning as he had.'[8] Robert was made of different stuff. His abilities attracted the attention of the Duke and Duchess of Marlborough, by whose favour he was preferred in 1715 to the rectory of Bladon, near Woodstock, and he later enjoyed the office of chancellor of the diocese of Gloucester. Three of his sermons were published, and many others survive in manuscript. From these writings it is

---

[6] For the Cookes of Highnam, see Sir Robert Atkyns, *The Ancient and Present State of Glocestershire . . .* (2nd edn.; London, 1768), p. 176; Mary Frear Keeler, *The Long Parliament, 1640–1641: A Biographical Study of Its Members* (Memoirs of the American Philosophical Society, 36; Philadelphia, 1954), 141; F. A. Hyett, 'The Civil War in the Forest of Dean, 1643–1645', *Transactions of the Bristol and Gloucestershire Archaeological Society*, 18 (1893–4), 95; HC 1660–90, ii. 120.

[7] Monumental inscription, St Peter's, Dumbleton, printed in Ralph Bigland, *Historical, Monumental and Genealogical Collections Relative to the County of Gloucester. Part Two: Daglingworth–Moreton Vallence*, ed. Brian Frith (Bristol and Gloucestershire Archaeological Society, Gloucestershire Record Series, 3; 1990), 502.

[8] Sir Richard Cocks, *Over Shoes, Over Boots: Being a Second Part of the Church of England Secur'd . . .* (London, 1722), 7. Mr Somers Cocks has pointed out to me that by the time this pamphlet was published Charles Cocks was dead and the rectory given over to his successor Thomas Baghott (the son of William Baghott of Prestbury, Glos.), but the sense of the passage makes it clear that Charles must have been meant, for Baghott was of a younger generation altogether, having matriculated at Oriel in 1711, aged 18.

possible to form an idea of his religious and political principles.[9] The brand of Protestantism to which he subscribed may best be defined as 'Low Church': stiffly anti-Catholic but tolerant of Dissenters (of whom there were none in Dumbleton itself though thriving communities existed in the vicinity),[10] possibly to the extent of wishing for a comprehensive settlement by which sundered brethren might be drawn back into the established church.[11] In this and in several other significant respects, he followed a very similar path to Sir Richard. Certainly in secular politics he was firmly committed to the Whig cause. According to the Jacobite antiquarian Thomas Hearne, Robert was 'a lewd, impudent fellow', who at Oxford in 1688–9 had been 'one of those rascally people . . . who were for discarding King James and receiving Dutch William'.[12] The more obviously politically oriented of his sermons extolled the triumphs of his patron Marlborough, rejoiced in the defeat of Jacobite plots to destroy 'liberty, property and religion', and repeatedly denounced the pernicious influence of High Church faction: 'of all prejudices, that of a party, under pretence of advancing Holy Church, is the strongest; tho' perhaps religion has the least share in it'.[13]

Principles and sympathies which had been instilled into Sir Richard around his family hearth were reinforced by his wedding, in October 1688, to Frances, daughter of Richard Neville of Billingbear in Berkshire. The Nevilles were of sound Puritan stock, and retained the godly enthusiasm of their forebears. Cocks's nephew by marriage, Grey Neville, an MP under Queen Anne, acquired the nickname 'the bishop' from his keen interest in theology; his devotion to the ideal of union among Protestants led him to break from the established church, attend an Independent congregation, and foster close

---

[9] Robert Cocks, *The Great Importance of a Meek and Merciful Spirit. A Sermon Preached at the Temple Church, July 4, 1714* (London, 1714); id., *Nothing but Religion Can Secure Our Peace and Happiness . . . A Sermon Preached at the Last Warwick Assizes . . .* (London, 1715); id., *The Beauty and Necessity of the Duty of Praising God: A Thanksgiving Sermon at Woodstock* (London, 1716); Bodl. MS Rawlinson E. 215–16 (two volumes of Robert Cocks's sermons, c.1695–1734); BL Add. MS 61468, fos. 168–74.

[10] Anne Whiteman (ed.), *The Compton Census of 1676: A Critical Edition* (British Academy Records of Social and Economic History, NS 10; London, 1986), 538; Glos. RO, Q/SO3 (quarter sessions order book 1702–14), 520–2, certificates issued for Dissenting meeting-houses 1689–1711.

[11] See e.g. Robert Cocks, *The Great Importance of a Meek and Merciful Spirit . . .* , 15–16, 20; Bodl. MS Rawlinson E. 216, fos. 254–60; and below nn. 51, 62.

[12] *Remarks and Collections of Thomas Hearne . . .* , i. 304. See also L. K. J. Glassey, *Politics and the Appointment of Justices of the Peace 1675–1720* (Oxford, 1979), 213.

[13] Robert Cocks, *The Great Importance of a Meek and Merciful Spirit . . .* , 15–18; id., *Nothing but Religion . . .* preface and 6–9, 13, 23–4; Bodl. MS Rawlinson E. 216, fos. 244–6, 256; BL Add. MS 61648, fos. 168, 170–1.

personal ties with Scottish Presbyterians.[14] Frances herself proved well able to match the self-conscious piety of her husband, if the tablet erected in her memory in Dumbleton church is to be believed:[15]

She was eminently pious and zealous for the established government and religion, which was demonstrated by the many hours she daily spent in her private devotions, and her constant attendance, even to the hazard of her health, upon the service of the church. She was an ornament to the honourable family from which she descended, and was esteemed an honour and a blessing to the family she came into.

These transcendent virtues recall Cocks's tribute to his sister Dorothy, while the joys of marital companionship are captured in Sir Richard's inimitable style: 'she lived more than 35 years in praise, harmony and tranquillity with her husband, as far as human imbecilities common to the best of mortals would permit'.

The connexion with the Neville family, however, offered more than simply a reinforcement of a Puritan tradition. For Frances was a niece of the Commonwealth political theorist Henry Neville, author of *Plato Redivivus* and doyen of the Grecian Tavern 'circle', which in the 1690s sought to revive and adapt the doctrines of classical republicanism for the new world of post-Revolution Whiggery, repackaging the works of Harrington, Milton, and Sidney, and the Civil War memoirs of the regicide Edmund Ludlow, for a new audience of 'polite' Augustans.[16] Cocks regarded 'the learned and ingenious Mr Neville' with something approaching veneration, though whether the two men ever enjoyed much contact is open to question.[17] After Neville's death in 1694 Cocks received a legacy of £3,000 in the great man's will, in belated fulfilment of the terms of his marriage settlement. However, he

[14] *HC 1715–54*, ii. 292; Scottish RO, GD 205/36/6 (Ogilvy of Inverquharity MSS), Neville to William Bennet, 30 Dec. 1707, 4 Jan., 11 July, 14 Sept. 1708, 19 Mar., 14 May 1709; Craig Rose, 'The Origins and Ideals of the SPCK 1699–1716', in John Walsh, Colin Haydon, and Stephen Taylor (edd.), *The Church of England c.1689–c.1833: From Toleration to Tractarianism* (Cambridge, 1993), 176.

[15] Printed in Bigland, *Historical . . . Collections . . . Part Two*, 502.

[16] For Neville, see *DNB* and Caroline Robbins (ed.), *Two English Republican Tracts* (Cambridge, 1969), 5–20. For the 'Grecian Tavern' group and post-Revolution civic humanist political writing in general see Caroline Robbins, *The Eighteenth-Century Commonwealthman* (Cambridge, Mass., 1959); J. G. A. Pocock, *The Machiavellian Moment: Florentine Political Thought and the Atlantic Republican Tradition* (Princeton, 1975); id. (ed.), *The Political Works of James Harrington* (Cambridge, 1977), 135–47; id., 'The *Machiavellian Moment* Revisited: A Study in History and Ideology', *Journal of Modern History*, 53 (1981), 49–72; id., *Virtue, Commerce and History* (Cambridge, 1985), 230–4; H. T. Dickinson, *Liberty and Property: Political Ideology in Eighteenth-Century Britain* (London, 1977), ch. 3; Edmund Ludlow, *A Voyce from the Watch Tower. Part Five: 1660–1662*, ed. A. B. Worden (Camden Society, 4th ser., 21; London, 1978), 17–55; J. B. Duke-Evans, 'The Political Theory and Practice of the English Commonwealthsmen 1675–1725', D.Phil. thesis (Oxford, 1980).   [17] MS Eng. hist. b. 209, fo. 36.

had no personal reminiscence to record.[18] What can be said with certainty is that Neville's influence was powerful enough to have permeated the Billing-bear household. Cocks's brother-in-law and occasional parliamentary com-rade, another Richard Neville, manifested a similar zeal for Country Whig principles and a disposition to apply the precepts of classical republicanism to issues of contemporary politics.[19]

The figure of Henry Neville would in any case stand out sharply in an account of Cocks's intellectual development, because of the flatness of the surrounding terrain. From his formal education Cocks drew meagre suste-nance. In 1667, while still a child, he had been admitted to the Middle Temple, as a favour to his father, then a bencher, but he does not appear ever to have taken up residence.[20] At best the influence of the temple was indirect. Some of his father's colleagues may have transferred their friendship to him, most notably John, later Lord, Somers, the Junto Whig leader (and Lord Chancel-lor 1697–1700), who was also a distant connexion by marriage, Somers's brother-in-law, Charles Cocks, MP for Worcester, being a cousin of the Dumbleton branch of the family. At various times Somers's presence may be detected on the fringes of Sir Richard's biography, though the exact nature of their relationship eludes definition. We find 'the knight of Dumbleton' apply-ing to Somers for help, attending a high-powered political cabal at which Somers was also present, and later, when out of Parliament, receiving mes-sages of encouragement allegedly entrusted by Somers to a third party.[21] Certainly, in his defence of the Lord Chancellor in the Commons against impeachment in 1701, Cocks claimed an intimate, and long-standing, acquain-tance: 'I live in the neighbourhood near him [Somers hailed from Worcester-shire], I have known him as long as I have known anybody, in all the parts of my life.' This may, however, have been a tactical, and thus in the circumstances pardonable, exaggeration.

University, which he did attend, scarcely made a greater impression. In 1677 Cocks matriculated at Oriel, Oxford, staying there for at least a year.[22] The

---

[18] PRO Prob. 11/421, fo. 305. I am grateful to Miss Frances Kelly for supplying me with this information.

[19] Geoffrey Holmes, *British Politics in the Age of Anne* (London, 1967), 141, 143, 222; and a contemporary panegyric in Berkshire RO, D/EN F47/2 (Braybrooke MSS), 'Threneleusis . . .' [1717].

[20] H. A. C. Sturgess, *Register of Admissions to the Honourable Society of the Middle Temple* (3 vols.; 1949), i. 175.　　　　[21] MS Eng. hist. b. 209, fo. 38; *Hervey Letterbooks*, i. 199.

[22] C. L. Shadwell, *Registrum Orielense* (2 vols.; London, 1893–1902), i. 356. The buttery books in the college archives show that Cocks remained in residence from May 1677 until at least Sept. 1678. The next book is missing, and by the time the series resumes, in Sept. 1680, Cocks had evidently gone down. (Information kindly supplied by the college archivist, Mrs Elizabeth Board-man.)

political complexion of the college at this time is difficult to judge. An analysis of the party orientation of the MPs whose names were placed on the college's books during the sitting of the Oxford Parliament in 1681 shows a majority of Exclusionists over Court loyalists of seven to three, though this may say more of the sentiments of Oriel men of the previous generation than of the atmosphere in the late 1670s.[23] Among a varied company of fellows could be found at least one future nonjuror, Henry Gandy, but the temper of the governing body was probably better represented by the man who may have been Cocks's own tutor (and in that capacity stigmatized by him as a sot), George Royse, a protégé of the future archbishop John Tillotson, a chaplain to the Earl of Berkeley, and later chaplain-in-ordinary to William III. Royse represented Low Churchmanship and Whig politics, but it was a kind of complacent, establishment Whiggery at which Cocks often bridled.[24]

Without any obvious mentor, Cocks was thrown back on his own devices, and it may be in this area that Neville was most influential, as a distant inspiration and even an example. By any standards Cocks was a voracious reader, and his diaries and other papers show evidence, not only of the customary familiarity with the ancients (which in his case expressed itself in the recitation of familiar stories and popular, often misquoted, Latin tags),[25] but of a wide acquaintance with more modern authors. He prepared a translation (from the French) of at least part of a lengthy history of the French wars of religion, and of Spon's *Lettre* to Père La Chaise; composed an answer to the third Earl of Shaftesbury's reflections on humour; and in his diaries quoted, with or without acknowledgement, a number of contemporary political works, the pamphlets of Davenant and Trenchard, for example, the essays of Sir Thomas Pope Blount, and more substantial fare such as Ludlow's *Memoirs* or Algernon Sydney's *Discourses*. (Oddly, perhaps, one author to whom he made no direct reference was Neville himself.) The effects of long periods of private reflection were easily visible in his speeches and writings, the political beliefs that he professed embodying the eclecticism, and occasional incoherence, of an ardent autodidact.

Any survey of the ideas embodied in Cocks's various writings and speeches would reveal a patchwork of borrowings and influences. Clearly he took his

[23] Shadwell, *Registrum Orielense*, i. 364–6 (political alignments derived from *HC 1660–90*).

[24] G. C. Richards and C. L. Shadwell, *The Provosts and Fellows of Oriel College Oxford* (Oxford, 1922). For Royse see Anthony à Wood, *Athenae Oxonienses . . .* (4 vols.; London, 1820), iv. 506–7.

[25] It is possible that his ability to relate stories from 'the Romish history' benefited from an acquaintance with a modern English account derived from classical authorities: Laurence E(a)chard, *The Roman History, from the Building of the City, to the Perfect Settlement of the Empire by Augustus Caesar . . .* (London, 1695), which was, incidentally, dedicated to Somers.

fundamental political principles, relating to the origin and limitations of monarchical power and the subject's right of resistance, from various Whig commentators, in particular Sydney and John Locke. When inveighing against 'corruption' in court and Parliament he often expressed himself in a style characteristic of those writers whom Professor J. G. A. Pocock has termed 'neo-Harringtonian' (after the mid-century republican James Harrington), emphasizing the rough-hewn civic virtue of the country squire, and warning of the danger that constitutional balance might be upset by the expansion of executive power. In matters of religion he followed Locke's *Letter on Toleration* at least part of the way in his own passionate denunciation of persecution; and echoed James Harrington and Henry Neville, as well as more recent writers such as Sir Robert Howard, Robert Molesworth, and Walter Moyle, in his violent opposition to 'priestcraft'.

He did not always acknowledge these sources, however. Indeed, on many issues he seems to have regarded it as his duty to find his own way. His publications, almost invariably essays on religious subjects, bristle with appeals to reason. He presented himself as a 'plain man', locked in combat with pedants and sophists who wrote 'to puzzle rather than inform'. To find true religion, he wrote, one need only apply oneself to a study of Scripture (or even apply one's intellectual powers to a consideration of the abstract circumstances of Creation).[26] As in matters spiritual, so in matters temporal: in many of his set speeches Cocks adopted the standpoint of an unsophisticated country squire, working through problems on the basis of his own observation and reasoning. This was particularly noticeable in economic questions, which (like most of his parliamentary colleagues) he pondered from a vantage point of 'common sense' rather than theory. The result was, in his opinion, 'truth' decked out 'in a homely country dress'.[27]

In reality, the consequences of Cocks's rustic reasoning were as likely to be occasional absurdity and blatant contradiction. For example, having propounded a crucial role for the lay magistrate in social reform, and indeed in the spiritual regeneration of the English people, he could disarmingly admit that 'being a magistrate gives men no more sense or inspiration'; or, having denounced the House of Commons as a sink of corruption and self-interest, he could recommend the notion that Parliament be made the sole arbiter of disputes over religion within the realm, on the grounds that whatever was done there must inevitably be in the public interest, MPs' 'private views'

---

[26] Sir Richard Cocks, *A True and Impartial Inquiry Made into the Late Bloody Execution at Thorn* . . . (London, 1727), 51; id., *Over Shoes, Over Boots*, 10.

[27] MS Eng. hist. b. 209, fo. 37ᵛ.

carrying no weight.[28] There are nevertheless several major themes which do recur consistently in his speeches and writings: pillars, so to speak, around which a sometimes ramshackle superstructure was constructed. Since these principles appear to have been fully formed by the time of Cocks's entry into adulthood, it may be useful to give some account of them before embarking upon a discussion of his public career.

III

For Cocks the preservation of 'the true reformed religion' was the most important function of civic life. Fundamental to his political beliefs and allegiances was a passionate antipathy to Roman Catholicism, which, in ascending power of invective, he described as a 'ridiculous and detestable religion', 'certainly the reverse of Christianity', 'a mere delusion of Satan's', and a 'deadly poison' corrupting state and people. Indeed, like many contemporaries, he regarded 'popery' as no religion at all, but a parasitic political system, an exotic tyranny, sustaining itself by 'ensnaring and deceiving the ignorant' and oppressing its enemies with unscrupulous violence. And naturally it always appeared as the handmaiden of despotic state power. Wherever popery became established, liberties were extinguished. Such was the assumption which underlay his 'vulgar Whiggism': liberty was associated with Protestantism and Englishness, whereas despotism was essentially Catholic and foreign.[29]

From this root grew two important branches in Cocks's thinking: on the one hand an extension of his antipathy to Roman Catholicism to encompass High Church Anglicanism, which he regarded as a kind of pseudo-popery; on the other a devotion to the Glorious Revolution and the consequent constitutional settlement, which had saved England from the nameless horrors of a popish tyranny.

The 'meditations' and prayers Cocks composed for his own private consumption in the 1690s, and the various pamphlets he published in later life, were imbued with the enthusiasm characteristic of late seventeenth- and early eighteenth-century Protestantism. Among both clergy and laity there had arisen a powerful movement for a new 'reformation', drawing ideas and

---

[28] Cocks, *Over Shoes, Over Boots*, 7; id., *A Perfect Discovery of Longitude* (London, 1721), 12.
[29] MS Eng. hist. b. 209, fo. 84ᵛ); Cocks, *A True and Impartial Inquiry* . . . , 18–19, 30, 34; Duncan Forbes, *Hume's Philosophical Politics* (London, 1975), 138–50. On English anti-Catholicism in general, see J. P. Kenyon, *The Popish Plot* (London, 1972), ch. 1; and Colin Haydon, *Anti-Catholicism in Eighteenth-Century England, c.1714–80: A Political and Social Study* (Manchester, 1993), ch. 1, esp. 3–11.

example from German Lutheran theologians, and issuing forth in the foundation of voluntary evangelical societies, in campaigns to regulate the morals and manners of the poor, and in philanthropic educational initiatives.[30] Cocks participated fully, exploiting his position as a justice of the peace in order to suppress 'vice and impiety', notably in the areas of public blasphemy, sabbath-breaking, and drunkenness. As lord of the manor, he also established a charity school in his parish.[31] All this, he assumed, was part of a mission to return English Protestantism to the purity of the early church; and the prime purposes of the 'new reformation' were not only to imbue the people of England with principles of 'true religion and morality', but to purge the church of 'the dregs of popery'.

In his view, the most persistent and most pernicious of popish survivals within the Church of England was the exalted role claimed for its clergy. For Cocks, as for so many English Puritans of the sixteenth and seventeenth centuries, true religion consisted in an individual's direct relationship with his Maker, for which the mediation of a priest was superfluous. To interpret the word of God no third party was needed; the faculty of reason, applied to Scripture, would lead a man infallibly to the truth. With the exception of the eucharist, in which he partook regularly, praying for God's grace to resist temptation, Cocks refused to regard the sacraments as meaningful; more often than not, they were only the mumbo-jumbo of 'horrid, impudent priest-craft'.[32] To accept a fully sacramental theology, and the notion of an apostolic succession, would in his view bind the Church of England to Rome and deny the Reformation. 'Good God!', he once exclaimed, 'to what absurdities

[30] D. W. R. Bahlman, *The Moral Revolution of 1688* (New Haven, 1957); Eamon Duffy, 'Primitive Christianity Revived: Religious Renewal in Augustan England', in Derek Baker (ed.), *Studies in Church History*, iv, *Renaissance and Renewal* (Oxford, 1977), 287–300; A. G. Craig, 'The Movement for the Reformation of Manners, 1688–1715', Ph.D. thesis (Edinburgh, 1980); Tina Isaacs, 'Moral Crime, Moral Reform and the State in Early Eighteenth-Century England: A Study of Piety and Politics', Ph.D. thesis (Rochester, NY, 1979); id., 'The Anglican Hierarchy and the Reformation of Manners, 1688–1738', *Journal of Ecclesiastical History*, 33 (1982), 391–411; C. M. Rose, 'Religion, Politics and Charity in Augustan London, *c*.1680–*c*.1720', Ph.D. thesis (Cambridge, 1989); id., 'Providence, Protestant Union and Godly Reformation in the 1690s', *Transactions of the Royal Historical Society*, 6th ser., 3 (1993), 151–69; id., 'Origin and Ideals of SPCK', 172–96; David Hayton, 'Moral Reform and Country Politics in the Late Seventeenth-Century House of Commons', *Past and Present*, 128 (1990), 48–91; John Spurr, 'The Church, the Societies and the Moral Reformation of 1688', in Walsh, Haydon, and Taylor (edd.), *The Church of England c.1689–c.1833*, 127–42.

[31] MS Eng. hist. b. 209, fos. 24–5, 27ᵛ, 28ᵛ, 30, 96, 95ᵛ, 94ᵛ; b. 210, fos. 32, 46ᵛ; *An Account of Charity Schools . . . in Great Britain and Ireland . . .* (London, 1709), 19. See also Anthony Fletcher, *Reform in the Provinces: The Government of Stuart England* (New Haven, 1986), 172, 273–7. Robert Cocks's sermons identify him as coming from the same mould: Bodl. MS Rawlinson E. 215, fos. 196–202, 257–69; E. 216, fos. 181–203, 259–70, 273.

[32] MS Eng. hist. b. 209, fos. 21ᵛ, 25–6, 30–2, 104ᵛ.

has our pride and ambition reduced us; we must support our succession, or we are no church; if we support it, we must receive our orders from Antichrist and the Whore of Babylon.'[33]

It followed that High Churchmen, with their correspondingly exalted interpretation of the theological importance of the priesthood, were little more than Romanists in disguise. The 'common speech' among them, wrote Cocks, was 'that "I had rather be a papist than a Presbyterian" '.[34] Their political ambitions too, in hoping to secure the independence of the church from lay authority, and to enforce a slavish uniformity of preaching and liturgical observance, were no different from those of their Catholic counterparts. Although in general the Anglican clergy had not advanced so extensive a claim for jurisdiction as had the papacy, this was only out of 'modesty, for their power is really as ample as any popish priest'.[35]

Like many another Whig writer, provoked by the political utterances of high-flying parsons and looking back in admiration to the 'civil religion' of the ancients, Cocks expressed a profound Erastianism and a hatred of the clerical-inspired oppression of Dissenting Protestants.[36] Never so explicit as to call in his pamphlets for the abolition of the Anglican clergy (he seems to have accepted their functions in marrying and burying parishioners, if not in baptizing them), he would have downgraded their role and brought the clerical estate firmly under lay control. With church courts abolished, moral supervision would become the province of the secular magistrate alone; and to this end he recommended that the civil government appoint 'teachers and overseers' to instruct the people. Above all, Parliament rather than Convocation ought to determine questions of ecclesiastical organization, liturgy, and doctrine, for the Church of England derived its position from Parliament; it was only 'that form of worship which is established by Act of Parliament'.[37] He even went so far on one occasion as to describe Parliament itself as 'a great church after the pattern of the small primitive ones'.[38]

---

[33] Sir Richard Cocks, *The Church of England Secur'd; the Toleration Act Enervated; and the Dissenters Ruin'd and Undone* (London, 1722), 26.

[34] Ibid. 27.   [35] Ibid. 19.

[36] Mark Goldie, 'The Civil Religion of James Harrington', in A. Pagden (ed.), *Ideas in Context: The Languages of Political Theory in Early-Modern Europe* (Cambridge, 1987), 206–22; id. 'Priestcraft and the Birth of Whiggism', in Nicholas Phillipson and Quentin Skinner (edd.), *Political Discourse in Early Modern Britain* (Cambridge, 1993), 209–31; J. A. I. Champion, *The Pillars of Priestcraft Shaken: The Church of England and Its Enemies, 1660–1730* (Cambridge, 1992), esp. ch. 6. The most notorious anticlerical in the Whig parliamentary party was probably Sir Robert Howard, author of *The History of Religion . . .* (London, 1694).

[37] Cocks, *A Perfect Discovery of Longitude*, 19; id., *The Church of England Secur'd*, 38.

[38] Bodl. MS Eng. misc. b. 433, fo. 32.

If properly established, this 'civil religion' should have been able to inspire allegiance. In principle Cocks did not approve of separation from the established church. 'Let me sum up the tenets of my religion', he once wrote:[39]

I must love God above all things, and my neighbour as myself . . . by that head of loving my neighbour as myself I am in a particular manner obliged not to disturb the peace of that country in which I live. I will therefore for conscience sake comply with the usage and forms of the people amongst whom I live . . . I will for convenience sake receive the sacraments and hold communion with those Protestant churches which are established in the country I live in . . .

A true established church would not be so narrow in its 'longitude' as to oblige sober Protestants to become schismatic. Comprehension was his aim; and even after the failure of this scheme at the Revolution he still hoped in time to repeal the 'odious' Toleration Act of 1689 so that 'all Protestants' could be brought together into 'one sheepfold'.[40] But not even a comprehensive church should be intolerant, for persecution was associated with popery, and Cocks was implacably opposed to 'dragoons, galleys . . . faggots', 'animosities, bloodshed and inquisitions'.[41] In reality, he argued, the 'chief occasion' of all discords among Protestants was 'the pride of the priests'. Authoritarian clerics were demanding assent to an orthodoxy of their own devising. All that a Christian needed to know and to believe was contained within the New Testament. The 'articles of faith' upon which the clergy insisted were no more than an artificial instrument to secure the exclusion of any they wished to label as heterodox.[42]

In political terms Cocks's fear and loathing of popery naturally made him a resolute opponent of King James II, and a devotee of the Glorious Revolution. This was an attitude which did not require to be sharpened by the experience of living under a Catholic king, for fragments of earlier writings at the time of the Exclusion Crisis reflect his belief that the actions of Charles II and his ministers formed part of, and were controlled by, an international popish conspiracy that, unless prevented, would lead inevitably and rapidly to the extinction of England's 'ancient constitution'.[43] Little is known about Cocks's personal experience of the 'Stuart revenge' of 1681–6, or of the government of James II, except for a suggestion that he believed himself at one point to be the target of an assassination plot concocted by local papists, but the many references to events in the 1670s and 1680s with which his later writings are peppered show that the corruption and tyranny (as he understood them) of

---

[39] Ibid. 30. [40] Cocks, *The Church of England Secur'd*, 22–3.
[41] Ibid. 17; id., *A True and Impartial Inquiry*, 4; id., *Sir R–d C–ks' His Farewel Sermon* (London, 1722), 21; MS Eng. hist. b. 210, fo. 23.
[42] Cocks, *The Church of England Secur'd*, 10, 13. [43] MS Eng. hist. b. 209, fos. 17–20.

pre-Revolution governments formed a point of departure for his reflections on Williamite politics.[44]

It was a simple matter to take the view that the Revolution had saved England from popery, and thus from despotism; but a rather different, and altogether more challenging, exercise to extrapolate from that premiss a clear and satisfactory interpretation of the constitutional principles on which the Williamite regime was based. In an unpublished disquisition on the subject of oaths, written after 1689 as a reply to the nonjurors, Cocks showed that he had not himself remained immune from the confusions into which the events of 1688–9 had plunged so many of his contemporaries.[45] In the course of a rambling argument he gave almost every conceivable Williamite explanation of the Revolution: James had 'abdicated', 'deserted' the throne, committed treason against his people, even (though Cocks subsequently disavowed 'that detestable name') been conquered. The interpretation on which he at last settled was in line with what might be called the 'authorized' Whig version. James had violated his coronation oath, and finally deserted the throne: William owed his title to Divine Providence, and to 'the misgovernment of his predecessor'. Active resistance on the part of James's subjects was scarcely mentioned. Instead, Protestant Englishmen had for the most part 'sat quiet at home' while 'a foreign prince, in relation to injuries offered to himself, invaded the [kingdo]m and . . . offered to refer the matters in despite [*sic*] in relation to this quarrel between these two [James and William] to the people of the land invaded'. In any case, such right of resistance as the subject possessed was, in Cocks's view, limited to quite exceptional circumstances:

Nothing but endeavouring to subvert this government by dispensing with the laws or by a standing army [or] endeavouring to alter the constitution and *change the religion*[46] . . . nothing but this could have justified any subject of England to have taken up arms or to hold so much as a hand up against King James . . .

Thus far Cocks had gone no further than the moderate Whiggism professed by ministerialists such as Somers, for whose approbation the disquisition on oaths was submitted. More interesting, and potentially more radical, was the basis on which he rested his contention that King James had abdicated, and had absolved erstwhile subjects from their oath of allegiance. Repeatedly

[44] Ibid. 37–8.
[45] Ibid. 32ᵛ–37. There is other relevant matter at MS Eng. hist. b. 210, fo. 63ᵛ, and in *Sir Richard Cocks His Charge to the Grand-Jury of the County of Gloucester at the General Quarter-Sessions . . . April the 30th 1717* (1717), 13–17 (repr. in Georges Lamoine (ed.), *Charges to the Grand Jury 1689–1803* (Camden Soc., 4th ser., 43; London, 1992), 85–7), which asserts the right of resistance more positively. On Whig responses generally, see J. P. Kenyon, *Revolution Principles: The Politics of Party 1689–1720* (Cambridge, 1977), esp. ch. 4.   [46] My italics.

Cocks stated that by seeking to introduce 'popery and French government' the ex-King had broken the 'original contract'; and in doing so had ended not just his own reign but the entire line of monarchy, for 'if the King in possession is either by force beaten or by fear terrified or for misgovernment deposed, in all these cases the original contract is dissolved and it is not absolutely necessary that his next heir should succeed'. To supply the vacancy, William (and Mary too of course, whom Cocks for this purpose always ignored) had been 'chosen' by 'our representatives'. Parliament had the right to do so because, according to Cocks, royal power originated in the will of the people, who in the beginning had 'chosen' a monarch 'for their easy and advantageous government': 'the first occasion, or rather original, of kings was their extraordinary merit, or at least the opinion the people conceived of their virtue'. In origin, and in 1688–9 in practice, he believed the monarchy to be elective. William (and Mary) had been pitched upon not because of hereditary right but because, 'since we intended a monarchical government we could do no less in mere gratitude than set him upon the throne who gave us this choice'. In essence, therefore, his view of the relationship between monarch and people was closer to the republicanism of Algernon Sydney than to the modified contractarianism of Whig party polemicists. Put simply, it was that 'one man is set over them [the people] for their good and is made what he is by them and for them. He is made for them and not they for him'; 'salus populi suprema lex est'.

Such a radical philosophy of the origin and basis of political authority implied a rigorous limitation on the constitutional powers that monarchy was assumed to possess. Cocks regarded the King as bound, first and foremost by his coronation oath, but also by the law: in his view it had been James's assumption of a dispensing power which had signalled his abdication of the throne. As to the King's part in the making of law, 'whoever knows the constitution of the English government, knows the King may either dissent or assent to any bill, but that is nothing, no power to alter the meaning, word or sense of any bill. He can assent or dissent, but change he cannot.' It was of course this established constitution that James had attempted to 'subvert', and the inevitable outcome would have been a monarchical despotism on the model of Louis XIV's, a threat which still hung over post-Revolution England: 'if our late tyrant King James [should] ever return to sit on the English throne (which God forbid), instead of our ancient laws we should have the French king's will; instead of our constitution the French king's pleasure'.[47] There was no half-way house between the English constitution and tyranny.

---

[47] MS Eng. hist. b. 209, fo. 39.

Cocks seems to have been unaware that a distinction could be made between 'absolute' and 'arbitrary' rule, using terms like 'arbitrary power', 'absolute despotic power', and 'absolute tyranny' quite interchangeably.

Despite his deep-seated fear of monarchical tyranny, Cocks was no enemy to monarchy as such. With the odd exception (a generous allusion to the regicide Henry Ireton, and a tendency to idealize Neville and some other republicans),[48] references in his writings and speeches to the era of the Commonwealth and Protectorate were usually derogatory. The execution of Charles I he regarded as abominable; the Interregnum 'tedious'; Oliver Cromwell an arbitrary ruler who had 'dismissed the militia' and the Parliament 'in a pretended fanatical, furious zeal to hide his knavery'.[49] Despite stern disapproval of both Charles II and James II, he was decided in his preference for a 'monarchical government', or at least one with a strong element of the monarchical.[50] Like most of his compatriots he believed in the supreme excellence of the English constitution, which combined the best of 'monarchy, aristocracy and democracy' into a 'mixed government'.[51] As he told the Gloucestershire commission of the peace in 1696,[52]

There never was so excellent a [government] in the world as this. The ancients knew none such. They divided their government under three heads, monarchy, aristocracy and democracy; and of all these governments we have the best. We have the conveniency of all and by our mixture the evils, the insolency, the tyranny is taken away. It is the excellency of our government that is is subject to law.

Occasionally Cocks elaborated this idea of a 'balanced' constitution, expressing himself in the 'neo-Harringtonian' mode associated with Henry Neville and the other civic virtue theorists. 'A speech not spoke' in the Commons on the subject of bribery and corruption at parliamentary elections began[53] by asking his notional audience to

look into the wise observation of the ancients and you shall find their opinions to be that Athens, Rome and other popular governments owed the loss of their liberties and subversion of their constitutions to the largess and bounty . . . bestowed by the candidates among the people, and I hope I may without offence term our body the popular part of our noble constitution (composed of monarchy, aristocracy and democracy). If any of these assume too much power or have not their due shares allowed them, unless quick remedies are applied there must follow a commotion, a dangerous disorder to the whole.

---

[48] Ibid. b. 210, fos. 32^v, 45^v.   [49] Ibid. b. 209, fo. 36^v; b. 210, fos. 3, 49^v, 60–1.
[50] Ibid. b. 209, fos. 2, 4, 29^v, 95; b. 210, fos. 45^v, 53^v.
[51] Ibid. b. 209, fos. 27^v–28^v, 30, 39; b. 210, fos. 3^v, 53^v, 62^v; *Grand Jury Charge 1717*, 13 (printed in Lamoine (ed.), *Charges to Grand Jury*, 85). Cf. Bodl. MS Rawlinson E. 216, fo. 305, for the expression of similar views by Cocks's brother Robert.
[52] MS Eng. hist. b. 209, fo. 39.   [53]Ibid. b. 210, fos. 61–2. See also ibid. 43, 45^v, 63.

In this case what was feared was a reinforcement of court influence through the contagious venality of borough elections. The increasing number of placemen in the Commons was another source of anxiety. Cocks did not dispute the necessity for some government officials to have seats in the House; his main concern was to prevent wholesale corruption, with the consequent forfeiture of parliamentary independence. The presence in the Commons of a legion of office-holders, who 'generally vote in matters of state all one way', gave 'a handle to . . . people out of doors to believe there is a separate interest between the King and the country'.

At other times Cocks's use of the vocabulary of 'corruption' conveyed a more straightforward meaning; not the overturning of the constitutional balance but a debasement in the precious currency of private and public morality. Christian piety, and a veneration for the civic virtue of republican Rome, combined to produce in him something of an obsession with notions of moral value. All enemies were stigmatized as morally derelict, whether they were 'mischievous and ambitious' High Church clergymen or unscrupulous and self-seeking politicians such as Cocks's *bête noire*, the rakehell 'Jack' Howe. The House of Commons itself seemed to crawl with iniquities. Looking about him Cocks could see little but lust for self-advancement. There were the 'proud and ambitious', the 'fawning' preferment-hunters, those who 'bray and bawl against the government in order to be bought off', others (notably Howe) who 'aggravate matters by railing, and by hot, satirical, witty speeches', and in one memorable catalogue, 'the beaux of all ages . . . the wits, the half-wits, and those who need no lawmaker'. Thus, in denouncing the 'corruption' of the political process, he often focused on corruption that was specific and personal, an official abusing his trust, an elector selling his vote, a Member of Parliament putting self-interest or factional advantage before the public good: actions of the kind that Henry Neville, in an interesting combination of images of civic and personal vice, had labelled a 'politic debauch'.[54]

The sense of 'moral crisis' that permeates Cocks's commentary on the political behaviour of his day originated in a wider critique of the manners and morals, and the religious observance, of society as a whole. This was an important by-product of the evengelical zeal for a 'new reformation' which animated the members of Protestant voluntary societies and the founders of charity schools, and which in the aftermath of the Glorious Revolution was transmuted into a negative and repressive impulse through a fear of the

---

[54] Robbins (ed.), *Two English Republican Tracts*, 196. Cf. Hayton, 'Moral Reform and Country Politics', 85.

imminence of providential judgement.[55] Looming political insecurity worked upon pious sensibilities that were already strained by despair at the spiralling of vice and crime and revulsion at the spate of sceptical and heterodox literature released by the expiry of the Licensing Act. The outcome was an acute and generalized 'moral panic'. In some circles it passed for a common assumption that the sins of the nation, the widespread immorality and disregard of religion, cried out for divine retribution, and that this punishment might well take the form of the return of a Catholic king.

At the outset of William's reign leadership of the campaign for the 'moral reformation' of the kingdom had come from the court, through Council proclamations, and the sermons of royal chaplains. But within a few years the movement had gathered a momentum of its own, with quite widespread support among Members of Parliament (in both Houses), county commissions of the peace, and borough magistrates, reaching the zenith of its influence in 1699, in an unsuccessful attempt to obtain a statute to make adultery a misdemeanour. Not long afterwards partisan differences between High and Low Churchmen, and a waning of interest among the less committed of the laity, weakened the impetus for reform and gave the surviving groups of reformers a somewhat cliquish air. But on the politics of the later 1690s this moral imperative exercised a considerable force, especially on Country Whig politics of the kind professed by Cocks. An excessive concern for morality was not of course confined to opposition benches, but was always more likely to surface in minds already obsessed with political 'corruption' and 'politic debauchery'. In partisan terms, despite the many contributions of individual Tories and High Churchmen, the central proposition of the reformers' argument remained decisively Whiggish: that the Revolution, besides a providential deliverance from tyranny, had also been a providential judgement on the wickedness of Charles II and James II; and that the sinfulness of post-Revolution England constituted a standing invitation to a further providential visitation. Vice and profaneness were thus bound up with popery and Jacobitism as threats to the safety of the Williamite regime.

Cocks moved in a distinctly 'reforming' milieu. Several of his nearest political associates can be identified as strong supporters of the reformation of public manners: his nephew by marriage Grey Neville, fellow Gloucestershire MP Maynard Colchester, the future Lord Chancellor Peter King, and the

---

[55] For what follows, see the works cited above, n. 30.

godly Hampshire squire Thomas Jervoise.[56] Moreover, his own writings declare him to have been 'a reform[er]'. He penned various meditations on the evils of drink and 'debauchery'; devised prayers for the nation to avert a providential judgement, and for himself to be made 'a means by my advice and encouragement' to help in the task of 'suppressing vice'; read charges to Gloucestershire quarter sessions on the themes of drunkenness, sexual incontinence, swearing, and sabbath-breaking; and prepared a speech to the Commons in 1699, which he was unable to deliver, to move for a further bill 'to hinder profaneness and immoralities'.[57]

Preoccupation with moral reform determined Cocks's views on what one might term 'social policy', at the heart of which was his insistence on the duty of the civil magistrate to impose social discipline. The very word magistracy 'signifies command and authority over others moving in lesser stations . . . it intends that a man should like a schoolmaster correct faults, punish idleness and instruct all under our care'.[58] Vices that were perhaps indicative of incipient social insubordination, such as drunkenness and profane swearing, he singled out for condign punishment, while the general emphasis was on 'obliging others . . . in outward appearance at least, to conform to the rules of modesty and decency'.[59] Of course, the need for moral discipline was not confined to the lower orders. Even Privy Councillors, Cocks noted, swore and got drunk. Moral regulation was a pious duty; not simply, or even primarily, a means of controlling behaviour. Underneath there was also a significant political objective. A true sense of religion, he thought, would make men industrious; industry 'creates a property in us'; property in turn 'creates a courage'; and courage preserves liberty against 'foreign and domestic invasion'.[60] This combination of passions, a deep social conservatism and a desire to promote godliness, and through godliness a civic virtue for the defence of liberty, could impart a ruthlessness to Cocks's contemplation of social problems, which was seen at its bleakest in his various writings on poverty. Unlike other 'moral reformers', who advocated, and even gave financial assistance to, constructive projects for workhouses, Cocks proposed remedies of the utmost

[56] Hayton, 'Moral Reform and Country Politics', 55, 61, 64, 66–7, 83. For Colchester, see also Rose, 'Providence, Protestant Union and Godly Reformation in the 1690s', 165–6; and for King, Lord Campbell, *Lives of the Lord Chancellors . . .* (8 vols.; London, 1845–69), iv. 567–9; Robert Wodrow, *Analecta, or Materials for a History of Remarkable Providences . . .*, ed. [M. Leishman] (Maitland Club, 60; 4 vols., Edinburgh, 1842–3), ii. 7, 291–2, 328.

[57] See sources cited above, n. 31.   [58] MS Eng. hist. b. 209, fo. 39ᵛ.

[59] Ibid.; Cocks, *Grand Jury Charge 1717*, 404 (repr. in Lamoine (ed.), *Charges to Grand Jury*, 81); id., *A Charge Given to the Grand-Jury of the County of Gloucester at the Midsummer Sessions, 1723* (London, 1723), 20–2 (repr. in Lamoine (ed.), *Charges to Grand Jury*, 181–2).

[60] MS Eng. hist. b. 209, fo. 29ᵛ. See also fos. 29, 94ᵛ.

severity: flogging, imprisonment, and transportation for vagrants; 'houses of correction' where conditions would be so grim that families would do anything rather than be committed.[61] The explanation lay in his exaggerated fears of the moral and social consequences of poverty, and in his simple view of its cause — idleness and 'improvidence' on the part of the poor themselves (the latter concept implying some form of divine sanction):[62] 'The reason of the great charge of the poor is, first, the negligent ways of living of the poor families, their wakes, their frequ[ent ho]lidays, their fiddlers, their debaucheries, their liberalities to their children, with no other intent [than to] become chargeable themselves.'

In this area Cocks did at least have coherent arguments and a clear understanding of social processes, however poorly that understanding may have corresponded with reality. On economic questions he was usually unable to work his ideas through to a logical conclusion. In one instance he devised a step-by-step analysis which traced back industrial and commercial depression to the prevailing high prices for provisions, but then abruptly confessed himself at a loss as to how the root cause might be tackled. Two basic notions are evident in all his writings on economic matters: first, that what was happening on the land, in terms of use, productivity, and rents, determined general trends in manufacturing and trade; secondly, that it was vitally important to increase the volume of England's commerce, especially its international commerce, 'since we are an island and our very subsistence and mere being does in a manner depend upon trade'. 'The very life and visible soul of the universe', he enthused, was trade. The merchant was 'the heart' of the body politic.[63] He seems to have taken for granted the mercantilist precept that the quantity of material wealth on earth was finite, while conceding that wars inspired a 'necessitous ingenuity' by which men 'dug salt out of the rocks', mined more precious metal, and discovered hoards of treasure 'that lay rusting and sleeping in chests and holes'. In the long run, however, trade represented the only hope of future national prosperity. Its

---

[61] Mary Ransome, 'The Parliamentary Career of Sir Humphry Mackworth, 1701–1713', *University of Birmingham Historical Journal*, 1 (1947–8), 244–7; S. M. Macfarlane, 'Studies in Poverty and Poor Relief in London at the End of the Seventeenth Century', D.Phil. thesis (Oxford, 1983), 362, 378–82; Hayton, 'Moral Reform and Country Politics', 67–8; MS Eng. hist. b. 210, fos. 58ᵛ–60; Lambeth Palace Library, MS 640 (Tenison papers), 501–23, 'Abstracts of the Statutes Relating to the Poor &c. by Sir Richard Cox'.

[62] MS Eng. hist. b. 210, fo. 60. See also ibid. fos. 29, 95ᵛ; and Bodl. MS Rawlinson E. 215, fos. 257–69 (for another fraternal echo).

[63] MS Eng. hist. b. 209, fo. 87. The expression 'trade is the very life and soul of the universe' is a direct quotation from *Sir Thomas Pope Blount's Essays on Several Subjects* (3rd edn.; London, 1697), 178.

welfare depended upon the removal of all restrictions and customs duties, together with some positive measures to facilitate the operation of market forces; domestic consumption expanded through the encouragement of population growth; and prices pegged through a voluntary lowering of rents. Interestingly, the only stage at which Cocks envisaged effective intervention was in the relationship of landlord and tenant, according a peculiar responsibility to 'the nobility and gentry', the 'arms and shoulders' of his 'body politic' analogy.

If Cocks was a zealous promoter of trade, his response to the 'financial revolution' of the 1690s was equivocal. He found it difficult to come to terms with the concept of deficit financing. Supplying the 'deficiencies' in public funds, and servicing the general mortgages, were a constant anxiety of his parliamentary life. Like all country gentlemen he deplored the burdens that war finance imposed on the land, and was suspicious that in the struggles against Louis XIV a few individuals had made great profits while he and his fellow squires had suffered. At one point in 1701 he seems to have believed that the war had effected a redistribution of wealth: 'I have heard it said, that there were as great riches now in England as were before the last war; if so, that England is as rich now, though the riches have in some measure changed'. In another parliamentary speech he drew an even sharper distinction between differing economic interests, pressing the case that money rather than land or trade should bear the weight of taxation. Land had 'in a manner borne the whole charge' of the previous, ruinously expensive war. Trade was already 'in most parts sufficiently charged', while an excise would be 'as odious as it represented to be'. Trade was 'the life of England'; land was 'England itself '; money had no such saving grace, and could no longer be spared its contribution. Later still, in Anne's reign, he wrote caustically of moneyed men who had become so powerful that they would not permit the public interest to be preferred to the private. Yet this issue, no less than any other, was subordinate to the greater question of national survival and the safeguarding of the ancient constitution. Against his demand in 1701 for the taxation of money rather than land or trade, should be set another speech in that session, in which, after admitting, 'all my small fortune is in land, and I believe everyone that knows me knows that I will not easily part with my money', he went on to pledge his entire estate in defence of liberty:

We are threatened and in danger abroad from a malicious and potent enemy . . . Though I shall not be willing to raise more upon land, nor do I well like what is done, yet since there is a possibility that we may be forced into a war I would not give such great encouragement to our enemies . . . if there is a necessity I would willingly part with one half to secure the other.

IV

Cocks's public career began in earnest after the Revolution. He had had little part to play in the train of events which saw William and Mary installed on the throne (hence, perhaps, his comments that most of his compatriots had 'sat quiet at home'), nor does he appear to have been involved in the elections to the Convention. But with the death of his grandmother he came into full possession of his ancestral estate, and was able to assert himself. He set in motion the building of an entirely new residence (a process eventually completed in 1699), an imposing if not extravagant manor house surrounded by fashionable gardens in the Dutch style. No trace of house or gardens can be seen today, but their contemporary appearance is recorded in an engraving by Johannes Kip.[64] As the squire of Dumbleton Cocks was now able to take his place in the forefront of local society, and in 1692 he was pricked as county sheriff.

It was in his capacity as a magistrate that Cocks first made a reputation. He had been named to the commission of the peace for Worcestershire in October 1689, and was added to the bench for his own county at about the same time, making his first appearance at the Gloucestershire quarter sessions at Michaelmas that year.[65] Thereafter he was a regular attender, parliamentary business permitting, except for the Epiphany meeting, which he usually avoided, presumably because of the likelihood of inclement weather and the distance involved in travelling from Dumbleton to Gloucester.[66] The sessions afforded him a captive audience, and it was not long before he had taken possession of the chairmanship and was subjecting his fellow justices to regular harangues. Evidence for the election of quarter sessions chairmen (not only for Gloucestershire but for most English counties) is tantalizingly

[64] MS Eng. hist. b. 209, fo. 104ᵛ. The engraving is printed in Sir Robert Atkyns, *The Ancient and Present State of Gloucestershire* . . . (2nd edn.; London, 1768). In this book, first published in 1712, Atkyns reported that Sir Robert Cocks was 'lord of the manor and has a handsome seat near the church; the whole parish belongs to him' (p. 212).

[65] History of Parliament Trust, microfilm index of Crown Office Docquet Books (PRO Ind. 4213–15); Glos. RO, Q/SO2 (quarter sessions order bk. 1681–92), fo. 167.

[66] Evidence taken from Glos. RO, Q/SO2–4 (quarter sessions order bks. 1681–92, 1702–14, 1714–24).

uncertain,[67] but it would appear that he may have been chosen chairman as early as Michaelmas 1690.[68]

The first of the grand jury 'charges' which he proudly recorded for posterity was an 'extempore' oration at Easter 1694, provoked by the publication of a recent parliamentary speech by the notorious Jacobite MP for Bristol, Sir John Knight. In opposing the general naturalization bill in the previous January, Knight had resorted to the most virulent xenophobia, savaging the Dutch in particular, and ending with a call to the Commons to 'kick this bill out of the House, and then foreigners out of the kingdom'.[69] In reply Cocks offered his own definition of patriotism:[70]

it is not the eating of beef or the consuming the English corn . . . [or] breathing an English air from infancy that makes a man an Englishman: it is the mind and actions pursuant to such principles . . . [I] take him for an Englishman that is for the securing our properties and maintaining the liberties of Europe against the French king and t'other king his confederate [James II], and I take him for a Frenchman, a papist, a foreigner or anything, that being born here and enjoying the freedom of an Englishman can ever entertain the thought of changing this present government or making any interest for the French king or our late tyrant.

This simple political message, equating Jacobitism with tyranny and the Williamite regime with the defence of liberty, was repeated in successive charges. In the following Midsummer sessions, having warned against the danger to the moral fabric of society posed by alehouses and other resorts of the idle and dissolute, Cocks vehemently denounced attempts to undermine public trust in King William and Queen Mary as being part of a surreptitious design against English liberties. Far from aspiring to absolute rule, as some mischievous spirits had alleged, the King and Queen were, he declared, the most resolute defenders of liberty and property, at home and abroad.[71] Then at Christmas 1697 he felt obliged to defend William's reputation once again,

---

[67] I. E. Gray and A. T. Gaydon, *Gloucestershire Quarter Sessions Archives 1660–1889* (Gloucester, 1958), 86. See also Norma Landau, *The Justices of the Peace, 1679–1760* (Berkeley, 1984), 48–9, 279–81, 284–5. The suggestion by Gray and Gaydon, that after about 1710 the first justice to be named in the sessions order book may well have been the chairman, seems plausible, since this first name sometimes broke the otherwise strict order of precedence. However, the first-named justice in Gloucestershire from 1719 to 1728 was always a John Cocks, and we know that the (published) charge for Midsummer 1723 had been given by Sir Richard. A similar reservation must also cloud the other possible source, the estreat rolls returned to the King's remembrancer (PRO E. 137/13/10–12), where again the first name on the list of justices was frequently out of precedence. I am obliged to Dr P. J. Le Fevre for a helpful discussion of this point.

[68] Glos. RO, Q/SO2, fo. 191, has him named in the first place on that sessions roll, when he had previously appeared in fifth, fourth, and second places.

[69] Knight's speech is reprinted in *Somers's Tracts*, x. 591–6. There is a short biography in *HC 1660–90*, ii. 696–7.   [70] MS Eng. hist. b. 209, fos. 27–8.   [71] Ibid. 28–9.

against the 'indefatigable malice and industry' of Jacobite critics who had
accused the King of wishing to maintain a standing army 'to deprive us of our
liberties'.[72] Such forthright and vocal partisanship naturally attracted attention, from both sides. The pungently Whiggish remarks he made at the
sessions of Easter 1696, after the discovery of the Assassination Plot and
the adoption of the loyal Association, met with open disapproval from
some (presumably Tory) justices,[73] and when he was eventually returned to
Parliament as knight of the shire in the general election of 1698, he was
described by one opponent as 'an ill-favoured orator of that county'.[74]

Cocks had been involved in parliamentary elections since at least the winter
of 1689/90, when he had taken part in the complicated manœuvres that had
preceded the Gloucestershire poll, at first active in support of the old
Exclusionist and Country Whig Sir John Guise of Elmore but then, surprisingly, making promises to Guise's opponent, James Thynne, brother of the
High Tory Lord Weymouth.[75] He had been a candidate himself in 1695, for
the borough of Tewkesbury, where there was a conflict between opposing
Whig interests: on one side a faction headed by Sir Francis Winnington and
supported by leading members of the corporation, which probably represented
the proprietorial interest of Henry, Lord Capell, the Lord Deputy of Ireland;
and on the other Capell's traditional rivals the Dowdeswells of Pull Court,
assisted by the lord lieutenant of the county Lord Dursley (later to succeed as
second Earl of Berkeley). Prior to the 1695 general election the Capell/
Winnington party had attempted to secure a new charter for the town, with
the assistance of Secretary of State Shrewsbury. The successful resistance
mounted by their opponents had included an appeal by Cocks to Lord
Chancellor Somers to delay the process.[76] At the poll Richard Dowdeswell
was returned without difficulty, and possibly without opposition, but there
was a stiff contest for the second seat in which Cocks found himself defeated
by Winnington. He petitioned the Commons against Winnington's return,
claiming that Sir Francis's agents had brought undue pressure to bear on
the freemen and freeholders who constituted the borough's electorate, 'not
only by threatening those who had voted for the petitioner, to turn them out of
their houses, if they did not withdraw their votes; but also by detaining the

---

[72] Ibid. 95ᵛ–94ᵛ.   [73] Ibid. 39.
[74] G. Davies (ed.), *Autobiography of Thomas Raymond and Memoirs of the Family of Guise of
Elmore, Gloucestershire* (Camden Soc., 3rd ser., 28; London, 1917), 140.
[75] Bath MSS (the Marquess of Bath, Longleat House, Wiltshire), Thynne papers, vol. xiii, fos.
256–7, James Thynne to Weymouth, 11 Feb. 1689/90.
[76] MS Eng. hist. b. 209, fo. 38; *CSP Dom.* 1694–5, pp. 462–3, 486; HMC, *Downshire MSS*, i.
473, 477–8, 550; Frances Redmond, 'The Borough of Tewkesbury, 1575–1714', MA thesis
(Birmingham, 1950), 57–64.

town book, wherein all the names of the freemen are entered that had a right to vote'. The petition was duly referred to the committee of privileges and elections, but no report was made.[77]

The county election three years later, at which Cocks was returned, was a similar scene of intra-party confusion.[78] At the original canvass there were no less than six candidates, of whom only one, Jack Howe, could be described as a Tory. Three went as far as a poll. Howe secured the first place on the return and Cocks the second, ahead of an unidentified rival, probably the Country Whig Thomas Stephens of Lypiatt. Which, if any, of the principals ran in tandem is unclear: most likely the election was a genuine three-cornered contest. There is even the possibility that Cocks, despite what we have heard of his political beliefs, may have appeared on this occasion as a ministerial candidate, in a general election which elsewhere was fought as much between representatives of 'Court' and 'County' as on Whig and Tory party lines.[79] After all, one of the major issues of the campaign was the continuance of a standing army in peacetime, and Cocks had defended King William on this very point in one of his sessional charges. His much-trumpeted connexion with Lord Chancellor Somers certainly persuaded the compiler of a contemporary analysis of the new House of Commons to assign him to the government rather than opposition side, though events were to prove this assessment to have been quite mistaken.[80]

V

The parliamentary scene which now opened offered peculiar opportunities to a back-bench Whig blessed with audacity, a strong voice, and a clear sense of political rectitude.[81] The administration established in 1693–5 by the so-called Whig 'Junto' — comprising Somers, Admiral Edward Russell (created Earl of Orford), Comptroller Thomas (second Baron) Wharton, and Chancellor of the Exchequer Charles Montagu — an administration which had successfully provided King William with the money and material resources to pursue a costly Continental war, retained its grip on power. However, it was being

[77] *CJ* xi. 343.   [78] *CSP Dom.* 1698, pp. 343, 377.

[79] Earl of Hardwicke (ed.), *Miscellaneous State Papers, from 1501 to 1726* (2 vols.; London, 1778), ii. 435; James (ed.), *Letters Illustrative . . .* , ii. 142–3; B. W. Hill, *The Growth of Parliamentary Parties 1689–1742* (London, 1976), 77–8; Horwitz, *Parliament, Policy and Politics*, 237–40.

[80] Henry Horwitz, 'Parties, Connections and Parliamentary Politics, 1689–1714: Review and Revision', *Journal of British Studies*, 6 (1966–7), 64.

[81] The following general account of the 1698–9 session relies heavily on Horwitz, *Parliament, Policy and Politics*, 247–57.

forced on to the defensive by an increasingly active and confident opposition, essentially Tory in its composition but calling itself the 'New Country Party' and possessing a leaven of anti-ministerial Whigs and ex-Whigs sufficient to give a surface respectability to this claim to non-partisan patriotism. Having survived a series of potentially damaging attacks in the winter of 1697/8, on such questions as the size of the army establishment and the scandal over the false endorsement of Exchequer bills, the Junto seemed to have held their ground in the 1698 election, for when the new Parliament met they secured a surprising victory in the contest for the Chair of the Commons, replacing the outgoing Speaker, Paul Foley, a former stalwart of the Country opposition, with the Treasury lord Sir Thomas Littleton. Whether because at bottom most observers still considered the ministers to be secure, or because the Peace of Ryswick had encouraged a temporary lull in alarms of Jacobite conspiracy and French invasion, the government's self-appointed Whig critics were not afraid to indulge themselves, and the 1698/9 session saw a continuation in the level of Whig disaffection, specifically Country Whig disaffection, which had been a marked feature of the preceding Parliament. The issues which dominated debates, a standing army, the inquiries into malversation in the navy and corruption in the granting of forfeited estates, could not have been more finely calculated to arouse the consciences of principled Whigs; and the House was, besides, consumed with the righteous fervour which produced the 'Immorality Bill' to criminalize adultery. It was a propitious time for Cocks to make his parliamentary début.

According to his own testimony, Cocks waited until 4 January 1699 to speak in the Commons, when he opposed a Court-inspired motion to confine the scope of the Disbanding Bill, the measure intended to reduce the size of the army in the aftermath of the peace. Although the statement that this was his maiden speech must probably be taken at face value, the 'parliamentary diary' itself nevertheless contains further evidence which would cast it into question; and indeed, Cocks appears already to have made some impression on the House as early as the previous 17 December, a day on which he was distinguished with nomination to four committees, including the all-important drafting committee on the Disbanding Bill.[82] Once he had broken the ice with an intervention on a major issue, his peculiar brand of oratory became a regular feature of debates. In several respects the 'maiden speech' set the tone. Its forthright denunciation of a standing army firmly established his position on the Country wing of his party, while the subsidiary arguments stated themes which would frequently recur: 'the frailty and imbecility of

---

[82] *CJ* xii. 358–9.

human nature [and] how many unthinking creatures there are over the virtuous and wise'; the destructive self-interest of 'proud and ambitious' place-seekers; and his own disinterested public spirit — 'I am guided by reason, not party'.

Preening himself on rational non-partisanship was, however, an act of self-delusion. It was true that from his earliest days in Parliament Cocks associated himself with such cherished 'Country' causes as place bills, projects for the reform of electoral abuses, and the inquiry into King William's grants of Irish forfeited estates to favourites and ministers, and that his observations on the forfeitures strayed far enough from Whig orthodoxy to permit even the expression of some sympathy for the defeated Irish Catholics—'methinks it is a great hardship to be reckoned a traitor for only adhering to one's natural prince'. But while he readily joined in any wholesale condemnation of courtiers, he none the less reserved specific, *ad hominem*, abuse for Tories rather than Whigs: the veteran government financier Sir Stephen Fox, treasurer of the Ordnance Charles Bertie, and above all the Master of the Rolls, Sir John Trevor, who had compounded the heinous crime of accepting bribes when in the Speaker's Chair with his steady obstruction of the godly work of the societies for the reformation of manners, and thus earned Cocks's undying enmity. In supporting the Place Bill Cocks went out of his way to propose an additional clause 'to exclude some few . . . that did refuse . . . the voluntary Association'; and he was willing to divide from the Country opposition if he felt its conduct to be merely factious, or if some deeply held Whig principle, prejudice, or connexion had been transgressed, as was the case with the malicious attacks of 'ill-humoured' Tories on the employment of foreign Protestants in the armed forces. Significantly, he seems to have played little or no part in the prolonged campaign to expose maladministration in the Admiralty, which was such a feature of the winter of 1698/9, and which paved the way for Orford's resignation in the summer of 1699 and, ultimately, the disintegration of the Junto ministry.

There was, of course, much more to parliamentary proceedings than the high political drama of set-piece debates, and in the daily round of business Cocks was soon an assiduous participant, regularly appointed to select committees to examine petitions or to draft, or consider, bills. The record of his legislative activity in his first session (as entered in the Commons' *Journals*) was in many ways typical of his parliamentary career as a whole.[83] Besides the pet projects of 'Country' Members, he involved himself

---

[83] Ibid. 349–658, *passim*. Interestingly, throughout his parliamentary career Cocks never once served as a teller in a full division in the House (divisions in committee were not recorded in *CJ*).

in various enterprises of moral and social reform, such as the Immorality Bill, a proposal for the suppression of lotteries, and other bills aiming to tackle what was perceived as the increasing incidence of poverty, vagrancy, and crime; in a raft of measures designed to foster economic development and protect trading and manufacturing interests, especially the woollen industry that was so vital to his native Gloucestershire; and in numerous private estate and naturalization bills. In common with other 'Country' enthusiasts, he regarded the promotion of social and economic 'improvement' as an essential element in the exercise of that public virtue which it was his duty to pursue and which was distressingly absent in the behaviour of so many of his parliamentary colleagues.[84]

VI

For one who had so clearly cherished an ideal vision of the purpose and function of Parliament, a glimpse of the reality in this first session was clearly a profoundly disillusioning experience. 'Before I was one amongst them', wrote Cocks,

I fancied the fools were awed, governed and had respect for those that were famous and renowned for their worth and parts, and that the knaves, for indeed I knew some such there were, would disguise themselves and be in fear of being censured . . . upon these considerations I expected, if not a judicious, honest, sober and grave assembly, at least in appearance, I mean one that would seem to be such: instead of judicious and honest I found them all upon parties, in so much that if they did not totally banish judgment I am sure they did honesty. . . then as for the gravity and sobriety it is intolerable, there is such a noise one can scarce hear or mind what is said, and indeed what is particularly minded is private business, to make parties, to make court, etc. . . . there [are] few that mind or understand the true integrity of the nation; in most of our public business men are biassed by private ends.

The next session, however, saw Cocks himself 'upon parties' much more consistently, and openly, than before. The defeats which the Court party had sustained during the winter of 1698/9, over the disbandment of troops, and the establishment of a commission of inquiry into grants of Irish forfeited estates, had inflicted serious political damage and left the battered Whig Junto

---

[84] For the public bills and petitions with which he concerned himself, see *CJ* xii. 358–60, 368, 390–1, 393, 402, 449, 484, 521, 524, 541, 551, 591, 620–1, 635, 641, 651, 656. The link between economic and social improvement and political and moral 'reform' is illustrated in the list of necessary bills which the Welsh Tory Sir Humphrey Mackworth (himself an active 'reformer') drew up in June 1701 to be 'prepare[d] against next Parliament': National Library of Wales, MS 14362E (Mackworth's diary 1696–1705), 124.

clinging grimly to power.[85] Afterwards the King reshuffled a number of offices, and even began discussions with the Tory leader Lord Rochester, but the general effect of his various changes made little difference to the party complexion of the ministry. Although appointments such as Lord Jersey to be Secretary of State, the veteran Lord Lonsdale as Lord Privy Seal, and Rochester's protégé Richard Hill to the Treasury commission, represented the intrusion of a new Tory element, at the same time the remnant of the former Court Tory connexion headed by the Duke of Leeds (Charles II's Lord Treasurer Danby) was winkled out. Rather than radically altering his 'scheme' of management, William had opted to stand 'on the defensive'. In practice this meant that the Whigs still constituted the Court interest in the House of Commons, and the principal targets of the (largely Tory) opposition remained the reputations, and indeed the persons, of the leading members of the Junto. Orford and Charles Montagu had both stepped back from the front line, the former from the Admiralty board and the latter from the Treasury to a more lucrative but less prominent place as auditor of the Exchequer. Others, most notably the Lord Chancellor, Somers, remained in place. But events were to show that none were safe from direct parliamentary attack.

Repeatedly during this session Cocks found himself smothering censorious impulses in his anxiety to come to the rescue of party colleagues. In each case the dominating motive seems to have been aversion to Tory opportunism as much as loyalty to fellow Whigs, and it may well be that his anger at the Tories was deepened by resentment at the failure of his own corresponding efforts to secure the condemnation of Sir John Trevor.[86] The first fury of the opposition onslaught fell on 6 December 1699, on the scandal surrounding Captain Kidd's piracies, the captain's dubious enterprise having originally been afforded ministerial sponsorship at the highest level. Among those who had stood to benefit personally from any seizures Kidd was to make of privateers' booty, and who were now implicated by association in his subsequent misadventures, were Orford and Somers, former Secretary of State Shrewsbury, and the master of the Ordnance and Court favourite Lord Romney.[87] The debate was opened by Jack Howe, whose denunciation of the patent was echoed in a succession of rousing speeches, with a notable contribution from the veteran Tory chieftain Sir Edward Seymour. On Cocks this tirade produced a strong reaction. Having entered the chamber feeling

---

[85] For the 1699–1700 session I have relied on Horwitz, *Parliament, Policy and Politics*, 257–69.

[86] James (ed.), *Letters Illustrative . . .* , ii. 369.

[87] The fullest discussion of the Kidd affair is to be found in Robert C. Ritchie, *Captain Kidd and the War against the Pirates* (Cambridge, Mass., 1986).

that the patent 'ought to be condemned and those concerned in it highly censured', he now

had time to consider and strip truth stark naked from the dregs of oratory and filth of satire with which she was defiled and disguised, [and] I found no more in it than that these gent[lemen], when the government was in distress for men, ships, and money, set out a ship at their own cost, not to get . . . treasures but to serve the nation at their own loss and hazard.

And when he considered the refusal of the Commons to do anything about Trevor's iniquities, the injustice of the motion seemed all the more glaring: 'Shall I, who could not get this instrument of slavery and arbitrary power censured, censure these tribunes of the people, these true Englishmen . . . What, sir, will you remove my Lord Chancellor and put Trevor and such as he in his place?' Another, similar, conversion occurred a week later, over a proposal made from the ranks of the High Tories to address the King to remove Bishop Gilbert Burnet as tutor to the Duke of Gloucester (Princess Anne's only surviving child and heir presumptive to the throne). Again Howe was among the speakers in favour of the motion, and again Cocks reacted strongly to the excesses of Tory rhetoric. 'When I came this day', he told the House, he had thought Burnet 'the fittest' to be addressed against, 'except one'. However, 'the incomparable character I have heard of him from . . . gent[lemen] who I am sure know men and on whose judgement I much rely I own I have altered my opinion and believe [him] the fittest man in the world for the place he is in.'

The weakest point in the ministry's defence was the issue of the confiscated estates and other Crown properties that King William had given away to courtiers, servants, and political friends. On this subject Cocks nurtured his Country principles through the initial debates, but eventually succumbed to the requirements of party solidarity. Interest centred on the Jacobite forfeitures in Ireland. When, in December 1699, the Commons received the report of the commissioners of inquiry appointed in the previous session, it became apparent just how extensive were the lands involved, especially the estates made over to the King's Dutch favourites Portland and Albemarle, and to William's alleged mistress, Elizabeth Villiers, Lady Orkney. A bill of resumption was promptly ordered, Cocks speaking third in support of the motion. After the Christmas recess things went from bad to worse. Court spokesmen failed to amend the Resumption Bill so as to reserve a proportion of the estates to the King's disposal. Then, in order to forestall possible interference by the House of Lords the resumption was 'tacked' to the most important of all the supply measures, the bill to renew the land tax. At the same time, in response to Court-inspired amendments at the second reading in the Commons, and to lay a foundation for future proceedings against individual ministers, Jack Howe successfully proposed resolutions declaring that 'the advising, procuring and passing the grants' had not only occasioned 'great debts upon the nation, and . . . heavy taxes upon the people', but had constituted a dereliction of public 'trust and duty'.[88] For his own part, Cocks took the opportunity to temper continuing support for the bill with a second-reading speech in which he went out of his way to record his boundless gratitude and admiration for King William, and corresponding detestation for King James. He was, moreover, becoming increasingly unhappy with the trend of the opposition campaign, the next stage of which was a barrage of personal attacks on Montagu and Somers, mounted on 15 February 1700 in a committee of the whole House on the state of the nation. 'I will not do anything that has any private look or end in it', Cocks told the committee. As for the Junto ministers, he admitted subsequently, 'I owe I like them better than I did'; 'I know no way to judge of men but by comparing them. They are as good or bad only comparatively as they are better than others.'

Events were now moving towards a climax. Not content with merging the Irish forfeitures resumption with the Land Tax Bill, Tories in the Commons added a further insult by inserting a clause to disqualify excise officers from sitting in Parliament. The Lords could scarcely fail to see the measure in its entirety as a calculated infringement on royal prerogatives, and a deliberate challenge to their own constitutional role, and whether out of loyalty to party or to the Crown, a substantial majority of peers resolved to respond. On 6 April the upper House took the near-fatal step of amending the bill, by the excision of the place clause, thus provoking a constitutional crisis. The Commons promptly rejected the amendments, denounced those Privy Councillors who had secured 'exorbitant grants' for themselves, and even talked of impeachments. Then, in a dramatic dénouement on the 10th, the Lords gave way, and William was able to register his assent to the bill and close the session. Simultaneously the Commons, in closed sitting, narrowly decided against calling for Somers's dismissal but did pass an address, aimed chiefly at Portland and Albemarle, which demanded the removal of all foreigners from the King's councils (except, that is, for Prince George of Denmark, the ineffectual consort of the Princess Anne).

---

[88] *CJ* xiii. 130.

VII

So ended a session that William considered to have been 'the most dismal . . . I have ever had'. The King was left with little choice but to change the composition of his ministry and, after accepting Somers's resignation, he proceeded, slowly and painfully, to carry out a major reconstruction.[89] To many contemporaries, especially Whigs such as Cocks, it seemed that what was happening was a straightforward transfer of power to the Tories. The reality was more complex. The titular leader of the Tory party, Lord Roche-ster, did indeed come into office, but peripherally, as Lord Lieutenant of Ireland. Although it suited Whig propagandists to depict Rochester as chief minister,[90] the centre of gravity in the new ministry was really located else-where, in an alliance between the experienced finance minister, Lord God-olphin, brought back to be a Treasury commissioner, and the man who had led the opposition in the preceding Parliament, Robert Harley. A politician of infinite subtlety, Harley had ridden to power on a surge of 'Country' rhetoric, skilfully exploited so as to sweep along some Whigs together with Tories in its wake. But although he posed as an incorruptible patriot, and even as a tribune of the people, his deeper political instincts were managerial.[91] In the new Parliament which the Tory ministers advised the King to summon, Harley would be the linchpin of the Court party in the Commons, chosen (with William's prior approval) to the Speakership, where his command of parlia-mentary procedure and precedent, and his familiarity with the personalities of his fellow Members, enabled him to exercise a powerful influence over the transaction of business.

Harley's very considerable political talents — 'the crafty Speaker', Cocks called him — were all the more necessary because of the vital importance of the issues which the Parliament of 1701 had to resolve. First, and most immediate, was the question of the line of succession to the Crown, fractured by the death in July 1700 of the Duke of Gloucester, only surviving child of Princess Anne. The obvious solution, which William and his new ministers would recommend, to declare for the Electress Sophia of Hanover as the

---

[89] The following account of the ministerial changes of 1700–1 is based on Horwitz, *Parliament, Policy and Politics*, 275–80.

[90] *The True Patriot Vindicated; or, a Justification of . . . the Earl of Rochester . . .* (London, 1701); *The Apostates; or the Noble Cause of Liberty Detected . . .* (London, 1702).

[91] Of the two modern biographical studies of Harley, Angus McInnes, *Robert Harley, Puritan Politician* (London, 1970), is on the whole to be preferred to B. W. Hill, *Robert Harley: Speaker, Secretary of State and Premier Minister* (New Haven, 1988), though neither could be described as definitive. See also Edward Rowlands, 'Robert Harley's Parliamentary Apprenticeship: 1690–1695', *British Library Journal*, 15 (1989), 173–86; and David Hayton, 'Robert Harley's "Middle Way": The Puritan Heritage in Augustan Politics', ibid. 158–72.

nearest Protestant heir, was by no means certain to receive unanimous support. Gloucester's death had excited the ambitions of those High Tories whose attachment to the principle of hereditary right extended to a desire to encompass the restoration of King James or his son, 'the pretended Prince of Wales', and a few enthusiasts were reported to have paid clandestine visits to the exiled court at Saint-Germain.[92] Scepticism about a Hanoverian settlement was also to be found in the ranks of the Whigs, the more radical among them hoping to seize the opportunity to establish a 'commonwealth' or at least to hammer home their interpretation of the nature of the monarchy as elective.[93]

The other major issue to be put before the Parliament was the ratification of the second Partition Treaty, concluded the previous year between William, the Emperor Leopold, and Louis XIV, in order to settle the disputed succession to the ailing king of Spain, Carlos II. The signatories had agreed to parcel out the territories of the Spanish monarchy between the rival claimants, Bourbon and Habsburg, with Louis being given the kingdoms of Naples and Sicily outright in compensation for his abandonment of the prospect of one of his grandsons inheriting an undivided Spanish empire. Subsequently, however, the situation had been complicated by the French decision to repudiate the treaty after the death of Carlos II in October 1700, in favour of recognizing the will which the Spanish king had made, leaving all his dominions intact to the Bourbon claimant. Anxious for the security of the United Provinces, and for the maintenance of the balance of power in Europe, William was intent on bolstering the Grand Alliance which had withstood the power of France during the Nine Years' War, and to prepare, if need be, for another conflict. But as with the succession to his own crown, he could not be sure that Parliament would agree. The prospect of a further expensive and disruptive Continental war brought out the isolationist sentiments which recent party polemic had fostered in the consciousness of Tory backwoodsmen. Moreover, there were sound strategic arguments, espoused by Godolphin and Rochester among others, for regarding a Bourbon king of a united Spain as less of a long-term threat to international stability than a partitioned Spanish empire.

The problems faced by the new Court party were severe. The general election of January 1701 witnessed the return of more Tory Members than Whig, but, thanks to the strenuous pecuniary efforts of the Whig-dominated New East India Company in various venal constituencies, the margin of

---

[92] Paul Monod, 'Jacobitism and Country Principles in the Reign of William III', *Historical Journal*, 30 (1987), 306–7.

[93] Horwitz, *Parliament, Policy and Politics*, 277. This perhaps explains Cocks's otherwise eccentric description of the Commons in this Parliament as divided into three factions, Jacobites, Commonwealthmen, and the 'honest party' (to which he himself belonged).

victory was by no means as clear-cut as optimistic Tories had assumed it would be.[94] Indeed, the end result appeared in some places to be no more than a stalemate: for example, in Gloucestershire, where Cocks and Howe were re-elected, after a three-cornered contest involving an independent Whig, Sir Ralph Dutton.[95] Ministers would thus need to draw support from the customary sources — placemen, and the dependants and clients of courtiers — as well as from amenable Tory back-benchers, in order to be sure of a comfortable working majority in the Commons. In the early days of the session there were signs that Harley's personal influence was capable of attracting some Whigs to vote with the Court.[96] However, everything depended on keeping the Tories in line, and in this respect it was unfortunate that the King's expectations, a settlement of the succession in the house of Hanover, the ratification of the Partition Treaty, and a pledge of moral and financial backing for a firm resistance to French ambition, cut across the grain of High Tory prejudice. An additional complication was the rumbling presence within Tory ranks of several loose cannons of heavy calibre, in the persons of such formidable and experienced parliamentarians as Howe, Sir Christopher Musgrave and, above all, Sir Edward Seymour: men who had been accustomed to regard themselves as leaders of the Tory interest and who resented their continued exclusion from office under the new dispensation.

In essence, the story of the 1701 Parliament was of the ministry's failure to restrain the partisan violence of its Tory supporters.[97] At first, things had seemed to go well. Harley was duly chosen Speaker, by a two-to-one majority, and, despite a strident exhibition of pacifism by Howe during the debate on the Address, the Commons agreed on 18 February to stand by the terms of the 1678 treaty with the States-General, and such further commitments as the King might consider necessary for 'the preservation of the peace of Europe', excited into doing so by anger at the (calculated) exposure of an intercepted letter in which James II's adviser Lord Melfort had claimed that there was active French support for another Jacobite invasion. Equally gratifying was the fact that the Bill of Settlement began its parliamentary progress with near

---

[94] Ibid. 280; Robert Walcott, 'The East India Interest in the General Election of 1700–1701', _English Historical Review_, 71 (1956), 223–39.

[95] Beaufort MSS (the Duke of Beaufort, Badminton House, Glos.), [?Charles] Hancock to Beaufort, 1 Jan. 1701; HMC, _Portland MSS_, iv. 11.

[96] This much is apparent from the list of supporters of the new Court party in the Commons compiled in Feb. 1701 (BL Add. MS 28091, fos. 179–80), which may refer to a question in the House on 22 Feb. concerning a resolution of the committee of supply to make good the deficiencies of parliamentary funds.

[97] Again, I have based my account of this Parliament on Horwitz, _Parliament, Policy and Politics_, 280–93.

unanimous support for a Hanoverian succession. The Jacobite alternative figured only once in the debate at which the Hanoverians were named: a political solecism which earned the perpetrator, the Tory John Granville, a sharp rebuke from the Chair.[98]

There were straws in the wind, however. Tories may have accepted the Hanoverian succession, but many were unenthusiastic, to say the least, and in electing to the chair of the second-reading committee on the bill the tragi-comic figure of Sir John Bolles they sent out a signal which was interpreted by Whigs as a declaration of distaste for the settlement.[99] At the same time, Country Tory and County Whig back-benchers (of whom Cocks was one), exploited the opportunity to append to the bill a series of clauses to entrench upon the royal prerogative, designed to take effect at various stages: on the Hanoverian succession, on the death of King William, even in some cases immediately.[100] Included was a sweeping exclusion of placemen from the Commons, precisely the kind of measure which Cocks's friend Sir Edward Hussey had repeatedly proposed, in vain, since 1694, and several limitations on a future king which were by implication insults directed at William: making prior parliamentary consent necessary for royal journeys abroad and for waging war in defence of dominions not attached to the Crown; and prohibiting the appointment of foreigners to membership of the Privy Council and to civil and military office.

Worse was to follow. Tory criticism of the second Partition Treaty culminated in a vote in the Commons to begin impeachment proceedings against the Earl of Portland, and in probing for evidence Members stumbled upon the previous, secret, Partition Treaty of 1698. Potentially this left William himself exposed, but at the same time Somers and the other Junto lords were closely implicated, and it would seem as if the leaders of the new Court party may have consciously decided to turn the Tory back-benchers loose on the former ministers in order to divert attention from the King. In a memorable debate on 14 April, during which Somers descended to the lower House to make a personal statement, impeachments were voted against the ousted Lord Chancellor, and against Charles Montagu (now Lord Halifax), and Lord Orford. The vote to impeach Somers, the first to be taken, was carried at 11 o'clock at night, by only ten votes in a House of nearly 400.

---

[98] BL Add. MS 30000 E, fo. 63; Archives Nationales, Paris, K. 1301, no. 42, 'Extrait d'une Lettre de Rotterdam du 24 Mars 1701'. I owe these references to Dr Eveline Cruickshanks.

[99] William, 1st Earl Cowper, 'An Impartial History of Parties', in Campbell, *Lives of the Lord Chancellors*, iv. 425; [M. J. Routh (ed.),] *Bishop Burnet's History of His Own Time* (2nd edn., 6 vols.; Oxford, 1833), iv. 499–500.

[100] Dennis Rubini, *Court and Country 1688–1702* (London, 1967), App. C.

If the new Court party had gambled on focusing resentment against their Whig adversaries, they had failed to take account of the dangers involved in permitting the political temperature to rise so rapidly. The impeachment proceedings dominated much of the remainder of the session, giving rise to extended procedural wrangles between the two Houses, until at length the Whig majority in the Lords dismissed the charges. Not only did this take up valuable parliamentary time: even more unfortunate, as far as ministers were concerned, was the stimulus the impeachments gave to Tory extremism. It became harder to obtain a supply sufficient for the King to undertake the kind of forceful foreign policy Parliament had previously sanctioned, and early in May, in a debate which revealed divisions in both parties, the Commons 'put our ministry into very great disorder' by agreeing to a proposal from Jack Howe to retrench the civil list.[101] In revealing their reluctance to take the necessary steps towards another war, Tory back-benchers handed the Whigs a propaganda advantage that was quickly exploited, by means of county addresses pressing Parliament to make good its earlier promises; and when the Commons, in high resentment at the presentation of one such address, from Kent, imprisoned the five sponsors — known as the 'Kentish Petitioners' — another line of argument was opened, relating to the liberty of the subject, on which Whig writers could outflank their opponents.

The effect on Cocks of this train of events was to bring out his party loyalties to their fullest extent. As the wife of Bishop Burnet observed at the end of the session, there was no doubt that this time Cocks had 'voted well' throughout.[102] He had begun by speaking against Harley's election to the Chair, but on the grounds that the King's involvement, in persuading the outgoing Whig Speaker, Sir Thomas Littleton, to absent himself from the House for the vote, had been an unprecedented interference, and a 'pollution' of the '*sacra* of the House'. His committee-appointments early in the session reflected traditional 'Country' concerns: the regulation of elections, and introduction of a landed qualification for MPs; the preservation of the integrity of the jury system; and the resumption of Crown grants.[103] And over the additional clauses to the Bill of Settlement he not only spoke vigorously but on one occasion even found himself seconding Howe. Soon, however, the sheer factiousness of the Tories — 'the angry party', as he called them — drove him to exasperation. He deplored the fact that the Kidd affair, raised anew by the critics of the old ministry, had become 'a party cause', and

---

[101] The Under-Secretary of State, John Ellis, quoted in Horwitz, *Parliament, Policy and Politics*, 289.

[102] Surrey RO (Kingston), Somers MSS O/1/1, Mrs Burnet to Lady Jekyll [*c.* Nov. 1701].

[103] *CJ* xiii. 345, 350, 358, 367, 426.

for the same reason stood back from accusations against the Whig Chancellor of the Duchy of Lancaster, Lord Stamford. On the issue of the impeachments he took up arms as a forthright upholder of 'moderation and justice', in defence of the four lords. Delighted with the eventual outcome, he observed acidly that, 'were those little, villainous, poor wretches that hatched these evils against the lords tried for their former ills in Westminster Hall, there would have been as many demanding justice and rejoicing at their condemnation as were at these lords' acquittal'. But it was not merely revulsion from Tory vindictiveness that propelled him back into the ranks of what he himself termed 'the honestest party'. There were important principles at stake, notably the high priority he accorded to safeguarding the Protestant succession at home and the liberties of the allies abroad. Fear of Louis XIV, and sympathy for the plight of the Dutch, produced just such pledges of wholehearted support for the King as those on which the Whig party as a whole prided itself.

Meanwhile, having been compromised by the behaviour of some of their nominal adherents in the Commons, leading Tories, both inside and outside the administration, began to try to put matters right. On 9 May, in a debate arising from yet another appeal from the Dutch, Howe, of all people, joined in a motion pledging to do whatever was necessary to 'maintain the liberties of Europe'. Later that month Seymour, backed by the Speaker and various of his cronies, initiated a reconsideration of the civil list settlement which left William better off in theory, if not necessarily in practice, and paved the way for a satisfactory completion of the outstanding items on the supply agenda. This was enough to persuade the King to look more favourably on the ministers, and to acquiesce in a parliamentary stratagem devised by Godolphin to close the session on a positive note, and steal back the propaganda initiative from the Whigs. When giving the Royal Assent to the Act of Settlement and other measures, William was prevailed upon to express his gratitude to both Houses for the backing they had given the Dutch and other allies; and in return Tories in the Commons carried a resolution acknowledging the King's approval of their proceedings, and repeating generalized promises of support.[104]

VIII

As things turned out, not even this belated show of solidarity was enough to save the Tory ministry. During the autumn of 1701 the two parties each sought to convince the King that they rather than their rivals would be better able to 'serve him'. The Tories emphasized their control over the existing House of

[104] Ibid. 626–7.

Commons, as proved by the passage of the impeachments. The Whigs argued both from their entrenched majority in the Lords, and their supposedly greater popularity in the kingdom at large (as demonstrated by a co-ordinated campaign of county and borough addresses), which would enable them to overturn the Tory domination of the lower House should Parliament be dissolved.[105] Advised by Lord Sunderland, still 'the minister behind the curtain', William was predisposed to favour the Whigs, given the Tories' traditional reputation for queasiness on the succession issue, which outside observers naturally magnified, and his own recent experience of the truculence and xenophobia of Tory back-benchers.[106] Eventually Somers was admitted to the royal closet, and given the opportunity to press the case for a dissolution. The combined weight of opinion presented by the former Chancellor and by Sunderland made up the King's mind. His decision to call a new election was not accompanied by any immediate ministerial reshuffle, William preferring to wait on the polls. None the less, Godolphin promptly resigned. Harley, though publicly confident about his friends' electoral prospects, was privately furious, believing that the Tories' mulishness had cost them a game that at the beginning of the Parliament had seemed comfortably within their grasp.[107]

The second general election of 1701 was preceded by bitter exchanges in the press. Especially damaging to the Tories was the publication of a 'black list' of those MPs who had opposed making preparations for war with France. The unfortunate discovery of three outgoing Tory Members (including the pamphleteer Charles Davenant) ensconced in a Westminster tavern with the French chargé d'affaires, Poussin, smeared the party as a whole as tools of the French: either mercenary and corrupt, or, what was worse, actively Jacobite and traitorous. The results were to be seen in some spectacular Tory defeats in the election: two of the so-called 'Poussineers' (Davenant and Anthony Hammond) lost their seats, and in Gloucestershire Cocks and his partner, the pious philanthropist and charity-school enthusiast Maynard Colchester, took the scalp of Jack Howe, after an uninhibited campaign.[108] But the Whigs could not claim an overall victory. Although contemporary analyses differed, the best modern assessment would be that the Tories still held a narrow majority of seats.[109] From the King's point of view, the gamble had worked well enough to justify a decisive shift in the direction of his political manage-

---

[105] Horwitz, *Parliament, Policy and Politics*, 294–7.

[106] J. P. Kenyon, *Robert Spencer, Earl of Sunderland 1641–1702* (London, 1958), 321–4.

[107] BL Loan 29/128, draft by Harley on reverse of letter from William Bromley, 20 Sept. 1701; Loan 29/165, Misc. 97, 'Large Account, Revolution and Succession', 13–15.

[108] *Mems. of Family of Guise*, 143; BL Loan 29/69, Lady Anne Pye to Abigail Harley, 22 Nov. 1701; BL Add. MS 17677 WW, fos. 254, 319; James (ed.), *Letters Illustrative . . .* , iii. 158.

[109] Horwitz, *Parliament, Policy and Politics*, 297–9.

ment. Believing that the Court interest would be substantial enough to tip the balance in the Commons, he appointed a Whig, Lord Carlisle, to succeed Godolphin at the Treasury, and let it be known that he hoped to see Sir Thomas Littleton chosen instead of Harley to the Chair.[110]

The election of the Speaker, on 30 December 1701, must therefore have given William an unpleasant surprise.[111] With no less than 428 Members present, Harley carried the day by four votes, thanks to a number of Tory office-holders who were willing to defy royal displeasure, most notably Secretary of State Sir Charles Hedges and Admiral Sir George Rooke. The closeness of the division presaged a session marked by continual squabbling between the parties: over disputed elections (in which Cocks behaved as partially as any other Member of what he himself priggishly denounced as 'the most corrupt court in Christendom'); over the imposition of an oath to abjure the Pretender; and, most dramatically, over the attempts by each side to justify in retrospect their conduct in the preceding session. The most highly charged debates occurred in February, in a committee of the whole House on 'the rights, liberties and privileges of the House of Commons', when MPs voted down a Tory motion that the Commons 'had not right done them in the matter of the impeachments' and vindicated the right of the subject to address the King for a dissolution. At the same time, however, both parties showed that they had learned the lessons of 1701, and seemed to vie with each other in their eagerness to forward the King's business. Events in Europe were now moving inevitably towards another war, with a revived and renegotiated Grand Alliance placed before the Commons in January 1702. Tory isolationism would have been futile as well as politically counter-productive. Moreover, the death of King James II in September 1701 had cooled the allegiance of many lukewarm English Jacobites. There was genuine resentment in both parties at the French king's peremptory recognition of 'James III', and when an address was proposed in the Commons to ensure that in any new treaty 'reparation' would be demanded for this gratuitous insult, the motion came from none other than Sir Edward Seymour.

William's unexpected death on 8 March 1702, from a fever and respiratory illness sustained after a fall from his horse in Richmond Park in February, dealt a shattering blow to Whig expectations. Some sense of the psychological impact may be derived from reading the heartfelt panegyric which Cocks inserted at this point in his parliamentary diary. But although political

---

[110] Ibid. 299.
[111] For the course of this Parliament, at least until the death of William, my account rests on Horwitz, *Parliament, Policy and Politics*, 299–304.

prospects were transformed, the effect on the atmosphere at Westminster was not immediate. Tories assumed that the sympathies of the new Queen, Anne, would lie with the 'Church party'. Unlike her predecessor, she was English, and a staunch Anglican, facts which were indiscreetly proclaimed in her first speech from the throne;[112] and her political confidence reposed in the formidable duumvirate of Godolphin and the Earl (later Duke) of Marlborough, who, if they could be given any party label at this time, could only be described as Court Tories. Certainly, after Godolphin was installed as her 'premier minister' in domestic affairs, the political balance of the administration shifted back towards the Tories. But the 'duumvirs' were committed to continuing William's vigorous foreign policy, and in preparing for the now inevitable Continental war. There would be no going back on the course William had set.[113] So for the remainder of the Parliament, until the prorogation on 25 May 1702 (followed by a dissolution in June) matters went on much as before: the settling of supply to fulfil the terms of William's treaties concluded with the minimum of fuss, unaffected by the continuing rumbles of party hostility.

In what was destined to be his last parliamentary session, Cocks had been busier than ever. Early on he had been nominated for the first time to the committee on the Address, and he subsequently served on five other major committees, including that of 18 March on the abjuration oath.[114] As before, much of his work arose from private bills, and from questions relating to trade and manufacture, with now and then a local flavour, as when he helped bring in a bill to regulate the 'water-measure' of fruit, in response to a petition from the Gloucestershire grand jury, or when he presented another petition from Gloucestershire clothiers.[115] He also took a special interest in proposals for the relief of Quakers, acting for a time as their parliamentary agent, though in a characteristically ham-handed manner.

Interestingly, the session also witnessed a recrudescence of the 'Country' enthusiasm which had been such a feature of his earlier contributions to parliamentary debate. He assisted in the preparation of yet another bill to prevent corruption at parliamentary elections, and was also nominated to the drafting committee on the public accounts bill, offering a clause of his own 'to

---

[112] Edward Gregg, *Queen Anne* (London, 1980), 152–3.

[113] Ibid. 151–3; Horwitz, *Parliament, Policy and Politics*, 304; I. F. Burton, *The Captain-General: The Career of John Churchill, Duke of Marlborough, from 1702 to 1711* (London, 1968), 22–3.

[114] *CJ* xiii. 647, 654, 683, 782, 808, 830. The other major committees were to prepare the Public Accounts Bill and a bill to prevent corruption at parliamentary elections (6, 17 Jan.), and to draft the addresses of condolence on the death of King William and thanks for the new Queen's speech from the throne (8, 30 Mar.).   [115] Ibid. 657, 710, 740.

inquire into the briberies and corruptions used amongst the officers concerned in managing the King's treasure'.[116] Attempts to resurrect other favourite themes of former sessions met with less success: a motion of his on 11 February for a resumption of 'all the grants made since the Revolution' failed to find a seconder; and a month or so later he was joined only by Sir Edward Hussey in seeking to investigate the revenue actually produced by the duties appropriated for the civil list. But he was still aware of the need to temper constitutional principle with a careful regard for the wider implications of any weakening of English power at this crisis in European affairs. His swansong was a speech on 4 May 1702, on a subject which had frequently exercised him in the past, the narrow-minded ingratitude of Tories who would refuse to employ any 'foreign' army officers in the Queen's forces, even though these 'foreigners' were themselves refugees from French, or French-inspired, persecutions abroad, and in many cases had already given sterling voluntary service in defence of English liberties. 'We are engaged in a war with France', he reminded the House,

and I hope we shall reserve all our malice and envy for France, and not spend it upon one another. I know the hopes and desire to get places has been the only thing that has so long supported party among us and I hope that those that have had the places so long will be satisfied with their so long enjoyment of them, and those that have them now will be satisfied with the possession of them, and that we that never had nor expected places shall all of us join to support our common country. I am sure for my part, though my estate is not a great one, yet it serves my turn, and I don't spend it all every year; if other gent[lemen] would do so too there would not be such hunting after places . . . I am of opinion that it will be more dangerous to our constitution not to reward those who have served us faithfully, and much more not to pay those that have shed their blood for us in a former war . . . I will therefore preserve that part of the constitution, and venture the other as the less dangerous . . .

IX

In common with the rest of his party, Cocks faced an uphill fight to secure re-election when the country went to the polls again in the summer of 1702. Queen Anne's remodelling of the ministry in favour of High Churchmen of her own kidney transmitted a clear message to the constituencies, and voters responded by returning a new House of Commons dominated by the Tories. Cocks's own position in Gloucestershire had been shaken as early as March, when he was defeated by Jack Howe in a contest for foreman of the grand jury. He therefore needed little prompting to abandon the county

---

[116] Ibid. 654, 683.

election, and instead turned his eyes back towards the borough of Tewkesbury, but in the event did not pursue his candidacy there either, and found himself without a parliamentary seat.[117] He remained active in local affairs, attempting without success to exploit grand jury presentments to make party-political points, and beseeching ministers and men of influence to reverse the recent Tory purge of the Gloucestershire commission of the peace. Personal connexions with the Junto lords were re-established, even though he was still enough of an 'old' Whig to retain some suspicion of 'courtiers' and professional politicians. (As always Somers was the exception: it was easy to flatter Cocks with a report that Somers himself would welcome his return to Parliament.)[118] Surprisingly, he avoided the county election again in the more favourable circumstances of 1705, deciding to try his luck in the borough of Evesham, where he was rejected after a contest marked by 'a great deal of foul play', as he himself described it.[119] Three years later, having unsuccessfully sought the recommendation of the Gloucestershire Whigs for a county seat, he stood against the two candidates who had been selected, only to meet with a decisive defeat.[120]

Compulsory rustication turned Cocks's mind towards contemplation, and literary composition. In about 1705 he wrote: 'I have since the last Parliament of King William retired and lived mostly in the country, where I have [?none] to advise or consult with, but to reflect on things past and to make my conclusions that, if such and suc[h] causes had formerly such and such effects, the same causes will have the same effects probably again.'[121] His pen was never still: there were essays and 'meditations', translations from foreign authors, a history of the reign of Henri III of France which ran 'almost parallel with more recent transactions', as well as the customary charges to grand juries. He even tried his hand at poetry, and a satirical playlet on the theme of the ministerial revolution of 1710.[122] But aside from the captive audiences at quarter sessions, these writings reached a readership no wider than a coterie of like-minded acquaintances, such as John, Lord Hervey (the future first Earl of Bristol), with whom Cocks carried on a regular and evidently prolix correspondence. Sadly, only Hervey's letters have survived, but they are enough to suggest the frequency of the exchanges and the tenor of

---

[117] BL Loan 29/154, Robert Price to Robert Harley, 30 Mar. 1702.

[118] Boston Public Library, Boston, Mass., MS K.5.5. (Somerset papers), Cocks to [Halifax], 11 Aug. 1703, Halifax to [Somerset], 17 Aug. 1703, Somers to [Somerset], n.d.; HMC, *Portland MSS*, iv. 86–7; *Hervey Letterbooks*, i. 182, 199–200.

[119] George Harris Healey (ed.), *The Letters of Daniel Defoe* (Oxford, 1955), 111.

[120] Bodl. MS Ballard 31, fo. 50, William Bishop to Arthur Charlett, 21 July 1707; BL Loan 29/158, Nathaniel Stephens to Robert Harley, 13 Dec. 1707; *Flying Post*, 18–20 May 1708.

[121] MS Eng. hist. b. 210, fo. 30.   [122] *Hervey Letterbooks*, i. 335–6.

Cocks's contribution, which ranged over a great variety of topics — not only politics, but economics and, increasingly, matters of religion. After receiving one 'discourse' in 1704, Hervey wrote admiringly (and perhaps with a tinge of unappreciated irony), 'though I always took you to be an honest, good man, I should never have believed you so able a divine, so skilful a merchant, and so general a statesman as I find by your writings'.[123]

In common with other 'Country Whigs' or 'commonwealthsmen', Cocks now gave first priority to the successful prosecution of the war, and was prepared to overlook many previous grievances against an over-mighty executive in order to fulfil the more urgent necessity of defeating 'the great coward tyrant France'.[124] There was still room in his mind for indignation over corruption at elections, and against placemen, or 'moneyed men', who put private concerns before the public interest, but the single most important theme of all these effusions was the danger to religion and liberty presented by the growth of 'popery': abroad through the extension of French military power; and at home through the underhand activities of Catholics and Jacobites, aided by the factionalism of the Tories. His grand jury charge in 1706 called for unity among Protestants, and an end to the persecution of 'our Dissenting brethren', while at the same time defending the continuance of penal laws against Catholics, whose 'bloody principles, their massacres, their assassinations, make them uncomeattable [*sic*] by reason and render them criminals and malefactors'.[125] Naturally he lionized Marlborough, whom he portrayed as a reincarnated Scipio Africanus, and praised the merits of the Duchess; while vilifying their Tory critics as 'incendiaries' and opportunists.[126] Harley, the modern Machiavel, and fellow conspirators Jack Howe and Sir Christopher Musgrave, were either Jacobites or, worse still, latter-day Catilines: men motivated by greed and malice, whose ambition was to rule or destroy the state.[127]

The great crisis over the royal succession in the last years of Queen Anne's reign inspired Cocks to new bursts of creative energy. He drew up addresses for the Gloucestershire freeholders, which they declined to adopt; drafted an 'imaginary speech' in favour of the house of Hanover; urged Whigs in Parliament to petition for an invitation to the Electoral Prince to come over

---

[123] Ibid. i. 182, 199–200, 205–7, 215–20, 229–30, 262–6, 270–5, 302–3, 335–9, 389–90; ii. 11–12. The quotation is taken from i. 216.

[124] A point made originally in Duke-Evans, 'English Commonwealthsmen'. The quotation is from MS Eng. hist. b. 210, fo. 32v. [125] MS Eng. hist. b. 210, fo. 32.

[126] Ibid. 33, 52ᵛ. The comparison was not without a hidden sting, for Cocks's version obliged Scipio/Marlborough to admit that 'in my security I misapplied public money'.

[127] Ibid. 30ᵛ, 44–5, 52–3, 60–1.

to Britain before Queen Anne should die.[128] In 1714 he resisted the 'persuasions' of one of the outgoing Whig knights of the shire, Matthew Ducie Moreton, to join in contesting the general election, but once the 'happy accession' had been accomplished reconsidered the offer. 'Truly, sir', he told Moreton, 'I have a desire to appear once more in public in order to take leave of my old friends, and to put a helping hand to part with some enemies to my country.' Sadly, he found that he had missed the boat, and his noble efforts in his party's cause passed unrewarded. The Gloucestershire Whigs, who in any case probably regarded him as too much of a maverick, had already settled upon other candidates.[129]

X

Although he was no longer even a candidate for Parliament, Cocks still had a part to play on the public stage. He held on to his position as chairman of the Gloucestershire quarter sessions, and the charges he gave were no less trenchant and politically oriented than ever. Also, at long last, he began to see some of his writings published. The history of Henri III had previously aroused some literary hopes, only to disappoint,[130] but in the panic-ridden atmosphere of early Hanoverian politics, Cocks's strident anti-Jacobitism had a strong polemical value. Hervey recommended publishing 'your excellent discourse you entertained your countrymen with' at the sessions in 1715,[131] and two years later one of the charges did find its way into print. Although he began it by expatiating on the duty of the civil magistrate to enforce the law, 'to secure property' and 'to oblige men, out of fear of penalties, to live honestly and justly', Cocks developed his harangue into a full-blown defence of the Hanoverian Succession, a justification of the right of resistance, as exercised at the Revolution, and a virulent denunciation of the Pretender, who, he wrote, had been 'educated in arbitrary French principles [and] instructed in all the cruel arts of popery'. Catholics suffered their customary verbal lashing, but so too did the 'High Church plotters', whose real motives were shown to be self-interest, a devotion to 'arbitrary power', and even crypto-Catholicism.[132]

After a period of complete withdrawal from 'all public business', even the routine duties of a justice of the peace, a retreat occasioned by 'the great infirmities of my body', Cocks returned to print in 1721. This time he offered

---

[128] Ibid. 63–4; *Hervey Letterbooks*, i. 389.
[129] Glos. RO, Ducie MSS D340a/C22/10, 12, Cocks to Moreton, 17 Aug. 1714, Richard Mariett to same, 4 Oct. 1714.   [130] *Hervey Letterbooks*, ii. 12.
[131] Ibid.   [132] See above n. 45.

a belated postscript to the 'Bangorian controversy', the paper and pulpit war over the relationship of church and state provoked by a sermon preached in 1717 by the then Bishop of Bangor, Benjamin Hoadly, which had seemed to deny all ecclesiastical authority.[133] Cocks's argument was predictably downright. In *A Perfect Discovery of Longitude* he claimed to 'prove' that Parliament was 'the fittest body of men to be entrusted with the government of the Church'. Once again, it was the High Church party, that 'generation of vipers' with neo-papist ambitions, who were the principal objects of his loathing, and a comprehensive union of Protestants his ultimate aim.[134] These ideas were elaborated the following year in a second pamphlet, *The Church of England Secured . . .*, which judged the established church by the law of reason and the pattern of primitive Christianity. In a two-pronged attack, Cocks denounced persecution, and the very notion of an apostolic succession: both were derived from popery, and in their different ways demonstrated that the High Churchmen were seeking to emulate Antichrist. As the invective gathered pace, Cocks launched into a violent condemnation of 'priestcraft', which he regarded as entirely distinct from real religion. Some passages were simply abusive. The pamphlet ended with a call for 'another reformation' in the hearts of men, to be encouraged by a series of specific measures enacted by Parliament, a manifesto which was a mixture of 'Low Church' theology, evangelical zeal, and brutal Erastianism. Recommendations included the prohibition of genuflection at communion; a tightening-up of ordination procedures; penalties for pluralism and non-residence; the abolition of ecclesiastical courts; and, lastly, the appointment by the secular authorities of teachers and 'overseers' to instruct the people in the principles of true religion and morality.[135]

It was inconceivable that self-respecting Anglican clergymen of orthodox bent should permit this kind of attack to pass without a response, and Cocks soon found himself overtaken by a squall of controversy. Some of the buffets to which he was subjected were particularly sharp, most notably perhaps when the scholar and antiquarian Zachary Grey, of Trinity Hall, Cambridge, produced a direct reply in the form of a tract entitled, *The Knight of Dumbleton Foiled at His Own Weapon . . .*, which was a thorough demolition of Cocks's shaky theology and dubious patristics.[136] Undaunted, Cocks fired off a third volley of his own, a pamphlet with the somewhat eccentric

---

[133] John Hunt, *Religious Thought in England from the Reformation to the End of the Last Century* (3 vols.; London, 1870–3), iii. 32–49; Norman Sykes, *William Wake Archbishop of Canterbury 1657–1737* (2 vols.; Cambridge, 1957), ii. 161–5, 181–2.

[134] See above, n. 28.   [135] See above, n. 33.

[136] [Zachary Grey,] *The Knight of Dumbleton Foiled at His Own Weapon . . .* (London, 1723).

title, *Over Shoes, Over Boots*.[137] This contained nothing new, but the tone became, if possible, even more scurrilous and offensively anticlerical. Further rejoinders followed, including the anonymous, *A Pair of Clean Shoes and Boots for a Dirty Baronet, Who Was Lately Terribly Mir'd by Wading beyond His Depth in Controversy*, which repaid him in kind; Cocks's own works were reissued in new editions; and in 1723 he published yet another restatement of his views, cast as a *Farewel* [sic] *Sermon*, the formula emphasizing his conviction that he was himself as good as any parson.[138] In it he drew heavily on an unpublished paper he had drafted at the time of the debates on the Schism Bill in 1714, to demonstrate, first and foremost, that 'the Christian religion was not introduced by power and force'.[139] Farewells were a little premature, however, for in the wake of the Atterbury Plot, and perhaps revived by the taste of battle, and the notoriety he had won for himself as a valiant opponent of priestcraft, he returned to the Gloucestershire quarter sessions in 1723 to deliver another powerful charge. Reminding his audience, should they need reminding, of the continuing perils of popery and Jacobitism, he pleaded for all true Protestants to 'leave off faction', that is to say, become Whigs. In so doing he betrayed the considerable distance he had travelled from his former dedication to 'Country' virtue by the casuistry with which he now exonerated government ministers from criticism over their involvement in the South Sea Bubble.[140]

Despite the disabling mortifications of gout, which necessitated a trip to Bath in the last year of his life,[141] Cocks maintained a hectic pace to the end of his days. Hardly had he buried his wife Frances in 1724 than he remarried, by November of the same year, Mary Bethell, sister of Hugh Bethell of Swindon in Yorkshire, Whig Member for Pontefract in the 1715 Parliament.[142] The will he prepared in order to provide for her also charged his estate with some £20,000 to be raised for portions for any daughters of the marriage, but in the two years of wedlock which the couple were vouchsafed no children appeared.[143] There was, however, one more literary production, eventually published posthumously in 1727 as *A True and Impartial Inquiry Made into the Late Bloody Execution at Thorn* . . . [the summary justice meted out by Augustus II of Poland in December 1724 to ten of his Protestant subjects in

[137] See above, n. 8.

[138] *A Pair of Clean Shoes and Boots for a Dirty Baronet, Who Was Lately Terribly Mir'd by Wading beyond His Depth in Controversy* . . . *By a Lover of the Clergy* (London, 1722).

[139] Bodl. MS Eng. misc. b. 433, fo. 30.   [140] See above, n. 59.

[141] MS Eng. hist. b. 210, fo. 23.

[142] J. W. Clay (ed.), *Dugdale's Visitation of Yorkshire* . . . (3 vols.; Exeter, 1899–1917), iii. 135.

[143] See above, n. 4. Parts of the will are quoted in Somers Cocks, *Hist. Cocks. Fam.*, pt. 3, p. 110.

'Thorn' (Torún) who had attacked a local Jesuit college], *together with a Vindication of Some of the Tenets of the Quakers . . .* , in which neither subject was so much as mentioned in passing. Instead the pamphlet was simply a stale reprise of past polemics against popery and High Church priestcraft, the flavour of which is adequately conveyed by the following description of an Anglican ordination:

We often see an ignorant, immoral dunce, because he was a relation of the bishop's or his wife's, or for marrying a poor relation or an old servant maid, or sometimes without that drudgery, by making a present to the wife or steward, it will open a way, and prevail upon an old, doting fellow to lay his hands on him, and by that means imprint on him an indelible character, and give him credentials to be from thenceforth an ambassador of Heaven.[144]

Cocks died about 21 October 1726,[145] and was buried in Dumbleton parish church. Besides the *True and Impartial Inquiry Made into the Late Bloody Execution at Thorn*, he had left another political testament, in the form of a curious coda to his will. In characteristic style, he had already included in the preamble some unsolicited advice to his beneficiaries, including a declaration of the uselessness of deathbed repentance, and more mundanely practical advice as to the desirability of making one's will in good time, since 'in weakness and disordering of body and mind lawyers and divines are uneasy company'. What came at the end was a request to

my friends and relations to serve God in a manner worthy of Him, and not to disturb the peace of their country with party and idle distinctions, which in weak persons is only the effect of their folly in cunning of private interest and ambition. I desire them to love one the other, to be kind to their neighbours, and be faithful and loyal to King George and to have more regard to the Protestant interest than to any private views whatever.

The most important material provision of the will concerned the succession to Dumbleton. Since Cocks had died childless, the baronetcy was inherited by his brother Robert, the rector of Bladon. But the estate was to descend immediately to Robert's second surviving son, another Robert, thus bypassing not only the new baronet himself, but his first son (and heir apparent to the title) Charles. The male children of the eldest son were the last in the immediate line of remainders. If the Dumbleton family failed completely to produce a male heir, the succession shifted over to cousins, in the first place to Charles Cocks, the son-in-law of Lord Somers and formerly MP for Worcester. There was also

---

[144] See above, n. 26 (the quotation is from p. 9). Cf. Henry Neville's remark, questioning the power of ordination 'to metamorphose a poor lay idiot into a heavenly creature': Robbins (ed.), *Two English Republican Tracts*, 118.   [145] *The Historical Register*, 1726, Chronicon, 40.

a clause recommending that the third baronet's youngest son, if ordained a priest, should be presented to the living of Dumbleton; a sharp irony in view of Sir Richard's previous strictures on clerical nepotism.

Sadly, the detailed provision in the will for contingent remainders proved to be prescient. By the time Cocks's nephew Robert had succeeded his father, and united baronetcy with estate, his brothers were all dead, and his own son represented the only surviving male line in the family. In 1750 a 'cruel distemper' swept through the fourth baronet's household, killing his wife and three of his four children, and leaving only a daughter, Dorothy. So when in 1765 Sir Robert himself sustained a fatal injury from a fall from his horse the title became extinct and Dumbleton passed to a John Cocks, younger son of Charles Cocks of Worcester. Further dynastic accidents reunited in the person of this John Cocks other family lands in Herefordshire, and then the Somers inheritance, and in 1784 his son was raised to the peerage as Baron Somers of the second creation. Dumbleton was now only one property in a vast conglomerate estate, and under the first Lord Somers the house was demolished.[146]

THE DIARY

What happened to Cocks's personal papers after his death is a mystery. They may ultimately have been inherited, along with the estate, by John Cocks of Worcester, but although the present seat of Baron Somers's descendants, Eastnor Castle in Herefordshire, contains portraits of Cocks himself and his brother Charles, the Dumbleton branch of the family seems not to be represented in the archive.[147] The readiest alternative explanation would be that they passed to Sir Richard's great-niece Dorothy, the only surviving child

---

[146] Somers Cocks, *Hist. Cocks Fam.*, typescript of revised chapter on 'The Cocks Family of Dumbleton' (a copy of which is deposited in the Eastnor Castle MSS (Mr J. F. S. Hervey-Bathurst, Eastnor Castle, Ledbury, Hereford and Worcester), 16–21. Once again I must record a very considerable obligation to Mr Somers Cocks, for permitting me to see and make use of the important new material in his revised account of the family.

[147] National Register of Archives, Report 5461, Somers Cocks MSS at Eastnor Castle, lists only a few deeds relating to Dumbleton (p. 2). I am grateful to Mrs Julia Page for further information concerning the muniments. On Eastnor, see the articles by Alistair Rowan: 'Eastnor Castle, Herefordshire', *Country Life*, 7, 21 Mar. 1968. Mr Somers Cocks has suggested to me that perhaps the likeliest vendor of manuscripts from Eastnor would have been Lady Henry Somerset (d. 1921), daughter and heiress of the 3rd (and last) Earl Somers, who was responsible for the sale of various items from the castle, including a family portrait. But this of course must remain speculation.

of the fourth baronet. She died unmarried in 1767, leaving only one close relation, a maiden aunt, Sarah, who was the very last of the Dumbleton line.[148]

At any event the provenance of the 'parliamentary diary' itself remains obscure. The two volumes in which it is contained were purchased by a Devon bookseller, Richard Gilbertson, at an auction in Torquay in the summer of 1964, and sold by him a few months later to the Bodleian Library, where they were catalogued as MSS English hist. b. 209–10.[149] The second of the two volumes had suffered the loss of at least ten folios, which at some point had been torn out.[150] Interestingly, the volumes purchased by Mr Gilbertson had included six loose folio leaves, consisting of writings by Cocks of a somewhat later date, but these were not part of the missing section. The six leaves were subsequently purchased by the Bodleian, and incorporated into MS English misc. b. 433 (as fos. 30–5).[151]

Originally the two volumes had been intended as account books. The first (MS Eng. hist. b. 209) was inscribed on the cover, 'Randall Brisco. Liber Receptorum' and dated 1642/3;[152] the second (MS Eng. hist. b. 210), which contains various personal and estate accounts of Sir Richard's father, from 1660 to 1664, was similarly inscribed, 'Richard Cocks. A booke of account concerning . . . my estate as alsoe severall observacions thereupon since . . . 1655', and, 'Richard Cocks His observations upon those severall observacions since . . . 1679'.[153] In these barely used account books Sir Richard had entered up many of his writings, beginning with essays and verses composed in the early 1680s and ending in about 1714, though with the addition of a prescription for gout, 'wrote at Bath' in 1726.

As a general rule the contents of the volumes follow chronological order. The first begins with a series of essays, meditations, and prayers: many are without a specific date but those that can be dated all come within the years

[148] Somers Cocks, typescript of revised account of Cocks family of Dumbleton, p. 19.

[149] The trail runs cold at the auctioneers, Bearnes of Torquay, whose existing records do not go back far enough to enable the vendor to be identified. I am very grateful to Bodley's Librarian for permitting me to see items of correspondence in the library's archives between his predecessor and Mr Gilbertson in Sept. and Oct. 1964, dealing with the purchase of the manuscripts; and to Mr Gilbertson himself for sharing with me his memories of the circumstances of the auction sale.

[150] Fragments of fos. 15–22 remain adhering to the spine of the volume. The fact that Cocks's account of the Parliament of 1701/2, which opens at fo. 1, omits the first four weeks of the session and begins in what appears to be the middle of a sentence would suggest that a number of preceding leaves had also been excised.

[151] Photocopies of these separate leaves, made before some words were lost from the corners of the originals, are kept at Bodl. MS Facs. b. 18, fos. 119–30.

[152] Parchment cover kept as MS Eng. hist. b. 210*/1.

[153] Cover kept as MS Eng. hist. b. 210*/2.

1682–96, except perhaps for a history of France, which may be identical with the account of the reign of Henri III sent to Lord Hervey in 1712.[154] Starting anew, and this time running from back to front, is the sequence that I have called the 'parliamentary diary' of 1698–1701. This begins with a series of speeches made by Cocks in the 1698/9 session, often placed in context with a brief account of the surrounding debate or some autobiographical reminiscence, and occasionally departing from strict chronology. Cocks then enters a number of commentaries on particular topics — the question of the poor, proposals to reform the centralized system for selling woollen cloth, the conduct of business in Parliament, and so on — some of which may well have been intended as Commons speeches. The next parliamentary session follows, represented by a series of accounts of set-piece debates, all featuring a contribution of some kind from the compiler, and this time in strict chronological sequence. After four folios of miscellaneous matter (this time clearly not versions of speeches) Cocks begins his account of the Parliament of 1701, starting out in autobiographical fashion but quickly settling into a different format as a diary of the session. The second volume is more straightforward in arrangement, picking up where the other left off with a diary of the 1701/2 Parliament (of which the first 28 days are missing).[155] Then come more essays, letters, and diverse items, disposed chronologically and covering the period 1705–c.1714.

The date of composition of the volumes cannot be established with certainty, but the shape of the first two parliamentary sections is inconsistent with a regular practice of diary- or journal-keeping, and implies instead a retrospective compilation. Moreover, the handwriting seems uniform, which would also argue against piecemeal construction over a long period. Alterations can occasionally be observed in the colour and intensity of the ink, but insufficient to imply any serious interruption to the process. It may be suggested, therefore, that at some stage in his life, public and estate duties permitting, Cocks began entering items into these volumes, most probably making fair copies from drafts or separate documents, such as the 'abstracts of the statutes relating to the poor', which he sent to Archbishop Tenison of Canterbury in May 1700, and which were included in the first of the volumes at an appropriate point, after the prorogation of the 1698–1700 Parliament and before the opening of the next, in January 1701.[156]

Examples of other such albums or copybooks of the period would allow for a date of compilation later (possibly much later) than the date of the

---

[154] *Hervey Letterbooks*, i. 335–9.   [155] The Parliament had assembled on 30 Dec.
[156] Lambeth Palace Lib., MS 640, pp. 501–23; MS Eng. hist. b. 209, fo. 81ᵛ.

documents being copied. The memoranda- or commonplace-books of the MP and minor *littérateur* Anthony Hammond include within the same covers material some ten to fifteen years apart.[157] Still more telling, perhaps, are the Irish parliamentary diaries of Sir John Perceval, later first Earl of Egmont, which were clearly reconstructed some years after the event from notes or copies of letters written at the time.[158] In Cocks's case there are hints, scattered across the diaries, of a delay before compilation. His own contribution to the debate of February 1699 on the Irish forfeitures resumption, for instance, manages to include a quotation(unacknowledged) from Charles Davenant's subsequent pamphlet, *A Discourse upon Grants and Resumptions*, while disparaging remarks on Jack Howe, inserted into Cocks's account of Commons proceedings in April 1701, echo another unpublished tract, *Jura Populi Anglicani*, which appeared later that year. It is also possible that his accounts of the speeches on Captain Kidd's affair in March 1701 included material properly belonging to the previous debate on the same subject in December 1699, a confusion which would be most satisfactorily explained by his having muddled his notes long afterwards; most likely in the period of retirement from active political involvement, after 1702, when we know from other sources, especially Hervey's testimony, that Cocks withdrew to his study and devoted himself largely to the exercise of his pen.

Assuming that Cocks compiled his 'parliamentary diaries' in retrospect, what materials would have been available to him? In the first place, there would be versions of his own speeches, and observations he had made on the proceedings in the House, preserved either in note form or written out in full, and occasionally, perhaps, included in letters of Westminster news sent to friends in the country, copies of which he may have kept.[159] Comparison with other parliamentary reporting in these sessions would invite the conclusion that Cocks probably relied more on copies of his letters than on notes taken in the Chamber, for his accounts of debates often focus on the more important exchanges, which also feature in contemporary correspondence.[160] In the case of the debate of 13 February 1700 on Crown grants, for which a set of notes survives in the papers of another Member, the Junto Whig Edward Clarke, Cocks's version is markedly inferior, recording fewer contributions than

---

[157] Bodl. MSS Rawlinson D. 174, 360, 386, 738, 968.

[158] David Hayton (ed.), 'An Irish Parliamentary Diary from the Reign of Queen Anne', *Analecta Hibernica*, 30 (1982), 106.

[159] See e.g. BL Add. MS 34730, fos. 238–9, 250, Cocks to Mariett, 22 Feb. [1700], 18 Mar. 1698[/9].

[160] See e.g. the letters of James Lowther in the Lonsdale MSS at Cumbria RO (Carlisle), the reports sent back to Liverpool corporation in the Norris MSS at Liverpool RO, and the various despatches of Dutch, French, and Prussian diplomats.

Clarke and generally telescoping proceedings. Nor can Cocks's reporting
compare with that of another Commons note-taker, the future Whig Lord
Chancellor William Cowper, during the 1698/9 session.[161] However, both of
these were special cases: Clarke in 1700 was presumably acting for his patron,
Lord Chancellor Somers, a principal target of opposition speeches, and was
therefore required to be as comprehensive as possible; while Cowper made his
notes while seated in the chair of the committees of supply and ways and
means, enjoying ampler freedom and opportunity to write than a back-
bencher jostling for space and, we may assume, anxious over his own
participation in the debate. Other notes of debates were conspicuously less
full than Clarke's or Cowper's. Robert Harley's archive, for instance, contains
many sets of notes on Commons debates, usually scribbled in pencil in the
little time that was available to him, and giving scant information on the
content of individual speeches.[162]

Besides records of this kind which he had made himself or perhaps had
obtained from some other observer of the proceedings of the House, Cocks
would have had access to various auxiliary materials with which to jog his
memory, supply gaps and even possibly to enable him to cover a period when
he was himself absent from Parliament. It would appear that he left Westminster before the end of the 1701 Parliament, since he was given leave of absence
(for a fortnight) on 3 June and his name does not appear again in the *Journals*
during the remainder of that session. Yet his 'diary' continues until the closing
day, the 24th.[163] While still a Member of Parliament he would have been able
to consult the draft *Journals* kept by the clerk of the House; afterwards he
would have had to rely on the published *Votes*, less detailed than the *Journals*
— omitting all mention of divisions, for example — but providing a skeletal
account of the day's proceedings. It seems significant that the contents of the
diary for the last three weeks of the 1701 Parliament, when he was almost
certainly absent, fail to improve on the basic information to be found in the
Votes, and indeed follow the spelling of the name of one Member, James
Brydges, as 'Bruges', from the official record.[164] However, if Cocks used the

---

[161] Published in 'Debates 1697–9', 392–401.

[162] BL Loan 29/10(1), notes, 31 Jan. 1695/6, 14 Apr. 1696, 'Breviat to the Lugg'; 29/10(2), notes
7/8, 11 Jan. 1697/8; 29/31, 'East Grinstead election . . .', 'East Grinstead', case of Weobley
election; 29/35(1), notes, Dec. 1697 and n.d.; 29/35(2), notes, 1699 (two sets); 29/206, fo. 328;
29/207, fos. 10, 21, 29; 29/215, fos. 137, 203, 357; 29/278, notes, n.d. (two sets); 29/280, notes, 20
Oct. 1696; 29/285, notes, 16 Dec. 1698; 29/286, notes, 1699; 29/290, notes, n.d.; 29/290, notes, n.d.

[163] *CJ* xiii. 592.

[164] *Votes* for 1701, nos. 93, 99 (pp. 195, 210). Once again I must record a debt to Miss Kemp, for
passing on to me photocopies collected by her of the *Votes* for the period 4 Jan. 1699–5 May 1702.
With her permission these have been deposited with the History of Parliament Trust.

Votes at other times as a supplementary source, he cannot have done so consistently, since he differed from them on many occasions. Contemporary pamphlets, and broadsheets on particular cases, provided an alternative means of filling out the bare outline of a debate,[165] as distinct from the newspapers of the period, which did not report parliamentary debates and seem to have given the diarist little if any assistance.

More intriguing is the possibility that Cocks may have used the many newsletters current at the time. One of these, which was sent on a regular basis to former Secretary of State Sir William Trumbull,[166] was a strictly parliamentary edition; essentially the same as the *Votes* but sometimes giving more information about debates, with a tendency to summarize the less interesting proceedings. The coincidence of one such summary in May 1701 with an identical comment by Cocks on the day's business promotes the notion that Cocks may have resorted to them when drawing a blank elsewhere. No such coincidence attends the other surviving newsletters of the period, but the inclusion of snippets of parliamentary proceedings in the daily digests of news prepared by annalists such as Narcissus Luttrell argues that there may have been other such parliamentary newsletters in existence, which are not yet known to us.[167] Moreover, the hypothesis put forward in the most detailed modern analysis of the parliamentary reporting prepared for foreign courts, namely that different diplomats sometimes drew on a common source, may also imply that there was at the time an unofficial agency or service for parliamentary news.[168]

Whatever Cocks's sources (and it is worth repeating that the little we know can only be deduced from comparative textual analysis, for there is no direct evidence for his methods of compilation), the importance of the diary remains undiminished. Besides the fact that it covers four parliamentary sessions in which vital questions of state were decided, and significant developments took place in the evolution of English party politics, it is the only substantial

---

[165] Most notably, perhaps [James Drake,] *The History of the Last Parliament* . . . (London, 1702), a lengthy political narrative of the Parliament of 1701.

[166] BL Trumbull Add. MS 130.

[167] The best surviving runs of newsletters are in the Newdigate collection in the Folger Shakespeare Library, Washington, DC; in the Earl of Strathmore's muniments at Glamis Castle; and in the Harley papers in the British Library (Loan 29/8, 358 — Dyer's newsletters). See Henry L. Snyder, 'Newsletters in England 1689–1715 with Special Reference to John Dyer — A Byway in the History of England', in Donovan H. Bond and W. Reynolds McLeod (edd.), *Newsletters to Newspapers: Eighteenth Century Journalism* (Morgantown, W. Va., 1977), esp. 6–7. Snyder claims that Luttrell, Hearne and others produced 'little more than a paraphrase of contemporary newsletters' (p. 12).

[168] J. F. G. Lowe, 'Parliamentary Debates in 1701, from the Reports of Foreign Observers', MA thesis (Liverpool, 1960), 18–34.

parliamentary diary yet to have been discovered between Narcissus Luttrell's and Anchitell Grey's reports of debates in the early 1690s, and Sir Edward Knatchbull's in the 1720s.[169] There is an incomplete account by William Cowper of the session of 1698/9, and brief and sparse relations of the 1710/11 and 1711/12 sessions by the Yorkshire Tory Sir Arthur Kaye;[170] otherwise, all we have are scraps of notes on separate debates, and descriptions of proceedings scattered across contemporary correspondence. Furthermore, although far skimpier in his reporting of individual speeches than Luttrell or Grey, Cocks gives a unique insight into events in the commons by describing the course of debates and the political context of motions and divisions which would otherwise be inexplicable, and by vivid character-sketches of those with whom he crossed swords in the Chamber. Unlike some other diarists, he also showed a keen interest in the details of procedure. At a stage in the evolution of Commons rules in which the authority of precedent was beginning to be superseded by formal codification through the passage of standing orders (the first standing orders date from 1678),[171] Cocks's references to the accepted rules of Commons procedure, some of which have not been found in any other contemporary source, possess an extraordinary value.

It remains to consider briefly Cocks's motives in constructing his 'parliamentary diary'. Naturally enough, these are not easy to disentangle from his wider purposes in making an album of his various writings and speeches, and may be seen as largely autobiography and self-justification: the desire to preserve a favourable account of his life and achievements. Nevertheless, his 'diary' invites comparison with the writings of other parliamentary reporters of the period. There may well be significance beyond mere accident of survival in the clustering of recorded debates at times of high political tension: in 1698/9, for instance, and again in 1714. Much as historians have explained the peaks and troughs of parliamentary reporting earlier in the seventeenth century as a function of varying popular interest in what Parliament was doing,[172] so one might attribute Cocks's interest in putting down for posterity

[169] Henry Horwitz (ed.), *The Parliamentary Diary of Narcissus Luttrell, 1691–1693* (Oxford, 1972); Anchitell Grey, *Debates of the House of Commons from the Year 1667 to the Year 1694* (10 vols.; London, 1769); A. N. Newman (ed.), *The Parliamentary Diary of Sir Edward Knatchbull (1722–1730)* (Camden 3rd ser., 94; London, 1963).

[170] 'Debates 1697–9', 361–79; D. Szechi (ed.), 'The Diary and Speeches of Sir Arthur Kaye, 1710–12', *Camden Miscellany XXXI* (Camden 4th ser., 44; London, 1992), 327–39.

[171] See Betty Kemp, *Votes and Standing Orders of the House of Commons: The Beginning* (House of Commons Library Document 8; London, 1971).

[172] For a useful survey, see John Ferris, 'Before Hansard: Records of Debate in the Seventeenth Century House of Commons', *Archives*, 20 (1992), 198–207.

his observations of the Westminster scene to a keen appreciation of the drama and significance of the events of which he was a witness.

However, Cocks shared several characteristics with other contemporary parliamentary diarists. Those who recorded debates in the House were often new Members, fascinated by the strange scene which had opened up in front of them: Cocks's nephew Grey Neville took notes in the House in his very first session in 1705/6, as did the Whig MP Oley Douglas in 1714.[173] The more ambitious kept records for themselves of debates and proceedings in the way that an apprentice lawyer would approach a major legal case; so that they might gain a mastery of Commons procedure (as was avowedly the intention of the young Salwey Winnington in 1695–8),[174] or to assist in the promotion of a parliamentary or official career, which was presumably the objective of William Cowper. The fact that a good many were themselves lawyers might indicate that what we have here is often little more than a professional habit extended to the parliamentary arena.[175] Cocks had enjoyed the briefest of legal trainings, and was never called to the bar, but, on the other hand, he was a new and enthusiastic Member of the 1698 Parliament, and a man determined, if not on high office, at least to cut a figure in the 'grand inquest of the nation'.

One other notable feature was shared by almost all the 'parliamentary diarists' of the period 1689–1714. They hailed from families which were, or had been, Puritan in their religious outlook, where diary-keeping was a recurrent phenomenon — a natural development from the spiritual self-examination in which Puritans are said to have habitually indulged. Active scholarly debate still surrounds the notion that the practice of keeping a journal was a specifically 'Puritan' trait; after all, many seventeenth-century diarists were devout Anglicans and High Churchmen (John Evelyn is only the most famous example). But, at least as far as these parliamentary diarists were concerned, the weight of evidence would bear out the thesis. Luttrell, Winnington, Cowper, Neville, Douglas, and Cocks: all came from families which had been, and often still were, Presbyterian in their religious affiliations, and striking examples of godly piety at that; and, in the case of the Winningtons and Cowpers, families with a strong history of diary-keeping in the domestic as well as the political sphere.

---

[173] Neville's notes were printed by W. A. Speck in 'An Anonymous Parliamentary Diary, 1705–6', *Camden Miscellany XXIII* (Camden 4th ser., 7; London, 1969), 29–81, though without identifying their author correctly. The attribution to Neville (confirmed by a comparison of handwriting) is the work of Mark Knights. A xerox copy of the Douglas diary (originally part of the Blackett of Matfen MSS) is in the possession of the History of Parliament Trust.

[174] For Winnington see 'Debates 1697–9', 347–8, 356–60, 379–92, which prints some of his notes on debates, from 1697/8 and 1698/9.   [175] A suggestion I owe to Mark Knights.

In preparing Cocks's diary for publication I have endeavoured to preserve as far as possible the idiosyncratic spelling, capitalization, and punctuation of the original. This has not always been possible, however. Cocks's handwriting frequently fails to distinguish upper and lower case; indeed, in some instances, notably with the leter 's', he may have made use of a 'half-capital' in a no-man's-land between the two. When in doubt I have opted for the standard modern form. Puctuation presents another area of difficulty. Cocks rarely used full stops, preferring colons, so on occasion, where the unambiguous sense of the prose requires it, I have followed the colon with a capital letter, to separate out what were clearly intended as discrete sentences. Proper names have been left untouched (Cocks may occasionally have employed variant spellings as a means of showing his contempt for political opponents), except for some abbreviations of Christian names, which have been expanded or corrected. For convenience sake, superior letters have been lowered, thorns modernized, and a few of the most common abbreviations silently extended. The cipher 'ℋ', to denote pounds sterling, has been replaced by 'li', the more usual contemporary form. On the other hand, the lines inserted by Cocks above some words, generally to indicate abbreviated or omitted letters, have been retained. Reconstructed passages are given within square brackets, in roman type; editorial insertions also within square brackets but italicized. Intentional gaps in the text, left by Cocks, appear as '. . .'; editorial excisions as '[. . .]'. A word lost or rendered illegible by damage to the manuscript has been indicated as '[–]'. In places where the extent of the loss cannot be gauged precisely, a question mark precedes the dash(es) within square brackets: in general, however, some attempt has been made to estimate the number of missing words. Erasures and interlinings made by Cocks have been omitted from the printed text but recorded in the footnotes.

In the introduction, and in editorial matter generally, spelling, capitalization, and puctuation have been standardized in quotations from contemporary documents and in the titles of books cited. Dates are given in Old Style (unless otherwise stated), although the year has been taken to begin on 1 January. According to contemporary practice, diplomatic dispatches have been cited in both Old and New Style. Finally, in a vain effort to prevent acute elephantiasis overcoming the editorial footnotes, biographical information on Members of the 1698–1702 Parliaments whose names occur in the diary has been gathered in an appendix.

Chronology of Debates Reported in the Diary

THE PARLIAMENT OF 1698–1700

The Session of 1698/9

4 Jan. 1699	Disbanding Bill: motion for an instruction to the committee (Cocks's speech)
5 Jan.	Disbanding Bill
10 Jan.–27 Mar.	Inquiries into the state of the navy
3 Feb.	Committee of supply (naval estimates)
15 Feb.	Committee of whole House on the price of guineas
18 Feb.	Report of committee of supply (naval estimates)
24 Feb.	Place Bill: committal (Cocks's speech)
8 Mar.	Place Bill: report
9 Mar.	East India Company Bill: 2nd reading
11 Mar. or 20 Apr.	A multiple naturalization bill
13, 15 Mar.	Buller's case
?21 Mar.	Committee of supply (deficiencies)
28 Mar.–12 Apr.	Land Tax Bill: report, or 3rd reading
18–19 Apr.	Land Tax Bill: report (tack of Irish forfeitures clause)

The Session of 1699/1700

27 Nov. 1699	King's Speech: committee of whole House
28 Nov.	Motion for a committee to inspect commissions of the peace and of deputy lieutenants
	Motion for supply
1 Dec.	Committee of whole House on trade (East India Co., Ireland)
6 Dec.	Committee of whole House on trade (Captain Kidd)
12 Dec.	Prince of Denmark's debt

THE PARLIAMENT OF 1701

27 or 30 May	Committee of ways and means (paymaster of navy)
28 May	Dartmouth election: report
	Winchester election: report
	Honiton election: report
30 May	Committee of ways and means
31 May	Box Divorce Bill: 3rd reading
	Committee on impeachments: report (replication to Somers's answer; precedents of Lords' message)
	Lords' message (trial of Orford)
	Trustees for Irish forfeitures: memorial
2 June	Vexatious Suits Bill: 2nd reading
	Motion to read report from committee on impeachments (replication to Somers's answer)
	Land Tax Bill: committee of whole House (appointment of commissioners)
3 June	Motion to read report from committee on impeachments (replication to Somers's answer)
	Committee of ways and means: report (paymaster of navy)
4 June	Committee to inspect precedents of Lords' message: report
5 June	Dillon Divorce Bill: report
6 June	Lords' message on impeachments: order for conference
9 June	Committee on impeachments: report (Halifax)
16 June	Peterborough election: report

THE PARLIAMENT OF 1701/2

27 Jan. 1702	Maldon election: report
28 Jan.	Quakers' Affirmation Bill: 2nd reading
	Abjuration Bill: committee of whole House
29 Jan.	Malmesbury election: hearing; censure on Lord Peterborough
31 Jan.	Fuller's letter
	Committee of supply (marines; deficiencies)
2 Feb.	Bill of Attainder: Lords' amendments
	Committee of supply (marines)
3 Feb.	Committee of supply: report; address for Allies to

28 Feb.	Committee on Freeman's petition (government of Leeward Is.): request for directions
	King's message (Anglo-Scottish union)
	Irish forfeitures: petitions (Keightley; Lady Tyrconnell; Mrs Macdonnell)
2 Mar.	Royal assent to bills: Speaker's report
	Public Accounts Bill: committee of whole House
	Calne election: committee hearing
3 Mar.	Land Tax Bill: 2nd reading
4 Mar.	East Retford election: committee hearing
5 Mar.	Malt Tax Bill: report
6 Mar.	Committee of ways and means (wine duty; Crown grants)
	Bishop's Castle election: committee hearing
7 Mar.	Motion for adjournment
	Cloth Manufactures Bill: 2nd reading
	Prisons Regulation Bill: instructions to committee
8 Mar.	Conference with Lords (proclamation of Queen Anne)
9 Mar.	Address of condolence and congratulation: report
	Committee of ways and means (naming chairman)
10 Mar.	Irish forfeitures: petition (Luttrell)
13 Mar.	Felons Punishment Bill: 1st reading
	Motion for papers concerning civil list
	Public Accounts Bill: report
	Committee of supply: election of chairman
14 Mar.	Motion 'to encourage popery in Ireland'
	Appreece's bill: report (point of order)
16 Mar.	Committee on petition to oblige Jews to maintain their Protestant children: report
	Committee of supply (civil list)
17 Mar.	East Retford election: report
	Ballot for commissioners of accounts
18 Mar.	Committee to investigate complaint against Queen's brewers: report
	Motion to take abjuration oath
19 Mar.	Public Accounts Bill: 3rd reading
	Anglo-Scottish union: order for bill
20 Mar.	Civil List Bill: 2nd reading
	Land Tax Bill: committee of whole House

Text of the Diary

1698 Parliament, 1698/9 Session

[*Bodleian Library, MS Eng. hist. b. 209, fo. 93ᵛ*]
My first speech in parliament spoken the 4th day of jan[uary] 1698 [/9] upon disbanding the army[1]

Mr Speaker[2]

Sir it has been very well observed that if you govern with the hearts and Affections of the people they are your best defence and security:[3] and I can say both from letters out of the country and by my conversation in this place that the very discours of the disbanding the army has much obliged the people I am sure without the peoples affections an army is but a small security.

Sir when I consider the frailtyes and imbecillityes of human nature how many unthinking creatures ther[e] are over the virtuous and wise: without going back to historyes or fetching examples from forreign parts or indeed without so much as remembring the late King James: wee may easily conceive that the th[ro]n[e] may be again fild with a weak and an impotent prince: and it is the interest of the people and the duty of a virtuous and good King rather to shelter us than expose us to future storms that m[?ay] and will arise

Sir I have heard those Gent[*lemen*] that are for not disbanding any part of the army both within doors and without compare these times to the unhappy divisions between the houses of york and Lancaster compa[r]in[g] as I believe his present Majesty to one and the late King James to the other faction:[4] but these Gent[*lemen*] read historyes to little purpose they only remember the names which is the hard and laborious part and Loose the sence I would feignn know if the earles of March had not as good a title in H[*enry*] 4ths time as the duke of york had in H[*enry*] 6ths time: and it is very demonstrable that

---

[1] In the debate on a motion for an instruction to the committee of the whole House on the Disbanding Bill, to reconsider the number of troops to be retained (7,000): *CJ* xii. 387.

[2] This speech was summarized in Salwey Winnington's notes as 'a bad K[*in*]g must have them': 'Debates 1697–9', p. 381. The Speaker was Sir Thomas Littleton.

[3] A sentiment variously expressed by Machiavelli, whom Cocks may have been intending to quote. The entire speech has Machiavellian overtones, and also shows the influence of more recent writings against a standing army, notably John Trenchard's *The History of Standing Armies . . .* (London, 1698). Dr A. B. Worden, in his introduction to Edmund Ludlow, *A Voyce from the Watch Tower. Part Five: 1660–1662* (Camden Society, 4th ser., 21; London, 1978), 47, 50, suggests that Cocks may also have drawn on the 1698 edition of Ludlow's *Memoirs*. This would be more readily apparent in the commentaries on the history of the Civil War and Interregnum, below pp. 25, 31–2.

[4] For example, *A True Account of the Land Forces in England . . .* (London, 1699), 37–9.

the title could not be much mended by lying so lo[ng] dormant so that it is very plain sir that the best title the house of york had was the evill administration of the house of Lancaster Sir I think I may venture to affirm that a good king never had a bad title and a bad one can never have a good one:

others tell us of our discontents in relation to those I suppose the world runs now much as formerly it did: proud and ambitious men allways valued their parts and merits a[t] a great rate, and if their rewards and preferments did not answer their expectation and the opinion [they] had of themselves, they were angry and disobliged: I beleive some here may be angry they are not Admira[ls] others that they are not Secretaryes of State, and some are disappoynted that they are not in your Chair and wee poor mortalls that move in meaner stations, when the humour of envy and ill nature seises on the property of these men: when the humour of flattery and obsequiousnes possesses us then we are lea[?d] and governed by the contrary party

Some people also mention the Jacobites their notion is that they are King Jameses catle[5] their party is [as] inconsiderable as their notion

Sir the nature of man is aspiring and ambitious and a wise and good man will not subject himself to ma[?ny] temptations and a weak one certainly cant resist them: and if the throne should be again filled with a weak and impotent prince, and he should have an army at his command does any one think he would be mended by his power: and who should then say to him pray sir dismis your army you are not so virtuous so good as K[ing ?–][6] they will incourage [?you] to do what otherwise you would not by their means you may at first take of[f] some of the daringest and bra[?zenest] and forwardest of your people: but at last the side of the people will joyne the army and will ruine you Sir if this must not be said then, we must now take care now that we may then have no occasion to say so

Sir it is agreed by everyone that this is a great concern to our country I have therefore tho unable and unwilling to speak in so great an assembly ventured to give my thoughts and reasons for my opinion to shew you that I am guided by reason not party and if anything should happen otherwise [?than] I foresee since I am guided only by my conscience I mean reason I hope I shall be the easier pardoned by God and man and the better satisfyed myself [. . .][7]

---

[5] Presumably in the sense of 'chattels', i.e. the Jacobites think that they *belong* to James and thus owe him unconditional and immutable loyalty.

[6] 'you are not so virtuous so good as K[ing ?–]' interlined.

[7] Omitted: calculations of wool imported from Ireland 1696–8; 'returns of 4415 parishes which paid to the poor 1695'.

[*10 Jan.–27 Mar. 1699*][8] The admiralty were accused of severall faults but not many reall ones proved[9] it was therefore mere malic[e] or a desire to have them out and others in then anything els than brought them upon the stage; their allowing preistman a salary for being cheif de squadre in K[*ing*] Charleses time was a fault the summ allowed was 390 li but the president was ill:[10] as for their not sending a fleet sooner into the Streights was no fault for they might ha[ve] been blamed then for having left the Kingdom naked and moreover they acted by superior orders:[11] [?the] busin[ess] in relation to price and Aylmere was nothing but mere malice nothing in it at all:[12] papilion to save himself discovered secrets in relation to my Lord Orphord,[13] and undoubtedly my Lord ought not to have been cheif of the admiralty and treasurer of the navye: those places were inconsistent in one: as to my Lord

---

[8] The committee of the whole House on the state of the navy met first on 10 Jan. 1699 and subsequently on 28 Jan., 2, 6, 9, and 17 Feb., 10, 13, 15, and 22 Mar., reporting on 27 Mar.: *CJ* xii. 392, 465, 479, 485, 495, 516, 561, 584, 590, 609, 618.

[9] For the opposition's muck-raking campaign against the Admiralty, see in general J. A. Johnston, 'Parliament and the Navy, 1688–1714', Ph.D. thesis (Sheffield, 1968), 92–6; Horwitz, *Parliament, Policy and Politics*, 252–3; and 'Debates 1697–9', 351, 387–92.

[10] Henry Priestman (*c.*1647–1712), Lord of the Admiralty 1690–May 1699, and MP New Shoreham 1695–8, for whom see J. Charnock, *Biographia Navalis* . . . (4 vols.; London, 1794–6), i. 400–2. On 12 Sept. 1695 the Admiralty board had granted a warrant for back pay of his salary (of 10*s.* a day) as commander-in-chief of a small squadron stationed off Morocco in 1684. Opposition MPs argued that the number of vessels concerned had been insufficient to qualify him for the rank. E. Chappell, 'Henry Priestman', *Mariners' Mirror*, 20 (1934), 115–19; BL Add. MS 17677 TT, fo. 88. According to Secretary James Vernon the total sum involved was about £400: James (ed.), *Letters Illustrative* . . . , ii. 259. The subject was raised in the committee on 2 Feb., when a resolution was passed declaring the order 'very unreasonable' and 'a misapplication of public money': *CSP Dom.* 1699–1700, pp. 40, 42; 'Debates 1697–9', 387–8; HMC, *Portland MSS*, x. 35–6; BL Loan 29/215, fos. 202–3; *CJ* xii. 618.

[11] The delay in the sailing of the Mediterranean squadron, from its receiving orders in the winter of 1697/8 until the following autumn, was discussed in the committee on 10 and 28 Jan., and voted a 'great mismanagement': BL Add. MS 40773, fo. 98; Add. MS 17677 TT, fos. 84–5; Add. MS 30000 C, fo. 26; *CSP Dom.* 1699–1700, p. 37; Luttrell, *Brief Relation*, iv. 477.

[12] John Price (d. 1709), capt. RN, for whom see Charnock, *Biographia Navalis*, ii. 282–5; and Matthew Aylmer, MP, vice-admiral and c.-in-c. Mediterranean squadron 1698–9. The complaint here was that Price's ship the *Centurion*, loaded with silver for England, had been detained at Cadiz in the autumn of 1698 by Aylmer, 'contrary to the King's order', and sent to cruise the North African coast until Price would agree to concede to Aylmer a large share of his profits: 'Debates 1697–9', 390; HMC, *Portland MSS*, x. 36. Price was examined by the committee on 9 Feb. and the matter was discussed at length on 10 Mar., but dropped: 'Debates 1697–9', 389–90; Bodl. MS Carte 130, fo. 399; *CSP Dom.* 1699–1700, p. 90.

[13] Thomas Papillon, MP, commissioner for victualling, who had made himself vulnerable by passing his accounts by Privy Seal rather than in the usual manner, was the first witness examined by the committee on the alleged victualling scandal: HMC, *Portland MSS*, x. 32; BL Add. MS 40773, fo. 151. For Edward Russell (1652–1727), 1st Earl of Orford, treasurer of the navy 1689–May 1699, Admiral of the Fleet 1693, and 1st Lord of the Admiralty 1694–May 1699, see *DNB*.

Orphords charge it was that he had cheated the nation in victualling at Cales[14]
and by setting down th[?at] at 1s that cost but 9d this papilion made out, by
letters and unvoys for my lord it was said he had sworn to his account: and
that excused him but by one: if my Lords oath was true this he was innocent: if
not it is likely he has got 2000 li by it: it was said and beleived by those that
had a mind to beleive what they would have true that my Lord had victualled
them for 6d: 39 [?s which] was 1d [?pd] cheaper per man per diem than they
were ever victualled before: this is fal[se] for with what they had on the Kings
account it come to 9d per diem, as for the contingent account [it] was
something scandalous for a man that had such great places to set down so
extrava[gant]ly for phisick and coach hire: viz 300 li each:[15] Churchill[16] said he
had known other ad[mirals] take diet drink but not set in on the publick
account: my Lord Orphord has done a great deale of good and has got himself
great riches many friends [?–]

[fo. 93]

the reason I and many more were for so few forces: was becaus we intended to
have 3000 marines[17] and uppon a great debate in the committee [3 Feb. 1699]
Sir C: Musgrove after we had agreed to have 15000 men for services at sea
would have added the word men to sea: but could not carry it then:[18] [18 Feb.
1699] the house agreed with the report from sea service it was carried by six:
and then when the quaestion was over and it was proposed to have a quaestion

---

[14] Cadiz.
[15] The complaint of the victualling of the Mediterranean squadron in 1694/5 was discussed in
the committee on 17 Feb., and again, more fully, on 15 Mar., when, according to Cocks, Lord
Orford was 'brought on the stage and accused by Papillon of setting down 12d. per gallon for wine
which cost him but 9d., and so for oil etc., by which computation he had gained from the public
£20,000'. L'Hermitage, the Dutch agent, reported Orford's alleged profit at between £15,000 and
£20,000. The committee resolved that it was 'inconsistent with the service of the Navy' for Orford
to hold simultaneously the posts of Admiralty commissioner and treasurer of the navy, but a
motion specifically criticizing the victualling accounts was defeated by a single vote, 141 : 140. BL
Add. MS 34730, fo. 250 (Cocks to Richard Mariett, 18 Mar. 1698/9); Add. MS 17677 TT, fos. 103,
125; Luttrell, Brief Relation, iv. 484, 494; CSP Dom. 1699–1700, p. 102; CJ xii. 618.
[16] George Churchill, MP, a former naval captain, appointed to the Admiralty board himself the
following October. He was absent from the House on 15 Mar.: Horwitz, Parliament, Policy and
Politics, 254.
[17] Towards recovering ground lost in the disbandment debates, ministers sought provision for
additional soldiers on the naval establishment through the inclusion of 3,000 marines: BL Add. MS
40773, fo. 89; Bodl. MS Carte 130, fo. 396; Suffolk RO (Ipswich), Gurdon MSS M142(1), ii. 29, 37,
Sir William Cook to Thornhagh Gurdon, 28 Jan., 23 Feb. 1698[/9]. In a curious rationalization,
Cocks espouses this scheme himself and uses it to justify his own support of the Disbanding Bill.
[18] In the committee of supply. According to the Under-Secretary, John Ellis, this was 'a long
debate' (CSP Dom. 1699–1700, p. 40). There are reports in 'Debates 1697–9', 388–9, 393–4;
Luttrell, Brief Relation, iv. 479; and Northants. RO, Montagu (Boughton) MSS 47/140, James
Vernon to the Duke of Shrewsbury, 4 Feb. 1698[/9]. Sir Christopher Musgrave's motion was in fact
the opposite to that recorded by Cocks, namely to add the prefix 'sea' to 'men'.

for 3000 mariners: it was lost by a few some dining others going to tell the news at Kinsington:[19] as for the marines some say they are better at fire arms and that many of our ships have been lost at the very first onset by the french having the advantage over us in that matter: others say they breed abundance of seamen:[20] the contrary say they are sick and nauseous at sea that seamen cant abide them that throw their nastines they breed distempers in the Ship that they do more harm then good[21]

There was a bill bill [*sic*] brought in to restrain the number of officers from sitting in the hous[22] there were great debates at the committing it [*24 Feb. 1699*]. I spoke for the committing it extempore as follows Sir were we assured or could we beleive that this government and this ministry should or could continue for ever wee should then certainly have no occasion for any law of this nature: Sir it is uneasye to us and in regard it Looks so much like a mistrust of the present government to make laws that seem to reflect upon the present government in order to prevent future evills: but sir when we consider that in bad reigns good laws cant be obtained I hope that will make our excuse and that we shall rather seem by offering a law that would never pas in a bad reign rather to commend then disparrage the present government: Sir there are two familyes I always opposed from sitting within these walls the one I have heard in other parliaments[23] is the family of the obliged the other the family of the disobliged: the one by fawning and flattery does every thing he is bid and more to get preferment the other brays and bawles against the government in order to be bought of[f]: if places were not to be the rewards of our actions here men of small or no estates would never try to get in and the [c]heif aym of

[19] At the report there were two divisions, both on amendments, the first to reduce the number from 15,000 to 12,000, which was defeated 189 : 184, the second that this complement comprise only seamen, which was carried 187 : 178: *CJ* xii. 518. The debate lasted from noon till 6 p.m., and Cocks's conviction that the opposition's success on the second amendment was owing to the early departure of a number of Court supporters was shared by both L'Hermitage and the Prussian resident, Bonet: Suffolk RO (Ipswich), M142(1), ii. 37, Sir William Cook to Thornhagh Gurdon, 23 Feb. 1698[/9]; BL Add. MS 33572, fo. 158; Add. MS 17677 TT, fo. 105; Add. MS 30000 C, fo. 53.

[20] i.e. that in due course experience would turn the marines into sailors: BL Add. MS 17677 TT, fo. 105. This argument was also put forward by Admiral Sir Clowdisley Shovell, MP for Rochester: BL Loan 29/35(1), Robert Harley's notes on this debate.

[21] Reference to the marines' weak stomachs was also recorded by L'Hermitage: BL Add. MS 17677 TT, fo. 105. Cf. 'Debates 1697–9', 394. For the extent of hostility to the marines, see Johnston, 'Parliament and the Navy', 367–8; and a contemporary pamphlet, 'A Letter to a Member of Parliament Concerning the Four Regiments Commonly Call'd Marines' (1698/9), repr. in *William III State Tracts*, ii. 680–4.   [22] Entered in *CJ* under this title.

[23] 'I have heard it in other parliaments' interlined. For the history of place legislation in this period, see Betty Kemp, *King and Commons 1660–1832* (London, 1965), 51–7; and D. Hayton, 'The Reorientation of Place Legislation in England in the 1690s', *Parliaments, Estates and Representation*, 5 (1985), 103–8.

every one would more probably be the true interest of their country since they could propose to make no other advantage to themselves. I am therefore for committing it to see if it may be amended I cant say I am for it as it now stands: this bill was committed and [*a*] very partiall bill it was it picked out men[24] and particularly Mr Charles Bertye was excepted under the name of the present secretary of the ordinance as being a very Honourable Gent[*leman*] and a very honourable Gent[*leman*] he was for he was paymaster to C[*harles*] 2ds pensioners and left the Kingdome rather than he would discover their names when the bill was reported:[25] and this amendment [*8 Mar. 1699*] I said sir I cant agree with [*the*] committee in this amendment[26] for the reason then given which was that he was a worthy man and an honourable Gent[*leman*]: Sir this is no reason in making of a law all laws are hard to some people and the only thing that makes them tolerable is their equality and impartiality: it is the nature of a law not to relate to private affections good or bad to aym at things and not men the definition of law is this Lex est mens sine appetitu:[27] and this amendment savours so much of appetite that it contradicts the very intention[28] of a law and therefore I cant agree with the committe: they cried agree nobody seconded me some in private said it was true then when the bill was reported [*8 Mar. 1699*] I offered this following clause and opened it after this manner Sir I was for committing of the bill in order to make it a good one: the bill provides against the obliged and I have here a clause to hinder the disobliged[29] which I desire I may bring up: they cried open it Sir I have heard you and others it may be remember the pensioner parliament[30] I have heard

---

[24] The bill provided for a general exclusion of placemen, with a number of offices specifically exempted: HMC, *House of Lords MSS*, NS iii. 382–3.

[25] As secretary to the Treasury 1673–9, Bertie had been responsible for the issue of secret service money, and after the Commons in the first Exclusion Parliament had twice interrogated him on this matter and committed him into custody for contempt in withholding information, the King had appointed him in 1680 as envoy extraordinary to the German states, where he had remained until after the dissolution of the Oxford Parliament in the following year: HC 1660–90, i. 641–2. Nothing in the present bill touched upon Bertie's honour. Cocks may have been thinking of the reference to 'His Majesty's most honourable Privy Council' (HMC, *House of Lords MSS*, NS iii. 382–3), although see the reference later in this speech to an argument in favour of exempting Bertie. The office Bertie held in 1699 was treasurer, not secretary, of the Ordnance.

[26] Possibly the treasurership of the Ordnance had been added in committee to the list of exceptions.

[27] Aristotle, *Politics*, 3. 15. 7, rendered in Latin as 'mens absque appetitu lex est' or 'quidem sine appetitu intellectus est', and quoted in these forms and in a similar version to Cocks's on several occasions in Algernon Sydney's *Discourses*, which had only recently appeared in print and had clearly made a significant impact upon Cocks's thinking: Sydney, *Discourses Concerning Government* (London, 1698), 103, 230, 316.

[28] Originally 'being' in MS.   [29] See above, p. 5.

[30] Charles II's long Parliament acquired this opprobrious nickname in the 1670s during the administration of Lord Danby.

they would get out of the way in the night shift sides and make a thousand severall shifts rather than [w]rong their country but pray sir who ever saw a private or a publick enemye ever neglect an opportunity that offerd it self, what pray sir brought the Moors into Spain the french into england in King Johns time I could tire you with instances of this nature my clause intends no more than to exclude some few few [*sic*] that did refuse subscribing the voluntary association[31] from sitting in the next parliament only: this put the house in a great rage on both sides[32] some said take it up others no: Seymour[33] spoke against and reflected on me and said there are some people not worth the obliging others that nobody values the disobliging: I answered sir this gent[*leman*] has forgot to tell you one thing that it has cost more to oblige some then it was worth: How[34] was in a great rage and all that party at last the Speaker put the quaestion whether I should bring it up or not and said the noes had it: the clause was as follows:[35] provided and be it enacted by the authority aforesaid that no person or persons having enjoyed or been in any place of profit or trust in the last year of King James the 2d who did not voluntarily subscribe the association entred into by the house of commons for the preservation of his Majestys person: before the said association was passed into a law and is not or hath been since in the service of his present majesty King W[*illia*]m shall be capable of being elected or to serve as a member in the ensuing Parliament which shall be called after the dissolution of this present parliament and also that no person or person [*sic*] or persons who shall have been in any place of profitt or trust since the reign of his present majesty and shall have been displaced and shall not have subscribed the voluntary association aforesaid within the time aforesaid shall be capable of being elected or to serve as a member in the next Parliament which shall be called after the dissolution of this present parliament.

[31] To defend King William and his government 'against the late King James and all his adherents'. Drawn up by the Commons on 25 Feb. 1696 to be tendered to Members, then imitated widely throughout the country: *CJ* xi. 466, 468; Lord Macaulay, *History of England from the Accession of James the Second*, ed. C. H. Firth (6 vols.; London, 1913–15), v. 2602–4, 2615. It was later embodied into the 1696 Security Act (7 & 8 Gul. III, c. 27), as a compulsory test for civil and military office, and membership of Parliament.

[32] L'Hermitage reported the House's anger at a speech (from a Member whom he did not identify) in support of this clause, in which it was said that those who had been loyal to James II during that king's reign were still so in their hearts. Some among the audience had called for the speaker to be brought to the bar. BL Add. MS 17677 TT, fos. 118–19.

[33] Throughout the diary, 'Seymour', may usually be understood to mean Sir Edward.

[34] It may fairly be assumed that Cocks generally intends 'Howe' to refer to John Grobham ('Jack') Howe, his great antagonist in Gloucestershire politics.

[35] The abortive clause was noticed by Luttrell, who recorded it as having provided that 'no person should ever be a Member of Parliament that had been in King James's service, or that had at first refused to sign the voluntary Association': *Brief Relation*, iv. 491.

[*n.d.*] I did this sessions intend to have desired Leave to bring in a bill to have disabled Sir John Trevour[36] from executing any place of profit or trust: How heard of it and told me if I had not [?had] blood enough he might dig up Sir John Fenwick[37] and eat a rib bone of him and that he would defend [h]im: my answer was he might have spared that speech for he well knew I never feared him [n]or valued his threats: I was much sollicited by Sir John Trevours friends to give over those [thoug]hts but that did not in the least prevaile with me: in so much that I appoynted a time [?for t]hose I thought zealous in the matter to meet in order to agree how wee should

[*fo. 92v*]

proceed none met except Mr Neville and Mr Jarvais:[38] many excused them-selfes becaus of the late [sit]ting of the house: I had a mind to try if this was excuse or earnest and in order to it I made an offer of another meeting but I found that proposall not forwarded: there were most in the house thought this fit to be be [*sic*] done and wished it might without their help or appearing in it: which occasions many things fit to be redressed to have more wishes than hands: but I was in earnest and drew up this following speech to ha[ve] shewed the Gent[*lemen*] if they had met

Sir we have spent much time in prying inquiring and fishing to find faults and have neglected to pun[ish] those crimes that are found, owned and proved to our hands such faults that are a scandall and an offence to the people of England such crimes that were abhorred and abominated by the very heathen the scandall I poynt at is bribery the man I mean is Sir John Trevour: I need not bring witnesses to atte[st] the veracity of what I have said and complained of the records before us will justifye my allegations:[39] Sir I have heard some go about to mitigate the fault by saying it was done openly: which in my opinion aggrevats the matter, for I think when such crimes have got head to that degree that they dare appear openly by daylight without a mask it is high time to check them others say it was long since past: t[o] part of which I answer becaus justice is not speedily executed therefore do the sons of men give themselves over to work wickednes, as to his having suffered allready for the same fault it is to that I cheifly speak: I

---

[36] (*c.*1637–1717), Master of the Rolls 1685–9, 1693–d., chief commissioner of the Great Seal 1690–3, Speaker of the Commons 1685–7, 1690–5 (when expelled the House for corruption). For Trevor himself, see *DNB*; and, for an explanation of Cocks's obsessive animosity towards him, above, p. xxxix.

[37] 3rd Bt. (*c.*1644–97), executed under an act of attainder, for his part in the Assassination Plot against King William. See *DNB*.

[38] Richard Neville, Cocks's brother-in-law; and Thomas Jervoise.

[39] i.e. the report on 12 March 1695 of the Commons committee investigating the charge of corruption against Trevor, and the vote on 16 Mar. following to expel him: *CJ* xi. 269–70, 274.

dare affirm if he was not guilty of what he stands charged with by the records of this house they went then to[o] farr to displace him and after they had went so farr gu[i]lty or not guilty they did not go far enough: Sir it is an uneasines and a dissatisfaction to the nation in generall a dishonour to this house to have a man displaced from your chair for bribery and after that to be permitted without any molestation to sit in a place of as great honour and trust as any is in the Kingdom: tis a greevance to the commons of england to be forced to have thei[r] rights and properties tryed and setled by a man so stigmatised by you: for the satisfaction therefore of the people for the preservation of the honour and reputation of this house and to let the wor[ld] see that tho the heat of business and the thoughts of[40] war made you let these sleep, yet that in times of peac[e] and leysure such things such practises shall be further inquired into the terror of ill magistr[a]tes and for an example to yourself I mean those that shall succeed in your chair: now the tower and the great bell is removing out of the sight and hearing of Westminster hall and this place whi[ch] was given upon a much lesser occasion:[41] I desire therefore that I may at least have [*leave*] to bring in a bill to disable Sir J[ohn] T[revor] from executing any office or place of trust in this Kingdom

[*after 9 Feb. 1699*] Sir B Shores[42] lost the bill and so I lost my speech that follows against immoralitie[s]

Sir you have given leave to bring in a bill or bills to hinder profanes and immoralities I am not [*at*] all discouraged at the fate [*of*] the first bill and the disappoyntments your worthy and well meaning member met with:[43] and if I and my bill meet with no better fortune if I cannot make it go into a law for myself for I am sure I shall have both the severest censures and most observing eis upon all my actions and behaviour to discover in order to

[40] 'thoughts of' interlined.

[41] The 14th-century clock tower, with its great bell, had recently been presented by King William to the parish of St Margaret's, Westminster, which demolished the tower and sold the bell to the dean and chapter of St Paul's: H. M. Colvin (ed.), *The History of the King's Works* (6 vols.; London, 1963–82), v. 385.

[42] Sir Bartholomew Shower's brother, John, a Nonconformist divine, was a keen supporter of the movement for the reformation of manners: *DNB*; and John Shower, *A Sermon Preach'd to the Societies for Reformation of Manners in . . . London and Westminster, Nov. 15 1697* (London, 1698).

[43] The 'Immorality Bill', designed to suppress prostitution, and adultery in general, had failed in committee on 9 Feb., when a motion to report was rejected: *CJ* xii. 494; Luttrell, *Brief Relation*, iv. 481; HMC, *Portland MSS*, iii. 602. Cocks had been a member of the small drafting committee (*CJ* xii. 368), but the 'worthy and well meaning member' who had been the bill's principal sponsor, was Sir John Philipps, 4th Bt. (*c.*1666–1737), of Picton Castle, Pembs., MP Pembroke Boroughs, for whom see *HC 1715–54*, ii. 344–5.

divulge the faults of a reform[er] I will therefore endeavour to be circum-
spect and continue honest myself and I have here a bill which if it passes
into a law will I hope in some measure oblige others to consider and in
outward appearance at least to conform to the rules of modesty and decency
I mean those whom the fear of god and the sence of religion does not
influence I remember the saying of a good old heathen conscientiis satisfa-
ciemus nihill in famam Laboremus vell si mala sequatur si bene marearis.[44] I
rely therefore upon these thoughts and will venture to expose my bill to the
beaus of all ages to the wits the half wits and those that know no Lawmaker
I mean out of doors in order thereto I desire I may have leave to bring it up

The reasons that induced me to be for the tacking of the clause to the
money bill [*18–19 Apr. 1699*][45]

the very transports to reduce Ireland cost this nation more the[n] 34000 li[46]
to transport our army: besides the charge of keeping the army there and the
Loss of so many brave lifes: if this land[47] had been divided amongst the
conquering army they would there have planted colonies and bred up people
in the religion and interest of England and would have defended ireland
without the charge of a standing army[48] and I bele[ive] the commons neither
in nor out of parliament would have complained or thought themselves hard
dealt with at all: but I am of an opinion that the people of Engla[n]d next to
the army deserve to have the Irish Land I mean that it ought to be sold to
defray the publick charges and pay the debts of the publick which have been at

---

[44] Seneca, *De Ira*, 3. 41. 1: 'conscientiae satis fiat, nil in famam laboremus: sequatur vel mala,
dum bene marentis'.

[45] The clause providing for the taking an account of the Irish estates forfeited after the Jacobite
war, which was first offered to be added to the Land Tax Bill at the report on 18 Apr. Debate was
then adjourned to the following day, when the amended clause was accepted. *CJ* xii. 651–2. For
this inquiry, see J. G. Simms, *The Williamite Confiscation in Ireland, 1690–1703* (London, 1956),
ch. 9.

[46] An error for £340,000: see below, p. 44. The debts incurred for transports during the war in
Ireland in 1689–91 remained unpaid, a scandal which provoked some satirical lines in a verse
'Encomium upon a Parliament' in 1699: repr. in George deForest Lord *et al.* (edd.), *Poems on
Affairs of State* (7 vols.; New Haven, 1938–75), vi. 55. The amount had been calculated at over
£325,000 in an account submitted to the Commons in Dec. 1697 (*CJ* xii. 9), and by Feb. 1700
interest had added a further £5,000 (*CJ* xiii. 182).   [47] The Irish forfeitures.

[48] The enthusiasm for colonial projects of this kind by writers such as Charles Davenant and
Walter Moyle, in the classical republican tradition, is discussed in Caroline Robbins, 'The
"Excellent Use" of Colonies. A Note on Walter Moyle's Justification of Roman Colonies, ca.
1699', *William and Mary Quarterly*, 3rd ser., 23 (1966), 620–6.

such vast expence of blood and treasure to recover it;[49] I beleive upon a [?trye]
of the matter it would not be adjudged to be an hardship to have all those
lands in ireland that did not belong to the rebells pay some years valew to
England at whose charge and expence the owner and proprietor injoys them
now: this as reasonable as the paying of the charges and the lawyers bill in an
action or sute: and it is less hard for them[50] to pay some years purchase in
acknowledgment of the advantages they have received: then for the poor irish[51]
who stood by their naturall prince whose cheifest fault and misfortune[52] was
his being of their religion of their understanding and being extremely partiall
and favourable to them on all occasions mythinks it is a great hardship to be
reckoned a tra[i]tour for only adhering to ones naturall prince whom oaths
and natulall [*sic*] allegiance and particular s[?–] dues and obligations force
one to adhere to, but I had almost forgot that the traitour is still he that [?is]
beaten well then since the irish are traytours it is more reasonable that they
should be traitours to [the] people of england then to a few court minions:
well but why should the grants of this King be rescinded [?rather] than the acts
of the former kings will it not be as just to have an act to reassume those lands
that were [?given] by the former kings to their favourites pimps and whores by
princes who by their designs and example [?by] their Luxury and Lasci-
viousnes endeavoured as far as in them was to ruine the government destroy
[?the religi]on, established and the very foundation and being of your constitution: is it fit that these m[en] should posses and injoy their grants and
estates obtained by such base mean[s?–] su[ch]
[*fo. 92*]
[?thing]s and that the grants made by a good King to men of merrit and virtues
who have lost their best blood spent the best of their time and spent all their
thoughts in rescewing you from popery slavery and the fre[n]ch power should
be vacated first and rested from the grantees by an act of parliament: in answer
to which I first say that had those Kings been extravagant and foolish in their
grants unpolitick and profuse in their expences we had most certainly been

---

[49] This phrase is so close to Charles Davenant's comment, in what was subsequently to become
the standard 'Country party' text on the forfeitures question, *A Discourse upon Grants and
Resumptions* . . . (London, 1700), that the people of England had 'repurchased' the Irish lands
'with so much blood and treasure' (p. 405), as to prompt the thought that Cocks may have
embroidered his speech while preparing the text of the diary. There is, however, a similar wording
in John Trenchard's 1698 pamphlet, *A History of Standing Armies* (reprinted in *William III State
Tracts*, ii. 677), and it may already have been a cliché before Davenant used it.

[50] Irish Protestants.

[51] i.e. James II's Catholic supporters in Ireland, 'Old English' as well as 'Old Irish' by race, who
were generally lumped together as 'the Irish' by Protestant commentators.

[52] 'and misfortune' interlined.

ruined so that those grants saved us in a manner and reduced our princes to
necessityes by which means sometimes by gratifying them with a sum we put a
stop to some designes formed against us and it may be got some new law to
strengthen and secure our liberties and besides these Kings are dead or exiled
and their names and memoryes are perished and corrupted past retreiving but
the case stands thus with us in relation to the new grants and the irish lands:
as for the new grants and indeed those grants made by former Kings are not
allt[o]gether upon the same bottome with the Irish lands; for all Kings have
given forfeited and escheated estates to their favourites and courtiers without
much uneasines and regret of the people and the reasons why they have been so
little set by, or taken notice of by the people is becaus they were seldom of so
great a valew or consideration as to be worth the publick I mean a parliamentary consideration, and especially when the people were not distressed
with so many taxes payments and reduced to such nationall necessityes, as to
have funds not answer and the debts contracted by credit of parliament no
otherwise provided for them by a deluding and not intending vote: I say at
such a time as this to have some ruined and undone, to have others feather
their nests and grow rich by grants is not altogether the same thing as
formerly: tho at any time it is an hardship upon the people to have the prince
give away the crown Land and to bring the Crown to so low an ebb that it cant
subsist but by precarious terms from the people: this is very injurious and
oppressive and must rais taxes on the people, tho the wiser sort and those that
are able to pay them may think their money well given: and may think it more
for the good of the Kingdom to have a prince necessitated to be beholding to
his people for his allowance and support: then to have [*him*] so rich as to want
nothing from his people and not stand in need of a parliament: but this is a
subject forreign to my busines and therefore to the matter in hand: now
therefore to restrain the prince from giving may be thought by some great
Kingsmen to call in question the understanding [o]f that King and to
invalidate grants already made may seem to reflect upon the honour and
conduct [o]f the donor: yet in time of trouble and danger men must not
Lose for want of asking and for nice [c]eremonies give way for the ruine of
the Kingdom: it is true that the prince is made for the good of the people and
is in strictnes but their steward:[53] and this does appear in fact, what is scarcely
fit to be named for many reasons for tho these are truths yet they are such

---

[53] The notion that kings are made for the good of the people may well be derived from
Algernon Sydney, who uses precisely this phraseology: Sydney, *Discourses*, 41, and more generally, 70, 92, 312. The analogy of kings to stewards was not unfamiliar in the 17th century (*OED*
has a citation from 1645), but perhaps was not common in the quasi-domestic sense that Cocks
seems to imply. The pun with 'Stuart' may be intentional.

truths that if they were common [t]hey would be profaned by the vulgar and
be of ill consequence to the governours: but it is obvious and plain if this is not
true, we cant justify our turning out our late steward and putting another in
his place: but it is strange to see how custome and practice has turned topsy
turvy these certain and undeniable truths, for in some countryes so many both
prince and people imagine, and beleive the prince to be a god at least
something above common man and the people to be his right and property:
and what is still wors where they do know better and have truer and more
generous notions yet are they very apt to forget or at least to act contrary to
their knowledg but to my purpose I therefore say that those things that may be
tolerable and law at one time may cease to be so at another time: I say
therefore that tho it was convenient and good for us to have C[*harles*] 2d
prodigall and did in a great measure save and preserve our liberties and
properties: yet at the same time I will affirm that if King william whome
we have chosen for a good King in these times of danger and necessities should
in this matter follow the example of that Late king he will both ruine himself
and us but then as to ireland the case is stronger for lands that escheat for
felonies or little treasons discovered without hasard or charge of the publick in
times of plenty and security to be given to a favourite or disposed of to a man
of worth and merrit is nothing: but to have part of a Kingdom gained by the
best blood of this, by vast expences, given by a good King to favourites or men
of great merrit and to have the transport ships unpaid[54] to have those
souldiers disbanded without their wages that hasarded their lives to reduce
it[55] is a fault, such a fault that would make a blot in the Escutcheon of this
great prince when dead whose design is to leave a name to be to him instead of
children and posterity: I honour this King and therefore I will endeavour to
make him be beloved whilst alive and honoured when gathered to his noble
wise and virtuous progenitors: I have often thought with my self how
foolishly those unthinking creatures about court generally live: they invite
Keep great tables have many attendants, liveries and other innumerable
fineryes: those they entertain scarcly think themselves beholding to them
they think it is on the publick, those that entertain oftentimes do it more to
shew their grandeur then to shew any particular respect to their guest and so
generally the guest and host part [on] as good terms as they first met on: I

---

[54] See above, p. 10, n. 46.
[55] From 4 February onwards the House had been inundated with petitions from soldiers (and
widows of soldiers) whose arrears from the Irish campaigns remained unpaid, and some of whom
had been demobilized. A committee had been established to investigate. *CJ* xii. 482, 485, 512, 514,
519–21, 526, 532, 535, 542, 562, 585, 602, 630. Cocks was added to the committee on 17 Apr.: *CJ*
xii. 646.

beleive there is no court but has some faults in the great and gloriou[s] reign
of our Elizabeth there were monopolies; and great men oppressed the people
with them, in this reforming age it is unseemly to see the privy Councill
Drunk to hear them sweare those who have sett forth proclamations against
profanes and immoralityes,[56] it is uneasy to see places given to men of no
abilityes no merrit only becaus their friends or relations are favourites: but
as for this government in generall I take it to be a good one becaus it is the
best I ever remember and many better I dont remember in History tho it is
the practice of all ages to admire whats past and condemn and despise what
is present the King is undoubtedly of our religion and in our interest and
designs our good it is therefore our duty to esteem him a blessing sent us by
the hand of providence it is our interest to bear up against evill practises and
endeavour to represent miscarriages fairly to the King who denies us nothing
and is never displea[sed] with the knowledg of miscarriages who generaly
passes all the bills offerd him: this will do the nation [mo]re good, then only
to aggrevate matters by rayling and by hot satiricall witty speeches set the
nation in a [fla]me and blow up those coales that now lye covered and
extinguishing in their ashes: to mend or to ende[avou]r to set [m]atters on a
right bottom and to heale breaches is becomming an englishman to exas-
parate and [?–] is the part of a malitious [?breedbate[57]] and a discontented
incendiary

[*fo. 91ᵛ*]

upon a debate in the bill for disbanding the army [*5 Jan. 1699*][58] the ill
humored part of the house were much against the forreign[ers] and would
not have so much as a naturall born Scot to have been capable of being any
part of the 7000 that were to b[e] kept up by act of parliament and as they
were very hot even against those that were naturalised[59] the buffoon Sir
Rob[ert] Napper[60] Sir Robert said sir the centurion [?tells] St paul with a

---

[56] The proclamation of 21 January 1692 against 'vicious, debauched and profane persons', and
that of 24 Feb. 1698, for 'preventing and punishing immorality and profaneness': R. R. Steele (ed.),
*Bibliotheca Lindesiana: A Bibliography of Royal Proclamations of the Tudor and Stuart Sovereigns
. . . 1485–1714* (2 vols.; Oxford, 1910), i. 489, 506.   [57] A mischief-maker.
[58] In the committee of the whole House on the Disbanding Bill. Dated from the evidence of
Luttrell, *Brief Relation*, iv. 468; *CSP Dom.* 1699–1700, pp. 6–7; BL Add. MS 17677 TT, fo. 62;
James (ed.), *Letters Illustrative . . .* , ii. 247.
[59] The bill as drafted excluded those who were not 'His Majesty's natural born subjects of this
kingdom of England'. In committee the phrase 'of this kingdom of England' was omitted,
specifically in order to exclude subjects born in Ireland, Scotland, or the Plantations, and those
who had been naturalized: 'Debates 1697–9', 372; *CSP Dom.* 1699–1700, p. 7. A later clause,
however, barred those who had been naturalized by act of the Irish Parliament: 10 Gul. III, c. 1, s.
ix.
[60] For other instances of Napier's misconceived attempts at wit, see *HC 1660–90*, iii. 128.

great sum he obtained his freedom: St paul said again but I was born free[61] he inferd if freedom was so valueable as to be purchased at such a rate why should we give it away for nothing I answerd sir I seldom answer that worthy member and as seldom talk scripture in this house but if you pleas[e] I will tell you of another passage in the Scripture: our blessed Saviour tells us in a parable[62] that a certain travelling Jew fell amongst theifs that the levite came by and seeing him wounded shakes his head at him that a goo[d] Samaritan passing by found him and set him on his hors and bound up his wounds and tooke him to an inne and ordered his host to provide for him and to take care of him and he would defray the charges of it and the quaestion is asked which of the two was neighbour to the Jew and it is there easily resolved; Sir the the [*sic*] kingdom of England was this jew that fell amongst theifs the theives were the jacobits the toryes the papist[s] etc: the good Samaritans were these outlandish men that came over with the prince of orange to assist us that helped us to make a stand to recover our liberties our religion and propertyes swallowed up and almost devoured by those ill sort of men Sir these men are better englishmen than the papist or jacobite and I hope sir wee shall make them as good.

upon the bringing in a bill to naturalise some 100dreds [*11 Mar. or 20 Apr. 1699*][63] Sir Xtopher musgrove who usually spoke last to set the house in an heat told us fi[r]st he hoped we should not go about to elude an act made the very first sessions[64] and to give way for strangers to be in place and our own countrymen[65] to starve for want in the streets; and to that purpose: I answered sir I hope Gent[*lemen*] will consider before they resolv[e] in this matter these poor men have leaft their religion at which the jacobite party Laughed and when that w[as] over I said sir these men have leaft their country becaus they would not leave their religion they have forsook their freinds their familyes their relation their estates becaus they would not forsake their god they are better englishmen than the Jacobite the papist and the other discontents why dont you laugh now: Sir I remember a sentence I learned [in] schoole that has

---

[61] Acts 22: 28–9.   [62] Luke 10: 29–37.

[63] Either the bill to naturalize Legge *et al.*, which was brought in on 11 Mar. and ordered to have a 2nd reading (*CJ* xii. 562), or that to naturalize Bernardeau *et al.*, brought in on 20 Apr., and the subject of a division on the motion for a 2nd reading (*CJ* xii. 655–6). The former, dealing with army officers in general, covered 105 persons, as against the 98 mentioned in the latter, comprising the foreign troopers in the guards regiments (HMC, *House of Lords MSS*, ns iii. 367–75, 401–7). However, the very fact of the division on 20 Apr., when the vocal opposition of MPs was recorded by at least two observers (Luttrell, *Brief Relation*, iv. 507; BL Add. MS 17677 TT, fo. 154), strongly suggests that it was the debate reported here.

[64] Musgrave was probably alluding to the Disbanding Act, the sense of his speech being that the House should not defeat the intention of that act in the very session in which it reached the statute book.   [65] Originally 'neighbours'.

ever since made an impression on me homo sum nihill quod humanum a me alienum est:[66] Sir these men have no country unless you will give them one they have fought against their naturall prince[67] for us they have shed their blood and spent the best of their time to preserve our lifes liberties and fortunes and [?now] we have by their help partly no occasion for them shall we turn them a wandring and expose them to the wide world and their merciles enemies: Sir this is so unnaturall so ungratefull so unbecumming the Eng[lish] temper I hope we shall not do it but give the bill a second reading in order to commit it

[*15 Feb. 1699*] Mr Hannington Frekue began the debate about Guineas[68]

Mr J. How spoke to this effect Sir I dont know what we have to do with this matter or who b[e]gan the debate but I do beleive it came from some friend to the court for it will have ill effect[s] it will hinder the disbanding of the armye and it will take sixpence in the pound out of the poor peop[le]s pockets Sir Ro[bert] Rich answered him in which he said something of Glo[u]c[este]rsh[ire]: Mr How answered him again then I said sir we are in a lamentable and deplorable condition we are bard from giving our reasons by hard words we are told if we are for lowring the guineas we are for taking money out of the poor peoples pockets tools to court and against the disbanding of the armye as for the disbandi[n]g of the army I have sufficiently declared my mind in that matter and as for injuring the poor tenants of Glo[u]c[este]rshire since that county has been named I have as much reason to take care of them as most in this house for I beleive I have as many there Sir I know it obliges the ignorant to be pittied and they think whoever pyttyes th[em] loves and they therefore love him again but as long as I am in this hous I will more endeavour to serve m[y] country truly then to please them: I will know whatever is good or bad for England in generall is good o[r] bad for Glo[u]c[este]rshire: and it is very demonstrable that if with gold of a les valew brought in we carry out silver of a better we must in time by often doing so ruine the nation Sir since we are told it will be ungratefull to the people it is not fitt the King should doe it unless addressed to by us and since it is good for the Kingdom it is fit we should address the King in the matter. Mr How replyed that Gent[*leman*] is pleased to tell of the number of his tenants I desire

---

[66] Terence, *Heautotimorumenos*, 1. 1. 23: 'homo sum; humani nihil a me alienum puto'.

[67] Louis XIV of France: the 'foreigners' were almost all Huguenots.

[68] Thomas Freke of Hannington, Wilts., MP Weymouth and Melcombe Regis, in a committee of the whole House 'to consider the price of gold'; in response to a recommendation from the Board of Trade that the value of the guinea be reduced from 22*s*. to 21*s*. 6*d*.: *CJ* xii. 511, 513.

to know who has most votes he or I[69] as for his motion I dont know what he means nor he neyther and so ridiculed what I had said. I replyed sir I litle thought the Election for the county of Glo[*u*]c[*este*]r would have been this [*sic*] quaestioned before this house but in answer to the quaestion asked me I would feighn Know who has most single votes but I beleive if we had neyther of us had more vites [*sic*] then our own tenants could have given us we had hardly now sat here then I renewed my motion: when this matter was first debated I thought the majority were against it but it was so argued and so cleared at las[t] especialy by a speech of my Lord mayours[70] who spoke against sinking of the guineas he said that if he brought gold from Holland and had it coyned here he could not get above eight pound per cent and that was but moderate gains but we computed that that that [*sic*] might be done six times in [?year] so that it was really six times eight pound loss to the nation in every 100 li used in that trade I neve[r] saw the house so turned at last when the quaestion was put few noes against it,[71] a little time a[f]ter [?*21 Mar. 1699*][72] they complained that money did not come in roundly upon the Land Tax why sais Sir Xtop[her] Musgrave I will tell you the reason of that is becaus of the sinking of guineas people [?will not] part with them[73] this he spoke by the by: I rose up to answer and said sir I rise not up to [?answer] any thing that Honourable Member said but to rectifye one mistake he was pleased to attribu[te ?the] slow bringing in of money into the Exchecquer to the fall of guineas Sir that was not the [?opinion ?–] some speeches that fell from some members that disparaged the Pa[rl]iamen[t ?–]

[69] In the 1698 general election Howe had topped the poll for knight of the shire, over 300 votes ahead of Cocks, though it was said 'he hath not a foot of land in the county': *CSP Dom.* 1698, p. 377.

[70] The lord mayor of London, Sir Francis Child, MP, a prominent goldsmith, for whom see F. G. Hilton Price, *The Marygold by Temple Bar* . . . (London, 1902), 79–85.

[71] Those who favoured keeping up the price had claimed that otherwise guineas would be 'sent beyond sea', where on the Continent the value was already 21*s*. 6*d*., but this argument was effectively answered by other Members, who pointed out that foreigners were bringing their guineas into England and 'carrying away our silver', resulting in a net loss of some 'four per cent' to the national economy: Luttrell, *Brief Relation*, iv. 483–4; Cumbria RO (Carlisle), D/Lons/W (Lonsdale MSS), James Lowther to Sir John Lowther, 14 Feb. 1698/9.

[72] Most probably in the committee of supply on 21 March, when the House debated raising funds to meet the deficiencies, and resolved on the issuing of Exchequer bills: *CJ* xii. 606, 611; Luttrell, *Brief Relation*, iv. 497.

[73] On 2 March Christopher Hatton had written that 'the bringing down guineas hath discouraged the loan for disbanding the army, and many do now hoard up guineas, expecting that in the spring of the year, when our gallants are going to travel abroad, the price will rise': BL Add. MS 29575, fo. 421.

[*fo. 91*]

Mountague seconded me and Seymour and how eat the words they formerly spoke[74] this occasioned two hours heat and then we came to our busines.

The words that occasioned this matter at first was what fell from Mr How first he said upon some occasion that we had no great occasion to rais money for any more than to supply the necessityes of the year [16]99 that this was a good parliament and that a good parliament was not obliged to maintain the credit of a bad one such a one as the last and that we were not obliged to make good the deficiencyes of what that bad and profuse parliament[75] did or gave seymour seconded it and said thos that had lent money were well paid considering the vast interest they had had: this past without answering at that time we expecting as I suppose that some one should answer and it coming in by the by when the other busines was reassumed it went of[f] for that time but it made a great noyse out of doors; and Mr How would feighn have perswaded us he was misunderstood or misrepeated: and standing up stood still till there was a profound silence: and looking towards me he said sir I have been misrepeated and therefore I desire that the house may be quieted that Gent[*lemen*] may hear what I say, and so he proceeded after his way: when he had done I answered and said

Sir I do not desire silence out of the least apprehension of being misrepeated for I have not the confidence to think anything I say is worth the repeating at all but there are other things I complain of Sir there are some Gent[*lemen*] are pleased to threaten those that differ with them in a vote that they shall never be chose again: I may venture sir to say if they could have helped it I had not sate here now and I am sure had it been [in] my power they had not been here now: if men are affraid it alters the freedom of their vote I thank God I do not Know what fear is: but sir if indignation possesses one that alters the reason of ones vote and byas[s]es one I will also endeavour to suppress that passion and speak as becomes me freely: this was becaus I did not vote with Mr H[o]w in the matter of the marines[76] he threatned me I mean told the great Morgan[77] I should never be chose again and said I durst not but vote so and laid a bottle of clarret with morgan

---

[74] Presumably on 15 Feb. Unless Cocks specifies an alternative Montagu, we may assume that he means the Chancellor of the Exchequer Charles (later Lord Halifax). As Chancellor, Charles Montagu had 'propounded' the vote on guineas: Suffolk RO (Ipswich), M142(1), ii. 35, Sir William Cooke to Thornhagh Gurdon, 16 Feb. 1698[/9].   [75] Of 1695–8.
[76] See above pp. 4–5; 'Debates 1697–9', 393–4; Northants. RO, Montagu (Boughton) MSS 47/145, James Vernon to the Duke of Shrewsbury, 16 Feb. 1698[/9].   [77] Thomas Morgan, MP.

[*9 Mar. 1699*] Of the bill to advantage the old E[*a*]stindia company[78]

the new E[*a*]st India Company lent money upon the credit of the act of parliament[79] many were for altering the law uppon pretence that the old E[*ast*] I[*ndia*] companye had hard play hard usage: in answer to which first they had the preference if they would have a[c]cepted it: 2dly they knew by their charter they were lyable to be dissolved at any time by the Kings giving them notice: 3dly if they were ill used it was not the new company that had any hand in it and certain[l]y those that lent their money upon the credit of an act of parliament ought not to suffer: Mr Poultney made a very tedious long oration[80] on the behalf of the old E[*ast*] I[*ndia*] company Mr Bruer said he was against the act at first and that he heard the Kings councill[81] say such things that he hoped he should never hear again at the passing of the act and tho he was against it then and did vote against it yet now it was an act he was for maintaining of it since so many people had lent their money on it: I said I beleived we had nothing to do to alter it [*it*] was not I hoped in our power I hoped we could not or at least would not do any thing that was dishonourable and unjust as I thought the altering of an act of parliament upon the credit of which so many people had lent their money, was without their consent we are the debtors and the people that lent their money are the creditors and if the debtor can alter the security without the consent of the creditor if he has power he may do it it is true but if he has such a power and will use [*it*] I presume nobody will be creditor for the future such ways will ruine the credit of parliaments for the future and destroy the publick faith of the nation: the debate lasted a long time whether we should give the bill a 2d reading at last it was carried that we should by a very few votes:[82] those that were for distressing the government were intirely for the old e[*ast*] i[*ndia company*] many also that were themselves concerned and many who had friends and

---

[78] The debate at the introduction of a bill brought in upon a petition from the Old East India Company, to enable the company to continue trading in its own right for the remainder of the 21-year term granted at the renewal of its charter in 1693, in spite of the royal notice to dissolve given after the establishment of the New Company: *CJ* xii. 526, 531, 557; H. Horwitz, 'The East India Trade, the Politicians and the Constitution: 1689–1702', *Journal of British Studies*, 17/2 (1977–8), 12–13.

[79] The 1698 act to set up the New Company (9 Gul. III, c. 44), for which see Horwitz, 'East India Trade', 10–11; and id., *Parliament, Policy and Politics*, 233–4.

[80] 'oration' scored through in MS.   [81] Presumably Privy Councillors.

[82] Cocks's account of the fate of this bill is utterly confused. In fact, the motion for a 2nd reading was lost by 149 : 139, the bill then being rejected on a second vote, 140 : 114: *CJ* xii. 557. The considerable duration of the debate is confirmed in Centre for Kentish Studies, Maidstone, U1590/O59/8 (Stanhope MSS), Robert Yard to Alexander Stanhope, 13 Mar. 1698/9. Unless otherwise stated, Cocks's account of parliamentary proceedings may be understood to agree with the record in *CJ*.

relations concerned in the old company were biassed: so that the bill had a 2d reading: it was read the 2d time the day that the tyger was baited and there was much labouring to have it committed but many that were for giving it a reading did [*so*] out of hopes to bring the old and new [*companies*] to some agreement but when they saw that would not do they insisted no longer upon the committment the Tiger had the credit of preserving the new and destroying the old company but that was nothing but a jest for there were as many of [?one] side in a manner as of the other side[83]

[*28 Mar. – 12 Apr. 1699*] whether we should give the Com[*mi*]s[*sione*]rs in the land tax a discretionall power to order the collecting of it[84] Mr Smith of the treasurye[85] said that it was a very unjust way to collect 3 4ths of [16]93 as it was then in the hundreds in every hundred[86] for that there were in some places honest and worthy Com[*mi*]s[*sione*]rs [and] assessors the one that brought in their assessments as they ought upon their oaths the others that asses[s]ed themselves and their fellow com[*missione*]rs as they ought and every papist and those that refused the oaths double;[87] and that now the jacobites had taken the oaths it was very hard they should bear their own full share and part of their ill neighbours as the reward of their justice and integrity and that those that were disaffected and negligent of their oaths and Dutye should be gainers by their perjury and neglect and that it would be affronting the Com[*mi*]s[*sione*]rs to mistrust their justice and integrity

I answered

Sir since we are upon justice I hope we shall begin to do justice here there is one county in relation to another is the same as [*one*] hundred in relation to

---

[83] The Tory Robert Price reported that 'the Court lay a snare for our young gentlemen and had a tiger baited towards Westminster that afternoon, which drew fifteen of one and about five of the other party, which occasioned a jest about town, that baiting the tiger without doors gave the lion Montagu an opportunity to prey within': Bodl. MS Carte 130, fo. 401. James Vernon, who more accurately located the event at the Cockpit, recorded 'a pretty many Members . . . present of both sides': Northants. RO, Montagu (Boughton) MSS 47/154, Vernon to Shrewsbury, 9 Mar. 1698[/9]; BL Add. MS 40773, fo. 225. The affair was a nine days' wonder: see e.g. *The Cock-Pit Combat: Or the Baiting of the Tiger on Thursday, Mar. 9, 1698[/9]* (London, 1699).

[84] The committee of the whole House on the Land Tax Bill met on 28 Mar., and 1, 3, and 12 Apr., reporting on the 14th. Subsequent debates were taken up by the Irish forfeitures inquiry clause (see above, p. 10, n. 45): *CJ* xii. 628–20, 640, 643.

[85] John Smith, MP Andover, Ld. of the Treasury.

[86] The bill followed the 1698 act in returning to the principle of a 'monthly assessment', taking as each county's quota the yield from the 1693 land tax but levying 3*s*. in the pound as against the 4*s*. paid then: see J. V. Beckett, 'Land Tax or Excise: The Levying of Taxation in Seventeenth- and Eighteenth-Century England', *English Historical Review*, 100 (1985), 287–95.

[87] The principle that Catholics and others refusing the oaths of allegiance and supremacy should pay double had been established by the 2*s*. Aid Act of 1690 (1 Gul. & Mar., sess. 2, c. 1), and continued in land tax legislation thereafter. The 1699 act (10 Gul. III, c. 9) did in fact provide a renewed opportunity for them to swear.

another there are as many more Jacobites as many more papists as many more
good as many more bad as many more well as many more ill affected [a]nd
negligent com[*mi*]s[*sione*]rs in one county over another proportionably as
there are in the hundreds one [ove]r the other and if we are so much for an
equality let us begin to alter the proportions of the [count]yes in this house
and then we shall have done that we shall all easily consent to give li[?berty] to
alter the hundreds: in the making of laws we ought to consider the conveniencyes and the incon[ven]iencyes if the inconveniencyes are most we ought to
say it shall not be a Law if the conveniencyes then [?we] ought to enact in most
things our weak foresight and judgment cannot see the events but [?we can]
k[?now] by experience: as for example in worcestershire in the neighbouring
county
[*fo. 90ᵛ*]
to me they used their discretionall power and rated some one way and some
another and their moneys are not [?yet] paid into the exchequer[88] as for the
county where I live we went exactly after 3 4ths of [16]93 and we are all friends
and ou[r] money is all paid in:[89] pray sir what is aymed at by this discretionall
power Shall the com[*mi*]s[*sione*]rs new rate the whole countye again if so
when will the rate be setled and the money collected or is the meaning of it to
go after 3: 4ths or the m[on]thly assesment at their choyce as for the monthly
assesment it is so notoriously unequall it has been long sin[ce] decried and
laid aside[90] and I hope it will never be used again: then sir as for the reflecting
upon the Com[*mi*]s[*sione*]rs by not giving them a discretionall power Sir I
know country busines much better than the busines of this ho[use] and I
beleive I should hardly be censured should I say I had observed partiality in
committees here and what[?ever] you may think I can assure you when we meet
in bodyes we are not much honester in the country

[88] For partial confirmation, see *Cal. Treas. Bks.*, xiv. 112; and W. R. Ward, *The English Land
Tax in the Eighteenth Century* (London, 1953).

[89] Cocks was a commissioner for Gloucestershire under the 1698 act. What is more, the
receiver-general for the county was a Richard Cocks, possibly a relation: *Cal. Treas. Bks.*, xiii.
304, 399. Interestingly, the assessments for 1699 did provoke conflict between the commissioners:
Ward, *Land Tax*, 35.

[90] The method of proceeding by 'monthly assessment', which dated back to the Interregnum,
had been followed in 1689–92, but the debate on the 1693 tax revealed great resentment at the
inequitable and out-of-date quotas, and a rate per pound on the value of property was substituted.
This experiment was abandoned in 1698. See Ward, *Land Tax*, 2–10; Beckett, 'Land Tax or
Excise', 287–95; and Horwitz, *Parliament, Policy and Politics*, 111–12. The amount paid by
Gloucestershire was actually higher under the pound rate, and the use of this figure as the basis
for the quotas of 1698/9 made the return to assessment even less palatable to Cocks and his
constituents: Ward, *Land Tax*, 8.

[n.d.] of the parliament[91]

the parliament is the representative body of the nation and before I was one
amongst them before I knew what they did there I fancyed the fools were awed
governed and had a respect for those that were famous and renowned for their
worth and parts, and that the Knaves for indeed I knew some such there were
would disguise themselves and be in fear of being censured by the honest
judicious and better part of our representatives upon these considerations I
expected if not a judicious honest sober and grave assembly att least in
appearance I mean one that would seem to be such: instead I found them
all upon parties insomuch that if they did not totally banish judgment I am
sure they did honesty for I think a man may averr tho it may be art and
cunning to be of and to maintain a par[ty] yet it is hard[l]y honest for men
who are chose to serve their countryes to go throw stick right or wrong with
such a party: and I beleive in all matters of moment reasoning does no more
than spend time for let but musgrove of one side or mountague of the other go
but out to divide and mu[?ch] the major part of the House will follow their
leader as well without as with reason then as for the gravity and sobriety it is
intollerable there is such a noyse one can scarce hear or mind what is said and
indeed what is particularly minded is private busines, to make partyes to make
Court etc: when I observed this after I was there a little time I much wonderd
our acts were penned so well as they are as befor[e] I admired how they could
have any faults; this bred in me a malancholy fear least this age had degen-
era[ted] but this fear vanished upon reading the journalls of the happy times
of Elizabeth there I found they co[m]plained of the same things of the noyse
and tumults wors then ever:[92] there are few that mind or understand the true
interest of the nation in most of our publick busines men are biassed by private
end[s] as to the fishery which is the undoubted and the best and most
profitable trade of the nation I mean to the Kingdom[93] and so for the woollen
manufacture[94] you shall find a private bill to serve some littl[e] inconsiderable
member by the craft and subtilty of a member to create himself a private
interest by the inadvertencye of the majority Steale into an act by this means

---

[91] What follows seems unlikely to have been a speech in the House.

[92] For some choice examples, see Hayward Townshend, *Historical Collections: Or, an Exact
Account of the Proceedings of the Four Last Parliaments of Q. Elizabeth* . . . (London, 1680), 205,
220, 229; and Sir Symonds D'Ewes, *The Journals of all the Parliaments during the Reign of Queen
Elizabeth* . . . (London, 1682), 640, 644. See also Sir John Neale *Elizabeth I and Her Parliaments* (2
vols.; London, 1953–7), ii. 270–3, 404–5.

[93] A reference either to the bill to give statutory establishment to the Royal Fishery Company,
brought in on 20 Mar. (*CJ* xii. 603), or, more probably, the bill to make Billingsgate a free market,
brought in on 21 Jan. (*CJ* xii. 446), which involved a number of local interests among east coast
boroughs.   [94] See below, pp. 26–30.

Sir W: Young procured the pas[si]ng of an act to prohibit the importation of flanders lace into the Kingdom[95] which never exce[e]ded 50000 li which made them prohibit the importation of our English woollen and other manufactures into flanders where there was imported from us goods manufactured to the value of 500000 li per annum:[96] it was this private interest which made the prohibiting the Irish cattle pass the house and stand so long unrepealed[97] it is undoubtedly the advantage to every place of England to have the Irish cattle brought in here: by that means the Irish would trade only with us and they would lay out the money they sold their cattle for upon our manufactu[res] by this means we should have the manufacturing of their tallow and hides and the sole serv[?ing] of the plantations with powderd[98] beef this would employ abundance of our people besides it would encreas our navigation: I remember I complimented Sir A: Kek[99] after he had been chosen to serve in parliament and had sate some time I told him the nation expected som[e] great things from him: this put this great and wise man in a rage to find he should not answer the expectations the world had of him and in his passion he expressed himself thus Sir you are mistaken in your thoughts of the house the house of commons is a bear garden you would do more good there then I can: we seldom get an house with 11 or 12 and a house is only 40 if there is a tyger or a great bear or some monster to be seen or baited wee have generally a very thinne house: and at committees for elections which begins 3 hours generally after the house rises there you shall see some of the members come in drunk some sleep and some tumultuous and seldome any mind the justice but his friend or the party: I remember one gent[*leman*] whose election was contested desired me to attend at the commi[t]tee and he told me he had a very just good

<hr>

[95] For Sir Walter Yonge's contribution to the passage of the 1698 Lace Act (9 Gul. III, c. 9), see *CJ* xii. 16, 41. His constituency, Honiton, was a noted centre for the manufacture of 'bone-lace in imitation of the Antwerp and Flanders lace': Christopher Morris (ed.), *The Journeys of Celia Fiennes* (London, 1949), 271.

[96] After a petition to the Commons from clothiers in Salisbury, linking the passage of the Lace Act directly to the recent slump in the woollen trade, Cocks himself, as the representative of another woollen-manufacturing district, introduced on 14 Apr. 1699 a bill to set a term to the prohibition of lace imports: *CJ* xii. 635, 641.

[97] The Irish Cattle Act of 1667 (18 & 19 Car. II c. 2), which expired only in 1679: see Carolyn A. Edie, 'The Irish Cattle Bills: A Study in Restoration Politics', *Transactions of the American Philosophical Society,* NS 60 (1970), 5–66.   [98] Salted.

[99] Sir Anthony Keck (1630–95), commissioner of the Great Seal 1689–90, MP Tiverton 1691–d., for whom see *DNB*. Like Cocks a Gloucestershire man, Keck was a strong supporter of such 'Country' measures as triennial bills, and allegedly believed the best form of government to be 'a republic, or, which was the same thing, a king always in check': Henry Horwitz (ed.), *The Parliamentary Diary of Narcissus Luttrell 1691–1693* (Oxford, 1972), 413; Roger North, *The Lives of . . . Francis North . . . Sir Dudley North; and . . . Dr John North*, ed. Augustus Jessopp (3 vols.; London, 1890), iii. 169.

cause I told him sir I have been now some little time in the house and I can easily tell the right without examining the merrits have you voted in the great poynts with the majority if so you have a just and consequently a safe and a good cause one would think by this relation that we should expect no good from a body so composed and so disposed but by such a body by such a government we have continued and have done [?so] this many 100d years and I hope we shall do so many 100d more there are the same nu[mber] of good as formerly and I beleive not one bad one less: and I beleive in other countryes thi[?ngs are] hardly better and if we are not wors then our neighbours I hope we shall do well god w[?illing]

[*fo. 90*]

[*13, 15 Mar. 1699*] There was this sessions a complaint reade in the house by a member that as I remember one Mr Buller had never petitioned the house and yet brought an action against the mayor for a falls return:[100] some said we never endeavoured to mend elections and settle the rights of them but we made them wors others said that if we let this proceed to a tryall we shall subject the rights of this house to the judgment of westminster hall[101] others affirmed that the remedy given by the late statute was a very good one and a certain rule and that if the sherriffe or mayor would voluntarily offend gent[*lemen*] would hardly think it worth time to be at the charge of petitioning the house, since elections were managed there with so much charge and uncertaintye: and since the law had given a rule to the officer to return by the same way and votes as formerly if he would do otherwise let him suffer and if this was tryed in westminster hall before the Kings bench and from thence by appeall brought before the Lords yet it [*would*] not make them masters of our priviledges but yet the officer was punished by the law made: H: neville[102] 1656 brought a speciall action against Strode the sherriff of Berks for a fals and malicious return mr neville recovered 1500 li

---

[100] John Buller (*c*.1668–1701), of Morval, Cornwall, MP Lostwithiel Jan.–Mar. 1701. Having contested Liskeard at the 1698 general election, and been denied his rightful seat, or so he alleged, by the partiality of the mayor, Richard Roberts, Buller was advised by counsel not to risk the uncertainty of a petition to the Commons but to sue the mayor in the common law courts for the £500 damages to which the 1696 Election Regulation Act (7 & 8 Gul. III, c. 25) entitled him: Buller MSS (Antony House, Cornwall), BO/23/72/3, 4, Buller's case, 'instructions . . .', and John Buller, sen., to [–], 26 Aug. 1698. The House, being informed of this proceeding, debated it at length on 13 and 14 Mar., but did not come to any resolution: *CJ* xii. 584, 590. The action was used as a precedent in the more controversial case of Ashby *v.* White: Eveline Cruickshanks, 'Ashby *v.* White: The Case of the Men of Aylesbury, 1701–4', in Clyve Jones (ed.), *Party and Management in Parliament, 1660–1784* (Leicester, 1984), 89, 94.

[101] i.e. the courts of common law accommodated in Westminster Hall.

[102] Henry Neville, Cocks's uncle by marriage, for whom see above, pp. xviii–xix.

damages:[103] and followed it throw all the courts in spight of Oliver and when he had made the example he forgave the sherriffe

Business to be done next sessions

of the poor[104]

The poor are those I mean that will not or cannot maintain themselves by their Labour and I am of opinion that the reason that has made many leave an honest labour and endeavour to support themselves in idlenes by begging is this provisions have of late been very dear and many of these poor have eyther not had full employment or have worked at such moderate rates that their wages would not find them necessaries which has obliged many of them to seek their fortunes and leave their work would not keep them: formerly 1d would buie a busshell of wheat and 6s and 8d an ox undoubtedly then there was more plenty of corn great scarcity of money and hardly so many people to labour undoubtedly when corn and money bore so great a disproportion the poor labourers had not so much wages as would find them or buie them a busshell of wheat with one days labour: as corn and provisions grew dearer which did not proceed at all from the scarcity of corn but from the plenty of money: tho I will not say but that in a year of great plenty corn may be cheaper and so in a year of great scarcity dearer but I dare venture to say that corn beef mutton chees wool and all necessaryes and provisions will never be so cheap as formerly: the wars have made mankind necessitous these necessityes have

---

[103] William Strowde (*c.*1614–*c.*1667), of Northbury, Ruscombe, Berks., sheriff 1655–6, for whom see *The Berks., Bucks. and Oxon. Archaeological Journal*, 12 (1906–7), 22–4; Victoria County History, *Berkshire*, iii. 204. After failing to secure election for Berkshire in 1656, Neville brought an action against Strowde in Common Pleas, on the basis of the statute 23 Hen. VI, c. 15. His case was in turn cited as a precedent in 1674, in Barnardiston *v.* Soame. *CJ* vii. 598–9, 672, 823–4; J. T. Rutt (ed.), *Diary of Thomas Burton . . .* (4 vols.; London, 1828), iii. 51–2, 498. Dr Worden (Ludlow, *Voyce*, ed. Worden 73) observes that here Cocks seems to be following the published version of Edmund Ludlow's memoirs: *The Memoirs of Edmund Ludlow . . .* (3 vols.; Vivay, 1698), ii. 600–2. See also below, pp. 31–2.

[104] Whilst the title of the following passage suggests an essay or memorial, the inclusion of a term of address indicates that it may also have served as the draft of a parliamentary speech. On 20 Dec. 1698 a committee had been appointed, including Cocks, to consider ways of reforming the poor law. If the speech had been intended for that debate it cannot have been given then, since by Cocks's own admission his maiden speech occurred on 4 Jan. 1699 (see above p. 1). The reference to 'next sessions' suggests that what we have here may be a draft for a speech at the beginning of the following session, on 19 Nov. 1699, when the committee was reconstituted, again with Cocks among its members (this time accompanied by all the Gloucestershire representatives). *CJ* xii. 360; xiii. 405. The subject was one which preoccupied Sir Richard. In May 1700 he was to send the Archbishop of Canterbury a lengthy disquisition on the problem of the poor and the best way to achieve a legislative remedy: Lambeth Palace Library, MS 640 (Tenison papers), fos. 501–21, copied into the memoranda-books at MS Eng. hist. b. 209, fos. 82–80. On the general question of poor law reform in this period, see S. Macfarlane, 'Social Policy and the Poor', in A. L. Beier and R. Finlay (edd.), *London 1500–1700* (London, 1986), 252–77; and Paul Slack, *Poverty and Policy in Tudor and Stuart England* (London, 1988), ch. 9.

made them sharp and industrious and this necessitous ingenuity has not only
supplyed with oak wood to dy with instead of Galls: these wants have not only
forced them to dig salt out of the rocks but allso more gold and silver out of
the mines, and has discovered more that lay rusting and sleeping in chests and
holes then the mines have of late produced this has probably made money
more plenty and consequently corn eatables and necessaryes dearer and the
first thing to be considerd of for our poor is not only to employ them but when
wee have employed them to order them so much wages for their work as they
may maintain themselves by their Labour: the wages of the poor ought to bear
a proportion to the prices of commodities this ought to be done but how to
have it so ordered I know not: Sir, The poor are a burthen to the rich a charge
and damage to the nation a scandall to the Xtian religion: wherefore I desire
you will appoynt a committee to consider of what laws we have proper and of
what Laws are wanting with a power to repeale all the old laws and to make
one Law in the place of them and that wee may send for persons papers and
records.

of woole

of woole manufactured.[105]

there is no dispute but we ought to incourage the wool of all parts to be
brought in here and to work here into the severall manufactures it is proper
for, and to export the manuf[a]ctures and not the wooll, which is so much
clear advantage to the nation a pound of woole manufactured brings more
then ten unworked: some Gent[*lemen*] have a notion that wool would be
dearer could we have liberty to export it, it is possible it may be so for a
season whilest they buie our wooll to mix with wooll otherwise uncapable of
being wrought into which [?when] will make the more plen[?tiful]:[106] but I

---

[105] As with the previous passage, it is unclear whether this is a draft of a speech, and if so, when
it was meant to be delivered. On 17 Dec. 1698 a committee had been appointed to consider ways to
prevent the export of wool and to encourage the woollen manufacture, and Cocks had been one of
the Members nominated (*CJ* xii. 358). This committee eventually reported on 28 Feb. 1699 and a
resultant bill was presented on 15 Mar., only to founder (*CJ* xii. 532, 588). Three other bills on the
same subject were also put forward during the session: Sir Edward Seymour's, introduced on 20
Dec. 1698 and, after a false start, reintroduced the following day, which eventually reached the
statute book as 10 Gul. III, c. 16; Lord Fairfax's, introduced on 20 January, which came to nothing;
and a somewhat different measure, sponsored by Gloucestershire and Wiltshire interests and
including Cocks in its drafting committee, which was concerned with reforming abuses in the
wholesale cloth market at Blackwell Hall (see below, p. 33): *CJ* xii. 360, 364, 444, 449, 520. Anxiety
in Gloucestershire over the depression in the clothing industry is evident from the three petitions
that came in from the county in this session: *CJ* xii. 423, 525, 530–1. It may be, however, that
Cocks is still referring here to business to be done in the next session, when on 27 Nov. 1699
another committee was appointed to consider methods of protecting the manufacture, including
Cocks himself and the rest of the Members for Gloucestershire.
[106] 'whilest they buie', to 'the more plen[?tiful]' interlined.

cant see the advantage even the landed men, (I mean the proprietour, not the tenant) can have or rationa[ll]y propose to himselfe having the product of the land at such great rates: indeed it would be of great advantage to the owner of the land to have fixed rates for the product of land: for according to the rates of things do we set our land: if corn bears a great price and so for catle cheese [?and but]ter when we sett land we shall have many tenants offer themselves but very few that [wi]ll offer any advance of rent: for these commodityes having been of late of Lower value the [tena]nt sais to himself I will venture to give no more rent then I can make if commodityes were of [?the] Lowest price I have known them:, so that if that should happen I am safe if the present price [co]ntinues I am then a gainer; now in this case if the prices of things continue the te[na]nt grows vastly rich and the landlord poor: the poor is reduced to extremityes: the usurer is [?well ni]gh worsted and trade not incouraged: no man in the kingdom but the occupier of land van[?taged] for instance the landlord sets his land for so many pound of beef mutton chees

[*fo. 89ᵛ*]

and wool:[107] to explain this every man that gets land considers with himself thus: my land will probably produce so many quarter of corn so many 10d of wooll so many 100d of cheess will fat so many beefs, so many muttons, and at such a rate the busshell, and at such a rate the pound, my tenant may live by his labour, and pay me so much rent, now in case these commodityes rise or fall by plenty or scarcity then there is no great damage or advantage to me or my tenant: if they [?sink] and continue so to do Lower then we expected, without that reason when we made the bargain, then hee is broke: if they rise and continue to do so then I am at a loss: for tho men have their rent paid in silver and gold, it is in effect but wool beef muton butter and cheese: and when commodityes are very low my tenant pays me more wooll etc. then he could rais of my land: which must ruine him: when corn wool beef etc. rise without any visible cause, as scarcity, or the unseasonableness of the year: then my tenant does pay me it is true in law so many busshell pounds etc. as we agreed to but this advance of price is a cheat that is come between us and has taken one halve away: for as the landlord really beleived his ren[t] would bring him such and such things, which he knew his tenant might pay him, now he finds he is mistaken and he has not halve and yet his tenant from the goodnes of the bargain well able to have payd the whole: the poor that thinks the parish is obliged in old age extremityes, and necessityes to provide for him, who in plenty and cheap times will eyther work little, or live without saving in hard

---

[107] 'for just half so many pound' erased.

times viz when the prices of every thing rises except his work is reduced to extreme necessityes: the usurer is in a wors case then the landlord: the landlord may eyther advance or occupy his land himself but the usurer if hee keeps his monye idle gets nothing: if he sets it out, if the prices of thing[s] run low he is the only true gainer: as in the other case hee is the only true looser of necesity: in a quick trade, where money circulates all commodityes will bear a tolerable good rate but for men to endeavouo[r] or desire to do anything to make necessaryes extremely dear is rather a damage then an advantag[e] to the publick, for as I have shewed before that the poor are made poorer the Landlord in effect have hi[s] rent and in short no gainer, but the Tenant gets all,: [*sic*] so when commodityes bear such high rates not only the Gen[?*tlemen*] etc. that set their estates but all mechanicks retailers merchants and all traders are at great expences more then usually which they must of necessity raise out of the advance of the commodity they trade in, or by liv[ing] less profusely or more saving (which we shall hardly perswade them to[)]: then if the commoditys are advan[ced] suppose 4s in the pound suppose I advance my land 4s in the pound am I a gainer no certainly I am in a manner if I spend my yearly incomb just where I was: id est I cant live 2d better for the advanced rent[108] indeed if I hord it all up I shall save more yearly: but so much for home trade: now as for our english manufactures, that are exported, if our manufacturers themselves are forced by reason of the dearnes of necessaryes to live at an higher and more expensive rate and if on the same reason our merchants are forced to do the same then of necessity our manufactures exported must be sold at forreign markets dearer by so much, as well as the retailer at home to sell[109] commodityes imported or manufactured at home: it may be for the interest as before of the occupyer of land to have the product advanced in price but it is prejudiciall to all the nation besides and very hurtfull to trade it self: as for trade it must flourish best undoubtedly where there is the most incouragement I speak cheifly as to manufactures and people have the most incouragement to settle work there where they can subsist comfortably by their work: and worked goods do bear a proportionable rate to the provisions of the country where they are manufactured: tis this makes the yorkshire stockings the welsh Flannings[110] so reasonable and so for many more: but had we no trade but with and amongst our selves it would be hardly worth our time to provide for these matters but to let chance take place and to let necessitye give rules and law, but since we are an island and our very

---

[108] 'id est I cant live 2d better for the advanced rent' interlined.
[109] 'the retailer at home to sell' interlined.   [110] Flannels.

subsistence and mere being does in a manner depend upon trade it is our interest and therefore our dutye to incourage trade which must be first by making such laws as are wanting repealing such as are inconvenient and in short to take care that speedy and cheap justice be done upon all occasions the next thing is if practicall to make sumptuary laws if possible[111] to hinder the expencive and vain way of living of our merchants and traders: by which profusenes if any losses happen by land or sea by fire or water they are feighn to turn Bankrupts to cheat their creditors and to give of[f] trading to the ruine of their own and other familyes and the great damage of the Publick: next to this we ought to take care that our provisions may bear such rates that our working people and those that buie from them may be able to subsist and when at Forreign markets to sell as cheap as good as any other nation that use that market, with the same goods there must therfore be no dutie on any comodity or relating to any commodity exported hence to foreign markets[112] now for the high prices of our wools if the price did proceed from the quicknes of the manufactured trade used amongst us and if our nation had monopolised the trade of the world so that they could afford to give what prices they would for unwrought wools, becaus they could sell ther manufactured woollen goods at what rate they would abroad: in that case if the price of wool did proceed from such causes if they did not set to[o] gr[?eat] a price upon their manufactured goods, so high as to force other nations to set up for them-selves this would undoubtedly be good from us: but if the high price of our wools does proceed from this reason becaus forreigners buie our unwrought wools to manufacture them at home with them and if that makes a quick trade by forcing our clothiers to advance price in order to keep our wools at home and to have them m[anufac]tured here it is no good to the nation: if there was a rent established between landlord and tenant a[?ccording] to the rates of goods I mean the product of the land: if money was setled at a low and proportionable r[?ent] and if the price of all the product of the earth was very moderate from our good husbandry and ple[?nty ?or] from want of trade and people: it would be no damage to us at home and an advantage to us [?abroad] or to a forreign trade: as for example if I set my land for a low rent and every body does so this low r[?ent ?will] bring me as much of every thing I want as the bigger rent did: gent[*lemen*] may fancy what they please b[ut ?by] examination and a wise inquiry it will be found: that the same estate will keep the master in the same condit[ion ?as] many horses as many servants as

---

[111] to be put in practice' erased.
[112] 'there must therefore be' to 'foreign markets' interlined.

good a table and every thing as plentifully if commod[i]ties produ[?ced]
[fo. 89]
[?are] cheap nay I dare affirm better then if at a great price: as for example if
all things are cheap if this is not from a decay of trade but plenty certainly I am
at no damage: no tho this plenty should proceed from the good husbandry of
improvements if my own land is not worsted I shall mow as much hay thresh
as much corn, fat as many cattle etc. and let the prices of the product sink or
fall I can live the same as ever I could, so it is the same thing to me: but in
relation to trade if provisions are very dear the artificer must eyther starve or
work at a great rate so that when we come to a Forreign market the merchants
for example that live and trade in Ireland if it was permitted them to
manufacture cloth would undersell undo and ruine our english woollen
merchants:[113] upon which reasons it seems to me probable that if the Irish
catle corn and all their provisions came in hither if they should make ours
cheaper that would by no means hurt us but would vastly advance and
incourage our trade:[114] I have heard many tradesmen have left england and
went and setled in other more remote countryes merely for the more con-
veniancy of provision now if by any means provisions by a greater plenty
became cheaper I have made it appear the occupyer of Land would by no
means suffer and it is rather more then probable that such conveniencyes
would keep our own natives at home and invite forreighners to come from
abroad and settle amongst us: and that by the cheapnes of our victualls by the
conveniency of our scituation wee might be masters of the woollen manu-
fact[ure] and of all handicraft trades out do and excell and undersell all
europe which would do the nation more good then to sell her commodityes
unwrought at a vast expensive rate.
[. . .][115]

---

[113] A reference to the purpose behind Seymour's 1698/9 bill: see above, p. 26, n. 105; H. F.
Kearney, 'The Political Background to English Mercantilism, 1695–1700', *Economic History
Review*, 2nd ser., 11 (1959), 484–96; and Patrick Kelly, 'The Irish Woollen Export Prohibition
Act of 1699: Kearney Re-Visited', *Irish Economic and Social History*, 7 (1980), 22–43.
[114] See above, p. 23.
[115] Omitted: 'An account of Grants from [*William*] Lownd[*e*]s [*secretary to the Treasury*] lately
made' (fos. 89–8); abstract of revenue from excise, customs, Post Office, and 'small branches',
1693–4 (fo. 88).

[*fo. 87ᵛ*]

[*n.d.*] The design of the long parliament to regulate elections before oliver turned them out[116]

some of the principall cittyes should chuse one member for the most part except london the rest of the 400 to be chosen by the countyes besides those that served for Scotland and Ireland the electors to be worth 200 li in reall or personall estate[117]

[*n.d.*] of oliver in relation to a Standing Army[118]

whatever country or government is feighn to support it self by a standing army may observe the revolutions that hapned to us, may remember from oliver Crumwell not to trust a generall too long or with too much power crumwell filld the army with officers that were his creaturs or that had the same aspiring designes and after the crowning victory as he called it of worcester he dismissed the militia which had done him good service with scorn and anger:[119] knowing a militia w[o]uld never act against the interest of the country or be out of conceipt with[120] a parliament that had subdued their enemi[es] in England Scotland and Ireland had reduced portugall to the terms they desired and had beat the dutch:[121] but upon the confide[n]ce and assurance of the standing army he comes into the house of commons in a pretended fanaticall furious mad canting Zeale to hide his Knavery and tells the parliament they were no parliament I will put an end to your sitting abused severall members takes away the mace by the helping hand of Gen: Harrison[122] he pulls down the Speaker:[123] here you may see the army turne out

---

[116] This short passage is clearly not a speech by itself, nor even part of one, but it may have been a preliminary note towards some comments Cocks intended to offer the House on the subject of electoral reform. 'Country' activists were beginning to entertain the idea of disfranchising some rotten boroughs and merging their seats with the county representation (John Toland, *The Art of Governing by Partys* . . . (London, 1701), 76–7; Warwickshire RO, CR 1386/iii/57 (Mordaunt of Walton Hall MSS), Sir Charles Holt to Sir John Mordaunt, 24 Mar. 1700[/1]), a solution attempted in 1702 in an abortive bill to disfranchise Hindon, a measure with which Cocks's associate Thomas Jervoise was intimately concerned (HMC, *House of Lords MSS*, NS v. 202–3; Hampshire RO, 44M69/08 [Jervoise MSS], speech by Jervoise, 1702).

[117] As Dr Worden pointed out (Ludlow, *Voyce*, ed. Worden, 73), Cocks here paraphrases the recent edition of Ludlow's memoirs (*Memoirs of Ludlow*, ii. 435–6). On the Rump's proposed electoral reforms, see Blair Worden, *The Rump Parliament* (Cambridge, 1974), ch. 8.

[118] Words addressed to the Chair mark this as part of a speech, most probably concerning the Disbanding Bill. As Dr Worden observes (Ludlow, *Voyce*, ed. Worden, 47), Cocks is again quoting extensively from Ludlow, and indeed the burden of his argument follows the preface to the third volume of the 1698 edition: 'men may learn from the issue of the Cromwellian tyranny, that liberty and a standing mercenary army are incompatible.'

[119] Paraphrased from *Memoirs of Ludlow*, ii. 447.   [120] i.e. dissatisfied with.

[121] Paraphrased from *Memoirs of Ludlow*, ii. 452–3.

[122] Thomas Harrison (1606–60), the regicide.

[123] The story is taken from *Memoirs of Ludlow*, ii. 455–7.

their own masters the bravest and the wisest and the most fortunate and successfull government this nation had Known for some ages: then contrary to their oaths sence and duty they many of them designed and all most made oliver king: who could never get the civill authority to countenance his arbitrary power[124] oliver dyes leaving the army filld with his own creatures governed by his sone in law affectionate and obliged to his family yet in a few months after his death: they depose Richard Crumwel[l] protector of the common wealth as they proclaimed him after his fathers death declared also generall of the army by the parliament: the very same army also restore the commonwealth or long parliament: Soon after this the army place gaurds to hinder the members from coming to the house and appoynt a select number of themselves and their creatures called a com[*mit*]tee of safety to have the administration: and then by monks means and pretences the parliament met and then they brought in the excluded members and by their means and monks power they brought in the king:[125] and i[f] he had not had them disbanded it is more than probable they would in a short time have turned him a tr[a]velling again if they had not served him wors: pray sir was it the prince of orange or king jameses own arm[y] that were most instrumentall in expelling the tirant Ki[*ng*] J[*ames*][126] Sir I have not went to shew you out of old hist[ories] of the Romans how many Caesars the armys made and unmade or to tell what other countryes have s[u]ffered or theis governments of France Sweden or denmark have been altered by their armyes or to tell what has hapned heretofore to this kingdom the instances I have repeated are in some Gent[*lemen's*] knowledg and fresh in every ones memory, and I dare affirm that a good prince will not be safer nor better by having a standing army and an indifferent one will be abundantly wors: and a bad one will not long be acceptable to the very army he commands: but that after they are tired in obeying his unjus[t] Tirannicall orders they will be nauseated at blood a weary at unjustice and joyn with the tide of the people to expell or depose that very Tirant they themselves made so

---

[124] 'who could never get' to 'arbitrary power' interlined.
[125] General George Monck (1608–70) created Duke of Albemarle after the Restoration. The story is taken from *Memoirs of Ludlow*, ii. 615–83.
[126] Here Cocks quotes from John Trenchard and Walter Moyle's *Argument . . . against a Standing Army* (1697), repr. in *William III State Tracts*, ii. 575.

of Blackwell Hall[127]

our cheif care ought to be of the clothier, and first seller for if they are damaged and suffer loss it affects the very trade it self for it is impossible for him to maintain the workers under him and support the manufacturers if he shall not have good payment of the money he sells those goods for: if therefore the clothier has not ready money he ought to have notes which he may transferr or endors for another the said notes to go as bills of Exchange and subject to the same law and rules as bills of exchange are: this note would save all delays would serve the clothier instead of money for with this note can he supply himself wit[h] oyle Spanish wool and what he wants and it will prevent all reckoning law suits and controversyes which [are] the bane and ruine of trade: and further the wollen trade being the trade of most advantage to the nation both for the poor it employs at home and from the riches it brings from abroad ou[gh]t above althings to be considered and to have all the advantages no disincouragement no dutye upon it at home nor abroad but that no regard in comparison of the trade should be had of Christchurch hospi-tall[128] or the priviledges of the citty: but that the first seller may sell where he will: and the buier be he stranger or free of the citty or alien may buie in blacwell hall or where he pleases: it would also be of great advantage to trade to have some persons appoynted or care taken to have our cloths made well and that if any cheat should appear tha[t] every clothier should set his own mark as well as the seale of the office that there may [be] satisfaction given in our courts for cloth sould beyond the seas: and all unwrought wools ought to

---

[127] The principal London cloth market, in Basinghall Street, and the subject of long-standing grievances held by the provincial clothiers who were obliged to sell their goods to wholesale drapers and export-merchants through middlemen known as 'factors'. These factors had engrossed the trade, and their delays in payments to the clothiers were a source of grave complaint: E. Lipson, *The Economic History of England* (6th edn., 3 vols.; London, 1956), ii. 25–31. After several attempts at reform, an act had been passed in 1697 (8 & 9 Gul. III, c. 9), supposedly at the instigation of rich Gloucestershire clothiers (*The Blackwell Hall Factors' Case* . . . (1698); *Reasons for a General Liberty to All Clothiers to Sell Their Cloth when, where and as They Please* (1698); *The Reply of the Country to the Sound Reasons of the City for a General Liberty to the Clothiers* . . . (?1698)) to compel the factors to obtain 'notes of hand' from their wholesale customers for the convenience of the clothiers. On 25 Jan. 1699 a bill was ordered to make that act more effective, Cocks being included in the drafting committee. The bill, supported by a petition from Gloucestershire, was read on 21 Feb. and eventually passed the Commons, only to be held up in the Lords. *CJ* xii. 449, 520, 558, 640, 656, 675; HMC, *House of Lords MSS*, NS iii. 366–7, 377–8. Conceivably, Cocks is here still looking forward to the next session, at the beginning of which, on 24 Nov. 1699, a further bill was ordered to regulate the market. Cocks again appeared in the drafting committee. *CJ* xiii. 5.

[128] Blackwell Hall was the property of Christ's Hospital, which received a levy on goods brought into the market, a privilege that the House of Lords in the 1698/9 session had sought to enshrine in one of their amendments: E. H. Pearce, *Annals of Christ's Hospital* (London, 1901), 187; HMC, *House of Lords MSS*, NS iii. 367.

have no duty in Ireland before they are shipped nor no custome here but we ought to give all the incouragement imaginable to bring wool unwrought in hither from all parts

[*n.d.*] of seamen and sea affairs[129]

Sea captains ought not to be obliged to pay the mariners at every unlading port Sometimes the freight is lost and sometimes the ship sold in the furthermost parts of the world to pay the seamen by which means the men scar[*ce*]ly come over hom[e] and the ship is lost to the nation: good laws incourage the merchant the incouraging the merchant increases trade and sea men: the captain often abuses the necessitous seamen the ship is sometimes lost the captain dyes and his book is lost and the merchant sued and forced to pay over again and the seamen get nothing at all sometimes: the dutch h[?ave] a better economy for their shipping: their captains are obliged to pay no more then subsistence money: their having all their money paid them at forreign ports helps to debauch them makes them have no dependance on their captain who is obliged to bring them back makes them enter into any forreign service for a little [?better] wages since they have nothing to expect at home and they are unwilling to see a wife and children whom they have slighted and neglected and must find starving without hope of releif

[*n.d.*] of the prohibiting foreign iron

[. . .][130]

---

[129] Cocks repeated these observations in his memorial to the Archbishop of Canterbury in May 1700: Lambeth Palace Lib. MS 640, fo. 521.

[130] Omitted: 'of Trade in answer to my Cousin Ball Sep[*tem*]b[*e*]r 1699' (fos. 87–86ᵛ).

1698 Parliament: 1699/1700 Session

[fo. 85ᵛ]

parliament [16]99 No[vem]b[e]r 26 [recte 27][1]

Sir Ed[ward] Seymour said mr How had well anotomised the K[ing's] speech mr How reflected on the parting speech and on th[e] ministry he said they had not put the supply of[f] out of disrespect to the king but to put things in their antient channell:[2] hee laid open the luxury the vices the debauchery of the court he railed against the clergyes being in com[mi]s[sio]n of the peace: he said little men that had been tooles in all reigns were in com[mi]s[sio]n that none were within 15 miles of him:[3] he complimented the souldiery and said their pay ought to be certain[4] he railed against drunkennes and gaming[5] and said some people told storyes of him what he said at kinsington:[6] [I] answered and said I would ease that worthy member of one of the evills that troubled him by assuring him that there were a great man[y] justices in 3 or 4 miles of him and I hoped other Gent[lemen] would do the same as to what concerned their knowledge: the next day [28 Nov. 1699] after the resolutions were read for the laying the com[mi]s[sio]n of the justices and deputy L[ieutenan]ts before the house:[7] mr How said they ought to know how so many gent[lemen] came to be

---

[1] In the committee of the whole House to consider the King's Speech.

[2] In his speech at the close of the preceding session, delivered on 4 May 1699, William had remarked, 'If anything shall be found wanting, for our safety, the support of the public credit, by making good the faith of the kingdom, as it stands engaged by parliamentary securities, and for discharge of the debts occasioned by the war, I cannot doubt but effectual care will be taken of them next winter, and I wish no inconvenience may happen in the meantime': LJ xvi. 466.

[3] Howe's Gloucestershire seat was at Stowell Park near Northleach. His strong feelings were almost certainly due to the fact that recently he himself had been displaced from the county commission of the peace in a Whig purge: L. K. J. Glassey, Politics and the Appointment of Justices of the Peace 1675–1720 (Oxford, 1979), 123, 127.

[4] Possibly a reference back to the number of petitions received during the previous session over arrears of army pay (see above, p. 13 n. 55), though the issue remained a live one (see HMC, Portland MSS, iii. 615).

[5] On 28 Nov., on a motion from this committee, the House ordered an address requesting a proclamation against 'vice and immorality', and a bill against gaming and duelling. Howe was named first to the drafting committee on the bill (Cocks being also included): CJ xiii. 8. For Howe's uncharacteristic participation in the parliamentary agitation for a reformation of morals, see D. Hayton, 'Moral Reform and Country Politics in the Late Seventeenth-Century House of Commons', Past and Present, 128 (1990), 60, 69, 73.   [6] Kensington House, i.e. at Court.

[7] On a motion of the committee of the whole on the King's Speech, a further committee was appointed (including both Howe and Cocks) to inspect the commissions of the peace and lieutenancy over the preceding seven years: CJ xiii. 8.

turned out I said sir as to what relates to the county of Glo[u]c[este]r I can give
you an account in the incomparable reign of the good Elizabeth there were
plots to destroy her and to subvert the government the people of England
entred into a voluntary association for her preservation:[8] we sir in imitation of
that virtuous and good reig[n] when our King and country was in danger the
one of being assacinated the other by that of being undone entred into the like
association: their association was made a law and so was ours pray sir do you
beleive those that refused that association were intrusted with the government:
neyther were ours:[9] to which there was no answer: the next upon some
occasion Mr How said now wee are upon a generall reformation: after the
resolution for laying the justices com[*mission*]s was agreed with I rose up and
said: Sir I desire another com[*mi*]s[*sio*]n may be laid before the house: Sir it
was well observed to you that a worthy member had well and exactly
anotomised the kings speech and I might say he had well exposed the luxury
and voluptuousnes and vices of the court: Sir there are other vices that I know
of which were not mentioned: I would have spoke then to them had not a fit of
modesty seised me: Sir I knew my own faults and I hardly thought one that
had so many was fitt [*to*] reform others: but sir when I recollected that
without doors those that were sickly and in[?firm] usually railed against
drinking and those whom the long practice of wickednes had made impotent
usually railed against whoring: at this there was a quarter of an hours laugh:
Sir when I remember my tutor in Oxford who was allwais drunk would preach
incomparably well against all other sins but drunkennes:[10] I have taken the
confidence to spar[e] my own darling sin and raile at reproach the faults of
others: but before I lay my finger upon the sore I poyn[t] at I will say

[8] The Bond of Association of 1584.
[9] On the Association of 1696, see above, p. 7, n. 31. The consequent purges of the commission
of the peace are discussed in Glassey, *Appointment of JPs*, 118–34. Sixteen justices were removed
in Gloucestershire (ibid. 119).
[10] It has not been possible to identify the sottish tutor with certainty, but of the 17 fellows who
were teaching at Oriel while Cocks was an undergraduate the most likely candidate is George
Royse (*c*.1655–1708) later provost of the college, chaplain-in-ordinary to William III and Dean of
Bristol. He was Whiggish enough to have been considered suitable as a tutor for Cocks, had
Gloucestershire connections as sometime chaplain to the 2nd Earl of Berkeley, and according to
Hearne was reckoned 'a good florid preacher' and was 'always famed for eating and drinking': G.
C. Richards and C. L. Shadwell, *The Provosts and Fellows of Oriel College Oxford* (Oxford,
1922), 118; Anthony à Wood, *Athenae Oxonienses* . . . (4 vols.; London, 1820), iv. 506–7; C. E.
Doble *et al.* (edd.), *Remarks and Collections of Thomas Hearne* . . . (11 vols., Oxford Historical
Society; Oxford, 1885–1921), i. 214. I am indebted to the college archivist, Mrs Elizabeth
Boardman, for pointing my way in this search. The notion that philosophers are always most
eloquent against their own personal vices originated with the Latin author Minucius Felix, and
had recently been given an airing by the essayist and MP Sir Thomas Pope Blount: Blount, *Essays
on Several Subjects*, 55.

something in relation to the resolution for keeping a good understanding between the King and the parliament Sir your worthy member told you the king heard and that injuriously what he said here told him at Kinsington: Sir he must then know what is said and done at Kinsington: Sir to prevent this evill for the future I would propose that your member should tell the king who it was that told storyes from kinsington and then your member might hope that the king would tell who informed him of what your member said: Sir the sore I poynt [*at*] is Bribery a fault I hope I complain of because it is abhorred by me abhorred by me did I say Sir it is an abomination to the nation a scandall to this house to have a man stigmatised by the votes of this house turned of[*f*] your chair for bribery fill and sit in one of the most honourable and profitable places of judicature in the Kingdome.[11] Sir your worthy member told you of the extravagant and luxurious way of living of some of your great men Sir did ever man live more idely and extravagantly then this: Sir your worthy member speaking of little justices said some were in com[*mi*]s[*sio*]n that had complyed in all reigns did ever man do that more to better purpose then this gent[*leman*] Sir you have ordered the Com[*mi*]s[*sio*]n of the justices and dep[*uty*] l[*ieutenan*]ts to be laid before you to see who are turned out Sir a rig[*h*]t re[*veren*]d father in god told me this Gent[*leman*] when he was one of the Lords Com[*mission*]ers for the great seale turned out severall justices becaus they Suppressed vice and prevented the profanation of the Lord's day[12] Sir I desire the comm[*i*]s[*sio*]n of the master of the Rolls may be also laid before this house in order to consider what is fitt to be done in this matter: my Lord Cornbury who was then in the Speakers chamber promised to second me as did Mr Morgan of Tredego[13] and I beleive somebody had had not Sir Xto[*pher*] musgrave wispered the Lord Cheney to move for a supply who did so immediately so my motion was not seconded:[14] upon Sir Cha[*rles*] Howthams moving for a supply just after the K[*ing'*]s Speech was read [*16 Nov. 1699*] after some deb[*ate*] I said sir I have heard that it was the antient method of Parliament to redress greevances

[11] Another reference to the Master of the Rolls, Sir John Trevor: see above, p. 8.

[12] As one of the commissioners of the Great Seal in 1691/2 Trevor had consistently opposed the reforming faction on the Middlesex bench: A. G. Craig, 'The Movement for the Reformation of Manners, 1688–1715', Ph.D. thesis (Edinburgh, 1980), 48–52; Horwitz (ed.), *Luttrell Parliamentary Diary*, 94.   [13] Thomas Morgan, MP, of Tredegar.

[14] James Vernon's version of the debate was that Cocks 'bethought himself of a speech against this day, and declaimed against bribery, which was to set himself loose against Sir John Trevor . . . All he concluded with was, that his commission should be ordered to be brought hither, and then they might consider what to do with him. Nobody seconded him, so that thunderbolt is over. But my Lord Cheyney [Cheyne] rose up, and made the motion for a supply, which nobody opposed': Northants. RO, Montagu (Boughton) MSS 48/3, to Shrewsbury, 28 Nov. 1699, printed with some errors in James (ed.), *Letters Illustrative . . .* , ii. 369.

before they gave money: I am sure there is nobody more truly loves K[*ing*]
W[*illiam*] then I do: but sir I am not for making a bad president in a good reign
I desire therefore that things may go in their antient channell friday
dec[*em*]b[*e*]r 2d [*recte 1st, 1699*] we sat in a committe[e] of the whole house
for trade where it was proved that the obliging the E[*ast*] Ind[*ia*] company to
carry out our woo[l]len manufactures was a damage to that trade becaus they
put it of[f] into persia by a land carriage which choaked our Turkey merchants
trade: it was said that the acts made in relation to Ireland were prejudiciall to
both kingdomes:[15] and that we forced them by that means to make fine cloth:
mr montague said the Kingdom might be supp[l]ied with money at 4 or 5 per
cent would we maintain our credit: that the duty on salt ought to be b[?r]ought
of[f] for that would ruine us that the plantation trade was the best that they
ought to be incouraged but not per[?mitted] to plant corn etc.:[16] some said
money ought to be sunk in the interest: mr Mountague said that would be
higher or lower according to the more or les plenty of money:
    on wednesday the 6th of dec[*em*]b[*e*]r [*1699*]
there was a debate in the house[17] whether a pattent[18] made to the Lord
Bellamont mr Harrison mr Newto[n] Rowley Watson Rennalds[19] to destroy

---

[15] Especially the 1699 Woollen Act (10 Gul. III, c. 16).

[16] Charles Montagu had made precisely this point in a debate the previous session: 'Debates
1697–9', 399.   [17] In the committee of the whole House on trade.

[18] That of 27 May 1697, granting to those who had financed the expedition of Captain Kidd (d.
1701) the goods held by his captives. On this affair, see Robert C. Ritchie, *Captain Kidd and the
War against the Pirates* (Cambridge, Mass., 1986); Horwitz, *Parliament, Policy and Politics*, 261–2.

[19] Richard Coote, Earl of Bellomont [I] (*c.* 1655–1701).
    Edmund Harrison (knighted in 1698) (d. 1712), a director of the New East India Company.
    Samuel Newton, 'gent', who acted here as a trustee for Lord Chancellor Somers (*LJ* xvi. 705).
Probably identical with the Samuel Newton who in 1697–8 bought £600 p.a. worth of fee farm
rents at 16 years' purchase: *CJ* xiii. 207; *Cal. Treas. Bks.*, xii. 101, 108; xiii, 185, 308–18. He may
have been the mathematics master at Christ's Hospital appointed in 1695 on his great namesake
Sir Isaac's recommendation (Pearce, *Annals of Christ's Hosp.*, 120–1), but is more likely to have
been connected with the law or the business world. One of this name, with an address in St
Dunstan-in-the-West, London, was licensed to be married in 1702, at the age of 31: Joseph Foster
(ed.), *London Marriage Licences 1521–1869* (London, 1887), col. 971. A Samuel Newton, who had
died by 1733, was surveyor of St Katherine's Hospital 1712–19. Catherine Jamison, *The History of
the Royal Hospital of St Katherine by the Tower of London* (London, 1952), 200–1.
    William Rowley, a clerk or man-of-business to the Duke of Shrewsbury, for whom he presumably
stood as trustee: James (ed.), *Letters Illustrative . . .* , i. 42, 48, 241, 259.
    George Watson, an agent for Lord Romney in his personal affairs: Centre for Kentish Studies,
Maidstone, U1475/C163/2–3, 8–16 (De L'Isle MSS); U1475/A75/32; U1475/C2/13.
    Thomas Reynolds, of St Martin-in-the-Fields, Middx., an agent victualler under the commis-
sioners of victualling: *Cal. Treas. Bks.*,xi. 13–14, 276. Presumably he acted for Lord Orford. Folger
Shakespeare Library, MS X.d.451/111 (Rich MSS), contains a reference to 'Charles Reynolds,
steward to the Earl of Orford', who was 'receiver of the 6*d.* per month of every seaman's pay'.

and take the pyrats at Malagasky[20] was good in law: mr How said it was bad
in law that that and the avarice of the Great ones was the occasion of the
deficiencyes of the funds the reason the army was not paid and that men were
brought into plots some months after they were dead[21] Sir Ed[*ward*] Seymour
said that it was such a grant so fortifyed there was no releif against [*it*] if you
come into Chancery there was my lord Chancellor[22] if you aplyed to the
Admiralty there was my lord Orford if to the Secretaryes office there was
the D[*uke*] of Shreusbury[23] if to Newengland there was my Lord Bellamont:[24]
that this grant had beggerd Ireland set Scotland in a flame and ruined england:
Sir B: Shores began the debate[25] and asked me as he came by me what was the
name of my house I at first refused to tell him but after he told me twas for my
service and he would tell m[e] something I unthinkingly told him Dumbleton
he said the grant was unusuall ex nostra scient[a][26] and that the qualifying
claus did signify nothing granting quantum in nobis est[27] and then he asked a
quaestion whether we should suppose it a good grant to have the K[*ing*] grant
the manno[r]

---

[20] Madagascar.

[21] Possibly a reference to the publication the previous year of a government-inspired pamphlet
which purported to print a list of names found in the possession of the Jacobite agent Crosby in
1694, of men upon whom King James might rely in the event of an invasion. One of the names was
that of Sir William Portman, 6th Bt., of Orchard Portman, Somerset, formerly MP for Taunton
and Somerset, and a cousin of Sir Edward Seymour's, who had died in 1690 (see *HC 1660–90*, iii.
265–6). R. K[ingston], *A True History of the Several Designs and Conspiracies against His
Majesty's Sacred Person and Government* . . . (London, 1698), 81–9. Howe's leading role in the
attack upon the commission against pirates is confirmed in Yale University, Beinecke Library,
Osborn Collection, Manchester MSS, Robert Yard to the Earl of Manchester, 28 Dec. 1699: 'it has
opened the eyes of a great many well meaning gentlemen of the Country Party, who by this
infamous prosecution are convinced they ought to look on him more as a dicontented courtier
than as a patriot'.

[22] John Somers (1651–1716), 1st Lord Somers, Lord Keeper 1693–7, Lord Chancellor 1697–
1700.

[23] Charles Talbot (1660–1718), 1st Duke of Shrewsbury, Secretary of State (South), 1693–Dec.
1698.

[24] Bellomont had been appointed governor of Massachusetts in 1695, and of New York in 1697.
This argument may be found repeated almost verbatim in [James Drake,] *The History of the Last
Parliament* . . . (London 1702), 190–1.

[25] For confirmation of Shower's leading role, see the accounts of this debate by John Freke (in E.
S. De Beer (ed.), *The Correspondence of John Locke* (8 vols.; Oxford, 1976–89), vi. 754–5), and
James Vernon (in James (ed.), *Letters Illustrative* . . . ii. 378–9)

[26] The original patent is enrolled at PRO C66/3391/9; a copy presented to the Commons is
printed in *CJ* xiii. 13–14; both are in English. The preamble to the grant of captured goods
includes the phrase 'of our . . . certain knowledge'.

[27] According to Freke, Vernon, and another reporter, Robert Price (Bodl. MS Carte 130, fo.
403), the clause in the patent which provoked the most vigorous criticism ran, 'as far as the said
premises . . . do, shall or may belong to us or can and may be granted or grantable by us is or are
in our power to dispose of'.

[*fo. 85*]

of dumbleton in the County of Glo[*uce*]ster quantum in nobis est whether that
would be a legall grant then he complimented me for bringing in the bill for
quieting the minds of the subjects[28] he exclaimed much against the pattent and
proposed a quaestion that it was dishonourable to the k[*in*]g against the laws
and statutes of the realm against the law of nations destructive to trade and
commerce and invasive of property: mr Harcourt[29] and How seconded and
3ded him: mr Secretary[30] told the history of the matter and how Kid come to
be employed: the debate lasted 9 hours 40 spoke to it[31] at last I spoke as
follows mr Granvill an Honourable member near the barr told us as I suppose
to satisfye us how Kid came to [*be*] employed that he was recommended to my
Lord Bellomont Sir I think that needs no excuse it is a common english
proverb that you should set a theif to ketch a theif, and if you were to chuse
out of us one to expose and raile against these grants and pattents I suppose if
you could find such a one amongst us you would chuse out one that had had
[*sic*] been dabling in grants and things of that nature: Sir it would be happy for
us and the nation in generall if all our judges and representa[*ti*]ves were free
from hope, fear, envy, malice expectation and dependencyes these things
prejudice mens understandings and give their judgments a byas I confess sir
I love the people of england above all the great men in the world and that zeale
for my country so inraged me when I heard these grants and that I may not
misrepeat the Gent[?*leman*] the avarice of the great ones was the occasion of
the deficiencyes of the funds the non payment of the souldiers and that men
were accused and brought into plots after they were dead some months
another gent[*leman*] said that this pattent made Scotland in a Flame: Sir I
really thought they would have made it out that this grant was the occasion of
the French persecution[32] Sir these things so far inflamed me that I thought the
pattent ought to be condemned and those concerned in it hig[*h*]ly censured but

[28] On 24 Nov. 1699 Cocks and William Thursby, MP, had been ordered to prepare a bill 'for the
general quiet of the subject, against all pretences of concealments, encroachments and other
defective titles', a new verson of a measure that Cocks had brought forward unsuccessfully in
the previous session. Cocks was to introduce the bill on 8 Dec.: *CJ* xii. 389; xiii. 5 41–2. .
[29] Harcourt's position on the issue is confirmed by Freke.   [30] James Vernon, MP.
[31] Freke and Vernon agree with Cocks as to the duration of the debate. Tallard, the French
ambassador, reported that it ran from noon until 10 p.m., while other accounts only refer to the
sitting having ended at 9 p.m. One observer, James Brydges, noted that debate lasted seven hours.
PRO 31/3/184/104; Luttrell, *Brief Relation*, iv. 590; Cumbria RO (Carlisle), D/Lons/W, James
Lowther to Sir John Lowther, 9 Dec. 1699; Huntington Library, San Marino, California, Stowe
MSS 26(2), Brydges' diary, 6 Dec. 1699. Vernon wrote that 'everybody had a share in it that uses to
speak, good or bad'.
[32] The plight of the Huguenot and Vaudois refugees was much in the public mind, a brief
having been taken up for them earlier in the year: *CSP Dom.* 1699–1700, pp. 92–4.

when I had time to consider and strip truth stark naked from the dregs of oratory and filth of satyr with which shee was defiled and disguised I found no more in it then that these gent[*lemen*] when the goverment was in distres for men ships and money set out a ship at their own cost not to get certain immens treasures but to serve the nation at their own loss and hasard and so it proved[33] Sir you were told it would be an honour to the parliament to come up to some gent[*lemen's*] heigths Sir will it be an honour to the parliament when hereafter it shall be said we refused to pas a censure upon a man guilty of bribery by the books the records of this hous and which by our votes we have published all over the world[34] and at the same time to set a mark on these gent[*lemen*] whose characters are valuable as farr as his is infamous: Egone qui ne taravinium interim hunc Sicinium feram[35] Shall I who could not get this instrument of slavery and arbitrary power censured: censure these tribunes of the people these true Englishmen now sir one word to dumbleton I come not here to get any thing but to save dumbleton and I think the best way to save dumbleton is not to put a censure on these men who have deserved well of their country and are in no fault by the opinion of those lawyers I have the best opinion of: what sir will you remove my lord Chancellour and put Trevour and such as he[36] in his place I hope not will you censure them and let them remain in their places as Sir J: T[*revor*] does I hardly belive: I had rather trust my estate with these gent[*le*]men then any I know of I know no censure they deserve and therefore when the quaestion is put I will positively give my negative

upon Tuesday the 12th of Dec[*em*]b[*e*]r 1699 upon a debate how to give the P[*rince*] of Denmark his money for his land he parted with to the D[*uke*] of Holsten[37] Sir Jo[*hn*] Bols after a long oration after his way concluded that before we did anything further in this matter that we should addres to the K[*ing*] to remove the B[*isho*]p of Sarum from being preceptor to the D[*uke*] of

---

[33] 'and so it proved' interlined. [34] Sir John Trevor again.

[35] Livy, *Ab Urbe Condita*, 2. 34. 10: 'Egone . . . Tarquinium regem qui non tulerim Sicinium feram.' [36] 'and such as he' interlined.

[37] Prince George (1653–1708), consort to the Princess Anne. As mediator between Denmark and Sweden at the time of the Treaty of Altona in 1689 William III had persuaded the Prince to surrender to the Duke of Holstein mortgages held on the Isle of Femern and the villages of Tremsbüttel and Steinhorst, in return for William's guarantee to pay compensation (amounting to 428,000 rix dollars) and interest in the meantime. But even though George lowered his demand in 1691 nothing was done towards payment until the King's Speech at the beginning of this session, when provision for settlement of the debt was recommended to Parliament. Edward Gregg, *Queen Anne* (London, 1980), 77, 105, 118–19; *CJ* xiii. 1.

Gl[*oucester*]³⁸ this motion was seconded by Sir J packington who really made
a very hansome speech on the occasion but shewed his want of Judgment in
saying that the B[*isho*]p had said the D[*uke*] was so like him that the princes
he beleived thought of him in her conception he said if the D[*uke*] was so like
him and Educated under him he did not know w[hat] he might come to: in this
Sir J: did the B[*isho*]p wrong for he spoke not this of himself but of the
d[*u*]k[*e'*]s being like th[e] K[*ing*]³⁹ on wednesd[*ay*] the 13th [*Dec. 1699*] Sir J
P[*akington*] proposed it for the first day it came to no quaestion becaus the
motion was irregular⁴⁰ and Sir J: B[*olles*] seconded him Mr H[*o*]w thirded and
all for that he had wrote a booke asserting the conquest of the kingdom⁴¹ and
it might be dangerous to us to have the D[*uke*] educated in such principles I
really thought nobody would have spoke for him and that he had been gone
but at last R. Aires⁴² did and was handsomly s[e]conded by Mr pellam: Mr
Smith at las Sir C: M[*usgrave*] spoke: and mr Mountague answerd him Sir B:
S[*hower*] spoke als[o] and told us of the right wee had to addres on such
occasions and he had known us appoynt governours to our princes: I told Sir
B: S[*hower*] if he spoke I would answer him which I did as follows
Sir it is no dispute but the people of England have a right by their representa-
tives in parliament to ad[dre]s to the throne to remove those from their princes

---

³⁸ Gilbert Burnet (1643–1715), Bishop of Salisbury 1689–1715, for whom see *DNB*; T. E. S.
Clarke and H. C. Foxcroft, *A Life of Gilbert Burnett* (Cambridge, 1907); and [M. J. Routh (ed.),]
Bishop Burnet's History of My Own Time (6 vols.; Oxford, 1833). In 1698 he had been appointed
preceptor to William Henry (1689–1700), Duke of Gloucester, Princess Anne's only surviving child
and heir presumptive to the throne.

³⁹ Luttrell (*Brief Relation*, iv. 592) reported that Pakington moved the question and Bolles
seconded, but Cocks's version is supported by Bonet (BL Add. MS 30000 C, fo. 271) and Vernon
James (ed.) *Letters Illustrative* . . . ii. 386–7. Bonet called Pakington Burnet's 'sworn enemy' (BL
Add. MS 30000 C. fo. 272), and indeed in the previous session he had turned a speech in favour of
the Disbanding Bill into a virulent attack on the bishop: E. M. Thompson (ed), *Correspondence of
the Family of Hatton* . . . (2 vols., Camden Soc., NS 22–3; London, 1878), ii. 238; 'Debates 1697–
9', 386. In this renewed onslaught he railed that Burnet 'was but a bishop in name and a republican
in principle, whose merit was bottomed on trickery, betraying the Duke of Lauderdale his master,
one who wants morals and full of obscene rhetoric, who should tell the King that the Duke of
Gloucester was like him, which he could attribute to no cause, unless the bishop did think of His
Majesty in the act of conception': Bodl. MS Carte 130, fo. 406.

⁴⁰ On 12 Dec. Pakington's speech and other 'scurrilous' and 'severe' reflections on Burnet had
provoked an intervention from the Speaker, who had declared them out of order: James (ed.),
Letters Illustrative . . . ii. 386—7; HMC, *Hope-Johnstone MSS*, 114.

⁴¹ Burnet's *Pastoral Letter* had been burned by order of the Commons in 1693, for asserting the
theory that William owed his tenure of the throne to conquest; Horwitz, *Parliament, Policy and
Politics*, 262; M. Goldie, 'Charles Blount's Intention in Writing "King William and Queen Mary
Conquerors" (1693)', *Notes and Queries*, NS 25 (1978), 529–32. It had been the subject of remarks
on the 12th as well as on the 13th: James (ed.), *Letters Illustrative* . . . ii. 386–8; HMC, *Hope-
Johnstone MSS*, 114; HMC, *Portland MSS*, iii. 613.

⁴² Robert Eyre was recorder of Salisbury as well as MP for the borough.

they beleive may be dangerous and they have reason to beleive do not behave themselves as they ought in their respective places: Sir it may be of good use to bring this yong prince up in our customs and use him to our constitutions: that a great while henc[e] and I hope it will be a great while hence when he shall fill the throne the laws of the land and nature see[m] to have designed for him he will not be surprised when future Parliament[?s] shall addres to remove his Chan[*cellor*] or others they do not like: truly sir when I came this day first into the house I thought if one must be rosted this one was the fittest except one[43] but the incomparable Character I have heard [o]f him from these Gent[*lemen*] who I am sure know men and on whose Judgment I much rely I own I have altered my opinion and beleive [*him*] the fittest man in the world for the place he is in[44] Sir I was at leysure the other day and put my eye on titus livius where I met with this sto[ry] which I will make as short as I can:[45] Sir livye tells that when Anniball was in Italy there many of the little states that were uneasy under the Romans had a design to revolt amongs them[selves ?and] particularly the capuans who hated the senators the Romans had set over them

[*fo. 84ᵛ*]

he tells us that there was one pacuvius who had a great authority both with the senate and people he therefore comes to the senators and tells them the people are resolved to destroy you and you have no way left to preserve your selves unless you will trust yourselves with me and go into a rome and let me have they key and Lock you in: the senators agreed and when he had them safe in his custody he goes to the people and tells them sirs you cannot abid[e] the senate it is true they dont govern well you have long designed their ruine they are now in your power you may do what you will with them I have them under lock and key they are all together: this is better than to have attacqued them at their houses tho they are wicked men yet have they many Clients and friends and it would have cost many a bloody nose to have destroyed them in their own houses; Gent[*lemen*] sais pacuvius it is good to be wise as well as angry pray consider who you will have in their places will you have a king no that is an abomination to the free people of italy: what then will you have a senate Sir this is all the story that is to my purpose and my application is this will you

---

[43] Presumably Sir John Trevor.

[44] Cocks's defence of Burnet may not have been quite so disinterested in motivation. In 1707 he was to recall that the bishop had promised him at least five or six years previously to 'get some preferment for my brother' (Robert): Surrey RO (Kingston), Somers MSS 371/14/01/14, Cocks to the Bishop of Oxford, 16 Apr. 1707.

[45] The story of Pacuvius Calavius is told in Livy, *Ab Urbe Condita*, 23. 2–3, and retold in Machiavelli, *Discorsi*, 1. 47.

tu[rn] this B[*isho*]p out who will you put in his place: will you turn this
B[*isho*]p out Because he should look after his dioces: Sir my reason why I
insist so much upon this quaestion is because I know a B[*isho*]p who is or who
will quicly be at leysure that has been tutor and preceptor to many of your
worthy members and client to others Sir I do n[ot] know but they may design
him as preceptor:[46] I am sure till I know who they design I will not give my
affi[r]mative
friday the 15th of De[*cem*]b[*e*]r [*16*]99
      When the Irish report about the forfeited estates[47] was presented to the
house by Mr Annesley[48] Mr How began and complained of the neglect of
Gent[*lemen*] in attending and avoyding of quaestions mr harcourt stood up
and complained of such vast grants when the nation was in such want etc. and
concluded with a motion to have these Iri[sh] estates to go towards the use of
the publick Mr Sloan 2ded him and I thirded[49] and said sir it has cost us I
mean it would have cost us 340000 li. in the very transports had they been
paid[50] and what a vast sum must be expended in maintain[?ence] of our army
in Ireland[51] besides the more valuable Loss of so many brave English lifes: Sir
these lands were got by the English blood and treasure and they ought to go
towards the defraying our charges Sir I truly love and h[o]nour his majesty and
therefore I will speak what I thing [*sic*] will be for his service and interest: I am
sure it is more for his majestys interest to have the people of England his
courtiers then to have a few private men rich I am therefore for the bill: on

---

[46] Thomas Watson (1637–1717), Bishop of St David's and a former fellow of St John's,
Cambridge: in politics a high-flying Tory and a suspected Jacobite. Sentenced in 1699 in the
Archbishop's Court to be deprived for simony, he had made various unsuccessful appeals,
culminating in a writ of error in the Lords, which was pending at this time, and was eventually
disallowed in the following March: *DNB*; HMC, *House of Lords MSS*, NS iv. 115–17.

[47] The report of the commissioners of inquiry into Irish forfeitures, established the previous
session: see above, n. 45, and Simms, *Williamite Confiscation*, 101–5. A copy is printed at HMC,
House of Lords MSS, NS iv. 14–54.

[48] Francis Annesley (1663–1750), MP Preston 1705–8, Westbury 1708–15, 1715, 1722–34; for
whom see *HC 1715–54*, i. 414–15.

[49] Howe, Harcourt, and Sloane were appointed to the resultant committee to draft of bill of
resumption, though Cocks was not: *CJ* xiii. 66. Sloane, an Ulsterman, had been an old associate of
Annesley's in the Irish 'Country' opposition. In August 1699 Annesley had described him as one of
the inquiry commission's 'benefactors', and had noted his frequent visits to Ireland at that time:
Kenneth Spencer Research Library, University of Kansas, MS 143 Cz.3 (Moore MSS), Annesley to
Arthur Moore, 5 Aug. 1699. Evidence given in the debate on 15 Jan. 1700 on the commissioners'
report confirms that Sloane and Harcourt had been in correspondence with the 'Country' activists
on the commission: William Cobbett, *The Parliamentary History of England* . . . (36 vols.;
London, 1806–20), v. 1214.   [50] See above, p. 10, n. 46.

[51] Details of the military establishment for Ireland in 1699–1700, totalling £292,263. 2s. 11⅝d.,
can be found at *Cal. Treas. Bks.* xv. 149–57.

thursday the 14th [*recte* 18th] of jan [16]199 [/1700] the Irish bill[52] was read the 2d time and before it was com[*mit*]ted mr Se[*creta*]ry ver[*no*]n moved that it might be an instruction to the Committee to set apart a proportion for the King[53] he was 2ded and then my Lord Con[*ings*]bee said the King had ventured and exposed himself for the reducing of Ireland and repeated the history of Ireland:[54] Sir W[*illia*]m Drake began upon my word sir it is very uneasy for me and unpleasant to rise up unwillingly to speak[55] in this place: he spoke against the motion I said sir upon my word I never speak here but with great disorder and reluctancy: but I never rose up more willingly to speak then now for I own I owe so much to our great King that I am glad of any opportunity of acting or speaking anything that may be for his service I am glad of all occasions to express my gratitude: Gen[*tle*]men say they would have a pa[rt] set aside for the King to dispose of: I would have it all so disposed of that it might make the ki[*ng*] truly Rich and the riches true riches of a King are the heart the love and the affection of the people: Sir I sit here by virtue of those votes that a[re] heartly well and Zealously affected to his Majesty King william and his government: I beleive I may without vanity say they love K[*ing*] w[*illiam*] better then themselves I am sure they would hasard themselves and their all for his majestys safety and preservation and I will on this opportunity shew them they are truly represented: and I will have regard to nothing so much as to his Majestys safty and service: Sir it is not the name of w[*illia*]m that sounds or pleases the ears of the people more then that of james: but the one we hate and abominate becaus he did by an arbitrary power invade our rights liberties and properties, and because he would have introduced a ridiculous a strange and detestable religion amongst us we love the other becaus he as restored to us these only valuable and desirable things to the inhabitants of this world and we beleive as he has done us this good so he will be ready on all occasions to do more for us: Love begets Love and in this

---

[52] To resume forfeited estates in Ireland granted by the Crown since 13 Feb. 1689 and to apply them 'to the use of the public'; later tacked to the Land Tax Bill.

[53] 'As it was agreed by us', wrote Vernon, 'I made the motion'; the King himself being 'strangely bent' on the proposed additional clause to reserve a third of the forfeitures to his own disposal: James (ed.), *Letters Illustrative* . . . ii. 411–12. That it was supported by the 'courtiers' in the House is noted in Richard Chandler, *The History and Proceedings of the House of Commons from the Restoration to the Present Time* (14 vols.; London, 1742–4), iii. 123.

[54] Coningsby, who had himself been present at the Battle of the Boyne, had served as a lord justice in Ireland from 1690 to 1692 and still held important Irish offices (as vice-treasurer and paymaster) as well as having received a grant of forfeited lands. His supporting role in the debate is confirmed by Vernon (James (ed.), *Letters Illustrative* . . . ii. 411–20), though Bonet denied that Coningsby, nor any other grantee, dared speak directly to this clause, and that Coningsby merely defended himself from any imputation of having acted illegally (BL Add MS 30000 C, fo. 19).

[55] Originally just 'unpleasant to speak'.

time of necessityes poverty and deficiencyes of it will oblige the whole people
of England to have this act passed without separating a part it will confirm
them in their opinion of their wise and happy choice, it will ruine the very
hopes of the Jacobites if we have yet any amongst us it will also destroy the
very imaginations of the uneasye disaffected and ambitious: I hear some
Gent[*lemen*] say will you leave the King nothing to dispose of to men of
merrit Sir if they had estates and were men of fortune they have been very well
rewarded in having preserved their liberties their properties their religion and
themselves and they have an opportunity of shewing they deserved well in
serving the publick more then to inrich themselves:[56] I have read in the Roman
histories of their Dictators: and the dictators[*hi*]p signifies as ample a power
as is in our King Lords and commons vested in one man: I have read how these
dictators have been taken from the plough and have fought their battles and
done the busines of their country and have returned again to their plough and
that they have thought themselves well rewarded in having served their country
Examples to be admired it may be rather Laughed at then imitated in this
degenerate age of ours: if these men of merit had no estates their Country is
the more obliged to them and a good place might satisfye them in these times
of difficulties poverty and necessitye: the gifts and acknowledgments should
not only be esteemed for the greatnes of their worth and value but from the
abilitye of the giver and obliged: but sir I would have great regard to merit I
would remember [P]indergras Athlone Hamilton Galloway[57] and others I
would have great regard to merit I would have I would have [*sic*] these lands

---

[56] 'On the contrary if that these' erased.

[57] Thomas Pendergrass, Prendergrass or Prendergast (*c.*1660–1709), an English Catholic and
once an active Jacobite, who had helped to betray and incriminate the Assassination Plotters of
1696, for which service he had been rewarded with a grant of £500 p.a. out of the Irish forfeitures.
See *DNB*; and Jane Garrett, *The Triumphs of Providence* (Cambridge, 1980), 117, 135–9, 258.
Lord Hartington moved in this debate for a special 'saving clause' for Pendergras, and although
this was rejected by the House it was agreed 'that he deserved greater favour than the King had
conferred upon him', and that the Commons 'would take care to reward' him: Suffolk RO
(Ipswich), M142 (1), ii. 93, John Gurdon to Thornhagh Gurdon, 18 Jan. 1699[/1700].

   Godard van Reede, Baron Ginkel (1644–1703). 1st Earl of Athlone, Commander-in-chief of the
Williamite army in Ireland 1690–1 and granted in 1693 the forfeited estate of the Jacobite Earl of
Limerick. See *DNB*; and Wouter Troost (ed.), 'Letters from Bartholomew Van Homrigh to
General Ginkel . . . ', *Analecta Hibernica,* 33 (1986), 59–128.

   Gustavus Hamilton (1639–1723), of Stackallan, Co. Meath. Active in the voluntary associations
of Protestants in Ulster from the beginning of the Jacobite war; commanded a regiment at the
Boyne; and particularly distinguished himself at the storming of Athlone in 1691. Rewarded with a
substantial grant of forfeited lands. See *DNB*; and John Lodge, *The Peerage of Ireland . . .* (4 vols.;
Dublin, 1754), iii. 237.

   Henri de Massue, Seigneur de Ruvigny (1648–1720), 1st Earl of Galway. A cavalry commander in
the Jacobite war, after which he received a grant of forfeitures, and currently a lord justice in
Dublin. See *DNB*; and D. C. A. Agnew, *Henry de Ruvigny, Earl of Galway . . .* (Edinburgh, 1864).

given to those that best deserve them viz to the people of England: I would have these lands he[?–] to make good the deficiencyes and pay the souldiers and ease the publick: as for resumptions it is true they were usually made when eyther the present King or his predecessors had by exorbitant unreasonable grants so lessed the revenues of the Crown that they were forced to be burthensome to the people in those cases resumptions were applyed wholly to the use of the crown: the case is not so now for for [*sic*] all our wants, we did as in gratitude we ought resolve our good King to whom we owe more then to all the world besides[58] should want nothing: we have therefore established sufficiently for the civill List I am not one of that number that thinks it to[o] much these lands therefore that were got with our blood and treasure these resumptions ought to defray the publick Charge of the nation: the great Eliz[abeth] in some of her speeches to her parliaments has told us shee was no greedy grasper nor fast holder but what w[?as] given her shee had laid out for our service and advantage and abundantly more of her own[59] it was these wor[ds] these actions that made her adored when living and renowned and honoured here after shee had changed this throne for a better Sir this is for the honour of the King what our debts and wants force us to ask and what the country I serve for expects and therefore I must be against the quaestion: Harley[60] spoke best that day he said he wondred any body [?had] the confidence to demand only a part for we intended to give him all twas for his honour to have the publick [?funds] made good to have the debts of the nation paid and that we ought to be just before we were bountifull

[*fo. 84*]

Feb 11th [*recte 10th, 16*]99[*/1700*]

Sir Charles Hedges and Sir Thomas Felton were petitioned against by Sir Edward Bacon and mr Johnson the first lost it by: for them 171, against them 172 the poynt was whether a select number should elect[61] it was agreed upon

---

[58] 'to whom we owe' to 'world besides' interlined.

[59] In the 'Golden Speech' of 1601, which, as reported by Hayward Townshend (*Hist. Colls.*, 264), ran: 'I was never any greedy scraping grasper, nor a straight, fast-holding Prince . . . What you do bestow on me I will not hoard it up, but receive it to bestow on you again; yea, my own properties I count yours, and to be expended for your good.' There is a slightly different version in D'Ewes, *Jnls.*, 659. Cocks appears to have conflated the two.

[60] It is probably safe to assume that, unless otherwise specified, Cocks has Robert Harley in mind.

[61] The division took place on the first resolution of the elections committee's report, that freemen possessed the franchise at Orford alongside other members of the corporation, contrary to the arguments advanced in committee by the sitting Members that only mayor, portmen, and capital burgesses were entitled to vote: *CJ* xiii. 189–92. At the poll, however, it would appear that Hedges and Felton had insisted on an even wider qualification, including not only freemen but inhabitants; *The Petitioners' Case of the Corporation of Orford* . . . [n.d.]; West Sussex RO, Winterton MSS Ac. 454/973a–c, 'A True and Perfect Account of the Election of the Burgesses of Orford', 28 July 1698.

the debate that no charter could lessen the number electing by prescription: and that in a burrough by prescription all inhabitants paying scot and lot had votes: and freemen by charter Elections only: Hedges and Felton had a very hard case of it[62]

on tuesday the 13th of Feb: 1699[/1700] we considered of the state of the nation[63]

I did intend to have said

Sir I speake to order and I think before we pretend to rectifye the faults of the nation we should in some measure mend our own disorders at least for this day as to order in generall all our orders are founded upon sollid and substantiall reason and the better we observe them the more we shall maintain the honour and dignity of this house and our proceedings without doors will have the better reputation and esteem to begin first with the order of speaking but once in one debate sir I beleive the reason of this order was from the inconveniency of the lawyers and other nimble tongued Gent[*lemen*] that were fond of talking and by their often speaking disturbed the debates and prevented men of better judg-ments from delivering their opinions this order was made to prevent those inconveniencyes without reflecting upon those that were guilty of this fault and making particular orders upon them and pray sir what are our second and third speeches nothing generally to the purpose nothing but vain commenda-tions of our selves and disparaging of others it may be the house in Generall Gent[*lemen*] are uneasy at the length of our debates this occasions it: truly sir I have observed the 2d third and fourth speech of one Gent[*leman*] last an houre the next thing worth your consideration is the new way of preparing quaestions

---

[62] An opinion shared to two other Whigs, John Hervey and James Lowther: *The Diary of John Hervey, First Earl of Bristol* . . . (Suffolk Green Books, 2; Wells, 1894), 31; Cumbria RO (Carlisle), D/Lons/W, James to Sir John Lowther, 10 Feb. 1699[/1700]. At the election Felton and Hedges had been seen as representing a Court Whig interest, Bacon and Johnson the Tory 'gentlemen of the country' (W. Sussex RO, Ac 454/839, 974, 1151, Lord Hereford to Sir Edmund Turnour, 19 July 1698, Nathaniel Gooding to same, 17 Oct. 1698, Thomas Palmer to same, 25 July 1698), and in the House the case naturally took on partisan overtones (BL Add MS 30000 D, fo. 47).

[63] The debate on Crown grants in the committee on the state of the nation began on 13 Feb., when the House rejected on a division a motion to condemn the procuring of such grants by 'public ministers' and instead ordered a bill of resumption. Two days later the committee sat again and reopened the issue, resolving on an address concerning Irish forfeited estates. (*CJ* xiii. 207–8, 211–18.) Two other lengthy accounts survive of the debate reported by Cocks on the 13th, in the form of notes taken in the Chamber by Edward Clarke, MP for Taunton (Somerset RO, Sanford MSS DD/SF 4107 (a), 'notes of the debate on my Ld. Chancellor the 15th Febr. 1699') and a letter written by an official in the Secretary of State's office to the diplomat Lord Manchester (Yale Univ., Beinecke Lib., Osborn Coll., Manchester MSS, Robert Yard to Manchester, 15 Feb. 1700). Both claim to be recording the second of the two days' debates, but in this instance it is clear from the evidence of the *Journals* that Cocks must be in the right.

before hand I have seen gent[*lemen*] that could not form the quaestions from the debate that could not remember what they had agreed on bring their quaestions out of their pockets and read them this is not parliamentary[64] I have heard gent[*lemen*] deservedly speake agai[*n*]st undertaking for parliaments I thinke this is no small fault this is a kind of undertaking in parliament:[65] I think sir I have heard you say you cant keep us in order you see the least amongst us will pretend to keep you to order pray sir do but exert your self and try if those that have the courage to keep you in order will not have the justice to assist you in keeping others to order: you never see the wisest and the ablest amongst [*us*] speake twice to any thing even to matter of fact or to inform us but they do it with great deference to you: you may be sure they will assist you: the Speaker puld of[*f*] his hat as I rose up to speak this and so prevented me by speaking to order himself I beleive he partly knew what I intended to speake to

Mr How began the debate[66] and said he desired wee might be kept in order as for his part the motion of a finger should check him at any time he said it was an invidious part to begin but his country laboured under the grants and the abuses of the ministry: Major Stringer sat by me opposite to How and he said he knew not what gent[*lemen*] meant that he had coppyes of grants in his hand were worth their notice grants of lands in most part of england to one mr Bertye in trust for some great men as he supposed[67] that some men were not content with small demands but that they had begged vast things for small values that would be lords of Soho:[68] And then when they were disappoynted

---

[64] P. D. G. Thomas, *The House of Commons in the Eighteenth Century* (Oxford, 1971), 169, notes that 'pocket motions' were still being attacked in George II's reign. For a near-contemporary example of parliamentarians' aversion to the practice, albeit from Dublin rather than Westminster, see D. Hayton (ed.), 'An Irish Parliamentary Diary from the Reign of Queen Anne', *Analecta Hibernica*, 30 (1982), 140.

[65] On the use of the term in general, see Clayton Roberts, *Schemes and Undertakings: A Study of English Politics in the Seventeenth Century* (Columbus, Ohio, 1985); and for particular examples, ibid. 115, 188.

[66] Confirmed by both Edward Clarke and Robert Yard (see above, p. 48, n. 63). The latter wrote that Howe 'complained of general mismanagements in all offices and officers about the court . . . and at last mentioned the grants that have been made since this reign as very exorbitant and fit to be inquired into'.

[67] An obscure remark, which may allude to the fact that a 'Charles Bertie' (and three others) had acted as trustees for a grant made to the Duke of Leeds in June 1696. Details of this grant had been reported to the Commons on 3 Dec. 1696 and were to be included in subsequent reports on 12 and 15 Feb. 1700. *CJ* xi. 608; xiii. 199, 215. I am obliged to Dr P. L. Gauci for this suggestion.

[68] Lands in the parish of St Anne's, Westminster, 'lately called by the name of Soho, or Soho fields', had been granted to Portland in January 1698: *Cal. Treas. Bks.*, xiii. 218; *CJ* xii. 50; C. L. Kingsford, *The Early History of Piccadilly, Leicester Square, Soho and Their Neighbourhood . . .* (London Topographical Soc. 55; Cambridge, 1925), 65. Jack Howe had been a competitor with Portland in soliciting the grant: [James Ralph,] *The History of England during the Reigns of King William, Queen Anne and King George the First* (2 vols.; London 1744–6), ii. 336–7; *Cal. Treas. Bks.* ix. 548.

like the snake in the fable they fled in their masters face and would have bit them to[o][69] and that he said nothing but what he would justifye without doors:[70] Cook of Darby[71] wrote down the words and how stood up and said he wanted not bread before he came into the Ki[ng's] service and had bread since he left it[72] that his busines was not to go into the field: Cook complained of Stringers words he said Stringer said fled in the Kings face: Stringer vindicated himself this put us in a warmth they said merily in the house that I had plante[d] my great gun opposite to Jack how and discharged it full at him indeed Stringer did lay about him with hand and tongue this heat lasted near an hour:[73] Mr Bridges my Lord Chan[dos's] son spoke next[74] he down right railed against the government and every part of it the great guns went of[f] whilst he was speaking for the 12th year of the inauguration of K[ing] W[illiam] I said sir I do not know if I am awake or in a dream if I am awake these guns put us in mind of the 12th year of the inauguration of King W[illia]m and I think I see your gold gown and you in the Chair in a parliament cald by K[ing] w[illiam] if that is true I hear that Gent[leman] speak I am in a dream and this is the 16th of King J[ames']s reign: you have forbad reflections I will not therefore tell that Gent[leman] that he is dis-appoynted of a place he asked for and therefore angry:[75] Sir as for grants it is the undoubted right of the crown to grant and the King and we may resume them again that would be for the publick service and I will do as much for the publick and go as far as any but I will not do any thing that has any private looke or end in it:[76] Bruges proposed the quaestion which was to this sence that in these times of poverty it was injurious to the publick a dishonour to the King to make such great grant and a failure of the trust reposed in them to

[69] Another obsurity. Cocks may be intending to refer to the snake that bit its rescuer, in Aesop's *Fables*, the *locus classicus* of proverbial ophidian ingratitude: alternatively, he may at some stage have confused 'serpent' with 'servant'.

[70] Clarke's notes of Stringer's speech run as follows: 'some have asked grants of £800 worth £40,000 . . . not to regard such reformers, £3,500 p. ann. Post Office', an allusion to Howe's unsuccessful request for a grant from King William in 1689, for which see Horwitz, *Parliament, Policy and Politics*, 31.   [71] 'of Darby' interlined.

[72] Howe had served as vice-chamberlain to Queen Mary 1689–92.

[73] Clarke noted several speeches occasioned by this incident, including Coke's, before Stringer 'explained himself, very well'. The length of the entire debate was variously estimated at two hours (BL Add, MS 17677 UU, fo. 150) and six (Cumbria RO (Carlisle), D/Lons/W, James to Sir John Lowther, 13 Feb. 1699[/1700]).

[74] James Brydges. His intervention at this point and authorship of the motion are confirmed by Clarke and Yard.   [75] See below, pp. 95, 168.

[76] Clarke noted Cocks's speech as: 'By what has been said he thinks he had been in King Jac: reign, proposes resuming all grants'.

take grants to themselves[77] Sir R gwin said this was aymed at my Lord Chan[*cellor*] Bru[*ges*] said it was fals for which he was called to the barr but evaded the expression poorly: mr newport maintained the Kings power of granting and the just liberty of the lord Chan[*cellor*] in taking by many presidents from most reigns to this very time[78] and said that Mi[*chael*] de: la: poole mentioned in a late author with a postscript[79] had never been impeached for his grants had not his whole administration been corrupt R: Harly said he did not know how de: la: poole came to be talked on there was nothing said of him so that was no answer to any thing said before he inforced the quaestion: Newport said it was to the purpose for the very quaestion was in print in that booke that treated of de: la: pool:[80] they all denied my Lord Chan[*cellor*] to be concerned in the quaestion and not meant nor intended:[81] tho it was very plain the words inten[d]ed no other or him cheifly: Seymour said he did not know how he came in nor why he went out but that if [*he*] would have done as those gent[*lemen*] that succeeded him he beleived he might still have kept his post this was in answer to Jack Smith who said they had trode in pathes beaten for them by others: and then Smith answered Seymour that he had got more by his places then ever he had that he would be willing to take a moyety of what he sold one place for for which when he was impeached he pleaded his pardon and that he never had any ten 1000 li. for salt petre: Seymour made no return[82] Sir W[*illia*]m Blacket mr

[77] Specifically, 'that the procuring or obtaining of grants of estates, belonging to the Crown, by any public minister, concerned in the directing or passing such grants to or for their own use or benefit, whilst the nation lay under the heavy taxes of the late war, was highly injurious to His Majesty, prejudicial to the state, and a violation of the trust reposed in them' (*CJ* xiii. 208).

[78] Clarke noted several intervening speeches before Gwynne's, which both he and Yard recorded, and several speeches between Brydges' apology and Newport's remarks. Interestingly, Newport owed his office as customs commissioner, to which he had been appointed in the preceding November, to a joint recommendation from Somers and Charles Montagu: James (ed.), *Letters Illustrative . . .* , ii. 315.

[79] Michael de la Pole (*c*.1330–89), 1st Earl of Suffolk, Lord Chancellor 1383–6. He had been impeached in 1386 on numerous charges, including the receipts of grants and estates from the King. The 'late author' was Charles Davenant, in *A Discourse of Grants and Resumptions* (pp. 317–33).

[80] Harley's cavil and Newport's reply are confirmed by Clarke's notes, which also include a reference to a speech by John Pulteney prior to Harley's.

[81] The general praise bestowed on Somers was noticed by Bonet and L'Hermitage in their accounts of the debate, respectively BL Add. MSS 30000 D, fos. 52–4, and 17677 UU, fo. 158.

[82] Sir Edward Seymour had been the subject of an attempted impeachment in 1680, but the charges had not included the selling of places (*CJ* ix. 658–9). Clarke, Bonet, and L'Hermitage all record this exchange, and confirm that John Smith, identified as Lord of the Treasury and MP for Andover, had accused Seymour of accepting bribes for assisting in the passage of grants while himself at the Treasury earlier in William's reign. The reference to saltpetre recalled the committee

Harvy[83] and every one reflected on the impudence of How who had such a grant and so deceived the King in it to arraign others for for [*sic*] the fault he would have been as guilty of as they:[84] How said no dirt would stick on him: the lawyers spoke very fine particularly Haules who answered all that was pretended to be law Hooper spoke against [?the l]egality of grants Harcourt Coxe[85] Shores Scobell[86] Broderton Mumpessons[87] divided against for the quaestion[88] How commended the Lord Chancellour spoke last and spoke for the quaestion[89] upon the division for the quaestion 182 against it 232 then Sir Rich[*ard*] onslow moved for a bill of resumption of all grants made since the warr I seconded the motion but after some short debate it was ordered to resume from [16]84:[90]

on thursday the 13th [*recte 15 Feb. 1700*] the state of the nation was again the busines of the [?day] How began the debate with reflections on tuesdays votes how agreable those things would appear to the world [?and in] the same [?maner] he exclaimed against putting those out of Com[*mi*]s[*sio*]n that refused the voluntary association and [?he] talked at [?rand]om and concluded without ayming at any thing particularly his last words were against vice and immorality I answered [?and] said sir to considering men our quaestions upon the paper will seem very deliberate it will app[ear ?from the] negative passed on the first quaestion that there was an hot party ayming at private

[*fo. 83ᵛ*]

ends and by the leave to bring in a bill it will appear that the greatest and wisest part were for doing the nation se[rvice] without ayming at particular

of inquiry in 1695 into bribery of MPs by the Old East India Company. One of its investigations concerned a contract of 1693 by which a cargo of saltpetre imported from India was to be purchased at £10,000 above face value, the beneficiary being Thomas Coulson, a close friend of Seymour and widely suspected of having acted as an agent for Sir Edward in this matter, though nothing could be proved. *CJ* xi. 268; Horwitz, *Parliament, Policy and Politics,* 151. Seymour's silence in response to this speech was confirmed by L'Hermitage.   [83] Confirmed by Clarke.

[84] See above, p. 50, n. 70.

[85] Almost certainly Charles Coxe (MP Cirencester), barrister and serjeant-at-law, and a Tory. The Whig Charles Cocks (MP Droitwich), although never entered at an inn of court, had practised as a solicitor in his native Worcester before being returned to Parliament: Hereford and Worcester RO (Worcester), Worcester Clothiers' Company MSS 705:232/BA5955/7/v, receipt for legal services, 1686. I owe this reference to Dr Stuart Handley.

[86] Confirmed by Clarke.

[87] Roger Mompesson, a barrister of Lincoln's Inn and recorder of Southampton.

[88] Divided against the legality of the grants, i.e. for the question.

[89] Both Bonet and Clarke confirm Howe's closing tribute to Somers.

[90] According to Yard, Onslow had moved for a resumption of all grants since 1684, which Howe and Musgrave had opposed. The drafting committee comprised Cocks, Onslow, and Treasury Secretary William Lowndes: *CJ* xiii. 208.

men: as for those gent[*lemen*] left out of com[*mi*]s[*sio*]n of the peace for not subscribing the voluntary association I beleive there was reason for it for I beleived I might say there were none that refused the voluntary association but those that exclaimed against the legall one and as for vice and immorality that the Gent[*leman*] last mentioned I am affraid of all is true I hear without doors of those entertainments and clubs and caballing of some within doors at the master of the Rollse I fear vi[ce] and immoralitye will find some patrones within doors:[91] Sir Ed[*ward*] Seymour stood up next and said sir I own I dined at the ma[s]ters of the Rolls last Sunday and I would have had that worthy gent[*leman*][92] invited if I could have had my will on purpose to have h[ad] him acquainted with the master of the Rolls for I am confident if he knew him he would like him better but sir to the busi[ness] I shall move nothing but I must speak plainly we cannot expect good to England under this set of ministry they ha[ve] surrounded the King hee sees and hears with their ears and eis only and by that means the best and most part of his people are become useles to him I think this worth your consideration: mr Cook of Darby moved to have Railtons grant read and that wee might proceed on that and see if the grant was made to any one in a place of trust a[nd] to put that Gent[*leman*] upon his tryall if he had not broke the trust reposed in him the Lord Renelagh said he desired that they would turn to such a page and such a folio and there they would see who Raylton was trustee for and so they did and it there appeared it was inquired into the last sessions of parliament and that Raylton was on[?ly] a trustee for mountague that that parliament was satisfyed with the grant: and gave mountague thanks for his ser[vi]ces[93] (he deserved well but the thanks was unusuall but Sir w[*illia*]m St Quintain got a custome house place by the motion of thanks [)][94] the grant was valued at 13000 li. but did arise to no more than 1500 li. as Mr Lownds made it appear: mr Hamon[d] moved that mountague might withdraw but they saw the aversnes of the house to that poynt: then Mum[pes]sens said he had known a thing done in one parliament and quoted presidents where the whole proceedings were vacated and jingled

---

[91] Sir John Trevor again.   [92] i.e. Cocks himself.

[93] A grant in April 1697 to one Thomas Railton of Crown debts in Ireland to the value of over £11,000 had been investigated by the Commons on 16 Feb. 1698, when Charles Montagu, who admitted that Railton was acting on his behalf, had none the less escaped censure. After a motion for Montagu's withdrawal had been rejected on a division, a resolution had been passed declaring that the Chancellor of the Exchequer had deserved royal favour by his 'good services'. *Cal. Treas. Bks.*, xii. 102; *CSP Dom.* 1698, p. 96; *CJ* xii. 50. For Railton (d. 1732), a minor Exchequer official living in Westminster, see H. W. Turnbull *et al.* (edd.) *The Correspondence of Sir Isaac Newton* (7 vols; Cambridge, 1958–77), iv. 212; BL Eg. MS 3252B, fos. 6, 24; Add. MS 38856, fos. 147–8, 150; *Historical Register*, xvii (1732), 'Chronicon', 36.

[94] That St Quintin had proposed the resolution is confirmed by *CSP Dom.* 1698, p. 95. He had been named a customs commissioner in the following September: *Cal. Treas. Bks.* xiv. 121.

pretily upon numbers and reason: but this would not do so they gave up this: and poor C[ook] was so foolish and childish as to say this should be the last motion he would ever make and went down th[e] stayers cursing all house meeting dogs meaning Ro[*bert*] Harley: then mr How held forth against the corrupt[i]on of the ministry and particularly at the justices of peace he could prove it that they made orders o[n] purpose to oblige and disoblige[95] those that were for them or against them and then he run into his usuall way of divisions: after that I said sir I speake to matter [*of*] fact I can demonstrate to that G[ent*leman*] that it is impossible to be as he sais for the Chairman[96] at the sessions has no more then [?*one*] vote and he can no more make the justices do what he would have them then a chairman at the committee here can, nor is he any more to answer for the miscarriages:[97] to which mr How shewed his dislike aloud: I said farther sir here are many things said which I beleive would not, had the Gent[*lemen*] inquired into matter of fact: as particularly an Honourable Gent[*leman*] near the bar[98] told us that a judge in his charge arraigned the proceedings of Parliament I am certain had he inquired into the truth he would have been of another opinion: I thank that Honourable Gent[*leman*] for his kind intentions of inviting me to dinner but to the busines before us a worthy member my very good fr[i]end told us that all ministryes are the same if so where would be the good of changing this: but I am n[ot] of his opinion: I know no way to judge of men but by comparing them nor no way of judging of mi[nis]ters but by comparing them they are good or bad only comparatively as they are better or wors then others Sir for all that has been said against this ministry I own I like them better then I did and if yo[u] will have patience I will shew you my reasons but first one word to what the Honourable Gent[*leman*] nea[r] the barr said he told us we could not be safe under this ministry that they incompassed the King that he saw and heard only with theire eis and ears and by that means was deprived of the services of on[e] half and that the best of his subjects I desire he would explain himself what would he hav[e] no ministry or would he have this ministry removed and another put in their places: or would h[e] have half the ministry of one sort and half of another and will he lett the King choose them or w[ill] he lett the King chuse for himself and if there is a new ministry will not the King see as much wit[h] their eis etc.: as he dos with the present: Sir to give you my reason why I Like this present mini[s]try better then I did: Sir I have seen an old great minister of K[*ing*] C[*harles*] whose abilities and reputatio[n]

---

[95] 'punish' is written above 'disoblige' in the MS. [96] Originally 'one just[ice]'.

[97] Cocks had probably served as chairman of the Gloucestershire bench from at least 1694 to 1699: see above, pp. xxxiv–xxxvi.

[98] From what follows it is clear that this must refer to Sir Edward Seymour.

recommended him to the service of his present Majesty this minister is now how he came in I kno[w] not nor why he went out: but I saw this old minister weighed fairly in the Scales in this house this great minister with one of least of K[*ing*] W[*illiam'*]s ministers now in place I cant flatter I think him one of the least this little minister was fairly put in the scales with this great on[e] and this little minister turned the scales with such a violence that he knocked the old ministe[r's] head against the beame:[99] after this[100] Sir X: musgrove said when they could ma[ke] nothing they liked go that they would lay the votes made the 15th of Feb [*recte 18th of Jan.*] before the King: and let him do what he pleased with them the sence of the votes was that the great[101] grants in Ireland was the occasion of the deficiencyes and poverty here:[102] my Lord Hartington said if we did remove this ministry he desird to know who should succeed them he hoped none of the ministry of K[*ing*] C[*harles*] non that were for the regency[103] none that had refused the association none behind the curtain etc.: Robyn Harley said he was not for removing this ministry but for laying down such rules that might prevent these evills for the future[104] then after some discourses in which Sir B: shores thought himself obliged to vindicate himself, he said what he did was occasioned by his youth that he was but 27 years old but poor and the great offers tempted him at that age that the cheif thing to be laid to his charge was the hangin[g] of a souldier[105] that my Lord C[*heif*] J[*ustice*] Treby had done the same in my Lord Russels case he commended Treby: this made the house laugh:[106] after this my Lord

[99] Possibly an allusion to the diminutive Charles Montagu's orchestration of the impeachment proceedings against the Duke of Leeds (formerly Lord Danby) in 1695, for which see Horwitz, *Parliament, Policy and Politics*, 152.

[100] 'Mr Cook', then 'R Harley said' erased.   [101] 'great' interlined.

[102] Resolutions 'that the advising, procuring and passing the grants' of the Irish forfeited estates had resulted in the 'contracting great debts upon the nation, and laying heavy taxes on the people'; that the 'advising and passing the said grants is highly reflecting on the King's honour'; and that those responsible had failed in their duty: *CJ* xiii. 130.

[103] In the Convention of 1689.

[104] Bonet reported Harley's speech in the same terms: BL Add. MS 30000 D, fo. 56. 'My brother spoke wonderfully', was Edward Harley's opinion: BL Loan 29/78, Edward to Sir Edward Harley 'Thursd. 11 clock' [15 Feb. 1700].

[105] In Sept. 1686, after the then recorder of London had delayed judgment on a convicted army deserter, doubting whether the offence was capital in time of peace, the judges were summoned and gave their opinion for the death sentence, which was then pronounced, in the recorder's absence, by his deputy, Shower: *The Autobiography of Sir John Bramston, K. B. . . . * (Camden Soc., 32; London, 1845), 245–6.

[106] Sir George Treby (*c*.1644–1700), recorder of London 1680–3, 1688–92, Solicitor-General 1689, Attorney-General 1689–92, Chief Justice of Common Pleas 1692–d. As recorder Treby had sentenced to death the Whig 'martyr' William, Lord Russell, in July 1683; *DNB* (Russell, William). He was, however, Whiggish in his own political sympathies: he subsequently lost the recordership through his resistance to the surrender of London's charter, and in due course became a pillar of the Williamite regime; hence the general amusement. See *HC 1660–90*, iii. 582–3.

Hartington commended the ingenuity of Harley and desired him to propose a quaestion upon what he offered Goodwin Warton did the same and then mr Harley said he could propose nothing better then to second that motion made by Sir Xto[*pher*] musgrove: afterwa[rds] that was debated some time[107] and then the quaestion was put and carried without a division and the Kings answer [*26 Feb. 1700*] was to this sence that he had disposed of some of the lands conquered by hi[m] and forfeited to him as he was moved by his inclinations and justice that he thought the great occasi[on] of the poverty was the long and necessary wars that he desired they would by just means provide for the deficiencyes which would be for the honour and safety of the Kingdom:[108] this answer was very hig[h]ly resented by the house[109] which occasioned this following vote that the advisers of it endeavoured to [?ma]Ke a misunderstanding between the King and the parliament[110] in this debate the cheif exceptions were the word m[e] they said it should have been us[111] they further said that if the grants were justly granted it would b[e] unjust to resume them and that the latter part of the answer intimated so much. they said by this answer the King said the lands were his and the debts and deficiencyes were ours

[fo. 83]

[? . . .] to clauses nothing relating to the bill if they are of consequence: they ought not be added for something inconvenient may pas with out due

---

[107] According to Abel Boyer it was 'a very hot and long debate': *The History of the Reign of King William III* (3 vols.; London, 1702–3), iii. 433. James Vernon wrote, 'we sat this evening much later than we did on Tuesday (James (ed.), *Letters Illustrative* . . . ii. 431); while Lord Basil Hamilton reported that the House 'have sat very late' (Scottish RO, GD406/1/4583 (Hamilton MSS), Lord Basil Hamilton to the Duke of Hamilton, 15 Feb. 1700).

[108] In *CJ* xiii. 228, it reads:

I was not only led by inclination, but thought myself obliged in justice, to reward those who had served well, and particularly in the reduction of Ireland, out of the estates forfeited to me by the rebellion there.

The long war, in which we were engaged, did occasion great taxes, and has left the nation much in debt; and the taking just and effectual ways for lessening that debt, and supporting public credit, in what, in my opinion, will best contribute to the honour, interest and security of the kingdom.

[109] No sooner had the Speaker finished reading then a great noise erupted: BL Add. MS 30000 D, fo. 69. Edward Harley, for one, considered the anwer 'very extraordinary': BL Loan 29/189, fo. 164. According to Sir William Cook, 'there was a very long and warm debate . . . wherein a great deal of plain English was spoken, and Mr Montagu and the other courtiers did not think it convenient for them to speak a word': Suffolk RO (Ipswich), M 142(1), ii. 65, Cook to Thornhagh Gurdon, 7 Mar. 1699[/1700].

[110] 'That whosoever advised His Majesty's answer . . . has used his utmost endeavours to create a misunderstanding and jealousy betwixt the King and his people': *CJ* xiii.228.

[111] Bonet and L'Hermitage confirm that this was the principal objection, i.e. that the Irish lands had been forfeited to the King personally and not to 'the public', and identify Howe and Musgrave as the chief objectors: BL Add. MSS 30000 D, fos. 69–70; 17677 UU, fos. 168–9.

consideration but bills on purpose ought to be brought in for such matters for then they will have the first and 2d reading and its right progres that men may consider of them: [*8 Mar. 1700*] the Bankers debt[112] was talked on when they were appropriating the overplus of the revenue [(]after the[113] civill list was provided for) to the publick service Mr Hamond [be]gan and said the overplus of the additionall excise was setled to pay the bankers debt[114] Mr Lownds talked a great while to [th]at purpose: Mr How said it was a just debt due to the widows and orphans and that the overplus belonged to [t]hem that we had given great sums to the D[*uke*] of Zell and other forreign Dukes and that this was more worthy of our Consideration: that there was 50,000 li. allowed out of the civill list for K[*ing*] J[*ames*][115] which was not paid and that that ought to go to the Bankers that he was against the giving of the civill list for life: that he was not for the abdication nor of an opinion that Kings could not forfeit:[116] Mr Mountague said since the Lords had reversed the Lord Chan[*cellor's*] decree: it was fit we should consider of the matter and tell the poor people if they should be paid or not: Sir Xtop[*her*] Musgrove said he did not know how the bankers were in the quaestion that the Bankers had often in the pensioner Parliament[117] endeavoured to get their debt setled by act of Parliament but that parliament would never come up to it and that the Honourable Gent[*leman*] near the bar had had such offers of that value that would have

---

[112] In origin loans to King Charles II advanced by Sir Robert Vyner and other goldsmith-bankers on the security of the public revenue, and consolidated in 1677 by the issue of annuities on the hereditary excise, the interest on which had not been paid since 1683. This debt had been the subject of various lawsuits since 1691, and of a judgment by Lord Chancellor Somers (as Lord Keeper) against the bankers and their assignees, in Williamson *v. regem* in 1696, reversal of which had been confirmed by the House of Lords on 23 Jan. 1700. T. B. Howell, *A Complete Collection of State Trials . . .* (34 vols.; London 1816–28), xiv. 1–114; HMC, *House of Lords MSS*, NS iii. 407–8; *LJ* xvi. 499–501. [113] 'additionall' erased.

[114] The Civil List Act of 1698 (9 Gul. III, c. 23) had stipulated that none of the surplus accruing from the further subsidy of tunnage and poundage granted for this purpose could be disposed of without parliamentary consent, but had said nothing specifically about the bankers' debt. At the report stage a clause had been proposed 'for saving the rights of those concerned in the bankers' debts' but had not been accepted by the House: *CSP Dom.* 1698, p. 289. See also E. A. Reitan, 'From Revenue to Civil List, 1689–1702: The Revolution Settlement and the "Mixed and Balanced" Constitution', *Historical Journal*, 13 (1970), 576, 578.

[115] Strictly speaking, for Queen Mary of Modena, but, as a speaker in a debate the previous year had noted, 'for K. J[ames] by intend[ment]'; 'Debates 1697–9', 397. The gist of Lowndes's and Howe's speeches is confirmed by James Vernon: Northants. RO, Montagu (Boughton) MSS 48/43, Vernon to Shrewsbury, 9 Mar. 1699[/1700]. Lowndes, he observed was the 'great champion' of those concerned in the debt.

[116] In the debates in the Convention on the transfer of the Crown. In fact, Howe's claim to have opposed the adoption of the concept of 'abdication' is contradicted by the evidence of his speech on the Indemnity Bill in 1689, quoted in *HC 1660–90*, ii. 609.

[117] Charles II's long Parliament of 1661–79, which had acquired this sobriquet in the 1670s.

tempted any man living that had not had steddy principles:[118] others said it was impossible to speake to this matter without speaking to the bankers case: old Thirsbee [s]aid it was a just debt and used the arguments the councill used to the Lords: I said after Thursbee: Mr Coniers I thou[g]ht you were used to sit in the resuming chaire but now I think by the debate you are in the chair for confirming of grants but I think the busines of the day is ways and means:[119] I hope the next time the house is in [?Je]wish humour for providing for the duke of Zell and other forreign dukes they will take some care of the bankers debt a gent[*leman*] near me said it is a just debt but I am sure it ought not to be paid I hope this parliament will never give such a blow to our liberties and properties as to seem in the least to provide for debts contracted by any King without the consent of Parliament I am sure we have many debts contracted by the credit of parliament I am sure it is both our Duty and interest to provide them and in order to it I hope you will appropriate the overplus of the [e]xcise to the publick use How stood up after and partly unsaid in relation to the bankers what he said before Sir Ed[*ward*] Seymour calld me to him and told me I remember how this debt was contracted the bankers would buie notes of credit from the crown for ten shillings in the pound it may be at a time to the value of 10000 li. and then they would take those notes and ten thousand pound more and make a debt of 20000 li.

[*5 Mar. 1700*] as to the union

the bill[120] came with a speciall recommendation from the Lords which upon searching the presidents upon Sir Xto[*pher*] musgroves motion did appear to be usuall[121] particularly from the Com[*mo*]ns to the Lords when they sent them the bill for quieting the minds of the people in K[*ing*] James the I[*s*]ts time:[122] The Scots had been hardly used in relation to Darien and were highly

---

[118] Presumably Seymour, as Speaker 1673–9. Vernon reported that Musgrave and Robert Harley 'were not for putting the bankers into any better condition than the law had left them': Northants. RO, Montagu (Boughton) MSS 48/43.

[119] John Conyers, the chairman of supply, and ways and means, had served in the chair of the committee on the Irish Forfeitures Resumption Bill.

[120] For appointing commissioners to treat for an union with Scotland.

[121] With the bill, delivered to the Commons on 28 Feb., the Lords had sent a message to recommend it 'as . . . of great consequence'. This was immediately referred to a committee to search for precedents (which included Cocks in its number and had Musgrave in the chair). The report, on 5 Mar., related five similar examples from the *Commons'* and *Lords' Journals,* all dating from 1621–4. *CJ* xiii. 236, 267.

[122] A measure from 1624 relating to 'concealments', which had been recommended 'as a bill concerning the general good and quiet of the whole kingdom': *CJ* xiii. 267.

incensed and when a treasonable book printed[123] was quaestioned in the house
of Lords my Lord Peterborrow proposed a union.[124] this was then Looked
upon as a jest but the court came into it on this account:[125] first it not coming
from the throne there was no occasion for inquiring into the miscarriages of
Darien: if the commons rejected the bill it might probably turn the anger of
the Scotch from the court on the Parliament if the bill was accepted it would
amuse the Scots at least but that I beleive they hardly expected: There was Mr
How began who railed against the usage of the Scots and against the K[*ing'*]s
going beyond sea and that this was not for any good intent but commended an
union upon good terms:[126] the matter of the union was hardly touched on: but
the coming of it to our house some said it should have come from the
throne[127] others that the Scots should have desired it all agreed it to be
convenient if practicable: Sir B: Shore spoke [?also] to it and repeated in
other terms what How said: I said I come with an intention to be against
the union but the gent[*leman*] that spoke last had changed my opinion for I
thought if they were in such distres and so uneasye we could [n]ever treat with
them to more advantage
[. . .][128]

---

[123] *An Enquiry into the Causes of the Miscarriage of the Scots Colony at Darien . . .* (Glasgow,
1700), repr. in *William III State Tracts,* iii. 520–65. The subject of a debate in the Commons in
January 1700, when it had been ordered to be burnt: *CJ* xiii. 123. For the history of the failure of
the Scottish settlement at Darien, see *The Darien Papers . . .* (Bannatyne Club; Edinburgh, 1849);
G. P. Insh, *The Company of Scotland . . .* (London, 1932); and John Prebble, *The Darien Disaster*
(London, 1968).

[124] Charles Mordaunt (*c.*1658–1735), 3rd Earl of Peterborough, had himself 'introduced' the
subject of the pamphlet into a Lords' debate on the Darien affair on 10 Feb. 1700, in order to make
the case for an union: HMC, *House of Lords MSS,* NS iv. 106–7; *LJ* vi. 512; HMC, *Hope-Johnstone
MSS,* 115. On this episode, see P. W. J. Riley, *The Union of England and Scotland: A Study in
Anglo-Scottish Politics of the Eighteenth Century* (Manchester, 1978), 23–5.

[125] The chief spokesmen in favour of union on this occasion were 'some of the Court',
especially Charles Montagu and James Vernon: Cumbria RO (Carlisle), D/Lons/W, James to Sir
John Lowther, 5 Mar. 1699[/1700]; BL Add. MSS 17677 UU, fo. 178; 30000 D, fo. 83. Robert Harley,
on the other hand, called it 'the sham union bill': HMC, *Portland MSS,* iii. 616.

[126] According to Bonet, Howe had argued that before an union was agreed the wishes of the
Scots should be ascertained, through the calling of 'a free Parliament' in Edinburgh: BL Add. MS
30000 D, fo. 83.

[127] The principal opposition argument, in L'Hermitage's account: BL Add. MS 17677 UU, fo.
178.

[128] Omitted: a standing order made 13 Feb. 1700[/1] relating to privilege (fo. 83); 'An abstract of
the laws relating to the poor' (fos. 82ᵛ–82ʳ); 'Of the Originall of the poor' (fo. 81ᵛ); 'Of the
increase of the poor' (fo. 81ᵛ–81ʳ); 'How to remedy these growing Evills' (fos. 81ʳ–80ᵛ); 'The
Charge I gave Mich[*aelmas*] sessions 1700' (fos. 80ᵛ–79ᵛ).

1701 Parliament

nota I called at Sir Thomas Littletons and dined with him the 5th of feb[*rua*]ry [*1701*] as I came to town I found him very uneasy in his mind, but till the poet Durfy[1] withdrew he said no great matter but then I told him the occasion of my coming to town was to give him my vote, and to make what Little interest I could for him; he told me that he had been with the King to acquain[t] him that he was ready to serve him as Speaker if the King approved thereof: the King desired him to absent himself[2] for it would be more for his interest to have Mr Harly: These things were adjusted between the K[*ing*] and Mr Harley who is now Spea[ker] by the Lord Rochester now prime minister of state an Ecclesiasticall com[*mi*]s[*sione*]r in King James time and a privy councellour in the French and arbitrary Councills of King Charles the 2d: one that would never own this King to be King de facto, was for the Regency, against the association;[3] this was the true cause I mean the cheif why we agreed and met at the Rose[4] in orde[r] to oppose mr Harley: becaus we did not like the preceptor at all nor the pupill very well god bles us from the ills they may do:[5] tho for all the opinions of many I cannot believe Mr Harley in the main to be in any interest but that of th[e] country tho I confes I do not approve of many of his words and actions prima pars Historie est ne quid falsi

[1] Thomas D'Urfey (1653–1723), for whom see *DNB*.

[2] According to [Ralph,] *Hist. Eng.*, ii. 908, and James Vernon (Yale Univ., Beinecke Lib., Osborn Coll., Manchester MSS, Vernon to Manchester, 3 Feb. 1700[/1]) this interview had taken place on the 3rd. See also T. Heywood (ed.), *The Norris Papers* (Chetham Society, 9; 1846), 55.

[3] Laurence Hyde (1642–1711), 1st Earl of Rochester, 1st Lord of the Treasury 1679–84, Lord President 1684–5, Lord Treasurer 1685–6, Lord Lieutenant of Ireland 1700–2. Burnet (*Own Time*, iv. 470) recorded that he had 'the chief direction of affairs' at this time. Rochester had spoken in favour of a regency in the debate in Jan. 1689 on the transfer of the Crown (Macaulay, *Hist. Eng.* iii. 1278); he had refused to subscribe the 1696 Association voluntarily, though had signed under compulsion (Cobbett, *Parl. Hist.* v. 993; *LJ* xv. 685).

[4] The Rose Tavern, in Russell Street, Covent Garden, at the corner of Bridges Street: Bryant Lillywhite, *London Coffee Houses . . .* (London, 1963), 487–9. The venue for meetings of a Court Whig club since at least 1694: Lord *et al.* (edd.), *Poems on Affairs of State*, v. 501–2; Macaulay, *Hist. Eng.*, vi. 2658;, Horwitz, *Parliament, Policy and Politics*, 209.

[5] L'Hermitage (BL Add. MS 17677 WW, fo. 152) noted that some Members opposed Harley's election because they looked upon him as Rochester's friend and the ministry's servant; while the Duke of Hamilton was informed that Harley 'hath been hand in glove with my Lord Rochester some time' (Scottish RO, GC406/1/4809, Gawin Mason to Hamilton, 8 Feb. 1700/1). There is first-hand evidence that Godolphin at least was actively promoting Harley's candidature: HMC, *Portland MSS*, iv. 14.

dicere audeat, deinde ne quid veri non audeat:[6] (we were about 125 that met at the Rose tavern)[7]

At the sessions of Parliament met the sixth of Febr[*uary*] 1700[/01] and prorogued[8] to munday the tenth we met on the sixth and were sworn in the little roome by the Lord Steward[9] and pror[o]gued to munday Some said and truly, out of the house, that the teste of writ for prorogation bearing date before we were sworn that we were not legally sworn and ought to be sworn again but that was not mentioned in the hou[se] when we met on munday [*10 Feb. 1701*] in the house. after we were a full house the black rod said the King commands this Honourable house to attend him in the house[10] [*of peers*] Sir Edward Seymour stood up after the King had sent for us and the house returned, and said that the King had ordered us to chus[e] a Speaker, he said the King had power to refuse, and that we ought to chuse a man of abilityes and knowledge in the laws and parliamentary affaires,[11] and as such he recommended mr Harley:[12] Sir John Luson [*Gower*] and the Lord Hartington stood up to[ge]ther: Sir John Luson after a great calling on my Lord Hartingtons name was first seen by Mr Joderill the clerk[13] for he was ordered as we beleived to see those that named Harley first so Sir John Luson seco[nded] Sir Edward Seymour:[14] and then my Lord Hartington complimented Mr Harley for his abilityes but said Sir Thomas Littleton was commanded to absent [*himself*] by the King and it was done in order to promote Mr Harleys e[lec]tion: that it was against the orders of the house and invasive of our rights which we were intrusted with, and then he proposed Sir Richard

---

[6] Cicero, *De Oratore*, 2. 15. 62: 'Nem quis nescit primam esse historiae, legem, ne quid falsi dicere audeat? Deinde ne quid veri non audeat.'

[7] Words in brackets are boxed in the MS. The Whig Member for Liverpool, William Clayton, reported on 8 Feb. that 'Mr Harley was generally talked of for Speaker till this week 70 of the chief members at the Rose pitched upon Sir Richard Onslow': Liverpool RO, 920 NOR 1/71 (Norris MSS), Clayton to Richard Norris.   [8] Originally 'adjourned'.

[9] In the inner Court of Wards (*CJ* xiii. 324) by William Cavendish (1641–1707), 1st Duke of Devonshire, Lord Steward 1689–d.

[10] From 'black rod' to 'in the house' interlined. Sir David Mitchell (*c*.1650–1710) was Gentleman Usher of the Black Rod 1698–d.

[11] 'in the laws and parliamentary affairs' interlined.

[12] An account of this debate in the papers of Charles Sergison, the Clerk of the Acts, confirms the outline of Seymour's speech. National Maritime Museum, Ser/103, fo. 63.

[13] Paul Jodrell (d. 1728), Clerk of the House of Commons 1683–1724.

[14] That Seymour proposed Harley is confirmed by L'Hermitage (BL Add. MSS 17677 WW, fo. 152). After Harley's election Seymour and Sir John Leveson Gower conducted him to the Chair (*CJ* xiii. 325).

onslow as a man capable of the busines and beyond exception:[15] Sir William[16] Stric[k]la[nd] spoke angrily, but nothing to the purpose against Harley: Sir Charles Sidley spoke for Harley foolishly: S[ir] Xtopher Musgrove spoke for harley, and said nothing appeared to him of the courts appearing for mr Harley if there were any ground for it, for all his respect friendship and value for mr Harley he would have been against him: Mr Clerk in answer to Sir John Luson said you perswade us to unanimity that is you would have us be of your opinion if you are so fond of unanimity why cant you come over to us, he spoke more to the purpose: I answered and said sir I have as great an opinion of Mr Harley as any one: I have hea[rd] it said without doors that Sir Thomas Litleton was spoken to absent himself, in order to promote Mr Har[ley's] pretension to be Speaker, and what I have heard since I came here confirms me in that opinion: Sir Tho[mas] Littleton is absent and Mr Harley is proposed: Gent[le]men say hee is a wise learned and judicious ma[n]: truly this manage[ment] had we never heard of him before makes that out, it is no easy matter to keep old fri[ends] to get new ones, and remove the only obstacle out of his way: this shews him to be a man of parts to[o] good and cur[?ious] parts for a Speaker of this house: the other Gent[leman] Sir Richard Onslow is an old long experienced member[17] (here the house interrupted me with a great laugh thinking I had jested upon Onslow he being very long and slim)[18] whom neyther his own seeking, nor a constant opposition to publick affairs nor a sinister mean complyance behind the curtain made acceptable to the court, and the only reason we are for him, the only thing that recommend[s] him to us, is the opinion we have that he loves both King and country as he ought: this debate puts me in mind of a story in the Romish history; which is as follows:[19] there were certain foolish ceremonyes and religious rights performed amongst the heathens at which it was unlawfull for a man to be at, these ceremonyes w[ere] observed at Julius Caesars house before he was dictator[20] Clodius

---

[15] Proposal confirmed by L'Hermitage (BL Add MS 17677 WW, fo. 152), who noted that Hartington was seconded by Charles, Lord Spencer. The exchange between Leveson Gower and Hartington, and the latter's proposal of Onslow 'as a more indifferent person' are again confirmed in Nat. Maritime Mus., Ser/103, fos. 63–4, where further speeches are noted: in favour of Harley by Sir Christopher Musgrave and Sir Charles Sedley; and in favour of Onslow by Charles, Lord Spencer, Sir John Mainwaring, Sir William Strickland, Edward Clarke, and Cocks himself.

[16] Originally 'Richard'.   [17] Onslow's continuous parliamentary service dated from 1679.

[18] Words in brackets interlined in MS, Sir Richard was described by his nephew, Speaker Arthur Onslow, as 'tall and very thin': C. E. Vulliamy, *The Onslow Family . . .* (London, 1953), 27.

[19] The story of Publius Clodius Pulcher's scandalous escapade at the Bona Dea festival in 62 BC is told in Plutarch, *Caesar,* 10 and id., *Cicero,* 28–9.

[20] The ceremonies were taking place at Caesar's house because at that time he held the office of praetor and chief priest.

another Roman dresses himself in womans cloaths and by that disguis[e] gets
into the house, but by his size and gate he was soon discovered and turned out:
Common fame carried this story to the senate: and they decree that there
should be an inquiry made de pollutis sacris:[21] Caesar turns away his wife[22]
tho shee was innocent as they told him, saying Caesars wife ought not only to
be inno[cent] but free from scandall: Sir my application is this the sacra of this
house are our Freedom of speech and ou[r] attending the service of the house
and whoever shall by bribe, menacyes, or any other art perswade a mem[ber] to
absent himself from the service of the house or not to speak what he thinks for
their good, does poll[ute] the sacra of the house, and as such (I hope) when the
Chair is filld, will be censured, this is like the prac[tice] in King Charles the
seconds time, and I beleive the advice came from one of his ministers:[23] Sir we
ought t[o] have as great a regard to the reputation of our Speaker as Caesar had
to his wifes and as he repudiate[d] her only for the report so I hope we shall
repudiate mr Harley when the quaestion is put I mean give a negative: pompeia
was innocent and I am confident Mr Harley knew no more of this matter than
shee did of Clodiuses coming: Mr Harley denyed any Knowledg of any practice
disabled himself as unfit and said in answer to Stricland who said he would
never give a vote for a man with whom he had never voted for ten [?years][24] that
he had never given a vote he repented of, nor had he done any thing under hand:
as for the story he did n[ot] remember it but he reme[m]bred a saying that
C[l]odius accused mcchos[25] he excused himself from the service, tooke the
chair[26] [?wh]en [?his ?excuse ?was] not allowed and then the mace was laid on
the table and we adjourned

[. . .][27]

[*fo. 78ᵛ*]

Shepperds case

[*13 Feb. 1701*] Sir Ed[*ward*] Seymour gave a charge against Shepperd for
having procured himself returned and others at Andover Malmsbury Ilchester

---

[21] Plutarch, *Cicero*, 28. 3: 'Is postea de pollutis sacris accusatis'.   [22] Pompeia.

[23] Probably a reference to the incident at the beginning of the First Exclusion Parliament in
March 1679, when Charles II had rejected the Commons' first choice as Speaker: *HC 1660–90*, iii.
416; Ronald Hutton, *Charles the Second* . . . (Oxford, 1989), 368–9. Cocks's innuendo is
presumably directed against Lord Rochester.

[24] Both Harley and Strickland had first entered the House in 1689. There is a draft of Harley's
disabling speech at BL Loan 29/161, Misc. 17.

[25] The reference is obscure; perhaps some allusion to Cicero is intended.

[26] There was in fact a division on Harley's election, carried by 249 votes to 129, in which
Onslow was his opponent: *CJ* xiii. 325; Luttrell, *Brief Relation*, v. 16; [Ralph,] *Hist. Eng.* ii. 908.

[27] Omitted: copies of votes of the House 'Concerning the pensioners', 22–24 May 1679 (fo. 79);
a MS copy of the list of Court supporters, 1679, originally published as *A List of One Unanimous
Club of Voters* . . . [1679] (fo. 79).

[?and *Bramber*] Shepperd had a day given him and [*3 Mar. 1701*] councill allowed[28] contrary to orders Sir Edw[*ard*] Seymour said: but councill was allowed him and Sir Ed[*ward*] Seymour had councill against him: the thing that brought an odium upon Sheppard was a letter found out: wrote to Bramber by one Clifton:[29] Mr Sheppard it appeared had endeavoured to get Mr Pascall of the prize office[30] chosen to serve for that place: and Clifton was ordered by Sheppard to abscond: millman had been tampered with to deny Sheppards being concerned Lawton had dealt between them:[31] when this matter appeared it reflected hard upon Sheppard before his tryall at the tryall [*14 Mar. 1701*] Mr Dobyns and Mr Brown[32] were councill for Sir Ed[*ward*] Seymour they said Sir Edward Seymour retained them out of a generous temper to serve the publick: they began with wootton Basset:[33] Dobbins opened the intreague of the new company: that an apothecary one lawrence was to go northward and a surgeon to go westward and endeavour to fix the

---

[28] Samuel Shepheard, sen., MP Newport (I.o.W.). That Seymour preferred the allegation is confirmed by, among others, Burnet, *Own Time,* iv. 476. On Shepheard's electoral activities, part of a wider campaign by New East India Company interests, see Robert Walcott, 'The East India Company Interest in the General Election of 1700–1701', *English Historical Review,* 278 (1956), 228–30, 234–6. After an information had been laid before the House on 13 Feb. of his involvement in bribery at several elections, and he had initially rebutted the charge, the case was appointed to be heard at the bar of the House on 11 Mar. However, in the meantime, on 3 Mar., it was ordered that Shepheard be heard by counsel. *CJ* xiii. 327, 374.

[29] This letter, from a William Clifton, promising £200 to Bramber to assist with the election of Shepheard's nominee, was brought to the notice of the House on 1 Mar., when an investigative committee was appointed (including Cocks): *CJ* xiii. 367. At the report on 12 Mar. the letter was condemned and several of Shepheard's agents were ordered into custody, but Clifton himself had absconded: ibid. 399–400; *CSP Dom.* 1700–2, p. 279. Clifton's full identity is unknown, but he may have been the attorney of the same name ordered into custody by the Commons on 3 Mar. 1705 for failing to attend the committee of inquiry into the legal proceedings on the Aylesbury case (Ashby *v.* White): *CJ* xiv. 558; Luttrell, *Brief Relation,* v. 527.

[30] John Pasc(h)all, commissioner of prizes 1694–8, officer for managing arrears of prizes 1699–1703 *(Cal. Treas. Bks.,* x. 763; xiv. 98,301; xvii. 296). Possibly the younger son of John Pascall of Great Baddow, Essex: *Transactions of the Essex Archaeological Society,* NS 23 (1942–5), 60, 64. A John Pascall, identified as a 'mariner', had been resident in Stepney in 1669–72: G. J. Armytage (ed.), *Allegations for Marriage Licences Issued by the Vicar-General of the Archbishop of Canterbury, 1669 to 1679* (Harleian Society, 34; London, 1892), 6, 71.

[31] William Millman (*c.*1650–1714), of Ormond Street, Middx., a barrister who had made a fortune by stock-jobbing. Knighted in 1709. 'A worthless person by the general character of him': G. W. Marshall (ed.), *Le Neve's Pedigrees of the Knights* (Harleian Soc., 8; London, 1873), 492. Millman was evidently a financial associate of Shepheard. He and his agent, Lawton, were examined at the bar on 12 Mar., when Lawton was ordered into custody: *CJ* xiii. 400.

[32] William Dobyns and John Brown, barristers and benchers of Lincoln's Inn.

[33] There had not in fact been any contest in this constituency, where the Tories Henry Pinnell and Henry St John had been returned unopposed. However, Shepheard's agent Lawrence was found guilty by the House of 'endeavouring by bribery and corrupt practices, to procure an election of a burgess' there, and was committed to Newgate: History of Parliament Trust, 1690–1715 section, draft constituency entry; *CJ* xiii. 407.

design of getting the members of the new E[*ast India*] Companys being chosen
to be mentioned by Sheppard at the Court: but it was not made out in the
least, it was proved that Lawrence gave money at Wooton Basset, and that he
promised if they would elec[t] Shepperd to deposite 250 li. in any 3d hand it
was made out that Old Sheppard[34] was first mentioned there: yong Shepperd[35]
was met by the Freemen[36] he said he would give nothing for the writs were
out,[37] many proved that old Sheppard had been first mentioned and that he
said if the money had been laid down he had had no occasion to have went
down: Lawrence gave ten shillings a man to those that met yong Sheppard:
after the evidence was over seymour summed it up dexterously and said that
we were in danger of ruine from bribery and corruption and that we ought to
extirpate the roots and fibers of it: I spoke afterwards and sai[d] sir I agree
with that Honourable Gent[*leman*] that the very roots and fibers of bribery
ought to be extirpated but briberi and corru[pti]on have long since taken deep
root in this house before Sir Stephen Fox was ordered to name such members
of the last parliament he could remember had received any money for secret
service[38] at this Mr How rose up and said to orders sir you should not let him
mention that Honourable gent[*leman's*] name [(] I knew I had transgressed
orders when I spoke and was provided to bring myself of [*f*)]:[39] at which the
Speaker very readily tooke me down to order and told me I should not
mention that Honourable gent[*leman's*] name: I said sir what I said I tooke
out of your journalls[40] and I can desire it to be read [?as] part of my speech
this was 20 years ago and I did not know this to be the same Sir Stephen Fox:
and then I went [?on] and said sir Bribery and corruption have been established and have taken firm root here (I must not name names for [?fear] it
should be a members) long before the Old East in[*dia*] Company endeavoured
to corrupt this house the house of Lords Kings Quee[ns ?Du]chesses and every
body, corruption and bribery have been long established in this house before
an honourable gent[*leman*] was expe[lled from] your chair for Bribery and
now sits in one of the cheif seats of Westminsterhall:[41] Sir I dont speak this to
reflect [?but] out of the sorrow and bitternes of my soule to complain that

[34] Samuel Shepheard, sen.
[35] Presumably Samuel Shepheard, jun., MP Malmesbury.
[36] In fact, Wootton Bassett was a scot-and-lot borough.
[37] The 'Treating Act' of 1696 (7 & 8 Gul. III, c. 4) provided that no gifts could be made or
entertainment supplied to the voters by a candidate after the *teste* of the writ.
[38] On 23 May 1679 Fox, then paymaster of the forces, had been interrogated by the Commons
on secret service payments after he and other officials had obstructed requests for documentary
evidence to assist inquiries into corruption. For this incident, see *HC 1660–90*, ii. 358.
[39] Words in brackets interlined in MS.   [40] *CJ* ix. 629–30.
[41] Sir John Trevor once more.

these things were not Looked into then and censured [?as] they ought: had that been done then I beleive verily we had had none now: I really beleive the bribery of the old com[pa]ny to be the occasion of this corruption of the new, for the new found that the old had bribed members, and the ne[w] were [*in*] a manner forced to bring some in by bribing to make a ballance to the interest of the old:[42] but to the busines I h[a]ve heard it said one might know Hercules by his foot[43] I can trace the footsteps of Old mister Shepperd thro all the eve[nts] and therefore when the quaestion is put I must say he is guilty: up stood mr Speaker again Sir I dont know what you mean by Bribery in my Chair I am sure I am guilty of none,[44] I dont know what you mean by ripping up old businesses and what is pardonned: to w[hich] I said sir I never heard that you were guilty of Bribery I never heard that you were nor do I beleive you ever will fo[r] I beleive you have more witt: nor do I think that you beleived I mentioned any thing relating, or with an intention to yo[u] and tho this crime is pardonned, I may say that pardon was not for the service of my country: after this Jack How said sir I do not know what is the meaning of the ripping of these old storyes and the bringing of that unfortunate Gent[*leman*][45] upon a[ll] occasions uppon the stage, I may say that had his worst enemies no more estate than what was gotten by rog[ue]rys and villany they would not have had enough to have brought them from their own Houses to town: the[n] the quaestion was put and passed.)[46] the next day [*15 Mar. 1701*] S[*he*]p[*hea*]rd was upon his tryal for Malmsbury there was his youngest son Cha[rles][47] recommended by the lords Wharton and Ferrers[48] and nothing appeared foule uppon Shepperd or his son it only appeared t[hat] the town was mercenary and had offered it to sale: so that the officers of the town were com[*mit*]ted and then they said that th[e] officers could do no fault unles incouraged by somebody and that somebody must be Shepperd, the house was very

[42] L'Hermitage (BL Add. MS 17677 WW, fo. 192) reported that during these debates Whig Members had in general supported the New Company, Tories the Old.

[43] From the Latin proverb, 'ex pede Herculem'.

[44] 'I am sure I am guilty of none' interlined. [45] Trevor.

[46] Two resolutions, in fact: first, that Shepheard, sen., was 'guilty of endeavouring, by bribery, and corrupt practices, to procure an election of a burgess . . . for . . . Wootton Bassett', then against Lawrence to the same effect: *CJ* xiii. 406.

[47] No trace has been found of this third son, who does not figure in Shepheard's will (PRO Prob. 11/567, fo. 123). Cocks presumably means the second son, Samuel, jun., who was indeed returned for Malmesbury at this election.

[48] Thomas Wharton (1648–1715), 5th Baron Wharton. Comptroller of the Household 1689–1702 and a member of the Whig Junto; high steward of Malmesbury (with intervals) 1690–1714. Robert Shirley (1650–1717), 8th Baron Ferrers. Their recommendation of young Shepheard is confirmed in A. L. Browne, 'Lord Halifax and the Malmesbury Election of 1701', *Wiltshire Archaeological and Natural History Magazine*, 47 (1936), 501–3; and BL Add.MS 28886, fo. 204.

i[n]different upon the quaestion[49] Sir Ed[*ward*] Seymour said that he hoped
every one was instigated against corruption and bribery and that the[?ir] zeale
was not cooled and so made the most of Little or nothing that was against
Sheppard: I understood many thought mr [How] reflected the last day upon
me so I said: Sir I have as great a detestation against Bribery and coruption as
any man within these walls or without I hope, I hate estates gotten by
roguerys and villanyes and have no great respect for those [?–] owed their
very originalls to,[50] but my Zeale shall not transport me beyond my reason:
had not She[p]perd been recommended by the Lords Ferrers and Wharton I
would have presumed corruption but I do not n[ow] see any reason for such
presumption: Sir I am not new East Indian enough to acquitt them when I
beleive them guilty nor am I old East Indian enough to find them guilty when
the evidence is not suf[fici]ent: Shepperd was undoubtedly guilty in relation to
the hindering the evidence from giving evidence in relation to Bra[m]ber by
sending away clifton etc. which being accidentally inquired into and falling
hard upon Shepperd blemished him in relation to his tryall: he and his two
sons were turned out himself and one justly enough the other to bear them
company becaus his name was sheppard there were more things I beleive
proved upon him than he was Guilty of and yet he was to[o] guilty to sitt
there: on tuesday the 25 of Mart: 1700[/01] the consideration of Sheppards
business was referred[51] then they proceeded against his agents and those that
promoted his interest some were Com[*mit*]t[*e*]d some proclama[ti]ons issued
out against: some of them being Custome house officers occasioned this
quaestion not regular but very necessary that no custome house officer should
be capable of being a Parliament man: the further Consideration of what was
to be done with Shepperd was put of[*f*] for one week longer[52]

---

[49] The House resolved that Shepheard, sen., had again been guilty of 'bribery and corruption'
in this election, and passed the same vote on William Ady, former deputy steward of the borough
(*CSP Dom.* 1696, p. 433; Beaufort MSS 602/17, Malmesbury election case [1698]), who was taken
into custody. The election at Ilchester was then considered, in which one of the candidates, the
New East India Company director Edward Allen, was found guilty of bribery but Shepheard was
cleared. *CJ* xiii. 407–8.

[50] 'I hate estates' to 'originalls to' interlined. It would appear that this insertion, begun half-
way across the page, could not be fitted into the space available, and thus 'owed their very
originalls to' appears on the left-hand side (but on the same line) as a continuation. No other
reading of the passage makes sense.

[51] In the meantime, on 17 and 18 Mar., the Commons had debated the evidence in the cases of
Andover and Newport (I.o.W.), after which Shepheard, sen., had been committed to the Tower: *CJ*
xiii, 410, 413.

[52] After the House had been informed of the abscondment of various persons ordered into
custody as a result of investigations into elections at Bramber and Newport, and at Grimsby,
where Shepheard had not been personally involved, an address was voted for a proclamation

Tuesday the 11th of feb. 1700[/01] was spent in swearing the members[53]
Wednesday the 12th [*Feb. 1701*] partly in delivering Petitio[ns] and debates
arising from those petitions[54] thursday [*13 Feb. 1701*] petitions and swearing:
on friday [*14 Feb. 1701*] Sir R Gwin Moved to take consideration of the
Kings Speech on Saterday Sir Xto[*pher*] musgrove proposed tuesday at last
there was an ag[re]ement nemine Con[*tradicente*] for Saterday on Saterday
[*recte Friday*] it was proposed[55] that we should vote that we would stand by
[the] King and support the government for the safety of England the
preservation of the protestant religion and for [the] peace of Europe[56]
some said this would insensibly bring us in and ingage us in a war[57] others
said that it was necessary to shew that we valued our religion etc. (liberty
and freinds and allies above our money)[58] this cost many an hard word and
two hours debate and at last a division the ays 181 the noyes 163[59] then we
ordered it to be put into an addres; as to the successio[n] the best part of the
house I mean the honestest were for it: the Jacobites against it and the
commonwea[*l*]ths men the one out of a des[*ign*]ing for one government and
the other for the other, these two partyes joyn in every thing and so they did
now to oppose the settlement of the crown[60] and instead thereof to have the
time prolonged to a year for the Parliament to sit aft[er] the death of the
King and princes many that wished for a comonwealth could not trust [t]he
virtue of their par[?ty] and feared the designs of the Jacobites in conjunction
with them least if such an interval [sh]ould happen the money of the Jacobites
would prevail over the honesty of the commonwea[*l*]ths men and tha[t] we

against them. Arising from the evidence in the Grimsby case resolutions were also passed against
customs officers sitting in Parliament or 'concerning themselves' in elections in the future. Further
consideration of Shepheard's case was adjourned for a week. *CJ* xiii. 427.

[53] And in hearing the King's Speech: *CJ* xiii. 325–6.

[54] According to *CJ* xiii. 326, and Luttrell, *Brief Relation*, v. 17, the sitting on the 12th was
entirely taken up with the swearing in of Members.

[55] By James Vernon: Luttrell, *Brief Relation*, v. 18; PRO 31/3/187/43.

[56] The wording of the motion was 'that this House will stand by and support His Majesty and
his government; and take such effectual measures as may best conduce to the interest and safety of
England, the preservation of the Protestant religion and the peace of Europe': *CJ* xiii. 332.

[57] Bonet and L'Hermitage noted that this was the principal argument against the wording: BL
Add. MSS 30000 E, fo. 40; 17677 WW, fos. 162–3. According to Salwey Winnington, 'the friends of
the old ministry and most of the courtiers did vote for it to procure a war, the Country Party
against it for fear we should run headlong into a war and become principals in it': House of Lords
RO, House of Commons Library MS 12, fo. 63. The opposition was led by John Granville, Jack
Howe, Sir Christopher Musgrave, Thomas Pelham, and Sir Edward Seymour: [Ralph] *Hist. Eng.*,
ii. 911; PRO 31/3/187/43–4.   [58] Words in brackets interlined.

[59] James Lowther reported that it had been 'a long debate': Cumbria RO (Carlisle), D/Lons/W,
James to Sir John Lowther, 15 Feb. 1700[/1]. The division was on an amendment to omit the phrase
'and the peace of Europe'.   [60] 'of the crown' interlined.

should be exposed to sale to the best bidder or where they could have the best terms: there are some [at] the head [?of them] are Jacobites but when the mask is of[f] that is but a thin party: and this fe[ar ?–] kn[ow ?– –]
[*fo. 78*]
[?– ?danger] so when grumbling and artifices to delay our proceedings[61] could no longer prevaile then we came to settle our rights and I hope not to[o] much but it maybe only to give our posterity an opportunity of complimenting the successor that is to be

friday the 18th of febr[*uary, recte Monday the 17th of February, 1701*] Secretary vernon opened to the house the discovery of a letter from the E[*arl*] of Melford to the E[*arl*] of Pyrth: he opened it as a providentiall great discovery, there were more chances that attended the bringing of it to hand then seemed merely accidental, and the inside contained nothing extraordin-ary but what every one knew that K[*ing*] James and his papist would be glad to come again.[62] this was to[o] much magnifyed by the Secretary and to[o] little on that accom[pt] minded or regarded by any one else, and made the ill natured wits sharp: Sir Xto[*pher*] Musgrove all this sessions was contriving ways to put of[f] our supplys and destroying our credit March 23d [*recte 24th, 1701*] speaking of the partititon [*sic*] treaty after we had censured it by addres[63] Mr How come in and said sir I understand the addres is over and I fear I came to[o] late but I hope I may speak yet in order to it and then moved for a day to consider the treaty: he said sir I cannot call this a treaty but a Combination of 3 robbers to rob the 4th to make a private a comparison it is as if 3 men with a [f]elonious intention should agree to break open the house of another person that was sick when he died[64] and one of the 3 was to have all the goods, the sick man dyes and gives all his goods to one of them, he that is executor will no longer consent to [th]e robbery having a better right and a great deale of

---

[61] Burnet (*Own Time*, iv. 497–8) also alleged that the settlement of the succession was repeatedly postponed for 'the most trifling matters', though he blamed the Tories alone, and Robert Harley in particular.

[62] John Drummond (c.1650–1715), 1st Earl of Melfort (and 1st Duke of Melfort in the Jacobite peerage); and his brother James (1648–1716), 4th Earl of Perth (and 1st Duke in the Jacobite peerage), governor to the Prince of Wales. The letter is printed in *CJ* xiii. 335–6. A copy, it had been intercepted in the Post Office: Luttrell, *Brief Relation*, v. 19. As many as forty MPs claimed that they could identify the hand (BL Add. MS 17677 WW, fos. 164–5), and the French authorities eventually admitted that it was genuine (N. Tindal, *The Continuation of Mr Rapin de Thoyras's History of England* (2 vols.; London, 1751), i. 445).

[63] An address had been agreed on 24 Mar., laying out the 'ill consequences of the second Partition Treaty (of 1700): *CJ* xiii. 425.   [64] 'when he died' interlined.

such stuff[65] this Gent[*leman*][66] talked, at last Coll Warton [r]ose up and said such words as these were never given nor used in an ale house bawdy house or tavern: the [S]peaker said the Gent[*leman*] had a low voyce he was ill and at a distance and that he could not hear him this caused more reflections and heats;[67] mr How said Kings can do no harm and that he reflected only upon the ministry and others did uppon the king: upon which Sir w[*illia*]m Strickland said if Kings can do no wrong then we have injuriously expelled K[*ing*] J[*ames*] if his councellours are to blame then are we more in fault for they are councellours now: and then [w]e appoynted a day for Kid[68] the bill for succession was read the first of Aprill [*1701*] the bill was read and the severall [ri]ghts therein mentioned were debated and ordered by the Committee to be reported and upon the report [*10 May 1701* ag]reed to by the house without much opposition[69] [*5 Mar. 1701*][70] they read the bill of rights and the[71] report of our rights by Treby upon the revolution[72] read Mr How complained that many necessary things in that report were omitted by the selfish designs of members in the bill of rights [M]r Harcourt said the best of the heads in the report were provided for; but since our successor was to come from abroad that [w]e could not do better than see and admire the great wisdom of our ancestors in the time that phi[*lip*] of Spain married our q[*ueen* M]ary and desired that to be read: in which it was enacted that no forreiner should be capable of a grant or place in this [K]ingdom[73] and upon this he grounded his

---

[65] The gist of these remarks by Howe is confirmed in BL Add. MS 17677 WW, fos. 200–1: and Devon RO, 1392/D/L/18/01/1 (Seymour of Berry Pomeroy MSS), Sir T Aleyne to [?–], 29 Mar. 1701. They were taken up in Defoe's 'Legion Memorial': *Somers's Tracts*, xi. 257. The contemporary historian Tindal, however, recorded that Sir Edward Seymour, Sir John Bolles, and others 'had compared the dividing another man's kingdom to robbery on the highway', while Howe had used the expression 'a felonious treaty': Tindal, *Continuation of Rapin's Hist.*, i. 451–2.

[66] Originally 'fellow'.

[67] Another observer reported that Howe 'was taken up very sharply. . . and had been called to the bar of the House had the Speaker heard the words, who being asked by a Member then sitting, how he could sit there, and hear that reflection, was pleased to say (as before) he heard them not, so all was hushed up': Devon RO, 1392/D/L/18/01/1. Later in the session Howe was observed by Cocks to be afflicted with breathing difficulties (below, p. 139). By June he had retired to the country, 'seized by a very troublesome disease almost continually upon me': BL Loan 29/393, Howe to [Robert Harley], June 1701.

[68] *CJ* xiii. 425, states that the address was agreed after the day for Captain Kidd's examination had been fixed.

[69] *CJ* xiii. 524–5, records no division, though two amendments were put forward.

[70] In the committee of the whole upon the Bill of Settlement.

[71] 'bill of rights and the' interlined.

[72] Sir George Treby's report on 2 Feb. 1689 from the committee to prepare heads of what was to become the Declaration of Rights (*CJ* x. 17). Sir John Verney referred to the Bill of Settlement as a new Bill of Rights (BL Add. MS 29568, fo. 9).

[73] A clause in Queen Mary I's Marriage Act (1 Mar. I, st. 3 c. 2). Bonet noted this reference back (BL Add. MS 30000 E, fo. 70).

motion: I 2ded him saying sir revolutions are very chargeable and seldom answer the ends and expectations of those that have ventured their lives the ruine of their familyes their alls to compass them: therefore we ought to settle upon such good foundations that there may be as little occasion as may be for another revolution: I observe in the reading of the report that the Eclesiasticall commission is censured I beleive very few gent[*lemen*] that hazarded [t]hemselves their lives and fortunes to bring about this last revolution expected to destroy only the commission and that one of the first of[74] that com[*mi*]s[*sio*]n should be made in this reign prime minister of state[75] and I beleive others that fought in that cause little thought [t]hat the forfeitures should have been shared and grants made to forreiners, the wisdom of our ancestors prevented and provided for this and our negligence upbraids us so this was quickly agreed to,[76] then mr How moved and spoke very well upon it that the things the matters of state should be debated and transacted in councill and the councill to put their names that consented. he said that this often caused heartburnings towards the King when any thing was done amiss and we Knew not on whom to put the fault that the king could do no wrong and a great many more good arguments I 2ded him and said sir there are many footsteps of the reasons of this, that it is now the law, even the very common proclamations I said more and concluded that if mens actions appeared above board if they had not so much religion as they ought yet shame would in som measure help to keep them honest and so I 2ded How upon which Seymour said and made it appear that of old [th]e privy councill were used to put their names and that it was the law tho disused that he was glad my brother [?h]as agreed to easily but the wording of the Quaestion was very difficult and took up time and not approved of as to [th]e words tho the sence when agreed was understood:[77] the matter of the judges was also debated and the matter pretty warmly argued some were against their being quam diu se bene gesserint[78] and to have their salaryes fixed for that they were very apt to be proud and rude in their circuits and this would encrease their incivilities: others said as long as they [d]epended upon the court absolutely their judgments were not free so that was agreed to [(] this was in the committee [)][79]

---

[74] 'the first of' interlined.					[75] Lord Rochester.

[76] Passage of a resolution that no foreigner be capable of receiving any office or Crown grant, is confirmed in Luttrell, *Brief Relation*, v. 24.

[77] Passage of a resolution to this effect was noted by Luttrell: *Brief Relation*, v. 24. Seymour had himself been a Privy Councillor 1673–89 and 1692–6.					[78] During good behaviour.

[79] To inspect and sort the papers submitted by the Admiralty concerning Kidd. Cocks was not a member of this committee, according to *CJ* xiii. 416. Words in brackets interlined.

Of the Com[*ission*]s granted to the Lords by which Kid acted

[*27 Mar. 1701*] Kid was brought before the house[80] sometime after his examination before the admiralty, in which was nothing reflecting on the Lords the owners, nothing but how levingston[81] recommended him to my Lord Bellamont that he had seen my Lord Orphord and my Lord Rumney but never Sir John Summers nor the d[*uke*] of Shrewsbury: and when he was brought to the house he said the same thing and no more to the disappoyntment of the old ministry now the new one, who would feighn disgrace those they have turned out and cannot see in any tolerable favour with King or people least they should be restored to their former places. [*28 Mar. 1701*][82] mr Hamond observing a great silence in the house moved to have two clauses in the bill of rights read which condemned the granting of felons goods before conviction Sir B: shores who is the litlest maliciousest man living desired to have some votes read relating to grants and reflecting upon my Lord Chancellour:[83] Sir Bart[*holomew*] Shores talked of patents passing the seales regularly and with all his malitious foolish oratory reflected upon my Lord Chancellour particularly for his scill and Knowledge and that the others might be seduced, he insisted upon the reason of felonye and that pyracy was subject to the same rules[84] Sir John Holles answered Shores who had also said that this was not intended personally only to censure the thing sais Sir John Holles I cannot forbear shewing my indignation When I hear that said only to censure the thing and to proceed no further I remember this was said when the deserting souldier was tryed in King Jameses time they would not hang him but if he was found not guilty the army would disert: but this fellow was hanged and by that example [1]00ds more murthered (*nota Holt was recorder of London and refused to condemn him, Shores was put in his place and did it [sic]*)[85] [t]hen as for patents passed he said in many cases it might be don[e] without passing the great seale and all the other pla[ces] as to instance that

[80] After the committee's report had been heard: *CJ* xiii. 441.

[81] Robert Livingston (1654–1728), of Livingston, N Y; Speaker of the New York assembly 1718–25, and a partner in the syndicate financing Kidd's voyage.

[82] A further debate on the Kidd affair: *CJ* xiii. 444.

[83] The former Lord Chancellor, Somers.

[84] In his account of this debate Cocks may well have muddled his notes, for a very similar version of Shower's speech, and also of the replies of Hawles and Cowper, was reported in a debate on the same issue in the previous session, on 6 Dec. 1699 (for which see above, pp. 38–41): Northants. RO, Montagu (Boughton) MSS 48/7, James Vernon to the Duke of Shrewsbury, 6 Dec. 1699. In the diarist's favour, it should be noted that a Tory pamphlet described how Hawles had 'made the same speech, word for word, in two Parliaments' on the Kidd affair: *A Letter from the Grecian Coffee-House, in Answer to the Taunton–Dean Letter* . . . (London 1701), 13. However, Cowper should not in any case have been permitted to speak twice in the same debate, as Cocks's account suggests he did. [85] See above, p. 55, n. 105.

Gent[*leman*] had a patent in King Jameses time to be Kings Councill which
never passed all the seale[86] and he had another patent which dispensed with
the taking of the sacrament and subscribing the test with a non obstante.[87] he
said that this grant appeared now in a better light then when it was formerly
examined: that the grant had nothing extraordinary in it: that the law of
piracy was not the same as the law in other cases: that pirates were hostes
humani generis[88] and were so treated in all that had to do with them: others
shewed that even the goods and persons of enemies were the captors and much
more pirates, mr Cowper instanced in one example of Caesars who was taken
by the pirates and after he had redeemed him self he armed a navall strength
and retooke the pirates and asked the proconsull[89] to have them executed the
proconsull would not unles he might be particeps of the booty upon which
Caesar crucifyed them himself this sais he Caesar did when a private man, and
nobody quaestioned it he said the granting the bona depredata was not a good
grant [b]ut that the granting quan[t]um in nobis[90] made all pass the King
could grant: that pirates goods when taken were adjudged by the [a]d[mi]ralty
and then if the owner could make proof of his right to them he might have
them: the other side said as positive[ly ?that ?the ?granting q]uant[um in]
nobis est shewed that they knew the grant was of no validity by putting those
words in it and [?th]is di[d ?not] much mend the matter nor make the grant
voyd in itself any thing the better that it
[*fo. 77*[v]]
was an unjust illegall grant and ought to be censured Mr H[91] said that a better
parliament might call over again things det[er]mined in a bad parliament that
this was a better parliament: that they discoursed of these gent[*lemen's*] merits:
but that when they did we[ll] they were to be gratifyed and rewarded but when
ill they were to be condemned: that the Romans gave manlius a gratuity for
saving the Capitoll and afterwards threw him headlong thence when they
perceived he had a design upon their libertyes: and then when one of[92] the

---

[86] Shower had been appointed a King's Counsel in Feb. 1688 and reappointed on 3 Nov.
following, but had not been continued in office after the Revolution: Sir John Sainty (comp.), *A
List of English Law Officers, King's Counsel and Holders of Patents of Precedence* (Selden
Society, suppl. ser. 7; London, 1987), 89.

[87] The beginning of the formula in royal dispensations: 'non obstante aliquo statuo in contra-
rium'. Shower, though by this time a strong Tory, came of a Dissenting background.

[88] Pliny the elder, *Natural History*, 7. 6: 'hostem generis humani'.

[89] Marcus Junius, governor of Asia Minor. The story of Caesar's capture by Cilician pirates at
Miletus in 75 BC, and its aftermath, is told in Plutarch, *Caesar*, 1. 8–217; 3. 1.

[90] See above, pp. 39–40.

[91] Probably either Anthony Hammond, the instigator of this debate, or Cocks's *bête noire*, Jack
Howe.   [92] 'one of' interlined.

Horatii had beaten the Curii[93] afterwards when he had Killed his sister he was not by his merit. protected from coming upon his tryall: that they had ascribed to themselves many great actions as that of Le Hogue[94] done by others and that not done as it ought or might have been: I could name those that for what they did there have since had no great thanks and a great deale of such loose stuff I answered as Loosly: Sir I am sorry this debate was ever began without doors if a man has escaped judgement tho deservedly the inferiour courts never try him again there is so[?me] favour allowed to honour Life and liberty and tho wee are not obliged by any such strict rules here yet wha[t] is just in one place is in another, and we ought rather to set them good examples then bad: as for the Gent[leman] saying this is a good parliament the other was not so the same may be said the very next sessions when we have tur[ned] out those we will I mean those that have no right to sit here nothing I think can justifye us Looki[ng] a great way back but to put a mark upon those men and crimes that have threatned our very constitution [?I] mean if oratory and a dexterity in speaking can make right wrong black white writing [?figur]ing and every thing other wise then it is[95] nothing should make us put a man upon a second tryall that had the fortune to escape one: I mean by thos[e] things that threaten our constitution the bribery the corrypting of our members that sit here I will name no names I will observe your orders I am pretty near your chair I have a[96] loud voyce I am sure you will hear me[97] Gent[lemen] talk of the Romans I have heard them say an English souldier was as good as a Roman I would we could say an English senatour was a[s] good as a Romane would a Romane senatour have asked why an honourable Gent[leman] was turned out[98] that endeavoured to corrupt this house by pensions and bribes was turned out of his place:[99] no sir a Romane senatour would have desired to know why such a Gent[leman] was put into a place unles they intended the same practice again: a Romane senato[ur] would have asked why such an one sate here I think these things worthy of your consideration and I hope yo[ur] justice will remove them if their own modesty will not make them withdraw: I think a man that wi[ll] give pensions and distribute bribes to corrupt this house is as great a criminall as the gunpow-

---

[93] *Recte* Curiatii. The stories of Marcus Manlius Capitolinus and Horatius are told in Livy, *Ab Urbe Condita*, 1. 24–6; 5. 47; 6. 11–21; and recapitulated in Machiavelli, *Discorsi*, 1. 24. The latter is being paraphrased here.

[94] The naval battle off Cape de la Hague in 1692, in which the English and Dutch fleets under Lord Orford (then plain Admiral Russell) had defeated the French.

[95] From 'oratory and a dexterity' to 'then it is' interlined.   [96] 'pretty' erased.

[97] A reference to the incident on 24 Mar., when the Speaker had claimed not to have heard some compromising remarks from Jack Howe: see above p. 71.

[98] 'of his place' erased.   [99] Sir John Trevor.

der treas[on] plotters or the regicides and as dangerous to our constitution: Gent[*lemen*] say that these matters of our gran[?ting] that the validity of this patent is controverted without doors in all conversation it is true sir and my a[c]quaintance without doors lyes much amongst the learned Gent[*lemen*] of the long robe: If I meet with any of them that have been favourites or councill in the late reigns they are unanimously for damning and censuring this grant other[s] are of another opinion and for defending it this without doors is a party cause I will not say that it is so with[in] and I really beleive that were the names concerned in the patent changed were the present ministry in the patent I mean others I beleive those that arraign and condemn it would justifye the legallity of it and the others would censure it: as for the reasons that are given to justifye it are strong and I do not like the often tryalls of the same matter I never had an opinion of the understanding of the judgment of the integrity of the councill of the late reigns I am sure their opinions shall never influence me I will therefore wheneve[r] you put the quaestion give my negative: Mr Cowper spoke very finely about pyracy and the distinction betwee[n] the rules of law in pyracy and felony[100] Mr finch spoke long and maliciously at last the quaestion was put[101] and the noes 198 the yeses 185: the next day [*29 Mar. 1701*] the house fell upon the partition treaty[102] there was nothing said a great while at Last it was moved by Sir John Luson [*Gower*] that that treaty was very prejudi[*ci*]all to our trade and destructive to our commerce: and that the making of it was a great crime and misdemeanour and then Sir John Luson [*Gower*] named the Lord Portland to be the maker of it and put the quaestion on him[103] Sir B Shores moved that it m[ust] be added to the quaestion and others concerned and consenting thereto: were guilty of great crimes and misdemeanours: Sir Xto[*pher*] musgrove said truly he thought none but the Lord Portland was concerned and that quaestions of this nature ought to be p[ut] singly and that every one ought to bear his own burthen and that he was never for nor could ever endure the thou[ght] of

[100] There is a copy of this speech, 'taken in shorthand in the House', in Hertfordshire RO, D/EP F 36 (Panshanger MSS), Lady Cowper's commonplace-book, no pagination. Cowper had been pressed by Sir Joseph Jekyll, MP, to attend this debate in order that he might 'contribute to prevent' the Tories' 'design' of 'falling upon' Somers: ibid D/EP F55, fos 59–60, Jekyll to Cowper, n.d.

[101] That the grant to Bellomont *et al.* was 'illegal and void': *CJ* xiii. 446. The vote took place at 8 p.m. 'and somewhat longer' (Luttrell, *Brief Relation*, v. 33; BL Add. MS 7074, fo. 7), after a debate of eight hours' duration (PRO/31/3/188/11).

[102] In the committee of the whole House on the state of the nation: *CJ* xiii. 450.

[103] Hans-Willem Bentinck (1649–1709), 1st Earl of Portland. The question was that Portland, 'by negotiating and concluding the Treaty of Partition, which was destructive to the trade of this kingdom, and dangerous to the peace of Europe, is guilty of an high crime and misdemeanour': *CJ* xiii. 465.

constructive treason this was in answer to Sir Ge[*orge*] Hungerford who
moved for constructive treason[104] so the quaestion w[as] according to the
Rules of Parliament put singly upon the Lord Portland and carried nobody
speaking one word for him[105] upon whic[h] Mr How said he could not but
reflect upon the instability of humane affairs that that great Lord that so lately
had so many obeysances from the Gent[*lemen*] of this house so many respects
paid him that even gent[*lemen*] of good quality thought it a[n] high honour to
drink chocolate with his footmen and that now this great man had not one
freind to speak [for] him this was in imitation of the history of Sejanus this
caused some heats and reflections[106] and afterwards Sir John Luson [*Gower*]
moved an impeachment against him and [*1 Apr. 1701*] he was ordered to
impeach him of high crimes and misdemeanour[s] before the Lords:[107] When
he returned: [*29 Mar. 1701*][108] Sir B Shore said if this was such a wicked
treaty there must be more then this Lord this st[ran]ger concerned in it, and
that the putting the great seale was an illegall and dangerous thing to our
constitution sitting the par[?liament] and so he moved after his usuall orang[109]
to put the same quaestion upon John Lord Sommers:[110] Sir R Gwin excused
the levity of his author but said that Gent[*leman*] bringing my Lord Sommers
upon the stage on all occasions[111] put him in mind of a famous story in
Hudibras which tels of a silly fellow who fancyed that if he could Kill a wise
great beautifull man he should posses his qualityes,[112] and after that he was
against the quaestion that Lord having not been privy to the treaty and only
putting the seale by virtue of his office: this was a long debate[113] and Sir

[104] As deduced from circumstances rather than by the application of the letter of the law.

[105] The vote was 'without opposition': Cumbria RO (Carlisle), D/Lons/W, James to Sir John
Lowther, 29 Mar. 1701.

[106] The notorious L. Aelius Sejanus (d. AD 31), Prefect of the Praetorian Guard and favourite of
the Emperor Tiberius. L'Hermitage reported that Howe had made 'par plaisanterie, un discours
de morale pour réprésenter la vicissitude des choses de ce monde, et dit quantité de choses fortes
envenimées': BL Add. MS 17677 WW, fo. 213.

[107] At the report of the committee: *CJ* xiii. 465.

[108] Luttrell (*Brief Relation*, v. 33–4), and James Lowther (Cumbria RO (Carlisle), D/Lons/W,
James to Sir John Lowther, 29 Mar. 1701), indicate that this debate took place in committee on the
29th.   [109] Harangue.

[110] According to the French ambassador this was Jack Howe's doing: PRO 31/3/188/12.

[111] 'on all occasions' interlined.

[112] Samuel Butler, *Hudibras*, I, ii. 23–6:

> So a wild Tartar when he spies
> A man that's handsome, valiant, wise,
> If he can kill him, thinks t'inherit
> His wit, his beauty and his spirit . . .

[113] Confirmed by Luttrell (*Brief Relation*, v. 33) and James Lowther (Cumbria RO (Carlisle), D/
Lons/W, James to Sir John Lowther, 29 Mar. 1701), who respectively claim that the sitting lasted
until 9 or 10 p.m.

Jos[*eph*] Jekiell[114] said my Lord Summers was against the treaty never approved of it but put the seales ministerially as he was obliged by his office: Mr Finch said he was not obliged ministerially to affix the seales but he should have desired the advice of the councill and not to have ventured to have acted without it and instead of that he should have laid down his seales all of them expressed a great regard for my Lord Sommers but that they could not endure that such pernicious destructive presidents should be made: of the other side they said th[at] the law in affixing the seals to a treaty of peace was not the same as in grants that the King could make peace or warr as he pleased and that if it was in the Chancellours power to refuse the affixing of the seale to ratifye it he was more then the King like the former major domus to the French King who quickly assumed the Regall name[115] so tha[t] the Kings of England could heretofore not only make peace or war but fight without the assistance of the Parliament they had such great estates it was true now the power remained tho ineffectual becaus the fortunes of our kings were lessened and they could do nothing without the assistance of Parliament but the law was still the same that in the passing of grants one office was a checq upon another and so from office to office the other side moved and argued cheifly from the ill consequences that would attend that proposition that the odium would light upon the Kin[g] if we could not punish and censure the ministers that the Lord Portland was a poor stranger ignorant of our laws and customs a freind to his own native country[116] to be rather pittied and excused then punished that my Lord Chancellour was an Englishman knowing in our laws and customs that they were sorry that he had committed so great crime but that it must be for the president[117] sake censured, up stood Mr Speaker then i[n] the Committee Mr Harley[118] and said I am sorry this debate ever began: it is of the greatest consequence to England imaginable: I would you would eyther rise without a quaestion and do nothing in it or censure it I have a great honour for the lord concerned but if this quaestion should be carried in the negative farwell England farwell Constitution for god sake let gent[*lemen*] consider what they are doing I earnestly press the consideration of this matter it is no less than putting the ax to the very roots of our constitution our posteri[t]y will curs us and our children here after blame us I would not have and I desire no thing may be d[on]e farther then the censuring of this

---

[114] Somers's brother-in-law. For his anger at the impeachments, see Surrey RO (Kingston), 371/14/01/10, Jekyll to [Somers], 30 Apr. 1701.
[115] Pepin, the first Carolingian king of the Franks, crowned in 754.
[116] The United Provinces.   [117] Precedent.
[118] The Speaker had left the Chair when the House went into committee.

practice[119] and no severityes used Jack Smith said he had as mu[ch] regard for the englis[h] Constitution as that Gent[*leman*] but that without a cause he would not put the [?question ?on] that lord [?–] and then when all had spoke and were tired the quaestion was put and the noes [?were 1]87 y[eas 182][120]

[*fo. 77*]

[*13 Feb. 1701* t]here were these orders made in relation to bribery this sessions that whosoever should by briberi and corrupt means procure himself to be returned a member of parliament should be highly censured

another that whoever should endeavour it should be[121] highly censured[122]

nota [*6 Mar. 1701*] a tryall at the barr with councill

More petitioned against Coatsworth for Grymsbee: there was pretty plain proof that coatsworth had come in by brebery and that mr Shepperd had used an interest for him:[123] but all the whilest the cause was trying by the rules of the house the members Cannot debate the house was very full of strangers, but when ever any thing was heard upon Coatsworth there were debating [o]bservations made by Mr How mr HarCourt mr Coxe[124] especially and by others this reflected upon the house much without [do]ors for when mr Moors tryall came on[125] these Gent[*lemen*] behaved themselves very partially in their words and behaviour: I remember particularly that mr moors agents were proved the night before the teste of the writ[126] to go to many houses just before [1]2 and left 2 li. 10s at an house and told them it must be drunk out before 12 in drinking mr Mores health this [w]as clearly proved to be done in

[119] Originally 'grant'. Both Bonet and L'Hermitage note that Harley abandoned his usual 'prudence' in this debate and showed his partisan colours. In Bonet's account he is said to have claimed that, if this crime should go unpunished, the ruin of English liberties would inevitably follow. BL Add. MSS 30000 E, fo. 121; 17677 WW, fos. 212–13.

[120] Bonet (BL Add. MS 30000 E, fo. 121), and Luttrell (*Brief Relation*, v. 33), agree that the figures were 189:182.   [121] 'guilty of' erased.

[122] In fact, a composite resolution: 'That in case it shall appear, any person hath procured himself to be elected, or returned, as a Member of this House, or endeavoured so to be, by bribery, or any other corrupt practices, this House will proceed with the utmost severity, against such persons'.

[123] Cotesworth was 'a very busy man in the New East India Company': Grimsby Central Library, G727/324/COA, 'The Case of Mr Coatsworth's Election' (typescript copy of a document which in 1964 was in the possession of Sir Geoffrey Harmsworth). The petitioner, Arthur Moore, MP for Grimsby in the preceding and succeeding Parliaments, was a director of the Old Company.

[124] Probably the barrister Charles Coxe, MP: see above, p. 52, n. 85.

[125] Counsel for Moore were heard first, after which resolutions were passed to declare Cotesworth not elected and to send him to the Tower for bribery. Then came the question as to whether or not Moore had been duly elected, which was also negatived (thus voiding the election). A motion to commit Moore as well for bribery was defeated. *CJ* xiii. 379.

[126] See above, p. 66, n. 37.

severall places: but Oh sais mr How this was spent in drink: my patience was tired after some hours[127] and I calld over the way and asked him if that was not all one upon which he medled no further at last Coatsworth was committed to the tower and his agents disposed of to other places,[128] and then we came to consider of Arther moor who was undoubtedly as criminall as Coatsworth,[129] and the proofs as full viz what I have mentioned and the forgiving old debts which he contracted with the electors on purpose for an interest: but this was argued some time at last we had but one Candle[130] and up stood mr How behind me his was but an indifferent speech and an indifferent cause so he humd and hawd and made a long pause and up stood I so the Gent[*lemen*] cryed my name and as I was speaking they cryed mr How again and down I sat: he before he went on said he had a long way of speaking and was not so happy to express himself as short [as] some Gent[*lemen*], but that he could stay till they had done and then go on. I said sir I could not see the Gent[*leman*] stopt I thought he [h]ad done I meant no harm, and begged pardon so on he went Humdrum again: at last when he had quite done I said sir The Gent[*leman*] tells you he speaks long I think so to[*o*], and that makes me speake as short as I can, least if, I should spe[a]ke as long as he dos wee might seem to engros to[*o*] much of your time more then came to the share of one County [ev]erybody is against corruption and think it dangerous to our constitution if so they must resolve to forget freinds and party [fo]r if some will maintain their freinds, and others will do so to[*o*] and must: I was truly sir very uneasy to see this house [s]hew so much partiality before strangers: how was everything reflecting on Coatsworth contrary to reason and rules all [?cr]ost in debates magnifyed; how was everything relating to mr moor after the same partiall manner extenuated; Sir I will not repeat the Evidence it is late if Gent[*lemen*] beleive mr Moor by the Evidence has endeavoured to procure him[s]elf Elected they will say so, if not the contrary: it went very hard a great while with mr Moor but at last by the Majority of the noes without a division he was acquitted[131]

---

[127] The hearing and ensuing debate lasted 'all day', until 8 p.m.: Luttrell, *Brief Relation*, v. 25; Cumbria RO (Carlisle) D/Lons/W, James Lowther to Sir John Lowther, 6 Mar. 1700[/1].

[128] 'to other places' interlined. Five of Cotesworth's agents were committed to the custody of the Serjeant: *CJ* xiii. 379.

[129] According to James Lowther 'there appeared the most notorious bribery in this case that has been heard of these many years in both their agents . . . besides great expenses in treating': Cumbria RO (Carlisle), D/Lons/W, James to Sir John Lowther, 6 Mar. 1700[/1]. See also *CJ* xiii. 329; Grimsby Central Lib., G727/324/COA.

[130] Eventually there was a motion that candles be brought in: *CJ* xiii. 379.

[131] i.e. he was cleared of bribery, without a division; *CJ* xiii. 379.

[8 Mar. 1701][132] *Of Sir John Packingtons bill to hinder the translation of Bishops [sic]*[133]

he made a very eloquent fine oration long but admirably witty some few things he had better not said this tickled [J]ack how so much[134] that he moved for a clause to prevent occasionall communion with dissenters he said he did not Know [*how*] to express it but he meant that those that received the communion according to the Church of England to qualify themselfs for a place should be uncap[*ab*]le of that or any other place if they ever after returned to their meetings[135] and so he 2ded Sir John packingtons motion; at which the Speaker put the quaestion to have Packington and How bring in the bill: How frighted and twined his body like an eele the house laughed Mr How desired to be excused the Speaker seemed as much pleased as any man in the house and told Mr H[*owe*] the business [*was*] over and the quaestion put and carried: but the next day Packington was singly in the votes and Hows name not entred in the journall[136]

---

[132] '7' in a box at left-hand edge of page. A debate immediately following an order to lay before the House an affidavit concerning further evidence in the Grimsby election case: *CJ* xiii. 388.

[133] A motion for leave for a bill 'for the better preservation of the Protestant religion, and for preventing the translation of bishops', intended to restrict the prerogative of the Crown in ecclesiastical appointments and provoked, allegedly, by a rumour of Bishop Burnet's impending translation to Winchester: *CJ* xiii. 388; Mark Goldie, 'The Nonjurors, Episcopacy, and the Origins of the Convocation Controversy', in E. Cruickshanks (ed.), *Ideology and Conspiracy: Aspects of Jacobitism, 1689–1759* (Edinburgh, 1982), 29, 35. For Pakington's personal animosity towards Burnet, see above, p. 42, n. 39.

[134] According to Bonet, Howe intervened out of spite towards Burnet: BL Add. MS 30000 E, fo. 75.

[135] On the origins of the controversy over 'occasional conformity', see John Flaningam, 'The Occasional Conformity Controversy: Ideology and Party Politics, 1697–1711', *Journal of British Studies*, 17/1 (1977) 38–62.

[136] Confirmed in *CJ* xiii. 388. There was, however, no mention of occasional conformity, the title of the bill being given as in n. 133 above. Cocks offers an alternative account of this debate in MS Eng. hist. b. 210, fo. 17, where, referring to the campaign against occasional conformity, he notes that

its rise and original was [?base] begot by lechery heat of blood without consideration its parent was ashamed of it and it was [?thrust] up and down as bastards used to be the very father of her was more ashamed of her than of any illegitimate issue in his life: the very original of her and the heat that begot her was this: Sir J. Pac[*kingto*]n had spoke a very witty speech in the House of Commons to introduce his bill to prevent the translation of bishops. Mr H[*owe*], to ingratiate himself with his new friends in the Church or to be revenged upon his old friends the Dissenters, moved that a clause should be added to the bill to prevent hypocrisy the worst of crimes, viz occasional confirmity. After a few more words, there was leave to bring in the bill and Sir Jo. Pa[*king*]ton and Mr J. H[*owe*] were ordered to bring in the bill. Mr H[*owe*] after it was ordered desired to be excused and would have had the university members [CAMBRIDGE: Henry Boyle, Anthony Hammond; OXFORD: Heneage Finch (*other seat vacant*)] joind they said they knew nothing [of] the matter. The Speaker Harley laughed extremely to see H[*owe*] catched: How who had a mind to humble and not disoblige his old friends the Dissenters and knew if his name was in the votes it would be in vain to deny it prevailed with the Speaker to have his name struck out of the journal. And so the Speaker made Sir John Packington's name appear in the

[137]Of Furnace and Heathcoate

Whether they were in the meaning of the clause for hindering those concerned in collecting or managing the revenue [f]rom being members of parliament[138] Sir Joseph Hern the last time was the same and his name in the list:[139] but then these very men that said Hern was not in the meaning said Heathcoat and furnace were Furnace was first tryed [*19 Feb. 1701*][140] for I beleive [i]f Heathcoat that was well beloved had been tryed first they had both escaped; in this there was one thing [v]ery remarcable when it appeared well for Furnace sais the Speaker I would not have Gent[*lemen*] think that mr [H]eathcoat and Sir Harry Furnace was the same case the one was a circulator of the Exchequer bills for the [K]ing the other for the people[141] he brought in this pretending to form a quaestion and looking upon the last journalls this caused some words between the late and present Speaker: it was a near division[142] and the next day [*20 Feb. 1701*] the [S]peaker said he was mistook he made no difference between Heathcoat nor was there any made in the judgment

Aprill the 1st 1701 the bill of succession was first read

world [?*singly*] with these two most ungrateful things both to the bishops and Dissenters and one would have thought both parties disobliged would have been a load no man could have bore (but his great virtue and piety surmounted all difficulties) it was a precedent without a precedent to have one man to be ordered to bring in a bill, but it is so upon the journals of the House of Commons for which I have heard Sir John curse the Speaker so near he must have heard him: but this bastard proved very serviceable and handy and has been since taken care of for special purposes.   [137] '8' in box at left-hand edge.

[138] The Salt Duty and Excise Act of 1694 (5 Gul. & Mar., c. 7) included a clause to prevent Members from being concerned, directly or indirectly, in the collection or management of this and subsequent parliamentary revenues, except those who held places on the Treasury commission or the commissions of customs and excise. Furnese and Heathcote were adjudged to have come within the bounds of this act in their capacities as trustees for Exchequer bills.

[139] In Feb. 1699, during a purge of MPs holding prohibited offices, in which Furnese among others had been expelled the House, Herne had been reported as a trustee for Exchequer bills but no action had been taken against him; an example, according to James Vernon, of the 'partiality' of the Country Party opposition: *CJ* xii. 511–12, 515–16, 519; James (ed.), *Letters Illustrative . . .* ii. 266. Herne was a Tory; Furnese and Heathcote Whigs. For the involvement of one Tory, Anthony Hammond in the present witch-hunt, see James Brydges to William Cadogan, 10 Dec. 1708, quoted in Henry L Snyder, 'The Contribution and Limitations of Division Lists to the Study of Parliamentary Parties', in Aubrey Newman (ed.), *The Parliamentary Lists of the Early Eighteenth Century: Their Compilation and Use* (Leicester, 1973), 80.

[140] Furnese's right to sit had first been called into question in the petition preferred by his defeated opponent in the Sandwich election (*CJ* xiii. 332). On 17 Feb. a copy of the commission to the Exchequer bills trustees was presented to the House, in which the names of Furnese and Heathcote (and Herne) appeared (ibid. 337); and two days later Furnese's case was taken up (ibid. 344).

[141] In the commission Furnese (and Hearne) were among the trustees 'on the part of the King'; Heathcote was a trustee 'on the part of the contractors': *CJ* xiii. 337.

[142] The vote went for Furnese's expulsion by 186:181: *CJ* xiii. 344. Heathcote was expelled a few days later, on 22 Feb.: ibid. 352.

[143]the Lord Fairfax made a report from the committee[144] by word of mouth which was wrong[145] and so nothing done [?in] it: upon the Kings message[146] which was considered Aprill 2d [*1701*]: Mr Bridges[147] said he[148] first opened as the yongest to give others the cu, and that[149] the wiser might be kept to sum up all at last: he lightly reflected upon all miscarriages and said he would not say anything to widen our breaches when we should unite he spoke of our debts of our inabilityes and at last concluded with the danger of having France in possession of all Spain: Seymour was for saving his stake in the hedge and he and his all upon occasion should be offered to the Publick he was not for declaring against war nor being to[o] forward in it, but[150] for supporting the dutch[151] according to the treaty[152] to be 2ds not principalls: Mr Finch spoke to the same purpose and proposed the quaestion which after many houres debate was at last agreed: the words insisted upon to be added were proposed to be added by the Lord Cuts viz the peace of Reswick not being sufficient seconded by the Lord Hartington and after many hours debate the Lord Cuts would have waved the words but could not the house being possessed of them but at last they were agreed to be waved: and then Sir B Shore said he was glad to find Gent[*lemen*] at last come to a little reason: this foolish sawcy expression caused great heats and [r]eflections but at last we agreed unanimously to the vote[153] and went into a committee of supply to vote that we would support the king [and] maintain that treaty[154] Aprill 7th 1701 Nothing materially said or done in relation to busines or order the most was that [th]e committee could not alter any resolution tho never so unreasonable but by recommitment:[155] in the evening there was the merits of the election of

---

[143] '9' in box at left-hand edge.

[144] Not the committee on the Bill of Settlement, which did not meet until 12 Apr. and of which Sir John Bolles was chairman: *CJ* xiii. 487. Probably the committee to examine petitions from imprisoned debtors, from which Fairfax eventually reported on 3 Apr. : ibid. 466–7.

[145] Bills to be reported were delivered to the clerk, who in turn read them to the House: W. Hakewil, *Modus Tenendi Parliamentum . . .* (London, 1671), 148–50, *Lex Parliamentaria . . .* (3rd edn.; London, 1748), 334–5.

[146] Of 31 Mar., regarding the answer given by the French ambassador at The Hague to the demands put forward by the States-General of the United Provinces: *CJ* xiii. 462.

[147] Of the three MPs in the House of the name Brydges or Bridges, James Brydges was by far the youngest (at 27). He was also the most prominent political figure. As recently as 24 Mar. his diary records a dinner with the Speaker: Huntington Lib., Stowe MS 26(2), unfoliated.

[148] 'said he' interlined.   [149] 'that' interlined.   [150] 'but' interlined.

[151] 'and' erased.

[152] The Treaty of Nijmegen of 1678: *CJ* xiii. 462; Luttrell, *Brief Relation,* v. 34.

[153] 'unanimously to the vote' interlined.

[154] Confirmed in Luttrell, *Brief Relation* v. 34; and in BL Trumbull Add. MS 130, 'Proceedings in Parliament' 12 Feb–17 June 1701, unfoliated, 2 Mar. 1701. As reported to the House, the resolution was for a supply to 'enable' the King 'to support and maintain the treaty': *CJ* xiii. 467.

[155] Not recorded in *CJ*.

Redford in Not[t]ing[ham]shire[156] between mr White and Sir Willoughbe
Hickman: White had a very good cause as to numbers upon the poll but
upon qualifying and disqualifying I could not exactly remember the numbers:[157] but the endeavours to bribe [a]nd corrupt votes was very notorious of
Sir Will[oughby] Hick[man's] side[158] yet the committee viz 93 against 50 were
for Sir Will[oughby] Hick[man] that he [w]as duly elected, never was a more
corrupter place then this fountain of justice: in other places it seldom happens
that there are upon tryalls party juries to byass their reasons and direct their
judgments

Aprill 8th 1701 nothing extraordinary[159] but a motion of mr John How not
2ded that every one of such an estate should be a justice of peace, and the
Speaker acquainted the house that Sir John Cotton whose library was worth
15000 li. did desire an act of parliament to make it unaliñable and to setle his
house and that on the publick[160] the Speaker said it was the repository of the
records that preserved our liberties:[161] Sir edward Seymour speaking in
commendation of the bill to regulate elections[162] said, he would proceed no
further in mr Shepperds fine till he saw the success of the bill if the bill passed
he should have prevented it for the future and should deale the more moder-
ately with Sheppard if the bill did not pas they must m[a]ke an example of him

---

[156] East Retford. Confirmed in Luttrell, *Brief Relation*, v. 36.

[157] White outpolled Hickman by 24 to 17 on the traditional franchise of resident freemen,
increasing his majority by four through objections against the qualifications of some of Hickman's
voters. The petition, however, argued that the franchise belonged to freemen at large, and the
House agreed. Hickman claimed that this would have given him a majority by 32 to 28, but White's
further objections removed 15 of his votes. *CJ* xiii. 492–5; BL Loan 29/31, 'Mr White's case'
[1701].

[158] Hickman alleged various 'indirect practices' on the part of his opponent, including the
cancellation of a debt, but stopping short of outright bribery. White's evidence, however, proved
bribery against Hickman's agents. *CJ* xiii. 492–5.

[159] The *Journals* record, *inter alia*, a report from the committee of supply and resolutions for an
address to request copies of various treaties, instructions, and papers: *CJ* xiii. 477.

[160] Sir John Cotton, 3rd Bt. (1621–1702), of Stratton Park, nr. Biggleswade, Beds. The library,
amassed by the great antiquary Sir Robert Cotton, 1st Bt. (1571–1631), of Conington, Hunts., was
kept at Cotton House in Westminster. See 'The House, Library and Garden of Sir John Cotton',
Wren Society, 11 (1934), 48–59; Bodl. MS Ballard 38, fo. 131. The bill, for which permission was
given, eventually passed onto law as 12 & 13 Gul. III c. 7.

[161] On the political uses to which the library had been put in the earlier 17th century, see F.
Smith Fussner, *The Historical Revolution: English Historical Writing and Thought 1580–1640*
(London, 1962), ch. 5; and Kevin Sharpe *Sir Robert Cotton 1586–1631: History and Politics in
Early Modern England* (Oxford, 1979), 48–83. Harley, as a noted bibliophile, had a particular
interest in the matter, and indeed in Apr. 1701 was given a copy of the catalogue of the library:
HMC, *Portland MSS*, iv. 16.

[162] The bill for the better preventing bribery, and other undue practices at elections, which
received its 2nd reading and was committed that day: *CJ* xiii. 477.

to deter others from such practices and more to inforce the bill:[163] Ap 9th
[*1701*]

this day was full of [ex]pectation the busines we were to go uppon was that
the house should resolve itself into a committee [of th]e [w]hole house [to]
consider of the trade of the nation and the publick debts: Mr How the day
before [*8 Apr. 1701*] complained of the [?–]miser[able] state we were in and
told us that he had somthing to propose to us that was for the pub[lic ?service
?not] ed the sale of the Forrests and a seperating of a fourth part of all places
for the pub

[*fo. 76ᵛ*]

lick remove him[164] from the house of Commons to hinder him from leading
the party that opposed them and from opposing [?their] interest: in the
preamble of his patent his vanity appeared which added fewell to the fire
Kindled in the brests of his enemies:[165] envy and malice can make great faults
of nothing and ambition lays it self to[o] open upon these disadvantages these
Gent[*lemen*] came upon the stage: and [*14 Apr. 1701*] the letters the Secretary
vernon brought being translated were read[166] the first letter was signed
portland dated from Loo the 14th and 24th of Aug: [16]98[167] which sais
Count Tallard[168] said that the death of the King of Spain was expected and
that an accommodation he thought might be found out to prevent a new war

---

[163] Consideration of Shepheard's case was adjourned a week: ibid.

[164] Charles Montagu, since created Lord Halifax. The sudden change of direction in Cocks's
narrative at this point might be explained by accidental omission of some material.

[165] For a copy of the preamble to the patent of Halifax's barony, see BL Add. MS 27440, fo. 20;
and for an example of an outraged reaction, Yorkshire Archaeological Society, Copley MSS DD38,
box B–C, Robert Molesworth to Sir Godfrey Copley, 19 Apr. 1701: 'If you will take the pains to
inquire after the preamble of my Lord Halifax's patent I believe both you and Jack Howe must
agree with me that since the Creation there never was anything so insolent, arrogant and
assuming; and highly dishonourable to Parliaments. It deserves in my opinion an impeachment
itself, for nobody (if you will believe that preamble), nor the two Houses joined, did anything
considerable to save the nation but his lordship. I saw it but t'other day, and it turned my stomach
so terribly I cannot think on it with patience and wonder that none of your House has spoke
anything on it yet.'

[166] By order, Secretary James Vernon had presented to the House on 12 Apr. copies of all letters
that had passed between himself, Lord Portland, and Sir Joseph Williamson relating to the
Partition Treaty. These were referred to a committee to be translated, where necessary, and
were reported on 14 Apr., when the translations were directed to be 'bound up with the papers
of the session' *CJ* xiii. 484, 487, 489. Although the letters are listed in the *Journals* (ibid. 487),
their contents are not detailed. Burnet (*Own Time*, iv. 487) paraphrases them, and some are
printed in N. Japikse (ed.), *Correspondence van Willem III en van Hans Willem Bentinck, Eersten
Graf van Portland* (5 vols.; The Hague, 1927–37).

[167] Portland to Vernon, 14/24 Aug. 1698, printed in Japikse (ed.), *Correspondentie*, ii. 88.
Written from William's Dutch palace at Het Loo.

[168] Camille d'Hostun (1652–1728), Comte de Tallard; French ambassador to England, 1697–
1700.

in Europe and that the King had a mind to have this matter discussed in England with my Lord Chancellour: that it might be prudent not to confine Jennings[169] for that he might do service: the Secretarys [(] Vernon [)] answer[170] Whitehall Aug: [16]98[171] that my Lord Chan[cellor] was gone to tunbridge[172] and the letters sent after him both the Kings and my Lord portland that it would be very Lucky if my Lord Chan[cellor] should make the Duke of Shrewsbury[173] a visit and he should be of the party:[174] that we were not in a condition for a war and that it should be avoyded if possible: that the Parliament would be satisfyed if the Indyes and Spain were not in French hands Whitehall Aug 21: [16]98[175] that he had my Lord Chancel[lor's] answer that Mr Mountague[176] and my Lord Chan[cellor] thought it a secret and would communicate it to nobody but the D[uke] of Shrewsbury, that they are of opinion that we are not in a condition for a new war: they are sensible of the designs of France to extend itself on the sea ports but that they beleive it may be best for England and that it was necessary for an order for my Lord Chan[cellor] to affix the greate seale signed Vernon [(] Whitehall [16]98 Aug:[177] that the ratifications were dispatched and that Sir . . .[178] would fill up the blanks[179] signed James Vernon: the 5th and 15th Oc[to]b[e]r [16]98[180] tells of the filling up of blanks and of sealing letters and Commissions and advises the acquainting the emperour with the treaty for that he would take it ill to hear of it from other hands and to have us take no notice of it: and then is spoke of recommending Codrington to be governour of the West Indye plantations[181]

---

[169] William Jennings, son of the former sea-captain, now a Jacobite exile, Sir William Jennings. Having been convicted in an English court earlier in 1698 on charges of piracy, the younger Jennings had been the subject of appeals for clemency from the French. Once pardoned by King William, he had sought to curry favour with the English government by persuading his father to return to England and himself inform against fellow Jacobites. See *CSP Dom.* 1698, pp. 216, 232, 254–6, 264, 270; Japikse (ed.), *Correspondentie*, i. 302; Luttrell, *Brief Relation*, iv. 392; James (ed.), *Letters Illustrative . . .* ii. 199–200.   [170] Words in brackets interlined.

[171] Vernon to Portland, 19/29 Aug. 1698, printed in Japikse (ed.), *Correspondentie*, ii. 89.

[172] Tunbridge Wells.

[173] At this time Shrewsbury was still Secretary of State for the Southern Department.

[174] A gathering of leading Whigs at Lord Wharton's house at Winchendon in Buckinghamshire.

[175] Vernon to Portland, 21 Aug./1 Sept., printed in Japikse (ed.), *Correspondentie*, ii. 89–91.

[176] Charles Montagu, MP, then Chancellor of the Exchequer.   [177] Not a new letter.

[178] At the end of the letter Vernon gives the result of the parliamentary election for Exeter, at which Sir Edward Seymour and Sir Bartholomew Shower were returned; confusingly, the defeated candidates also possessed knighthoods or baronetcies.

[179] It is clear from the letter that the commissioners' names were to be inserted by Vernon himself, and only known to him and to Lord Chancellor Somers.

[180] Portland to Vernon, 5/15 Oct. 1698, printed in Japikse (ed.), *Correspondentie*, ii. 106–7.

[181] Christopher Codrington (1668–1710), appointed in May 1699 as captain-general and c.-in-c. in the Leeward Islands, a post his father had held before him: see *DNB* ; and Vincent T. Harlow, *Christopher Codrington . . .* (Oxford, 1928).

and of the untoward temper of the Irish parliament and of his sons my Lord Woodstocks estate gave him by the King in Ireland[182] signed Portland S [*sic*] this where The stroake Comes after[)][183] Whitehall the 30th of Aug: 1998 [*recte* 1698*][184] The lord chancellour will write his own thoughts to the King: the people of England are neyther willing nor able to maintain a new war that the parliament of england would never consent to make any war but by sea which would expose hol[l]and and Flanders that we should not be much concerned at the Italians having an ill neighbour: that the king in this treaty ought to avoyd the scandall of preferring interest before his faith: the 2d name should [*be*] filled up for form sake that orders should be sent to the lord chan[*cellor*] to affix the great seale ⌈ [*sic*] 7b[*e*]r [*i.e. Sept.* 16*]98[185] signed Portland that France would get all if the King of Spain should dye that these things ought to be managed with all the secresy imaginable postscript: to desire the secretaryes advice if he s[h]ould venture to medle with business after hi[s] retirement and to desire his opinion to know if it would be gratefull to the English nation:[186] Whitehall 2d Sep[*t. 16*]98[187] signed James Vernon my Lord Chancellours letter to the King would give him the best information, that it was his opinion that those that prevented a war would mos[t] oblige England, that the nature of the busines required a man they could confide in: that all the danger was that the French should make the world beleive that this was only an amusement and so create jealousies and fears amongst one another: that if the King of Spain live[d] it would ruine France to keep up his armyes at so great a charge: the rest related to the augmentation of mr Priors salary[188] 9 [*i.e. Nov.*] the 9th [*recte 7th* 1698*][189] loo signed Por[*t*]land that Sir william jennings only endeavoured to deceive that it was more convenient and reasonable for a rebell to trust [a]

[182] Henry Bentinck (*c.*1682–1726), Viscount Woodstock; later 2nd Earl and 1st Duke of Portland. In 1697 he had been granted the forfeited estate of Lord Clancarty in County Cork, amounting to over 135,000 acres: Simms, *Williamite Confiscation,* 87. The Irish Parliament, then in session, was to be presented with a bill to confirm this grant.

[183] Passage in brackets enclosed within box in MS.

[184] Vernon to Portland, 30 Aug./10 Sept. 1698, printed in Japikse (ed.), *Correspondentie,* ii. 96–7.

[185] Portland to Vernon, 5 Sept. 1698, printed ibid. *94–5.*

[186] What Portland asked was whether he should sign the treaty, not whether he should 'medle with business after his retirement', which is not mentioned in the original letter.

[187] Vernon to Portland, 2 Sept. 1698, printed in Japikse (ed.), *Correspondentie,* ii. 97–8.

[188] Matthew Prior (1664–1721), poet and diplomatist, then secretary to the English embassy in France: see *DNB.*

[189] Portland to Vernon, 7 Nov. 1698, printed in Japikse (ed.), *Correspondentie,* ii. 108–9.

King than for a king to trust a rebell[190] Dec[em]b[e]r [*recte September*] 16
signed Portland [16]98[191] he desires the secretarys advice in the matter and sais
there are no better conditions to be had, that a war was to be avoyded and a
double armey must be maintained now we were seperated from th[e] emperour: that France would posses all when he no longer feared England. ([*sic*] the
13th of Dec[em]b[e]r [*recte September 16*]98[192] signed vernon sais that the
Spanis[h] Queen and the Germans[193] began to be odious to the Spaniards no
conjecture to be possibly made of the new parliament that the partyes w[ere]
very sower that a very little thing would turn the scales: that the discours of
this treaty would be apt to prevaile with the Spaniards to throw all their
dominions intirely upon the D[*uke*] of Berry[194] to Keep their Countries intire
that we could not Keep force to maintain our treatyes that he must put him in
mind of Sir Ed[*ward*] Seymours observation why do you make a treaty you
cannot trust to ([*sic*] Whitehall 27th of 7b[e]r [*i.e. September 16*]98[195] signed
vernon: he commends secrecy above all things and does at all wonder at my
Lords concern and apprehensions: but that the continuing the peace of Europe
and a publick good would jus[ti]fy every thing: that my Lord Chan[*cellor's*]
opinion was that neyther we nor the states should communicate this to the
e[m]perour that ill consequences might attend such a discovery but not good
ones (the 28th of 7b[e]r [*i.e. September 16*]98 instructions to Stanh[ope] not to
be opened till the king of Spains death[196] and that then he should address
himself to the[197] 4 grandees and tell them the bargain[198] White hall signed

---

[190] Sir William Jennings (for whom see above, p. 86, n. 169) had been persuaded by his son to
come over from France in Oct. 1698 to present to the English administration what was evidently a
cock-and-bull story of an imminent Jacobite 'enterprise' against England. James Vernon paid little
heed to this information and placed Jennings, sen. under arrest, though he felt 'pity for an old man
trepanned into danger by his own son'. Subsequently Sir William was permitted to travel to
Portugal, where he settled. *CSP Dom*, 1698, p. 403; Luttrell, *Brief Relation*, iv. 444, 451; James
(ed.), *Letters Illustrative . . .* , ii. 199; HMC, *Bath MSS*, iii. 284, 292; BL Add. MS 40772, fos. 201–
2, 301; 59480, fo. 6.

[191] Portland to Vernon, 16 Sept. 1698, printed in Japikse (ed.), *Correspondentie*, ii. 99.

[192] Vernon to Portland, 13/23 Sept. 1698, printed ibid. 99–100.

[193] Maria Anna (1667–1740) of Pfalz-Neuburg, 2nd wife of Carlos II of Spain, and a sister-in-
law of the Emperor Leopold. In the original letter 'the Germans' appeared as 'the German party',
i.e. supporters of the Austrian Habsburgs.

[194] Charles (1686–1714), Duc de Berri, youngest of the three sons of the Dauphin.

[195] Vernon to Portland, 27 Sept. 1698, printed in Japikse (ed.), *Correspondentie*, ii. 104–5.

[196] Alexander Stanhope (1638–1707), envoy extraordinary to Spain 1689–99. There is a draft of
these instructions at BL Add. MS 40772, fo. 145.

[197] 'Gove[rn ?ment]' erased.

[198] According to his instructions, Stanhope was to inform the Spanish Council of State of the
existence of the Partition Treaty.

vernon) 8b[e]r [*i.e. October 16*]98[199] whitehall signed vernon orders repeated
to repeated [*sic*] not to open it till the K[*ing*] of Sp[*ain's*] death and that, if he
did not dy then to return them sealed as delivered) [*sic 16*]98 7b[e]r [*Sept.*][200]
signed portland and williamson and they send to have the treaty sealed and
ratyfyed and not to be communicated with any but my Lord Chan[*cellor*]
that a large blank should be left for the Com[*mi*]ssion[*e*]rs of the States[201]
for that they had not yet been acquainted with it and therefore it could not
be Known who they would na[me] loo the 18th of 7b[e]r [*i.e. Sept. 16*]98[202]
Sir Joseph williamson and I send you this letter: that the duke of Bavarias
son[203] was but six ye[ars] old and that if he should dy we should be never
the better for this treaty: of Sloans good luck at gaming[204] postscript I
h[ave] sent the warrant for the ratification and for affixing the great seale, to
be sent the minute it comes ([*sic*][205] now comes in ov[?er] the Marked place
and after that as follows (Oc[*to*]b[e]r the 7th [*16*]98)[206] that the emperour
would be the single person against the treat[y] that Kings princes and states
for all Sir Edward Seymours remark to keep forces to support them[207] signed
Portland

8b[e]r [*i.e. Oct. 16*]98[208] signed James vernon that nothing but a necessity
and force could justifye this treaty, and that now our army was dismissed it
was doubtfull how it would be maintained: the next parliament would hardly
be for a war: Oc[*to*]b[e]r [*16*]98[209] signed James Vernon Whitehall my Lord
Chanc[*ellor*] will assist the Lord portlands bill when it comes:

[199] As detailed in the list of documents in *CJ* xiii. 487, this must either be the set of parallel
instructions sent out on 28 Sept. to Paul Methuen, envoy extraordinary to Portugal (draft at BL
Add. MS 40772, fo. 143), or one of the covering letters dispatched to Stanhope and Methuen on 8
Oct.

[200] Portland and Sir Joseph Williamson to Vernon, 27 Sept. 1698, printed in Japikse (ed.),
Correspondentie, ii. 101–2. Williamson, MP Rochester, was at that time ambassador to the United
Provinces.

[201] The States-General of the United Provinces.

[202] Portland to Vernon, 18/28 Sept. 1698, printed in Japikse (ed.), *Correspondentie*, ii. 102–3.

[203] Joseph Ferdinand (1692–9), Electoral Prince of Bavaria.

[204] James Sloane, MP, who had recently been reported as winning 700 guineas from 'the
sharpers' at Tunbridge Wells: James (ed.), *Letters Illustrative . . .* ii. 167.

[205] 'Whit' erased.

[206] Portland to Vernon, 7 Oct. 1698, printed in Japikse (ed.), *Correspondentie*, ii. 106.

[207] In the original letter the response ran, 'All that is to be said is, that kings, princes, and states
do make and have ever made, treaties, and kept forces for the maintenance of them'.

[208] Probably a letter from Vernon to Portland of 7 Oct. 1698, going by the list in *CJ* xiii. 487.

[209] Probably a letter from Vernon to Portland of 18 Oct. 1698, again going by the list ibid.

that there were many difficultyes, of the Broderick party in Ireland[210] that the
Spaniards grew jealous of Mr Stanop: that the emperour being acquainted with
it will quickly notifye it to the Spaniards: that mr Stanhop ought to provided
with answers to the quaestions the Spaniards would ask: that Codrington was a
fit man for the West Indeis: of some other mans busines: of my Lord Chancel[*lor*] being acquainted with Sir william jennings['s] affair ([*sic*] the 28th of
8b[*e*]r [*i.e. Oct. 16*]98 Whitehall signed vernon that the treaty had been kept
close but that it was discoursed that Count Tallard had given proposalls: that
Count Avesburg[211] who was a man of wit and part knew well enough to expose
the treaty and some reflections on the Irish Parliament after this the treatyes
were read by which the duke of Bavarias son was to have Spain and the Indias and
flanders and if the son dyed the duke[212] and his heirs were to have it: the
Archduke Charles[213] was to have Millan, and the French Naples and the rest
of Italy: Sir B Shores reflected upon the treaty that it was wors then that that was
censured[214] becaus of the unjustnes of giving these dominions to the d[*uke*]
of Bava[*ria*] in case his son dyed: down he sat and then rose up in disorder and
said he did not fear being beat down he sat again and up again the Speaker said
he should name him: but I beleive by what I heard that nobody said so he in
private[215] put it on Sir Charles Hotham but those near him said he said not one
word Shores aggravated the matter and spoke of sealing the powers with great
blanks and moved that John Lord Somers was guilty of great crimes and
misdemeanours. Sir Tho[*mas*] littleton said this peace had some difference
from the other and that the ministry had a fine time of it that if they had
disswaded this treaty and war had ensued that they might have been censured
for neglecting to make use of such an opportu[ni]ty: Mr Harcourt reflected upon
the Lord Sumers for his mean originall for his great riches for his grants and
2ded the quaestion for his being guilty of great crimes and misdemeanours:[216]

[210] The Whiggish faction in the Irish House of Commons, headed by the brothers Alan (*c.*
1655–1728) and Thomas (1654–1730) Brodrick, for whom see *HC 1715–54*, i. 489–92; and Wouter
Troost, *William III and the Treaty of Limerick (1691–1697): A Study of His Irish Policy* (Leiden,
1983), 166, 175–6.

[211] Leopold (1663–1705), Count Auersperg, Imperial envoy to England 1694–1700.

[212] Maximilian Emanuel (1662–1726), Elector of Bavaria.

[213] Charles (1685–1740), Archduke of Austria; 2nd son of the Emperor Leopold.

[214] The second Partition Treaty of 1700 had been censured in debates on 21, 24, 26, 29 Mar.,
and 1 Apr. (*CJ* xiii. 419, 425, 434–6, 465; above, pp. 70–1, 76–9). What was under discussion now
was the first Partition Treaty of 1698.   [215] 'in private' interlined.

[216] For Somers's humble origins (among the lesser gentry of Worcestershire), and conspicuous
consumption at the height of his career, see *DNB; HC 1660–90*, iii. 451; and W. L. Sachse, *Lord
Somers: A Political Portrait* (Manchester, 1975), 1–5, 68, 70–1, 192–7. According to the young
Robert Walpole, Harcourt 'began with extremely fallacious but as plausible remarks, as the
subject could admit'; William Coxe, *Memoirs of the Life and Administration of Sir Robert
Walpole* . . . (3 vols.; London, 1798), i. 14.

all the councill of the late reigns finch shores[217] and the disc[on]tented in this
argued the King can do no wrong that he had consulted with his Councill that
the reason of that maxim was t[hat] there should be nothing done that was
blame worthy but that somebody should be punished for it, to satisfye the wrath
of the people who would otherwise censure the king, and at last cause revolutions: they urged from the [lett]ers that my Lord Chan[*cellor*] must be privy to it
that the sealing it with a blank was a crime in itself: others that defen[ded] it
said my lord Chanc[*ellor*] had wrote to the king himself that it was probable he
would desire to stand and fall by his ow[n] letters that we should not be over
hasty in censuring least we should incur the very same fault we had so latel[y
?censured] viz we had addressed to the King concerning his not making use of
English councill[218] now we were satisfyed he ha[d ?made] use of no other I think
it was littleton said it was to be wished that we might see the letter the king
wro[te] to my Lord Chancel[*lor*] and his answer: for then we should be masters
of the thing: Sir [X]to[*pher*] Musgrave ridiculed th[?e] proposall as if a motion
made in earnest as ridiculous and not fit to be mentioned Little[to]n said he did
not propo[se] it as fit to ground an addres upon: some said the leaving the blank
was nothing but what [mi]ght be justifyed it bein[g to] be filled up in the
presence of the King and it being only names whilest we were debating this
matter pretty war[mly] up stands my lord Hartington and acquaints the house
that Lord Summers was without and desired to be heard befo[re the] quaestion
passed: all the discontents opposed this: but they were overruled in it by the
directions of the [?hou]se[219] and the [?Speaker ?said ?the]

[*fo. 76*]

[precedents] were many viz of the duke of Buckingham the duke of Leeds[220]
who had wrote what my Lord desired by my Lord Hartington some urged that
we should proceed in this vote and then let him defend himself that was
thought very hard that he should acquit himself after he was foun[d] guilty
and condemned so we agreed that he should come in: but the methods were
setled the preliminaries viz that there should be a Chair set with in the bar for

---

[217] Heneage Finch had served James II as Solicitor-General; Sir Bartholomew Shower as a
King's Counsel.
[218] The address of 24 Mar. on the second Partition Treaty regretted, *inter alia*, that the treaty
had been entered upon without the King 'taking the advice of your English councils', Parliament
not being in session at the time: *CJ* xiii. 425.
[219] Bonet noted that several Members opposed it (BL Add. MS 30000 E, fo. 142); Burnet that
there was 'some' opposition, but that the granting of such requests was too well precedented to be
denied (*Own Time*, iv. 490).
[220] George Villiers (1628–87), 2nd Duke of Buckingham, had been admitted to the House on 13
and 14 Jan. 1674 to speak in response to demands for his dismissal from office: *CJ* ix. 292–3.
Thomas Osborne (1632–1711), 1st Duke of Leeds had been heard on 27 Apr. 1695 relating to his
impeachment: *CJ* xi. 327.

my Lord to sit down in: the mace lay on the table[221] and Seymour desired that when my Lord had done speaking that he might be asked who informed him[222] with what was doing, this was a little opposed but at last agreed to and my Lord was called in he boughed as he came in and whent to the chair sat down[223] rose up again and stood behind the chair the Speaker said my Lord Somers this house has heard that you have somthing you desire to say in relation to the busines before us the house is ready to hear you, he spoke very fine[224] he said he had heard that the house had justly condemned the treaty of partition and that he was strangely surprised to hear that he was like to be censured as the adviser of it that Secretary vernon might write what he pleased that he was certain he had no authority to write what he did that he desired to stand and fall by his own letters and that the King had given him leave to have coppyes of his majestys letter and of his letter to the king in order to make his defence: he said he was not affraid of the justice and favour of the house of Commons which on severall occasions he had experimented and for which he thanked them that he had thro the whole cours of his life behaved himself as became an englishman and particularly when he was a member of this house[225] as many there Could testifye: that he was assured that the narrowerly his actions were examined and looked into the fairer and better they would appear: and then he desired leave to read his letter to the King[226] which was to this purpose first read the Kings as follows to my Lord Chan[cellor][227]

that count Tallard had formerly told my Lord portland that there might be some way found out so to settle matters that there might be peace in case the King of Spain should dye: that he had now sent the proposalls to my Lord C[hancellor] which he desired might be Kept as a great secret and desired his opinion in the matter and withall left it to him to consult with whom he pleased and that he had Communicated it to no body but vernon and that if he approved of it that he should get the instructions wrote as secretly and the powers as possibly, and affix the great seale: the Lord Chancellour Summerses letter to the King

Tunbridge Wells Aug [16]98[228]

that he was there by the kings favour for the recovery of his health that the waters had disordered his head and made him the l[e]ss Capable of judging:

---

[221] 'the mace lay on the table' interlined.   [222] 'him' interlined.

[223] 'sat down' interlined.

[224] The gist of Somers's speech is given at *CJ* xiii. 489, and in Burnet, *Own Time*, iv. 490–1. Bonet noted that he spoke 'avec beaucoup de grace at d'eloquence' (BL Add. MS 30000 E, fo. 142).

[225] Somers had sat as MP for Worcester 1689–93.

[226] According to *CJ* xiii. 489, Somers withdrew, and then returned to present the letters.

[227] The King to Somers, 15/25 Aug. 1698, translated from the French and printed ibid. 492.

[228] Somers to the King, 28 Aug. 1698, printed ibid. 491–2.

that he had sent the letter to London where it would probably[229] meet my
Lord orford: the duke of Shrewsbury and Mr Moun[t]ague together, that the
entertaining the thoughts of such a treaty was dangerous considering the
nature of the prince we had to [d]eale with: but that he referred wholly to
the king on whose nice judgment he relyed on for that matter that what was
done was to be done quickly because of the likelyhood of the King of Spains
death and then the french who had such forces in readines would be in
possession of the whole dominions: that there appeared a more then expected
aversnes in the English [b]y the Choyce of the new parliament: that if this
treaty tooke it would open a new and easye way for france from Italy t[o]
invade Spain: but that we must make the best conditions we could for it was
not to be expected that so great a prince [a]s the french King would part with
such just pretensions to so many great countryes for nothing: that it would
make it the more acceptable to the english if they had some advantages in the
west Indies: that it does not appear whether wee are to be newters or what
part we are to act postscript[230] that he had the instructions and powers wrote
with so much secresy that the man thad [*sic*] wrote it Knew not what it was:
and that he had affixed the great seale: (nota I was the Ap[*ri*]ll the 26th [*1701*]
with my Lord Sumers Orford and Hallifax and the Lord Summers said the
treaty he knew of was not the treaty he saw viz that there were severall articles
in the treaty as that of assisting the French that he never heard of before it was
conCluded: Orford said he knew nothing of it and so said Hallifax: but state
affairs are like childrens playthings wound up so high that some times they
break and often times their overstreyning makes them go with a swing back
again)[231] and then when he came to the postscript he said that was another
matter but he would read it presently but then he spoke more in his own
vindication he said he desired that these things might be communicated to my
Lord orford and mr Mountague and that he was so far from advising for it
that he advised the contrary as he had done the Speaker said my Lord I am
commanded by this house to ask your Lords[*hi*]p who it was that told you
what we were doing[232] my Lord Somers said that was so strange a quaestion
he beleived it was never asked any one before who told him, that there was
nothing he more feared [t]hen the censure of the house but that he would
suffer any thing rather then injure the poorest creature in England that [h]ad
told him any thing to serve[233] and so made his legs and away he went:[234] he

---

[229] 'probably' interlined.   [230] 'postscript' interlined.
[231] Passage within brackets partly boxed in MS.
[232] *CJ* xiii. 489, records this exchange as having taken place between Somers's first speech and
the reading of the letters.   [233] Somers's remark is recorded ibid.
[234] To return with the letters: ibid.

spoke and behaved himself so well to the satisfacti[on] of some that were
before his enemies and to the surprise of all that the debate languished and
there was no great life in it[235] [M]r How spoke after my Lord was gone
commending the King and reflecting upon the ministry that did ill things
and were so base [a]nd ungratefull as to put all the blame upon the king:
others argued that the Lord Chan[*cellor*] had done all he Could do he advised
against it [a]nd gave his reasons against it: mr Finch said he should plainly
have wrote to the King that he could not approve of it and [?if] that would not
do he should rather have given up his seales then have complyed and after
much debating between [?–] and 12 the quaestion was put[236] ays 198 noes 188
and then they put the same quaestion upon Edward Lord Orford and [?for] that
there was a greater majority of the yeas and then the same quaestion was put
upon Charles Lord Hallifax and [th]e majority of the yeas still increased and
then we adjourned ([*sic*] there was no debate relating to my Lord Orford or
Hallyfax only the question put[237]

April the 15th 1701

after the impeachments were carryed up it was moved to addres the king to
remove these lords from his Councils and presence for ever[238] and mr Boyle
said that was not regular nor presidented that now they were impeached which
was no more then accused to put [a] censure upon them which would be part
of the sentence if they were found guilty: but with us where majority is law
and the reason is what will most Humble our enemies this had no great weight
and so the addres was ordered and a Committee appoynted to draw it: after
this the Lords hearing of our addres went into a committee and made an
addres reported agreed it and carried it immediately to the King to desire that
no Lord impeached might be removed from his presence and councill till tryed
and found guilty:[239] my Lord devonshire and Rumney[240] were ordered to

---

[235] Cocks's observation is confirmed by Burnet (*Own Time*, iv. 491), L'Hermitage (BL Add. MS.
17677 WW, fo. 229), Ralph (*Hist. Eng.* ii. 943), Sir John Verney (BL Add MS 29568, fo. 13), and
Robert Walpole (Coxe, *Walpole*, i. 13–14). The one discordant voice is that of Lord Dartmouth, in
a note to Burnet's history, who claims that he 'never saw the House in so great a flame as they were
upon his [Somers] withdrawing' (*Own Time*, iv. 491).

[236] According to Luttrell (*Brief Relation*, v. 39), Somers had been admitted to the House at 8
p.m. and the debate had lasted till 11. The question was that Somers, by 'advising His Majesty. . .
to the Treaty for Partition of the Spanish Monarchy. . . is guilty of a high crime and misdemeanour': *CJ* xiii. 489.

[237] The same question was put, and carried, successively against Lords Orford and Halifax:
ibid. 489–90.

[238] The question was put first against Lord Somers, and only after this had been carried was it
put separately against Orford, Halifax and Portland: ibid. 491.

[239] This occurred on 16 Apr.: *LJ* xvi. 654–5.

[240] Henry Sydney (1641–1704), 1st Earl of Romney.

present it Rumnee went with it to which the King gave no answer at which the lords were very warm in their debates but concluded with nothing[241] Nota Mr Bruges the Lord Chandois son[242] carried up the impeachment against Charles Lord Hallifax who did frequent his levy formerly and all the Lords of the Treasury about 3 years ago with humble bows and fine reverences in order to be a com[*mis*]s[*ione*]r of the excise telling them he should be a parliament man shortly[243] that he suffered for being a Williamite his father being a Jacobite[244] Nota at the last division my Lord Cuts absented himself and Mr Neville told the house of him and said he was at the quaestion he said he was not and so was not at the division of the 188 and 198[245] but except Godfery yong Stringer St. Quintan[246] and two or 3 More a souldier that can Look death in the face cannot a quaestion[247] and for the courtiers they prefer the rising sun before god Country friend and every thing: this day [15 Apr. 1701] Sheppard was brought by our warrant and received the sentence of expulsion at the bar of the house on his Knees:[248] and then they debated how they should deale with him further: Mr Lowns said about 100 years ago Tippars was

---

[241] The King's non-reply was reported and debated on 17 Apr.: *LJ* xvi. 655, 657. A committee was appointed by the Lords 'to consider whether formerly, upon an address to the King there has been no answer', but no record of any proceedings of that committee seems to have survived: HMC, *House of Lords MSS*, ns iv. 296.

[242] 'the Lord Chandois son' interlined. James Brydges, MP, was the son of James Brydges (1642–1714), 8th Lord Chandos.

[243] Brydges carried up the impeachment on 14 Apr.: *CJ* xiii. 490. There is ample evidence in his diary of his assiduous attendance at ministerial levées in 1697–8, especially at Charles Montagu's: Huntington Lib., Stowe MS 26(1), *passim*. Some of it is discussed in C. H. Collins Baker and Muriel I. Baker, *The Life and Circumstances of James Brydges, First Duke of Chandos . . .* (Oxford, 1949), 18–20, 30. For specific reference to Brydges' ambition to secure an excise commissionership, see the diary entries for 8 Feb. and 24 June 1697. Cf. below, p. 168.

[244] In February 1698 the then Speaker, Paul Foley, had noted that Brydges' political leanings were 'otherwise' than those of his Jacobitishly inclined father: James (ed.), *Letters Illustrative . . .* ii. 17. Cf. Paul Monod, 'Jacobitism and Country Principles in the Reign of William III', *Historical Journal*, 30 (1987), 306, which gives a contradictory interpretation of this evidence.

[245] [John Hatsell,] *Precedents of Proceedings in the House of Commons . . .* (London, 1781), 129, observes that, 'as no Member ought to be told in a division who was not in the House when the question was put, so all Members who were in the House must be told on one side or the other, and cannot be suffered to withdraw'. The precedent was from 1624. Cutts was later to claim that during the last years of William's reign he had acted in Parliament in concert with Robert Harley and the Tories and had 'made such steps . . . that I was become obnoxious to the ministry then reigning': Huntington Lib., Stowe MS 58 (1), p. 33.

[246] Charles Godfrey, formerly colonel of the 5th Dragoon Guards, was currently master of the jewel office; Sir Walter Yonge a commissioner of customs; Thomas Stringer a lieutenant-colonel in the 1st Foot Guards; Sir William St Quintin also a commissioner of customs. 'they [?dare]' erased.

[247] Cutts was a major-general, and colonel of the 2nd Foot Guards.

[248] On the 15th it was resolved to expel Samuel Shepheard, sen. He was informed of the sentence the following day. *CJ* xiii. 491, 493.

brough[t] to the bar for taking an 100 broad peices of gold for a parliamentary busines that he was fined but the fine never levied[249] as he heard of or could find out neither was there any way to Levy it but that they must bring it to be determined in the inferiour courts and at last upon an appeale before the Lords: that he had found an order to have an untoward Lackey whipped:[250] that no fine could [b]e levied becaus none had and that the Judges must have the determination of it before them which would subject the authority of the [s]uperior courts to the inferior: in the midst of this debate Sir B— Shores good nature moved him to desire that the impeached [l]ords might give security for their appearances: Sir Edward Seymour said that was not usuall but for High treason: Sir John Bolles for impeaching Sheppard as the best way and as he thought by his grinn afterwards reflected upon the proceedings against Sir Charles Duncomb[251] Sir Thomas Powis said he had seen bills brought in upon such occasions but that he never liked such pro[c]eedings and that such presidents were dangerous: that a fine could not be maintained nor levyed and that westminster hall was beneath the offence that impeachments were a proper parliament[ary] way for a Parliament[ary] offence Sir Edward Seymour said we want power to punish these offences as they ought to be that he was against the way of a bill from ill president that he had searched presidents and that the fines were never paid unles they were so small, that the prisoner had rather pay them than be confined [lo]nger: and that if there was a fine it must come at last before the Lords that he was for an impeachment rather, as not mistrusting the justice of the lords, that he beleived that the impeached lords had a hand in Sheppards Election, for that one Sheppard told him he wished his name had not been Sheppard: for that messages coaches and six horses, and servants about the time of the Election mistaking his house for the other Sheppards would not let him rest day or night (Mr Harcourt said he had impeached John Lord Somers and had acquainted the lords that in a short time they would make good their impeachments:[252] Mr How sais the letters my Lord Somers [p]roduced accuses

[249] Originally 'collected'. For the case of William Typper, a patentee for defective titles, accused in May 1604 of taking money for 'following and procuring' passage of the bill for the better making of hats and felts, see *CJ* i. 199–200, 206, 210–12, 965, 969, 972.

[250] Presumably a reference to the case of Edward Floyde, who in May 1621 had been punished by both Houses of Parliament for having spoken 'basely' of the King. The Lords' sentence had included whipping; the Commons' not, though some Members had argued for it. *LJ* iii. 133–4; *CJ* i. 599–604, 607–8.

[251] In Jan. and Feb. 1698 Duncombe, a Tory, had been investigated by the Commons in connection with frauds over Exchequer bills. He was expelled the House, and then proceeded against by a bill of pains and penalties. When this failed in the Lords, legal action was taken against him, with equal lack of success. *CJ* xii. 63, 78, 91, 101, 123, 132–3, 147; Macaulay, *Hist. Eng.*, vi. 2758–66.

[252] According to *CJ* xii. 491, this occurred before the consideration of Shepheard's case.

the Lords [a]s the advisers of the treaty and demonstrates that the king to his honour had acted by English councils and exclaimed against th[e] vilenes of the Lords in endeavouring to make the King the author of their faults: Mr Speaker sais [th]e lette[r]s should not be coppyed: and if the Kings letter was coppyed it should not be made publick so that was a tacite or[?d]er of the house not to be put in the votes:[253] Sir Edward Seymour to order: he said we were in the midle of a debate and that debate ough[t] to be over before any new matter should be began Mr attourney[254] was for impeaching Sheppard [*fo. 75ᵛ*]

so that was tacitely agreed to but not ordered) the Speaker said I must put you in mind that when Mr Sheppard is impeached he [?–] Sir Xto[*pher*] Musgrove it is said the lords may take baile and so may we: when we commit a man to the serjeant he may be impowered to take bail[e] then Mr How moved to have my Lord Summers letter read[255] he said that if the letter and the postscripts had been read intelligibly in the house we h[?ad] had never a negative the letter was in French so after some debate mr How and mr Bruges were ordered to translate the letter which they did and then the letter was read | [*sic*] it bore date in Aug[*ust 16*]98 from tunbridge[256] my Lord complains of the indisposition of his head ([*sic*] as is set down on the other side and after that the addres mentioned before was agreed: [*14 Apr.*] this day in the morning Sir Rob[*ert*] Davers reported the bill of Mr Rider which was unjust and unreasonable as contrary to law taking from warner 1600 li. he had laid out to serve deale with fresh water[257] Mr Br[*e*]wer opened the unjustnes[258] I seconded it but mr Rider was a Jacobite[259] and a sportsman so that nobody heard Brewer or minded me mr How and one or two more spoke for Riders bill so it was ordered to be ingrossed: [*15 Apr.*] The day was far spent but they Called for the report of east Redford in nottingam shire and we that were used to desire busines to be dispatched were for putting of[*f*] the report others that were used to be for delaying all things especially supplyes upon pretence of Long sittings the day before were for having it reported presently we that were for delaying it moved

---

[253] It was, however, printed in the *Journals*: see above, p. 92, n. 227.   [254] Sir Thomas Trevor.
[255] After Shepheard's case had been heard: *CJ* xiii. 491.
[256] Cocks is referring to Somers's letter to the King: see above, p. 92, n. 228.
[257] In fact on the 14th: *CJ* xiii. 489. The bill concerned was the Deal Waterworks Bill, introduced on behalf of William Rider or Ryder, and intended to favour his scheme against a more recent project undertaken by William Warner (who claimed to have spent £1,600 on the workings). For details of the case, see *CJ* xiii. 137, 180, 269, 376, 441; HMC, *House of Lords MSS*, NS iv. 364–6.
[258] John Brewer was recorder of Deal corporation, which had given Warner a lease for his waterworks: J. Laker, *History of Deal* (Deal, 1917), 240; *CJ* xiii. 441.
[259] Ryder's involvement with the waterworks dated from a patent granted by James II in July 1688 to him and his partner, Edward Burdett: *CSP Dom.* 1687–8, p. 223.

and 2ded an adjournment insisted upon the quaestion but we lost it upon the division there was proved upon the petitioner Sir Willoughby Hicman by his agents many notorious briberyes but the party[260] were resolved to carry every thing with a swing littleton spoke for White the sitting member and made out the bribery and said it was proved by one witnes that the reason of his voting for Sir Willowby was becaus he was for the country and not for the King that in the 4s taxes the Nobles had 2s 6d the publick 1s 6d[261] the bribery was substantially proved: Sir Xto[*pher*] musgrove sp[o]ke for Sir Willoubee extenu[a]ting the bribery and justifying his Election: So White was voted not duly Elected and Sir Willowbe duly Elected: this day Mr How moved that a busines heard and determined before the Lords of the treasury between Mr John Dutton Colt and one Ballad might be examined in parliament this was very new, but a Committee was appoynted:[262] this was said to be done in order to pas a vote upon the Lord Tankervile[263] who is a great friend of the impeached lords but I rather beleive it to be done to oppres Colt to oblige the Speaker and his brother:[264] Apr 16th 1701

this day another new motion was made by Mr Gorges to have some part of the leominster report read[265] in which it appeared that one Bub[266] an agent of Mr Colts had not obeyed an order of the Charman of the Committee of

---

[260] The Tories.

[261] One of White's witnesses, William Bellamy, testified that a Mr Hoar had said that 'he was for Sir Willoughby and were [*sic*] for such gentlemen as were for the country and not for the King; for . . . when the Parliament gave 4s. in the pound, the country had the advantage of not more than 2s. 6d': *CJ* xiii. 494.

[262] An attempt to reopen the inquiry held by the Treasury board in 1698–1700 into accusations of corruption and embezzlement against John Dutton Colt in his capacity as collector of customs in Bristol. Colt had responded by throwing the blame for all irregularities onto his deputy and accomplice, Daniel Ballard, and although he had lost his office had by this expedient avoided repaying his debt to the Crown. See *Cal. Treas. Pprs.* 1697–1702, pp. 260–1; *Cal. Treas. Bks.*, xv. 279; xvii. 22, 210, 276: Luttrell, *Brief Relation*, iv. 529, 532, 535, 618; J. M. Price, 'The Tobacco Trade and the Treasury, 1685–1733: British Mercantilism in Its Fiscal Aspects', Ph.D. thesis (Harvard, 1954), 572–84. Secretary Vernon had evidently done all he could to avert Colt's dismissal, and claimed the Treasury commissioners had only acquiesced in it because they 'thought they could not withstand the clamour that would be raised on this occasion': Northants. RO, Montagu (Boughton) MSS 48/38, Vernon to the Duke of Shrewsbury, 29 Feb. 1699/[/1700]. Cocks was included in the committee: *CJ* xii. 491.

[263] Ford Grey (1655–July 1701), 1st Earl of Tankerville, a Lord of the Treasury June–Nov. 1699, First Lord Nov. 1699–Nov. 1700.

[264] Colt had defeated Edward Harley at Leominster in the general election, but had been unseated on petition on 3 Apr.: *CJ* xiii, 470–4.

[265] Gorges had been supported by Robert Harley in the county election for Herefordshire: BL Loan 29/190, fo. 35.   [266] 'that one Bub' interlined.

Elections in giving coppyes of some levy[267] and it was said to make the thing
look better that he had spoken scandalously of the house since so that being
seconded he was ordered to be take[n] into custody: great power and authority
seldom forgives opponents and in [*the*] long run by many unjust actions ruines
itself this day the addres was reported by Mr Bromely for removing these
lords[268] from the Kings Councill and presence the word ever the Speaker
kindly helped them too: Sir Humphery Mackworth offered as an addition
that we should assure the king of our readin[ess] to support the King and his
government against all his enemies at home and abroad[269] this was said to be
to undeceive peop[le] abroad that tho we had impeached the lords we would
support the King and to let the world see that it was their faults and not any
disrespect to the King others said it would be convenient to have something of
that nature to satisfye the jealousies of some at home: Sir Ba[*rtholomew*]
Shores spoke in great commendations of the King and reflecting upon the late
ministry and conclud[ed] for the words: Sir Thom[*as*] powis also highly
Commended the King. they sate opposite one to the other and their speeches
were taken not[e] of as if they both made their court to be acceptable to the
new ministry and to outdo each other so this addition passed withou[t]
opposition then mr Munckton moved to have these words added that they
would support the King in preventing the union of France and Spain and in the
maintaining of the trade and commerce of this Kingdom:[270] Sir Xto[*pher*]
Musgrove said he did not know What these words did mean we had in the
former additionall words said we support him viz the King against all his
enemi[es] at home and abroad if the words meant no more they were
insignificant if they meant more it was more then was intended that he tooke
them to be a kind of a declaration of war: and desired to know if we were in a
condition fo[r] a war Considering the great Load and vast debts we groaned
under: Col: Stringer 2ded the words and moved as an amendment to have this

---

[267] 'John Bubb', according to the entry in *CJ* for 16 Apr. (xiii. 496), but referred to earlier, in the
report of the elections committee, as 'Mun the overseer' of the poor, who had refused to comply
with an order of the committee to produce the 'lewn' or roll of the poor rate, in effect a register of
those entitled to vote in this scot-and-lot borough (ibid. 471).

[268] Halifax, Orford, Portland, and Somers.

[269] To add the clause 'And we humbly crave leave, upon this occasion, to repeat our assurances
to Your Majesty, that we will always stand by, and support, Your Majesty, to the utmost of our
power, against all your enemies, both at home and abroad': *CJ* xiii. 497. Mackworth noted in his
diary that he had brought in this clause himself, which he felt 'will in all probability be fatal to his
[Somers] interest, and demonstrate to the King that the Parliament are resolved to stand by His
Majesty while they pull down his enemies': National Library of Wales, MS 14326E, p. 119.

[270] 'And to prevent the ill consequences that seem to threaten the peace of Europe, and the
interest and trade of this nation, by the present union of France and Spain': *CJ* xiii. 497. Bonet (BL
Add. MS 30000 E, fos. 147–8) ascribes the moving of this amendment to Lord Hartington.

word added the unjust union of Spain and France Sir Ba[*rtholomew*] Shores
seconded Stringer as to the amendment upon which Stringer not liking his 2d
waved the motion this made the house merry: Coll: Wart[on][271] mr Smith and
I stood up together and mr Speaker poynting to Coll wharton who began to
speake upon which the hous[e] was in a disorder and many went out; when the
house was settled Goodwin warton made a long oration declaring the
n[e]cessity of some vigorous votes that the eis of Europe were upon us and
that our slow motions were censured Mr Smith spoke for the words it was his
opinion since we had made such steps at home that we should show w[e] were
only angry at the treaty as giving so great dominions of Spain to france and
that we would not be satisfyed to have France have all: then I spoke: after mr
Cooper who was for the words and had called one the Bavaria[n] treaty the
other the treaty of partition and mr How had said if one was the Bavarian
treaty the other he w[?ud] call the Archducall treaty[272] he made a long oration
with more wor[?s] words then sence: then I stood up a[nd] said sir I desired to
have spoke some time ago when the house was in a tumult and disorder I have
a particular fancy to speak at such a time I do not desire a quiet house nor that
you should attend to what I say I speake not here with any assurance to
convince any one but to satisfye my own conscience I am well en[ough]
satisfyed to have nobody hear me: I will not spend your time in giving this
treaty the title of Bavarian or archducall trea[t]y[273] which made a greater
silence then if I had desired it: I said sir I am not to discours of war or peace
that not being our subject but without entring upon that matter give me
lea[ve] to answer something said just now: are we in a condition? Sir I have
heard it said lately upon another occasion that there were as great Riches now
in England as were before the last war: if so that england is as rich now tho the
riches have in some measure changed the first owners yet England is in a
condition: an[d] we in a condition to know that we must not only compare our
selves with what we now are in comparison of what we were: but our busines
to Know our strength is to compare ourselves with franc[e] if we are richer
comparitively then France we are in a condition, are we in a condition pray sir
if by our supines all those that would joyne us make seperate leagues and
treatys with France shall we be i[n] a condition to make war singly with France

---

[271] Goodwin Wharton, MP, held a lieutenant-colonelcy in Lord Macclesfield's regiment of
horse.
[272] By the first Partition Treaty of 1698 the crown of Spain and the Spanish possessions in the
Indies were to go to the electoral prince of Bavaria. However, he had died in the following year,
and by the second treaty in 1700 his intended share of the Spanish inheritance was redistributed to
the Emperor's second son, the Archduke Charles.
[273] 'I will not spend' to 'archducall trea[ty]' interlined.

which is like now to be our case: if we say we will have no war we shall be forced to have a war: if we say we will engage in a war if we cannot without it have what we think necessary for our preservation it is very probable our terms may be complye[d] with and I dont see these words intend further: I am therefor for them: mr Ward spoke next he said we ought not to go hastily into a war and these words might ingage us further then we intended he desire[d] to have them waved)[*sic*] munckton who moved them first[274] told us the condition we were in in relation to the union of Spain and france and discouraged handsomely in relation to our trade how that must be ruined if we permitted this union to t[ake] place and France to be setled in the dominions of Spain the Speaker interrupted him by pulling of[*f*] his hat and stan[ding] up (for then all sit to hear him)[275] he said that he[276] should open the Clause first and then give arguments to maintai[n] it: muncton said he was a true Englishman and had a flaming Zeale for his country and would no[*t*] betray it: tha[?t] word made some grumbling and then he poynted over the house in his Zeale that gent[?*leman*] said so then that was dis[or]derly and he was taken down to order: but this did not discourage him or disturb him but on he went after he had spoke the sence of the Clause he discoursed handsomely of our condition in relation to every part of Spain of the West indies and trade: Sir Thomas meres would have this quaestion waved for he said this would be proper [?for] a day to consider of it on purpose he would not come into a war by a side wind but that by what he hear[d] and beleived we Could not be long withou[*t*] a war declared mr paget said we all meant the same thing and was against dividing for words he spoke handsomely to that purpose and moved that the previous quaestion should be fir[st] put viz that this quaestion be not now put Lord Coningsbe would have the words insisted on and put and not carried for the world it might be a thing of dangerous consequence to England so he secon[ded] the previous quaestion and the house divided for the previous quaestion 170 against 70 but all this w[as] by generall consent omitted out of the votes so that in the votes there is [*no*] mention of any quaestion [?of] this nature[277]

---

[274] See above, p. 99, n. 270.

[275] By an order dating from 1604, 'when the Speaker desires to speak, he ought to be heard without interruption', and 'when the Speaker stands up, the Member standing up, ought to sit down': *Lex Parliamentaria* . . ., 280.   [276] i.e. Monckton.

[277] On the contrary, the *Journals* record that the previous question was put, and defeated by a margin of 208:120: *CJ* xiii. 497.

[fo. 75]

Aprill 17th 1701 private bills in the morning and then at 12 we went into the
last committee of supply[278] when we ordered that a[279] committee should be
appoynted to see what officers should be allowed half pay the committee
generally agreed to use them civilly now since there were but a few and that
we did not know how soon we might have occasion for them again:[280] then we
discoursed of Exchec[quer] bills and all agreed that they would sink the nation
unles they were sunk Sir Xto[pher] musgrove was but for sinking half now but
he did not understand what he said for every hundred costs us one way or
other as it appeared by the debate 50 per cent: Lowns proposed that if it was a
private mans case that could have money at 5 per cent whether the world
would not esteem him mad to give 50 li. Scobell proposed as a fund to give 1s
per pound for two year on which we might borrow enough to pay of[f] the
bills at six per Cent: and at last we agreed to pay them of[f] but not by
mortgaging our land for two year[281] mr Smith and many more spoke against it
and it was not a regular motion but a proposition this being a committee of
supply not of ways and means and then we adjourned till wednesday the 23d
of Ap[ri]ll 1701 this morning was spent in reading private bills, the Bill to
hinder the translation of Bishops was read and com[mit]ted by the majority of
the [?house] upon the division: then they debated about exchequer bills[282] and
were for having 50000 li. voted for that service raised in order to sink them
this was debated and mr How proposed to raise money out of those that had
passed their accounts without regular vouchers for so much and by reducing
the great places in the exchecquer: muncton moved that no place should be
worth 1000 li. per an: this was all irregular for the Lord Coningsbee said as
for the sinking the exchecquer bills it was agreed to but this morning and
therefore by the orders of the house we could not go the same day into ways
and means for that service Sir Xto[pher] mu[s]grove said it was true: Mr
Smith said this had been ordered before and tho it was but reported this day
they might proceed upon it: and so that bill fell: the Speaker then mr Harley[283]
said it was requisite to sink the Exchec[quer] bills and if we did we must raise
a good fund a certain fund for that purpose and that since [l]and must be

---

[278] i.e. the last meeting of the committee of supply. After reporting its final resolution on 23
Apr. that committee was transformed into the committee of ways and means.

[279] 'the' erased. The committee which was appointed included Cocks among its members:*CJ*
xiii. 500.

[280] The committee resolved to continue the half-pay to disbanded officers for a year from
Michaelmas 1700: ibid. 501.

[281] The resolution as reported was simply to grant a supply to pay off the Exchequer bills: ibid.

[282] In a committee of ways and means: ibid.

[283] As the House was sitting in committee of the whole.

raised he would not propose any thing certain but said it would be best to
begin with Land: mr Hows notions were all loose and so were Sir Charles
Sidleys and Sir George Hungerfords in relation to their discourses and at last
they agreed to 3s in the pound and the words not exceeding were added but
they lost those words by near 100:[284] Ap[ri]ll 24th [1701]
the Speaker was ill and there were some private bills read,[285] nothing worth
writing or observing said or done:[286] mr Coniers reported from the Committee for ways and means the 3s in the pound on land the word[s] not exceeding
were moved and seconded this tooke up some time in debating: the case was
this if the words not exceeding had been added then whatever occasion we had
had there Could no more money have been raised upon land this sessions so
that if we had had wars or any [n]ecessity we had not foreseen and could no
way provide for but by Laying more upon land, we must have had a prorogation to have come at the land again: mr How made a long speech first to know
gent[*lemen*']s thoughts [?next th]e 2d against the word the 3d for them: we
agreed without a division the only remarkable thing in this day was the
divi[s]ion I mean the unusuall proceedings as to matter of speeches: for those
that were used to be against taxes were now against the words those that were
used to promote taxes were many of them for the words:[287] I have here set
down what I said on this occasion becaus I heard it was reported to my
disadvantage viz sir I wish all our affairs could be managed without taxes
and especially land taxes which has [*sic*] so long born the Burthen: we are
threatned and in danger abroad from a malitious and potent enemye and at
home from vast and immens debts and as for my part all my small fortune is
in Land and I beleive every one that knows me knows that I will not easily part
with my money: I am against charging land I mean for charging it with as little
as possible, I am also against the words for tho I shall not be willing to raise
more upon Land nor do I well like what is done yet since there is a possibility
that we may be forced into a warr I would not give such great incouragement
to our enemies as to let them perceive our BaCkwardnes and that if there is

[284] Confirmed by Luttrell (*Brief Relation,* v. 41), and L'Hermitage (BL Add. MS 17677 WW, fos.
238–9), who each give only the number of votes in the minority (68 and 56 respectively).
L'Hermitage identifies the Whigs as the authors of the amendment, and the Tories as its
opponents. As reported, the resolution was for a tax of 3s. in the pound on lands, offices,
pensions, and personal estates: *CJ* xiii. 507.
[285] 'read' interlined. Harley was suffering from inflammation of the throat, caused by a
'quinsy': BL Add MS 30000 E, fo. 161; Cumbria RO (Carlisle), D/Lons/W, James Lowther to
Sir John Lowther, 26, 29 Apr. 1701.
[286] Cocks omits to mention, *inter alia*, the 2nd reading of the public accounts bill, and the
report of the King's answer to the Commons address of 16 Apr.: *CJ* xiii. 506–7.
[287] 'Ap[ri]ll 25' erased. This point was also observed by Bonet; BL Add. MS 30000 E, fo. 158.

occasion that we will rather take any indignity then raise more money: I am
against a land tax if we can possibly be without it, but if there is a necessity I
would willingly part with one half to secure the other Aprill 25th [*1701*]
There were some private bills read and the prisoners with the serjeant for
bribery were dismissed[288] the Speaker was ill and we adjourned till Tuesday[289]
the 29th of Aprill 1701 we met and appoynted When severall bills should be
read and when we should go into committees the Speaker was not recovered
enough to proceed upon busines and therefore they presently agreed to
adjourn: there was nothing remarkable but one usuall thing I could not but
observe viz that if we have any rogue in the house he will be sure to make an
occasion to raile against the roguery he is particularly guilty of as for example
it is reported and I think agreed of by all that there is not one man in the house
that has received greater bribes and been more corrupt then Sir Ed[*ward*]
Seymour[290] yet no man [r]ailes against bribery and corruption more then he as
he did particularly this day when he desired the bill for [p]reventing corruptions and bribery to be ordered[291] a day to go into the Committee of the whole
house to be considered of there is no man in England has done wors thing to
raise himself then Sir B: Shores yet no man railes against rogues like him as he
did this day when perks[292] C [*sic*] who was concerned in some of the Elections
for Sheppard was to be discharged: he said let them stay in custody till they
have spent their ill goten moneys: this would have become an honest man: but
the foul mouth it came from blasted the sence and made me think it was pitty
but the man that said so should be so served: Charles Bertye allso who has
given near 100000 li. to corrupt members[293] rayled against bribery: Jack How
who was ingaged in the most shamefull grant that ever passed always rayles
the most against grants.[294] in consideration of the Speakers illnes we
adjourned till fryday the 2d of May 1701 this day we read private bills or
publick one reading in the morning the first remarkeable thing that hapned
was a petition delivered from Sir John Luson Gow[*e*]r from severall traders in
and about London complaining of the hardships they suffered from parliament[*ary*] priviledges: that some of them had 8000 li. owing them from

---

[288] Jeremy Boreman, George Clayton, John Jeffreys, and John Story, committed into custody on 6
Mar., as a result of the proceedings on the Grimsby election: *CJ* xiii. 379, 508, see above, pp. 79-80.
   [289] Originally 'Friday'.   [290] See above, p. 51.   [291] Originally 'rea[d]'.
   [292] John Perks, also committed to custody on 6 Mar. after the hearing of the Grimsby election:
CJ xiii. 379, 509.   [293] See above, p. 6.
   [294] See above, p. 50, n. 70. Cocks had made this general point himself on a previous occasion
(see above, p. 36), but here he is echoing some comments in the Whig tract, *Jura Populi Anglicani*
. . . (1701): 'if we consider the men, and compare what they have done with the pretended
principles of their party, 'twill hardly seem odder to see Sir Ed—rd Sey—r bring in a bill to prevent
bribery, or Mr J—n H—w exclaim against exorbitant grants' (*William III State Tracts*, iii. 260).

Members as appeared by the books that they shewed him and many said they had as much to their utter ruine and undoing: Sir B: Shores[295] said they would get in here on purpose to be secure from arrests and then they would in six years time they would [*sic*] plead the Statute of limitations:[296] Sir John luson [*Gower*] moved from the votes of the house which declared that in the prorogations of parliament no member should have priviledge but for his person[297] he moved upon this vote to have leave to bring in a bill: Seymour said [t]his was to[o] good to pass but that the bill should be brought in for the other house as well as for this[298] that it was true that no vote in generall could take away any mans private interest and priviledge[299] which was vested in him by being a member of this house: then after a little while we ordered the Speaker to leave the Chair and then mr Coniers tooke the chair of ways and means mr How spoke first and said tho he was for leaving out the words [*not*] exCeeding yet he should be very unwilling unles absolute necessity obliged him to lay 12d in the pound more on the Land he enumerated the places the forrests and hoped Gent[*lemen*] would try every thing first: I said Mr Coniers[300] I do not [d]eny but I was one of those that were against having the words not exceeding left out of the question but I was for it upon no other account but becaus if absolute necessity required we might barr no way that would help to our preservation: we Ly under many difficulties almost insuperable and under many allmost invincible deplorable necessityes both from at home and abroad from abroad we are threatned[301] and it is almost absolutely necessary for us to be engaged in a chargeable war for the preservation of our liberties our propertyes and that that is dearer to all thinking [a]nd considering men our religion it self: we are surrounded and overwhelmed with vast clamorous and just debts [c]ontracted by the late expensive and unnecessary war I mean unnecessary if we will permit France to grow [g]reat with the un[io]n [o]f Flanders and all the Spanish Countrys and dominions: we have had an ill hand a great while and like [l]osing gamesters we have thrown away our cards: I should have been glad that we had tooke a new pack; [bu]t instead of that we have taken an old pack so marked that every one can tell what will be the trump w[?]hen the card is turned up: but be this as it will whoever are ministers we must take care to provide

[295] Shower was to be named, along with Leveson Gower and 'Mr Pelham', to the committee appointed to bring in a bill on the subject of this petition: *CJ* xiii. 509–10.

[296] The Act of Limitations of 1623 (21 Jac. I, c. 16) limited to six years the period in which an action could be brought for debt.

[297] On 13 Feb. 1701 the Commons had declared a standing order that no Member might claim privilege in a lawsuit against a commoner, 'except for his person only': *CJ* xiii. 326.

[298] The resultant bill (eventually the act 12 & 13 Gul. III, c. 3) did extend to the House of Lords.   [299] 'and priviledge' interlined.   [300] Originally 'sir'.   [301] 'with an' erased.

[fo. 74ᵛ]

for what is necessary for our support and safety: if we neglect to do that, if
there is any thing amis it is our fault if [?we] provide sufficiently it is theirs,
and if we provide and it is mis applyed I beleive and hope we shall call them to
an account for [?it] we are now sir in a committee of ways and means in order
to raise money for these purposes and I think we have four ways and means
only proper to rais money on: that is trade land money and excise as for trade
I take it to be the life of England[302] and the land to be England it self: the trade
I thinck is in most parts sufficiently Charged where it may be charged more I
leave it to other Gent[*lemen*] that are better able to inform you: and before I
speake of the land give me leave to say something of taxes in Gen[*era*]ll as for
taxes in gen[*era*]ll they are odious and greeveous to the people and there is
nothing can make them tolerable but their Equality upon this foot I discours
of the land tax is there any tax more unequall first in relation to its self: for
how much higher is one county rated then another: nay often in places hardly
distinguished by an hedge in one place they pay 4s in the pound in another not
one but was this all the inequality I would have been silent and not have
troubled you but pray sir give me leave to set before you a country gent[*leman*]
of an 150 per an: charged with 1000 li. debt: why the use of that comes too 60
his tax a 4s per li. comes to 30 li. and we may allow for repairs Church and
poor ten which makes 100 and then Consider in times of war and scarcity the
50 li. will not bring him so much as 35 li. per an in times of peace and plenty
thus you see the condition of the landed man whilest the man that has 3000 li.
in money has[303] 180 li. per an[304] incomb pays nothing and if he lends his
money to the publick he makes it may be between 2 and 300 li. per an and pays
nothing to the support of the Publick is this Equall to have the Landed man
undon the proprietor of england ruined whilest others live in plenty and
luxury and reap the fruit of his labours: now sir as for money it has paid
Nothing allmost all this war Land has in a manner born the whole charge: it is
certainly reasonable that money should be charged and land eased, but
gent[*lemen*] say how will you come at it: I beleive that may be easily found
out: but I am sure I know a way to reach it but that is not proper for this place
I will therefore only mention it that gent[*lemen*] may think of it and that is to
sink interest of money from six to five:[305] this would make money pay this
would eas[e] land that is when it was sold it would make it more valuable it
would also advance trade the 4th way is excises and as for my part as odious as

---

[302] Originally 'the being'.   [303] '90' erased.   [304] 'per an' interlined.

[305] Since 1651 the maximum rate of interest on loans between private persons had been fixed at
6 per cent: P. G. M. Dickson, *The Financial Revolution in England: A Study in the Development of
Public Credit 1688–1756* (London, 1967), 39.

it is represented to be I shall sooner come into them then to undo the poor land hold[er] of england: Mr Harley the Speakers brother proposed the sale of the kings lands and the forrests and then Mr Lownds[306] told us the damage that would be in that the wrong the commoners would have done them the time these things would take to be adjust[ed] and then that kings land was fitt for nobody but the King that he had nothing left but the principality of Wales and th[e] Dukedom of Cornwall that the prince of wales which might be would repine at the sale of these things: at las[t] upon the debate we allowed to have one shillings of the three on land[307] appropriated for the sinking of exchecquer bills: and then we had 800000 li. to rais: mr Bruges offered at many things and indeed he had taken great pains to inform him self of them unles they were done for him[308] he offered to raise money by taking of the prohibition off indian wroght silk[s] he said this would sink our Customs 200000 li. per an: if they were not permitted to come in this was received with no manner of approbation but rather with disdain thinking this gent[lemen] was not in the interest of his country in the mai[n], the many things mr Bruges offered at came as he said to about 400000 li. lownds allowed them to come near to so much then there was four hundred thousand pound to be raised: mr How said since he saw Gent[lemen] seemed to be agains[t] Charging land any more he hoped that they would help him in abating the Extravagant luxuries and debaucherys of the Court by abating their pensions and salaries by lessening the fees of the Exchequer that rose from the money we gave he said he did not speak this out of any particular spleen or envy to any[309] man[310] but out of service to his country and that he wished he had served god half so well as he had don his country since he satt here and then he spoke of the 700000 li. allowed for the civill list he said there was 50000 li. allowed for King James[311] 30000 li. for the duke of Gloucester and that 2[0] was put in to make it an even sum;[312] he exposed the manner of[313] giving of it and all was true he said as I was told by honest Gent[lemen] that sate by me and that were of that parliament[314] he

---

[306] William Lowndes was Treasury Secretary.   [307] 'on land' interlined.

[308] James Brydges recorded in his diary for 27 Apr. that he had 'discoursed with' Lord Godolphin 'about the raising of what we had voted': Huntington Lib., Stowe MS 26 (2).

[309] 'spleen or envy to any' interlined.   [310] Originally 'mans'.

[311] Strictly speaking, for Mary of Modena: see above, p. 57, n. 115. That Howe was the originator of the motion to apply part of the civil list to the payment of the public debts is confirmed in BL Add. MS 17677 WW, fo. 246; and Hereford and Worcester RO (Hereford), A81/IV/23/a (Brydges MSS), William Brydges to Francis Brydges, 6 May 1701.

[312] L'Hermitage picked up this point, that according to Howe the original calculation of the sum to be granted, £680,000, had been rounded up to the nearest hundred thousand: BL Add. MS 17677 WW, fo. 245.   [313] 'manner of' interlined.

[314] The civil list had been settled in the last session of the 1695–8 Parliament.

desired to know if the princes[s][315] should be Queen whether shee should not
abate for the 50000 li. per an shee had he said it was to[o] much for a future
prince that it was enoug[h] to ruine our liberties that he had discoursed this
with Gent[lemen] that were against that theyr arguments he thought ha[d] no
weight in them: and therefore he moved that wee might Consider of this,
before we proceeded on to anythi[ng] Else and bring in a bill for that
pu[r]pose: Nota Mr Speaker Sir Ed[ward] Seymour Harcourt Hammond
and some others were let into the secret to oppose or divert Hows
motion:[316] and to get 4s on the pound in order to establish and shew the
interest and credit of the new ministry in our house: so that mr Speaker made
a long oration first he ment[io]ned the kings lands in the principality of wales
sais he if it is fitt to be begged it is fit to be sold[317] and will sure bring some
thing then he gave an hint of the Indian wrought silks and said it would
prejudice our customs then he spoke of the forrests and also of ale and beer he
spoke long and to many things in order to divert us from mr Hows motion:
but when he had done I that was upon some reasons not alltogether so fond of
Mr Hows motion but yet I could not well endure to see the house tricked and
the party made so ill an use of as only to support one or two I mean a fewe
Gent[lemen's] interest at the price of our land I said: Sir I beleive there may be
greater advantages from the forrests then only raising of money I beleive it
would rais a great sum to[o] to the content of all it woul[d] also employ many
poor and raise many men: the gent[leman] that spoke last but one said we had
a good king and a good ministry as for a good king I knew it before he told me
so as for the ministry I do not Know it yet bu[t] I will for argument sake [take]
it for granted I beleive the gent[leman] meant by a good ministry a wise
ministry and if so sir what will they advise they will say sir you and your
people are all in the same interest you are their head and the people are the
body Sir you must help them in what you can and they must support you you
will have enough left for your occasions when you have parted with this
100000 li. per ann: more then they have for theirs and it will be more your
interest to have the people of england your Courtiers th[an] to have a few mean
rascally spendthrifts live in Luxury: Sir if I should perceive that this good

---

[315] Princess Anne.

[316] According to William Brydges, 'most of his [Howe] party', considered the motion to be 'ill
timed': Hereford and Worcester RO (Hereford), A81/1V/23/a, William to Frances Brydges, 6 May
1701.

[317] William's grant to Lord Portland in 1695 of the lordships of Denbigh, Bromfield, and Yale
had provoked a storm of protest from 'Country' MPs in north Wales and the Welsh marches: *Cal.
Treas. Bks.*, x. 1046–52, 1374–5; *Cal. Treas. Pprs.* 1557–1696, pp. 437–8; Robert Price, 'Gloria
Cambria: Or the Speech of a Bold Briton in Parliament, against a Dutch Prince of Wales' (1702), in
Somers's Tracts, xi. 387–93.

ministry should give such good advice if we did receive any benefitt by the result of such councills I sho[uld] then think this a good ministry: I think this 100000 li. may be spared we have great occasion for it what way [?we] come at it eyther by addres or bill I leave that the Gent[*lemen*] to consider of it: Sir Edward Seymour to put of[*f*] this moved a tax of 100000 li. upon the Jews Harcourt something else at last after much foolish and some other debates it was moved to have Coniers leave the Chair and that it should be presently moved for leave to bri[ng] in a bill this was said to be irregular so late to make a new motion:[318] and at last the committee chair[*man*] was ordered t[o] ask leave of the house for leave to bring in a bill for the repeale of the civill list act[319] and [?th]en we adjourned) [*sic*] May 3d [*1701*] the lady Angleseys bill was read as also my Lords petition against the bill[320] it was debated when the [pe]tition was to be received and heard the Speaker said there was one president in my Lord northamptons case[321] where [?it] was referred to a prior Committee but that was afterwards in a committee of the whole house and that would be the p[?rop]er time for my Lord t[o] be heard then the house gave my lady the protection of the house during the time of the dependanc[e][322]

[*fo. 74*]

[o]f the busines before the house: then we went into a committee about Seymours bill for regulating corporations[323] this concerned half the house ten were up at a time, it was like a knocking at a wasps nest every one talked for the publick but all had a private end in it at last we adjourned from Saterday the 3d to munday the 5th of May 1701
and then we had abundance were up at a time for motions knowing the house was eager for the business of the Civill list at last Mr Coniers reported that it

---

[318] In 1695 it had been established as a standing order that no new motion should be made after 1 p.m.: [Hatsell,] *Precedents*, 120.

[319] Confirmed in Luttrell, *Brief Relation*, v. 45; and BL Trumbull Add. MS 130, votes, 2 May 1701. More specifically, the request was for a bill to apply £100,000 of the sum allowed for the civil list to the public debt.

[320] Catherine (*c.*1682–1743), née Darnley, an illegitimate daughter of King James II, married to James Annesley (1674–1702), 5th Earl of Anglesey. The bill, sent down from the Lords, was to enforce a legal separation between husband and wife. Lord Anglesey's petition requested a hearing by counsel prior to the 2nd reading, his argument being that the cause ought more properly to be heard by an 'inferior court': *CJ* xiii. 511.

[321] William Parr (1513–71), 1st Marquess of Northampton, whose marriage act of 1552 (5 Edw. VI, c. 30) had frequently been cited as a precedent in recent divorce bills: *The Case of My Lord Roos*[n.d.]; HMC, *14th Report*, vi. 18; HMC, *House of Lords MSS*, NS iii. 57–8. Harley possessed an extensive collection of parliamentary journals: Baker and Baker, *Chandos*, 38.

[322] The House ordered that the petition lie on the table until the 2nd reading of the bill: *CJ* xiii. 511.   [323] The bill to prevent bribery and corruption at elections.

was the opinion of the Committee that[324] he should ask leave to repeale one part of the act that established the civill list and appropriate 100000 li. thereof to the use of the publick:[325] Sir R Gwin spoke long against first that it was irregular he could not tell whether it was a report or a motion: if it was report the committee had done what they had no power to do for that they had nothing to do to repeale an act of parliament without leave[326] then he commended the merit of the King and spoke of the great things he had done for us and concluded that we should not proceed in this matter Lord Cunningsbee spoke to the same purpose only added that if this was referred to the people of England there was hardly a man of 20 li. per an: would be for this and that it would sound ill abroad:[327] How spoke for going on presently and against hitting us in the teeth with the merrit and honour of the King: Brewer said he that was allways for giving of taxes and for that reason was esteemed a courtier was since the reason for this was given ceased viz the death of the D[*uke*] of Gloucester[328] and the non payment of K[*ing*] James for applying this to the use of the publick: I said sir I beleive this will sound very well abroad to have both king and people mutually joyn in bearing the burthen and charge[329] of the nation but since it has been mentioned to know What opinion they are of abroad in relation to this matter I can give you some account just before I came from home severall of my country neighbours came to see[330] me where after we had discoursed over the badnes of the weather and the difficulties of that election I asked them since I had the honour to serve them what it was they would have me do, why sais one of them make warr with France and pay our just debts I said this is very wholesom seasonable good directions but shall we be able to bear the Charge: why sais [*he*] dont lett some live voluptuously and in luxury by great places and pensions and others bear all the burthens sett us all upon one bottom let us pay equall and bleed us as long as you please pray sir sais he will you give me leave to make a comparison you know my estate it requires six horses to plough it now sir sais he supose I should give all my corn to two of my horses and do the work with the four those two that eat all the corn would be very unlucky they would run away with my cart break my tackle and be full of diseases and do me more harm then good, and my other horses that bore all the burthens and [d]id all the work and lived upon straw and offill would be strarved and wore out why sir sais he we are the poor working horses that do all the work and live poorly

---

[324] 'they' erased. The report was from ways and means.   [325] See above, pp. 108–9.
[326] Poussin confirms that this was the principal argument used by Court spokesmen in the debate: PRO 31/3/188/53.   [327] 'and that would sound ill abroad' interlined.
[328] Prince William, who had died on 30 July 1700.
[329] 'and' erased.   [330] 'see' interlined.

and the courtiers and those that have great pensions are the horses that eat all the corn: abate their corn and bring down their stomackes and make them work as we do and wip the corn they have eat out of them and we will refuse nothing I promised them I would do so and now I have this opportunity I will be as good as my word: I will say nothing to the debate till I have heard others speak first: Sir Ed[*ward*] Seymour spoke to order and said it was a regular motion: we were abundance that spoke on both sides there was nothing remarkable those that were for applying it to the publick insisted that the occasion for which it was given ceased upon the death of the Duke of Gloucester the non payment of King Jameses pension and the other was given to make up some [*of*] us insisted that this would oblige the people that the hearts of the people were the true treasure of the prince and that the king and people were and ought to be in the same bottom: I said amongst other things that a dying king of Numidia said this to his sons – non thesauri non exercitus praesidia regni verum amici[331] and that Quaen E[*lizabeth*] had spoke the same in English to her parliament there is no Jewell that I price like your loves I can tell how to set a value upon a jewell but love and thanks I account inestimable:[332] those of the other side said this would be a disrepute to the king beyond sea a disparragement to him at home: and the great occasions he[333] had for money for intelligence that he intended to lay it out upon many necessary occasions for the publick that he was in debt to his servants that his civill list was not so great as his predecessors[334] at last when we had all spoke the speeches we had made before hand the quaestion was put and those that were for applying 100000 li. for the paying of the publick debts and for the use of the nation the reasons ceasing for which it was given were 294 those against 169:[335] this was the oddest division that ever was in the house the two Tredenhams and Hammond spoke against the quaestion that was against themselves for it was evident gifts or hopes altered them: Sir Ed[*ward*] Seymour who endeavoured to put it of[*f*] in the Committee spoke

---

[331] Sallust, *Jugurtha*, 10. 4: 'non exercitus neque thesauri praesidia sunt, verum amici'. The Numidian king was Micipsa.

[332] Another quotation from the 'Golden Speech' of 1601. 'There is no jewel, be it of never so rich a price, which I set before this jewel; I mean, your love: for I do more esteem it, than any treasure or riches; for, that we know how to prize, but love and thanks I count invaluable'. D'Ewes, *Jnls*, 659; Townshend, *Hist. Colls.*, 263. See above, p. 47.   [333] i.e. King William.

[334] This remark was probably based on the abstract of the expenses of King James II, 1685–8, presented to the Commons on 20 Mar. 1689, with accompanying notes referring back to Charles II's reign. The average yearly total of James's expenditure had been calculated at just under £1,700,000 (though this included military accounts). *CJ* x. 55. For a modern estimate of Charles II's average expenditure, at between £1,100,000 and £1,250,000 p.a., see C. D. Chandaman, *The English Public Revenue 1660–1688*(Oxford, 1975), 267–8.

[335] Division of 214:169 in *CJ* xiii. 513.

hansomely for it[336] Harcourt divided for it for they were ashamed to do otherwise harcourt said never a word: Powis spoke[337] against taking: here was honour interest hopes fears and severall passions that biassed reason: and then the lords sent a message to hasten the impeachments:[338] and the answer was that wee would send up articles in good time: it was said and it may be truly that many voted for the taking away 100000 li. becaus they were dissatisfyed with the Kings giving up the lord Summers:[339] May 6th [*1701*] The only memorable thing was this morning a complaint of the ill usage of the seamen Sir Rich[*ard*] Onslow moved it[340] and said they were turned on shore without money without cloaths that they begged thro Surrey[341] that some of them were starved and most of them reduced to the last extremity by this ill usage and made so desperate that they declared they would rather serve the turk or the french then England: he said they ought to have been paid at their ships according to the cu[st]om of the navy[342] and if they had had no money to have paid them off that then they should have been k[ep]t on board till they could have been paid: others said they were paid in tickets and that [t]hey sold a twenty shilling ticket for five shillings and that by these means those that belonged to the admi[r]alty got vast expe[nses][343] littleton said then was no money but exchequer bills but that he had six thousand [p]ound appropriated [?to] other uses which he had let go for exchequer bills without leave of the house[344] others said they w[e]re pay[i]ng of[f] as fast as they did come: at last it was agreed to addres the King to have them paid [?out ?of] the bounty money money [*sic*]: nobody went about to excuse the not paying them of[f] at their

---

[336] Bonet noted that Seymour supported the motion (BL Add. MS 30000 E, fo. 173), but Poussin named him as one of the speakers on the Court side (PRO 31/3/188/53).   [337] 'For it' erased.

[338] To remind the Commons that they had not yet exhibited their articles: *CJ* xiii. 513.

[339] Somers had been dismissed as Lord Chancellor in April 1700. Lord Shaftesbury's view was that the Whigs 'would not oppose' the motion 'because they desponded of the King's intentions as to a war': PRO 30/24/20/57–8.

[340] Confirmed in Luttrell, *Brief Relation*, v. 46. Onslow was the first Member named to the commitee appointed to inquire into the complaint: *CJ* xiii. 514.

[341] Onslow was one of the knights of the shire for Surrey. The committee expressly included all the Members for the seaports and for constituencies in Surrey and Hampshire: *CJ* xiii. 515. For details of the suffering of the discharged seamen, see the report by L'Hermitage in BL Add. MS 17677 WW, fos. 247–8; and [Drake,] *Hist. Parl.*, 165–6.

[342] Onslow had been an Admiralty commissioner in 1690–3.

[343] On the practice of paying seamen by ticket, see R. D. Merriman (ed.), *The Sergison Papers* (Navy Records Society, 1949), 167–70, 195–204.

[344] Sir Thomas Littleton was treasurer of the navy. [Ralph,] *Hist. Eng.*, ii. 972, confirmed that when, on 26 Apr., the number of seamen in Royal Navy ships was ordered to be reduced to the lowest complement, the treasurer had been unable to pay each man in cash because he was only able to issue money in Exchequer bills and these could not be divided into small enough amounts for the purpose.

[*fo. 73ᵛ*]

ships: Mr How said he was glad to see the house in this temper that all were ready to find faults this [?–] time he longed to see that the late ministry were upon a sadle pitched to the back that it was impossible to p[u]ll of[f] the sadle without the hair and scin: that they had left a str[?i]ng behind them that would ruine two or three succeeding ministrys viz that of the exchecquer bills: my Lord Hartington said the Checquer bills when they were first made were of great use and service to pay of[f] the fleet and army when there was no money: at last th[ey] agreed also to appoynt a Committee with power to send for persons papers and records to inquire into the miscarriages and to report the same to the house:[345] and then we went into a committee of the whole house to cons[i]der of the succession bill which was very slenderly attended[346] we went thro the bill and nothing remarkable only a do[?ubt] as to order whether the committee could leave out a clause of the bill commited to them it was agreed they could but that if the house did not agree to the amendment then the clause was to be again inserted: May 7th [*1701*]

Nothing worth observing[347] May 8th [*1701*] this day at the committee in the Speakers chamber to whom we referred to inquire why the seamen were discharged and not paid Mr Churchill one of the Lords of the admiralty[348] said they represented to the king that it would save 300 li. per diem to discharge them that they did it according to the usuall method of disCharging them that there was not money to pay them becaus of the exchequer bills:[349] the matter of fact was that those they pressed from all parts were discharged and set on shore in Surrey or some where many miles of london and more of many of their habitations without money without cloaths and they had only billets for their money which they were to receive at Broad Street[350] many of these poor creatures perished by the way those that lived were exposed to the

---

[345] Cocks was named to this committee: *CJ* xiii. 514.

[346] Burnet, *Own Time*, iv. 500, recalled that the number attending the committee on the Bill of Settlement seldom ran to 50 or 60. The point was also made in a contemporary pamphlet: see Tindal, *Continuation of Rapin's Hist.*, i. 497.

[347] The parliamentary newsletters preserved in Sir William Trumbull's papers also reported that on this day 'there passed . . . nothing material in the House of Commons': BL Trumbull Add. MS 130, votes, 7 May 1701. The *Journals* record, *inter alia*, the 1st reading of the JP Qualification Bill, and the report from the Irish forfeitures trustees: *CJ* xiii. 516–17.

[348] George Churchill, MP.

[349] These remarks are taken from a paper prepared by the Admiralty board and delivered into the committee by their secretary: *CJ* xiii. 564. In fact the Admiralty had not pointed out the likely saving in their representation to the King, but in a separate memorial of 26 Apr.: ibid.

[350] The 'Pay Office' of the Navy, i.e. the office of the treasurer of the Navy, was situated in Old Broad St.: Daniel A. Baugh, *British Naval Administration in the Age of Walpole* (Princeton, 1965), 30.

greatest hardship[s] many sold a ticket of 20s for 3s some[351] for 5s one or two hanged themselves: Churchill owned they gave orders to discharge them before they ordered money to pay them: I beleive this barbarous inhumanity was comitted in order to disparrage my Lord Hallifax by reflecting on the exchequer bills: there were some private bills read in the house and then there was a petition delivered I mean offered from the Kentish Gent[lemen] Justices and Grandjury of Maidston signed by 200[352] mr Meredith K[nigh]t of Kent said he had a petition of an extraordinary nature to offer for the said Gent[lemen] that he was unwilling to do any thing against the sence of the house and very modestly asked the advice and direction of the house:[353] the Speaker after some insignificant speeches of mr How and others[354] asked Mr Mer[e]d[i]th if any of those that subscribed it were there to own it he said there were five at the door[355] upon which they were called to the bar and the petition was shewed th[em] viz to two mr Culpepers to Mr Hambleton to mr Pollhill and to Mr Champnes[356] very honest worthy Gent[lemen] Sir Edwa[rd] Seymour said it was very seditious and that these Gent[lemen] were the tooles of the[357] late ministry[358] who had had their money and were supporting their interest: and that it was high time to Looke into the Com[mis]s[io]ns of the peace and to put a stop to such proceedings which would destroy our constitution and bring us to 41[359] many more spoke to the same purpose:

[351] 'some' interlined.
[352] Drawn up by the grand jury of Kent at Maidstone on 29 Apr. 1701, and signed by 22 justices and around 250 gentlemen: *CJ* xiii. 518; Boyer, *Hist. Wm. III*, iii. 484. For an account of this episode, see 'The History of the Kentish Petition' (1740), in *Somers's Tracts*, xi. 242–54.
[353] Confirmed in [Ralph,] *Hist. Eng.*, ii. 946; and *Somers's Tracts*, xi. 246–7.
[354] The 'history' of the petition notes speeches by Jack Howe, Sir Edward Seymour, Sir Theophilus Oglethorpe, and 'several other gentlemen': *Somers's Tracts*, xi. 246–7.
[355] The chairman of the grand jury, William Colepeper, had been requested to present the petition to Parliament, and four others had volunteered to accompany him: ibid. 245.
[356] William Colepeper (1665–1726), of Hollingbourne, Kent, for whom see J. Cave-Brown, *The Story of Hollingbourne* (privately printed, 1890), 76; Foster (ed.), *London Marriage Licences*, col. 365; *Somers's Tracts*, xi. 244–5. Thomas Colepeper (b. 1669), William's younger brother, also of Hollingbourne, for whom see Cave-Brown, *Hollingbourne*, 77; and Edward Hasted, *The History and Topographical Survey of the County of Kent* (2nd edn., 12 vols.; Canterbury, 1797–1801), iv. 438. William Hamilton (d. 1737), of Chilston Park, Kent, a brother-in-law of the Colepepers: see John Lodge, *The Peerage of Ireland* (4 vols.; Dublin, 1754), iii. 163–4. David Polhill (1674–1754), of Chipstead, Kent, MP Kent 1710, Bramber 1723–7, Rochester 1727–41, 1742–54: see *HC 1715–54*, ii. 359. Justinian Champneys (1670–1754), of the Middle Temple and Ostenhanger, Kent: see William Berry, *Pedigrees of the Families of the County of Kent* (London, 1830), 39.
[357] 'governmen[t]' erased.   [358] 'late mini' interlined.
[359] i.e. 1641. The pamphlet *Jura Populi Anglicani . . .* (1701) noted Seymour's comment that the petition 'smelt of forty-One', and also speeches by Anthony Hammond, Simon Harcourt, Jack Howe, and Sir Bartholomew Shower, arguing for the petitioner's incarceration: *Wm. III State Tracts*, iii. 258–9.

the thing that angred them in the petition was to desire the parliament to[360] Loyal addresses into bills of supply:[361] the other part was nothing that could be found fault with: viz to provide for our common safeties and to set forth the great service and regard they had for the king: then mr Harcourt moved that it was insolent seditious and tending to the subversion of the constitution of parliament Mr Harvy said he could not say it was seditious for if we did not follow those methods it would tend to our perdition and as[362] for tooles he was a building a little box and pulling down another and that he found there needed as many and as sharp tooles to pull down the old hous as were to sett up the new at last we[363] put the quaestion[364] and it was carried without a division:[365] and then Mr How moved as he said from his good nature said he was willing if these gent[lemen] would acknowledge their Error that the Speaker should repremand them and that they should be discharged: many of us went to perswade them and very hardly could we perswade them to any submission, and when we had done that mr [How] retracted his motion of accepting their submission he said his compassionate good nature which was a fault but in very few besid[e] himself had led him in to that error: but the reasons of the house had convinced him of the contrary so the quaestion was put an[d] carried for their being taken into custody without a division: then there was the Secretary Hedges at the bar with a lett[er] from the king[366] and a memoriall from the States under pensioner Fagells hand[367] and a letter from Stanhope our Envoy there[368] and Sir B Shores with impeachments against my Lord Orford:[369] and by the rules of reason and order undoubtedly the Secre[ta]ry ought to have the preference yet many silly warm fooles cryed out of Sir Bart[holomew] but the Secretary brought up th[e] papers in which was set forth the miserable deplorable condition of the States Gen[era]ll: that they were forced to drown part of their country to save another part: that they Expected every minute to be invaded and that they were in a great deale wors

---

[360] 'let alone their' erased.   [361] To 'turn' loyal addresses into supply bills.
[362] 'as' interlined.   [363] 'divided' erased.   [364] 'put the quaestion' interlined.
[365] Confirmed in *CJ* xiii. 518. The 'history' of the petition estimated the duration of the debate at five hours: *Somers's Tracts*, xi. 248.
[366] To the Commons, 8 May 1701, communicating letters from the States-General and from the English envoy to The Hague, and laying before the consideration of the House the 'hardships' and 'great pressures' the United Provinces were suffering: *CJ* xiii. 518.
[367] States-General to William, 13 May [n.s.] 1701, signed by François Fagel (1659–1746), the *greffier* or secretary to the States, whom Cocks seems to have confused with a namesake, the former Grand Pensionary Casper Fagel. The letter is printed in *CJ* xiii. 519–20.
[368] Alexander Stanhope (1638–1707), envoy extraordinary to the United Provinces 1700–6, to Sir Charles Hedges, 2/13 May 1701, printed ibid., 520.
[369] The report of the committee appointed to prepare articles of impeachment against Orford: ibid. 520–1.

condition then if they were in an actuall warr: that they would do nothing but in concert with england and that the French would treat seperately: this was ordered to be conside[red] of to morrow: then Sir B Shores reported his articles from the Barr: and then they were read by the Cle[rk] and then Sir Bar[*tholomew*] Shores endeavoured to maintain them which he very easily did having a majority to suppor[t] him and Sir Tho[*mas*] Meres[370] saying we ought to agree with them if we had but a tolerable reason to induce us to beleive them: the articles were that he got great grants which impoverished the King and greeved the commons with taxes[371] and other barbarous falshoods not one thing but what had been examined and cleared but the party prevailing things were carried with a swing: I remember my Lord orford told me Pen the Qua[ker][372] desired to meet him after the le Hogue victory and pen said Give me leave to call thee freind Russell when that was easily grant[ed] sais he freind Russel you have beat the French once if ever you beat them again you will be hanged, I see what danger [you] are in for what you have done:[373] may the 9th [*1701*]: the articles of impeachment against the lord Orford[374] were read after ingrossed Bierly carried it up to the Lords by order of the house[375] and there was many went with it: and then we read the kings letter and at the name of W[*illia*]m Rex according to order we all uncover and continue bare till it is all read:[376] assoon [*sic*] as that was over Bierly reported

---

[370] A member of the committee which prepared the articles: ibid. 491.

[371] One of the charges in the articles was that in consequence of Orford's grants 'the standing revenues of the Crown of England, which ought to be applied to the service of the public, are greatly diminished and the people of England thereby burdened with debt, and subjected to grievous taxes': ibid. 520.

[372] 'the Qua[ker]' interlined. For William Penn (1644–1718), see *DNB*.

[373] Presumably Penn's meaning is that the Tories, whose real loyalty is to King James II, will exact vengeance upon Orford for destroying the prospects for a Jacobite restoration. Certainly, by the time of the admiral's return to England in the autumn of 1692 it seemed likely that the Tories in Parliament would attack his failure to follow up his victory with an amphibious landing on the French coast. Russell had also quarrelled bitterly with Tory members of the administration, notably Secretary Nottingham. John Ehrman, *The Navy in the War of William III 1689–1697* . . . . (Cambridge, 1953), 392–408; Henry Horwitz, *Revolution Politicks: The Career of Daniel Finch, Second Earl of Nottingham, 1647–1730* (Cambridge, 1968), 127–36; Nottingham University Library, PwA 2792a (Portland (Bentinck) (MSS), [?–] to Portland [1 Nov. 1692]. Ironically, both Russell and Penn had themselves corresponded with King James, though the latter was at this point 'sick, inactive, and . . . possibly trying to break with the Jacobites': P. A. Hopkins, 'Aspects of Jacobite Conspiracy in England in the Reign of William III', Ph.D. thesis (Cambridge, 1981), 303. I am grateful to Dr Hopkins for a lengthy discussion of the implications of this passage of the diary.　　　　　　　　　　　　　　　　　　　　　　　　　　　[374] 'Orford' interlined.

[375] Byerley had also served on the committee to prepare the articles: *CJ* xiii. 491.

[376] According to Speaker Arthur Onslow later in the century, a message from the sovereign had always to be read first to the House by the Speaker (or the chairman, if the House was sitting in committee of the whole), with the Members bare-headed. If any further reading proved necessary, this could be done by the clerk, and Members were not required to keep their hats off: [Hatsell], *Precedents*, 236.

that [*he had*] Carried up the impeachments and Lodged them with the Lords then the Speaker asked him if that was all and put him in mind of demanding security for his appearance to answer them, this was ordered upon a motion of Sir B: Shores who said it had been done in other cases, and that it was necessary to[*o*] to use and revive those presidents for tho this Lord had a good stake in the hedg[e] yet some of the impeached Lords were forreigners[377] and had but litle interest in England and might easily withdraw them[selves] from justice: and then we went upon the kings letter and the States memoriall which was very moving it complai[ned] of their miserable condition that they were in a manner beseiged by land and had no way open but the sea: and that the[y] would do nothing seperate but in concert with England that they would suffer any thing first and that our [?and their] interest were the same: the Kings letter told us that he knew this to be the state of their present case Mr St[an]hops letter complained of the triffling ill usage of France that they would admitt of him no more then as a [?ci]pher[378] Mr How began the debate and said that now there was occasion we should shew the world that we were mis[re]presented and demonstrate to them that we were neyther to be affrighted nor bribed, but that we would manag[e] things so that we would not be principalls and yet not neglect any thing that was necessary for our safety that the breach of our originall[379] treatys with the emperour[380] was a great occasion of our present misfortunes: that the Sta[tes] were not yet formally attacked but that they were in that condition that they must attack or be overwhelm[ed] that the liberties of Europe were in danger from france that it was a just quarrell to defend our injured n[ei]ghbours: that the tooles of the late ministry were very impudent in their lyes and reports and that tho evill [?–] may prevaile for a season yet that god was above all and these things would at la[st ap]pear: that he w[as] for a generall resolution that we should be unanimous w[h]ere we ought to be and then [?–] h[e mov]ed and offer[ed] at some thing for a quaestion but he could only tell the sence of what he would have t[?hat] o[?thers] should put

[*fo. 73*]

[?into?form]: Sir Rob[*ert*] Davers that he had given great attention to the debate that he was sensible of the bad condition the dutch were in [t]hat we

---

[377] Only Portland, a Dutchman, could be so described.

[378] Stanhope's letter (*CJ* xiii. 520) complained of the refusal of the French to admit him as a full participant in conferences with the States-General, but did not define the status they were prepared to allow him. In fact, what the French had said was that Stanhope might be present 'to assist and support any pretensions of the States but not to propose or demand anything for England in the King's name': Centre for Kentish Studies Maidstone, U1590/C9/1, Alexander Stanhope to James Stanhope, 29 Apr./10 May 1701.

[379] 'originall' interlined.   [380] The Grand Alliance of 1689.

had had gen[*era*]ll quaestions enough and that we should particularly say that
our ships our men and our money were ready for the Dutch: Sir John Bolles
talked a long time foolishly against a war and of our debts mr Singeons[381] was
against generall quaestions and that we should resolve to secure and encourage our allyes abroad and our selves at home that we were like a bundle of
Faggots in the fable that we were easily broke stick by stick but when bound
up together not so easily broken[382] mr Boyle that the fate of Europe was at
stake that we should resolve to maintain the ballance of Europe and send the
Dutch our men and ships according to the treaty of 79[383] Sir Godfery Copley
was for sending the army out of Ireland that they were ready raised and
disciplined[384] and wee might presently recruit if occasion: Sir Theo[*philus*]
Oglethorp was for sending men or money presently if we sent money that they
would have presently if men not till they had occasion if we sent men they
might be cloathed here and our half pay officers employed Sir Row[*land*] Gwin
seconded Boyle Sir Ed[*ward*] Seymour said it was a matter of the highest
consequence that the fate of Europe was at stake and wished that we had been
in a committee where these things might have been spoken to more then once
if occasion offered[385] that he would say nothing of our poverty for if there was
occasion a a [*sic*] man must venture his all: that he was for providing and
preparing as if we were[386] to enter into a war tho to avoyd a war if possible
that the dutch had ill neighbours and that our own safety depended on theirs
that the minute we entred into a war we should be 3 millions more in debt:
that we should send those forces we were obliged by the treaty and no more
least it should be ill interpreted that if we made war we should drive Spain
more intirely into the interest of france: that the dutch had no ground to draw
an army out he was against the Ballance of Europe to be put in: being words
to[*o*] extensive that might engage us further then we intended: here I stood up
to speak but I saw the house by the Gen[*era*]ll demand of the quaestion so
unanimous that I said no more then that I saw since I rose up to speak such a
gen[*era*]ll consent that I thought it needed no further inforcement and there-

---

[381] Henry St John's early parliamentary career is covered in H. T. Dickinson, *Bolingbroke*
(London, 1970), 25–7. Though the first intervention to be recorded by Cocks, this was evidently
not his maiden speech.   [382] Aesop's fable of 'the bundle of sticks'.
[383] The Treaty of Nijmegen.
[384] For the size of the Irish military establishment, see Charles Dalton, *English Army Lists and
Commission Registers, 1661–1714* (6 vols.; London, 1892–1904), iv. 216, 255–62; and PRO SP 63/
362/91–106, 123–40.
[385] It was an order of the House that 'no Member should speak twice to the same question',
unless in committee, when 'every Member may speak as often as he pleases': [Hatsell], *Precedents*,
66–7.   [386] 'as if we were' interlined.

fore I would say nothing to keep Gent[*lemen*] from the quaestion:[387] and indeed I thought the quaestion would have been presently put: But that impertinent fellow Shores stood up and prated againts [*sic*] the treaty of partition in the conclusion of his speech and reflected upon the impeached lords and the treaty of partition as the cause of all our ills: and Jack Smith answered him in a long premeditated discours and said he would not reflect but did reflect cursorily upon all the miscarriages and heats of the angry party and spoke of the necessity of our exerting our selves at this time: this occasio[ned] an hours debate Sir Xto[*pher*] musgrove in a sedate speech laid before us the inconveniencys of the war the necessity of preserving the Dutch but was against those Gen[*era*]ll words as dangerous and unnecessary and too extensive as unnecessary for that it did not appear that the emperour desired our alliance or that any other princes were in our interest:[388] Mr Paget said he could not help differing from those Gent[*lemen*] he did seldom differ from:[389] but that he could not agree with the honourable Gent[*leman*] near the war [*sic*][390] that we should fear angring france or fear making Spain more in the French interest that he though[t] it was our interest to animate those by a gen[*era*]ll vote that were ready to come into the common assistance and to encourage our friends and to make as many more as we could he spoke very handsomely:[391] Secretary hedges told us that the [E]mperour and severall others courted our allyance that the Emperour had rejected the popes[392] mediation of a peace and expected to see what we would do Sir Jeffery Jefferys talked like a madman according to his custome[393] and said amongst other stuff that the petitioners of Kent knew more then the Secretarys of State: at last the quaestion was put and the word ballance altered for the libertye of Europe[394]

---

[387] Sir Charles Hedges recorded that in this debate the House proceeded 'with more spirit and unanimity than has appeared on any subject these many years': Centre for Kentish Studies, Maidstone, U1590/019/1, Hedges to Alexander Stanhope, 9 May 1701. Gilbert Heathcote likewise wrote that the resolutions 'came without struggle': *CSP Dom.* 1700–2, p. 320.

[388] According to Poussin, Musgrave was the only Member to represent 'les conséquences d'une resolution si précipitée, voulant fair connoître que d'embrasser le maintien de la liberté d'Europe, c'étoit se mettre dans de grands embaras, et faire même plus que les Etats Généraux ne demandoient': PRO 31/3/188/57. [389] The Tories.

[390] *Recte* bar.

[391] An opinion shared by Lord Shaftesbury, who considered that Paget had spoken 'beyond all others for the interest of Holland, the Protestant religion, and Europe': PRO 30/24/20/56.

[392] Giovanni Francesco Albani (1649–1721), Pope Clement XI.

[393] As late as 1714, a report of a disastrous maiden speech in the Commons noted that its perpetrator had 'blundered so badly that he was the jest of the House, and . . . made so ill a beginning that he would ever after be the standing jest of the House whenever he rise up to speak, like Sir Geoffry Geoffrys': James J. Cartwright (ed.), *The Wentworth Papers 1705–1739* (London 1883), 358. See also below, p.276.

[394] To assist the King in supporting the allies, and 'in maintaining the liberties of Europe': *CJ* xiii. 523.

and carried nemine Contradicente: then Jack How to shew his parts reflected
upon Smith and others that had spent the time of the house after all was agreed
rather then they would loose their speeches then Smith said angrily that this
was against the order of parliament to Reflect upon any thing that had been
said in a debate after the debate was over: Sir will[*iam*] Strickland said such
liberties were not to be endured and would occasion differences without doors
reflected upon Hows impudence: How Grinned: and then there was a debate
whether this should be presented by the whole house or the privy councill it
was carried by the whole house after some debate: and then the councill for
those that had lent money on the fund of Coale and Culm taken away by act of
parliament without their consent[395] were heard this was hard and unjust: May
10th[396] [*1701*] Bolles reported the bill of succession in a very thin house all
went of[*f*] as if it had been a land tax bill there was no amendmend but when
he came to that parted [*sic*] that excluded persons in places from being
members of Parliament littleton opposed it in a vehement long oration
shewing the Jealousies that this claus would perpetually make between the
king and the people for future ages as well as the time Present he asked if it was
impossible to be an honest man and the kings servant: Boyle seconded him to
have this Clause omitted I thought the house had been set to throw it out, and
then I spoke to Sir Godfery Copley to answer them Copley said to me[397] he
could not speak when he would and could not help it but he moved to have the
serjeant go into the court of requests and the hall to call the members in this
being a great quaestion Ned[398] Harley 2ded him[399] when the serjeant came in I
was not prepared and staid to see if any one else would and when I saw that
nobody else would I said: Sir there is nothing that a true and good Englishman
ought to endeavour more then to prevent and hinder all jealousies and
misunderstandings[400] that shall and may[401] arise between the King and his
people the debate is about the clause that hinders a member of parliament to
have a place: by what I have heard of those that sate before me by what I have
observed in my own time there is nothing has occasioned so much Flattery so
much rayling envy[402] and satyr as this thing place which is often the bane of[403]

[395] Creditors on the fund established by the act of 1695 imposing duties on glassware, stone and
earthenware bottles, coals and culm (6 & 7 Gul. III c. 18). This had been removed by the 1696 Salt
Duty Act (7 & 8 Gul. III c. 31), but a year later another fund had been constituted in its place by
the Leather Duty Act (8 & 9 Gul. III c. 21). When the creditors had protested that this new duty
would be insufficient to meet the debt, they had been promised an 'enacting clause' in the next
session to make up the shortfall, and now renewed their request: *CJ* xiii. 512.
[396] 'May 10th' boxed in MS.   [397] 'to me' interlined.   [398] 'Ned' interlined.
[399] The order was made: *CJ* xiii. 524.   [400] 'and misunderstandings' interlined.
[401] Originally 'must'.   [402] 'envy' interlined.   [403] 'the' erased.

kingdoms and ought to be avoyded above all things:[404] I compare the rayler and the flatterer to two travailers upon the same roade the one rides a pacing hors and the other the trotter, but at night they come both to the same inne and the trotter often safest: Gent[*lemen*] say are all people in place influenced? we all know that those in places generally vote in matters of state all one way and this can hardly proceed from conscience to have a body of men intirely all of one mind it must have something more then chance and wee have seen men vote and talk one way before they have had places another way when in places and then alter again when they have been out: it gives a handle to Gent[*lemen*] to reflect, to people out of doors to beleive that [t]here is a seperate interest between the king and the country when the one in quaestions divide from the other tho the court should and did act by consciens:[405] it will mend parliament the most of any thing for if we have none sit here that have places none of small fortunes will endeavour to be returned it will not be worth their times and this house will be filled with men of the best fortunes Character and esteem which will be an honour to the house and a service to the king and kingdom: there was one word mended without any opposition: both instead of eyther house may addres the king to remove a judge: then the Chairman reported the Election of litchfield we proposed to adjourn and divided for it it was past 3 and at 4 we were to go to Kinsington with the vote we lost it: and so they proceeded and they would hear no reason but agree agree to one of which agree we could not agree and divided again it was to hinder those Freemen from voting who were not inrolled by the townclerk [*sic*] in a new roll tho they were freemen: Diot was voted duly Elected and Wormly not duly Elected and when Wamsly the other sitting member had the quaestion put upon him he stood up to make his dying spech [?t]hen the Speaker desired us to adjourn and the quaestion was put and mr Harcourt said the noes had it but then [u]pon the division we carried it for adjourning so the debate was adjourned[406] May 12th

---

[404] 'above all things' interlined.   [405] 'and not par[*liamen*]t[*ar*]y' erased.

[406] The Lichfield election had been contested by, on the one hand, Sir Michael Biddulph and Richard Dyott, and, on the other, William Walmesley and Humphrey Wyrley. Their respective party political alignments are not altogether clear, but evidently the latter pairing represented a 'Church' interest (HMC, *Cowper MSS*, ii. 419). One of each side had been returned, and the two defeated candidates thus petitioned separately, Wyrley against Dyott and Biddulph against Walmesley. The committee, however, had considered both cases together. According to the *Journals*, the report began with a consideration of Wyrley's petition, which was rejected by the House. It was then the turn of Biddulph's, wherein the committee had adjudged neither of the two candidates concerned duly elected. After the first resolution had been ratified by the House, voiding Biddulph's election, a motion to adjourn was defeated. Further resolutions were then accepted, including one arising from Wyrley's petition, which had sought to establish that freemen of the Taylors' company of Lichfield whose names were not enrolled in the new register begun after the regulation of the company in 1698, were still entitled to vote on the basis of their

1701[407] [N]othing worth observing the day was spent in debating whether we
should send the Dutch men [o]r money Harley the Speaker began the debate
we being in a committee of the Whole house[408] he told [u]s that it was a thing
of great Consequence that nearly concerned us otherwise he had not troubled
us but that if we sent men it would ipso facto ingage us in a war that we
should not Know how to disband them again he spoke very pressingly long
and as I thought [?b]y directions from Court: but I found afterwards that the
court were for men it was answered by Sir Ed[*ward*] Seymour: who said if we
did send the dutch assistance we should send them the most effectual that
th[ey] wanted men and not money, that we might spare some men out of
ireland and m[ak]e th[em] up with recruits out of england all that was
remarkable in this debate was that [S]eymou[r] How and Shores were against
Harly musgrove and Harcourt:[409] the debate

[*fo. 72ᵛ*]

lasted 5 hours[410] but nothing considerable said more but of the courage of the
english souldiers and how[411] much they we[re es]teemed abroad: above
others:[412] then there was a complaint of the destruction of the yong timber
in Enfeild Chase a Committee appoynted to examine it:[413] Nota the reason the
Speaker in the committee mr Harley was for money and not men was becaus if
we sent men out of Ireland it would lessen the standing army: but that was an
argument he Durst not give but tho the king had rather have us send men then
money into Holland yet he had rather have the money sent into Holland then
lose 5000 men from his army: and the reason Sir Edward Seymour was for
sending the men out of Ireland was because if in time of war and danger

appearance in the old register. However, to prevent the House from deciding upon the last of the
committee's resolutions, to declare Walmesley's election invalid, a second adjournment motion
was passed. *CJ* xiii. 525–30. Earlier, before the House had embarked on the hearing of the report,
Sir Charles Hedges had informed Members that the King had appointed a time (4 p.m. that day) to
receive at Kensington Palace the Commons' resolutions of 9 May: ibid. 525, 532–3. Of the four
candidates at this election, the only one not to sit in Parliament during the period covered by the
diary (indeed not at all) was Wyrley (1648–aft. 1705), of Hamstead, Handsworth, Staffs., for
whom see Sir George J. Armytage and W. Harry Rylands (edd.), *Staffordshire Pedigrees* . . .
(Harleian Soc., 43; London 1912), 259; and Stebbing Shaw, *The History and Antiquities of
Staffordshire* . . . . (2 vols.; London, 1798–1801), ii. 111, 116.

[407] '12th 1701' boxed in MS.   [408] Of ways and means.
[409] L'Hermitage confirms that Harley spoke in favour of sending money, and that the opposite
point of view, for sending troops, was put chiefly by Seymour: BL Add. MS 17677 WW, fos. 257–8.
[410] James Brydges noted in his diary that the House rose at 6 p.m.: Huntington Lib., Stowe MS
26 (2), 12 May 1701.   [411] 'how' interlined.
[412] The committee resolved that 12 battalions from the Irish establishment should be brought
up to strength and sent to the aid of the States-General: Luttrell, *Brief Relation*, v. 49; BL Trumbull
Add. MS 130, votes, 12 May 1701.
[413] 'May 13th' erased. The committee included Cocks: *CJ* xiii. 533. See below, pp. 148–50.

ireland could be safe it might be as safe in time of peace with as few forces: so that the sending of men out of Ireland would both lessen the standing army and gett the Scotch regiments out of Ireland (which nation he fears and hates) and would also lessen the charge that nation is at in keeping so many forces: for his son has a great estate in ireland:[414] thus you may see men argue upon one reason and have another and the silly and undiscerning part of the house are led by the reasons given and never see nor know the reason[?s] those that argue go upon May 13[415] 1701 Sir Rouland Gwin reported formerly[416] Mr Wamslys election for Litchfield the which was adjourned becaus of our going to kinsington and there is no dispute but had we then had time to have gon[?e] thro the election Wamsley had been turned out as the house was then set filled and humoured but now it was a pretty thin house and att the division against agreeing with the Committee 113 for agreeing 96[417] Hindon Election was next reported and Coultrop[418] put out without a division: his agent had given 70 li. to 70 persons to appear for him the day of the Election at the Cross it was proved at the Committee and owned by mr Coultrop:[419] I moved to have the agent voted guilty of endeavouring by distributing money to procure mr Coultrop to be returned but the house would not hear of it: then came on Bishop castle election Sir w[*illia*]m Brownlo deceased had petitioned against Mas[on] the sitting member at the Committee Mason had no councill nor no witnesses but stood in the bar in the councills pla[ce] and behaved himself foolishly for he was but an indifferent fellow of no great parts or integrity:[420]

[414] Francis Seymour Conway, MP Bramber, who in 1699 had succeeded his elder brother Popham to the property of their mother's cousin, Edward Conway, 1st Earl of Conway (d. 1683), including a substantial estate at Lisburn, Co. Antrim.

[415] 'May 13th' boxed in MS.   [416] 'formerly' interlined.

[417] Confirmed in *CJ* xiii, 533. The rejected resolution was that Walmesley had not been duly elected.   [418] Reynolds Calthorpe.

[419] 'The Cross' was the place of election at Hindon, though the borough consisted 'chiefly of one long street': Sir Richard Colt Hoare, *The History of Modern Wiltshire: Hundred of Mere* (London, 1822), 194. Mention of the £70 said to have been spent by Calthorpe's agent Burlington occurred twice in evidence reported for the petitioner, but the total of 70 for the number of recipients of this largess cannot be found in the report, which similarly contains no admission of bribery on Calthorpe's part, though one of his witnesses did let slip that he (Calthorpe) had been informed of the expenditure before the poll. *CJ* xiii. 533–6.

[420] As with Lichfield, there were two separate petitions over the Bishop's Castle election, which the committee heard, and reported on, together: that of Sir William Brownlow, 4th Bt., against Charles Mason; and one preferred by Sir Gilbert Gerard, 2nd Bt., against George Walcot. Brownlow had already died on 6 Mar. 1701. For Mason, 'a staunch but disreputable Whig', who left his office as joint comptroller of the mint in 1701 'under a cloud' and later as receiver-general and paymaster of transports embezzled some £6,000 of public money, see *Cal. Treas. Bks.*, xvi. 8–9, 135–6; *Cal. Treas. Pprs.* 1697–1702, pp. 424–5; Shropshire RO, Walcot MSS, John Walcot to George Walcot, 18 Dec. 1698; and *HC 1715–54*, ii. 245. No evidence given on Mason's behalf is reported in *CJ* (xiii. 537).

the Committee agr[eed] that he was not Duly elected and guilty of bribery and corruption: at the report he said he desired to have hi[s] cause recommitted thinking it against the orders of the house to have a dead mans petition heard and on that accou[nt] he was not provided with Councill or witnesses to make his defence: the debate was very inconsiderable: and the Speaker told us a lord called up to the upper house upon the death of his father had tryed the validity of his petitio[n] here[421] and one instance where a man had been turned out at the petition of a dead man:[422] so that poynt was over ruled and mr Mason who had withdrawn whilest this matter was debating and had desired if he was overrul[ed] in it to be heard to the merits of his Election was called in and he not appearing for I beleive he took that ocCasion to run away he was voted not duly Elected: and then voted gui[l]ty of bribery and undue practic[e]s and then ordered to be committed to the serjeant:[423] then Mr Walcuts election came on[424] and Coll Stringer repeated many notorious ill practices and briberys he had observed at the Committee and said he hoped the house would not a[gree] with the Committee he could not: Sir Thomas Powis Commended Walcuts family and their interest and concluded Contrary to Stringer:[425] Then the Speaker in his Chair said that no imputation might be upon Walcut that the burrough was near him in his neighbourhood that the walcuts were an antient honourable family that wou[ld] scorn such practices that they did not want such an interest that he knew walcut was free from such pra[c]tices and Mason Guilty of them:[426]

---

[421] Although not according precisely with the details of the precedent reported by Cocks, it is probable that the case in question was that of Lord Ossory (eldest son of the 1st Duke of Ormond), who in Sept. 1666 was created Lord Butler in the English peerage, and was thus rendered unable to sit any longer as MP for Bristol. But, rather than risk a by-election, his defeated opponent in 1661, Sir Humphrey Hooke, revived a dormant petition against the previous return, and on 30 Oct. 1666 was declared elected on a report from the committee of privileges: CJ viii. 644; HC 1660–90, i. 237–8, 756–7. I am very grateful to my former colleague, Mr J. P. Ferris, for assistance on this point.

[422] Francis Gratwick had been unseated on 10 Feb. 1671 following a petition against the return of a by-election at Seaford, by which time both he and the petitioner, Robert Morley, had both died: HC 1660–90, i. 502. Again I owe the identification of the precedent to the expert advice of Mr Ferris.

[423] Charles Allestree noted that Mason had been expelled 'ignominiously and with one consent', i.e. unanimously: BL Add. MS 27440, fo. 165.

[424] In fact, the *Journals* record that the reports on both petitions were made first, and then the House voted to agree with all the resolutions of the committee, and to order Mason into custody: CJ xiii. 536–8.   [425] Powys sat for a Shropshire constituency.

[426] The Harleys had many connections with the gentry of Shropshire, and indeed some interest of their own at Bishop's Castle (Victoria County History, *Shropshire*, iii. 300). On 22 May Walcot's father wrote to thank the Speaker for 'your great kindness to my son . . . and more for the good character which you have given of myself and family': BL Loan 29/160, John Walcot to Harley, 22 May 1701. See also Loan 29/306, George Walcot to same, 13 Dec. 1701.

Nota this was extraordinary[427] then the Speaker told us something he had heard concerning the Kentish men an[d] that the serjeant would tell us more: the serjeant Powell[428] told us that mr Culpiper wrote him a letter from Maid[stone] that he would be in town in 3 or four days and that Mr Pollill sent him word if he intended to keep him in Wendsay night he must have 50 men to do it he said he had beat his man for letting Culpeper go that they were very unruly and that he could not keep them safely:[429] this occasioned a debate at last a division but mr Harco[urt] proposed to have them Committed to the gatehouse others to the tower that quaestion was put and carried by a great majority:[430] then the quaestion was put to addres the king to put them out of the Comissions of the pea[ce] and leiuetenancy and that was carried:[431] then it was proposed to addres the king to issue forth a proclamation to apprehend Culpeper: and that was carried:[432] then Jack How and Sir B Shores in long historicall oratio[ns] from Canterbury to paris and Germany at last came to kent and concluded that the petitioners were inst[ru]ments of the impeached lords and that their being still privy councellours was the occasion of it they cō[m]plained tha[t] they had thanked the King for his gracious answer and that nothing was done Seymour said he could not but observe that all that were against impeaching the lords staid in at the quaestion for sending the Kentish men to th[e] gatehouse I answered and said I must give that Honourable Gent[leman] observation for his observation I cannot but observe that some[433] of those gent[lemen] that went oud [sic] did beleive that Kid was at my Lord Hallifaxes invisibly[434] Mr Boyle spoke against the

---

[427] 'Nota this was extraordinary' interlined.

[428] Samuel Powell, serjeant-at-arms 1693–1709: Philip Marsden, The Officers of the Commons 1363–1965 (London, 1966), app. D.

[429] William Colepeper's letter, though not mentioned in the Journals, is confirmed in several other sources, which also refer to the threatening behaviour of the other detainees, without giving Polhill's exact words: Somers's Tracts, xi. 248–9, R.C., 'Extract from an Old Diary', Notes and Queries, 2nd ser. 10 (1860), 324–5; Liverpool RO, 920 NOR 1/116, William Clayton to Richard Norris, 13 May 1701; National Archives of Ireland, Wyche MSS 1/221, Maurice Annesley to Sir Cyril Wyche, 13 May 1701. Powell's own account, as delivered to Robert Harley in the following Sept., adds some more details and confirms, inter alia, the allegation that he himself had beaten the messenger responsible for guarding Colepeper: HMC, Portland MSS, viii. 90–1.

[430] The first of the two motions was put and carried 169:93: CJ xiii. 538.

[431] Without a division: ibid. 539.

[432] Again without a division, but the Journals record that this question preceded the motion to remove the five from the bench and lieutenancy: ibid.   [433] 'some' interlined.

[434] When on 31 Mar. Sir Edward Seymour had proposed that the House send for Kidd a second time, he had grounded his motion on information that he claimed to have received (from the brother of one of Lord Halifax's maidservants), that on the way back to Newgate after his first appearance before the Commons Kidd had stopped off at Halifax's house, where Somers had also been present. The tale did not, however, stand up to examination. Tindal, Continuation of Rapin's Hist., i. 458–9.

quaestion handsomely Sir w: Stricland angrily reflected upon How for his grant and said some gent[?*leman*] had called the dividers of the treaty called the partition treaty robbers but he thought that gent[*leman*] that would have had a gran[t] of great value and begged if for a small one tho he went without was as criminall intentionally as thos[e] that had them:[435] as put the case if an highway man should come to rob me and attempted it if I was to[o] strong and he could not must that be imputed to his honesty: they Carried the quaestion for it 133 against 111[436] – Nota this was very extraordinary to address to the King, and to return him thanks for his gracious answer and in so short a time to addres for the same thing. May 14[437] [*1701*]

The orders of the day were read and we were in a committee for the land tax[438] and in the midst of busines Sir Ed[*ward*] Seymour moved that Conyers should leave the Chaire that was 2d and done and the Speaker took the chaire and then Sir Ed[*ward*] Seymour moved that the mace should go into the court of requests and westminster hall[439] which was ordered for the members to attend then he moved to have a letter and a paper stiled a memoriall inclosed in it since printed and here to annexed[440] read and it was read accordingly: it was very reflecting and sharp it complained of our ill usage of the kentish men, and of our committing them contrary to law that we tooke a power over our fellow subjects more then we had a right to that the king could not keep[441] the assasinators in pri[son] but by act of parliament:[442] that we were immorall atheists and debauched persons: that tho there was no na[me] to it that they were 200000 that there name was legion[443] that tho they pet[*it*]ioned they Could command that we ought to pay the just debts of the nation: that we were unjest in punishing some for briber[y] and excusing others: that we should expell that scandall of Parliaments John How or [?oblige ?him ?to ?ask][444] the kings pardon upon

---

[435] See above, pp. 49–50, 70–1.

[436] 'May 14' erased. The result of the division if given as 134:111 in *CJ* xiii. 539.

[437] 'May 14 [*1701*]' boxed in MS.

[438] A committee of the whole House on the Land Tax Bill.

[439] i.e. the serjeant-at-arms, bearing the mace.

[440] 'since printed and here to annexed' interlined. The antiquary Abraham de la Pryme attributed the authorship of this motion to Jack Howe: *The Diary of Abraham de la Pryme* . . . (Surtees Society, 54, Durham, 1869), 243. The presentation of the memorial is discussed in James Sutherland, *Defoe* (London, 1937), 71. It is printed in *Somers's Tracts*, xi. 255–64.

[441] 'keep' supersedes a word erased and now illegible.

[442] The act of 1697 to continue the imprisonment of those accused of involvement in the Assassination Plot (8 & 9 Gul. III, c. 5).

[443] Mark 5: 9: 'My name is Legion, for we are many.'

[444] Bottom right-hand corner of folio missing.

his knees for calling him robber or they would come and demand [?what ?they ?had ?petitio]ned for in another manner: that we minded triffling things and neglected greater as mrs [?Stout's ?petition ?and ?a][445] great deale more: Mr How said he tooke it to be an honour to him to have these men thin[?k ?ill ?of] him that he would ask any the meanest mans pardon had he injured him he said something [?more] of cur dogs and of being affraid that we heard of petitions in the Citty[446] that we were not safe [?he ?would] adjourn into the country and that in Gloucestershire they would not think the worse of him th[?at ?–] should be put into better hands: Sir william Stricland said something reflecting upon how [?he ?–] in long foolish oration said we must not take notes in the house:[447] Sir Theo[*philus*] Oglethorpe De[?manded ?that Strick]land's words might be wrote down: Mr How said if any body said he said he was aff[?raid ?but ?the] Speaker interposed and said we must not have such heats and spoke to prevent it [?–] and then Shores talked a long time for adjour[*n*]ment of the petition in the citty[448] [? –

. . . [449]

fo. 71]

[?– ?petitio]n nothing materiall: Sir Ed[*ward*] Seymour said Gent[*lemen*] were mistaken that being called to westminster we could not adjourn without leave:[450] Sir Robert Clayton said he beleived Furguson wrote this letter[451]

---

[445] One of the complaints in the memorial was that while the House had heard 'trifling petitions' on elections it had put off a petition from the widow Stout of Hertford, concerning the murder of her daughter, a crime of which the young Whig Spencer Cowper, brother of William Cowper, MP, stood accused: [Ralph,] *Hist. Eng.*, ii. 952.

[446] The common council of London had appointed a committee to prepare a petition along the lines of the Kentish Petition, though this vote was subsequently rescinded: Gary Stuart De Krey, *A Fractured Society: The Politics of London in the First Age of Party 1688–1715* (London, 1985), 201–2.

[447] In 1588 Members had been admonished against publishing outside the House any notes of proceedings: *Lex Parliamentaria*, 283; W. R. McKay (ed.), *Observations, Rules and Orders of the House of Commons: An Early Procedural Collection* (House of Commons Library Document 17; London, 1989), 55. Cf. Thomas, *House of Commons in 18th Cent.*, 204–5.

[448] A speech by Shower on 14 May on the subject of the Kentish Petition is noted in Scottish RO, GD 406/1/6508, Earl of Orkney to Duke of Hamilton, 14 May 1701.

[449] Fo. 72 was originally left blank by Cocks, but subsequently he added 'I mistooke and turned over two Leaves in my writing of these journalls and here I have inserted things worth observing'. This admission is followed by: accounts of privy purse and civil list expenses. 1683, 1695; 'Neat produce of Civill list', 1700–1, presented 14 Mar. 1702. Remainder of fo. 72 and fo. 71 ᵛ blank.

[450] Presumably Seymour is suggesting that once Members had been summoned by the serjeant the House could not adjourn without leave from the sovereign, though such a ruling is not suggested by any standing order or manual of procedure.

[451] Robert Ferguson (d. 1714), for whom see *DNB*, and J. Ferguson, *Ferguson the Plotter* (Edinburgh 1877). Following a contemporary identification by John Oldmixon, the author is now generally assumed to have been Daniel Defoe: Sutherland, *Defoe*, 71–3; J. R. Moore, *Daniel Defoe Citizen of the Modern World* (Chicago, 1958), 105–6.

and that we did it too much honour to take notice of it if he had had it he would have dropt it in a place fit for it: and then they agreed to have an addres to the king to take care of the publick safety and to put the militia of london in better hand[s] Sir Xto[*pher*] musgrove opposed those words and so the words[452] were in order (to addres) to take care of the publick safety: and a Committee was appoynted to inquire into the encouragers of these things:[453] Mr Culpiper returned to the keeper and was committed to the gate house.[454] nota all wise men thought the poynt was carried to[o] high and that they had better have called these gent[*lemen*] in and have admonished them and so have dismissed them after a repremand for the using them so was making them too considerable like burning a booke that was foolish, and not worth the taking notice off [*sic*] which receives a value from the mark of infamy spreta exolescunt si Irasceris agnita videntur[455]

  May 15th [*1701*]

the land tax bill was partly read and nothing said or done worth observation mr Richard How[456] forced me to move to have a clause received to bring the receivours of the money for mending[457] Burlip hill to an account the Speaker told me what I before told mr How that it would not be received for that nothing but a necessity should make us offer at a tack so we waved it and it was agreed to be brought into the bill for the repair of Minhead[458] the Lords desired a conference about the bill for regulating the prisons[459] in which they would give their reasons for the amendments drawn by the judges: and indeed there were amendments for nothing but the preamble of our bill was left: and the amendments were unjust and impracticable: Nota the judges spoyled our bill for fear they should lose their new years gifts of 200 li. from the Keepers of the Kings bench and Fleet and the bill they had drawn would

---

[452] 'ran' erased.

[453] In fact, to prepare an address to lay before the King 'the endeavours of several ill-disposed persons to raise tumults and sedition', and to request that he would 'provide for the public peace and security'. Cocks was included in the committee, of which the first Member to be named was Jack Howe: *CJ* xiii. 540.

[454] 'to the gate house' interlined; 'May 15th' erased. The serjeant had reported Colepeper's surrender, whereupon the House ordered that the prisoner be conveyed to the gatehouse: ibid.

[455] Tacitus, *Annals*, 4. 34. 5: 'namque spreta exolescunt: si ira scare, adgnita videntur'.

[456] Howe sat for Wiltshire, but owned a Gloucestershire estate.   [457] 'move' erased.

[458] The bill for the repair of Minehead harbour was reported on 16 May: *CJ* xiii. 544. Cocks had not been named to the 2nd-reading committee: ibid. 517. In its final form, as 12 & 13 Gul. III, c. 9, this measure included provisions (ss. xiv–xvi) to make the Gloucestershire justices responsible for administering the tolls levelled on the road from Birdlip to Gloucester, thus amending the Birdlip Turnpike Act of 1698 (9 & 10 Gul. III, c. 18): *Statutes of the Realm*, vii. 647.

[459] The King's Bench and the Fleet.

have been more advantageous then 500 li. per annum for licences for the prisonners to go out in case of sickness

May 16th [*1701*][460]

[(]Nota I forgot to insert may the 14th [*1701*] that after the foolish heats between the two warm gent[*lemen*] Mr How and Sir w[*illia*]m Stricland mr mr [*sic*] How went out of the house and Sir Ed[*ward*] Seymour moved that he might be sent for in again he said the king gave us [l]iberty of speech but that we used that liberty sometimes to[*o*] much which occasioned heats and warm words the quarrell is not worth writing mr How said somthing of our not being safe or fearing the mob and removing to Glo[*u*]c[*este*]rshire wher [th]e people would not think ill of him for his words and that the petitioners were no more to be regarded then barking [c]ur dogs Sir w[*illia*]m Stricland stood up Palms his father [-*in*-] law[461] beckoned with his hand often to have him sit still: but up he [ro]se and said some insignificant thing of Hows being affraid: and then How said he said no such thing and that it was a ly:[462] So before the adjournment upon Sir Ed[*ward*] Seymours motion who said they were both men of spirit and resentment and that ill consequences might ensue if they were not ordered to prosecute the quarrell no further How stood up first and complained of Sir w[*illia*]m Stricklands ill usage severall times and told a long wrong story of his grant and promised to prosecute the quarrel no further and so did Strickland[)][463]

May 16th [*1701*] private bill[*s*] were read and we added a clause for the better regulating of the moneys collected and to be collected for Burlip hill to the bill for repairing the harbour of minhead: we read the Lord Orfords reply to the articles of impeachment in which I thought he cleared all objections: then they were referred to the committee that drew up the articles: and then mr Thompson stood up and said it would reflect upon the justice of the house to have some punished and others as great criminalls esccape without notice

---

[460] 'May 16th [*1701*]' boxed in MS. [461] William Palmes, MP.

[462] L'Hermitage reported the exchange as follows: Howe 'voulu faire son apologie, et s'attirer comme la protection de la chambre contre les divers murmures qu'il sait qu'on forme contre lui; il dit, qu'il ne pouvoit plus y avoir de sûreté, puis qu' on excitoit le peuple contre les plus zélés défenseurs de la liberté de leur patrie. Le Sr. Strickland, qui prétendoit ne ceder rien en zèle, dit qui s'il y avoit des gens comme réprésentoit le Sr. Howe, il y en avoit d'autres qui étoient ingénieux à former les phantomes pour avoir le plaisir de les combattre, et à supposer des craintes et des alarmes quand il n'y en avoit point, et que des gens de ce caractère ne pouvoient passer que des poltrons, et que leur timidité rendoit méprisable, mais que les véritables défenseurs de la liberté n'avoient rien à craindre du peuple, parce qu'il en étoit le plus ferme appuy': BL Add. MS 17677 WW. fo. 264. Cf. [Ralph,] *Hist. Eng.*, ii. 953.

[463] Passage within brackets is boxed in MS.

and that therefore he impeached my Lord Jarsy:[464] Sir Ba[r]t[*holomew*] Shore
said to order to the last busines and then moved to proceed upon the
impeachment I mean the articles against my Lord Somers: my Lord Hartington said Mr Thompson was regular and that he ought to proceed the house
was in a great uproar some for Coll Thompsons motion some against it the
Speaker pulled [o]f[f] his hat which made silence[465] and he said the articles
against the Lord Somers were the order of the day and therefore we ought
regularly to proceed upon them this forced a consent: and it was done in order
to screen my Lord Jarsey: if it had been against any of the lords already
impeached it would have been regular enough, malice knows no rules nor
seasons: witnes the addres ordered to be[466] made the 2d time upon the rising
of the house to remove the impeached lords from the kings councill and
presenc for ever:[467] after the articles were read at the bar and brought up
the two former were complyed with which was for sealing a power with blanks
to be filled up and about the partition treaty:[468] the third article was for
passing of great grants and upon this the debate arose the next article was for
taking great grants to himself and this was debated tho not read: Sir B Shores
said this tended to the disherison of the king and to burthen the commons
with taxes and ought not to be done at any time especially in times of such
wants and expences: Sir Joseph Jekiell vindicated my Lord Chancell[*our*] and
said it never was a crime before and was alwais practiced by Lord Chancellours and Lord Treasurers and that had raised most of the great familyes of
England:[469] Sir Edward Seymour said Michaell delapoole was impeached for it
and quoted R[*ichard*] 2d[*'s*] reign:[470] Sir Jo[*seph*] Jekiell rose to speak again
and they cryed spoke spoke[471] but the Speaker quieted the house and he
proceeded Mr Boyle said this was never reckoned a fault before and that
the Lord Southhampton[472] from [*sic*] had great grants and it was never
esteemed a fault in him and that considering the great post this lord was in
and taken from it and made a lord he could not think but there ought to be
some recompence made him from the publick and that what he had done both

---

[464] Edward Villiers (*c*.1656–1711), 1st Earl of Jersey, ambassador to the United Provinces 1697–
8, to France 1698–9; Secretary of State 1699–1700; and jt.-plenipotentiary for the second Partition
Treaty. Poussin confirms that the author of the motion was Colonel Thompson: PRO 31/3/188/
66.   [465] See above, p. 101.
[466] 'ordered to be' interlined.   [467] See above, p. 94.
[468] The first article charged Somers with affixing the great seal to the first Partition Treaty
(1698), the second with affixing the seal to the commission for plenipotentiaries to negotiate the
treaty when the commissioners' names had been left blank: *CJ* xiii. 546–7.
[469] For Jekyll's role in assisting Somers's defence, see HMC, *Downshire MSS*, i. 803; and above,
pp. 77–8.   [470] See above, p. 51.   [471] See above, p. 118, n. 385.
[472] Thomas Wriothesley (1608–87), 2nd Earl of Southampton, Lord Treasurer 1660–d.

in passing of grants and in taking of grants to himself was allwais practiced as it did appear to him and that Honourable Gent[*leman*] meaning Seymour had done the same thing[473] Seymour reflected upon boyle as if he vindicated these things having a mind to follow such examples and said that Boyle knew nothing of these things himself and that he always spoke against it otherwais he had not been removed: Smith said that Seymours hand was to the passing of all the great grants[474] and reflected upon Jack How for saying formerly that he should not censure my Lord Chan[*cellor*] for having a moderate grant: Seymour said it was true that he had put his hand but had alwais spoke against it and said my Lord Chan[*cellor*] had rose to a great estate from a mean originall:[475] How said he was not formerly for censuring my Lord Chan[*cellor*] for a moderate grant if that had been all but that [h]e since found him guilty of severall crimes: I said Sir the Honourable gent[*leman*] near the Bar[476] mentions this lords originall now in the debate before us, I live in the neighbourhood near him I have known him as long as I have known any body in all the parts of his life[477] he has merited esteem from good men and been honoured and at last as he well merited he became honourable in the reign of King Charles he never addressed nor complyed in the reign of King James he behaved himself as became an Englishman he defended the church and the Bishops for nothing when others betrayed our libertyes and attacqued them for profit and preferment[478] and after this revolution he was deservedly made attourney Gen[*era*]ll and in great Esteem and in an honourable post of getting a great fortune without malice or envy he was taken from this place and made Lord keeper and afterwards lord Somers and chancellour in no way possible to encreas or advance his fortune but by the favour of his prince and since he had leaft his busines and dedicated himself wholly to the publick I cannot think it unreasonable that he should be provided for out of the publick I do not think any one is obliged to be a looser by serving the publick: Sir John Hawles said it was never a crime to take grants or to pas them and that it was the same thing no difference for that they both tended to the disherison of the crown and that many of the Lords enjoyed great estates got by those means and that it was very hard to punish it as[479] a crime before it was made and that if the lords were satisfyed that this was a crime he hoped that they would restore the estates they had owned their fathers had ill gotten: Sir Humphery

---

[473] See above, p. 51.   [474] As a Lord of the Treasury, 1691–4.

[475] See above, p. 90.   [476] Sir Edward Seymour, See above pp. 118–19.

[477] For Cocks's long-standing association with Somers, see above, p. xix.

[478] Somers had appeared as junior counsel for the defence at the trial of the Seven Bishops in 1688, when Sir Thomas Powys and Sir Bartholomew Shower among others had acted for the prosecution.   [479] 'to punish it as' had originally read as 'for punishing'.

Macworth said if we rejected this article it would prove of very dangerous consequence and that it would be the first time such an article was ever rejected: Roger mumpesson said there was an act in H[*enry*] the 8th time which commended the kings making of grants and said he had the statute in his hand[480] he spoke warmly and made the house merry Sir Xto[*pher*] musgrove said we had allowed this article in my Lord Orfords impeachment lately[481] and if we should deny it in this case it would seem very partiall: it was said in the debate that neville D[*uke*] of Bedford was degraded for [?want] of estate[482] that this lord had no necessity of being a lord and that it was better to have him degraded t[han ?en]riched by the publick much more was said but it was yeilded without a division

[*fo. 70ᵛ*]

May 17th [*1701*] this day after the private bills were read mr How moved to have the report made by Sir Hump[*hrey*] Mackworth received [?on] a project of the old company to pay the new off, and to have all the trade to themselves and to lend the money to the publick at five per cen[t][483] assoon [*sic*] as the report and proposall was read mr Hamond spoke for it in commendation of the old they they ought to have the thanks of the house for their proposall and in the condition we were that we ought to be good husbands and lessen our interest and pay of[*f*] our debts and to the proposall[484] my Lord Hartington agreed that we should be provident but just and that we ought with contempt to reject the Cla[*use*] Mr How began for it, talked of war what the mob: did: of the inconveniencys of tumults that the Citty would have the worst of it: that he was for war: that the old East India company were forced to bribe to have justic[485] that the new East india were the tooles of the late ministry that he did not know what he was for that he desired it might be waved and hoped that that noble lord would not insist of [*sic*] having any quaestion about it that might reflect: this so far qualified the debate that the proposall was given

---

[480] The act of 1535 concerning the clerks of the Signet (27 Hen. VIII, c. 11), a precedent cited later in the year in the pamphlet *Jus Regium: Or, the King's Right to Grant Forfeitures* (1701), a ministerial production which has been conjecturally ascribed to Somers himself: *Wm. III State Tracts*, ii. 744.   [481] Reported on 8 May: *CJ* xiii. 520.

[482] George Neville (1457–83), Duke of Bedford, degraded by Act of Parliament in 1477 after the attainder of his father and consequent forfeiture of the family estates.

[483] Mackworth reported from the committee to receive proposals for paying off the public debts and advancing the credit of the nation. The Old Company's proposal to assume responsibility for the loan to the Crown of £2,000,000 made by the New Company on its establishment in 1698, at the lower rate of interest of 5 per cent, is printed in *CJ* xiii. 551–2. See Horwitz, 'East India Trade, Politicians, and the Constitution', 15–16.

[484] Hammond had purchased some £500-worth of East India stock (presumably in the Old Company) in August of the preceding year: Baker and Baker, *Chandos*, 32.

[485] See above, pp. 65–7.

up[486] and then mr Smith moved to have a quaestion proposed to this purpose that we would maintain the credit of parliament: the Cunning K[487] [*sic*] Speaker would feighn have made us beleive that this was a new quaestion after the hour of 12:[488] then I 2ded Mr Smith and said sir I will not debate of war or peace that not being the subject before us but I must say this proposall has disturbed the generall quiet of the nation and some vote must be necessary to settle it I will not reflect it has been told you that the new Comp[a]ny are the tooles of the late ministry[489] and you have been told of the bribery of the old it is very plain that whatever Gent[*lemen*] do not like they presently call the tools of the late ministry I may say the old company are the tools of the present ministry[490] Gent[*lemen*] talk of their Joyning[491] if these companys these tooles were in one interest they would Like the sons ser[?v]ia to[o] hard for you[492] the reference to the committee was to consider to lessen the publick debts and to advance the credit of the nation:[493] it was just instructions to pay the debts [?bu]t so as we might advance credit this proposall violates an act of parliament[494] destroys credit and instead of paying the [d]ebts will increas them for nobody will trust us and I think we have need of a vote as was proposed by the Honourable Ge[nt*leman* o]ver the way[495] I therefore second the motion: the house partly called for a quaestion partly for the order of the day some said they would put a previous quaestion, all said if this quaestion was put and not carried it would be of fatall consequence to us all and the same for the previous quaestion: mr Attourney said there was no need of any quaestion it would appear by the vote[?s] that the proposall[496] was not received that our votes would be no strengthning to the security he was for the order of the day: S[ir] B Shores who often mimicks Jack How spoke to the commotions of the Citty[497] that it would light most severely upon them [?if] we could find our Land Sir Xto[*pher*] musgrove spoke against the quaestion

---

[486] Luttrell reported that, after several speeches on both sides, the Old Company's proposal 'was ordered to lie on the table, lest, if it should pass, it should destroy the public credit': *Brief Relation*, v. 51. [487] 'K' interlined.

[488] 'after the hour of 12' interlined. One o'clock was the deadline for any new motion: see above, p. 109, n. 318. [489] 'I may' erased.

[490] The Whig John Dolben observed that in Parliament the Old Company was 'publicly owned and protected by the Tory interest'; PRO C110/28 (Pitt MSS), Dolben to Thomas Pitt, 19 July 1701.

[491] Negotiations in fact began during the summer: Horwitz, 'East India Trade, Politicians, and the Constitution', 17.

[492] The analogy is presumably to the fate of the King of Rome, Servius Tullius, murdered by his son-in-law Tarquinius Superbus, at the alleged instigation of his own daughter Tullia, after Servius had allowed her to take Tarquinius, her sister's widower, as her second husband: Livy, *Ab Urbe Condita*, 1. 45–7. [493] 'of the nation' interlined.

[494] That of 1698 establishing the New East India Company (9 Gul. III, c. 44).

[495] i.e. Smith. [496] Original word erased and now illegible. [497] See above, pp. 127, 132.

but said there was no withdrawing it but that some quaestion must be, or that it must ly upon the table[498] he spoke against the quaestion proposed and talked artificially and discouraged spending thei[r] time in discoursing of what was said or done without doors, then mr Cooper said he did not intend to speak to th[e] debate but that he was of mr attourneys opinion that there was no need of the quaestion: so that we wen[?t] u[p]on the order of the day by consent after we had spent two houres to know how we should part with a waved quaestion before that[499] Sir Richard Onslow said that when K[*ing*] James went off the revenue of the crown was 2 millio[ns][500] and if we had kept that up and had raised two millions more upon land we might yearly have maintained the charge of the natio[n] without running into such great debts and deficiencyes as we did upon funds: then we went into the land tax and the house [t]hinned to that degree as usually they do when the committee of the whole house for the land tax that there was scarce an house May 19th 1701 the first thing of moment was the reading of the impeachment Engrossed against the lord Summers and there is never any dispute upon or after the reading then because they have been debated before:[501] it was moved by Sir [B]: Shores to have an instruction given to mr Harcourt to desire that he might be kept to baile[502] and the reason was give[n] by him that tho this lord had a stake in the hedge and there was no danger of his absenting himself, yet there were forreigner[s c]oncerned and might be impeached and they might pack up their fortunes and withdraw from justice and besides it was what we have had done sometimes and we ought not to lose our rights for want of Claim and usage and [t]hat the same was done in the case of my Lord Orford lately:[503] and that it could be no prejudice nor delay to our busines for that if the Lords did not do it we needed not insist upon it: the Speaker told us that in some cas[es] this had been done in others omitted: it was agreed that in cases of High treason where they have been imp[eac]hed a commitment has been insisted on but that after the articles were carried up it was never deny[ed] When this was setled by the house and mr Harcourt had his impeachments to go to the lords some called for the order of the day and

---

[498] 'or that it must ly upon the table' interlined.

[499] 'May 20th 1701' erased, and 'before that' inserted.

[500] A figure almost certainly derived from the computation presented to the Commons on 1 Mar. 1699, which, taking an average of the yield of royal revenues from 1685 to 1688, would have produced a total of just over £1,900,000: *CJ* x. 37–8.

[501] In fact, according to the *Journals*, some amendments were proposed and accepted: *CJ* xiii. 553.   [502] i.e. to 'give sufficient security': ibid.

[503] When on 9 May the articles against Orford had been taken up to the Lords, the bearer, Robert Byerley, MP, had been ordered to demand that Orford 'do give sufficient security to abide the judgement of the House of Lords': ibid. 523.

then my Lord Hartingdon stood up and mr Thompson the Lord Hartington to desire the time being Lapsed for the Election of Totnes it being a very undue election and corrupt practices a[?nd] so it was but reasonable to have a day appoynted for the hearing[504] and that he did not move this upon hearsay only but that as he was coming into the house the letters the originall letters of Sir Edward Seymour and Mr Coulson were put into his hands by one — [sic][505] at the door who would prove them Sir Edward Seymour desired this election m[ig]ht be heard in its due time and not upon this motion for that would be a reflection upon him as if he had not desird [t]o have the Totnes election come on out of apprehension of this matter and that it was brought on in order to ex[p]ose him he desired that the letter might be read and there was a great disorder some hoping some fearing and [s]ome saying that it was an ill president to have a man charged in the house with his own letter what never [d]id before appear upon our books Sir Edward Seymour desired he might see the letter before it was read to see if [it] was his own hand he owned it and the letter was read and no great matter in it so the party rejoyced and then the [h]ouse were uneasye to come at the order of the day which was to deliver petitions in relation to Ireland and the lett[ers] were ordered to be given to the Chairman of the committee to be kept as evidence when the Totnes cause was to be heard [b]ut one word drew on another my Lord Hartingdon said mr Coulsons letter would explain Sir Ed[ward] Seymours so that was read Seymours spoke of an organ to be given to totne[s][506] Coulsons talked of a the [sic] dissolution of the Parliament and of perswading them to be recon-Ciled to Sir Ed[ward] Seymour: and perswading them to bring in Frank Gwin

[504] On 10 Apr. two related complaints had been made to the House: first, of a breach of privilege committed against Sir Edward Seymour by the arrest of one of his servants, in an action for *scandalum magnatum* involving one of the principals on the opposing side in the Totnes election, in which Seymour, recorder of the borough, had been actively engaged on behalf of the Tory candidates, Thomas Coulson and Francis Gwyn; secondly, and by way of response, allegations of 'threats and indirect practices' in that election. The two complaints had each been referred to the committee of privileges and elections. On 19 May the committee was discharged of its responsibility to hear both causes, but a further complaint was then entered by the defendant in the privilege case, James Buckley, concerning the conduct of Seymour and Coulson before the election, in sending letters to the corporation in support of Gwyn, which had included various improper promises of benefactions. *CJ* xii. 480, 553. For Seymour's strong interest in this constituency, see HMC, *3rd Report*, App. 349; HMC, *Portland MSS*, iv. 270; Devon RO, Exeter diocesan MSS, Bishop Trelawny to 'Mr Cook', 18 Jan. [1701] (a reference I owe to Professor H. G. Horwitz); and for Buckley, mayor of Totnes in 1693–4, see Edward Windeatt, 'Totnes: Its Mayors and Mayoralties: Part II', *Transactions of the Devonshire Association*, 33 (1901), 546–7.

[505] James Buckley.

[506] Reference was made to Seymour's letter in a Whig squib published prior to the next general election, in November, where it was said that he had 'promised a pair of organs to the town of Totnes': *A List of One Unanimous Club of Members of the Late Parliament . . . that Met at the Vine-Tavern in Long Acre* (London, 1701), 2.

and promising them to [d]o the town a Kindnes in relation to the buing mills
that did incommode them: there were other[507] perswading practices and
prom[is]es that would have not[508] been bribery in Sir Ed[*ward*] Seymour
which would in Shepperd[509] How moved and talked too foolishly too[510]
loose[?ly ?d]own, viz[511] to commit . . .[512] to the serjeant[513] for reflecting
upon a gent[*leman*] that had so lately had the thanks of the hou[se f]or
detecting bribery at his own cost and charge[514] he said this was a good
occasion to renew our thanks to him and [?much] more of such empty stuff
he said his taylour told him of it a fortnight ago. this was 2ded and thirded
and not strongly opposed so that the man was committed and I do beleive had
the busines been heard by imparti[al j]udges the thing had not went of[f] so
easily for Jack How said the fellow in some discourses had said he would
apply himself to mr Shepperd in the tower[515] this he said to shew the malice of
the fellow but to me it shewed the merits of the caus for I could not conceive it
that a man could be so si[*m*]p̄le to tell an[?y] unfortunate[516] man in prison a
story that was not so plain that it could maintain its own credit for what
assistance Could mr Shepperd give it nothing but disparagement and that
every one must know and then we went upon the order of the day which was to
receive petitions from those that thoug[ht] they were injured in Ireland by the
late act of Parliament these petitions were by an order of a former day to be
received and referred to the Com[*mi*]s[*sione*]rs in England to report their
thoughts upon them to us:[517] so the petitions were received and the title
read and so another till we adjourned[518] memorandum this day Mr Dyot
moved to have the 29th of May observed by the house and that we should
appoynt a sermon the Speaker shooke his head and hand at him but he insisted

---

[507] Originally 'this was the'.   [508] 'not' interlined.

[509] Seymour had been the prime mover behind earlier inquiries into the corrupt electoral
campaigning of Samuel Shepheard, sen.: see above, pp. 64–8. According to Abraham de la
Pryme, Lord Hartington told Seymour to his face in the House of Commons that 'he was as
guilty as any of bribery': *Diary of Abraham de la Pryme*, 243. Seymour's hypocrisy in this respect
was a theme of subsequent Whig propaganda: e.g. *Wm. III State Tracts*, iii. 260; Lord *et al.* (edd.),
Poems on Affairs of State, vi. 325.

[510] 'too' interlined.   [511] 'viz' interlined.   [512] James Buckley.

[513] Originally 'gatehouse'.

[514] On 19 Mar. Seymour had received the thanks of the house for his 'great services' in
'detecting the bribery and corruption . . . practised at elections': *CJ* xiii. 415.

[515] Samuel Shepheard, sen., for whom see above, p. 65, n. 28.   [516] Originally 'poor'.

[517] On 7 May the House had appointed the 13th as the day to receive all petitions concerning
Irish forfeitures, but then had adjourned to the 19th: *CJ* xiii, 517, 539. The three trustees,
appointed under the Land Tax and Irish Forfeitures Resumption Act of 1700 (11 Gul. III, c. 2),
who had come over to England were Francis Annesley, Sir Henry Sheres, and John Trenchard: PRO
Northern Ireland, D. 1854/2/20 (Annesley MSS), entry-book of petitions, 1701–4.

[518] 'May 20st [*sic*]' erased.

that [th]e day was appoynted by act of parliament[519] but nobody seconded
him and it past as a rediculous m[?otion ?:] M[?–

fo. 70]

[N]ota that to shew the hardnes of James Bucles case[520] the Gent[*lemen*] that
wrote the letters owned their hands owned the letters and there was nothing
proved upon or against Bucle only what was suggested: but this is a president I
hope too bad to be followed: May 20th 1701[521] ([*sic*] the house went into a
Committee upon mrs Boxes bill[522] the CounCill for mrs Box argued her
innocence and that shee permitted sentence of divorce to pass against her
becaus shee lived uncomfortably with him and that shee was willing to be
divorced and therefore made no opposition that they had agreed to terms
which were that[523] Mr Box should pay her forty shillings by the week till the
divorce was perfected by act of Parliament and that mr Box should refund to
her 3000 li.:[524] they proved the sentence in the spirituall court[525] and
produced evidence to prove her in bed with one . . .[526] and also they offered
to prove more Mr Chase was in the Chair[527] and went thro the bill they for mr
Box[528] answered the evidence against him by proving the adultery and that
they never made any agreement for that they were advised against that, by the
Council who told them it might prejudice the bill but that they were willing to
give that or anything rather then to Keep such a vile creature[529] but that they
would submit all to the parliament and that 3000 li. was in the bill but altered

[519] The act of 1660 (12 Car. II, c. 14) for a perpetual thanksgiving on 29 May, Restoration Day,
had appointed church services but no commemoration sermons.

[520] James Buckley, for whom see above, p. 135, n. 504.   [521] 'May 20th 1701' boxed in MS.

[522] The bill to confirm the dissolution of the marriage of Ralph Box, Grocer and 'druggist', of
St Mary Colechurch, London, and his wife Elizabeth. See HMC, *House of Lords MSS*, NS iv. 175–
7; Luttrell, *Brief Relation*, iv. 709; and Lambeth Palace Lib., Court of Arches records, B13/107/3.

[523] 'they' erased.

[524] The bill as originally presented to the Lords had provided for a payment of £3,000 to Mrs
Box in part-compensation of the £4,000 which had been her marriage portion: HMC, *House of
Lords MSS*, NS iv. 176–7.

[525] Box had secured a sentence in the Court of Arches on 15 Feb. 1701: Lambeth Palace Lib., Ct.
of Arches recs., B13/107/2.

[526] The principal (among several) co-respondents was one Henry Wells 'of Hampshire', against
whom Box had obtained a verdict for crim. con. in Kings Bench in 1700: HMC, *House of Lords
MSS*, NS i. 175–7; Luttrell, *Brief Relation*, iv. 709; *The Case of Ralph Box, Citizen of London* . . .
[London 1701], He was probably the Henry Wells of Bambridge, Hants, who died in 1735: John
Hutchins, *The History and Antiquities of the County of Dorset* . . . (4 vols.; Westminster, 1861–
70), i. 668.

[527] James Chase was Ralph Box's brother-in-law, having married Box's sister in 1677: J. L.
Chester (ed.), *The Marriage, Baptismal and Burial Registers of the* . . . *Abbey of St Peter,
Westminster* (Harleian Soc. 10; London, 1876), 15.

[528] His counsel, including James Sloane, MP: HMC, *House of Lords MSS*, NS iv. 475.

[529] 'creature' interlined. See below, p. 155.

by the Lords who thought adultery should not receive such incouragement this
was ordered to be reported and then the Speaker tooke the chair and Mr
Thompson moved to have the Lord Jarsey impeached for that it would shew a
great deale of partiality in the hous to impeach some and not those that were
cheifly concerned as it did appear my Lord was by the setting his hand to the
treaty:[530] nobody 2ded Thompson for none of those that were against
impeaching the other lords could with any Confidence do it, and none of
the others would: mr Paget said his father was an Embassadour abroad[531] and
that he thought he was obliged to consent to and to put his hand to what he
was ordered by his prince and very prettily upon that subject so they called for
the order of the day: which was the committee of the whole house for the land
tax:[532] mr Coniers took the Chaire there was a small debate about a clause to
be tacked for hindering the com[mi]s[sione]rs of the customs from being
members of Parliament:[533] Boyle said the hard passage the last tack had
and the unwillingnes the Lords shewed to it[534] should in these times of
danger shew [u]s the[535] inconveniency of pressing it: Shores offered it Boles
told Boyle how he was altered by being a lord of the Treasury and Chancellour
of the exchecquer:[536] Boyle said jestingly he thanked that gent[leman] for his
advice the clause was put and carryed in the Committee then there was a
clause offered to excuse vickars of small vicaridges from being [r]ated to the
land tax the committee divided about bringing it up and it was by the division
brought up: then the Materiall Blank was filled with 40 li. per añ: the
arguments for it were the incouragement for learning the better Education
of the clergy the inconsiderablenes of the Charge to the Parish: the arguments
against it was [sic] the envy it would make them the hardnes of men of small
fortunes to pay for them: the difficulties it would make in collecting and rating
the taxes and would occasion deficiencys: Mr How said he was against
excusing them for another reason which was not given[537] for he was satisfyed
the reason that made so many dissenters was they paying of Tyth and that they
had no other reason for absenting themselves and that this thing alone had

[530] See above, pp. 129–30.
[531] William, 7th Lord Paget (1637–1713), ambassador to Vienna 1689–92, and to Constantinople
1692–1702.
[532] i.e. on the Land Tax Bill.
[533] Eventually embodied into the resultant act as 12 & 13 Gul. III, c. 10 s. lxxxvii.
[534] The clauses, to resume the Irish forfeitures, tacked to the Land Tax Act of 1700, for the
passage of which see Horwitz, *Parliament, Policy and Politics*, 266–8.
[535] Originally 'that'.
[536] For Boyle's transition from Country party stalwart to courtier, see Horwitz, *Parliament,
Policy and Politics*, 125, 144, 146, 150, 166, 179, 226, 229, 252, 258, 261, 282, 284.
[537] 'which was not given' interlined.

made them such stiff disenters that they would hardly receive the sacrament according to the usage of the Church of England for a place and that the excusing the parsons and vicars from taxes would occasion more ill blood and make more dissenters since the parishioners must pay it the quaestion was put ([*sic*] the ays and the noes each 75 so that mr Coniers vote determined it[538] and amongst those that voted for the claus was mr John How who spoke against it: I could not forbear telling him that he had the advantage of me for he might tell the free holders that he spoke against the clause and might tell the clergye that he voted for it May 21 [1701][539] this day the Lords sent to hasten the reply to my Lord Orfords impeachment after the masters in chancery[540] had made their three bows and were departed Sir Ed[*ward*] Seymour said when he was impeached his impeachment lay one month and desired the Speaker to have it read the Speaker waved it for he knew it lay but 2 days:[541] the answer was they would return an answer by messengers of their own: then we came into the Committee of ways and means and mr How began and it was to me very remarkable to see a man that had broke thro all the rules of justice and morall honesty in order to impeach and sacrifice the old ministry to the new so abandon the new as to break all their measures and sacrifice those he had so lately exalted and in whose interest he was: this must be that men are in somethings strictly honest in others latitudinarians he spoke from the bar with a low voyce and complained [*of*] his lungs[542] and repeated severall arguments used in the late debate, he spoke long with little spirit he said he beleived some were altered their reasons he knew not but he was still the same and concluded for the 10000 li. [o]ut of the civill list[543] next to him Sir Ed[*ward*] Seymour that he was for taking the 10000 li. but in another method, that he had [*a*] proposall not to give one penny more upon land nor to rays money by excises which was the only ways left that what we were to rais this year with the paying of the Exchecquer bills was 2 million four

---

[538] The chairman's casting vote is defined in McKay (ed.), *Observations, Rules and Orders*, 136.

[539] 'May 21 [1701]' boxed in MS.

[540] Thomas Gery (*c*.1663–1727), formerly MP for Coventry, and later to resume his seat for the borough; and Sir Robert Legard (*c*.1633–1721).

[541] Seymour's case, in 1679–80, did not, strictly speaking, furnish an appropriate precedent. He may himself have been thinking here of the month that had elapsed between the presentation of the articles against him to the Commons and their communication to the Lords; Harley of the three days between the Lords' receipt of the articles and their return to the Commons of Seymour's answer. *CJ* ix. 658, 684, 692.   [542] See above, p. 71.

[543] See above, pp. 109–12; a reference to the resolution of ways and means, reported on 5 May 1701, for a bill to repeal part of the Civil List Act of 1698, and appropriate to 'the use of the public' £100,000 of the sum allowed for the civil list.

hundred thousand pound[544] so that we wanted a million that the severall small expiring branches of the revenue would produce 34000 li. so that there was still 700000 li.: that he hoped gent[*lemen*] would pardon if they did not approve of what he proposed that instead of taking 100000 li. from the king the king should have all those funds that were established for the civill list and pay us weekly 3000 li. that we should mortgage that for 3 or four years and upon that security raise 700000 li.[545] and that then we had done all and might go home: Mr Lownds in other words explained this and inforced it: Mr How answered and spoke many times I seconded him and spoke twice my lord Hartington[546] Mr Hervy of Berry Sir Godfery Copley and Sir Rich[*ard*] Onslow and others spoke against our arguments were that this was given for purposes which now were not as the d[*uke*] of Glou[*cester*] King James etc.:[547] that we would not mortgage nor anticipate our revenue but make each year bear its own charge that the King and people were in the same interest and ought to help each other on all occasions that we designed to take 10000 li. from the crown and that by this proposall the crown would get above 100000: Speaker Harley Sir Xto[*pher*] muggrove [*sic*] Mr Bruges Mr Harcourt Lord Coningsbee and many others spoke for it their arguments as to Bruges and Hartcourt were that they would not have been for taking it at first but that they thought there would have been no occasion for a land tax or excises if this had been but now that must be they would not be for this:[548] we replyed that we never pretended to take this for one year only or that it would prevent land taxes but that we thought unles we saved what we could and what might be saved the people would never be contented to pay their taxes: Sir Xto[*pher*] musgrove said that he was for a certain good bargain that if there were wars which were likely that then the king would be a looser that he was for a certainty when it might be had: to this we answered that wee were not for doing anything hard upon the king nor would we make a bad bargain for the country we were resolved the king should want nothing we were resolved to demonstrate our Zeale for his service by providing him with what was

[544] A total presumably reached through adding together the sums stated in the various resolutions of the committee of supply, not all of which are detailed in the *Journals*: *CJ* xiii. 357, 360, 425, 467, 501.

[545] In L'Hermitage's opinion this proposal of Seymour's was designed by the Tories to reverse the previous vote on the retrenchment of the civil list: BL Add. MS 176677 WW, fo. 267.

[546] Poussin confirms that Hartington was one of the most vehement opponents of any move to go back on the previous decision to retrench the civil list: PRO 31/3/188/70.

[547] This and some of the succeeding arguments had been advanced in earlier debates: see above, pp. 107–12.

[548] James Lowther's account claimed that Seymour's proposal was intended in particular to 'save the 4th shilling in the pound on land': Cumbria RO (Carlisle), D/Lons/W, James to Sir John Lowther, 21 May 1701.

necessary and more: indeed all those that had discovered their change their [n]ew principles did argue but aukwardly but at last the quaestion was to be put and Mr Coniers had two upon his book the one the first[549] that we should take 100000 li. out of the civill list: the other other [*sic*] that the king should pay us 3000 li. per week as Seymour proposed we debated an hour which quaestion we should have the first quaestion Mr Coniers had taken we insisted upon as the right quaestion as having leave from the house to proceed upon it: viz[550] to alter an act of parliament[551] in that case and that the other altered the sence and meaning of the whole act but that they had no leave so to do this was true: but that they urged that what they tooke was the 100000 li. and the surplusage which was not setled by act of Parliament but in this we had the better for they could not tell what the surplusage would come to:[552] both partyes were eager for the quaestion they insisted also that Sir Ed[*ward*] Seymour proposed and that Lowns 2d it then Sir Hum[*phrey*] Mackworth proposed that the King should give us 4000 li. per week: this they seemed not fond of and we would not accept of: so at last mr Coniers gave it that Seymour moved first and that Lowns 2d then we fearing how this would go framed these additiona[l] words that after the 3000 per week the King should have 600000 per an: and the rest to [b]e appr[opr]iated to the use of the publick: nobody spoke against these words but lowns nobo[dy ?spoke ?to] the quaestion but it was put and agreed to[553]

[*fo. 69ᵛ*]

May 22d [*1701*] after the private bills were read the house to dissolved [*sic*] itself into a committee of the whole house to consider of the Lady[e] Angleseys bill which came ingrossed from the Lords to cause a seperation between my Lord Anglesey and Catherine Countes of Anglesey (king Jameses daughter by my lady Dorchester) till she should signify before so many of the privy Councill that shee was willing to cohabite with him again: this was to be under her hand:[554] they proved that my Lord had used her barbarously as

---

[549] 'the first' interlined.   [550] 'viz' interlined.   [551] The Civil List Act.

[552] In the preceding year it had amounted to over £80,000: *CJ* xiii. 421.

[553] L'Hermitage observed that some Whig Members, suspecting trickery from Seymour, adapted his scheme by insisting that the surplus of the civil list revenue, above and beyond the sum of £600,000, should be applied to the public debts (BL Add. MS 17677 WW, fo. 268). Passage of the resolution, which provided first for the sum of £3,000 per week to be taken from the revenue, and then for the appropriation of the surplus, is confirmed in Luttrell, *Brief Relation*, v. 52.

[554] See above, p. 109 and for details of the case, HMC, *House of Lords MSS*, NS iv. 149–51, 188–205; *A Letter from a Peer to a Member of the House of Commons, about the Countess of Anglesey's Bill* [1701]; and *A Vindication of the Earl of Anglesey* [1701]. The reconciliation was to be signed before two witnesses and delivered into a court of record or to the Lord Chancellor or Lord Keeper: HMC, *House of Lords MSS*, NS iv. 205.

before she was brought to bed Locked her up by her self in a cold rome: beat and pinched her at that rate that he was ashamed to have her smock changed when she lay inn by candle light, becaus the widwife [*sic*][555] and those that waited should not be witnes of the ill usage shee had Met with by seeing the black and blew spots he had made in her arms: the wifive [*sic*][556] and the servants gave an account of the Crueltyes and barbaritys he used towards her after she was brought to bed as the forcing her to shift her selfe without having the cloaths ayred and that he forced her to rise in four days time and to walk in the Cold in short it was evident that he had a mind to destroy her and kill her in such a manner that the law might not take hold of him that he might be rid of her without the danger of being hanged for her: the councill for my Lord[557] urged that my Lord would wave his priviledge and that the law in Doctors Commons in the spirituall courts were open and that we should not break in uppon the constitution but in cases of necessity and that since my Lord had waved his priviledge there was not necessity so that they hoped the house would not medle in the matter: the Councill of the other side[558] said my Lord might resume his priviledge when he pleased and the barbarous usage my lady had met with might make her reasonably beleive if shee ever was again under his power shee should be destroyed the house was of the same opinion so they easily went through the bill[559] after the councill were ordered to withdraw and the bill was ordered to be reported: then we went into a committee of the whole house to consider of the bill to appoynt Com[*mi*]s[*sione*]rs to state the accounts and so we adjourned May 23d 1[*701*][560]

Sir B Shores who was Chairman of the committee to draw a reply to my Lord Orfords answer[561] discoursed about presidents that they had searched them all, that sometimes the replication was by word of Mouth which became matter of record when it was entred in the Lords Journalls and sometimes in writing in paper: the Speaker stood uncovered[562] and told us that in my

---

[555] Mrs Elizabeth Cotton, a midwife from London engaged to attend the Countess, and in the case a witness on the Countess's behalf: HMC, *House of Lords MSS*, NS iv. 194; *A Letter from a Peer . . .*, 8.   [556] Midwife.

[557] James Sloane, MP, and the civilians John Ayliffe (1676–1732), William King (1663–1712), and William Oldys (1636–1708): HMC, *House of Lords MSS*, NS iv. 190–201. Sloane seems to have been the family lawyer: HMC, *Rutland MSS*, ii. 170.

[558] The barristers John Beresford (*c.*1668–1705), and Constantine Phipps (1656–1723), and the civilians John Cooke (1666–1710), and Stephen Waller (*c.*1655–1707): HMC *House of Lords MSS*, NS iv. 190–201.

[559] According to one report, there were 'not . . . above two against it': Cheshire RO DCH/L28 (Cholmondeley of Cholmondeley MSS), Robert Critchley to William Adams, 22 May 1701.

[560] 'May 23rd 1[*701*]' boxed in MS.

[561] Originally appointed to prepare the articles of impeachment.   [562] See above, p.101.

Lord Staffords tryall everything was adjusted but that all those proceedings were raced and lost[563] except private mens[564] books that the replication was suddenly demanded in 48 hours time which was not very usuall: that the reply ought to bee in paper and then ingrossed: Sir Ed[*ward*] Seymour sais the lords have used us in an extraordinary manner: by saying it was hard to impeach the Lords and when they had answered not to reply to their answer: Somebody I think Shores said that this was appealing to the people for that since what came from the lords by way of message was entred upon our journall and sent abroad in our v[otes][565] what the lords said was made publick and so should our answer to[o]: The replication was that the house will be ready to prove the same, and the w[ord] house was altered and commons incerted in the place thereof as being a more parliamentary word: at such convenient time as shall be appoyn[t]ed here was a litle debate they said the word appoynt Lodged to[o] much power in the Lords and then it was moved that after the word appoynted These words and agreed should be added but then upon debate they said time convenient signifyed all that, and some were for leaving out the word appoynted but at last it remained without any other alteration:[566] then Sir B Shores Moved to have power given to the Committee to send for persons papers and records in order to make use of them of the same in the most private manner imaginable at the tryall[567] he moved again that the committee may have a sollicitor and that they should not pay for stā[*m*]ping the copyes of the records they should have occasion to use and that they had occasion to examine Mr Shepperd in relation to a bargain drove between some lords and the french lustring merchants which occasioned them to confes and submit upon the account that the said Lords had agreed and promised them that upon those terms their fine should be the easier that they were silly wretches and would confes but were frighted with the rough ill usage they met with but they

---

[563] 'and lost' interlined. William Howard (1612–80), 1st Viscount Stafford, had been impeached by the Commons on 5 Dec. 1678, when a committee was appointed to draw up the articles, but no further action had been taken in that Parliament. Proceedings were revived two years later, on 10 Nov. 1680, and carried through to Stafford's conviction and execution. *CJ* ix. 553, 650–87 *passim*: *LJ* xiii, 404, 662–706 *passim*. [564] 'mens' interlined.

[565] The Lords' message on 21 May to remind the Commons that no answer had yet been made to Orford's replication: *CJ* xiii. 559.

[566] 'At such convenient time as shall be appointed for the purpose': *CJ* xiii. 562.

[567] According to the *Journals*, Shower reported that he had been directed by the committee to move 'that they may have power to send for persons, papers, and records, that shall be thought necessary to be used at the trial of the said Earl, and to proceed in the most speedy and secret way they can for the advantage of the prosecution': a motion to which the House agreed (ibid.).

beleived Mr Shepperd drove the bargain and that he might do service:[568] mr
How said there were words that fell from Shepperd in answer to what he said
that moved him to beleive that Shepperd would discover: the Speaker told
them they had no occasion to have a Committee for that purpose but that they
might delegate any 3 or 4 of the committee to go to the tower to him:[569] then
upon some motion it was ordered that mr Shepperd should be asked if any
member had been with him to prepare him before hand[570] Nota this was all
done with an intent only to throw dirt, for they well knew there never had
been any such practices that Shepperd knew nothing and that if he had known
he would discover Nothing he did Know: then Bierly[571] moved to have an
instruction to the committee to inspect presidents in relation to the Lords
messages: and then Sir R Davers[572] reported the Countes of Angleseys bill and
that was immediately read[573] and then Conier[s] reported the resolution of the
committee viz that out of the funds established for the civill list there should
be 3000 li. per week paid for the use of the Publick that the king should have
600000 out of them and the overplus to be g[sic] appropriated to the use of the
public[k] Scobell began that what a good bargain we should have that he
thought it might come to 3500 that it would save 1s in the pound mor[e][574]
that the revenue would be better managed more improved when it was
managed for themselves: to this I answered I desired no good bargain that
what they called a good bargain for us they meant an hard bargain for the
King that I was for a certainty to have the Ki[ng] have six 100d Thousand
pound per annum certain and we to have the new overplus that I was of
opinion that our businesses were not managed at that ra[?te] that I thought
the King loved us and had such a regard for the publick good that it would be
managed as well for us as for himsel[f] Sir Thomas Duvall said tho the
Customs in case of war might lessen yet in any time the excise would rise
so that it would advan[ce] 150000 more so that he was for allowing the King
11500 li. per week and we to have the overplus: Mr J How who used to
excl[?aim] against the great revenues of the king that they enabled him to raise

---

[568] The smuggling of French lustrings (a type of silk manufactured principally at Lyons) had
been investigated by the Commons in 1698 at the behest of the recently constituted Royal Lustring
Company, after which an act had been passed (9 & 10 Gul. III, c. 43) to confirm the company's
charter and extend its monopoly: *CSP Dom.* 1700–2, p. 552; *CJ* xii, 210–35, 241; Cecil T. Carr
(ed.), *Select Charters of Trading Companies* . . . (Selden Soc. 28; London, 1913), pp. cxi–cxiii,
231–4.

[569] It was ordered that the committee have the power to send some of their number to examine
Shepheard in the Tower.   [570] Not recorded in *CJ* xiii. 562.

[571] A member of the committee: *CJ* xiii. 491.   [572] 'reported that the E' erased.

[573] It was read for the 3rd time and passed: *CJ* xiii. 562.

[574] On the land tax, see above, p. 140, n. 548.

an army if he pleased to ruine our liberties and it would be a president for future kings and that if we had not good laws under good Kings we could not expect them under bad and that it would hardly be said to the next king that he was not so good as king w[*illia*]m and therefore must not Expect it:[575] now he began in a long Canterbury story incoherent that he heard it was said he was so great a jacobite that they tosted his health in France that that was all the account we had of the negotiation that he was allways against the civill list as not liking the unjust and unusuall[576] way it was obtained, that he was not for lessening the kings incomb and that now he had confounded that project he was as willing as any one to help to maintain the Kings grandeur that he was against the latter part of the quaestion and never liked it that he was for having the king have the surplusage: Sir Robert Claiton spoke against mor[t]gaging before hand that it was a practice that had brought us into all these inconveniencyes Mr Bugnell exclaimed against the man[a]gement of the revenue by two many offices he had a paper in his hand and in a long winded speech he amongst other things said the excise would raise a great sum more then it did Sir Edward Seymour was up before Bucknell but sate down to let Bucnell speak first he said viz Seymour that he was willing to let that worthy member speak first becaus he spoke by booke and he without booke he said that he gave great heed to what two worthy members had spoke before him meaning Clayton and Bucknell he beleived that they spoke in earnest becaus they spoke against their own interest the one against mortgages the other against the brewers (nota *Claiton was a scrivener and Bucknell a brewer* [*sic*])[577] that he was against hard bargains that they never proved well that he remembred a great while ago when wee had peace with the Algerines the treaty was discoursed of in councill and much approved of, that one Lord of the privy councill said he did not like it it was to[o] advantageous to us to be long observed by the Algerines and so it proved for they quickly broke it and seised 100000 li. of our merchants goods[578] that he owned that he knew the inconveniencys of being under the displeasure of the crown that he would

---

[575] 'Debates 1697–9', 382, 397.   [576] Originally 'arbitrary'.

[577] Clayton's financial career is examined in F. T. Melton, *Sir Robert Clayton and the Origins of English Deposit Banking 1658–1685* (Cambridge, 1986). Bucknall's brother Sir William, MP Liverpool 1670–6, had served as master of the Brewers' Company in 1669–70, and he himself had been admitted into the company as a 'brother' in 1672: J. R. Woodhead, *The Rulers of London 1660–89* (London and Middlesex Archaeological Society; London, 1965), 40; HC 1660–90, i. 741–2; Guildhall Library, London, MS 5445/21, p. 197 (a reference I owe to Dr P. L. Gauci).

[578] The treaty with Algiers, made in 1664, had been broken by early 1669, when, after the caputure of goods and passengers from English ships, a ransom of 100,000 pieces of eight had been demanded by the Algerines: *CSP Dom.* 1668–9, pp. 179–80. A punitive expedition had proved necessary. Seymour himself had not been appointed to the Privy Council until 1673.

make his court to the crown by all means he could without prejuducing the country that he was therefore not for going to the extremity that there were severall motions the highest 4000 per week the lowes[t] 3500 the middle 3700 li. and that he was for that [?it] was first moved by Sir Thomas Meres and 2ded Sir Xto[*pher*] Musgrove so this quaestion was put and agreed unto without a di[*vi*]sion:[579] this was the most art I ever saw in the house: The new ministry as it was said had ingaged to hinder the taking of 100000 li. of[*f*] from the civill list and to get 4s upon land How had without any intent to have it succeed only to shew his own integrity and great spirit moved, to have this taken from the civill list, many that loved the king intirely were for lessening th[e] civill list not out of disrespect to the King but with an intention to destroy the new ministry: others becaus they thought w[ith] these difficulties that every one ought to beare a share and retrench thought it just to take this that was never designed to be given but for such purposes which are now ceased: those that were for supporting the new ministry who had launched forth in that bottom were resolved to try their utmost to save the 100000 li. from being dismembred from the civill list but when they found the reason was so palpable against them they fenced and did all they could to divert it and when they saw that impossible they were drove to the last extremityes which often make men ingenious, and that ingenuity and thier necessity obliged them to put their best thoughts foremost and then they invented this that the king should give us instead of our giving him and he to have the surplus: the sūm that it raised above the 700000 last year was 80000 so that reckoning that to be the highest it would rais we should get[580] 12000 by the bargain besides save the 100000 li. out of the civill list these were gre[at] motives besides the thoughts of rising sooner and saving 1s in the pound off of land this and other triviall motives made many run in to Musgro[ve] Seymour and the new court party: and the delays which is very dangerous to the country when engaged in an [op]posite party to [?the] Court gave the court an opportunity to perswade some and invite others by odd ways to ge[t o]ver others [?–]

[*fo.* 69]

[b]y this means by these arts where many seduced some ignorantly thinking we had a good Bargain others going in with a party they had so long followed there were some that saw we were bought and sold and were in their minds against it and cursed the contrivers and said in private that their old friends

---

[579] Poussin reported that Musgrave had moved for £4,000, and that Howe had also been prominent in pressing for this figure; PRO 31/3/188/73. The question agreed was for the amendment, for £3,700: *CJ* xiii. 562.   [580] '10' erased.

the new ministry were greater rogues then the late: and mr How being in private shewed the inconveniencys that would follow if the taking of the 100000 li. were insisted on and carried how it would advance the interest of his enemies and ruine his friends, retreated, as did Sir Godferry Copley so it was carried by a long debate without a division for the leaving out of those words that after that the overplus was to go to the publick[581] and then we adjourned May 24 [1701][582]

we read many private bills the last reading we went with 7 at one time up to the lords[583] memorandum the one was a bill of Pope and others in order to confirm by[584] an act of Parliament a decree made in chancery by the consent of all partyes Concerned[585] (nota[586] this was throw̅[n] out by the Lords becaus they said it would take of[f] the Benefit of Appeales)[587] the next thing was the report of the committee appoynted to examine the matter relating to the discharging the seamen they were all read all the papers relating to the matter,[588] and in the main it did appear to me that Churchill[589] and the admiralty had discharged them in that base disgracefull and pernicious manner on purpose if possible to bring more disgrace upon the author of the exchecquer bills by pretending that was the occasion they Could not [590] pay them off becaus there was no money only Exchecquer bills:[591] but there was money ready as it hapned but he ordered them to be discharged as it was proved[592] without ordering money to pay them, he told us at the Committee[593] there was no memoriall laid before the king only they took minutes upon which the king ordered them to discharge 3000 afterwards by an order from the Committee the memoriall he denyed, was laid before the committee[594] and

---

[581] Originally 'people'. According to Lord Shaftesbury, the Whigs had changed their minds because they had been reassured about the King's intentions in foreign policy. The Tories had 'made a compromise . . . to wash off the disgrace they incurred with the King before', and 'it went thus advantageously for the King, without any division, question, or so much as anyone speaking against it'. PRO 30/24/20/57–8.   [582] 'May 24 [1701]' boxed in MS.

[583] Six, according to the *Journals*, one of which was carried up by Cocks himself: *CJ* xiii. 563.

[584] 'by' interlined.

[585] A bill to confirm a judgment in Chancery in favour of one John Edwards, against Sir Francis Charlton, 2nd Bt. (1651–1729), and Roger Pope, MP Bridgnorth, sons-in-law of the late Alice Bromwich, and trustees under her will. In order to raise the purchase money for a new property Pope had borrowed from Edwards and a partner on the security of part of the existing estate, which Edwards wished now to be able to sell. Cocks had served on the 2nd-reading committee on this bill. HMC, *House of Lords MSS*, NS iv. 467; *CJ* xiii. 511.   [586] 'nota' interlined.

[587] The bill was rejected by the Lords that very day, at its first reading: *LJ* xvi. 706.

[588] Printed in *CJ* xiii. 564–7. See above, pp. 113–14.   [589] George Churchill, MP.

[590] 'not' interlined.

[591] As declared in the covering note sent by the Admiralty commissioners with the papers they submitted to the House: *CJ*, xiii. 564. The 'author' of the bills was Charles Montagu: See above, pp. 113–14.   [592] 'was proved' read originally as 'hapned'.

[593] Of which Cocks was a member: *CJ* xiii. 514. The speaker here is Churchill.

[594] Originally 'house'.

by them before the house[595] he told the committee he found some of their own
board had betrayed him he would therefore tell truth he said there was a
memorial laid before the king but that it was not exactly regular what was
done so that he denied it and this he must say in the house after these papers
were read they were laid upon the table to be perused by the members till the
other part of the report was made, I do not know what the fault was but the
Speaker found some fault with the report as not being in writing and not
giving the opinion of the Committee Sir R onslow[596] said that was not ordered
that he had pursued the powers delegated to him from the house George
Churchill said what he had done in relation to the discharging of them so
far of[f] Broadstreet the place of their pay[597] was according to the rules and
methods of the navy but that since that was thought inconvenient for the
future they should be discharged and paid at the same time and place: and then
they went upon the priviledge bill[598] which was sent from the lords with some
amendments all the amendments were agreed too with very little debate: but
the Clause [t]hat was added for taking away priviledge from those that were
the Kings debtors was so penned that it could not [b]e complyed with but with
some amendments the consideration Whereof was referred to Munday the 26th
of May 1701[599] [t]his day was appoynted for ways and means and for the
report of Enfeild Chase[600] but it being more the humour of the leading men to
ruine an enemye and remove a Lord they dont like and to put one they do in his
place: we went upon Enfeild chase report: the matter of fact was that there
were ridings ordered to be cut for the advantage of the sports and hunting and
this would have been very usefull and convenient [?–] and an order was
obtained by my Lord Stamford Chancellour of the Dutchy to whom the care
of this did belong for the doing the same and [h]e sent his directions to Mr
Westcoat his under officer to pursue the same according to the orders:[601]

[595] See above, p. 113, n. 349.   [596] The chairman of the committee: *CJ* xiii. 563.
[597] 'the place of their pay' interlined. The Pay Office was in Broad St.: see above, p. 113, n. 350.
[598] To prevent 'inconveniences that may happen by privilege of Parliament'.
[599] '26th of May 1701' boxed in MS. Two amendments to this clause (Clause A) were accepted
by the House, before others were referred to a separate committee, and consideration of the bill
adjourned to the 26th: *CJ* xiii. 567–8.
[600] On 12 May, following a complaint about the cutting down of timber in Enfield Chase the
Commons had addressed the King to put a stop to the practice, and had appointed a committee,
including Cocks, to make further investigations: *CJ* xiii. 533.
[601] In July 1700 the Chancellor of the Duchy of Lancaster, Thomas Grey (c.1653–1720), 2nd
Earl of Stamford, had ordered the Duchy's surveyor of woods in the south parts, Hugh Westlake
(b. c.1656), of the Middle Temple, to begin cutting rides and thinning timber in the chase, Sir
Robert Somerville, *History of the Duchy of Lancaster* (2 vols.; London, 1953–70), ii. 94–5; id.,
Office-Holders in the Duchy and County Palatine of Lancaster from 1603 (London, 1972), 82; *CJ*
xiii. 570–2. *The Case of the Earl of Stamford Considered, Relating to the Wood Lately Cut in
Enfield Chace* (London, 1701).

instead thereof the [*sic*] cut more ridings then [w]ere ordered and cut indentures in and out many a foot to come at a tree to cut down: Sir Basill firebras[602] came to my Lord Stampford to the house of lords[603] and told him of it: My Lord said if he would bring it in writing he would take care in it and should understand [?i]t: after some debate there passed a vote that there was a wast committed that was agreed to generally: and after wit and ill nature and good nature and friendship had been satisfyed we came to the next quaestion which was that the E[*arl*] of Stanford was guilty of neglect and breach of his duty in letting the yong oaks to be destroyed[604] the quaestion proposed was that he was guilty of a breach of trust and male administration and ought to be removed the Speakers quaestion was more soft and agreable, it came nearer the subject matter of the debate but I stood and looked upon those that came in against my Lord Standford and I dont beleive argument turned but party guided most that went out[605] and as a lover of truth I may say so for those that stayd in I mean for most: Cooper spoke finely[606] and said that Sir Basill firebrases speaking to my lord rudely[607] and not giving it to him in[608] writing was a design not to have my Lord mind it in order to give him the better opportunity of complaining in parliament Cooper spoke a great deale very well and Seymour commended his great parts and oratory and said he could make a bad cause seem a good one and that he hoped he would not take it ill if he shewed how he came to espouse my Lords cause viz to expres his gratitude for bringing him into the house: Sir John Holles[609] said amongst other things that he was willing to addres to the king to put in a man skilled in the laws and of experience in busines but that he saw no occasion for this quaestion unles they would let him Know who they intended to put in his place and then if he liked him he could agree to the quaestion and there were many of us that spoke of

---

[602] Sir Basil Firebrace (1652–1724), of London, and Enfield, MP Chippenham 1690–1, 1691–2, who as chief ranger of the chase had been the prime mover in the complaint. This was itself only the latest incident in a long-running feud between Firebrace and Stamford. The previous year a quarrel between Firebrace and the earl's crony, Sir Henry Belasyse, occasioned by the killing of a greyhound, had threatened to end in a duel, and had been brought to the attention of the Secretary of State and the Privy Council: BL Add. MS 40774, fos. 58–9, 62–4, 70–1; Northants. RO, Montagu (Boughton) MSS, 47/201, 207, James Vernon to the Duke of Shrewsbury, 22 June, 6 July 1699; Boston Public Library (Boston, Mass.), MS K.5.3, Robert Yard to William Blathwayt, 23 June 1699.

[603] In the Painted Chamber. The committee's report gives an account of the exchange: *CJ* xiii. 571.

[604] 'In letting the yong oaks to be destroyed' interlined. The question was that the destruction of the woods 'hath happened through the neglect of duty and trust of Thomas, Earl of Stamford, Chancellor of the Duchy of Lancaster': *CJ* xiii. 572.   [605] The yeas: ibid.

[606] William Cowper had been elected to Parliament on Stamford's interest: J. J. Alexander, 'Bere Alston as a Parliamentary Borough', *Trans. Devonshire Assoc.*, 41 (1909), 154–5.

[607] 'rudely' interlined.   [608] 'giving it to him in' interlined.   [609] Hawles.

both sides not worth writing[610] and the debate lasted four hours allmost: Gent[*lemen*] moved to have the[611] answer of John Lord Somers to the articles of impeachment read and the Speaker said the order of the day was ways and means and that would take a great time [?tha]t he would take this report which would take up no time: but he well Knew how long it would last: they declared in the discours of [m]y Lord Somerses busines that they could try which they pleased first and that they would try the lord Somers first: becaus in [h]is tryall there would be severall things discovered necessary to be used at the other tryalls: When the debate upon the [r]eport was over the quaestion was put and those for finding my Lord guilty of a breach of trust and neglect were 136 against it [1]02 and then we tooke our places Sir Ed[*ward*] Seymour said he was not for making that vote of removing men upon every little occasion from the Kings presence or their places[612] but he moved to have these votes laid before the king which was ordered accordingly and then we adjourned[613] Nota the reason they viz Seymour and that party did insist no further in their vote for removing my Lord Stanford was becaus the King ordered the Secretary[614] to acquaint the house that every thing that was done in Enfeild Chase was by his own particular order the Secretary did not come time enough to acquaint the house but told the new courtiers and ministry in private of the Kings message which made them more then their own temper and good nature soften the vote: The Secretary was ordered before in his answer to our addres[615] relating to enfeild Chase which was that what was cut down might [*be*] applyed to the use of the publick to tell us it was applyed but his answer was it should be applyed:[616] May 27th [*1701*][617] the busines of the day was ways and means and before we went into the Committee Mr How moved[618] that it might be an instruction to the committee to receive a Clause to lessen the salaries that did arise out of the great places that managed the revenue his meaning was particularly to abate my lord Hallifaxes place which he said was 7000 li. per an:[619] he inlarged upon this toppick about our poverty and

---

[610] 'not worth writing' interlined.　　　　　　　　　　　[611] 'articles' erased.

[612] As had been resolved on 15 Apr. in respect of the four impeached lords: see above, p. 94.

[613] 'May 27th' erased.

[614] Almost certainly James Vernon rather than the other Secretary of State, Sir Charles Hedges; but cf. below p. 165.　　　　　　　　　　　[615] Originally 'vote'.

[616] On 13 May Secretary Vernon had conveyed to the Commons the King's answer to the address of the 12th for an end to be put to the cutting of timber; in the version in the *Journals* this had not included any mention of applying the proceeds to public uses: *CJ* xiii. 538.

[617] 'May 27th [*1701*]' boxed in MS.

[618] Howe was to leave London for the country only two days later: HMC, *Cowper MSS*, ii. 427.

[619] The auditorship of the receipt in the Exchequer. For the controversial circumstances surrounding Montagu's appointment, see Stephen B. Baxter, *The Development of the Treasury, 1660–1702* (London, 1957), 137–8, where the value of the office is estimated at £4,000 p.a.

necessities: I said sir I think considering the great difficulties we labour under and the necessities of a war and other [*sic*][620] we strugle with it is necessary for us to retrench from the king to the peasant we that have estates must and others should to make it aequall, I think not only the salaries of the places but the great pensions ought to be considered of and abated Sir I usually speak short and only to the poynt and therefore if I deviate this once since I design to bring it to your service I hope you will give me leave and pardon me it was a great quaestion amongst the antients whether the vigour of the mind or the strength of the body was more beneficiall to ones country that was resolved according to our English proverb that policy goes beyond strength I had a doubt something like this in my own mind which was whether seamen or ships were most beneficiall to this Island I knew under god that our walls were our ships[621] I knew these ships could not be made without timber I knew when they were made they were of no use without men I knew also that seamen were of no use without ships whilest I was at this debate in my own mind there comes an accident that brought these matters regularly before the house to give their opinions in it I suspended my thoughts till I knew the opinion of the house: here was great wrong done to our seamen and great wast made of our timber and both matters referred to two [s]everall committees which report the one that our men were used at that rate that it was a disparagement to us a broad and a [s]candall to us at home their ill usage forced them to blaspheme and curs god and the king and renounce their affection to their Country some of them hanged themselves rather then they would live amongst such ungratefull Countrymen: this the Committee reported and it was proved the Committee of the timber reported the spoyle and the wast and that was censured justly as it ought and the other lyes upon the table so my quaestion is resolved but I wish my lord Stamford had had a place in the admiralty then then [*sic*] the ill usage of the men had also been inquired into but sir to make this come to the poynt here have been such neglects and male administration of the dutchy that I take this to be a good opportunity to take it away and subject it to the rules of the Exchequer by that means the salaries would be saved and they might be applyed to the use of the publick: Stringer seconded me and said the pensions[622] might be taken away as well as the places and that he knew one lord that had 3 or 4000 li. per an: out of the post house: How said his motion was that some should not grow rich by taxes whilest others starved that he made

[620] 'of a war and other [*sic*]' interlined.

[621] A common conceit, originally found in Herodotus (*History*, 7. 141). For a notable example of its use in the early 17th century, with which Cocks may well have been familiar, see Lord Keeper Coventry's speech of 1635, printed in John Rushworth *Historical Collections* . . . (7 vols.; London, 1659–1701), ii. 297.   [622] Originally 'places'.

no motion becaus he was angry (reflecting upon Stringer who was angry with
the D[*uke*] of leeds who has a pension of that value out of the post office)[623]
but for the service of his country and moved that it might be an instruction to
the Committee to receive a clause that there might be consideration of the
great places had: the Speaker said it was to[*o*] late for such an instruction but
that they might add at the end of every Clause that no poundage shoud be
paid the Speaker turned Hows quaestion how made mouths signifying his
thoughts of the Speakers honesty but he could not help himself for he is the
w[?ors]t at a quaestion in the world Mr Pellam said he did not know why
pensions should not be considered [?of] as well [as] places for for [*sic*] the one
men did some thing for the other nothing was done at all to deserve them
[*fo. 68ᵛ*]

at last Sir Xto[*pher*] musgrove said Hows motion was nothing more nor
intended any more then to hinder the officers of the Exchecquer grow[?ing]
and great out of the moneys that were raised more then usuall for our
preservation and use: Seymour said let them have what is usuall out of the
600000 li. for the civill list and make the best of it and that there was nothing
more designed by How but to prevent their having poundage of the new taxes
so they forced How out of the sence of his motion and agreed to the clause,
then we resumed the debate of the pensions and the Speaker told us they were
all paid out of the civill list that the king paid whom he ple[a]sed and not paid
whom he pleased: the pension was that that maintained the kings children and
charitys that they were all precarious and needed no taking away: so that fell
and we went upon ways and means but before this in the morning my Lord
Hartington after my Lord Somerses answer was read moved for the reply to
my Lord Orfords answer to be carried up to the lords Sir Ed[*ward*] Seymour
opposed saying it was time enough that the witnesses against my Lord Orford
were in the Fleet and abroad[624] and that it was necessary for them to impeach
my Lord Somers first for at his triall things would come out necessary to [be]
used at the tryall of the other lords that they would send up the reply to the
lord Somerses answer and that of my Lord Orford together that it was time
enough and then they the commons[625] might Chuse which they would try first
but if they sent up my Lord Orfords first the lords might appoynt a day for the

[623] Leeds had been granted in 1691 a pension of £3,500 p.a. (for 21 years) from the revenues of
the Post Office: Andrew Browning, *Thomas Osborne Earl of Danby and Duke of Leeds 1632–1712*
(3 vols.; Glasgow, 1951), i. 486–7.

[624] Maurice Annesley reported that 'Lord Orford's friends in the House pressed that a reply to
his answer might be sped to the Lords but, many of the witnesses against him being alleged to be
at sea and in foreign parts, that was put off': Nat. Archs. Ireland, Wyche MSS, 1/223, Maurice
Annesley to Sir Cyril Wyche, 27 May 1701.   [625] 'the commons' interlined.

tryall before they had replyed to my Lord Somers: Sir Tho[*mas*] Littleton said
he had heard in answers in Chancery that they had prayed for time becaus their
witnesses were beyond the seas but seldom in such cases as these and prayed
that wee might reply to morrow: Mr Hartcourt said they would be ready in a
day or two but that the lord Somerses answer was long and would require some
little time to which the house agreed: Nota the replication is nothing but matte[r]
of form that they will maintain or prove the truth of what they have alledged:
May 28 [*1701*][626] nothing remarkable nothing but Elections the first for Dartmouth no great busines Ball and vernon petitioned against the two Herns the
petitioners had no very good caus nor did they make any great friends to
support them:[627] next Dartmouth [*sic*] winchester election came on[628] Tilney
petitioned against my Lord William paw[lett] and mr Rodney Bruges[629] there
was never a fairer Cause so fair that at the committee my Lord left it without
making any defence: on th[e] evidence of the petitioner at the committee after
the report my Lord made a short speech and withdrew: I thought there would
have been noth[ing] said to it but Sir Edward Seymour said the Lord influenced
and produced a letter of Jack Smiths which he wrote to Tilney to let him know
he could not serve him being made free by the D[*uke*] of Boulton[630] and that he
might do as the duke would have him there were present allso the D[*uke*]s of St

---

[626] Date boxed in MS.

[627] 'Ball' was either William Balle (*c.*1635–*c.*1722), of Mamhead, nr. Chudleigh, Devon, or his
son William (b. 1669): J. L. Vivian, *The Visitations of the County of Devon* . . . (Exeter, 1895), 37;
Foster (ed.), *London Mar. Lics.*, col. 69. Balle sen., was a first cousin of Cocks through his mother.
The other petitioner was Thomas Vernon (bef. 1683–1726), of Twickenham Park, Middx., MP
Whitchurch 1710–21, 1722–6: *HC 1715–54*, ii. 499. The committee's judgment in favour of the
sitting Members, Frederick and Nathaniel Herne, was accepted by the House without a division:
CJ xiii. 581.   [628] 'winchester election came on' interlined.

[629] The petitioner was Frederick Tylney (*c.*1653–1725), of Tylney Hall, Rotherwick, Hants, MP
Winchester 1690–1700, Stockbridge 1701–2, Southampton 1701–5, Whitchurch 1708, 1710–15,
1721 (for whom see *HC 1715–54*, ii. 489); the sitting Members Lord William Powlett and George
Rodney Brydges.

[630] According to James Lowther, Seymour, Sir Christopher Musgrave, 'and their friends
laboured very had to turn out' Powlett, 'for lords appearing and meddling very much in the
election'. Seymour in particular was said to have taken 'a great deal of pains'. Cumbria RO
(Carlisle), D/Lons/W, James to Sir John Lowther, 29 May 1701. For the personal connection
between John Smith, MP Andover, and Charles Powlett (1661–1722), 2nd Duke of Bolton, MP
Hants 1681–98, and high steward of Winchester, see Bolton MSS (Lord Bolton, Bolton Hall,
Wensley, Yorks.), D/18, 27, Thomas Cobbe to Lord Winchester, 16 May 1698, George Rodney
Brydges to same, 8 Nov. 1698. Smith had been admitted a freeman of Winchester in 1693 'at a
public dinner, at which was the late [i.e. the 1st] Duke of Bolton' (*CJ* xiii. 582), and had voted for
Brydges and Powlett in the disputed election (Hants RO. Winchester corporation records,
ordinance book 7, fo. 127).

Albans and Richmond[631] this was contrary to a vote made this sessions[632] and therefore if it had been a[633] law, not subject to it being made before the offence was committed: but this was wonderfully insisted on but the quaestion was carryed by a majority of 40 for the sitting member:[634] then Sir Walter yo[nge's] Election for Hunnington in devonshire came on the case was this Sir W: yong had an undisputed majority no comparison the[re] stood one Sanford against him and Mr Courtney[635] Sir Walter yongs friends in london men that were obliged to Sir Walte[r] spent 200 li. as was said for him and they and others treated for him and one of Sir W Y[onge']s servants had said Sir Wal[ter] would spend any thing rather than then lose it[636] Sir W: had such an undoubted interest that there was no need of spending or treating for him nor was there any appearance of his spending or treating or incourageng [?but] this was a good handle for the party to make use of and urge a breach of the late act but after a prett[y] long debate Sir walter carried by twenty: Sanford never petitioned he came near Sir Wal[ter] Courtney had that petition had not 17 votes but relyed upon the strength of the party[637] May 29th [1701][638] observed as an holyday May 30th [1701][639] nothing remarkeable private Bills read and we were into a Committee of ways and means, where there was some witt not worth mentioni[n]g Sir John Bolles reflected upon my

[631] Charles Beauclerk (1670–1726), 1st Duke of St Albans; Charles Lennox (1672–1723), 1st Duke of Richmond. The presence of Richmond at the election was attested in the evidence to the committee printed in *CJ* xiii. 581–2. Both he and St Albans are recorded as having voted for Brydges and Powlett (Hants RO, Winchester corp. recs. ord. bk. 7, fo. 127).

[632] The resolution on 15 Feb. that for any peer to concern himself in elections to the lower House was 'a high infringement of the liberties and privileges of the Commons': *CJ* xiii. 333.

[633] 'it had been' interlined.

[634] 'for the sitting member' interlined. The first resolution of the committee, that Powlett had been duly elected, was carried on a division by 154 votes to 114; the second, in favour of Brydges, was not contested: *CJ* xiii. 582.

[635] John Sanford (1640–1711), of Basinghall St., London, and Nynehead Court, Som., MP Taunton 1685–90: see *HC 1660–90*, iii. 391. William Courtenay (1676–1735), of Powderham Court, Devon, later 2nd Bt.; MP Devon 1701–10, 1712–d.: see *HC 1715–54*, i. 587. Courtenay and Sanford had stood unsuccessfully against Yonge and Sir William Drake, 4th Bt., of Ashe, Devon, after which Courtenay had petitioned against Yonge's return.

[636] One of Courtenay's witnesses estimated that '£2 or 300' had been spent in treating on Yonge's behalf, and that Yonge's servant, John Cesse, had 'on the election day' declared, 'Let it cost what it would, Sir Walter would not lose it'. Yonge's supporters had included 'Mr Glanville . . . a laceman in London'. *CJ* xiii. 583. Honiton was centre of lace manufacture: see above, p. 23.

[637] James Lowther bracketed Yonge with Lord William Powlett as one whom Seymour, Musgrave, and the other Tories had sought to turn out: Cumbria RO (Carlisle), D/Lons/W, James to Sir John Lowther, 29 May 1701. The act concerned was the 'Treating Act' of 1696 (7 & 8 Gul. III. c. 4), for which see above, p. 66, n. 37. The figures at the division were 146:121: *CJ* xiii. 584. At the election Courtenay had polled 18 votes against Yonge's 191: ibid. 583.

[638] Date boxed in MS. Restoration Day.   [639] Date boxed in MS.

Lord Coningsbee[640] for hanging somebody without law: my Lord said Bolles might do any thing in any place safely for he allwais carryed his priviledge about him[641] we sate till 7n [*sic*] to expedite ways and means[642] May 30th [*recte 31st 1701*][643] the bill to divorce Mr Box from his wife was read the third time shee brought box 4000 li. portion shee was a very infamous woman the daughter of the worthy learned and good judge Ayres Sir Giles,[644] Mr Hoblin moved that in the press that allowed her one hundred pound per annum the word fifty might be added after hundred he said he had a great respect for the memory of her father and tha[t] shee brought 4000 li. and for that reason he made this motion that he had no knowledge of the yong lady: I answered Hobli[n] and said I knew Mrs Boxes father the worthy and learned judge that I had a value for his memory and that I knew him so well that I was assured were he now living he was a man of so much worth and pyety that he would abhor such practices in his daughter and would rather think it too much for her what was allowed her and that I thought it enough and that I hoped wee should agree with the Lords bill there was no more said and then we agreed: th[en] we were told the Lords messengers I mean that there was a message from the lords we knew the business it was to appoynt amongst other things (there were severall messages) a day for tryall for the Lord Orford and it told us we might reply[645] Sir B Shores was at the Bar with the reply for the Lord Somerses answer he said it was a shuffling answ[er] at which they might take exceptions but that the committee had drawed up a replication after he had done that he reported from the Committee that they had examined presidents in relation to the Lords message that they could find no praesidents like it and

---

[640] 'Coningsbee' interlined. As a lord justice in Ireland in 1691 Coningsby had ordered the summary execution of one Gaffney, a prosecution witness in the trial of a Jacobite charged with murdering Williamite soldiers. It was alleged that the accused man had bribed Coningsby's secretary to secure his acquittal. This had formed one of the articles of impeachment against Coningsby in 1693. The incident had earned him the sobriquet 'Gaffney's hangman'. See *CJ* xi. 33; *CSP Dom.* 1693, p. 205; Lord *et al.* (edd.), *Poems on Affairs of State*, vi. 20, 221.

[641] An allusion to Bolles's disordered mental state, which was eventually to degenerate into insanity: James (ed.), *Letters Illustrative . . .* ii. 337; Burnet, *Own Time*, iv. 499–500; BL Sloane MS 4078, fo. 303.

[642] The ten resolutions carried at this sitting of the committee are detailed in Luttrell, *Brief Relation*, v. 56.   [643] Date boxed in MS.

[644] See above, pp. 137–8. Particulars of Mrs Box's spectacular moral dereliction are provided in Lambeth Palace Lib., Ct. of Arches recs., B13/107/5, Ralph Box's case; Northants. RO, Montagu (Boughton) MSS, 48/51, James Vernon to the Duke of Shrewsbury, 28 Mar. 1700. Her father was Sir Giles Eyre (1635–95), of Brickworth, Whiteparish, Wilts., and Lincoln's Inn, justice of King's Bench 1689–d., MP Downton 1660, Salisbury 1689: see *DNB*; and *HC 1660–90*, iii. 287–8.

[645] The message was that the Lords had appointed 9 June for Orford's trial and 'this House may reply if they think fit'; also to remind the Commons that articles had not yet been exhibited against Halifax and Portland: *CJ* xiii. 587.

it concluded that it tended to breed a misunderstanding between the two houses[646] then the messengers were called in, they told us the severall bills the Lords had agreed too and at last that they thought it hard to impeach the Lords and not to bring up the impeachments against the Lords Hallifax and portland impeached weeks ago[647] and not to reply to my Lord Orfords answer: they called the messengers in again and said they would return an answer by messengers of their own: as to the first report made by Sir B Shores[648] in relation to the manner of the proceedings and presidents it was moved that it might be sent to the Lords by a message others Mr Boyle said it was the properest way to desire a conference: Sir Xto[pher] musgrove said we had said we would return an answer by our own messengers and therefore we were tyed down: So that was agreed to: then we considered of the lords message in relation to the Lord Orford: Sir Ed[ward] Seymour said it was unpresidented and that he knew of no president but in his impeachment When he was so unfortunate as to come under the displeasure of the house[649] but that that was another thing for that he was under bayle sequestred from the house and that these lords were under no restraint, that in his case it could not be a president for there followed a prorogation so that nothing was done that impeachments were very usefull but that they had not been practiced a great while that they were like a rusty sword in a scabbard that had lost its Edge that his was so long ago that his memory would not serve him to remember all the particula[rs] that it was very Extraordinary to appoynt a day and them to give us leave to reply what need was there of a replication then when the day was appoynted and that it was the undoubted right of the commons when there were severall impeached to try which they would first: there were severall warm speeches some to try my Lord Orford as appoynted but they said that how much soever Gent[lemen] were against those[650] impeachments at first that it was now the act of the house and that those that were against it were obliged to stand by the honour of the house and to take care not to lose our rights it was agreed by all who spoke to the purpose that we had a right to

---

[646] Shower was reporting from the (extended) committee on the impeachments, in this case to Somers's replication to the charges against him. In fact, the *Journals* record that the report from this committee on the reference to it of the Lords' message of 21 May (see above, p. 139) was made by 'Mr Bromely' *before* Shower reported on Somers's replication. The exact wording of the report was 'that it does . . . tend to the breach of that good correspondence betwixt the two Houses, which ought to be mutually preserved'. *CJ* xiii. 587. Maurice Annesley called this response 'a very round message': Nat. Archs. Ireland, Wyche MSS 1/224, Annesley to Sir Cyril Wyche, 31 May 1701.

[647] Halifax had been impeached on 14 Apr., Portland on the 1st: *CJ* xiii. 490, 465.

[648] *Recte* Bromley.

[649] On 3 Jan. 1680 the Lords had sent to the Commons to appoint a day for Seymour's trial: *CJ* ix. 697. See above p. 139.   [650] 'those' interlined.

impeach which we pleased first then it was moved to refer the consideration of these matters to the Committee that were to draw up the impeachments [?to] search for presidents and Mr Smith moved to have a new Committee he said this was no secret but that since all the house were ingaged in it that there might be a new Committee which was agreed too:[651] then it was moved to ha[ve] no more members go out of town without leave and afterwards for a call of the house on munday sen[*nigh*]t and that those that did not appear should be sent for into custody and that the Speaker should write circular letters [?to] the sherriffes: but all this was but a feint to amuse the people for they knew there was nothing against the lords and they were very uneasye to be pressed beyond what they intended and to have this appear in their votes to the people who were too much incensed against them before: afterwards they went upon the Irish report and the Commissioners for the sale of the Irish estates gave in a memoriall[652] which informed the house that to severall of the matters they had [?no] Knowledge of them as not having had any examination of them and not having their books or papers here as to those they had examined and so after a long debate about the hardsh[*i*]ps of many cases as particularly the tenants of the private estate who had taken leases under a good title not forfeited but made lyable by our act[653] and of the attainting of men after they were dead by the Irish law they provided for all the trustees knew and reported fit and referred the rest to be examined in Ireland by the Com[*mi*]s[*sione*]rs and then to consider of their report June 1st [*recte 2nd 1701*] Nothing remarkable private bills were read in the morning: a bill sent from the lords for preventing vexatious sutes not ordered a 2d reading: [?A]s being a design to bring all the triviall actions now tryed in the inferiour courts into Westminster hall[654] it tooke [a]way the hold[?ing] to baile in the inferiour courts in actions under 2: li. then there was a motion to read the ingr[osse]d reply to the [Lord] Somerses answer but the order of the day was called for before and the Speaker who was very backw[ard] in brin[ging]

---

[651] Including Cocks as well as Seymour and Smith: *CJ* xiii. 588.

[652] The report from the three members of the Irish forfeitures trust then in England, to whom petitions relating to the resumption had been referred on 19 May (see above, p. 136). Their memorial is printed in *CJ* xiii. 588.

[653] King James's private estate in Ireland, amounting to over 200,000 acres, granted by William to Elizabeth, Lady Orkney, the inclusion of which in the report of the commissioners of inquiry in 1699–1700, and thus in the ensuing resumption, had provoked some bitter wrangling: Simms, *Williamite Confiscation*, 85–6, 92–5, 102–9, 114.

[654] The bill 'for the more effectual restraining of trifling and vexatious suits'. A surviving draft, printed at HMC, *House of Lords MSS*, NS iv. 356–9, renders 'Westminster Hall' as 'the courts at Westminster'.

[*fo. 68*]

th]e [l]ords to their tryall for there was nothing against them would not lett
the reply be read but left the chaire Nota he was the principall man that had
all along contrived their ruine, then he left the chair and we went into a
committee of the whole house for the land tax and there was this Materiall
Frank Gwin moved to have one Chamberlain left out from being a
com[*mi*]s[*sione*]r of the land tax the reason he gave was that he was a
troublesome fellow: the true reason was that he opposed Gwins interest:
there were used as arguments for him that he was allways a
Com[*mi*]s[*sione*]r and a man of substance and a good one:[655] we divided in
the committee and those that were for turning out Chamberlain were 75 for
his being a com[*mi*]s[*sione*]r 51 then the same quaestion was put upon one
Trout that opposed Sir Ed[*ward*] Seymour both of Devonshire[656] and that was
carried without a division: then Mr Coniers said there were severall struck out
out [*sic*] of Denbyshire which he thought he was obliged to inform the house
of the County was over first Mr Bruerton said That he had a letter from the
K[*nigh*]t of the shire of Denbyshire to put in the old and some few new ones
that he Knew none of those that were put in but David Floyd Sir R Cottons
servant Sir Robert Cotton said they were men of account and recommended to
him by men of Estates Sir Robert was very angry and when the house rose he
struck Bruerton over the head with a little cane Just out of westminster Hall
Bruerton returned the compliment with two hard Blows over the face with the
head of his great Cane:[657] The Kentish peititioners were put in
Com[*mi*]s[*sione*]rs by the K[*nigh*]ts of their shire in the list which ocasioned
some warm words so they were lef out: on Tuesday the 3d of June [*1701*][658] Sir

---

[655] Probably Roger Chamberlain, a commissioner for Devon appointed under the 1698 Land
Tax Act, 9 Gul. III, c. 10 (*Statutes of the Realm*, vii. 317) but omitted two years later (ibid. 658–9).
Francis Gwyn sat for Totnes.

[656] Abraham Trout, who, when appointed a JP in Devon in 1693, had been described as 'zealous
for the government and ... always ... an opponent of the Tories'. He had subsequently been
removed from the bench after Tory protests at his low social origins. Lady Eliott-Drake, *The
Family and Heirs of Sir Francis Drake* (2 vols.; London, 1911), ii. 88; Glassey, *Appointment of JPs*,
116–17.

[657] The enmity between Brereton and Cotton arose from local political rivalry. At the previous
two general elections Cotton's son had stood against Brereton in Denbigh Boroughs, in contests
marked by considerable physical violence. Brereton enjoyed the support of the knight of the shire,
his fellow Tory Sir Richard Myddelton, with whom he kept in close contact. See National Library
of Wales, Chirk Castle MSS F1433, Myddelton *et al.* to Sir John Trevor, 6 June 1699; E1036,
Brereton to Myddelton, 18 Feb. 1700[/1]; Albinia L. Cust, *Chronicles of Erthig on the Dyke* (2
vols.; London, 1914), i. 59–61; and for the general background, P. D. G. Thomas, 'Wynnstay *versus*
Chirk Castle: Parliamentary Elections in Denbighshire 1716–1741', *National Library of Wales
Journal*, 10 (1959/60), 106–7.

[658] 'Tuesday the 3rd June [*1701*]' boxed in MS. On this day Cocks was granted a fortnight's
leave of absence (*CJ* xiii. 592), and indeed his name figures no more in the *Journals* during this
session.

Bart[*holomew*] Shores moved to have the reply to my Lord Somerses answer which lay ingrossed upon the table to be read he said this was an impeachment that they needed no wittnesses from Cales no victualler from the navy[659] and a many other nos in the way of oratory but that they all appeared upon record that this being a new matter would not interfare with the messages that passed between us and the lords: that he was for the reading of the ingrossed articles and a great deale more Sir Xto[*pher*] musgrove opposed it and said we ought to give up nothing of our rights that we ought to have this poynt setled in relation to the messages: that their appoynting of a time and sending word that it was [h]ard was unparliamentary and that if we should let it pas so it would be giving up the poynt: the Speaker said the occasion of all that hapned the reason of our misunderstanding was the going at first out of the way and that one step out of beaten path lead us quite wrong: Sir Ed[*ward*] Seymour that we ought to have had a conference and then a committee to setle the praeliminaryes that the Lords have a right to name the time and place but we to Chuse which we would try first and as for the time and place it is our right to have them altered shewing Cause Sir R Onslow said we had many presidents to try which [w]e will first as it appeared in the Case of the E[*arl*] of Danby and the popish lords that first the Commons agreed to try the E[*arl*] of [Da]nby first and after the prorogation then they would try the popish lords first[660] he said if we had been out of the way [i]t was time to come in and moved for a Committee Sir Rowland Gwin to the same purpose Sir Xto[*pher*] musgrove till the lords are willing to give up this we must not appoynt a committee the Lords have sent no satisfactory answer nor ought we till [t]hen to desire a committee Sir Jo[*seph*] Jechell to have the report read to morrow and that he hoped there would be no delay for that would be unjust and that since all appeared upon record he hoped that they would say they were ready to try my Lord Somers: Sir Bar[*tholomew*] Shores moved to have the report from the committee made to morrow about the presidents: Mr Attor[?ney] General said unnecessary delays were unjust but that we ought to proceed regularly in every step first in appoynting whom we would first try and that in the first place we should have the report from the committee and if we desired

---

[659] A reference to the articles of impeachment against Orford, which included charges that while at Cadiz (Cales) he had embezzled money provided for victualling: *CJ* xii. 520; J Ehrman, *The Navy in the War of William III 1689–1697* . . . (Cambridge, 1953), 538–9; Johnston, 'Parliament and the Navy' 92–6; above, p. 4, n. 15.

[660] The protracted impeachments in 1678–9 of Thomas Osborne, 1st Earl of Danby and later Duke of Leeds, and the 'five lords'—Henry Arundell (1608–94), 3rd Baron Arundell of Wardour; John Belasyse (1614–89), 1st Baron Belasyse of Worlaby; William Petre (*c.*1626–84), 4th Baron Petre; William Herbert (*c.*1626–96), 1st Earl of Powis; and the 1st Viscount Stafford. On the progress of impeachments, see *CJ* ix. 631–3.

to have a committee of lords and commons meet before that was setled we gave away the poynts we now claimed as our due: Sir Tho[*mas*] Powis sais we must be very exact this will not be the last impeachment the slip in Sir Ed[*ward*] Seymours impeachment gave this handle[661] the bill of treasons was well penned in which the prosecutor and prosecuted had equall advantage[662] delays gave people abroad occasion to say there is nothing against them and to Malign our proceedings Gent[*lemen*] say my Lord Somerses is another caus but they are all upon the same foot all the impeachments depending at the same time and no conference to be desired: the Speaker said the 16th of Dec[*em*]b[*e*]r 1678 there was a president in the lords house when it was voted that we had a right to try which we would first:[663] the error we made was to impeach and not carry up the impeachments so soon as formerly they did and then when we had replyed wee should have desired a conference and at that Conference have desired a committee to adjust the preliminaryes and the time this was well known by those that managed the impeachments for they were able men but [t]hey designed no more then to disparage and disgrace not to try the lords: and they did not imagine that the lords would have found so many friends in the Lords house and amongst the people: Wednesday the 4th of June [*1701*][664] the report from the Committee to inspect presidents in relation to what hapned between the two houses and particularly in relation to the Lords messages saying it was hard to impeach and not to bring up articles in so long a time after was made by Mr Bromeley[665] the report was read at the table and in it the Earle of Orford was stiled my Lord Orford litlton moved to have the places amended and the word Lord left out and the word Earle inserted which amendments were made accordingly: then there began a debate whether we should send the message as reported the Lords having in a manner receded and mollifyed the words we tooke exceptions at by a message just now read in which they said they could find no president in their books for such Long delays in exhibiting articles of impeachment after they had impeached a lord and that therefore they thought it hard[666] and that at the request of the lord

---

[661] See above, p. 156.

[662] Since the Revolution there had been six bills to amend the law relating to treason trials, culminating in the act of 1696 (7 & 8 Gul. III. c. 3): Horwitz, *Parliament, Policy and Politics*, 64, 74–5, 86, 98, 106, 124, 127–8, 137–8, 143–4, 147; James R. Phifer, 'Law, Politics and Violence: The Treason Trials Act of 1696', *Albion*, 12 (1980), 235–56.

[663] Not borne out by the *Journals*, though on 15 Dec. there had been a vote against sending a message to the Commons to raise the subject of the delay in sending up articles: *LJ* xii. 418.

[664] 'Wednesday the 4th June [*1701*]' boxed in MS.　　　　[665] Harcourt, in *CJ* xiii. 595.

[666] 'Having searched their own journals, they do not find that, after a general impeachment, there has ever been so long a delay of bringing up the particular articles of impeachment; and therefore . . . do think they had reason to assert, that it was a hardship to the two lords concerned'; *CJ* xiii. 594.

Somers they had waved their insisting upon the tryall of my Lord Orford[667] first and were willing to try my Lord Somers they put us in mind also again of the hardship my Lord Portland and my Lord Hallifax lay under they having been impeached so long and not so much as articles exhibited against them and no reply to my Lord Somers and Orford who were all impeached a great while ago:[668] the Speaker from the Chair informed us that we had went out of the way in not desiring a conference: Mr Boyle thanks the Speaker for putting us in the right way: that ever since we went out of the way we have been farther off our journeys end, that since the only way to Come to an good understanding was a conference and that messages tended only to widen the rupture and a conference may bring every thing right again he moves for a Conference the Speaker told us from the chaire that we were now upon the report from the Committee [?and] that when we had setled and agreed the report we might consider whether we would send it by message or desire a conference: Sir John Luson The Lords send these messages to upbraid us with delays and by the prin[ti]ng of our votes they will reflect upon us and libell us to the people[669] all over the kingdom that we ought to send a sharp message again which will also appear in our votes to be even with the Lords: mr Sollicitor[670] moved an amendment Sir John luson to order: if any word is amended there can no amendment be offered to amend a word before that but after it may[671] ([sic] Nota this was the amendment Sir Tho[mas] Litleton moved to have the word E[arl] inserted in the place of [?the] word lord: Sir Rowland Gwin tho you cannot move an amendment before an amendment made yet you may speak against the Clause and have it recommitted and there you may amend any part of: Mr Smith it will be very inconvenient to ty our selves up so strictly to order: that tho we might try which we pleased first yet it would seem but reasonable to try whom we[672] first impeached that giving some colour for mankind to beleive that we were the readier for those that we first impeached: that it was unparliamentary and a very unnusuall expression to say that the lords libelled us and that we should appeale to the people: that he knew of no president before the five lords that were tryed in King Charleses time for us to try which lord we pleased first that it was hardly possible before that to have a dispute on this subject[673] there being as he beleives but one lord before that impeached at one time: that the sending to us to put us in mind of our delais

[667] Originally 'Somers'.
[668] On 14 Apr.: *CJ* xiii. 489.
[669] 'and libell us to the people' interlined.
[670] Sir John Hawles.
[671] [Hatsell,] *Precedents*, 81, notes that it was 'an established rule of the House "that, when you have amended the latter part of a question, you cannot recur back, and make any alteration in the former part"'.
[672] Originally 'which we plea[sed]'.
[673] 'on this subject' interlined.

and to hasten us had been done by us to them that in the case of the Lord
mordant impeached by the Commons the commons sent to the lords to hasten
the said lords answer:[674] the Lords returned an answer that that was the day
appoynted for his answer Mr Bromely said the Lords messages were without
president or reason president he never heard of and there was no reason
cō[n]sidering the busines we were ingaged in besides the impeachments and
enumerated some of the great matters before us

[*fo. 67ᵛ*]

Sir Xto[*pher*] musgrove our debates are to no purpose[675] the clause having been
amended: then the claus was read vizt th[?at] the messages to hasten us were
unparliamentary and unpresidented in relation to the Lords Hallifax and
portland we having exhibited articles against two already Mr Smith that the
impeachments were grounded upon the treaty of partition but that when we
impeach for any thing we have a right to put what we please in the impeachment but that in reason we ought not to put in so many things as to occasion
delays that it was 9 weeks since my Lord portland was impeached and 7n [*sic*]
since my Lord Hallifax was impeached that gent[*lemen*] had mentioned the
three Lords that were impeached in the convention viz Salisbury peterborough
and Sunderland[676] that they had lain a great while longer and no articles
exhibited and yet no messages to hasten us that then wee were ingaged in great
businesses and that there was a difference and that a great one between those that
lay quietly under it and submitted and those that desired to come upon their
tryalls, that if w[e] did differ with the lords there must be a delay of justice and
that would be a fault and where that would ly he left them to judge: mr
Bromley we have already sent word that those words were unparliamentary and
without a president and that we Could not recede from them that Gent[*leman*]
had said that articles had not been exhibited for some time against the five
popish Lords becaus of the prorogations but that that was Equally hard and
injurious to the impeached lords as if the parliament was sitting that it was no
certain sign of ones innocence to desire to come to ones tryall that my lord
Stafford did the same who was afterwards condemned[677] Sir Joseph Jechiell[678]

---

[674] Presumably the message sent to the Lords on 16 Jan. 1668 to remind them of the
impeachment proceedings against John Mordaunt (1627–75), Viscount Mordaunt of Avalon,
which was followed within two days by the submission of Mordaunt's answer to the articles:
CJ viii. 677; *LJ* xii. 76–7.   [675] 'our' erased.
    [676] James Cecil (1666–94), 4th Earl of Salisbury, and Henry Mordaunt (1623–97), 2nd Earl of
Peterborough, had been impeached on 26 Oct. 1689 (*CJ* x. 275), though no further action was
taken against them. Robert Spencer (1641–1702), 2nd Earl of Sunderland, had not been impeached
during the Convention.   [677] See above, p. 143, n. 563.
    [678] See above, p. 78, n. 114. Henry St John claimed that Jekyll had helped Somers pen 'all the
messages and answers which have been sent down to our House': HMC, *Downshire MSS*, i. 803.

said there was a grea[t] difference between delays occasioned by prorogations
and those that were when the parliament was sitting he spo[ke] against those
words in another clause which said it tended to delay of justice he said it might
occasion disputes and he thought Gent[*lemen*] would not be glad of disputes
Sintgeons[679] said the honour of the house was concerned which was worth a
thousand of us and more warm stuff Sir Xto[*pher*] musgrove there are
exceptions taken to our proceedings as if they were dilatory but that it was
very unusuall and out of the way to send to hasten us: it is the right a[nd]
constant practice in impeachments for misdemeanour to add what more you
will that is not mentioned in the cause of the impeachment: the lords in their
words are very pressing but that when one consider[s] more of it it dos not
look like pressing there are some expressions that seem like a concession bu[t]
in reallity they are not so it is very new to say that at the instance of my Lord
Somers that is no concession to us but to gratify that Lords request that we
have had a great deale of busines as well as the Convention parliament which
may excuse our seeming delays: Sir John Luson the lords sent twice or th[?rice]
before we would take any notice of their unusuall messages that now we are
thus dealt with we Cannot be to[o] sharp and that the more we shew our
resentments the more and the sooner the lords will Comply: Sir Godfrey
Copley if we insist on more then what is our right we may be said to delay
oth[er] wise not as for impeachments sometime Lords have been impeached and
articles never exhibited and there may me [*sic*] be reason for it as particularly
when my lord Portland was first impeached it was becaus he did being a
forreigner make treatys to the prejudice of England without consulting [?of]
English councill and so it did then appear but looking further into matters
upon these other impeachments it does appear he [*h*]as acted nothing but by
and with the directions and advice of En[g]lish councills so that it dos appear
that he is not so guilty as at the first we had reason t[o] beleive him: Sir Robert
davers as long as he is a member will maintain the honour of the hou[se] Sir
Hum[*phrey*] Mackworth sais the lords may send for a conference in a
parliament[*ar*]y way as well as thi[s] house[680] mr Hamond I dont wonder to
see such things acted in the house of lords since those that are the criminalls
are the Judges also and the same reason is allso for our proceedings sin[ce] the
relations of the criminalls sit here[681] and are their advocates who ought to be

[679] i.e. St John.

[680] Mackworth was subsequently to publish a lengthy *Vindication of the Rights of the*
Commons . . . (1701), dealing with the arguments arising from the impeachment proceedings:
Somers's Tracts, xi. 276–315. His bitterness against Somers arose from a personal 'injustice' the
former Lord Chancellor had done him; Nat. Lib. Wales, MS 14362E, p. 121; see above, p. 99, n. 269.

[681] As is made clear below, Hammond is referring to Sir Joseph Jekyll, Somers's brother-in-law.

removed that i[t] did appear they were in great hast to come to their tryalls since the scaffolds were begun to [be] built on Sunday[682] Sir Tho[*mas*] littleton in all things the moderate ways are most secure and best and [?he] desires that the replication may be sent to the lords and a conference desired Sir Jo[*seph*] Jechiell sais he minds not what a private opinion is in relation to removing him but that as long as he sits here he will act and speak what is consistent with the trust reposed in him by his count[?ry] musgrove sais that Seymour who was vice admirall to the duke of Buckingham was sequest[*er*]ed from the service of the house when the debates related to that Duke[683] Sir John Holles sais in all cases it is the constant practice of all courts to give convenient time and place to the prosecutor and to the prosecuted Sir W[*illia*]m Stricland sais we should be more moderate and not[684] run things up too great heigths that we should send up our reply and go on with the tryall Lord Coningsbee I am[685] as much for the honour and dignity of the house as any body and that right will take place at last that messages tended to nothing more but to widen breaches and that conferences were first invented to prevent heats and to bring us to a right understanding: Sir Xto[*pher*] musgrove that we ought to be even with the lords first by way of message and [?that then] We may have an opportunity for a Conference after some more debating they agreed to the message to be sent to the lords and put of[*f*] the debate of the conference and the sending up of the reading of the[686] reply[687] by putting of a quaestion which was carried in the negative[688] and then they read the money bill[689] and so [?adjourned] nota they had great reason to delay the reading of the reply and to raise so many [?difficulties] to delay the tryall for they were sensible that they had no evidence to ground any just [accu]sation against the lord Somers and less against the rest wherefore they hastned the money bill a[?nd] the busines of the sessions and delayed the reply in hopes to be prorogued before the try[all] came on least this should appear upon the printing of the tryall to the whole world Nota I never hear the honour and dignity of the house mentioned but in order to inflame and heat our debates: but Certainly the honour and dignity of

---

[682] On Friday, 30 May, the Lords had given orders for the erection of scaffolds in Westminster Hall for the trial of Orford's impeachment; *LJ* xvi. 712; Luttrell, *Brief Relation*, v. 55–6.

[683] Possibly a confusion between the sequestration of Richard Dyott (MP Lichfield) on 9 May 1626 for words spoken in the debate on the message relating to the committal of the 1st Duke of Buckingham (*CJ* i. 858), and the accusations of partiality levelled at Sir Edward Seymour, as Speaker, when his former patron, the 2nd Duke of Buckingham, appeared before the Commons on 13 Jan. 1674 (*CJ* ix. 292; *HC 1660–90*, iii. 415). Seymour had been a commissioner of the navy, though not a vice-admiral.   [684] 'not' interlined.

[685] 'I am' interlined.   [686] 'reading of the' interlined.

[687] 'till tomorrow morning' erased.

[688] 'by putting of a question which was carried in the negative' interlined. To read the engrossed replication to Somers's answer: *CJ* xiii. 596.   [689]The Land Tax Bill.

the house is never kept up and maintained by any thing more then by moderation and justice: Nota may the 26th [*1701*] the Bishop of Salisbury told me that he heard Sir Charles Hedges tell my lord Stamford that he had orders from the king to acquaint the house that there was nothing done in Enfeild Chase but by his particular orders tho he never mentioned this in the house but told some of the members of it privately after the debate was Just Concluded why he did so quaere:[690] nota [*3 May 1701*] Sir John Luson brought in the bill to take away priviledge from those members that did make use of it to protect their estates in time of prorogations:[691] the Lord Rochesters son the lord Hide married lusons sister[692] [?the] the Lord Rochester had a grant of 1500 out of my Lord Tankerfeilds est[ate ?but] Could never come at the Lord[693] Tankerville standing upon Privile[ge][694] and it [?was] said the rise of this bill was to serve my lord Rochester

[*fo. 67*]

[695]nota Dorrington[696] was made paymaster of the navy by my Lord Orford and in the year [*16*]98 the parliament fell very hard upon my Lord Orford and he was saved but by one vote[697] and he had all the foleys and the Harleys and Winnington[698] for him they pretending that they aymed not at persons but things ([*sic*] tho the thing in reallity was that Tom Foley the son of Tom of Worcestershire courted mr [*sic*] Harbord my Lord Orfords neice[699] and therefore to promote that match they saved my Lord Orford from a storm

---

[690] See above, p. 150.

[691] The bill 'to prevent any inconveniences that may happen by privilege of Parliament': *CJ* xiii. 511.

[692] Henry, Lord Hyde, MP Launceston, married in 1692 Jane, daughter of Sir William Leveson Gower, 4th Bt. [693] 'Stanford' erased.

[694] Cf. Lord Clarendon to Rochester, 8 May 1686, printed in S. W. Singer (ed.), *The Correspondence of Henry Hyde, Earl of Clarendon and of His Brother Laurence Hyde, Earl of Rochester* . . . (2 vols.; London 1828), i. 374: 'I hope care is taken to secure your money before Lord Grey [the future Tankerville] was restored to his estate'.

[695] 'Thursday the 5th June' erased.

[696] George Dodington (*c.*1658–1720) of Eastbury, Dorset: cashier to Orford as treasurer of the navy, 1692–9; later Lord of the Admiralty 1709–10, 1714–17; MP Winchelsea 1705–8, 1713–15, Bridgwater 1708–13, 1715–d. See *HC 1715–54*, i. 615.

[697] In committee on 15 Mar. 1699, on the motion that victualling the Straits fleet without due proof of the purchase costs of the provisions was 'an ill example and prejudicial to the public', which was defeated 141:140: Luttrell, *Brief Relation*, iv. 494.

[698] Salwey Winnington, MP, son-in-law of Thomas Foley, sen. (MP Worcs. 1679–98, Droitwich 1699–1701).

[699] Thomas Foley, jun., MP Strafford, son of Thomas Foley, sen.; and Letitia Harbord (d. 1737), da. of William Harbord (MP Dartmouth 1661–79, Thetford 1679–81, Launceston 1689–92) by his 2nd wife, Orford's sister. Letitia eventually married in 1703, Sir Rowland Winn of Nostell Priory, Yorks., allegedly bringing with her a portion of £30,000: George Baker, *The History of the County of Northampton* (2 vols.; London, 1822–30), ii. 172; Luttrell, *Brief Relation*, v. 330.

which is now fell upon him and will[700] be for his honour when the truth
appears: but when they could not[701] hurt my Lord Orford they fell foule upon
Do[r]rington the paymaster of the navy the case was this he had by his place
12 in the pound to keep the seamens account Deadmens cloaths tobacko and
what els I Know not Called slop money this was allways paid by the seamen
and allowed out of the seamens wages to the paymaster for keeping their
account it was said that Dorrington got to[o] much and that he had by this
means 30000 li. and my Lord orfords freinds to save him gave up Dorrington
to shift for himself so there was a vote passed upon dorrington in that
parliament[702] [27 or 30 May 1701][703] Coll Bierley who is the most party
and ill natured man in the house desired to have that vote read in the
Committee of ways and means: that Committee divided and it was caried
by one vote only to charge Dorrington with the mony he had received for slops
and dead mens Cloaths they said the sum was 17000 li. yeats of Bristol and
[?me] divided with the angry party against dorrington for we were in the
parliament which gave Dorrington up in [or]der to turn the present[704] fury
from my Lord orford hoping I beleive withall that they might retreive
Dorrington at any time his being ajust and good case: Dorringtons case
was this (but I did not understand it at the division so I did absent myself
at the report[705] [3 June 1701], tho I think being convinced I rather ought to
have staid and have made him amends Knowingly for the injury I did him
ignorantly but busines hinderd me)[706] Dorrington had but 3000 li. per añ
[sa]lary and it cost him more amongst his Clerks the seamen allowed the other
shilling per li. out of their salaryes this was practiced time out of mind:
Dorrington by the death and running away of his Clerks [l]ost a great deale
with what it cost him more then his salary came to: and it being the usuall
perqui[s]its of his place suppose he had received such a great sum and had
spent what he thought was [h]is own will you by a retrospect law take from
him this he and all mankind thought to be his own and as such had used and

---

[700] 'will' interlined.   [701] 'not' interlined.

[702] On 22 Mar. 1699 the committee on the state of the navy resolved that passing the accounts
for money imprested for the contingent uses of the navy without regular vouchers was 'contrary to
the rules of the navy and of dangerous consequence', Dodington having paid several sums by privy
seal and without vouchers: Luttrell, *Brief Relation*, iv. 497. This was reported on 27 Mar., with
another resolution that the deduction of poundage taken by the paymaster of the navy for slop
clothes, dead men's clothes, tobacco, etc., was 'without warrant and ought to be accounted for':
CJ xii. 609, 618.

[703] There were meetings of ways and means on both these days, after which various resolutions
were reported (on 3 June), including one that the poundage deducted out of defalcations made by
the paymaster for slop clothing etc. be applied to the public funds: *CJ* xiii, 578, 586, 592–3.

[704] 'present' interlined.   [705] See above, p. 158, n. 658.

[706] 'but business hinderd me' interlined.

spent it: at the report the house divided and those for Dorrington carried it by 20[707] Jovis 5 die Jun[*ii 1701*][708] Sir John dillons bill[709] was read and it being proved that Sir John offered her his wife[710] money to defend her self to enable her if she pleased and she making no defence[711] the bill went easily thro and was ordered to be reported without any amendments: Nota that the Lord Anglesea was the occasion of two divorces this sessions of his own from his lady by his barbarous and villanous ill usage and he was the man that firs[t] took my Lady Dillon from Sir John[712] and both these ladys did sollicite the Lords at the same time which was an Extraordinary thing and I hope will never be a common case Nothing more extraordinary this day

Veneris 6th die [*June 1701*] Mr Harcourt reported from the committee of impeachments appoynted to consider of the lords message[713] the 4th of June [*1701*] and to draw up what shall be offered at a conference upon the subject matter of the [sai]d message which was that the Com[*mon*]s desired this conference upon your Lords[*hi*]ps message of the 4th of June in order to preserve a good Correspondence they desire a committee of both houses may be nominated to consider of the most proper and the best methods of proceeding upon impeachments according to the usage of Parliament Nota all these messages are allmost nothing but matter of form taken out of the Journalls upon such occasions nothing worth observing, but that at the report Singeons[714] said the impeached lords were not at the conference. Sabbati 7 Junii [*1701*][715] an addres to the King to prefer the Chaplain Mr Hern[716] and the second reading of bills and things of cours Lunae 9 Junii [*1701*][717] Mr B[*r*]uges[718] reported the articles of impeachment against Charles lord Hallifax: a message from the Lords:[719] In answer to a message of the

---

[707] Carried 104:86 according to *CJ* xiii. 593.   [708] Jovis 5 die Jun[*ii 1701*]' boxed in MS.

[709] The bill to divorce Sir John Dillon (d. *c.*1708), of Lismullen, Co. Meath, from his wife Mary, daughter of Murrough Boyle, 1st Viscount Blessington, who had 'eloped' from him in 1695 and had since been living, it was alleged in 'open adultery' in England. Lodge, *Peerage of Ireland*, i. 75; Sir Arthur Vicars (ed.), *Index to the Prerogative Wills of Ireland 1536–1810* (Dublin, 1897), 134; HMC, *House of Lords MSS*, NS iv. 304–6.   [710] 'his wife' interlined.

[711] Lady Dillon's petition to the Lords noted that Sir John had offered to pay the fees of her solicitor and counsel: HMC, *House of Lords MSS*, NS iv. 306.

[712] In December Anglesey and Dillon had fought a duel: Luttrell, *Brief Relation*, iii. 559.

[713] The committee originally appointed to prepare the articles of impeachment, and since extended. The message is printed in *CJ* xiii. 600.

[714] Henry St John had earlier been sent as the Commons' messenger to request the conference: ibid.   [715] 'Sabbati 7 junii [*1701*]' boxed in MS.

[716] John Herne (d. 1707), rector of East Shefford, Berks., chaplain to King William in 1690, and canon of Windsor 1690–d.: Donald Gray, *Chaplain to Mr Speaker . . .* (House of Commons Library Document 19; London, 1991), 60.   [717] 'Lunae 9 Junii [*1701*]' boxed in MS.

[718] James Brydges's name is spelt thus in the *Journals* (*CJ* xiii. 603).

[719] Printed ibid. 606.

house of commons of the 4th instant they declare they are ready to try any of the impeached lords which the commons will first: that the Lords have shewed their willingnes to comply in what is reasonable and therefore (as they conceive) the commons had no occasion to begin any dispute so the Lords are carefull to avoyd all controversies the Lords think it their right to appoynt a day for the tryall of any impeachment lying before them, if they see good caus for it, without any previous signification from the Commons of their being ready to proceed which right is made out by many presidents and reason and that they will allwais use that right in the administration of Justice and with a care to prevent unreasonable[720] delays: and the lords wonder the commons without any foundation for it use such expressions never used before: and which if the same were returned must necessarily destroy all good correspondence between the two houses: the last part of the commons message being but a repetition of the former of the 31 of may [1701] the lords having given a full answer to it allready, they need say no more: then that they cannot imagine with what colour their calling upon the hous of commons to send up articles against two Lords whom the commons have so long impeached in Generall terms can be said to tend to the delay of justice and therefore as the Lords think the commons ought to have forbore that reflection so their Lords[*hi*]ps in laying no more upon the occasion of this message of the commons think they have shewed their moderation and desire to keep a good Correspondence which is necessary for the publick security as well as doing right upon the impeachments) [*sic*] Nota that this mr Bruges who carried up the impeachment against my Lord Hallifax was used to sollicit my lord then mr Mountague and Sir Tho[*mas*] littleton and Mr Smith these 3 told me to get a place in the excise he was used to say his father was a Jacobite and used him hardly by the reason he was of contrary principles[721] and that he Knew these places were disposed of to none but to the parliament men that tho he was not now one he was sure he should the next sessions of parliament and that he would deserve his place by his voting Littleton said to him sir I dont know that the King expects any mans vote at the price of his place but I beleive this is an offer of the first impression to promise how will vote before you are chosen: my Lord Hallifax told me he was constantly at his levy and desired him speak to the King for him and that I might Know he was acquainted with him he bid me observe the stinking of his breath which was very offensive to him in a morning: he told me he had often spoken to the king to give it him and all the disobligation he knew was the kings not granting this request ([*sic*] Nota that upon the reading of the articles of impeachment against the Lord Hallifax Sir

---

[720] 'un' interlined.   [721] See above, p. 95.

William St. Quintain who formerly moved to have the thanks of the house given to mr Mountague then (now my Lord Hallifax) for his good services to the publick when there was a quaestion put upon Mr mountague for obtaining a grant of a small value I think of about 1200 li. and it was carried in the negative all which appears by the journalls of the house of Commons and the thanks of the house upon the motion of the said Sir william St Quintain were given him ([*sic*] for which good services Sir william was made a comissioner of the custome house[722] the said Sir william St Quintain after the articles were read in the house in order to impeach to maintain the impeachments [*sic*] of Charles Lord Hallifax said he was not against carrying up the said articles for he thought considering the great places of honour and trust that the said Lord had been in it would turn to his honour to have the world see what small and litle things only he could be accused of: for which he was in the heat and fury of the angry party called to the barr and after more heat and warm words in his place he explained himself that what he said was not as was suggested mentioned with the least intention to reflect on or to arraign the justice of the house only that he thought that lord could easily vindicate himself and that upon his tryall he would be acquitted upon which the heat abated and they proceeded upon other matters[723] Martis die 10th Junii [*1701*] Mr Harcourt reported the answer to the Lords message as followes:[724] the Commons to avoyd delays and inconveniencyes in the proceedings against the impeached lords have proposed at a conference that a Committee of both houses shoud [b]e nominated to consider of the best ways and methods of proceeding on impeachments think[ing ?they ?m]ight [justly h]ave expected your Lords[*hi*]ps complyance with the said proposition instead of the message

[*fo. 66ᵛ*]

the 4th of Instant: in which answer of your Lords[*hi*]ps tho many matters of great exception are contained a suttable [re]ply whereunto would inevitably destroy all good correspondence between the two houses yet the commons from an earnest desire to preserve the same as well as to shew their moderation and readines to bring the impeached lords to justice: at present only insis[t] on their proposition for a Committee of both houses to setle preliminaryes to the tryalls particularly whether the impeached Lor[ds] should appear on their tryalls as criminalls at your Lords[*hi*]p[*s'*] barr. Whether being

---

[722] See above, p. 53.

[723] John Ellis confirmed that 'Sir William St Quintin was so bold as to say they [the articles] would tend to his [Halifax's] eternal honour, for which he had like to have been called to the bar, but escaped, after a long debate': BL Add. MS 7074, fo. 29.

[724] The committee for the impeachments had been ordered to draft an answer to the Lords' message of the previous day: it is printed in *CJ* xiii. 614.

under accusation of the same crimes they are to sit as judges on each others tryalls for those crimes or can vote in their own cases as we find by your Lords[*hi*]ps journalls since their being impeached they have been admitted to do: which matters and some other necessary to be adjusted the commons cannot but insis[t] on a committee of both houses to be appoynted for that purpose: their departing from which would be giving up the rights of the com[*mons*] of England Known by unquaestionable precedents and the usage of Parliament and making all impeachments (the bulwarks of the laws and liberties of England) impracticable for the future:[725] ordered that mr Harcourt carry up this message to the Lords nothing more remarkable: Mercurii 11 die junii [*1701*] ordere[726] that the com[*mi*]s[*sione*]rs of accounts have no salaries and be members:[727] mr Harcourt repo[r]ted from the committee in answer to the Lords message munday last as follows:[728] the Commons last munday received a message that your Lords[*hi*]ps had appoynted friday next for the tryall of the Lord Somers they have observed your Lords[*hi*]ps have nominated no place for [the] tryall tho your Lords[*hi*]ps thought fit to make that matter[729] on the last impeachment for misdemeanours the subject of a lon[g] debate and they cannot but take notice that your Lords[*hi*]ps have taken as long a time to give your answer to the Commons desire of a committee of both houses delivered at a conference on friday last as you are pleased to allow the commons to have of the day appoynted by your Lords[*hi*]ps for the said tryall: Your Lords[*hi*]ps so short a day especially whilst the proposition made to your Lords[*hi*]ps for a committee of both houses was undetermined: the Commons take to be such an hardship to them and[730] such an indulgence to the person accused as is not to be paralleld in any parliament[*ar*]y proceedings The Commons must likewise acquaint you that their experience of a former tryall on an impeachment of misdemeanours for want of setling the preliminaries between the two houses obliges them to insist on a committee of both houses for preventing the like interruption And they conceive it would be very preposterous for them to enter upon the tryall of any of those lords till your Lords[*hi*]ps discover some inclinations to make proc[ee]dings thereon practicable and therefore they think they have reason to insist upon another day to be appoynted for the trya[ll] of the Lord Somers and the Commons doubt not but at a free Conference to satisfy your

---

[725] 'that' erased. [726] 'ordere' interlined.

[727] An adjourned debate on the qualification of commissioners of accounts, after the engrossment of the bill to appoint a commission: *CJ* xiii. 623.

[728] The Lords' message was to inform the Commons that they had appointed Somers's trial for 13 June: ibid 614. The Commons' reply is printed ibid. 623.

[729] 'the last' erased. [730] 'so unparalled' erased.

Lords[*hi*]ps of the necessity of having a Committee of both houses before they can proceed upon the tryalls: the other things were matter of form Jovis 12th junii [*1701*][731] Mr Bruges[732] who carryed the articles of impeachment against the Lord Hallifax was allso ordered to pray and demand that Charles Lord Halli[fax] do give sufficient security to abide the judgment of the lords ([*sic*] nota all this is for nothing but to blast this and the other lords reputation without doors in order to make the world beleive there are great matters against them: then the King by Asto[n] the usher of the black rod commanded the honourable[733] house to him [*in*] the house of peers and at their return the Speaker reported what bi[lls] the king had given his royall assent to and after that the Kings speech of which he had obtained a coppy[734] the substance of [?which] was my Lords and Gent[*lemen*] I thank [*you*] for your care in establishing the crown in a protestant line and he [*sic*] will not lose this opp[or]tunity of acquainting them of his sence of their assurances of supporting him in his alliances as shall be proper for the pr[e]servation of the liberty of Europe and the security of England and holland and he tels them their ready complyance with his desires to asssist the States generall is a great satisfaction to him and advantage to the common cause: and that nothing is so mu[ch] at[735] heart as the preservation of the liberty of Europe and the honour and interest of England, so I make no doubt of attaining those great[736] ends by the blessing of god and the continuance of your cheerfull Concurrence: my Lords and Gent[*lemen*] the season of the year makes it necessary for[737] to have a speedy recess and the posture of affairs abroad dos absolutely require my presence for the encouragement of our allies and for the perfecting of such alliances as may be most Effectuall for the common interest and therefore I must recommend a dispatch of the publick busines Especially of those matters which are of the greatest importance upon which the whole house went with this following addres to Kinsington[738] most gracious sovereign: wee your Majestys most Dutifull and Loyall subjects etc.: do with all imaginable cheerfulnes return your Majesty our humble thanks for your most gracious speech from the throne in which your Majesty is pleased to Express

[731] 'Jovis 12 junii [*1701*]' boxed in MS.

[732] James Brydges, whose name is spelt this way in *CJ* xiii. 625.

[733] 'honourable' interlined. Francis Aston was deputy usher of the black rod (*Cal. Treas. Bks.*, xvii. 1003); possibly identical with former fellow of Trinity College, Cambridge, born in 1645 and dying in 1715, who had served as joint-secretary of the Royal Society 1681–5.

[734] Printed in *CJ* xiii. 626.   [735] 'my' erased.   [736] 'great' interlined.

[737] 'your' superseded.

[738] Printed in *CJ* xiii. 626–7. The *Journals* record a resolution on 12 June that the address be presented to the King by the whole House (ibid. 627). Luttrell, however, dates the actual presentation, at Kensington, to the 13th (*Brief Relation*, v. 60–1).

your Royall Approbation of the proceeding[s] of your Commons and we do further unanimously assure your Majesty that we will be ready on all occasions to assist you[r] majesty in supporting such alliances as your Majesty shall think fit to make in conjunction with the emperour and St[ates] Generall for the preservation of the liberties of Europe the prosperity and peace of England and for reducing the exorbitant power of France: Nota I beleive the king knew before hand what the Commons would say for he had no reason to thank them much before: and truly so gracious a speech upon so small reason deserved the addres the Commons made: A message from the Lords by Mr Gery and Dr Newton[739] in answer to the message from the house of Commons of the 10th instant the Lords say that altho they take it to be unparliamentary in many particulars yet to shew the[ir] reall desire of avoyding disputes and removing all pretence of delaying the tryalls of the impeached lords they will only take notice of[740] th[at] part of their message wherein the commons propose some things as difficulties in respect of the tryalls which matters relating wholly to their judicature and to their rights and priviledges as peers they think fit to acquaint the commons with the follo[w]ing resolutions of the house of Lords:[741] first that no lord of Parliament impeached of high crimes and misdemeanours and com[ing] to his tryall shall upon his tryall be without the bar 2dly that no Lord etc.: can be precluded from voting on any occasion exce[pt] in his own tryall: their Lords[*hi*]ps further take notice of a mistake in poynt of fact alledged in the message of the commons it no way appearing in their journalls that the lords impeached have voted in their own case: the lords being well assured that all the step[s] that have been taken by them in relation to these impeachments are warranted by the practice of their ancestors and usage o[f] parliaments, have reason to expect the tryalls should proceed without delay: Also that they were comanded by the Lords to acquain[t] this house that: In answer to the message of the house of commons yesterday the lords say that they cannot give a greater evidence of their sincere and hearty desires of avoyding all differences with the house of Commons and of proceeding on the tryalls of the impeachments, than by not taking notice of the severall just[742] exceptions to which that message is lyable both as to the matter and expressions: The Lords have nothing further from their thoughts than the going about to do any thing which might [*have*] the least appearance of hardship with relation to the commons: But the answer of the lord Sommers to the articles exhibited against him having been sent down to the

---

[739] Henry (later Sir Henry) Newton (1651–1715), chancellor of the diocese of London, and judge-advocate to the Admiralty. For Gery, see above, p. 139, n. 540. The message is printed in *CJ* xiii. 627.

[740] 'notice of' interlined.   [741] '[?peers]' erased.   [742] 'impeachments' erased.

commons on the 24th of May last and they having by their message of th[e] 31st of may last signifyed to their Lords[hi]ps their intention of beginning with the tryall of his impeachment in the first place: the Lords considering how far the session is advanced thought it reasonable to appoynt the 13th instant for the said tryall: their lordships finding severall precedents of appoynting tryalls in impeachments within a shorter time: the Lords also think it incumbent upon them to indeavour to dispatch the tryalls of all the impeached lords before the rising of this Parliament: this is what Justice requires and cannot be looked upon as a matter of indulgency: nevertheless that the commons may see how desirous their Lords[hi]ps are to comply with them in any thing which may be Consistent with justice they have appoynted the tryall of impeachmen[t] against John Lords Sommers on the 17th of this june at 10 of the clock in the morning in the house of lords which will be th[en] sitting in westminster hall: Also that the Lords do agree to a free conference with the Commons as desired and do appoynt tomorrow at one a clock in the painted Chamber Ordered that the Members do prepare their lists of the names of 7 persons to be Com[mi]s[sione]rs to be incerted into the bill for appoynting and enabling Com[mi]s[sione]rs to take examine and state the publick aCCounts of the kingdom: the rest was matters of Cours: Nota I do beleive that this was Concerted that now upon the rising of the house the king should thank the house and seem satisfyed with the proceedings, and that the house should assure the king of their readines to support hi[m] and to curb the exorbitant power of France to prevent the addresses talked on as intended upon the rise of this Parliament to dissolve this parliament and to call a new one: there are many things that aime at one thing and give a look towards another but this is only my Conjecture veneris 13th [*June 1701*][743] the chancellour of the exchec[*quer*][744] acquainted the house that the king would take care to prefer our Chaplain Mr Heron: mr St John a forwar[d]ly yong fellow of a great Estate Whom the angry party have blooded [?with] taking notice of him reported from the committee to whom the messages from the lords yesterday were referred and is as follo[ws:][745] The house of Commons find greater reason to insist upon their proposall of a committee of both houses from the two messages received yesterday from your Lords[hi]ps for their ambiguity and uncertainty do shew the methods of former parliaments to be the most proper way for dispatch of business the Commons have been

---

[743] 'veneris 13th [*June 1701*]' boxed in MS.   [744] Henry Boyle.

[745] Henry St John certainly had the prospect of a 'great estate' when his father died, but at this time he himself considered his financial circumstances to be 'low', and this despite his recent marriage to an heiress: St John to Sir William Trumbull, 13 Aug. 1701, quoted in Dickinson, *Bolingbroke*, 13. The Commons reply is printed in *CJ* xiii. 629.

obliged to spend that time in considering and answering your Lords[*hi*]p[s] messages, which otherwise would have been spent in preparing for the lord Sommerses tryall so that the Delay must be Charged where the occasion ariseth but the Commons having desired a committee of[746] both houses to adjust the preliminaries of th[e] tryals can not but think it[747] strange your Lords[*hi*]ps should come to resolutions upon two of those poynts while the proposall of the house of Commons is under debate at Conference between the two houses the commons having other difficulties to propose which concern them as prosecutors and all other impeachments: And altho the com[*mon*]s leave the subiect of your Lords[*hi*]ps resolutions with other things to be debated at a Committee of both houses yet they cannot but observe that your Lords[*hi*]ps second resolutions [*sic*] is no direct answer to the commons proposall which was whether Peers impeached of the same crimes shall vote for each other upon their tryall for the same crime and the commons cannot beleive that any such rule can be laid down in plain words, Where there is a due regard to justice and as to what your Lords[*hi*]ps observe, that there is a mistake in po[ynt] of fact alledged by the comons that this house may take notice of the caution used by your Lords[*hi*]ps in wording that p[a]rt of yo[ur] message for they Know your Lords[*hi*]ps are too well acquainted with the truth of the fact that to affirm that the impe[a]cht L[ords] did not vote in their own cases and tho the appearing or not appearing upon your Lords[*hi*]ps jou[rn]all do[s] not

[*fo*. 66

m]ake it more or les agreable to the rules of justice: yet the com[*mon*]s cannot but add this further observation from your Lords[*hi*]p[*s'*] Journalls that the impeached lords presence is not only recorded When those votes passed but they also find some of them appoynted of Committees for preparing and drawing up messages and answers to the house of com[*mon*]s, which they do not think has been the best expedient for preserving a good correspondence between the two houses, Or adjusting what will be[748] necessary upon their tryalls and therefore the com[*mon*]s cannot think is [*sic*] agreable to the Rules of parliament for them to appear at a tryall till all necessary preliminaries are first setled with your Lords[*hi*]ps: then the managers went to the conference and being returned Mr Harcourt reported What had hapned in a speech of the Lord Haversham[749] they thought fit to withdraw from the Conference to acquaint the house therewith: Ordered that the managers withdraw into the

---

[746] Originally 'desired a conference'.   [747] 'hard' erased.   [748] 'proper' erased.

[749] John Thompson (*c*.1648–1705), 1st Lord Haversham. For details of this incident, see 'A True Account of the Proceedings Relating to the Charge of the House of Commons against John, Lord Haversham', in *Somers's Tracts*, xi. 334–9; and Burnet, *Own Time*, iv. 515–16.

Speakers Chamber and collect the matter thereof and report the same to the house: the report was made and it was resolved that John Lord Haversham hath at the free Conferenc uttered most scandalous and fals expressions and reproaches highly reflecting upon the honour and justice of the house of com̄ons and tending to the making a breach in the good Correspondence between the Lords and commons and to the interrupting the publick justice of the nation by delaying the proceedings of the impeachments: Resolved that John Lord Haversham be charged before the lords for the words spoken by the said lord this day at the free Conference and that the lords be desired to proceed in justice against the Lord Haversham and to inflict such punishment upon the said lord as so high an offence against the hous of com̄[*mon*]s dos deserve: and that Sir Xto[*pher*] musgrove do carry the said Charge and resolution to the lords: the Lords by message desire the Contimuance [*sic*] of the free conference and ar concerned at what hapned and desire the Com̄[*mon*]s to return presently as the best expedient to prevent misunderstandings: the commons will return an answer by their own messengers Sir Xto[*pher*] musgrove reported that he had delivered the Charge etc. and then the house adjourned Sabbati 14th [*June 1701*][750] the lords by a message[751] acquaint the house that upon occasion of the last message the Commons sent yesterday in order to continue a good correspondence the Lords did appoynt a committee to state the matter of the free conference and to search presidents and that the publick busines may not be delaid the time desired by their Lords[*hi*]ps being Elapsed for renewing the free Conference their Lords[*hi*]ps desire a present free Conference upon the subject matter of the last free Conference: Resolved that they will send an answer by messengers of their own: Resolved that the answer be: that the Com̄[*mo*]ns are desirous to preserve a good correspondence between the two houses and to expedite the tryalls of the impeached Lords but do conceive it is not consistent with the honour of the com̄[*mons*] to re[n]ew the free conference untill they have received reparation by their Lords[*hi*]ps doing justice upon John Lord Haversham for the indignity he offered the house of Com̄[*mon*]s yesterday: mr Speaker reported the kings answer[752] which was Gent[*lemen*] I thank you very heartily for the unanimous assurances you have given me of your readines to assist me in supporting such alliances as I shall make in conjunction with the emperour and the States Generall: it will be a great Encouragement to them to find the sence of this kingdom so fully expressed on this occasion and will Likewise contribute most Effectually to the obtaining of those great

---

[750] 'Sabbati 14th [*June 1701*]' boxed in MS. [751] Printed in *CJ*, xiii. 631.
[752] Printed ibid.

ends you have now mentioned on which the happines of Europe does so much depend: all the rest reading of bills and consideration of reports Lunae 16th die Junii 1701[753] Sir Rowland Gwin reported[754] Sidney mountague alias Wortley to be [d]uly Elected for peterborrow Which was agreed to by the house: and indeed there appeared nothing of a ground for a petition but tha[t] singeons the petitioner would have voted another way[755] and that in the case of white[756] and others was ground enough: A message from the Lords[757] by which the messengers are commanded to acquaint the house that the Lord Somers having informed the Lords that Sir Ste[phen] Fox mr Smith Hervey[758] Lownds and Gulston members of this house may be materiall witness for him at his tryall on Tuesday next in westminster Hall the Lords desire that they may have leave to attend and to give their testimonies at the said tryall and that a letter which his Majesty was pleased to write to him in 1698 being now in this house[759] will be necessary for his defence at his tryall they desire that the said letter may be produced on his tryall: resolved an answer be sent by Messengers of their own A message from the Lords[760] acquaints the house intending to try the Lord Somers on tuesday have prepared some rules to be observed at the said tryall which they thought fit to communicate to this house: Die Lunae 16 Junii 1701[761] That the Whole impeachment be read and then the answer, which being done the Lord Keeper is to tell the commons that now they may go on with their Evidence Then the Lord Keeper is to declare that now the court is proceeding to hear the evidence and to desire the peers to give attention: if any of the peers or the members of the house of com[mon]s that manage the evidence or the Lord impeached desire to have any quaestion asked they must desire the Lord keeper to ask the same: If any doubt doth arise at the tryall no debate is to be in the court but the question suspended to be debated in this house The members of the house of Com[mon]s to be there

---

[753] 'Lunae 16th die Junii 1701' boxed in MS.

[754] From the committee of privileges and elections.

[755] Francis St John (*c*.1634–1705), of Thorpe Hall, nr. Peterborough, MP Tewkesbury 1654–5, Peterborough 1656–8, 1660, 1679–81, 1698–1700. See *HC 1660–90*, iii. 381–2. Although a Presbyterian by upbringing (he was the eldest son of Lord Chief Justice Oliver St John), and a Whig during the Exclusion Crisis, St John had adhered to the Country party during the 1698–1700 Parliament (David Hayton, 'The Country Party in the House of Commons 1698–1699: A Forecast of the Opposition to a Standing Army?', *Parliamentary History*, vi (1987), 158), and had taken his Country allegiance so far that in this election he had stood with the Tory Gilbert Dolben against a Whig, Sidney Wortley Montagu (Cambridgeshire RO (Huntingdon), dd M56A/2 (Manchester MSS), electoral expenses of Dolben and St John, Jan. 1701). He had petitioned against Montagu's return (*CJ* xiii. 330, 632–3).

[756] In the East Retford election: see above, pp. 83–4, 97–8.

[757] Printed in *CJ* xiii. 633.

[758] John Smith, MP Andover, and Stephen Harvey.

[759] See above, p. 92.

[760] Printed in *CJ* xiii. 634.

[761] Part of the Lords' message; not a new heading in the diary.

before the peers come: None to be covered at the tryall but the peers That such peers at the tryall of the impeached lords who at the instance of the said lord or of the Com[mon]s shall be admitted witnesses are to be sworn at the clerks table and the Lord Keeper to administer the oath and to deliver their Evidence in [t]heir own places the witnesses that are Com[mone]rs are to be sworn at the bar by the Clerk and are to deliver their Evidence there the oath what is usuall in other courts: The impeached Lord may cros examine witnesses viva voce: orderd that the message or notes be referred to the impeaching Committee Another message from the Lords[762] acquaint this house that the Lord Hallifax had put in his answer and they were to deliver a copy as also to acquaint the house that the Lord portland was impeached and that as yet no particular articles are exhibited against him: the Lords think themselve[s] obliged to put the house in mind thereof: Another message from the Lords[763] that for the keeping a good correspondence between the two houses and to put the charges against John Lord Haversham in cours of justice at his Lords[hi]ps motion have ordered his Lords[hi]p a Copy of the Charge against him and that he do put in his answer in order to bring that Matter to a speedy judgement: nothing else but Reading of bills and reports from Committees Martis 17th Junii [1701][764] ordered that no member do[765] p[r]esume to go ī[n] to the place appoynted by the Lords for the tryall of the Lord Somers without the leave of the house: Mr Harcourt reported the reasons why they cañot this day proceed to the tryall of the Lord Somers[766] The com[mon]s in this whole proceeding against the impea[che]d Lords have acted with all imaginable Zeale to bring them to a speedy tryall and they doubt not but 'twill appear by comparing their proceedings with all others upon the like occasion that the house of Com[mon]s have nothing to blame themselves for but that they have not ex[p]ressed the resentment their Ancestors have justly[767] shewed upon much Les attempts which have been made upon their Power of impeachments: the Com[mon]s on the 31st of may acquainted your Lords[hi]ps that they thought it proper from the nature of the Evidence to proceed in the 1st place upon the tryall of the Lord Somers upon the first intimation from your Lords[hi]ps some days afterwards that you would proceed to the tryall of any of the impeached Lords whom the Com[mon]s should be ready first to begin with, notwithstanding your Lords[hi]ps had before thought fit to appoynt[768] which impeachment should be first tryed and affix a day for such tryall without consulting the Com[mon]s Who are the prosecutors the

---

[762] Printed in *CJ* xiii. 634.
[763] Printed ibid.
[764] 'Martis 17th Junii [1701]' boxed in MS.
[765] Originally 'go'.
[766] Printed in *CJ* xiii. 635–6.
[767] 'justly' interlined.
[768] 'a day' erased.

com[mon]s determine to try to expedite the tryalls to the Uttmost of their power in hopes of attaining that End and for the more speedy and easy adjusting of[769] preventing[770] any difference which had happend or might arise previous to or upon these tryalls proposed to your Lords[hi]ps a Conference; the most parliamentary and Effectuall[771] method for that purpose and that which in no manner intrenched upon your Lords[hi]ps judicature that a committee of both houses should be nominate[772] to Consider of the most proper ways and methods of proceeding upon impeach[m]ents according to the usage of Parliament in the next message to the Com[mon]s upon munday the 9th of june your Lords[hi]ps thought fit without taking the least notice of this proposition to appoynt the friday then following for the tryall of the said Lord Somers whereunto as well as to many other messages and proceedings of your Lords[hi]ps upon this occasion the house of Com[mon]s might justly have taken very great Exceptions yet as an evidence of their moderation and to shew their readines to bring the impeached Lords to speedy justice the Com[mon]s insisted only on their proposition for a Committee of both houses to settle and adjust the necessary preliminaryes to the tryall particularly whether the impeached lords shoul[d appear] on their tryals at your Lords[hi]ps bar as Criminalls whether being under accusation of the same crime [t]hey should sit as judges on each others tryall for those crimes or should vote in their own Cases as tis [noto]rious [t]hey have been permitted by your Lords[hi]ps to do in many instances which might be given

[*fo. 65ᵛ*]

To which particulars your Lords[hi]ps have not yet given a direct answer tho put in mind thereof by the Com[mon]s your Lords[hi]ps having offered some reasons why you could not agree to a Committee of both houses to adjust the necessary prelim[inar]ies, the Com[mon]s thereupon desired a free conference and your Lords[hi]ps agreed thereunto, at which it is well Known to many of your Lords[hi]ps who were then present what scandalous reproaches and fals expressions, highly reflecting upon the honour and justice of the house of Com[mon]s, were uttered by John Lord Haversham whereby the Com[mon]s were unde[r] a necessity of withdrawing from the said free[773] Conference for which offence the Com[mon]s have[774] with all regard to your Lords[hi]ps prayed your Lords[hi]ps justice against the Lord Haversham, but have as yet received no manner of satisfaction: the Com[mon]s restraine themselves from enumerating your Lords[hi]ps very many irregular and unparliamentary proceedings on this occasio[n] but think it What they owe to publick justice

---

[769] 'tryalls' erased. [770] 'preventing' interlined. [771] 'way' erased.
[772] Originally 'appoynted'. [773] 'free' interlined. [774] 'under' erased.

and all[775] the Com[mon]s of England whom they represent to declare some few of those reasons why they peremptorily refuse to proceed on the tryall of the Lord Somers the 17th of June

1st becaus your Lords[hi]ps have not yet agreed that a Committee of both houses should be appoynted for setling the preliminarie[s] a method never untill this time denied by the house of Lords when the Com[mon]s have thought fit to desire the same

2dly should[776] the Com[mon]s (which they never will do) be contented to give up these rights which have been transmitted to them from thei[r] Ancestors and are of absolute necessity to their proceedings in impeachments, yet whilest they have any regard to publick justice they never can appear as prosecutors before your Lords[hi]ps till your Lords[hi]ps have first given them satisfaction; th[at] lords impeacht for the same crimes shall not sit as judges on each others tryalls for those crimes

3dly because the comm[on]s have as yet received no reparation for the great indignity offered to them at the free Conferenc[e] by the Lord Haversham: the Com[mon]s are far from any inclination and cannot be supposed to be under any necessity of delaying the tryall of the Lord Somers: There is not any article exhibited by them in mantenance of their impeachment against the lord Somers: for the proof whereof they have not full and undeniable evidence which they will be ready to produce as soon as your Lords[hi]ps shall have don justice upon the Lord Haversham and the necessary preliminaries in order to the said tryall shall be setled by a Committee of both house[s]

The Com[mon]s think it unnecessary to observe to your lords[hi]ps that most of the articles whereof the Lord Somers stands impeached will appear to your Lords[hi]ps to be undoubtedly true from matters of record as well as by the confession of the said Lord Sommers in his answer to the articles to which the Com[mon]s doubt not but your Lords[hi]ps will have a du regard when his tryall shall regularly proceed: resolved[777] the reasons be carried by a message and the Lord Disert do carry the sam[e] mr Lawson reported[778] that the majority fell upon Sir Godfery Copley Jack How w[illia]m Bromley Sir Hum[phrey] Mackworth Sir Bart[holomew] Shower Ant[hony] Hamond Dr D Avenant to be com[mi]s[sione]rs of accounts Ordered that no member do presume to appear at the place erected for the pretended tryall of the impeachment of the Lord Sommers under the penalt[y] of incurring the utmost displeasure of the house: mercuriii [sic] 18th die junii [1701] A petition of parkus[t] and pascall relating to a claus concerning them was

---

[775] 'all' interlined.   [776] 'should' interlined.   [777] 'resolved' interlined.

[778] From the committee to scrutinize the ballot for commissioners of accounts: *CJ* xiii. 636.

not allowed to be brought up[779] Ordered that a Committee inspect the Lord[s'] journalls in relation to the proceedings against the impeached Lords and relate what they find therei[n] ordered the Committee of impeachments be the Committee Ordered no member presume to go out of town ordered that all the members attend the service of the house on friday and then the house adjourned till friday Veneris 20 die junii [1701][780] Mr Speaker acquainted the house that severall letters have been sent to the post house with his hand counterfeited for the franking of letters with libells inclosed in them:[781] Ordered that the postmasters take care to prevent and discover such practices: A message from the lords[782] to acquaint the house that the Lords have appoynted Monday the 23d of june at ten of the clock for the tryall of Ed[ward] E[arl] of Orford and that they were commanded by the lords to to [sic] deliver to this house a copy of my Lord Havershams answer to the charge exhibited against him that

The Lords in answer to the message of the com[mon]s of the 17th instant, say, the only true way of determining which of the two houses has acted with the greatest sincerity in order to bring the impeached lords to their tri[al] is to looke back upon the respective proceedings: The Lords do not well understand what the com[mon]s mean by th[at] resentment which they speak of in their message their Lords[hi]ps own the house of Com[mon]s have a right of impeaching and the Lords have an undoubted[783] power of doing justice upon those impeachments by bringing them to tryall and condemning or acquitting the parties in a reasonable time, this power is derived to them fro[m] their Ancestors, which they will not suffer to be wrested from them by any pretences whatsoever their Lords[hi]ps c[an]not but wonder that the com[mon]s should not have proposed a committee of both houses much sooner if they thought it so [neces]sary for the bringing on the tryalls no mention being made of such a Committee from the first of Ap[ri]ll to the 6th of june though during that intervall their delays were frequently complained of by the house of Lords

[779] John Parkhurst, MP Northants.; for Pas(c)hall, see above, p. 65, n. 30. The two men had been committed to the Tower on 28 Feb. for neglect of their duty as commissioners for prizes, in refusing to submit accounts to the Commons' accounts commission. A clause had been added to the current bill to establish a new accounts commission, requiring them to submit accounts by 1 Feb. 1702 and continuing their imprisonment until the end of the next parliamentary session should they fail to comply: *CJ* xiii. 365, 636–7; *Mr Pascall's Letter to a Friend in the Country, Stating the Case of Mr Parkhurst and Himself . . .* (1701).

[780] 'Veneris 20 die junii [1701]' half-boxed in MS.

[781] For the privilege, known as 'Members' Franks', by which letters under 2 oz. from peers and MPs could be sent free of charge within the British Isles, see Kenneth Ellis, *The Post Office in the Eighteenth Century . . .* (London, 1958), 39.

[782] Printed in *CJ* xiii. 637–8.

[783] 'right of' erased.

The manner in which the Com[mon]s demand this Committee the Lords Looke upon as a direct invading of their ju[dica]ture and therefore as there never was a Committee of both houses yeelded to by the Lords in case of any impea[ch]ment for high crimes and misdemeanours so their Lords[hi]ps do insist that they will make no new president on this occasion: many impeachments for misdemeanours have in all times been determined without such a Committee: and now if the Com[mon]s think fit by an unpresidented demand to form an excuse for not prosecuting their impeachments, it is demonstr[a]ble where the obstruction lies

As to the preliminaries which the com[mon]s mention in particular as proper to be setled at such a Committee they have received the resolutions of the house of Lords therein by their message of the 12 instant, from which being matters[784] relating intirely to their judicature their Lords[hi]ps can not depart

As to the last pretence the com[mon]s would make to shelter the delaying the tryall from the expressions whic[h] fell from the Lord Haversham at the free conference at which offence was taken their Lords[hi]ps will only observe 1st that they have omitted nothing which might give the com[mon]s all reasonable satisfaction of their purpose to do them justice in that matter, so far as is consistent with doing justice to that Lord and also to preser[ve] all good correspondence with them as appears by the severall steps they have taken

2dly that this busines has no relation to the tryalls of the impeached lords, and therefore their Lords[hi]ps [cannot] imagine why the com[mon]s should make satisfaction and reparation against the Lord Haversham a necessary co[ndition] for the going on with the tryalls and at the same time find no difficulty in proceeding on other busines

Resolved in answer to the Lords message appointing munday next for the tryall of the E[arl] of Orford:[785] that the Co[mmons] would proceed in the first place against the Lord Somers and they are ready to go to that Lords tryall assoon as ever they have received satisfaction for the affront at the free Conference offered by the Lord Haversham and the preliminaries are setled etc.

Mr Bruges[786] reported from the committee to inspect the Lords journall[787] the same was read and then it was resolved that the Lords have refused justice to the com[mon]s upon the impeachment against the Lord Somers by Denying them a Committee of both Houses which was desired[788] for setling the necessary preliminaries in order to proceeding to the tryall of the Lord

---

[784] 'that' erased.   [785] Printed in *CJ* xiii. 638.

[786] James Brydges' name is spelt this way in the *Journals*: ibid.

[787] Concerning the proceedings against the impeached lords.

[788] 'which was desired' interlined.

Som̄[ers] with effect and afterwards by proceeding to a pretended tryall of the said lord which could only tend to protect him fro[m] justice by colour of an illegal acquittall against which proceedings of the Lords the com̄[mon]s do s[o]lemnly protest as bei[n]g repugnant to justice and therefore null and void resolved that the house of Lords by the pretended tryall of John Lord Somers have endeavoured to overturn the rights of impeachments lodged in the house of com̄[mon]s by the antient constitution of this kingdom for the safety and protection of the Com̄[mon]s against the power of great [m]en and have made an invasion upon the liberties of the subject by laying a foundation of impunity for the greatest offenders resolved that all the ill consequences which may at this time attend the delay of the supplyes given by the Com̄[mon]s for the preserving the publick peace and maintaining the balance of Europe by supporting our alli[e]s against the power of France are to be imputed to those who to procure an indempnity for their enormous crimes have used their utmost endeavours to make a breach between the t[w]o houses
[*fo. 65*

Ord]ered that the message this day be referred to the impeaching Committee ordered that the committee do consider of the proceedings between the two houses relating to the impeached lords and state to this house the matter of fact in order to the justification of this house in their proceedings

in answer to the message of the house of Com̄[mon]s of this day the Lords do acquaint the Com̄[mon]s[789] that they might have Known by the records of the house of lords that the lords have proceeded to the tryall of the Lord Som̄ers[790] on tuesday last being the day appoynted, and the com̄[mon]s not appearing to maintain their articles against the said lord the Lords have by judgment of their house acquitted him of the articles of impeachment against him exhibited by the house of Com̄[mon]s and all things therein contained and have dismissed the said impeachment: And the Lords have appoynted Monday next for the tryall of the Lord Orford on which day they will proceed on the said tryall: The Com̄[mon]s still pressing for a Committee of both houses, which the Lords never can consent to, for the reasons allready given, their Lords[hi]ps can infer nothing from their persisting in that demand than that they never designed to bring any of their[791] impeachments to a tryall As to the Lord Haversham his answer is now before the house and the Lords resolve to do justice in that matter ordered that no member presume etc. to appear at my Lord Orfords tryall on munday and then the house adjourned till tuesday morning nine a clock Nota the Lord Sommers was acquitted by 56

---

[789] This message from the Lords is printed in *CJ* xiii. 639.
[790] 'this' erased.   [791] 'of their' interlined.

Lords there being but 31 non Contents:[792] the assembly was very great in westminster hall and before Lords rose from their seats the sentence was received with great satisfactory and lowd clamors of the assembly the ladys with their fans and feet others wit[h] hands and tongues made as great a noys as ever was in westminster hall: Nota one of the most angry passages in my Lord Havershams speech at the conference viz that the com[mon]s themselves must think the impeached lords inocent becaus they did permit severall Lords and others Guilty of the same crimes and fact to be near the kings [pe]rson and not impeached:[793] the Lord Orford was acquitted by forty and more votes the Lords not content in Lord Somm[ers]es tryall came not so he was acquitted nem: Con:[794] Where those litle villanous poor wretches that hatched these evills against the Lords tryed for their former ills in westminster hall there would have been as many deman[d]ing justice and rejoycing at their Condemnation as were at these Lords acquittall Martis 24 Junii 1701[795]

The Lords by a message acquaint the house that they have agreed to the bill entituled an act for appoynting commissioners to take state and examine the severall and respective accounts therein mentioned with some amendments to which they desire the concurrence of this house: The house proceeded to take the saide amendments [i]nto consideration and the same being severally read were upon the question severally put thereupon and disagreed [u]nto by the house: ordered that a committee do withdraw, and draw up reasons to be offered to the Lords at a con[fe]rence, for disagreeing to the said amendments and the committee was accordingly appoynted ordered that it be an instruction to the said Committee that they do in the said reasons shew the inconveniencyes by not passing the bill and particularly that by the not passing this bill the payment of the arrears due to the army must be delaied ordered that all the proceedings with relation to the impeachments[796] and what hapned between the house of lords and Com[mon]s be examined by the journalls and printed: Sir Tho[mas] Meers reported from the Committee appoynted to draw up reasons at the conference etc.: that they had drawn

---

[792] The division (before proxies were called) was 56:32: J. C. Sainty and D. Dewar (comp.), *Divisions in the House of Lords: An Analytical List, 1685–1857* (House of Lords RO, Occasional Publn. 2; London, 1976), fiche 1; *The Several Proceedings and Resolutions of the House of Peers in Relation to the Lords Impeached or Charged* (1701), 88–90; HMC, *House of Lords MSS*, NS iv. 300. [793] See above, pp. 174–5.
[794] On 23 June. After 43 votes had been given in favour of dismissing the impeachment, 'the Lord Keeper declared, that the votes were unanimous in the affirmative': *The Several Proceedings . . .* , 99–100; HMC, *House of Lords MSS*, NS iv. 300. No division is recorded in Sainty and Dewar (comp.), *Lords Divisions*, fiche 1. [795] 'Martis 24 Junii 1701' boxed in MS.
[796] Originally 'the impeached lords'.

up the reasons accordingly etc. which were agreed unto by the house and are as follows[797] becaus it is notorious that many millions of money[798] have been given to his majesty by the com[mon]s for the service of the publick which remain yet unaccounted for to the great dissatisfaction of the good people of England who cheerfully contributed to those supplies and their Lords[hi]ps first amendment prevents any account being taken of those moneys by the Com[mi]s[sione]rs appoynted by the com[mon]s for that purpose:

The Com[mon]s disagree to the 2d amendment made by the Lords: Becaus John parkust and John paschall Esqrs have for severall years been Com[mi]s[sione]rs of the prizes taken during the late war and are accountable for great sums of money arising thereby which ought to be applyed to the use of the publick that the said John par[khurst] and Jo[hn] pas[chall] were frequently pressed to account for the same by the Late Com[mi]s[sione]rs appoynted by act of Parliament but by many artifices and evasions de[lai]d and avoyded giving up such an account as was required by the said Com[mi]s[sione]rs that the Clause to which their Lords[hi]ps [ha]ve disagreed by their second amendment requires them to account before the 1st of 7:br [*i.e. September*] next but by their Lords[hi]ps ame[nd]ment the said Jo[hn] p.s [*sic*] are exempted from giving any such account which is highly unreasonable

The Com[mon]s disagree to the 3d amend[ment] made etc.: The com[mon]s cañt agree to the clause sent down by the Lords marked with an X because their Lords[hi]ps have therein directed the Com[mi]s[sione]rs to allow and certifye a pretended debt [t]o Coll Baldwin Leighton wheras the disposition as well as the granting money by act of Parliament has ever been in the [h]ouse of com[mon]s:[799] and this amendment relating to the disposall of money does intrench upon that right

The Com[mon]s do disagree to the 4th etc.

Because it is notorious that edward Whitmore mentioned in the rider left out by their Lords[hi]ps hath by colour of his employment as sollicitor to the admiralty received the sum of 25000 and upwards of publick moneys which without producing any just or reasonable vouchers for the Expence thereof and therefore ought to be accountable for the same[800] And that by reason of

---

[797] Printed in *CJ* xiii. 641. [798] 'of money' interlined.

[799] Baldwin Leighton (aft. 1650–aft. 1711), then a captain of horse, had in January 1689 been sent by the citizens of Londonderry to the Prince of Orange with a request for military assistance, after which the House of Lords had ordered a payment to him of £130 for his services: Dalton, *Army Lists and Commission Registers*, i. 242; ii. 15; iii. 103; Patrick Macrory, *The Siege of Derry* (London, 1980), 144, 147. For Leighton's petition to the Lords in 1701, which prompted the inclusion of this clause, see HMC, *House of Lords MSS*, NS iv. 394.

[800] Edward Whitaker (d. 1731), solicitor to the Admiralty 1692–9. For his petition, see *The Case of Mr Edward Whitaker . . .* [London, 1701]; HMC, *House of Lords MSS*, NS iv. 394.

their Lords[*hi*]ps disagreeing to the severall parts of the bill the supplyes provided by the com̃[*mon*]s for paying the arrears of the army must of necessity be ineffectuall till another session of Parliament By a message the King Commanded the house to attend him in the house of peers, where the Speaker in a most elegant speech told the king that the loyall com̃[*mon*]s had given the King more then was ever given to any of his progenitors in time of peace that they had answered th[e K]ings Speech and provided something towards the deficient funds setled the succession: raised necessary [sup]plys for the maintenance of the navy and army for the present year and that if the french king did not [ma]ke such concessions as were proper for the preserva-tion of the peace of Europe the Com[*mon*]s would stand [b]y the king and his allies in order to force him to terms of reason by a just war: The kings speech in parliament[801]

[M]y Lords and Gent[*lemen*]

The session being now come to a conclusion, I must return you my hearty thanks for the great Zeale you have expressed for the publick service, and your ready Complyance with those things which I recom̃ended to you at the opening of this Parliament: And I must thank you Gent[*lemen*] of the house of Com̃[*mon*]s in particular both for your dispatch of those necessary supplyes which you have granted for the publick occasions and for the encouragement you have given me to enter into alliances for the preservation of the libertyes of Europe and the support of the Confederacy in which as it shall be my care not to put the nation to any unnecessary expence so I make no doubt that wha[*t*]soever shall be done during your recess for the advantage of the Com̃on Cause in this matter will have your approbation[802] at our meeting again in the winter: My Lords and Gent[*lemen*] I shall conclude with recom̃ending to you all, the discharge of your duties in your respective countries that the peace of the kingdom may be secured by your vigilance and care [in y]our severall stations and afterwards the Lord Keeper of the great seale by his majestys com̃and prorogued the parliament untill tuesday the 7th of Aug[*u*]st next

---

[801] Printed in *LJ* xv. 700.   [802] 'aga[in]' erased.

1701/2 Parliament

[*MS. Eng. hist. b. 210, fo. 1*[1]
27 Jan. 1702

?no – – serv]ants go for [?m– – –] quaestion for bringing up [– – –[2] ?th]en we went upon the busines of the day which was two reports from the committee of elections [?the ?first ?Maldon ?in E]ssex Cummings was the sitting member and Coll[*onel*] Mountague[3] the petitioner: the right of the election [?was ?agreed ?to ?be ?in] the freemen etc. not receiving al[m]s and charity: Nota the lord Hallifax had formerly given weat in [– – – ?to ?the] Poor of Malden about a year ago was the last my Lord ordered the distributor to give it promiscuousl[y ?and] without regard to party or faction:[4] the bailifs had declared they would not return Coll Mountagu[e – ?be ?this] majority so ever[5] and when the poll was taken they rejected all those from voting for Coll mou[ntague ?who ?had recei]ved his brothers wheat and let the very same men viz those that had received wheat vote fo[r ?Comyns –] now if those votes had been allowed then mountague had had the majority but so it further was to[?ld ?that ?one ?voter] for mountague the very day of the election received nineteen shillings of mr Coe Coll m[*ontagu'*]s agent nine sh[illings ?for ?last] years wheat and ten for this and this was a scoundrill fellow to looke at but nobody blemished hi[s ?character[6] ?and] further Coll Mountague had treated

---

[1] Damage to the manuscript has resulted in the loss of the top right-hand corner of each of the first seven folios, to a depth of around 20 lines of text.

[2] On a report from the committee of supply, five amendments were carried to resolutions concerning the military establishment, to make the numbers allowed in various regiments inclusive or exclusive of servants: *CJ* xiii. 706.

[3] John Comyns, MP; and Irby Montagu, MP Maldon 1695–1701 (Nov.).

[4] In 1699 Lord Halifax, himself a former Member for the borough, had responded to representations from Maldon over the high price of corn, by ordering wheat to be distributed to the poor there on Christmas Day, 'without any distinction, only with respect to the poverty of the persons': *CJ* xiii. 707.

[5] The evidence to the House alleged this only of 'bailiff Taverner', who, on being told that Montagu would be returned, had reportedly remarked that 'he should not: he knew a trick worth two of that': ibid.

[6] The agent was William Coe (d. *c.*1711), one of the most important merchants in Maldon, and, though probably a Nonconformist, the owner of two inns in the town: *CJ* xiii. 707–8; HMC, *Cowper MSS*, iii. 161; J. R. Smith, 'The Borough of Maldon, 1688–1768: A Study in English Urban History', M.Phil. thesis (Leicester, 1981), 44–5, 74, 95, 97; Essex RO, Bishop of London's commissary court, registered wills, 208 BR 16 [reel 10] (a reference I owe to Dr M. J. Knights). The voter concerned was one William Wells: *CJ* xiii. 708.

in the town the night before the Election and would spen[d ?no ?money ?at]
any house that would not engage to vote for him on the account of his
spending money at their [?house ?this ?was] the short of the case and the
Committee voted Cummings duly Elected and after the report was first read
[– – –] then at the table the question was put, those that agree say ay Sir
Tho[*mas*] Littleton began the debate it lasted two [?hours[7] ?and ?at ?last]
agreed that tho Mountague had the majority yet he could not be Elected he
having treated Contrary [?to ?the ?act ?of ?Parliament] nota the act was so
penned that those that had treated after the order for the dissolution were
within n[ot ?only ?the] meaning of the act but the words also for the words are
the order for a dissolution[8] so that mountague [?could ?have ?no pre]tence to
be Elected: but the question was only if Cummings was duly Elected[9] the
debate last[ed] two hours [?and ?the] Cheif argument why Cummings was
duly Elected was this Suppose a man treats from this time to the setting of
[?the] new parliament and by treats procures himself a majority what a fine
case is another Candidate in for he cannot [?treat ?and] the other having the
majority must be returned, and if he petitions it must be a voyd Election the
other hav[ing ?the] majority: Others said the bayliffs had no other rule to go
by but the poors levy and the freemans roll and that [?they] had no other
power to judge and it was not fitt they should make to themselves any other
rule for the[?y] had no power to try the matter and therefore Could not be
judges in it and then of What a dangerous conseq[u]ence would it be to have
the bayliffs encouraged to take so much upon them: it was said in Sloans case
for Thetford he was turned out for treating and yet he having the majority
Soames could not be Elected without a new writt[?:][10] there was a great deale
more said and at last the question was put for agreeing with the Committee

---

[7] 'Three hours or very nigh', according to Thomas Johnson (Liverpool RO, 920 NOR 2/245,
Johnson to Richard Norris, 27 Jan. 1701[/2]), while Robert Yard merely noted that it was 'a long
debate in a full house' (Centre for Kentish Studies, Maidstone, U1590/O59/9, Yard to Alexander
Stanhope, 27 Jan. 1701/2).

[8] See above, p. 66, n. 37. The wording of the 1696 'Treating Act' prevented expenditure 'after
the *teste* of the writ of summons to Parliament . . . or the issuing out or ordering of the writ of
election': *Statutes of the Realm*, vii. 7.

[9] Confirmed in *CJ* xiii. 708. The Whig James Lowther observed that Montagu's objective in
petitioning had only been to void the election: Cumbria RO (Carlisle), D/Lons/W, James to Sir
John Lowther, 27 Jan. 1701[/2].

[10] The Thetford election of 1698, eventually decided on 17 Jan. 1700 against James Sloane, MP,
at the petition of Edmund Soame (MP for the borough in 1701), whose own case, however, had
been too weak for the House to do more for him on that occasion than declare the election void.

226 for not agreeing 208:[11] and then Came on the Hertford case their Case was this the town petitioned becaus of the inju[ry] done them about the Honorary freemen: they were an antient Burough and chose by prescription but by ch[ar]ter in Queen Marys time they were incorporated and in King Jameses time the Charter was confirmed and by th[?ese] Charters they had power to make three honorary freemen out of the vills: they have for the last 40 years exceed[ed] that power and made many freemen and of late years they have made the Six Clerks Clerks [*sic*][12] and many others freemen that [?they] knew would serve their turn and vote as they would have them:[13] the quaestion at the committee was whether these hono[ra]ry freemen should vote contrary to the Charter and it was agreed they should: this after the report was agreed to by the house without any division the others having before outvoted them:[14]

[J]an 28th [*1702*]

the bill for the quakers subscribing their asseveration[15] was read the second time and committed and no gre[at oppo]sition but Sir Ed[*ward*] Seymours spoke against it I answered him[16] and then the quaestion was put and the com[mittee ?resu]med and then after a few motions and bills made and read

[11] James Lowther, who voted for Montagu, claimed that at this division 'there were several brought in men's arms to vote. There was not one man that could get out of bed absent on the other side': Cumbria RO (Carlisle), D/Lons/W, James to Sir John Lowther, 27 Jan. 1701[/2]. According to a newsletter-writer, this was the greatest number 'that ever was known' in a Commons division, 'at least since the Revolution, there being one more than at the abdication, so that it was a perfect trial of the strength of both parties': Strathmore MSS (the Earl of Strathmore, Glamis Castle, Forfarshire), box 70, folder 1, bdle. 1, newsletter, 29 Jan. 1701[/2].

[12] The second 'Clerks' is interlined.

[13] There had been two petitions against the return for Hertford of the Tories Charles Caesar and Richard Gulston, one from the defeated candidate, William Monson, and the other from 'divers inhabitants' of the borough. Both had protested against the admission of 'honorary' freemen to vote: *CJ* xiii. 649, 655. Queen Mary's charter of 1554 (printed in Robert Clutterbuck, *The History and Antiquities of the County of Hertford* . . . (3 vols.; London, 1815), ii. app. 2–3) provided for the admission of resident freemen; King James I's of 1605 (abstracted in John Edwin Cussans, *History of Hertfordshire* . . . *Hundred of Hertford* (London, 1876), 57), enabled the admission of non-residents, up to a maximum of three at a time (*CJ* xiii. 708–9). The issue had come to a head in July–Sept. 1698, when over 110 'honorary' (and non-resident) freemen had been admitted, giving rise to a petition to the mayor from aggrieved inhabitants, and eventually a suit at Kings' Bench (Herts. RO, Hertford borough records, vol. 25, nos. 25–6, 37, 39, 42, 61, 100–2). At one point the number of 'honorary' freemen was estimated at 147, out of an electorate of 500–600 (ibid. nos. 27, 36). They included John Cheevely or Chievely (admitted 1697), and Everard Goodman (admitted 1701), clerks in the Six Clerks' Office in Chancery (ibid. nos. 36, 55, 98, 104). In fact, neither seems to have polled in this election (ibid. vol. 23, nos. 202–17).

[14] i.e. the Tories had just outvoted the Whigs in the Maldon case. Lady Cowper, wife of a former Whig Member for Hertford, noted in her commonplace-book that the Tories won their verdict 'against all reason and demonstration of right, say the Whigs, being outvoted by the diligent attendance of that party, and negligent absence of their own': Herts. RO, D/EP F29, p. 182.

[15] The bill to continue the Quakers' Affirmation Act of 1696 (7 & 8 Gul. III, c. 34).

[16] Cocks (but not Seymour) was named to this committee: *CJ* xiii. 710.

they called for the order of the day whi[ch ?was] for to go into a committee of
the whole house upon the abjuration bill Sir Charles hedges took the chair:[17]
and Sir J[ohn] Bolles began where we left of[f] to add words to the Clause: the
debate lasted above 4 hours[18] and the Clause [?he] would have amended was I
do swear that I will defend support and maintain the government in Kin[g]
lords and Commons as Established by law the addition moved was the
executive[19] power in the king and the Legislativ[e] in king Lords and
Com[mon]s: the arguments against the claus were that it was out of the
way to meddle with king Lords an[d] Com[mon]s in this bill which was
only to abjure the prince of wales that it would divide the people and that
the King had recommended to us to make no Distinction but French and
english, and papist and protestant and that many Jacobites would in disguise
shelter themselves under pretence that they could not take the oath as not
unders[tan]ding what the Establishment under King Lords and Commons
was:[20] that this was offered at in 1675 and that the Lor[d] Southampton
and many more threw it out saying they would never take such an oath by
which they C[?ould] never mend any thing that they saw wanted it:[21] that
there were now the Congee de Eslier[22] the spirituall cour[ts] that wanted
mending[23] that it would put us in confusion by disobliging the dissenters
who could never take a[?n] oath to maintain the Church of England: that it
was said in the committee that in the case of oaths we should n[e]ver have
them recitalls to acts of parliaments but be plain as every one might understand them and that we should say in our oath what the prerogative was and

---

[17] The bill 'for the further security of His Majesty's person, and the succession of the Crown in
the Protestant line; and extinguishing the hopes of the Pretended Prince of Wales and all other
Pretenders'. According to Burnet, the abjuration oath was 'drawn by' Hedges: *Own Time*, iv. 551.
[18] Edward Clarke reported that the debate lasted six hours, and Luttrell that it ended at 6 p.m.:
De Beer (ed.), *Locke Corresp.*, vii. 549; Luttrell, *Brief Relation*, v. 135.
[19] Originally 'Rego[–]'.
[20] L'Hermitage noted that the arguments used against the bill included its divisiveness, and the
impossibility of defining precisely the privileges of Lords and Commons: BL Add. MS 17677 XX,
fo. 193.
[21] The 1675 bill to prevent dangers from disaffected persons imposed an oath to oblige swearers
'to abjure all endeavours to alter the government in the Church'. The dissentient lords' protest at
its committal was not signed by Lord Southampton. Cocks may have been thinking of Shaftesbury,
or Stamford.
[22] *Congé d'elire*: royal permission to a cathedral chapter to fill a vacant see by election. The year
before, Sir John Pakington had brought in a bill 'to prevent the translation of bishops' (see above,
p. 81), and other schemes to reform episcopal appointment were in the air: Goldie, 'Nonjurors,
Episcopacy, and Origins of Convocation Controversy', 29.
[23] For contemporary dissatisfaction with the functioning of the ecclesiastical courts, see G. V.
Bennett, *The Tory Crisis in Church and State, 1688–1730* (Oxford, 1975), 14–15; and Susan Doran
and Christopher Durston, *Princes, Pastors, and People: The Church and Religion in England 1529–
1689* (London, 1991), 187–8.

what our liberties, to this it was said that we were in danger of common wealths men and that this was a test upon them that if they refused it there was someth[ing] in their brests that they would not discover: that it was hard to understand what the established gover[nment] was, and that it would be darker and very voluminous to explain it: at last when they found their arguments were weake they added the Liberty of Consciens as it is tolerated by Law:[24] and then when the questio[n] was mended it was put and was this: I will to the Uttmost of my Power support maintain and def[end] the Regall government of this Realm and the constitution of Parliament in King Lords and Com[mons] and the Church of England as by Law Established with liberty of Conscience as it is[25] by law tolerated[26] for it 158 against it 173[27] nota Sir Xto[pher] musgrove said he would never vote for liberty of Con-science to b[e] supported by an oath and when the question was put he gave his negative but upon the division he divided for it

Jan 29th [1702]

after some acts read and little motions made we came upon the business of the day which was th[e] petition of mamsbury (delivered by Coll[onel] Mordant my Lord Peterborows brother) from the inhabitants of Mams-bury[28] [?It ?was] delivered so late that they never intended to have it heard but only to put a Blemish upon Sir Charles He[dges] Now turned out of his employ of Secretary of State:[29] the consequence was just since the beginning was s[o in]solent and unmanlike to run a man quite down that was going down before: The petition was read which [?was] from Mamsbury inhabitants Complaining that one Ady an attorney did contract and constantly sell the election there[30] [?and] that mr Secretary Hedges and mr Pauncefoot were

---

[24] Bonet ascribed this amendment to the initiative of 'Mr Foley and others' (DZA, Rep. XI Eng. 25c, fos. 42–3); a newsletter-writer to 'Mr F[o]ly' alone (Strathmore MSS, box 70, folder 1, bdle. 1, newsletter, 29 Jan. 1701[/2]). Presumably this was Thomas Foley, MP Hereford, who, though a Tory, had not entirely divested himself of his Presbyterian sympathies and associations (Hayton, 'Moral Reform and Country Politics', 66). [25] 'it is' interlined.

[26] Originally 'established'.

[27] Four other witnesses agree on the figures 173 : 155 : Bonet (DZA, Rep. XI Eng. 25c, fo. 43); Edward Clarke (De Beer (ed.), *Locke Corresp.*, vii. 549); Luttrell (*Brief Relation*, v. 135); and an anonymous newsletter-writer (BL Add. MS 40803, fos. 14–15).

[28] Harry Mordaunt, MP, brother of the 3rd Earl of Peterborough. He had suffered a chastening experience as Lord Wharton's nominee at Malmesbury in the 1698 general election: James (ed.), *Letters Illustrative . . .* , ii. 148.

[29] Hedges had lost office as Secretary of State for the Northern department in Dec. 1701.

[30] William Ady, a local attorney and deputy to Lord Wharton as high steward, who claimed some interest of his own in the borough and in 1698 had tried to act as an electoral broker there: VCH, *Wilts.*, v. 218; Sir Richard H. Luce, 'An Old Malmesbury Minute Book', *Wilts. Arch. and Nat. Hist. Mag.*, 47 (1935–7), 324; Marquess of Lansdowne, 'Wiltshire Politicians (*c*.1700)', ibid., 46 (1932–4), 76; *CJ* xii. 351, 622–3; James (ed.), *Letters Illustrative . . .* , ii. 148; above, p. 68, n. 49. The

Elected by bribery and Corruption: mr dod and mr Sloan[31] [were] Councill for the town and they would have given evidence of Adys former villanyes the councill of the other sid[e] opp[osed] saying they were to defend their clients and not to support Adys former reputation that they were not ins[?tructed] the councill withdrew and upon the debate it was said it was needles to reflect upon Adys reputation for that [?every] one knew and that the meaning of the petition reached no further then the last [32] dissolution so they were order[ed to con]fine themselves to this Election: then the councill for the people of Mamsbury endeavoured to prove Escourt [?and ?—] agents for the sitting member[33] and that they had treated since the dissolution, the treats were not great [?then ?they ?asked] to have one Brown,[34] one that had subscribed the petition for a witnes the other councill refused him as being to [?give evi]dence for himself: but Sloan insisted and the Speaker asked Mr Dod if he did insist he said he did not it was[s ?—] and that he leaft it to Slone to make good so the house laughed and then we proceeded and [?—

fo. 1[v]

− − −] bill of 200 li. and 100 which he received to Elect a member as they were going to Elect a[?nd − −] a gent[*leman*] was produced and asked if he knew any thing of mr Adys offering to sell the Election of Malms[bury − − ?Ge]nt[?*leman*] who gave the money and the bill, and was charged with it and ordered to appear in order to make his defence hi[s ?name ?was ?Parke ?a] Coll[*onel*] in the west indies of a great estate:[35] the councill of both sides were willing to have him give evidence so [?that ?he ?was ex]amined and cross examined but mr Hartcourt desired that the Councill might withdraw Sir

petition against the return of Hedges and Edward Pauncefort, signed by 'several of the burgesses and inhabitants' of Malmesbury, claimed that Ady and 'other his accomplices did corruptly treat and contract with several persons, in order to their being elected': *CJ* xiii. 679.

[31] Samuel Dod (*c.*1652–1716), of the Inner Temple, knighted in 1714 and lord chief baron of the Exchequer 1714–d.; James Sloane, MP.   [32] Originally 'former'.

[33] Sir Thomas Estcourt (*c.*1645–1702), of Sherston Pinkney, nr. Malmesbury, MP Malmesbury 1673–9, 1685–7, Bath 1695–8: see *HC 1660–90*, ii. 275. Estcourt claimed that he had been drawn in by Ady 'to be concerned for my friend Pauncefort': Lansdowne, 'Wiltshire Politicians', 75.

[34] Edward Brown: *CJ* xiii. 711.

[35] The account printed in Cobbett, *Parl. Hist.*, v. 1337–8, notes that the hearing 'took a turn . . . which was altogether extraordinary: for Ady, in person, declared his concern in that affair had been in behalf of Daniel Parke, esq., another candidate for the said borough . . . in verification of which he produced, and delivered to the clerk of the House, a bag of gold, and a banknote of £200', which he said he had received from Parke. The delivery of the gold and 'a bank bill for £200' is confirmed in *CJ* xiii. 711. Colonel Daniel Parke (1669–1710), was of Whitchurch, Hants, Virginia, and Antigua, and was to be governor of the Leeward Islands 1706–d. His Hampshire estate was worth £500 p.a., and he held a mortgage of £6,000 on Gamble's plantation in Antigua, some 314 acres in extent. For Parke, see *DNB*; and Vere Langford Oliver, *The History of the Island of Antigua* . . . (3 vols.; London, 1894–9), iii. 2–3. Bonet (DZA, Rep. XI Eng. 25c, fo. 43) identifies him as a Whig, and Hedges and Pauncefort as Tories.

Thomas [— ?moved ?to ?have] the orders read in which parks was ordered to attend and another in which he was ordered to have Councill [– ?would ?not h]ave had him give evidence in this matter as not being a party: mr Smith was for having him give evidence in [– – – ?M]r Ady not to give evidence being as much a party: then the councill for the sitting members offered to bring in [?witnesses ?to ?pro]ve the undue practices of getting this petition: the evidence was hearsay and the councill for the sitting members [– – –] so the quaestion was put and no opposition: it went for the sitting members and then mr Freeman moved for the [?taking ?into ?custody ?the] petitioners: Coll mordant moved an amendment that was vexatious and frivolous as far as it appeared to [– – – ?b]y the evidence that was heard: then they moved to have one brown a man whose name they remembered taken [?into ?custody] for his name sake Sir Ed[*ward*] Seymour said if he was Brown they were all black and so moved to have them all [?given ?the sa]me fate:[36] Then came on parks: his councill made a very artificiall fine defence that he would confess and avoyd [– – –] fact but avoyd the crime that this gent[*leman*] did give the bill and the money that they were both marked and desired [– – t]hem the councill was Mr Cheshire:[37] he said Mr Parks was a man of fortune and did not value 300 li. to discover and ex[?pose ?su]ch a villany and villain that he never designed standing after he gave the money but that his aym was to oblige the town to choose him hereafter that my Lord Knew nothing of the matter till the bargain [?was] drove and that then my Lord was concerned and angry:[38] that he might have been Chose at Hindon for forty pound[39] and that it [was] not likely he would give three hundred for any other reason but to expose Ady that he had severall witnesses to prove that the [sa]me day he had given Ady this money and bill he declared he would not stand: all this he proved by witnesses then Ady was exami[ne]d his wife and severall others and they proved the bargain and that my Lord peterborow had threatned Ady: and Ady brought [w]itnesses that he had hid behind the wainscoat that proved the bargain between the Coll Parks and Ady: and that when Ady had dis[co]vered the matter that he did not intend to serve the Coll: the Coll threatned him and

---

[36] Five in all, including Brown: *CJ* xiii. 711.

[37] John Chesshyre (1662–1738), of the Inner Temple, and Hallwood, nr. Runcorn, Cheshire, Queen's serjeant 1711–14, King's serjeant 1715–38, Prime Serjeant 1738–d., knighted in 1713: Humphry William Woolrych, *Lives of Eminent Serjeants-at-Law of the English Bar* (2 vols.; London, 1869), ii. 504–11.

[38] Lord Peterborough, whose name had been brought into the case as having 'interfered' on behalf of Parke: Cobbett, *Parl. Hist.*, v. 1338.

[39] For Hindon's notorious venality, see VCH, *Wilts.*, v. 224–5. It was to be made the subject of an unsuccessful bill of disfranchisement on these grounds in the next Parliament: HMC, *House of Lords MSS*, NS v. 202.

said he would have his money again and a great [dea]le more such roguery and stuff was said and proved at last they withdrew and then they put the question upon parks that he was [g]uilty of Bribery etc.: and then it was moved by Robyn Dormir that if it was not against the orders of the house that my Lord Peterborrow might have leave to make his defence Sir Xto[*pher*] musgrove Rose up in a great rage and said there never was such an invasion of our rights to have a lord come into the house and prompt the councill as a sollicitor and stand with his hat on as a member that it was an invasion of our rights and that the lords in time would lay[40] a claim to this as a right and that we ought to make a vote to secure our rights: the Speaker said the door was open and nobody told him that there was a lord and he said he could Know him only by his face but that if the house did not like it it should not be so for he would take notice of it for the future: then Sir Edward Seymour said that [i]t was not to be endured to have a member of another house come here in such a manner that the Speaker should sum up the evidence and that if there was anything in the debate that affected my Lord when the quaestion was put then before it was carried my Lord should not be there as a member but that a chair should be set for him as a lord of another house: mr Speaker said he did not think [h]e was obliged to sum up the evidence and so was not provided otherwise he would, but that it was fresh in every ones memory and [s]o he hoped to be excused the house cryed ay ay: parks was voted guilty with little debate for Hartcourt said if he had designed it only to expose ady he would never have desired his money again and to deliver the bond he had from Ady to repay him the 300 li. so the question was put and easily carried that he was guilty: and then it was a little debated Where they should commit him some said to the sergeant some to the tower at last it was carried to the serjeant those that opposed the tower said it was too much honour those that opposed the sergeant [said] it was to[o] mean for a man of his fortune: his agent a scholemaster was commited to[o]: [41] nota that the house seemed willing to discharge [the pe]titioners after they were brought to the barr and repremanded but it was agreed to be the orders of the house that they must petition to be [?remo]ved after they were Committed[42] so they were kept till Saterday: the quaestion was put upon my Lord and then mr Clark moved that my lord might [?be h]eard and mr Dormir said my Lord desired it so a chair was set on the Speakers right hand near the barr and in came my Lord

[40] Originally 'have'.

[41] Found guilty of 'notorious bribery and corruption', Parke was ordered into the custody of the serjeant and the Attorney-General was ordered to prosecute. His agent, one Gould, was also committed into the serjeant's custody. *CJ* xiii. 711.

[42] For a digest of the standing orders relating to custody and release, see McKay (ed.), *Observations* . . . , 40–8, 115–21.

and set down [?and] rose up and spoke one hour and half by the Clock[43] he said Ady offered him without his seeking to Chuse whom he pleased and [tha]t he recommended Parks as a man of fortune in the west indies in order to have him inform the house of the affairs of the Country [tha]t so nearly concerned us that he knew nothing of any money: till the bargain was drove that he was angry at it: that he had an ho[n]our for the house of commons that upon his honour he was no way concerned in the bargain but astonished when he heard of it: that [he had b]een Lord l[*ieutenan*]t for 13 year[44] and never sollicited one vote that Ady was a rogue: that he had rather be impeached then censu[r]ed by the house that men of honour and fortunes ought not to be censured but upon better proof then Evidence given by ignorant people Without an oath that men of integrity gave the same evidence as if they were upon an oath that he would be willing they should give [a]n oath: he solemnly denied the having anything to do with any indirect means: that he could have had parks chose at Hindon for forty pound that he had a letter Which a worthy member would attest the hand of when he was gone that he knew nothing of the petition and that he told Sir Charles Hedges assoon [*sic*] as he knew he stood that park should not oppose him he appealed to Sir Charles to speak when he was gone after he was gone the member he appealed to was Morley[45] who made a long nonsensicall discours [?I] could not understand whether he owned or disowned the letter: when he had done Sir Charles Hedges disowned all [t]hat my Lord said and concluded with saying that if he Knew any thing more that he could say to serve my lord he would have said it and then we moved for an adjournment and divided: for it 57 against it 170: and then the question was put to [a]djourn the debate but that was carried in the negative without a division Resolved upon another division in which we got about 7 or 8[46] that my Lord was guilty of many indirect practices etc. and then the house adjourned this debate lasted about eleven hours[47] and when the king heard of it the next day he said he wished that we would take as much pains to preserve the whole as we would to ruine one another: the truth of the matter I really beleive was that Ady had some way or another more money

---

[43] Bonet computed the time at 'almost two hours': DZA, Rep. XI Eng. 25c, fo. 43.

[44] Peterborough had been lord lieutenant of Northamptonshire 1689–97.

[45] George Morley, MP Hindon.   [46] '7 or 8' interlined.

[47] The first motion, *to adjourn the House*, was defeated 156:76 according to *CJ* xiii. 712. L'Hermitage noted that those who hoped to spare Peterborough from blame voted in favour: BL Add. MS 17677 XX, fo. 194. Then, *after* the question had been put that Peterborough was guilty of 'many indirect practices, in endeavouring to procure' Parke's election, and carried 141:56, a motion *to adjourn the debate* was defeated 158:44: *CJ* xiii. 712. James Lowther reported that the House sat till 11 p.m. (Cumbria RO (Carlisle), D/Lons/W, James to Sir John Lowther, 10 Feb. 1701[/2]); Luttrell that the sitting ended at midnight (*Brief Relation*, v. 136).

of Sir Charles or some freind of his for him then parks did or would give nota
my Lord peterborrow and his son were the last sessions intirely in the opposite
party: and this year they changed their side which made them the more severe
against him because he was a renegado from them[48]

Jan ult [*i.e. 31st, 1702*]

We met in the morning and we had read to us fullers letter in which he
desired eight members might be sent to him and that he would discover great
matters and that he knew w[h]ere Jones was at mr Inglefeilds and that they
desired to be taken into custo[d]y for some reasons and that they would not
Come in otherwise:[49] and more in relation to his confinement and poverty etc.
[The] Speaker sat down after he had read his letter expecting to hear if any
member would observe anything at last uprose [?Low]ns and said Fuller had
drew two bills on him one of an 100 li. and another of 5 li. that he told the
people they were cheated [th]en when the Speaker found nobody stirred he
spoke to us and said he had another intelligencer which was one doctor
Strin[ge]r his letter was dated from his laboratory and his intelligence was a
man in prison that could tell of plots against the king [a]nd of money won of

---

[48] The Whig Lord Shaftesbury wrote in December 1702 that Peterborough 'this last year or two
threw himself so eagerly into the Tory interest, and prosecuted both the impeachments and all
those other fatal, obstructive, and unjust measures, with so much violence. He has now smarted
for it, having been barbarously treated by that party he went over to, who sacrificed him last year
in the House of Commons, where his son [John, Lord Mordaunt] . . . never gave us a vote till
about that time. My lord is now come back to his original friends and principles . . .': Benjamin
Rand (ed.), *The Life, Unpublished Letters and Philosophical Regimen of Anthony, Earl of
Shaftesbury* . . . (London, 1900), 313. See also PRO 30/24/20/135–6, where Shaftesbury recorded
Peterborough's censure by the Commons on 29 Jan. as the effect of 'the treachery and malice of the
Tory party'.

[49] William Fuller (1670–?1717), informer and *agent provocateur*, for whom see *DNB*. His letter
of 30 Jan. to the Speaker (his 3rd that month) is printed in *The Whole Life of Mr William Fuller
. . .* (London, 1703), 90–2, in which pamphlet a full account of the episode may be found (pp. 75–
107).

Thomas Jones was 'an intimate crony' of Fuller's, and allegedly the author of *A Secret History
of Whitehall* and *Detection of the Four Last Reigns*. He was identified by Fuller himself as a
gentleman with an estate of about £1,000 p.a., who had been 'long . . . an agent for the late King,
and had managed his [King James] concerns in England since the Revolution': HMC, *Portland
MSS*, iv. 18, 34; *The Life and Unaccountable Actions of William Fuller . . .* (2nd edn.; London,
n.d.), 141–2; William Fuller, *Original Letters of the Late King's and Others . . .* (London, 1702),
1–12.

John Englefield was presumably the 10th son of Anthony Englefield of Whiteknights, nr.
Reading, Berks., a member of a notable recusant family, who in 1708 was 'living and travelling
beyond sea': *CJ* xiii. 720; W. Harry Rylands (ed.), *The Four Visitations of Berkshire . . . Vol. II*
(Harleian Soc., 62; London, 1908), 124. On 5 Feb. Fuller told the Commons that Jones and
Englefield, the two witnesses to corroborate his information of a Jacobite conspiracy, were within
12 miles of London, and requested the appointment of a committee to take their evidence: Luttrell,
Brief Relation, v. 138.

Tallard[50] the Speaker said he tooke this to be such another busines as fullers but he knew had [n]ot he laid it before the house when the house rose he should have a story made of him as if he smothered it as [be]ing disaffected to the government: that he beleived he Knew who Fuller meant by Jones and that he might have [be]en taken he said he desired Dr Stringer to give the Secretary[51] Romans letters for that was the name of the intelligen[cer] who said he had been Emanuensis to Obediah Walker:[52] the Secretary said he had been visited by dr Stringer [wh]o told him of Roman[53] that he sent one, to Roman to examine him in prison but Roman would make no discoveryes [?but] at the Tavern and that he did not care to take him being so deep in debt from prison: the house at mr Speakers [?moti]on ordered the Secretary to examine the man and mr Speaker to give him the letters: the Secretary[54] undertooke the exami[nation] and to report it to the house; then they Cried the order of the day and mr Secretary proposed to the house the necessi[ty of] 10000 marines and shewed us the necessity of them and the use they would be to us to annoy france he did not [?make] it a motion for the committee to receive an instruction to go on with it but that he thought fit to mention it [before] we went into the committee[55] Sir Charles Hotham spoke well of the necessity of them and of the advantage: Sir Xto[pher ?Musgrave] said, it was a money matter and that money could not be given from the Chair that it could not be debated [?in ?the] Committee it not having been asked from the throne: and that if it must be debated he hoped it was not [?propose]d that we should go presently into it but that a day should be appoynted to consider of it:[56] at last after [– sp]eeches shewing it was demanded from the throne by generall words and all agreeing of the necessity of the ma[?rines ?we a]ppoynted munday by consent without an order to debate this matter and then the

---

[50] Moses Stringer, MD (1670–1713), of Blackfriars, London, a physician and chemist: Luttrell, *Brief Relation*, v. 138; P. J. and R. V. Wallis, *Eighteenth Century Medics* (2nd edn.; Newcastle upon Tyne, 1988), 577. (I am grateful to Dr J. A. I. Champion for help with this identification.) For Tallard, see above, p. 85, n. 168. Stringer claimed in his letter to have information of a plot against the King's government: Tindal, *Continuation of Rapin's Hist.*, i. 303.

[51] Presumably James Vernon: see below, p. 201, p. 82.

[52] Obadiah Walker (1616–99), master of University College, Oxford, 1676–89, and, as a Catholic convert, a principal agent for King James II within the university: see *DNB*.

[53] 'One Romaine, a prisoner in the Counter': *CJ* xiii. 720.   [54] Originally 'Speaker'.

[55] This proposal, made by Secretary Vernon, and intended to be partially offset by a reduction in the number of seamen provided for the navy, is conformed by Bonet (DZA, Rep. XI Eng. 25c, fo. 44), John Ellis (BL Add. MS 7074, fos. 85–6), and L'Hermitage (BL Add. MS 17677 XX, fo. 200). 'The committee' was the committee of supply.

[56] According to Bonet, Musgrave observed that this was in effect to demand a new subsidy, which, according to custom, could only be requested from the throne (DZA, Rep. XI Eng. 25c, fo. 44).

[*fo*.2]

Sp]eaker left the chair and mr Coniers took the supply chair and then the Speaker now m[r Harley[57] ?spoke ?to ?this] purpose that we should pay the charge of the warr every year and not run more in debt that this might easily h[ave ?been ?done ?at ?the] beginning of the first war[58] that the publick revenue as it then stood with a land tax would have done it that [– – ?instead ?of] troubling the committee[59] that we ought to secure and pay the interest and principall of all the old debts that that would increas[e – – ?and ?by] that means we might have money at easier terms: that it would do us but little service to look back and ref[lect ?upon ?what ?was] past but that it was our duty to prevent these evills for the future, that he thought the trade of stock jo[bbing ?was ?very] prejudi[*ci*]all to the publick that that trade was a cheat, and that he had not communicated his proposa[l ?in ?case] the knowledge of it would have promoted that trade: that he hoped we would vote to pay the principall [?and ?interest ?of] the deficient funds that he knew how it might be done and that was by continuing the generall mortgage [?for ?one ?year] longer if Gent[*lemen*] would come up to it[60] this was argued backwards and forwards every one was for paying the d[?eficient ?funds] viz mr Smith that the Speaker was against continuing the Generall mortgage[61] last year and allways before and that this was the only security w[e ?had ?to] raise money upon any exigency and now our necessityes were so pressing he did not well Know the [– ?of] it at this time: Sir Godfery Copley said we must accommodate the war to our conveniencys since we [?cannot accom]modate our conveniencys to the warr: I desired to know what he meant by accommodating the warr to ou[r convenien]cyes if he intended that we should send to the French King to let him know we could not conveniently b[ring] so many men into the feild and desire him to bring no more: after such discourses the Committee voted th[at ?we] should pay all the debts principall and interest that were unprovided for[62]

---

[57] i.e. in his private capacity as a member of the committee.

[58] The Nine Years War.   [59] 'the committee' interlined.

[60] The 'General Fund' to settle the public debts, established in 1697 by the act of 8 & 9 Gul. III, c. 20, from the proceeds of nine separate duties, soon became known as the 'General Mortgage' or 'Great Mortgage': Dickson, *Financial Revolution*, 353. Of this debate Thomas Johnson reported: 'The Speaker made a long discourse and truly very good, setting forth what had been told them in the beginning of the last war how they might prevent going into debt, and the occasions of running so deep into the same, and advised for the prevention of the like this, that we would provide for all deficiencies, raise the money necessary within the year, and the way of managing that money. He also proposed to put these deficiencies at the end of the General Mortgage, and that it would pay all off in the time proposed, 1706. The other side does not like this proposal; the reason I do not know.' Liverpool RO, 920 NOR 2/244, Johnson to Richard Norris, 31 Jan. 1701[/2].

[61] 'continuing the Generall mortgage' interlined.

[62] 'That provision be made for making good the principal and interest due on parliamentary funds, granted since his Majesty's happy accession to the Crown' (*CJ* xiii. 714). The passing of the resolution is confirmed in Luttrell, *Brief Relation*, v. 137.

and the Speaker tooke the chair and we ad[journed] Nota this proposall of the Speakers so contradictory to his and his partys former disposition was to ingratiate themselve[s] with the people against the next dissolution which they imagined would be shortly: for they well knew how they had Enraged the people by fooling them about their debts: and another reason was that this revenue might be mortgaged s[o] much that we might not be able to run further in debt having nothing to rais money upon or to make a fund for security: the Speaker in his speech told us very true that what we raised and what we paid yearly[63] was 7 millions wh[ich] was the whole silver money in england:[64] that is the interest that was paid upon the generall mortgage and what we mus[t] raise for the present service came to seaven millions

Feb 2d [1702] th[e] amendments [(] nota the amendtment the Lords would have made was Mary the dowager of the late K[ing)][65] frō[m] the Lords to our[66] bill of attaindour of the prince of wales[67] was read and debated we could [not] agree to it as being unpresidented and if presidented not fit to be followed: it being too summary: and attaindour[s] were never used formerly but [68] after tryalls and convictions:[69] Then the Speaker left the Chair and we went into a [com]mittee of supply to debate the case of the mariners, all agreed it was good for the sea service and that without the mari[nes] our navy would be insignificant for that the french would not come out to sea and then we should have nothing to [con]tend with but the waves and winds that they would put the french to great inconveniencys in Guarding their coas[t] or force them to sea: that the mariners bred seamen[70] and their small arms were necessary in close ingagements it was objected that it was against order that it ought to have been mentioned from the throne: that it should ha[ve] been spoke of at first and that we never Knew the end of our reckoning that we were kinder and had more regard to the Dutch then the english and that the Quota was not observed[71] that was the only thing m[ateri]all and the only

---

[63] 'yearly' interlined.

[64] The original deficiency in 1697 had totalled £5,143,459 and by 1702 a further £2,498,678 had been added: Dickson, *Financial Revolution*, 353–4.

[65] Words in brackets interlined.   [66] 'to our' interlined.

[67] The bill of attainder against the Pretender, to which the Lords had added an amendment to attaint the Queen dowager, Mary of Modena: *CJ* xiii. 713; HMC, *House of Lords MSS*, NS iv. 418–19.   [68] 'upon' erased.

[69] The Commons' reason for disagreeing at this stage, as communicated at a conference between the two Houses on 7 Feb., was that 'it may be of dangerous consequence to attaint persons by an amendment only': *CJ* xiii. 730.   [70] See above, p. 4–5.

[71.] The quota of troops to be provided by the Dutch according to the terms of the Treaty of Grand Alliance of September 1701 was 10,000: William Coxe, *Memoirs of the Duke of Marlborough . . .* (Bohn edn., 3 vols.; London, 1847–8), i. 91.

thing insisted upon at last by Sir Xto[*pher*] musgrove:[72] we expected great opposition but carri[ed ?it ?at] last without a division after some two hours debate[73] for my Lord Renelagh proposed one thing and Admir[al] Rooke another and it was demonstrated to us by the reducing the hors guards to foot and by reducing fi[ve] thousand seamen to mariners it would cost us but very Little

in this debate Seymour said reflecting upon the present ministry if you man boys and hors Colts you will never come to your Jou[?rney's ?end]

Feb 3d [*1702*] the report from the supply was a little contested but that was yeelded but it was insisted on that th[e] Dutch ought to find their quota and that we should address the King to that purpose Mr Secretary[74] said the five thousand that were abated out of the ships were proportionable to the abatement of the dutch that were in the sea service and that the other being mariners were upon the sea establishment and the house seemed satisfyed with the first 5 thousand but seemed dissatisfyed with the other 5000 so ma[ny] things were proposed to be inserted in the address but the Speaker turned it off saying you would a[dd]res to have the Quota observed if you all agree in that you will leave it to the King and the house acquiesced and the question was put:[75] then the bill for the stating and taking the accounts was put off[76] and the Irish Com[*mi*]s[*sione*]rs were called in and asked severall quaestions in relation to ireland and they brough[t] in the books [77] which they had not signed nota every written paper ought to be signed by the party that offers it:[78] and then there wa[s] a debate in relation to petitions first it was moved that

[72] Musgrave's opposition, along with that of Sir Edward Seymour and Heneage Finch, is noted in Cumbria RO (Carlisle), D/Lons/W, James Lowther to Sir John Lowther, 3 Feb. 1701[/2].

[73] The passing of the resolution to add 5,000 marines to the estimate for guards and garrisons (the remaining 5,000 to be drawn from the seamen whose numbers had already been voted) is confirmed by John Ellis (BL Add. MS 7074, fos. 85–6); Luttrell (*Brief Relation*, v. 137); Robert Yard (BL Add. MS 7074, fo. 176); and an anonymous newsletter-writer, who reported the decision as having been taken 'in a manner unanimously' (BL Add. MS 40803, fo. 16).

[74] James Vernon: Centre for Kentish Studies, Maidstone, U1590/O59/8, Robert Yard to Alexander Stanhope, 3 Feb. 1702.

[75] The reports of John Ellis (BL Add. MS 7074, fos. 85–6), James Vernon (Centre for Kentish Studies, Maidstone, U1590/O53/10, Vernon to Alexander Stanhope, 3 Feb. 1701[/2]), and Robert Yard (ibid. U1590/O59/8), confirm that the addition of 5,000 troops was opposed on the grounds that this would disturb the balance of the quotas agreed in the Grand Alliance, and that these objections were met by the expedient of an address. As voted, the resolution was for an address to the King 'that he will be graciously pleased to interpose with his Allies, that they may increase their quotas of land forces, to be put on board the fleet, in proportion to the numbers his Majesty shall have on board his fleet': *CJ* xiii. 715.

[76] The House voted a week's adjournment of the committee of the whole on the bill·for taking the public accounts: *CJ* xiii. 715.

[77] Francis Annesley (see above, p. 44, n. 48) and James Hooper were the two trustees for Irish forfeitures who were then in London: *CJ* xiii. 714, 717. Their 'books' are listed ibid. 717.

[78] 'that offers it' interlined.

none should be received then that none should be rece[i]ved till after the other that were referred were disposed of: the arguments against receiving them and for giving th[em] a day by which they were impossible to be heard and to receive the benefit were, first that we had given away 300000 li.[79] next that they never applyed to the grantees, and then that it would bring the act to nothing: the answer was that they had a right to petition and that was nonsense to say a man had a right unles that we ought to hear them that would be a right and non remedy was no right: that it was no argument, that becaus the trustees were unjus[t] and rapacious, that therefore the parliament should be so too,[80] neyther was it an argument that if we had given away 300000 [?li.] that therefore the others were uppon a juster bottom should receive no advantage in hard cases: and as for reducing the act to nothing, that we ought not to inlarge it by violence and injustice: so the petitions were ordered to be received: and the Com[mi]s[sione]rs Complained of undue practices used to Lessen the value of the act they produced coppyes of petitions, that were handed up and down to send to england and a chance letter w[hich] shewed some of the Irish rogueries the letter was signed J Lutterell[81] but no body proved the hand and we adjo[urned] Feb 4th [1702] Mr Fullers letter was read in which he promised to make great and serviceable discoveryes an[d] desired to be Called to the barr of the house he allso promised to produce Jones and Inglefeild he sa[id] he knew where they were he was ordered to be brought to morrow morning: and then mr Secretar[y][82] said he had sent to examine Doctor Stringer, who knew nothing but what Roman told him: and upon exa[mi]nation Roman knew no more then a popish letter carrier that was run away and not to be found t[?–] so that was soon over,[83] and wee went into a Committee of ways and means and setled the sum for the [or]dinance[84] and then adjourned to

Feb 5th [1702] Mr Fuller was brought before us, he made a very pretty shamming discours and we censured [?him] by a vote Mr Burnaby moved to have leave to bring in a bill[85] to have Fuller whipped in every coun[ty] town in

---

[79] Presumably an estimate of the value of the forfeited estates excepted from resumption under the terms of the act of 1700 (11 Gul. III, c. 2, ss. 4–6).   [80] 'be so too' interlined.

[81] According to the *Journals*, what Annesley and Hooper produced was a copy of a circular letter signed by forty Irish Protestant gentlemen (none of them called Luttrell) to promote addresses to the Crown against the Resumption Act, the so-called 'National Remonstrance', together with a copy of one such county address (from Westmeath): *CJ* xiii. 718; Simms, *Williamite Confiscation*, 124–5. The reference to Luttrell probably arises from confusion with a later statement of the trustees on 10 Mar. see below, p. 242.

[82] James Vernon: *CJ* xiii. 720.

[83] Luttrell recorded on 3 Feb. that a Frenchman and two Irishmen had been arrested on Stringer's information: *Brief Relation*, v. 138.   [84] Confirmed ibid.

[85] Originally 'an act'.

england that was not seconded and after some wise speeches and reflections we voted him as [so?–] a cheat[86] and we went thro the abjuration bill: and Harcourts clause to preserve the princes[s] of Denmark from treasonous designes[87]

[*fo. 2ᵛ: 6 Feb. 1702*

– – –] were read and [?com*mit*tee] motions made: when we went into the Committee of supply the Speaker tooke the [Chair ?to] receive a message from the Lords: and then he left the Chair again and mr Coniers tooke the supply Chair in which [?it ?was] debated about the charge the King had been at about making the treaties some of the considerable things were allow'd [– – –] greatest some little things that were thought properest for the civill list rejected[88]

[*7 Feb. 1702*

?ille scele]ris crucem tulit hic diadema:[89] Old garoway[90] was used to say no one could bear the fury of the [House of Com]mons: and these Kentish petitioners[91] had exasperated the Parliament viz the majority of this by[92] [– ?their be]ing censured abroad for their ill treating them and ill usage to them for their peti[*ti*]on last sessions

[– – –] a little time in the house Mr Bromeley proposed that we should addres the King [?tha]t the half pay officers should be first preferred[93] this was 2ded and agreed to by the [?Hous]e and was ordered to be presented to the King by the privy Councill[94] without any opposition [?then ?the] bill for punishing diserters and mutineers was read the 2d time and Com[*mit*]ted to a Committee of the [whole] house Mr Coe of Malden was discharged upon his submission and kneeling at the barr to receive a [repr]imand upon both knees and then Mr Finch moved that he might make a motion, tho after the houre of

---

[86] The House resolved that Fuller was 'a cheat, a false accuser, and an incorrigible rogue', and that he be prosecuted: *CJ* xiii. 730. 'Upon the whole', wrote the Tory William Bromley (MP Oxford University), 'I believe no person doubts his villainy, and that the contents of his books are false and scandalous': Bodl. MS Ballard 38, fo. 135, Bromley to Arthur Charlett, 20 Jan. 1701[/2].

[87] That this clause was added is confirmed by Robert Yard (BL Add. MS 7074, fos. 80–1).

[88] The line from '[– – –] greatest' to 'rejected', of which the first few words are missing, is underlined in the MS. Four resolutions were passed to allow for subsidies and payments for troops, under the terms of the treaties with Denmark of 1696 and 1701. Three further resolutions (for 'wagon money', incident charges, and provisions) were negatived. BL Add. MS 40803, fo. 17; *CJ* xiii. 738. James Vernon also noted that some points were disallowed as not being expressly stipulated in the treaties, and as belonging more properly to the civil list: Centre for Kentish Studies, Maidstone, U1590/O53/10, Vernon to Alexander Stanhope, 6 Feb. 1701[/2].

[89] Juvenal, *Satires*, 13. 105: 'ille crucem sceleris, pretium tulit, hic diadema'.

[90] William Garway or Garraway (1617–1701), MP Chichester 1661–79, Arundel 1679–90: see *HC 1660–90*, ii. 373–80.   [91] See above, p. 114–15.

[92] 'being cen[*sured*]' erased.   [93] 'In the recruits and levies now to be made': *CJ* xiii. 732.

[94] By such MPs as were Privy Councillors: ibid.

[one] in order to assert the rights and priviledeges of the house:[95] so the house agreed that this was an adjourned debate [?so ?th]at it might be taken up at any time then the report of maidston election[96] came on and after report I was against agreeing with the committee for that mr Bliss had treated Contrary to the act of parliament[97] and that [?this] would destroy the act mr Brewer answered me and said I had not mentioned particulars and in a long or[ati]on justifyed bliss throwt Mr Stringer mentioned the particulars Sir Edward Seymour answered Coll[*onel*] Stringer and reflected on him without cause as if he endeavoured to Justify the corrupt practices of malden tho he exposed this mr Brewer said that bliss sollicited nobody to go to the tr[e]ats mr Stringer contradicted this by matter of fact and referred himself to the report but the house cryed agree agree so the quaestion was put and Blis voted duly elected the case was thus Mr Blys stood at Maidston and Sir Robert Massum[98] and Mr Thomas Culpiper one of the kentish petitioners blis had treated the town after the teste of the writs with drink and had[99] besides his treats and had given money and a woman of good repute was asked by Mr Bliss for her interest one Mrs Watle[100] Shee told him that the king had dissolved the parliament because he did not like them, and that they would choose such as the king liked and particularly that shee had heard that mr Blis was against the Kings interest, that mr Blis answered her that the king was an usurper[101] mr Blis had not the majority of good votes: mr Colepeper was also guilty of Bribery and it was proved that he had dispersed many quires of reflecting papers amongst which was one that reflected upon the last Parliament for taking of french money that we had not the majority of above 18 at

---

[95] See above, p. 109, n. 318.

[96] A petition from Thomas Colepeper, one of the Kentish Petitioners (for whom see above, p. 114, n. 356), against the return of Thomas Bliss for Maidstone: *CJ* xiii. 653, 732–5. Finch, whose family had electoral associations with Kent, presumably intended to raise a question concerning the Kentish Petition, which would have prejudiced the outcome of Colepeper's election case. See his speech on 17 Feb. (below, p. 217). I am grateful to Dr S. N. Handley for suggesting this point to me.

[97] The Treating Act of 1696: see above, p. 66, n. 37. [98] Marsham.

[99] 'spent [*originally* given] money' erased.

[100] 'one Mrs Watle' interlined. Elizabeth Wattle or Wattell (b. 1662) was the wife of Richard, mayor of Maidstone 1688–9: John Meadows Cowper (ed.), *Canterbury Marriage Licences. Fourth Series: 1677–1700* (Canterbury, 1898), col. 606; J. Cave-Browne (ed.), *The Marriage Registers of the Parish Church of All Saints, Maidstone . . .* (London, 1901), 86; J. M. Russell, *History of Maidstone* (Maidstone, 1881), 411.

[101] Elizabeth Wattle's evidence was that Bliss had asked her for her electoral interest, 'upon which Mrs Wattle told him, that the King did not like him and had sent him home; and she desired to please the King: and Mr Bliss replied, "A usurper!" and "Kings would be arbitrary; and, he could not go out of his house, without being ready to tumble on a cess book" ': *CJ* xiii. 733. The rejection of Colepeper's petition was taken by contemporaries to have effectively disposed of this charge: BL Add. MS 28946, fo. 375.

the vote in which we declared that we would stand by the king in the defence of
the protestant religion and the libertyes of Europe, and that those eighteen were
easily bought [o]ff that they desired the freeholders to consider of the matter
and recommended the Kentish petitio[ne]rs as the Centinells, that had stood
for the defence of their Country and in this paper were inserted the names of
several members:[102] mr Colepeper also wrote a silly reflecting letter on the last
house of par[li]ament which exasperated the house, the letter was wrote to the
Speaker and was ordered to be read by the house and after that was read which
was before the report, it was declared that it was a new custome to read letters
and that it ought not to be followed; that the scribler gratifyed his humour if his
letter was read and that wee shoud [h]ave more such letters and that the time of
the hous would be wholly taken up in such fruitles matters:[103] after the report
was read they censured mr Colpeper that he had by base and indirect means
Endeavoured to get himself Elected[104] and then mr[105] Sombody moved to have
him taken into custody of the serjeant mr Harcourt said he was uneasy with the
gatehous, that he had sued the sergeant,[106] so that it was not likely they would
agree so he moved that he might be com[mit]ted to Newgate, which was
seconded and not opposed and so ordered [a]nd then the attourney generall
was ordered to prosecute him: then: they made a motion to vote tha[t[107] t]he
libell was scandalous reflecting and then it was added[108] that the Kentish
petition was procured by indirect means, and that [i]t was[109] seditious
etc.:[110] I said as for reflecting upon past parliament[s] it was a lesson I
had learned in this house that the first time I ever had the honour to come
here, I had learned it, that I beleived those proceeding[111] parliament and

---

[102] *A Letter to the Freeholders and Freemen of England* (CJ xiii. 734), no surviving copy of
which has been located. The division was that of 14 Feb. 1701 on a Tory amendment to omit the
phrase, 'and the peace of Europe', from the resolution to support the King and government in
measures to advance 'the interest and safety of England', and secure 'the preservation of the
Protestant religion': see above, p. 69.

[103] The purpose of Colepeper's letter was to 'bespeak clemency' of the House, but according to
L'Hermitage it angered even his friends, while the historian Ralph recorded that its reading
produced 'an angry motion' and 'a violent debate': BL Add. MS 17677 XX, fo. 207; [Ralph,]
Hist. Eng., ii. 1015.

[104] That he had been guilty of 'corrupt, scandalous, and indirect practices' in attempting to
secure his return: CJ xiii. 734–5.　　　　　　　　　　　　　　　　　　[105] 'H' erased.

[106] A reference back to Colepeper's clash with the serjeant the previous year, for which see
above, p. 125, and *Somers's Tracts*, xi. 249, where there is a hint of legal action to be taken against
the serjeant.

[107] Originally 'that: Coll[onel –] made a motion that since'.

[108] 'then it was added' interlined.　　　　　　　　　　　　　　[109] 'tending to' erased.

[110] An amendment was made to the resolution against Colepeper, to add the observation that
he had been 'one of the instruments in promoting the scandalous, insolent, and seditious petition,
commonly called the Kentish Petition': CJ xiii. 734.　　　　　　　　　　[111] 's' erased.

that[112] had taught people without doors the lesson that I had voted against sending the Kentish petitioners to the Gatehous; and the reason was becaus I did not think so hardly of their petition and that I had not since altered my opinion, and that therefore I Could not agree to those words added: Robyn dormir spoke somthing of the busines being transacted in the last parliament and not being a party that it was unusuall to vindicat their proceedings there being nothing before us: Sir Edward Seymour reflected upon Dormir for his knowledge in the law[113] and said the petition was before us and that Lawyers were used to make recitalls and then the question was put and carried: then mr Harcourt mentioned Dr Smith[114] as having been instrumentall in dispersing of libe[ls] and moved to have him taken into custody I opposed it, there being nothing said of the doctors dispersing the libells only that Mr Colepeper sent for some papers that he had left with doctor Smith: it did not appear that Doctor Smith had[115] seen the papers or that he knew what they were, only that he had kept What Colepeper had left with him, and had sent them when sent for: the question was urged and likely to go against the Doctor and Mr Smith said it would not be for the honour of the house to commit persons so easily, and that if the question was urged that he would move that before Smith was taken into custody he might be ordered [t]o attend and to make his defence So that fell then they moved to Censure those libells that reflected on the [l]ast Parliament for taking of french money that was done without any opposition and then Coll[onel] mansell How[116] moved to have it inquired into the matter of the members being at the blew posts with pousseen[117] after the Order[s] were out to forbid him tarrying any longer in England, and on an account which was very scandalous for an englishman [t]o be seen with him after he had been forbid becaus his master had owned and proclaimed the pretended prince of wales[118] that imposture king of England, that two of them

[112] 'parliament and that' interlined.

[113] Robert Dormer, a barrister of Lincoln's Inn, was later to be appointed a justice of Common Pleas: Edward Foss, *The Judges of England, with Sketches of Their Lives* . . . (9 vols.; London, 1848–64), viii. 29–30.

[114] Probably Thomas Smith, MD (*c*.1668–aft. 1719), a physician in Maidstone: Wallis and Wallis, *Eighteenth-Century Medics*, 555; Joseph Foster, *Alumni Oxonienses* . . . *1500–1714* (4 vols.; Oxford, [1892]), iv. 1383.   [115] 'left the' erased.

[116] Presumably Emanuel Scrope Howe .

[117] Jean-Baptiste Poussin, French chargé d'affaires in England from Apr. to Sept. 1701.

[118] 'as an' erased. The messenger sent to Poussin in Sept. 1701, to put into execution the order that the chargé d'affaires remove himself from England, had found him supping at the Blue Posts tavern in the company of three Tory MPs, Charles Davenant, Anthony Hammond, and John Tredenham, a discovery of which Whig propagandists had made much in the run-up to the general election: Macaulay, *Hist. Eng.*, vi. 2992–3; Horwitz, *Parliament, Policy and Politics*, 297–8.

had lost their elections by it and that one sat here[119] and that if it was fals they had an injury done them if it was true which he could not beleive then our worthy member[120] ought not to sitt here: the Speaker would have put this of[f] as a new motion after [o]ne[121] but Sir Francis Blake seconded it and I said indeed sir it will be but a jest to vote that it was reflecting [?and] groundles to say that the parliament had french gold: and not to inquire into a thing of this nature when it was [?m]oved at and to avoyd it under pretence of order: the Speaker insisted upon it that it was not order [an]d then Sir Ed[*ward*] Seymour said he was partly concerned in it (meaning his relation to Tredenham viz his [mo]thers brother)[122] and that he would take care to have it inquired into so the house was satisfyed and [the]n after some more reflections and hard words they adjourned the debate till tuesday [whi]ch was to Consider of the rights liberties and priviledges of the house of Commons

[*fo. 3*]

Feb 9th [*1702*] after we had delivered petitions and read a few bills we went into a Committee of supply [– – –] of the Court made some little extravagant demands that were not complyed with by the Committee [?I ?thought ?this] weak and ill manage[d] but I was told that they formerly used to bring in the accounts as they ough[t ?to ?and ?the] Committee used to[123] abate something which made them alter that way, I think to the [– – – de]mand of 20000 for Cloath given to Sweden was the only remarkeable thing this day[124] the treaty [?was ?brought ?in ?to] ly upon the table but that treaty had reference to another treaty which was not there[125] the Sec[retary[126] ?was ?informed ?of] the matter and told us that the treaty did confirm another treaty and by that other treaty we [?were ?to ?pay] the Swedes 20000 li. in Cloath: and that that was complyed with and part of the Cloath actually s[ent ?and ?the] rest contracted with Mr Stratford to send:[127] they reflected upon Mr Secretary for not shewing [?us ?the ?treaty] they said they Could not allow it without that and that it did not appear

[119] Davenant and Hammond had lost their seats at the ensuing general election; Tredenham, however, had kept his.   [120] 'had' erased.   [121] See above, p. 109, n. 318.
[122] Seymour was indeed Tredenham's uncle.   [123] 'bring in' erased.
[124] Besides the £20,000 advanced by King William for clothing for the Swedes, the House also approved the allowance of £7,000 for barrels of gunpowder for Sweden; further sums amounting to 275,000 rix dollars, arising out of the Swedish alliance; 6,556 rix dollars for the transportation of troops from Glückstadt to Celle; and £185,000 to the charge of circulating Exchequer bills: Centre for Kentish Studies, Maidstone, U1590/O53/10, James Vernon to Alexander Stanhope, 10 Feb. 1701[/2]; *CJ* xiii. 738; BL Add. MS 40803, fo. 18.
[125] The convention of Oct. 1701, subscribed by England, Sweden, and the United Provinces, part of which had confirmed the earlier treaty of alliance between the same powers signed in Jan. 1700.   [126] James Vernon: Chandler, *Hist. and Procs. of Commons*, iii. 187.
[127] Francis Stratford (1645–1704), MP Newport (Cornwall) 1699–1701, Hamburg merchant, governor of Hamburg Co., and director of Bank of England: W. Marston Acres, 'Directors of the

there was any such [?treaty ?and] if there was such a treaty, that it ought to have been laid on the table for the members to peruse [?Mr ?Secretary] was in great wroth and said he had the treaty in his pocket but then it was said by the order[s of the] house it could not have been read it not having been referred to the Committee by the house: it was told us unles this was complyed with we should have no treaty with Sweden which all a[greed] was necessary to have:[128] then it was proposed by Mr Harley (the Speaker) that we should vote a supply for th[e] Making good the treaty with Sweden: Some of the yong men proposed that mr Coniers should leave the Chair and that the Speaker should resume the[129] Chair and that then the treaty should be received but then by the orders of the hous[e] we could not consider of it that day Nota this was only a device to Elude the payment of the money: but att last it was Complyed with to vote a supply for the Swedish treaty not exceeding 27000: and then we called to Mr Coniers to leave the Chair and so the petitions of the Clothiers and souldiers for interest of their debent[ures] was [*sic*] Evaded without debating[130] and the Committee of supply was shut without asking leave to sit again

Feb 10th [*1702*] after Mr Coniers had reported 15000 li. for Circulating the last year[131] Sir John Bolles to the last bus[iness] moved that Sir Henry Furnass was a circulator and by the Claus in the salt act could not sit that the busines w[as] already heard and setled last parliament[132] Sir Ed[*ward*] Seymour said it was a known law setled and determined last parliament it was said we could not bring a new parliament take notice of the determinations of the last; it was urged that meggot was punished in the next parliament for an offence done in the last: but that was set right for me[g]got had committed an offence that parliament tooke notice of by shewing a man for giving Evidence to the

---

Bank of England', *Notes and Queries*, 179 (1940), 58; Jacob M. Price, 'The Tobacco Adventure to Russia', *Transactions of the American Philosophical Society*, 51/1 (1961), 109; *Cal. Treas. Bks.*, xvi. 65; xvii. 246.

[128] Vernon observed that the committee showed 'a great inclination to have a strict alliance with Sweden': Centre for Kentish Studies, Maidstone, U1590/O53/10, Vernon to Alexander Stanhope, 10 Feb. 1701[/2]. [129] 'treaty' erased.

[130] A petition from clothiers of the army for 1698–9, claiming that the debentures given them in payment were running at over £40 p.a. discount; presented to the House on 5 Feb. and referred to the committee of supply: *CJ* xiii. 721.

[131] The £18,500 to be allowed for the charge of circulating Exchequer bills, according to the report from the committee of supply: ibid. 738.

[132] The Salt Duty Act of 1696: see above, p. 82 and n. 138.

Committee of the last parliament[133] that was agreed too and the house
ordered the contract of the Circulators of the exch[e]quer bills to be laid
before the house and that then if there was occasion that he should answer it
in his place: the messengers Came from the Lords viz Sir Lacon Child and mr
Rogers they brought up a messa[ge] from the Lords:[134] they make three Bows
and Leave their message in writing after they have delivered th[?at] When the
Speaker has acquainted the house with the busines then the house comes to
some resolution an[d] they are Called in and acquainted with the answer
Sometimes the answer is that they will send an answ[er] by messengers of
their own: they return back making three congees [(]they turn at such a naile
to bow[)][135] as they did when they come in: sa[ve] When they bring in an
account of the agreement to or amendments in a bill they return without an[y]
waiting for an answer:[136] this day the Speaker was in his gold gown[137] in order
to attend the king in the house of Lords and he acquainted the house that he
had sent to the Lords to inquire if the bill of accounts that was to pass was not
a money bill and if so that it ought to be sent down to him to bring up wi[th]
him when the King came and the Lords said it was no money bill;[138] sais
Seymour the Lords told you true for I remember when I had the honour to be
in that chair the black rod came to summon the house to atte[nd] the King and
the Lords kept the money bill and I told them I would not stir till I had the
money bill from [the] Lords which at last they sent: then wee went upon the
order of the day which was the report of the abjuration bill:[139] Ned Harley
began and railed against and Exploded oaths in generall that they were only a

---

[133] Sir George Meggot of Horsley Down, Surrey, a Southwark brewer, had been committed into
custody in Dec. 1695 after the unsuccessful hearing of his petition over the Southwark election, for
previous remarks to the effect that he had sufficient friends in the House to guarantee his being
seated. He had subsequently taken legal action against those who had testified against him, for
which, in the next session, in Dec. 1696, he was found guilty of breach of privilege. *CJ* xii. 371,
613.

[134] Sir Lacon William Childe (c.1645–1720), of Kinlet, Salop, and Lincoln's Inn, master in
Chancery 1673–1710; William Rogers (1657–1734), of Lincoln's Inn, and Bray, Berks., master in
Chancery 1701–21. According to the Commons' *Journals*, messages came on this day from Rogers
and Thomas Gery, and from Francis Aston, the deputy usher of the black rod: *CJ* xiii. 737, 739.
The Lords' *Journals* record that Childe and Rogers were sent with a message to the imprisoned
informer William Fuller: *LJ* xvii. 32.

[135] Words in brackets interlined in MS. 'Congees' were retiring bows.

[136] The procedure is described in Erskine May, *A Practical Treatise on the Law, Privileges,
Proceedings, and Usage of Parliament* (London, 1844), 249–52.

[137] The state gown, of gold-embroidered black damask: Philip Laundy, *The Office of Speaker*
(London, 1964), 10.

[138] The King had given the Royal Assent to the bill to continue the act appointing commissioners to take account of the debts due to the army, navy, and transports (13 & 14 Gul. III, c. 1).

[139] The bill 'for the further security of His Majesty's person, and the succession of the Crown in
the Protestant line'.

snare to tender Consciences and of no signification to others that the very persons that abjured king Charles the second in less than 12 months brought him in,[140] that the security of the prince was whe[n] it was the interest of the people to support and therefore he moved to recommitt: I seconded hi[m] King thirded it and Cooper opposed if finely sais he it is true they swore to the other governments and that did not preserve them the other governments had navyes soulddiers etc. yet they miscarried wee therefore should say we would have no navyes no arms a little of all dos well King spoke of the little validity of oaths and as Harley said if it was recommitted it might be well and all the substance of it be brought into the association bill[141] which must be amended severall spoke against it[s] recommitment at Last Seymour said in the latter end of his speech that the pamphlets this summer marked us and designed us to be no more then hewers of wood and drawers of water[142] and that this test would perfect it: this altered the sence of abundance at Last the question was put for a rec[om]mitment the yeas 156 the noes 194[143] and then it was offered at by St Johns to disagree with the Committee in the leaving out of the Oath the King Lords and Commons:[144] and that was an Idle debate nothing said worth mentioning they said they would have the words in to prevent a Common wealth the others would not have them least it might spoyle the force of the bill by giving the Jacobites a shelter to hide themselves: at Last we divided for the amendment wh[ich] threw out the words 186 against 165[145]

Feb 11 [1702] this day was spent in the morning about the delivery of the Irish petitions those that were brought in becaus their ancestors were attainted after death tho they had been slain in battell were rejected, for it would have destroyed the Irish bi[ll] and tho it seemed hard yet it was said they must alter the law[146] or as the law stood n[?ow] it was not hard that it was the law of England often practised as particularly of thos[e] that were slain in

---

[140] Presumably those Councillors and MPs who had taken the oath of allegiance to the Protectorate, as directed in the additional petition of June 1657: C. H. Firth and R. S. Rait (edd.), *Acts and Ordinances of the Interregnum* (3 vols.; London, 1911), ii. 1185–6.

[141] According to Robert Yard, the opponents of the bill moved for its recommittal, with an instruction to the committee to omit entirely the oath of abjuration, and insert instead a version of the Association (as established by the act of 7 & 8 Gul. III, c. 27), amended so as to substitute the name of the Pretender for that of King James II: BL Add. MS 7074, fos. 182–3.

[142] From Joshua 9: 21: 'let them be hewers of wood and drawers of water unto the whole congregation'. Yard (BL Add. MS 7074, fos. 182–3) confirms that Sir Edward Seymour supported recommittal.   [143] Given as 158 : 193 in *CJ* xiii. 739.

[144] Yard, again, confirms that a debate ensued on a motion to omit from the commitment in the oath to defend the established constitution of government the qualifying words, 'in King, Lord, and Commons' (BL Add. MS 7074, fos. 182–3). The entire clause had evidently been added in committee: cf. the original draft of the bill in HMC, *House of Lords MSS*, NS iv. 414.

[145] *CJ* xiii. 739, gives the figures as 187 : 166.   [146] 'to' erased.

Boswoth feilds[147] then we went upon ways and means I spoke first and said Mr Coniers it was very lately that with great solemnity we observed the da[y] of the Martyrdom of that blessed saint King Charles the first[148] a day fatall to England, not that so good a King was murthered by cruell and merciles blood thirsty men but that [–] so good a King who might eyther have[149] outlived his two vitious successors or at least h[ave –

fo. 3ᵛ

– – ?to ha]ve made them better men more in the interest of their country and of a better religion: but [?his ?death w]ill be lamented many ages longer helped it cannot be: but the people of england grew soon weary of [?civil ?wars a]nd confusion and restored the monarchy which is the best of governments in the World composed [?of ?three ?par]ts of Aristocracy monarchy and democracy but there is nothing certain in this world when [?kingdoms ?reach t]heir top felicity at their heigh of perfection they soond decay and decline and so it then [?happened ?that ?in] a very little time we lost the right names of things and at last the things themselves [?we ?called ri]ght wrong and wrong right we called those that swore and drank and cursed good Churchmen [?and ?those t]hat lived soberly and went to Church constantly we termed dissenters and those that spent their [?time ?in] rioting and luxury that run in debt and paid nobody we called modish fine gentlemen and those [?that ?were] good and lived providently we reckoned[150] unsociable miserable[151] niggards but our greatest mis[?takes] were that we thought the extravagant luxury of our Kings their great grants and consuming [?the pub]lick treasure to be royall bounty and Princely munificence and Generosity and those that by pimping [?and ?other ?ba]se means pillaged the publick and Like the harpyes devoured all that was in their way we called your [?grace ?those] that by the same means got Estates and made fortunes not quite so good we called your Lords[*hi*]p: and the les[?ser] Rogues and pimps we called your Worships: by these means and methods[152] we languish and are brought to [gr]eat streights and necessitys: but our necessitys have made us I hope wiser and we have now learned this lesson that it is better to be Just then bountifull Sir I know it is better to look forwards and prevent evills for the future then to make unnecessary reflections on what is past and indeed I would not have reflected so far back did I not think it necessary for the publick to take some advantage by those

[147] See *Rotuli Parliamentorum* . . . (6 vols.; London, 1783), vi. 275–8. I am greatly obliged to my former colleague, Dr Carole Rawcliffe, for help with this reference.
[148] 30 Jan., which the Commons had marked by hearing a sermon from Dr George Smalridge: *CJ* xiii. 712.　　　　[149] 'have' erased.　　　　[150] 'fine modish gentle[*men*]' erased.
[151] 'unsociable miserable' interlined.　　　　　　　　　　　[152] 'methods' interlined.

reflections my motion is therefore that an ayd be given to his Majesty out of all the grants made since the revolution to this day this with the sale of the crown lands will rais 700000 li. no mean nor Contemptible sum: this is the time to make something of them the grantees will be no loosers their estates will be worth more to keep or sell they will be easy in being secured: and they will be willing to give something now for fear if this war continues you should lay your hands on all and if this war should be a short one as I hope it will we should then make nothing of them my motion therefore is that it is the opinion of this Committee[153] that an ayd be given to his majesty out of the pensions and Crown lands granted or given since the restoration of king Charles the second: Sir Rich[ard] Onslow mr Mart[154] mr Brewer and mr Byrch promised to second me [b]ut they were not there so Sir Jo[hn] Bolles moved the 4s on the pound and that was given[155] and we went on other ways and means

Feb 12 [1702]

We had busines of Cours: and Sir John Holland was ordered to acquaint the Lords that we desired a free conference[156] he delivered their answer and brought word that they would send an answer by messengers of their own: Sir Robert legard and Sir Rich[ard] Holford brought the message that the Lords desired then a free conference so the names of the managers was read and they ordered to go:[157] and Sir Rowland Gwin[158] acquainted the house that they had been at the conference and would report what passed when the house would receive the same, some cryed report report but it was agreed to be the [p]ractice of the house in these cases to have the Committee meet together amongst themselves and remember as well as they could what passed at the Conference and to set it down in writing and then report the same and bring it up [t]o be kept for a president in cases to come: then there was a petition delivered by mr palmer of Sommersetshire from the Gent[lemen] of the remoter parts of the county desiring that there might be other places appoynted to take the poll at for the conveniency of the county it was strongly opposed by Sir Ed[ward] Seymour: palmer had the right of his side by the

---

[153] Ways and means.   [154] Possibly Joseph Martin, MP.
[155] The land tax: confirmed by Luttrell (*Brief Relation*, v. 141), and Bonet (DZA, Rep. XI Eng. 25c, fo. 57).
[156] Concerning the Lords' amendments to the bill to attaint the Pretender: *CJ* xiii. 741.
[157] Those who had managed the previous conference with the Lords on the same subject: ibid. 738. Sir Richard Holford (*c.*1633–1714), of London, was a master in Chancery 1693–1710; for Legard, see above, p. 139, n. 540).   [158] 'reported' erased.

arguments but upon the division he lost it by forty viz 13[0] 170:[159] The cheif argument for adjourning of the poll was the reason of the act of Parliament which sais the poll may be taken and[160] adjourned to another place by the Consent of all the Candidates[161] which is unpracticable for to be sure no candidate will consent to adjourn for anothers advantage and his own detriment the arguments of the other side were cheifly the weight of the majority which is the best argument in the world.

Feb 13 [*1702*] Doctor Newton was in the morning in the Chair in a committee of the whole house upon the bill to prevent[162] Coyners and there was a clause which obliged Every one that tooke money under the value to discover it to the next Justice in days otherwise it was a felony this Clause was rejected as of dangerous consequence the taking of it was lawfull but the not discovering of it[163] penall: the claus was rejected and then we went into a Committee of ways and means Feb 14th [*1702*] We immediately went into a Committee of the whole house upon the bill to prevent deserters and mutineers:[164] Nota in publick Bills they always postpone the preamble in private bills not: there was a clause offered to hinder the souldiers from carrying Greyhounds and setting dogs up and down with them into their quarters but this was rejected as not being fit to be offered to gent[*lemen*] of worth who fight for their Country so the Clause was withdrawn[165] and then the mamsbury men that put in their petition upon a great debate for such a trifle were called in[166] to give an account of those that set them on work they denied any Knowledge of the matter they Knew nothing more but that they were perswaded there was bribery and corruption and that they had a mind to have it discovered they were all in the same tale and the house Could get nothing out of them: then the question was whether they

---

[159] A petition from the justices, grand jury, and other gentlemen and freeholders, at the Wells sessions, 13 Jan. 1702, praying that the poll might be taken at Taunton and Wells, as well as at Ilchester: *CJ* xiii. 741. Seymour's brother Henry had in 1690 succeeded to the Somerset estates of his cousin, Sir William Portman: *HC 1660–90*, iii. 423. Oddly enough, his seat at Orchard Portman was just south of Taunton. Seymour may, however, have been principally concerned to preserve the interest of his fellow Tory, Lord Poulett, which was centred at the eastern end of the county, near Ilchester. The vote is given as 132 : 173 in *CJ* xiii. 741.   [160] 'and' interlined.

[161] The fourth clause of the 1696 Election Regulation Act (7 & 8 Gul. III, c. 25).

[162] 'Clippers' erased. The bill to continue the 1697 act against counterfeiting coin (8 & 9 Gul. III, c. 26). Isaac Newton did not possess a doctorate. He was, however, Master of the Mint, and as such had an official interest in the measure, which he had himself introduced on 31 Jan.: *CJ* xiii. 712.   [163] 'of it' interlined.

[164] The bill 'for punishing of officers and soldiers that shall mutiny and desert in England or Ireland'.

[165] To be attempted again at the report stage on the 16th: see below, p. 214.

[166] Those burgesses and inhabitants of Malmesbury who had petitioned against the return of Sir Charles Hedges and Edward Pauncefort, and had been committed into custody on 29 Jan., when their petition had been voted 'scandalous, false, and vexatious': see above, pp. 191–6.

should be discharged or not Seymour was against having them discharged so was musgrove Mr Jacob had said he beleived it was fit to inquire into the matter and that it would appear as for his part he beleived they never chose but by bribery: this Called up Sir Charles Hedges who denied that ever he gave a farthing and was Clearly Elected as it did appear by the report: after some debates I said I had a great regard for what my worthy freind of my right hand had said that he was a gent[*leman*] of the Country and that when I reflected upon the methods used at the Elections for that place had I not known the modesty and virtue of the Gent[*lemen*] that were Elected I should have thought them the best bidders the Speaker spoke softly and said gent[*lemen*] should not say so I went on and Sir Godfery Copley spoke against reflections and said we·should not say things that would look ill one upon another would that Gent[*leman*] take it well to say that Sir Richard Cocks did not bribe the County but was Chosen for his great merit and virtue: after one or two more had spoke up I rose and said sir I would not have [s]poke the second time but to vindicate my self from that aspersion of reflecting I assure you sir I intendd [n]ot to reflect on the Elected but on the Electors but as for What the worthy Gent[*leman*] spoke he had the least rea[s]on to make the remark of any man in the house I live and am well known in the County I have the honour to serve for and my Country knows me better than his burrow I beleive dos him: nota he is chose forty miles from the place where he lives and so ill beloved in his own country that his house [w]as lately on fire and his neighbours got about it and cryed a bonefire and would hard help to put it out[167] and [aft]erwards Harry Blake in vindication of the fellows who were asked who would bear their

[*fo.* 4]

Charges[168] said the Honourable gent[*leman*] near the bar bore the charges of the last discovery of bribery and [?corruption ?for] Which he had the thanks of the house[169] and the fellows might think he would do so now to merit new tha[nks – –] the question was put to discharge them: and to discharge them

---

[167] Copley's seat was at Sprotborough, near Doncaster, some 50 miles from his constituency of Thirsk. The house had been built only recently: the date is given as *c.*1696–1700 in Howard Colvin, *A Biographical Dictionary of British Architects 1600–1840* (London, 1978), 300. When the antiquarian Ralph Thoresby visited in 1703 he did not record any evidence of fire-damage, though he referred to another mansion, 'at a little distance', which had been 'lately burned down by lightning': Joseph Hunter (ed.), *The Diary of Ralph Thoresby . . .* (2 vols.; London, 1830), i. 414–15.

[168] Blaake was a party to another electoral dispute involving Hedges, at Calne, where his partner Edward Bayntun had been obliged to petition against Hedges' return: see below, pp. 231–2. Blaake had also been involved in the Malmesbury affair himself, as an intermediary between Whig party magnates and local interests: Lansdowne, 'Wiltshire Politicians', 79–80.

[169] Sir Edward Seymour, see above, p. 136.

152 against 158: Sir R Gwin said they we[re – – –] but that it was not worth
the troubling the house with them for suppose you should run it up[?on – – –]
should light upon three or four lords and you should pas a vote upon them
that would be all that y[?ou ?could ?do] and the lords would not value that: to
which Seymour said he knew the time that a vote of this h[ouse ?would] Make
the greatest lord of them all fear and tremble and he hoped before wee laid
down to see i[?t ?again]

Feb 16th [1702] This day we went thro the bill to prevent mutineers and
diserters and we threw out a claus th[?at ?would ?have] hindered the souldiers
from taking dogs with them up and down the country and keeping them in their
qu[arters ?and] Upon the division for the clause 130 against it 126[170] Nota the
tellers mistook the noes for the ayes and were ob[?liged ?to ?go] to the barr and
come up again and rectify their mistake: then the order of the day was to call in
my Lord Abercorn [and Mr] Toppam:[171] the Irish nation[172] were uneasy at the
act of resumption for Ireland and well they might for severall acts that h[ad
been] Made in Ireland had confirmed the grant Made to the grantees and
severall protestants had bought those estates and laid ou[t] Whole fortunes
in building and improving of those Estates all which were resumed and put in
the possession of the trustees [?and] without any power to consider and allow
for these Costs and Charges and the private estate viz the late king Jameses
which was worth about 10000 li. per annum was resumed tho never within the
instructions of the parliament to inquire into the value of it but the trustees do
that voluntarily and officiously (nota this was a little to[o] much to be granted
to one mistris it was used to be the establishment and provision for them all for
all king Jameses were provided out of it) this estate was absolutely and
unquestionably in the King and he might grant it to whom he pleased and
the grant was good in law he had granted all this to the Countes of Orkenney[173]
and she[e] she [*sic*] had granted it again to her undertenants and it was pretty
hard that those that had bought those lands upon a good title such a title as
any Lawyer would approve of it was hard that those persons committing no
fault should by a humour of the house loose all their estates: these people were

[170] *CJ* xiii. 744, puts the majority at 124, and describes the clause as 'against officers keeping
greyhounds, and setting dogs'.
[171] James Hamilton (*c.*1661–1734), 6th Earl of Abercorn [S], and 1st Viscount Strabane [I], of
Baronscourt, Co. Tyrone; and James Topham (1677–1724), of Dublin, later a Member of the Irish
Parliament (on Abercorn's interest) for Strabane 1703–13, and St Johnston 1713–d.
[172] i.e. 'the Protestants of . . . Ireland': *CJ* xiii. 745.
[173] Elizabeth (d. 1733), née Villiers, who had married in 1695 her distant cousin, George, 1st
Earl of Orkney. Allegedly she was King William's mistress. For the dispute between the members
of the 1699–1700 commission of inquiry over the inclusion of James II's 'private estate' in their
report, see above, p. 157, n. 653.

the more uneasy becaus the outlawryes reversed were confirm[ed] by this law: under these and many more hardships and difficulties did these poor protestants labour especially becaus the reversing of th[e] outlawries confirmed the papists in the possession of their estates and made the protestants more uneasye becaus they thought they might expect greater favour from those of their own nation and religion: under their dissatisfaction they meet an[d] encourage one another to addres the king for a relaxation of this act: and in it they say they were directed so to do by their freinds in England I mean they wrote so in their letters that promoted the addres of which letters a coppy was laid bef[ore] the house which was subscribed by my Lord Abercorn and mr Toppam:[174] The addresses were presented to the king and the King ordered them to be laid before the house by mr Secretary vernon:[175] the addresses were full of bitter expressions co[m]plaining of the injustice in depriving innocent protestants of their estates and such as they had purchased by the advice of the best Lawyers and of establishing and confirming the papish interest and destroying the protestant The addresses were not drawn altogether so warily but rather the language of an injured and inraged people: when the order of the day was read which was to call in my lord Abercorn and mr Toppam the Speaker desired to know what questions he should ask them. first it was ordered to ask if it was his hand and if he signed it[176] and what the meaning of that expression was that they did it by advic[e] from their freinds in England:[177] but then they remembred that it was but a coppy of a coppy and that there was nothing to Charge them with uppon this Sir Ed[ward] Seymour when he found he Could invent no question and that it was upon the whole a foolish matter to send for them said sir you are out of the old method you ought to examine them to such things as offer themselves and if any Gent[leman] is not satisfyed with the examination then they [sic] are to propose further questio[ns] mr Smith I think it was told the Speaker he should tell them that they were not obliged to accuse themselves and that such questions should not be asked them upon this they were called in and asked first my Lord Abercorn if he had wrote such a letter my Lord said if he saw the hand he could tell and would make an answer the Speaker said he would know what was meant by their freinds in england my Lord said he had

---

[174] See above, p. 201, n. 81. Abercorn and Topham were only two out of 40 signatories.

[175] Ralph (*Hist. Eng.*, ii. 1013), and Bonet (DZA, Rep. XI Eng. 25c, fo. 59), confirm that Vernon was the Secretary in question. In all, ten county addresses (including one from the county borough of Galway) were considered: *CJ* xiii. 746. [176] Presumably Abercorn is meant.

[177] The circular letter sent out by the organizers of the remonstrance (see above, p. 201, n. 81) began with a statement of what was 'the opinion of our freinds in England', whose 'advice' the signatories claimed to have followed: *CJ* xiii. 718.

wrote severall letters and that he Could not remember what was in them if he
Could see them he would give the best answer he could[178] mr Toppam spoke
to the same Purpose and when they were withdrawn these petitions were
stigmatized and the promoters of them by a vote of this house,[179] and thanks
ordered to be given the King for laying them before the house

Feb 17th [*1702*] the Irish petitions were delivered in the morning and some
received and some rejected[180] at last there w[as] a petition delivered from the
E[*arl*] of Athlone setting forth that he had received the thanks of the house for
his services that his grants were confirmed by an act of Parliament[181] in Ireland
that he had sold his Esta[te] so granted and desired a consideration of his
petition this was delivered by Sir william Hustler and debated and at last the
question was put for referring it to the trustees 180 against 140[182] and then the
time was expired for taking the petitions and it was moved that we should
have another day to receive petitions but that was not carried[183] tho the
majority were for it becaus the Speaker who had given for the ays said the
ays must go out when the noes insisted that the noes had it but it was argued
that the time given for delivering of petitions was taken up in the private
busines of the house so that the leave was of little signification and in a
manner evaded and they did desire that the leave Might be prolonged by an
order of the house and that they might have leave to move it to morrow [*sic*] by
consent and then when this seemed to be Complyed with we went into the
order of the day after it was read which was to Consider how to maintain the

[178] Bishop Ashe of Clogher confirmed that Abercorn had refused to explain the letter on the
grounds that it did not have a signature: 'as to that copy, they could not tell whence it was had, nor
had nothing to say to it'. Trinity College, Dublin, MS 2001/879 (Lyons (King) MSS), Ashe to
Bishop King of Derry, 17 Feb. 1701[/2].

[179] The addresses were declared to contain 'scandalous and false expressions, highly reflecting
upon His Majesty's honour, and both Houses of Parliament'; the promoters were 'guilty of an high
crime and misdemeanour': *CJ* xiii. 746. Ralph reported 'many warm speeches' in the debate: *Hist.
Eng.*, ii. 1015.

[180] Only one received and one rejected, according to *CJ* xiii. 747.

[181] 'from England' erased.

[182] For Athlone's case, see above, p. 46, n. 57; Troost (ed.), 'Letters from Van Homrigh to Ginkel',
61–3; and *The Case of the Purchasers under the Earl of Athlone* (n.d.). Athlone had received the
thanks of the English House of Commons on 4 Jan. 1692 for his 'great service' in the Irish war,
and his grant of Lord Limerick's sequestered estate had been confirmed by an act of the Irish
Parliament in 1695: *CJ* x. 610. Earlier in the session his agent, Bartholomew Vanhomrigh, and
several of the principal purchasers, had applied to Robert Harley 'to name some worthy Member
that they may apply to for delivering their papers to the House': HMC, *Portland MSS*, viii. 95; BL
Loan 29/159, George Tollet to Harley, 15 Feb. 1701[/2]. The figures for the division are given as
164 : 140 in *CJ* xiii. 747, with Hustler a teller in the majority.

[183] According to *CJ* xiii. 747, the question negatived was 'that the House will now proceed in
receiving petitions relating to Irish forfeited estates'.

priviledges of the house which were indanger [*sic*] of being invaded:[184] Mr finch after Sir H Ashurst had made a long tedious oration that neyther he nor any one else knew what he meant stood up spoke against libells and reflections upon the parliament and Concluded without any motion but talked at random but at last in a second spee[ch] he re commended [*sic*] it to us to Consider how you sit here and what power you have and after a debate of only one part they voted that to assert that the house of commons was not the representative body of the[185] Com̄[*mon*]s of England tended to subvert the rights and fundamentalls of our constitution that to assert that the house has no right to commit any but their own Members tended to subvert etc.[186] there were severall instances of the houses using the righ[t] formerly: as in the case of Ferrers in H[*enry*] 8ths time by virtue of a verball order of the house of Commons they sent for the lord mayour and sherriffes and Clerks of the Counter and committed them:[187] and in Sir Thomas Sherleys Case vide Journalls the first o[f] King James the first they Committed the marshall of the kings bench to Little ease in the tower[188] and then they censured the writing of libells reflecting on the parliament:[189] and then mr Bromley moved to censure the Grand juryes that[190] addressed for a dissolution and reflected

---

[184] To consider 'the rights, liberties, and privileges' of the Commons: ibid.

[185] 'kingdom' erased.

[186] The first two resolutions were to condemn as subversive of the constitution the propositions (1) that the House of Commons 'is not the only representatives of the commons of England'; and (2) that the Commons 'have no power of commitment, but of their own Members': *CJ* xiii. 767. That these, and the subsequent resolution on libels (see below, n. 189), were moved by Heneage Finch and passed in this sitting of the committee, is confirmed in De Beer (ed.), *Locke Corresp.*, vii. 569; BL Add. MS 17677 XX, fo. 224; and Luttrell, *Brief Relation*, v. 143.

[187] After George Ferrers (*c.*1510–79), MP Plymouth, had been arrested for debt in 1542, the sheriffs of London, and the clerk of the Counter had been committed to the Tower for breach of privilege: H. C. Leonard, 'Ferrers' Case: A Note', *Bulletin of the Institute of Historical Research*, 42 (1969), 230–4; S. T. Bindoff (ed.), *The House of Commons 1509–1558* (3 vols.; London, 1982), ii. 129–31.

[188] Sir Thomas Shirley (1542–1612), of Wiston, nr. Steyning, Sussex, MP Sussex 1572–85, 1593, Steyning, 1601, 1604, for whom see P. W. Hasler (ed.), *The House of Commons 1559–1603* (3 vols.; London, 1981), iii. 375–6. Arrested for debt four days before the 1604 Parliament met, he became the subject of a writ of habeas corpus issued by the Commons. The warden of the Fleet prison, in which Shirley was held, was committed to the Tower on 7 May for refusing to obey the writ. See *CJ* i. 149, 167, 173–5, 181, 198, 200. I am grateful to Mr George Yerby for help with this point.

[189] The resolution was 'that to print, or publish, any books or libels, reflecting upon the proceedings of the House of Commons, or any Member thereof, for, or relating to, his service therein', was 'a high violation' of the rights and privileges of the Commons: *CJ* xiii. 767.

[190] 'mov[*ed*]' erased.

upon the parliament this cost many hours debate[191] and at last it was moved
to le[ave] the Chair for there was a great heat in the house many warm words
and the house would not censure those [?of] the grand juryes and when those
that had spoke for the addressers to be censured could not prevaile they
woul[d] have leaft out some parts of the question but others said that by
the rules of the Committee after the question for le[a]ving the Chair was put
and seconded they could not mend the question that they must eyther have the
questio[n] as it was put or the question for leaving the chair[192] so the question
for leaving the Chair was insisted on and yeelded without a division so all this
day was spent to no purpose for Mr Granvill being obliged to leave th[e] Chair
before he had asKed leave to report Could make no report so this day was
spent to very little purp[ose] only to vent their spleen and ease their minds
Just as the house rose Sir william Strickland fell down dead in all appearance
he had just spoke befo[re] a brisk hearty speech[193] and so we adjourned the
hous was very rude and bearish: nota mr Granville left the Chair very
irregularly and mr Speaker took his chair immediately and put the question
for adjournment and the [–

fo. 4ᵛ

– – –] cry was noes if Sir will[*iam*] Strickland had not fell down dead in
appearance of an appoplexy we had had wa[r]m [?speeches – –] it was
irregular in Granville and the Speaker to leave the Chair as they did: and it
would have been questioned:[194]

---

[191] Bromley's speech was noted both by Bonet (DZA, Rep. XI Eng. 25c, fo. 63), and
L'Hermitage (BL Add. MS 17677 XX, fos. 225–6). The grand juries concerned were those of
'Bedfordshire, Yorkshire, etc.': Strathmore MSS, box 70, folder 1, bdle. 2, newsletter, 19 Feb. 1701[/
2]. According to John Ellis, the debate continued for five to six hours (BL Add. MS 7074, fo. 91);
according to Robert Yard, until 8 p.m. (ibid. fo. 186).

[192] See [Hatsell,] *Precedents*, 75: 'It is a rule, that in a committee of the House there can be no
previous question; if therefore it is wished to avoid a question it is usual to move "that the
chairman do leave the chair"; which has the effect of a motion to adjourn.'

[193] Both Bonet (DZA, Rep. XI Eng. 25c, fo. 63) and L'Hermitage (BL Add. MS 17677 XX, fos.
219, 226), confirm that Strickland had spoken powerfully in response to Bromley, thereby bringing
on what James Brydges considered to have been an apoplectic fit (Huntington Lib., Stowe MS
26(2), Brydges' diary, 17 Feb. 1702). Another source reported that Sir John Bolles had 'mentioned
something of the impeachments', which was 'not seconded', and that Strickland was 'vindicating
the Yorkshire address' when struck down: Strathmore MSS, box 70, folder 1, bdle. 2, newsletter, 19
Feb. 1701[/2].

[194] What seems to have happened is that John Granville, the Tory chairman of the committee,
had refused to concede to the demand made by his party colleagues that he put the question to
leave the chair, for fear that the Whigs would prove too strong in the vote. He took advantage of
Strickland's collapse, and the consequent confusion as the stricken knight was 'carried out
attended by many Members', to make way for Speaker Harley, who then swiftly put and declared
carried a motion to adjourn. DZA, Rep. XI Eng. 25c, fo. 63; BL Add. MS 17677 XX, fos. 226–7;
West Yorkshire Archives, TN/C9/195 (Temple Newsam MSS), Thomas Smith to Lord Irwin, 19
Feb. 1701[/2] (partly calendared in HMC, *Various Colls.*, viii. 85).

[18 Feb. 1702 – ?Lord] Cuts letter was read in the house to choose cambridgshire: it was opposed by Sir Ed[*ward*] Seymour who moved [?for ?a ?committe]e to inspect presidents: we divided upon it the ays 106 – the noes 126[195] this was done to Sir Jos[*eph*] Williamson when he [?was ?abroad] in the kings service about 3 sessions ago: this was done before on the same accoun[t] to this lord Cuts: this was [?done ?to ?Mr] Howard who was travailing for his pleasure: this was denied mr Johnsons who went to the Indies for his profitt [?and ?left ?a] letter for the Speaker before he was chose at any place to tell at which place he would serve:[196] there are many [?other pres]idents of the like nature: then we went into the Committee of supply and tooke one day to breath to see if [?we ?could] find any thing in the room of malt or at least to ease the malt[197]

[195] Cutts had been elected both for Cambridgeshire and Newport (I.o.W.). As he was abroad on military service, he wrote to the Speaker from The Hague, 21 Feb. NS 1702, stating his wish to sit for the former constituency: *CJ* xiii. 749. James Vernon observed that the request 'met with more opposition than I expected': Centre for Kentish Studies, Maidstone, U1590/O53/10, Vernon to Alexander Stanhope, 20 Feb. 1701[/2]. Both Bonet and L'Hermitage noted that the opposition came from the Tories, Cutts himself being a Whig: DZA, Rep. XI Eng. 25c, fo. 63; BL Add. MS 17677 XX, fo. 223. The motion was to search precedents of Members 'beyond sea' exercising this prerogative: *CJ* xiii. 749.

[196] Sir Joseph Williamson had opted in 1698 to sit for Thetford rather than Rochester, for which he had also been returned. As acting ambassador at The Hague he was obliged to communicate his choice by letter. With the exception of a doubt expressed by Jack Howe as to whether service abroad excused attendance on the House, the Commons had accepted this practice without demur. *CJ* xii. 388; *CSP Dom.* 1699–1700, p. 5.

Cutts had chosen Cambridgeshire as his preferred seat over Newport after being returned for both constituencies in three successive general elections, from 1695 to 1701, but in none of these previous instances do the *Journals* indicate that his decision was communicated by letter: *CJ* xi. 338; xii. 367; xiii. 344. Indeed, there is evidence that in 1695 and 1701 Cutts was in England at around the time Parliament met: HMC, *Frankland-Russell-Astley MSS*, 86, 97.

William Howard's letter opting to sit for Northumberland, written from Paris, had been presented to the Commons by the Speaker on 4 Mar. 1701. The House had immediately appointed a committee to search precedents, but it had not reported by 19 May following, when Howard's choice was registered. *CJ* xiii. 380, 552.

William Johnson had been successful at Aldeburgh in the 1698 general election but had also stood at Orford, and, although defeated there, had entered a petition against the return. By November 1699 the petition had still not been heard, and Johnson was about to depart on a long trading voyage to the orient. He sent the Speaker a letter announcing his choice of Orford as constituency, should his petition be successful. After he had been seated for Orford in Feb. 1700 this letter was brought before the House. Again a committee was named to search precedents, but in this case no further action was taken. *CJ* xiii. 191–2, 278–9.

[197] The next day Luttrell reported that he expected the House to lay a duty of 6d. a bushel on malt when the committee met again on the 20th.

Feb 19th [*1702*] the bill for repairing and making good the harbour of Bridport
Mr Pitfeild and Mr Gulston serve for the place Sir Ed[*ward*] Seymour
Reflected severely upon them as being elected there by indirect means:[198] the
abjuration bill was read upon the reading[199] the order for its being read Mr
Finch said he did not oppose the reading of the bill but that if he had anything
to offer in the place of it that might be satisfactory to Gent[*lemen*] he hoped
they would hear him at Least and then it was offered by him a new strong oath
to support the king and to oppose the prince of wales:[200] my Lord Conningsbee opposed mr finches [s]peaking against the bill before it was read as irregular:
but the house said go on but all he offered was to propose some[t]hing in the
place of the bill that might satisfye Gent[*lemen*] and be as strong but that was
not agreed too: so the bill [w]as read and put and then the Lord Cheney
offered a clause for the quakers' Preachers to be exempted but the clause
[u]pon the debate was not received:[201] and then Sir Jo[*hn*] Bolles offered a
clause for the Church test and without any [d]ebating they went to the
question for receiving the clause 139 for not 203:[202] then mr Cummings[203]
made a [s]uperfine speech like reason against Passing[204] it Sir Jo[*hn*] Bolles[205]
and Sir Jeffery Jefferys did so to and then the bill was passed and Sir Charles
Hedges[206] was ordered to carry it up to the lords: the Lord Conningsbe
reflected upon mr Finches as he [(]Mr Finch[)][207] thougt so that made him
answer but this was before the bill was read my Lord said the new bill
looked as if it was made in another place fitted for the humour and pallate of
those that could not digest the abjuration oath Manly a silly hot fellow Cried
to the Barr but mr Finch endeavoured instead of complaining of the reflection
in an angry manner to say there was not one Equivoking expression in it and
then there was a little reflection of mr Har[c]ourt[208] upon Sir Walter yong
which was resented by Mr King and more of us were speaking to it but the

[198] 'as being elected there by indirect means' interlined. There is no evidence of a contest having
taken place at Bridport, though the circumstances of two Londoners being returned for a small
scot-and-lot borough would suggest that attention had been paid by the candidates to the material
wants of the voters.   [199] 'the reading' interlined.
[200] Burnet noted that Finch 'offered an alteration to the clause abjuring the Prince of Wales, so
that it imported only an oath not to assist him': *Own Time*, iv. 551. Robert Yard confirms that he
did so on this occasion: BL Add. MS 7074, fo. 188.
[201] *CJ* xiii. 750, notes merely a rider 'to exempt Quakers'.
[202] The *Journals* confirm that a rider, stipulating that 'persons who take upon them offices,
shall not depart from the communion of the Church of England', was defeated by this margin:
ibid.   [203] John Comyns.   [204] Originally 'engrossing'.
[205] Confirmed by Robert Yard: BL Add. MS 7074, fo. 188.
[206] 'and mr' erased.   [207] Words in brackets interlined in MS.
[208] Originally 'Hamond'.

Speaker diverted it by saying something to order so the matter Fell and we adjourned

Feb 20th [*1702*] nothing materiall but in the delivery of the Irish petitions there was this case a tenant that had a good leas forfeits an Irish popish lord puts in his cliaim to the estate after the term of the forfeiting person was expired and it was allowed my lord Haversham sais the Estate was his and desires time to be given him to put in his claim the publick got nor lost any thing let which of the lords would have the estate but if my Lord Havershams time had not been prolonged the estate would have been given absolutely to the popish lord[209] but they remembred my Lord Haversham behaviour last sessions[210] more then their own integrity so they made us divide for it and we were about 150 and they 130[211] and then came on the ways and means (after the remaining petitions were all brought up to the Clark and marked and an order to recive no more and these to be delivered on munday[*)]:* we then debated a malt tax some were quite against it [a]nd there were projectors at the door and a question for calling them and Carried against it and then a division after many words whether a malt tax or no for it 214 against 111[212]

Feb 21 [*1702*] Nothing materiall: but when the orders of the day was read they insisted to have the first Order which was to call in the Irish[213] trustees to give an account of the petitions[214] mr Boyle moved to have the report from the Chairman of the Committee of the ways and means: but it was said that report might be as well made on munday (the report was then a duty be laid on malt) that it was unreasonable to make the trustees wait and attend so often and to shew them so little respect from this house would make them appear but little without doors and would disparage them and the Com[*mi*]s[*sio*]n they acted by so the order relating to the Irish petitions and the trustees was Ordered to be first proceeded on: then mr Harcourt moved that wee should discours the trustees if the lands would not sell better if there were leases made and a term of years granted to the tenants for that then the trustees Could advance the rents and the estates would sell according to the advancement of the rents: Sir Tho[*mas*] littleton said that that matter could

---

[209] The estate, in Co. Tipperary, had been forfeited by one Thady Meagher: HMC, *House of Lords MSS*, NS v. 144. The identity of the 'Irish popish lord' remains obscure.

[210] See above, pp. 174–5, 177–9, 182–3.   [211] Given as 156 : 123 in *CJ* xiii. 752.

[212] The three other surviving accounts of this division give varying figures, none agreeing entirely with Cocks's: L'Hermitage (BL Add. MS 17677 XX, fos. 223–4) has 214 : 107; Luttrell (*Brief Relation*, v. 144), 208 : 114; and an anonymous newsletter-writer (BL Add. MS 40803, fo. 24), 207 : 114.   [213] 'peti[*tion?ers*]' erased.

[214] According to *CJ* xiii. 754–5, this was the penultimate item of business (followed by an adjournment of the report from ways and means). The two trustees then in London were Francis Annesley and James Hooper: see above, p. 200, n. 77.

not by your order be discoursed on now nor could the trustees be examined or asked any questions relating to that matter the order being only to read the petitions and to examine the trustees in such things that do relate only to the petitions the house agreed that Sir Tho[*mas*] Littleton was right as to order and so mr Harcourt who put of[*f*] the malt report was disappoynted and they proceeded and went thro six petitions and at five of the clock adjourned to munday

Feb 23 [*1702*] we went into the Committee of ways and means after a dispute whether the house should agree with that committee upon the report of the malt tax: it was opposed by Sir Ed[*ward*] Seymour Sir Xto[*pher*] musgrove and some of that side in order as we thought to distress and cramp the service. for tho they were against that they could Not invent any other ways to raise the money: then we went into the committee of ways and means and there it was moved to put four shilling on a quarter of Malt sixpence the bushell: that was opposed and we ran into great debates about the bank to tax them and complaints were made of the favour they had from the government to the prejudice of other merchants trading in exchange that they had the preference from the treasury and that they had been allowed 55000 li. over their bargain for remitting money into holland to serve the army in holland but this was the case they agreed to remitt money for the army and they were to receive money there and instead of money they were paid in tallyes which were at 50 per cent. discount and their bargain was to have money in specie so that tho they had the 55000 li. they were loosers this was Nothing When the truth appeared and nothing to the busines before: and then we ordered sixpence on the bushell of Malt and four shillings on 36 gallons of cyder[215] and adjourned

[*fo. 5*]

Feb 24 [*1702*] The house sat late and after some petitions the Speaker poynted to some at the barr to [– – –] the house Cryed out my lord Hartington the Speaker Continued his poynt and there hapned to be some debate [– –] about agreeing with the committee it was the Coynage bill[216] so that it was past one, and when that was over [?my Lord Harting] ton made his motion the Speaker told him it was past one and that the orders would not permit of any new [?motion[217] my] lord said considering the late sitting of the house and the Debates of agreeing with Committees after the reports [?were ?made ?of] a long bill it was impossible ever to make a[218] motion he therefore desired leave of the house to do so whi[ch was gran]ted and my lords motion was that it be

215 Confirmed by Bonet (DZA, Rep. XI Eng. 25c, fo. 67), and Luttrell (*Brief Relation*, v. 145).
216 The bill to continue the act of 8 & 9 Gul III, to prevent counterfeiting.
217 See above, p. 109, n. 318. According to *CJ* xiii. 759, 'it was then about two o'clock'.
218 'report' erased.

an instruction to the Committee that is to consider of the Rights li[berties and] Priviledges of this house that they then Consider of the rights and liberties of the commons of England:[219] [?there ?was] 20 up to second my Lord but Sir Rich[*ard*] Onslow did it Sir Edward Seymour opposed[220] and Mr Finch and musg[rove –] Harcourt Sir John Holland spoke his mayden speech which was very fine and much Commended it ref]le]cted [on] Powes and Finch in the late reigns[221] they insisted on it that the previous question should be first put but [Par]Ker who has more sence and temper then the whole party made angry faces att those that insisted on it [?and] so they found their Error: for had they divided the house upon the previous question it would have [?been] a wors list for them then the black list[222] viz that they had been against the rights and liberties of the [commons] of england: Seymour was very uneasy with himself for opposing this question and Looked out of humo[ur] and confessed at dinner that he was mistaken in speaking against it: so there was no division then was the Coventry Election reported and the question put that Sir Xto[*pher*] Hale was duly Elected.[223] Robyn Dormer said he had attended the Committee and that he hoped he should never have lived so long as to see such injustice at the committee confirmed at the house:[224] the case was very hard they refused Neale from disqualifying of Sir Xto[*pher*][225] Hales votes becaus they were not in the Lists of the charity they had tho they had all they demand[ed] or were ordered them, they gave in the Committee Hale leave to object against what votes he pleased of Neale but tyed Neale down to such restrictions that made it impossible for him to object as he ought and cou[ld][226] I seconded Dormir and said I could not say that I

---

[219] 'Of all the commons of England', in *CJ* xiii. 759. Hartington's responsibility for this motion is confirmed by a multiplicity of witnesses, e.g. [Ralph,] *Hist. Eng.*, ii. 1015; and Rebecca Warner (ed.), *Epistolary Curiosities, Consisting of Unpublished Letters of the Seventeenth Century, Illustrative of the Herbert Family* . . . (2 vols.; London, 1818), ii. 16.

[220] Thomas Johnson's account of the debate also recorded Onslow as seconding Hartington, and Seymour as opposing: Liverpool RO, 920 NOR 2/216, Johnson to Richard Norris, 24 Feb. 1701[/2].

[221] Heneage Finch had served as Solicitor-General 1679–86; Sir Thomas Powys as Solicitor-General 1686–7, and Attorney-General 1687–8.

[222] [Tristram Savage,] *A List of One Unanimous Club of Members of the Late Parliament* . . . *Who Ought to Be Opposed in the Ensuing Elections, by All that Intend to Save Their Native Country from Being a Province of France* . . . (London, 1701), for which see R. R. Walcott, 'Division-Lists of the House of Commons, 1689–1715', *Bulletin of the Institute of Historical Research*, 14 (1936–7), 26–7; Horwitz, *Parliament, Policy and Politics*, 297–8.

[223] Hales had been double-returned with Henry Neale (*c*.1660–1730), of Allesley Park, War., MP Bucks., 1696–8. The committee had found for Hales.

[224] Dormer was connected with the excluded candidate through his own electoral patron, Lord Wharton, who had assisted Neale's election for Buckinghamshire in 1696.

[225] 'musgroves' erased.

[226] For details of this election, see *CJ* xiii. 759–63; BL Add. MS. 11364, fos. 29–30; and BL Lothian MSS, 'Sir Christopher Hales Case . . . '.

wished not to live so long as to see such things I had seen them and I hoped
to live to see them rectifyed that I was at the committee and was witnes to
the sev[e]rall hardships complained of and that I did not see any right any
colour of a majority unles that his being one of the black list that I had
lately heard so much Commended within doors and without by the historian
of the late parliament[227] would create him right to be a member: this made
all the black liste[d] buss all over the house and Sir Xto[pher] musgrove in a
rage said I had[228] reflected on Gent[lemen] many of whom w[ere] of as good
quality estates and as loyall to the government as I was the house was very
Noysey and som[e] of the Fooles Cryed to the barr as they usually do if any
one angers their old ones: but I repeated wha[t] I had said and so that
Ceased and the question was put and Hale declared to be duly elected: then
Mr Bromley moved to have the sherriffe taken into Custody but after some
debate they were told that the[y] must first vote him guilty of some Crime so
that was done, but it was truly objected that the sher[r]iffe was guilty of no
fault for he could not tell that the house would disqualify so many and if
they had not it might have been even or neale might have had the majority
all would not do but they were ordered to be taken into Custody: then mr
Harcourt moved that the undersher[r]iffe might attend the high sherriffe for
that he was very busy at the Election and had said this should be the dearest
thing Sir Xto[pher] ever went about, and this was all as was said I opposed
it but the question being put and carried[229] and then we adjourned to
Feb 25 [1702]
We had members sworn read some private acts and considered the Irish
petitions that lay upon the table [–] and adjourned to the mamsbury men
were discharged who were Kept to see what Goodenough and goodman would

---

[227] Witnesses had told the committee how the appearance of Hales's name on the 'black list'
had been used against him: *CJ* xiii. 760; BL Add. MS 11364, fo. 30; Lothian MSS, 'Sir Christopher
Hales Case . . . ' [Drake,] *Hist. Last Parl.*, preface, pp. [xi–xxii], denounced the compiler of the
list, and praised the blacklisted as 'worthy patriots'.   [228] 'man' erased.

[229] In fact, there were two sheriffs, Abraham Owen, and John Collins, and both, together with
the under-sheriff, Edward Owen, were declared guilty of 'indirect practices', or 'illegal and partial
proceedings', and were ordered into custody: *CJ* xiii. 763. All were Dissenters. For Abraham
Owen, a capper and feltmaker, who served as mayor of Coventry three times between 1710 and
1727, and Collins (?d. 1711), a clothier, see Judith Hurwich, ' "A Fanatick Town": The Political
Influence of Dissenters in Coventry, 1660–1720', *Midland History,* 4 (1977–8), 35, 38; K. J. Smith
(ed.), *Warwickshire Apprentices and Their Masters 1710–1760* (Dugdale Society, 29; [Stratford-
upon-Avon,] 1975), 131; and Levi Fox (ed.), *Coventry Constables' Presentments* (Dugdale Soc., 34;
[Stratford-upon-Avon,] 1986), 69.

say w[?hen] they were kept on purpose for that and were discharged before:[230] this commitment was unjust as was the sending for goodeno[ugh]

This night was the norwich[231] petition examined by the Committee[232] which is certainly the most Corrupt Court in Xtendom nay in the world when they have a mind to d[o] an unjustice they will Call withdraw and then move that the Councill may withdraw and then the matter is debated and the major part that have a mind to carry any thing will put a question forreign to the matter and being the majority can have what question put they please but the truth they will never put for then they would be ashamed to vote in it Feb 26 [1702]

after the land tax was read the first time[233] that yong firebrand St: j[oh]n stood up and in Jack hows usuall place made a flaming oration of the great good qualities of the last parliament of what great things they had done for the Kingdom and how necessary it was to justify them in the matters of the impeachments and to assert our own rights to impeachments that he intended not to drive things to[o] far, not to go any farther then to vindicate our own Rights and not [234] to come to any persons, but things and then ended with this Motion: that the Commons of England have not right done th[em] in the late impeachments: Cooke in a weaker insipid dreaming way seconded St Johns motions this question was debate[d] six hours[235] and hardly any body shewed in what they had not right done them, but in generall in givin[g] Judgment before it was demanded and in appoynting a day without their consent and trying them without Joyning issue, to this it was answered: that in criminall matters it was not necessary to joyn issue that there was but one president of it and that the Judges when they had appoynted a day if the others would not prosecute ought in justice to acquit, or else what an inconveniency would that be to labo[ur] Continually under an impeachment: all the debate was nothing to the question some vindicated the partitio[n] treaty so condemned and

[230] See above, pp. 191–6, 212–14. Goodenough, an attorney, and John Woodman (not Goodman), had been summoned on 14 Feb., and kept till the 25th before being questioned and discharged.

[231] Originally 'norwige'.

[232] Confirmed in Luttrell, *Brief Relation*, v. 146, who reported that the petition of the defeated Whig candidate, Peter Thacker, against the sitting Tory Member, Robert Davy, was rejected in the committee without a division. For the case, see *CJ* xiii. 790–1; *The Case Relating to the Election of Members . . . for . . . Norwich* [1701/2].   [233] 'was read the first time' interlined.

[234] 'not' interlined.

[235] St John's role as proposer of this motion, and Coke's as seconder, were also noted by Robert Yard (BL Add. MS 7074, fo. 193), and L'Hermitage (BL Add. MS 17677 XX, fos. 234, 238), the latter reporting that St John had been taught his part by Jack Howe, and Coke by Sir Edward Seymour — either directly, or by emulation. According to L'Hermitage, the debate lasted eight hours (BL Add. MS 17677 XX, fo. 235). Rachel, Lady Russell, commented, 'the business in the House of Commons today makes everybody diligent' (HMC, *Rutland MSS*, ii. 168).

censured the last sessions some vindicated the lords and censured the last parliament very severely and justly the answer to that was we were not trying the lords but let the grounds be nev[er] so unjust let the impeachments be never so groundles that was nothing to the purpose for in the prose[cu]tion we had not right done us: and if we did not say so, we gave up our rights the R[*igh*]ts of the people o[f] England and that it was intended to go no[236] further: to this it was answered if we did proceed so far nobody could tell how much further we should go: that it might set the Lords and Com[*mon*]s together by the ears and throw down all that was done: the last parliament justifyed it self and printed their proceedings the Lords did so too, this was an appeale to the people:[237] if we made a vote, they would do so too and then we were b[?ack] just as we begun if we proceeded further there must be a rupture which would be a very malancholy sight for our freinds abroad and ruine our hopes and distract us at home: that a di[sso]lution was intended to compose our differences and if we would still persist and would not C[?ome ?to

[*fo. 5ᵛ*]

?a ?resoluti]on there was no other remedy but that we must fight it out, for there could never be an end of [?these ?differen]ces: or that according to what they had done in Sweden and Denmark we must give up our rights to the Mo[?narch ?:[238] t]hat the Lords had as much reason to beleive themselves in the right as we had: and that we had as much rea[son to belie]ve they acted with sincerity and if so they neyther would nor Could recede: and after a many re[?flections ?and h]ard speeches the question was put for it 221 against 235:[239] and then a question for leaving the Chair [?put ?and ?in] a division carried in the negative and so off went the 221: and then my Lord Hartington: that it is the un[doubted r]ight of the people of England to petition or Address

---

[236] 'no' interlined.

[237] *CJ* xiii. 641; *A State of the Proceedings and Resolutions of the House of Commons with Relation to the Impeached Lords, and What Happened Thereupon between the Two Houses* (London, 1701); *LJ* xvi. 746; *The Several Proceedings and Resolutions of the House of Peers* . . . See also Betty Kemp, *Votes and Standing Orders of the House of Commons: The Beginning* (HC Lib. Doc. 8; London, 1971), 25–7, 30, which discusses the disputes arising during the impeachment proceedings over the publication of the Commons' *Votes*.

[238] The iniquities of the absolutist regimes in Denmark, and (to a lesser extent) in Sweden, constituted a hobby-horse beloved of Whig parliamentarians, who drew their evidence from two highly popular works of travel description and contemporary history: [Robert Molesworth,] *An Account of Denmark as It Was in the Year 1692* (London, 1694); and [John Robinson,] *An Account of Sueden* . . . (London, 1694).

[239] Four witnesses agree with Cocks's figures: William Blathwayt (Yale Univ., Beinecke Lib., Osborn Coll., Blathwayt MSS, box 20, Blathwayt to George Stepney, 28 Feb. 1701[/2]); John Ellis (BL Add. MSS 28888, fo. 82); Peter King (De Beer (ed.), *Locke Corresp.*, vii. 577); and Luttrell (*Brief Relation*, v. 147).

to the King for the calling sitting or dissolving of [Par]liaments[240] Resolved
that it is the undoubted right of every subject of England under any accusation
eyther by [im]peachment or otherwise to be brought to a speedy tryall in order
to be acquitted or condemned: and then we ordered [?Col.] Granville to[241]
report[242] the resolutions and then he leaft the Chair and then the Speaker
re[su]med the Chair and some were for having these resolutions reported
immediately others for having them reported on Sa[t]erday and the question
was put for Saterday and the house divided we that were for Saterday went out
and were [ab]out 60 those that staid in were about 120:[243] so they were
reported with others made the day before[244] viz that to[245] [a]ssert that the
house of commons is not the only representative of the commons of England
tends to the subversion of the Rights and priviledges of the house of[246]
Commons[247] and of the fundamentall constitution of the government of this
kingdom: Resol[*ved*] that to assert that the house of commons have no power
of Commitment but of their own members tends to the subversion of the
house of Commons:[248] Nota it is very unusuall to report these resolutions that
are made the same day: but it was the first day that party had been victorious
and they were resolved to keep what they had got: and the reason they gave
was for the Keeping us in peace and preventing of heats: So we rose at ten at
night:[249] Coll[*onel*] Colchester mr Hopkins Lord mordant never spoke before
and did now speake very well: nota the first question that was carried in the
negative did not only reflect upon the lords but would certainly if it had been
carryed have brought in those that had advised the dissolution[250]

Feb 27 [*1702*]

a debate about regulating the distillers busines and trade made some debate
in order to repeale a clause in an act which obliged the sellers of those liquors

---

[240] 'for the calling, sitting, and dissolving, of Parliaments; and for the redressing of grievances':
CJ xiii. 767. That Hartington was the author of this motion is confirmed by Bonet (DZA, Rep. XI
Eng. 25c, fo. 69); and L'Hermitage (BL Add. MS 17677 XX, fo. 238). He was evidently seconded by
Sir John Holland (Strathmore MSS, box 70, folder 1, bdle. 2, newsletter, 26 Feb. 1701[/2]).
[241] 'leave the Chair and' erased.   [242] 'first' erased.
[243] Given as 102 : 62 in *CJ* xiii. 767. Bonet noted that the Whigs, anxious to strike while the iron
was hot, had favoured an immediate report, the Tories a postponement until the following
Saturday (DZA, Rep. XI Eng. 25c, fo. 70).
[244] A previous sitting of the committee, i.e. 17 Feb.   [245] Originally 'the'.
[246] 'house of' interlined.   [247] 'of Engl[*and*]' erased.
[248] In fact, voted on the 17th: see above, p. 217. Cocks omits a 4th resolution, against publishing
libels reflecting on the proceedings of the Commons and the conduct of its Members: *CJ* xiii. 767.
[249] Confirmed by John Ellis (BL Add. MS 28888, fo. 82), although Luttrell gives 'about nine
o'clock' (*Brief Relation*, v. 147), and L'Hermitage 9.30 (BL Add. MS 17677 XX, fo. 236). Burnet
(*Own Time*, iv. 548), recalled that this had been 'a long and hot debate in a very full House'.
[250] Blathwayt observed that the outcome of the debate 'has freed all the impeached lords in all
respects' (Yale Univ., Beinecke Lib., Osborn Coll., Blathwayt MSS, box 20, Blathwayt to George
Stepney, 28 Feb. 1701[/2]).

to take a Licence:[251] and then the Apothecaryes bill was passed after the offer Of ar [*sic*] rider or two which were not brought up[252] (Nota if a rider is interlined one letter it cannot be added to the bill [)] and then we went into ways and means and severall things were proposed but nothing further agreed to: it was proposed to sell the reversion of the Crown lands that were in reversions after the expiring of long leases: but that was not agreed to but it was agreed to bring in a bill not to alien them so the Committee rose without doing any thing[253] Feb ult [*i.e. 28th 1702*] After some bills were read mr Freeman who was Chairman of the Committee[254] that was to inquire into the Matter of the petition of Mr Freeman against Coll[*onel*] Coddrington the governour of the Lerward Islands for seising his plantation[255] desired the instructions of the house to know if they might read an affidavit: Seymour set forth the difficulties those people laboured under in relation to their distance and the unpracticablenes of their coming over hither that they could not come to complain unles their governours would give them a licence which they would never do to Complain against themselves and therefore he was for reading it: I was for maintaining the old usage of parliaments and not going out of the old way that if we should open such a gap the governours would get by it for they Could Easier get affidavits then the inferiour people and that they ought to be read in their favour as well as against them: mr Blathwait told us this busines was depending before the Com[*mi*]s[*sione*]rs of trade[256] and that there they did read affidavits but that their affidavits were not ex parte but that both sides did make the best of the matter and affidavits were made before a publick magistrate and that both partyes did make their answers and

---

[251] The report of the committee on a petition from the Distillers' Company (of which committee Cocks had been a member: *CJ* xiii. 748), one of whose resolutions was that the clause in the 1701 Low Wines Act (12 & 13 Gul. III, c. 11), requiring brandy-sellers to be licensed was 'a great hindrance' to the consumption of English brandies: *CJ* xiii. 769.

[252] The bill to revive the act exempting apothecaries from parish office and jury service. Two riders were offered: ibid.

[253] According to Thomas Johnson, the committee not only agreed to insert a clause in 'some bill' to prevent the alienation of Crown lands (duly reported on the 28th: *CJ* xiii. 770), but also to lay a duty on wines: Liverpool RO, 920 NOR 2/242, Johnson to Richard Norris, 28 Feb. 1701[/2].

[254] Of which Cocks had been a member: *CJ* xiii. 750.

[255] Captain William Freeman (*c*.1645–1707), of Godwyn, St Kitts, and Fawley Court, Bucks.: Vere Langford Oliver (ed.), *Caribbeana* . . . (8 vols.; London, 1910–19), v. 43; George Lipscomb, *The History and Antiquities of the County of Buckingham* (4 vols.; London, 1847), iii. 561, 563; *CSP Colonial* 1701, p. 687. (No relation to Ralph Freman, the chairman of the committee.) For Codrington, see above, p. 86, n. 181. Freeman petitioned on his own behalf, and on behalf of other planters who claimed the illegal seizure of their estates by the governor: *CJ* xiii. 750.

[256] Blathwayt, a member of the Board of Trade, had been delegated by the board on the 23rd to make their report to the Commons: *CSP Colonial* 1702, p. 98. Petitions from Freeman, and others, had been received by the board in the previous Dec., and were still under consideration: ibid. 1701, pp. 683–7, 694–5, 718–19, 722–5; 1702, pp. 9–12, 20–1, 23–4, 75–6, 78.

objections: and [t]hat upon such affidavits they did give judgement: Mr
Etherick did desire to know what they did mean by reading of the affidavit
if they intended to give credit to it and to send for the governour over upon the
strength of this affidavit to make his defence if so the governour would have a
very hard case of it that he beleived that if the house had Known the truth of
the matter when the petition was delivered that the Cause was depending in
another court and that Justice was not denied and that the cause was under
examination before the king they would then have hardly received the petition:
Sir Xto[*pher*] musgrove was against[257] the reading of the affidavit the question
was put for reading 122 against reading 142[258] then mr Secretary vernon
acquainted the house that he had a message to deliver from the King So[259]
it was brought up and read at the table and the Speaker acquainted the house
that the Kings name was to it so Whilest the letter was reading we all sat
bare:[260] the subject of the message was that there was nothing that the King
desired more then an union with Scotland that Considering how near the line
on Which the Scotch crown was intailed was expiring that he was very desirous
to make an union of the two Kingdoms in order to prevent the evills that
attended both nations before the union that he had met with an unhappy
accident which hindered him from Coming to the parliament to tell them this
from the throne:[261] mr Secretary moved to have this considered on[262] upon[263]
thursday which was seconded and agreed to by the house mr Lownds told the
house of a president in 1604 in which king James sent such a message to the
house and the president sais according to presidents in those cases used the
house ordered the Chancellour of the Exchecquer to inquire after the Kings
health and to express their sorrow for his misfortune which was from the kik
of his hors and that the King received the message very kindly and assured
them he would be allwais ready to ease their greevances[264] he moved that we
might send somebody on the message Sir Rowland Gwin seconded the motion
but Mr Smith proposed something new and so it dropped: then Came on the

[257] 'receiving' erased.
[258] The question was whether to read the deposition of Mr Cole, the Solicitor-General of the
Leeward Islands: *CJ* xiii. 769.
[259] Capital 'S' in MS, and by the context clearly intended to indicate the beginning of a new
sentence.   [260] Bare-headed: see above, p. 116, n. 376.
[261] For the full text of this message, see *CJ* xiii. 769.   [262] 'f' erased.
[263] 'upon' interlined.
[264] On 28 June 1604 the Commons was informed that King James I had been confined to bed
following a hunting accident, in which one of his feet had been injured 'by a stroke of the Queen's
horse'. The Vice-Chamberlain of the Household, accompanied by six other MPs (none of whom
was at that time Chancellor of the Exchequer) had thereupon been sent to inquire after the King's
health. *CJ* i. 247–8.

consideration of the Irish petitions the first was my[265] Lady Francis Kitelys
daughter[266] who was my Lord Chancellour Hides daughter and had a grant
from the Queen who was her cousin germin[267] this was within the words and
meaning of the act of resumption but it was urged in favour of her that shee
was the queens near relation and the only grant shee made the house divided
and wee that staid in were 65 those went out for to have it referred to the[268]
trustees were 140;[269] then came on my lady Tirconnells hers was a pretty hard
case viz shee was outlawed for being in France and the Queen would not give
her leave to come over: then of[f] Went the squadron that was set on purpose
to defend her[270] then was my lady Limricks petition shee was a Spanish Lady
and brought her husband 30000 li. assoon as her Cause was determined of[f]
went another squadron:[271] then was Mrs Mackdonnell woman to the Dutches
of potsmouth and assoon as her petition was determined in her favour off
went another squadron:[272] and then the house was very thin and one more was
determined all in favour[273] and so the house adjourned to munday[274]

---

[265] 'Lord' erased.   [266] 'daughter' interlined.

[267] In fact, the petition came not from Lady Frances Keightley (d. 1726), the daughter of
Edward Hyde (1609–75), 1st Earl of Clarendon and Lord Chancellor 1658–67, but from her
husband, Thomas Keightley (c.1650–1719), an Irish revenue commissioner, who in 1696 had
been granted some Irish forfeitures in lieu of the favourable leases he had previously held on
parts of his brother-in-law King James II's private estate. See HMC, *House of Lords MSS*, NS v. 24.

[268] Originally 'considered of [?by]'.

[269] More accurately, the question was whether to give leave for a bill on Keightley's behalf. It
was carried 140:65, those in favour 'going out'. *CJ* xiii. 770.

[270] Frances (c.1650–1731), née Jennings, widow of James II's principal henchman in Ireland,
Richard Talbot, 1st Earl of Tyrconnell [I], and also a sister of the Countess of Marlborough. The
petition had been presented by her two surviving trustees, and also resulted in a vote for a private
bill. Ibid. Bishop Ashe later reported that the bill 'was hurried with . . . unusual expedition thro'
both Houses, both Whigs and Tories striving who could favour it most': Trinity Coll., Dublin, MS
2001/901, Ashe to Bishop King, 2 Apr. 1702. See also Henry L. Snyder (ed.), *The Marlborough–
Godolphin Correspondence* (3 vols.; Oxford, 1975), i. 51.

[271] Euphemia Maria (d. 1703), widow of William Dungan, 1st Earl of Limerick. She was the
daughter of Sir Richard Chambers, but had been living in Spain prior to her marriage. After the
Battle of the Boyne she and her husband went into exile in France. He died in 1698, and in Nov.
1701 she was granted a licence to return to England. Again her petition gave rise to a bill. *CJ* xiii.
770.

[272] Hannah MacDonnell was in service to Louise de Kéroualle (1649–1734), Duchess of
Portsmouth, Charles II's mistress. The widow of a Jacobite, Sir Randal MacDonnell, she had
brought a fortune of some £7,000 to her marriage, but found herself after the Revolution in 'a very
necessitous condition'. She made a 'discovery' of her husband's forfeited property, and claimed not
only the quarter to which she was thus entitled, but also her jointure of £4,000. In 1696 the whole
estate was granted in trust to her. Again a private bill resulted from the petition. See HMC, *House
of Lords MSS*, NS v. 25–6; *The Case of Hannah Macdonnel* [1702]; PRO Northern Ireland, D.1854/
2/18, fos. 186–8; *CJ* xiii. 770.   [273] That of Maurice Annesley: *CJ* xiii. 770.

[274] The *Journals* record two sets of additional committee-appointments before the House rose:
ibid.

March 2d [*1702*]

This the black rod[275] Came and acquainted the house that the king by an unhappy accident had been prevented from coming [h]imself to the parliament and that therefore he had commissionated 3 lords to[276] give the Royall assent to those bills that [w]ere ready[277] and the Lords had sent him to desire the Speaker and the[278] Commons to be present at the passing of the bills and so he returned [and] the Speaker and the house went to the Lords and the Speaker when he returned told us that it was our right to see

[*fo. 6*]

the bills passed but that there were not very often presidents of this nature that the first was . . . [?the ?bills] passed were the attaindour of the W: p[279] the bill to prevent mutineers and diserters that he did not think it [?proper ?to] tell the Lords names that were commissionated: Sir Ed[*ward*] Seymour said sir you are right as to the presidents but we [?have ?gone ?a] great way out of the way formerly all the bills were passed together publick and private and the greevances fir[st –] before any bill passed and spoke idlely at last that the sending for us up to see the bills receive the kings assent was [– ?and] that the Lords ought not to have given judgment against the impeached Lords till the com[*mon*]s demanded it: then Sir Jo[*seph*] Je[kyll took] the Chair for taking and stating the publick accounts of the kingdom [280] I brought up a Clause to empower the co[mmissioners] to inquire into the briberys and Corruptions used amongst the officers concerned in managing the Kings treasure [?then] Mr Cooke brought up a clause to hinder the Officers in the dutch regiments from being paid till the . . . [Van]deryes had stated their accounts[281] this was very unjust in relation to the officers it was a little debated and mad[e ?a] part of the bill

in the Evening there was the Case of Cauln Election tryed for Sir Charles Hedges 7n voters and the und[er] Steward against Sir Charles for mr Bainton 7

---

[275] In fact, the deputy usher, Francis Aston (ibid.), for whom see above, p. 171, n. 733.

[276] 'consent' erased.

[277] Seven lords had been commissioned (any two of them being able to act): the Lord President (Duke of Somerset), Lord High Admiral (Earl of Pembroke), Lord Steward (Duke of Devonshire), Earl Marshall (Earl of Carlisle), Secretary of State (Earl of Manchester), Chamberlain of the Household (Earl of Jersey), and Lord Keeper (Sir Nathan Wright): *LJ* xvii. 52–3.

[278] 'Speaker and the' interlined.   [279] 'The pretended Prince of Wales'.

[280] The bill for taking the public accounts.

[281] The Dutch forces on the English establishment, whose paymaster was Jacob Vanderesche. A clause to this effect had been ordered on 16 Jan.: *CJ* xiii. 682.

and the High Steward:[282] and made a voyd Election tho Hedges his frein[ds]
divided for having him duly Elected. and that was lost and then the question
was put upon Baintons being du[ly] Elected and his freinds divided the
house[283] for him: it was made a voyd election[284]

March 3d [*1702*] This day private bills were read and the malt tax bill and the
land tax bill the second time and the amendments to the abjuration bill sent
from the lords[285] the amendments were agreed to with an amendment: in the
land tax there were debates relating to instructions to be given to the
committee for receiving of clauses one I moved that there should be no fees
paid out of the money given for the 4000 men to the officers of the Exch[e]quer
and that after some debate that was ordered with this alteration that no fees
should be paid ou[t] of the aydes given this sessions: and another instruction
made by Sir Ed[*ward*] Hussey that all lands given to Charity since 1693 to
charitys should be rated as they then were:[286] this was easily complyed with:
and then mr Smith moved that it might be an instruction to the Committee to
receive a Clause in favour of those that wer[e] oppressed by the burthen of the
taxes by reason of the non jurors who paid then double and the papist som[e]
of whom had taken the oaths and others were dead and their lands descended
to those that owned the gove[r]nment and so the double those lands were charged
with was taken off them and laid upon others the hous[e] divided for such an
instruction 140 against 83[287] and when they had carried it they Could not tell
what to do with it at last Seymour proposed that after the owners of those
lands had sworn that they paid[288] above 4s in the pound what was[289] above the

---

[282] All 16 voters at Calne had polled for one candidate, Henry Blaake, who had been returned
unopposed, but they had divided equally for the second seat between Hedges and Edward Bayntun
(*c.*1660–1720), of Hardenhuish, Wilts. (MP for the borough 1705–10). The 'senior' guild steward
at Calne, John Haskins, an innkeeper, voted for Bayntun; the 'junior', Richard Seager, seneschal of
the Crown manor of Ogbourne St George, voted for Hedges: *CJ* xiii. 791–2; Wiltshire RO, G18/1/1
(Calne borough records, guild stewards' book, 1561–1814), fos. 109, 171; G18/1/11 (election
papers), affidavit of Humphrey Townsend and John Haskins, 3 Feb. 1714, petition of James
Johnson, 10 Oct. 1710.   [283] 'the house' interlined.
[284] This sequence of divisions is confirmed by Robert Yard (BL Add. MS 7074, fos. 194–5); and
James Lowther (Cumbria RO (Carlisle), D/Lons/W, James to Sir John Lowther, 3 Mar. 1701[/2]),
who noted that the Whigs voted against Hedges, and the Tories against Bayntun.
[285] 'I mean' erased.
[286] In the resultant act (1 Anne, c. 6, s. lxv) this provision applied to hospitals, almshouses, and
the Corporation for the Sons of the Clergy: *Statutes of the Realm*, viii. 27. The 1692 Subsidy Act
(4 Gul. & Mar., c. 1), which came into force in 1693, had changed the basis of direct taxation from
a monthly assessment to a pound rate, and was assumed to have inaugurated the land tax.
[287] Given as 126 : 89 in *CJ* xiii. 774, which makes it clear that what was proposed was the relief
of lands formerly charged at a double rate according to the terms of the 1692 act, i.e. the property
of recusants and nonjurors, which now qualified for a single rate. See above, p. 20, n. 87.
[288] '4' erased.   [289] 'the' erased.

4s should be a surcharge upon the County[290] there were other clauses offered viz to ease those places that paid extraordinary by reason of personall estat[es] Which were removed but the Speaker put that the other motions off by telling them they were filling up the blanks in the bill[291] in the house which was the busines of the committee so wee adjourned[292]

March 4th [1702] we put of[f] all elections but four for this sessions,[293] and went thro the malt act in the Committee and adjourned to

at night the committee sat upon East Redford in nottingamshire Sir Willough-bee Hickman and levings[294] petitioners against Thornagh and white: the first thing the councill desired was to have the[295] report of the last parliament read[296] and this was debated above one hour they that were against it said we were not tyed down by the report of the last parliament this was a new cause and we were a new parliament and that it would not be decent to have opinions of parliaments read pro and con in the same Burrough that Sir Xto[pher] wren was chosen at windsor first by the select number and after-wards by the populacy the first time the parliament were of opinion that the right of Electing was in the populacy the 2d time they were of opinion it was in the select numb[er][297] and that there [were] other cases of the same nature:[298] the others said that we should not be guided by the[299] report of another parliament but that every Gent[leman] might have any thing in our journall read as part of his speech that it could not be evidenc[e] but that it should be read: the answer was why should it be read if it signifyed nothing: that tho we might have it read [?in] the house as part of ones speech yet there was difference between that and the having it read by the councill:[300] at last the

---

[290] 'That, where any persons, relieved for lands that have paid double, shall come to be charged more than four shillings in the pound, the same shall be levied by way of surcharge upon the whole county': *CJ* xiii. 774.   [291] 'before' erased.

[292] *CJ* xiii. 774, records one further instruction passed, for a clause 'for the more effectual payment of seamen's wages, and to prevent the discount upon their tickets'.

[293] i.e. the elections committee was 'discharged from hearing' more than four more cases in the current session: ibid. 775.

[294] William Levinz (c.1671–1747), of Grove, and Bilby, Notts., MP E. Retford 1702–6, 1708–10, Notts. 1710–22, 1732–4. See *HC 1715–54*, ii. 213.   [295] 'resolutions' erased.

[296] On 15 Apr. 1701, in accepting a petition of Hickman against White, the Commons had declared the franchise to lie with the freemen at large: *CJ* xiii. 495. See above, pp. 97–8.

[297] 'resolutions' erased.

[298] A misleading version of the outcome of the disputed elections for New Windsor in 1689 and 1690. In the first, the franchise had been declared to reside in the mayor, bailiff, and a 'select number' of burgesses, thereby allowing Sir Christopher Wren, the sitting Member, to remain seated. A year later, with Wren again returned by the 'select number', the House had reversed its previous ruling, and extended the franchise to scot-and-lot payers, with the result that Wren had been ejected. *CJ* x. 118, 419. For Wren (1632–1723), see *DNB*.   [299] 'resolutions' erased.

[300] i.e. legal counsel.

question was put for reading 156 against reading it 168: the next question was
whether the yonger sons of Freemen had a right to demand their freedom:[301] it
was proved that many of them had paid for their Freedom that question was
put that they had right 124 that they had none 168: then off went one side and
then they proved bribery in Sir Willoughbee Hickmans agents and about 2 in
the morning the question was put and Thorna[gh] and White were declared
duly Elected[302]

March 5 1701 [/]2
this day the report of the malt tax was made and a debate whether the
colledges should receive of their tenants the pr[?i]c[?e]s of malt advanced by
the duty or deduct 4s in the quarter: they said the tenants had good bargains
and might afford to pay Others said the tenants were used very hardly and that
the Colledges should not take the advantage of the tax that was imposed by an
act: Sir Xto[*pher*] musgrove said the committee had done what they had no
power to do that they had taken upon them to repeale an act which obliged the
tenants obliged by covenants to pay taxes according to those covenants and he
proposed that they should only pay two shillings in the quarter to this Mr
Smith said it would have been as contrary to their power to have impose[d]
two shillings as four: and the question was put and for agreeing with the
committee 126 against it 162 or thereabouts[303] and then we adjourned to

March 6th [*1702*] private bills and reports were made and we made a motion
to give leave to bring in a bill for the better encouragement of the Greenland
fishery but before that could be given it tending to the repea[l] of an act we
were forced to ask leave that that act should be read[304] and then we went into
the committee of wa[ys] and means where mr Lownds proposed to raise
money upon the wine in the vinctners hands by so much a quart but the
vincners freinds and the lovers of Clarit would not admit of this motion so it
was rejected[305] and [?off] went they when their drink was defended: and then
it was proposed to rais money by taxing the grants sin[ce] King Jameses time

---

[301] Hickman and Levinz had argued that the younger sons of freemen were entitled to their
freedom by right. For the case, see *CJ* xiii. 803–5.

[302] This day's entry underlined to separate it from the next. James Brydges left the committee
at midnight with the debate still in progress: Huntington Lib., Stowe MS 26(2), Brydges' diary, 4
Mar. 1702. According to Luttrell, the final decision went against the petitioners without a division:
Brief Relation, v. 148. The Whig James Lowther reported that his party had carried the 'cause',
and had 'settled the right contrary to the determination of the last Parliament, which was very
much censured': Cumbria RO (Carlisle), D/Lons/W, James to Sir John Lowther, 5 Mar. 1701[/2].

[303] In fact the question was carried for agreeing with the committee, by 166:103: *CJ* xiii. 777.

[304] The 1693 Greenland Trade Act (4 Gul. & Mar., c. 8).

[305] The rejection of a proposal for an additional impost on wine is confirmed by Bonet (DZA,
Rep. XI Eng. 25c, fo. 79), and by Luttrell (*Brief Relation*, v. 149), who defined the suggested duty as
£16 per tun, to be paid by the retailer.

but we agreed to tax them from 29th of[306] may 1660[307] and then we were upon other busines viz the securing and providing for the deficiencys and the Speaker told us of unfortunate accident that had hapned so that he must move that the Chairman might leave the Chair for a near relation of his w[as] dead or dying: it was his wife[308] nota that Mr Coniers was in the Chair of the Malt act and mr Boyle went with it up to the Lords tho Mr Coniers was ordered to carry it but mr Boyle said he did it by mr Conierses consent: this was ne[w] in the Evening there was Walcuts petition against Mason[309] walcut had no coppy of a poll only a paper s[ig]ned by the sherriffe Without any title to it and it was debated a hour whether it should be receive[d] as a coppy no body had examined it with the poll nor had any body there seen the sherriffe subscribe it so after the question for reading it as a coppy was put there were few ays and as we proceeded the[re] was a motion made by mr Ed[*ward*] Harley that mr Brewer and my Lord will[*iam*] Pawlett had had some words a[nd] were gone out together and desired we might adjourn the question was put and it was carryed by nine or ten for an adjournment:[310] my lord William was all this time in the house

[*fo. 6*ᵛ

7 *Mar.* 1702 w]e read private and publick bills and about 11[311] of the clock Sir John Bolles after many foolish undecent [?reflection]s as that the King was locked in a box and only in the hands of a few dutch lords and that we were of as good familys as [– –] for all which put together they called him after their usuall ways of resentment to the barr to the Barr: but on [?he ?went] and told of our bad circumstances by the illnes of the king and moved to adjourn at this time there was a message [?from ?the] Lords at the door and the Speaker said he would put the question for Calling them in and those that were for the ad[journme]nt would be against calling them in but the question was put and in they were called without a division: and th[?ey ?told] us the Lords did desire that this house would sit Longer: and then Seymour in more decent language seconded Bol[les's] motion he seemed sorry for the kings illnes and concerned for the effects it might have upon us and all Europe but he [th]ought when the King was so ill it was not fit for us to sit and that the acts passed by Com[*mi*]s[*sio*]n would not have that [for]ce and virtue and might be ques-

---

[306] '29th of' interlined.

[307] i.e. the restoration of King Charles II. This is confirmed by Bonet (DZA, Rep. XI Eng. 25c, fo. 79), Luttrell (*Brief Relation*, v. 149), and Robert Yard (BL Add. MS 7074, fos. 198–9).

[308] Mary Conyers, née Lee, whose remains were indeed buried at Walthamstow in 1702: Philip Morant, *The History and Antiquities of the County of Essex* (2 vols.; London, 1768), i. 49. Royal Commission on Historic Monuments, *Essex*, ii. 247.

[309] George Walcot's petition against Charles Mason, a rerun of an electoral dispute reported by Cocks a year before. See above, pp. 123–4.   [310] Not recorded in *CJ*.   [311] Originally '12'.

tioned as not having that sanction as they ought to have if it should happen
that [the] Kings understanding was lessened by the indisposition he laboured
under he said wee were not well dealt with in not [ha]ving been made[312]
acquainted with the Kings health so he moved for an adjournment till munday
and by that time [w]ee might see how god would dispose of the King: and
Bromeley thirded it:[313] but the necessity of an unanimity [w]ith the Lords in
this time of danger and the danger of adjourning for so long a time in this
great danger prevailed [w]ith the house (nota the reason these Gent[*lemen*]
would have had us adjourn was becaus they knew there was a power to be
delegated to some Lords to pass the abjuration act and the malt act the one
they feared at least for their freinds if not for themselves:[314] and some fancyed
they had no mind to have the Malt act passed that the government might be
distressed in case the king should dy. and that in that case they might Elude the
Abjuration act [*)*]: so we sent the Lords word that we would sit some time
longer and then we spun out the time in reading the bills and making reports
and debating upon trifles expecting to be sent for up to the Lords house by the
Lords Commissionated to pass the Bills; The[y] refused a bill a[315] commitment that made penaltyes upon those that were employed in the manufactures
of linnen Cotton and wool they said it discouraged the poor manufacturers:
we divided the house about it and lost it by 12:[316] and then there was a bill to
regulate the Fleet and kingsbench [*sic*] and it was proposed to give instructions
to the committee to report wha[t] they thought proper for that end to the
house and that it might be another instruction to raise money to pay of[f] the
mortgages that were on the prisonnes which debts obstructed the bills passing
in the Lords house the way to raise the money was sixpence upon every writt:
to this it was said they would not rais publick money to pay private debts and
it was further objected that this was not a power fit to be given to any
Committee but that of ways and means: but we divided upon the first
instruction,[317] Sir Ed[*ward*] Seymour proposed a new way which was to erect
new prisonnes and to take no notice of the old and to give the same

---

[312] 'made' interlined.

[313] Dr Richard West (fellow of Magdalen College, Oxford, and sometime chaplain to Bishop
Burnet) listed the principal speakers in favour of the motion to adjourn 'some days' as Seymour,
Bromley, Musgrave, and Bolles: Lambeth Palace Lib., MS 2564, p. 407, 'entry of historical
matters'. I am indebted to Stephen Taylor for this reference.

[314] Burnet too observed, with some malice, that the point of the Tories' adjournment motion
was to forestall the passage of the Abjuration Bill: *Own Time*, iv. 559.

[315] 'second reading' erased.

[316] *CJ* xiii. 781, records that the bill to prevent abuses and frauds by workers in the cotton,
linen, and woollen industries was lost by 90:79.

[317] The defeated motion was for an instruction to the committee to 'consider the best methods
for discharging' the 'encumbrances upon the said prisons': ibid.

Jurisdiction to the new ones and to establish them so that they might be free from the inconveniencyes we now laboured under: it was now past fower and very uneasy these gent[*lemen*] were least the black rod should come to summon us up to the Lords house before we were adjourned and so they desired the question and often Called out for it and when we Could no longer prolong the debate Coll[*onel*] Bierly moved the adjournment again nota the first adjournment was offered before one which was contrary to orders: Bierly said we had long enough complyed with the Lords message that the Lords were not now sitting and that we might adjourn Seymour and Bolles seconded and thirded it; others said we had often sat longer and that not only England but Europe was in danger and that we could sit up at committees till one that the lords had adjourned and were not sat yet that they could set at any time assoon [*sic*] as their Speaker was in the Chair they were an house that we could not do so Seymour proposed that the house should go to Kinsington and that the Speaker should only desire to be admitted to see the King others proposed to send the Speaker to see the King and that we should sit till he returned but at last when the adjournment was insisted on the Speaker said he could put no question by the orders of the house but of other days to adjourn till the morrow at nine of the Clock and of Saterday till munday nine of the Clock my Lord Ross[318] said the reason the Lords did not sit was becaus the Lord Keeper was at kinsington and that the King was a sleep [*sic*] others told us of presidents in the popish plot When the house adjourned and sat again the same day in few hours and that they sat on Sunday.[319] Mr pellam said we had no money in the treasury no army in England and that if Ever it was requisite to pass the abjuration bill it was now So the debate of adjournment languished and Sir Tho[*mas*] Felton[320] said the King was very bad and had not slept and proposed that in case of the Kings death we should vote that we would stand by and support the princes Anne of Denmark this was seconded by the Lord Cheney but not well received by the house so it was Evaded easily by a discours of mr Smiths at last we adjourned till six[321] and then as we met the black rod[322] told us the King had commissioned some lords to pass the bills that were ready and that the[y] desired the house to come to up to [*sic*] the Lords house where the com[*mi*]s[*sio*]n was read and the bill of abjuration

---

[318] John Manners, Lord Roos.

[319] Between 22 Oct. and 23 Dec. 1678 there had been nine examples of such adjournments, and two Sunday sittings (on 10 Nov., and 1 Dec.): *CJ* ix. 518, 522, 530, 532, 536–7, 542, 547, 551, 564.

[320] Master of the Household.

[321] According to Thomas Johnson, the adjournment was taken at 5 p.m.: Liverpool RO, 920 NOR 1/155, Johnson to Richard Norris, 7 Mar. 1701[/2].

[322] In fact, the deputy, Aston (*CJ* xiii. 781), for whom see above, p. 171, n. 733.

and the malt act and the Lord Orrorys[323] had the Royall assent and When the Speaker returned upon a little debate we adjourned till Sunday morning: it was very remarkeable in the motion of adjournment and the debate very few came into Seymour and musgrove who looked very well pleased, but most others very malancholy

March 8th [1702] on this day in the Morning about 8 of the Clock[324] dyed William the 3d his first ilnes was occasioned by a Fall from his hors as he was hunting a dear in hounslow heath his hors fell with him and threw him and broke or put out his collar bone and his dropsicall humours hindered his physitians from letting his blood this was uneasy to him but he seemed pretty well with it but in a few days after he fell into an ague and sometimes wee had hopes of his recovery but on Sunday morning his fits returned very often at four in the morning he received the sacrament[325] and dyed at eight hee was a prince bred up [i]n troubles born after his fathers death the States were Jealous of the greatnes of his family and birth and allyance and made him renounce solemnly his pretensions to the Statholders place which was allways enjoyed in his family but the misfortunes that after befell them made them release[326] that renunciation and him[327] accept of being Statholder he delivered his own country from the dangers and pressures they laboured under and afterwards When our rights and libertyes and religion were invaded by his father in law King James the 2d he made a descent into england and rescued us: he forced france to terms of peace and was now ingaged in the quarrell of Europe to defend them against france and to support the emperour and to preserve Holland from the invasion of the french tyrant and to defend us from the pretended prince of wales he was the supporter of the protestant religion of the libertye of Europe and an enemy to france the only obstacle[328] he had that hindred[329] him from being universall monarch: his life was uneasy between the ContenDing[330] partyes he now and then endeavoured to oblige them by trusting and employing them which was the misfortune and blemish of his reign with the neglecting for some short time his best and faithfullest freinds

---

[323] 'passed' erased. To permit Orrery to sell property to meet his debts.

[324] Besides the detailed narratives in two contemporary newspapers, the *Flying Post* (7–10 Mar. 1702), and *Post Boy* (7–10 Mar. 1702), Boyer, *Hist. Wm. III*, iii. 511–15, available in print from 1703, gave a lengthy account of the King's death, which concurred exactly with Cocks on this point (iii. 513). Richard West, whose information came from Burnet, is rather more precise, putting the time of death at 7.45 p.m.: Lambeth Palace Lib., MS 2564, p. 407.

[325] A detail confirmed in a letter of Sir John Cotton, 3rd Bt.: J. E. Foster (ed.), *The Diary of Samuel Newton, Alderman of Cambridge (1662–1717)* (Cambridge Antiquarian Soc. 23; Cambridge, 1890), 112–13.　　　　　　　　　　　　　　　　　　　[326] 'those' erased.

[327] 'him' interlined.　　　　[328] 'they' erased.　　　　[329] 'them' erased.

[330] The letter 'D' begins a new line in the MS.

but: [*sic*] that was soon over he was the justest wisest and bravest Prince of his age and his faults were as few as any his virtues more then any king now reigning those that opposed him living lamented his death [?and ?ha]d he lived longer it may bee hee might have lived more to our good then to his own glory [*fo. 7*]

and honour [(] virtutem inColumem odimus sublatum ex oculis querimus invidi)[331] Just before the king dyed he Called my Lord Rumney[332] to him a[nd ?said −] I pray god bles and prosper england: the King foresaw his aproachin[g ?end ?and] told my Lord Portland he shoud not live long some little time before his fall my Lord told him if he had no reason to say so he ho[ped − −] as to the posture of his affaires the King said they had been so ill that he would have been glad to part with them but that [?now ?they] were in such a posture that he expected to have succes and should have been glad to see the issue of them[333] Wee met on Sunday [*8 Mar. 1702*] and after prayers we satt gazing one upon another most m[elanc]holy presaging looks but at last the Speaker tooke the Chaire and wee ordered a committee to draw [?up ?an ?address] to the princes now Queen Anne to make good the allyances etc.:[334] and afterwards there came a message [from] the Lords to desire a conference upon an unfortunate accident that had befell us the house w[onde]red at the expression and they sent in word that they had mistaken the message and desired th[?at] they might be readmitted the masters were Sir Richard Holford and mr Pitt[335] the message was that the Lords desired a conference presently in the Painted Chamber upon an unfortunate occasi[on] that had befell us: Bolles talked att his usuall mad rate but the Conference was agreed too and the Com[mittee][336] appoynted my Lord Hartington reported that the Lords according a president when such [?an] unfortunate accident had befell us sitting the parliament had sent to the commons to acquaint them that they inte[n]ded to attend the proclaiming[337] of the Queen the Speaker told us that When Queen mary dyed the Lords sent the same message to the commons to proclaim Queen Elizabeth:[338] it was said we never could have a president of

---

[331] Horace, *Carminum*, 3. 24. 31–2: 'virtutem incolumem odimus sublatam ex oculis quaerimus invidi'. [332] Lord Romney.
[333] Burnet (*Own Time*, iv. 557), and L'Hermitage (BL Add. MS 17677 XX, fo. 246), confirm that the King imparted to Portland his conviction of impending death. West (Lambeth Palace Lib., MS 2564, p. 407) adds the reported royal comment, 'that time was, when he could have wished to die: but now his affairs were in so good a posture, that he could have desired to live'.
[334] The address of condolence on the death of King William, and congratulation on the accession of Queen Anne, which also included the pledge 'to maintain her alliances for preserving the liberties of Europe, and reducing the exorbitant power of France'. Cocks was named to this committee. *CJ* xiii. 782.
[335] Thomas Pitt (*c.*1656–1717), of the Middle Temple, master in Chancery 1694–1712; for Holford, see above, p. 211, n. 157. [336] 'agreed to' erased.
[337] Originally 'proclamation'. [338] On 17 Nov. 1558: *CJ* i. 52.

this nature for that all parliaments before this were dissolved upon the demise of the King and that we should act according to reason it was then moved that we should attend the proclaiming of Queen Anne as an house it was objected that the Lords did not do so and that we ought to do as the Lords did and that if we attended as an house there might severall difficultyes arrise Which we ought to avoyd as pa[r]ticularly the precedency of the Speaker whose place was undoubtedly next to the peers of England and that they perchance might Contest it and then that we might act in Concert with the Lords we sent Sir Rowland Gwin Sir Ri[*chard*] OnsLow and mr St Johns and Sir Ri[*chard*] onslow reported that there was Nothing entered on the lords Journall but that he had met some Lords who told him they did not intend to goe [as] an house that that was not ordered but that they intended to attend the proclamation some were fo[r] our going as an house for all that as being the most respect others moved that not receiving the approba[ti]on of the house that we should vote that we would attend and that it should be so ordered by the house but that was not complyed with but it was urged that such an order appearing upon the votes would make our unanimity appear abroad and would be a satisfaction to the people: and then the Speaker told us that we should attend the proc[*l*]amation first at St Jameses and then to Temple barr and to th[e] Royall exChange and this was aggreed too and so we adjourned till munday: and at St Jameses the Lords and wee met and went in a great body as aforesaid in coaches the streets were filled with spectators most see[med] more Curious then pleased: after the king had received the sacrament at the hands of the archbishop he said my lord I have lived a pretty[339] morall life and I dy in the Xtian faith

There were many things seemed to prognosticate this kings death as first all the addresses were delivered by the presenters in mourning for the late king James:[340] then Sir W[*illia*]m Str[*i*]ckland fell down dead in the house in appearance and Mr Coniers was forced to leave the Chair upon the illnes of his wife: if this had not hapned these things had not been regarded but now upon this occasion they are remembred I pray god to direct and preserve us: the King decayed sensibly and his doctor Sir Richard Blackmore[341] told me that it was rather a wonder he lived so long then that he dyed so soon he had his Cough 30 years and the king told him his indispositio[n] and what he had

---

[339] 'good' erased.

[340] Presumably the various addresses presented the previous autumn in response to the French king's acknowledgement of the Pretender as King James's successor: see [Ralph,] *Hist. Eng.*, ii. 988.

[341] Sir Richard Blackmore (d. 1729), of Cheapside, London, Physician-in-Ordinary to King William, 1697–1702.

observed did him good but that he knew how to observe but not apply a remedy: on thursday [5 Mar. 1702] he purged at the time of his fit[342] on friday [6 Mar. 1702] he vomited so that no[343] medicine could stay with him he vomited Collarick green stuff and a great dea[le] of corruption the wednesday before [4 Mar. 1702] he walked into the outward room to see a feild bed and sat down in the window the room he had kept was as warm as a box and he fell a sleep [sic] in the window which gave him cold and with the dropsey and the consumption of the Lungs this cold set these humours a float [sic][344] and as Sir Richard Blacmore said occasioned his death some days sooner his phisitians had said some time before that he could not last Long but that was not fitt to be divulged: never was prince more beloved nor more lamented some swooned when they heard of his death and could hardly be brought to life as my Lord Overkirks son[345] and others: in the house of Commons there were many eyes brim full and Many tongues not able to speak for greif the herald that proclaimed the Queen cryed

March 9th [1702]

we read private bills and the Committee reported an address expressing our sorrow for the death of our king of glorious memory which was moderated by the assurance we had of her[346] and assuring her that wee would support her to make good the alliances with the emperour and other potentates that were made, and that shee should make for the defence of[347] the liberties of Europe[348] and to humble and reduce France and to maintain the publick credit.[349] and then we ordered the privy councill to know when shee would be attended with it and then we went into the committee of ways and means and in the naming of the Chairman of the Committee the house cryed some mr Boyle others Mr Bromeley Mr Bromeley went dowwn to the barr to take the chair but the noyse continued and[350] so the Speaker tooke the Chair Sir Xto[pher] musgrove and mr Smith moved together the one for Boyle the other for Bromley my Lord will[iam] Pawlet seconded Smith the Speaker put the question on Boyle but they grumbled but the Speaker put the question and Boyle had hardly a negative: Bolles in this debate talked foolishly and they

---

[342] Confirmed by John Ellis (BL Add. MS 7074, fo. 97).   [343] 'no' interlined.

[344] These details of the King's last illness are confirmed by, among others, Boyer, *Hist. Wm. III*, iii. 512.

[345] Sir John Cotton wrote that 'the Lord Overkirk's son died away for some time in the King's chamber' (*Diary of Samuel Newton*, 112–13), though according to L'Hermitage it was the father himself who was overcome with grief (BL Add. MS 17677 XX, fo. 258). Hendrik van Nassau (1640–1708), Lord of Ouwerkeerk, had been William's Master of Horse.

[346] 'which was moderated by the assurance we had of her' interlined.

[347] 'our' erased.   [348] 'of Europe' interlined.

[349] The full text of the address is given in *CJ* xiii. 784–5.   [350] 'he' erased.

called him to the barr to the barr Bromley was to[o] forward in accepting of
the chair before it was given him and was ashamed that he was baffled and so
went out of the house in the Committee we mortgaged the great mortgage
four year longer to make good the deficiencyes[351] and then the Speaker tooke
the Chair and Mr Secretary told us the Queen would be attended with the
Addres a little after five and so we adjourned: the Members with the Speaker
went to St Jameses and p[r]esented their addres and kissed the queens hand
there was a great crowd and noyse and nobody heard her answer[352] shee
cu[r]tesyed When the members kissed her hand it was her left hand they
Kissed for her right hand had the goute

March 10th [1702]

This day mr Boyle reported the resolutions of the Committee of ways and
means with which the house agreed exCept[353] the longer continuance of the
duty on marriages byrths and burialls[354] and then we considered of the Irish
petitions and the Irish Com[mi]s[sione]rs[355] told the house they had a letter
that was found relating to Coll[onel] Lutterells Estate which was found in a
room with a superscription to . . . and subscribed [?L] Lutterell[356] Sir
Xto[pher] musgrove would have had it read but the house would not endure
it it not being proved to be his hand nor attested from whom it dropt The
Speaker reported the Queens answer which was that she tooke kindly their
assurances and the best way of expressing it would be to make a quick
dispatch of busines for the publick affaires required it[357]

[*fo. 7*]

March 11th *1702*] we had a debate about a welsh bri[?d]g and Clauses[358] and
were sent for up to house of Lords to hear the[359] Queens Speech[360] [?in ?which

---

[351] In ways and means. This report is confirmed by Bonet (DZA, Rep. XI Eng. 25c, fo. 82), and
Luttrell (*Brief Relation*, v. 151).
[352] On the next day the Speaker reported that, when he had attended the Queen with the
Commons' address, he had been obliged to ask for a written copy of her reply, 'the great crowd
occasioning much noise': CJ xiii. 787.   [353] The letter 'C' begins a new line in the MS.
[354] Originally granted by the act of 6 & 7 Gul. & Mar., c. 6.
[355] Francis Annesley and James Hooper, the two trustees for the sale of the resumed Irish
forfeitures who were available in London.
[356] When eventually presented to the Lords (as part of the evidence concerning the bill arising
from this petition), the letter was said to have been addressed to a Walter Delamer, and signed
merely 'Luttrell': HMC, *House of Lords MSS*, NS v. 30. For the case of Henry Luttrell (*c.*1654–
1717), of Luttrellstown, Co. Dublin, see Simms, *Williamite Confiscation*, 129–30; C. McNeill,
'Reports on the Rawlinson Collection . . . ', *Analecta Hibernica*, 1 (1930), 80–4. The petition was
supported by, among others, the Irish Whig Robert Molesworth: HMC, *Various Colls.*, viii. 226.
[357] Full text given in CJ xiii. 787.
[358] The report from the committee on the bill to amend the act of 22 Hen. VIII, c. 5, concerning
the repair of bridges on the highway. The only clause to be specified in the *Journals* related to a
bridge at Rochester in Kent: ibid. 788.   [359] 'King's' erased.
[360] The full text of this speech is given in CJ xiii. 788.

?she] Lamented the Death of K[*ing*] W[*illia*]m and her coming to the Crown immediately after such a king but that her care for our religion [?laws ?and ?liberties] and other good reasons made her undertake the Charge and shee promises her self succes from our good proceedings: and [?that ?it ?was] necessary in order to accomplish those great ends to dispatch our busines: she expressed great satisfaction at our [?– una]nimity recommended the consideration of an union with Scotland: and to the Gent[*lemen*] of the house of com[*mo*]ns to provide for the [civil] list according to the dignity of the crown and that her good administration should make amends for our regard for her [th]at she had an heart truly English[361] and was a protestant and a religious observer of her word: we voted thanks and [–]d ordered them to be presented by the privy Councill and the Speech to be considered to morrow [*sic*] and then wee ordered no [n]ew list of com[*mi*]s[*sione*]rs nor no addition of names but an amendments [*sic*] only of wrong names[362] and so we went into the committee of supply and adjourned to: nota people tooke exceptions at the word intirely English as if it reflected upon the kings having a regard for Holland and they observed the xpression of her word to be in her fathers speech he first spoke[363] Shee spoke or read it gracefully and well
March 12 [*1702*]

we read some Irish bills and ordered some clauses to provide their estates should go to protestants that their Children should be Educated in the protestant religion:[364] we considered of the Queens Speech and Cooke of darby Commended the word entirely English and moved to have it considered of too morrow [*sic*]: and a day was appoynted to consider of the union and the house agreed to agree with the committee in the elections of norwige and Caune[365]

March 13th [*1702*] Some bills were read and amongst the rest the alteration of the law as to felons viz to transport them to our plantations instead of hanging them[366] the house divided upon the giving it a second reading I beleive one half of the house did not know what they divided about: after that I made a motion that the produce of the duties that were given to support the Civill List should be laid before the house What it produced the last year and that the Establishment of the civill list in King Charles the 2ds time should

---

[361] *Recte* 'entirely English'.

[362] In a committee of the whole on the Land Tax Bill: *CJ* xiii. 788.

[363] Presumably King James's declaration at the first meeting of his Privy Council on 6 Feb. 1685, in which he had promised to endeavour to preserve the government in church and state 'as by law established', and the 'just rights and liberties' of his subjects: *London Gazette*, 5–9 Feb. 1684[/5].

[364] In the bill to make provision for the Protestant children of the Earl of Clanricarde, and Lord Bophin (see below, p. 263, n. 482): *CJ* xiii. 789.   [365] See above, pp. 225, 231–2.

[366] The bill 'for the more effectual punishment of felons and their accessories'.

be laid before the house:[367] my motion was received with great indignation by all those that had agreed to give up our liberties and to make shipwrack of their Conscienses in hopes to get places: but Sir Edward Hussey seconded me as he had promised me and said sir what are gent[*lemen*] affraid off must wee Lump it and give we do not know what I should be ashamed to go down into my Country and to be asked if such a motion was made and not put not 2ded so that was put but I was wrong in the other part for there was no Establishment in king Charles time I should have said Charge:[368] Before this there was a report[369] from the Chairman of the bill for taking the public accounts and in it on a debate it was ordered that members should be Com[*mi*]s[*sione*]rs the argument against it was that it would be giving places to our selves: the argument for it was that others would not have authority and the trouble of attending at the barr and door their going in and out would be very inconvenient that we found it so in other matters: then we went into the Committee for the supply and some Cryed Granville some Boyle and as they Cryed Granville went on one side of the house down to the Barr and Boyle on the other and both stood at the Barr and we some Cryed one some the other till the Speaker resumed the chaire and the question was moved and seconded first as the Speaker said for Granville and the question was put first upon him after some silly debate and the house divided the noes went out and were 154 the ays 179:[370] and then we went on in the committee of supply for the land tax then Mr Boyle had the chair as of right having had it before: Nota Granville staid in and voted for himself which was prety extraordinary Nota to shew the servile complyance of this house if I had not made this motion nobody would and if Sir Ed[*ward*] Hussey had not 2ded me nobody Else would: O hom[*ines*] ād ser[*vitutem*] par[atos][371]

March 14 [1702] Nothing remarkeable said or done Mr Lowns Laid the paper before the house which was ordered to be referred to the Committee[372] mr Manly moved to incourage popery in Ireland to keep up two partyes in order to continue them under the English yoake[373] Sir Edward Hussey has a Low voyce and reported from the Barr and being low those that came in neyther saw nor heard him which made them cross between him and the Chair which

---

[367] As eventually embodied in *CJ* xiii. 793, the motion called simply for the laying before the House of details of the produce of the funds given for the Civil List over the preceding year.

[368] The principle of the Civil List had not been established until 1690. Charles II had enjoyed a 'revenue' consisting of hereditary taxes, and others granted by Parliament for his lifetime. See Reitan, 'From Revenue to Civil List', 571–8.   [369] 'for h' erased.

[370] L'Hermitage (BL Add. MS. 17677 XX, fo. 254) confirms that Boyle was Granville's competitor.   [371] Tacitus, *Annals*, 3. 65. 11: 'O homines ad servitutem paratos'.

[372] The produce of the Civil List funds, 25 Dec. 1700–25 Dec. 1701, laid before the committee of supply: *CJ* xiii. 796.   [373] Not recorded in *CJ*.

made the house call often to order[374] Coll[onel] Web was the last and when he sat in his place he Laughed Seymour made a grave oration Concerning the breach of orders he said the breach should not pass so easily over with the only Calling to Order and sitting down and laughing at it when they had done but that some body should be punished that the not observing of orders was very dangerous many were caught Whilest Hussey reported they called him the order Trapp and then they went on reading the Irish bills

March 16 [1702] this was the day ordered for the committee of supply and after some private bills read and the report of the Jews and the report of a petition relating to a jew who would not own his daughter that was turned Xtian:[375] the report from the Committee was that shee had made out the allegations and proved her self [sic] his daughter: but some that attended the Committee said that the proof was not plain to them that shee was any more then his naturall Child: and this was in order to force them to keep their protestant Children to bring in an bill for that purpose the Jew had freinds and indeed it must be a very jew or wors that cant make a freind there I mean in the house of Com[mon]s: they urged the unreasonablenes of maKing their fathers allowing their children that turned protestants a maintenance this make their Children Hippocrites instead of protestants and make the Jews who were a trading people leave the Country that it was true they were accused of having betrayed us to the French in the late warrs but that was never proved: that they knew a Jew that had married a protestant and that the females were bred up after their mothers religion and the males after their fathers and that they agreed well together: to this it was answered that tho the Jew did peform the covenants of marriage with his protestant wife yet the whole people of the Jews were so uneasy with him that they would never employ him and that if the protestants had not found him work he would have been starved: why should we put a greater hards[hi]p upon papists then Jews

[374] It was a standing order that no Member 'coming into the House or removing from his place' should pass between the Chair and a Member who was speaking: McKay (ed.), *Observations . . .* , 56.

[375] A report from the committee appointed to consider a petition from various City parishes for a bill to oblige Jews to provide for such of their children as became Protestant. The issue arose from the case of Miriam, daughter of the Portuguese Sephardic merchant Jacob Mendes de Brito (d. 1747), of St Andrew Undershaft. Having converted to Christianity the year before, and been baptized into the Church of England, the girl had, allegedly, been disowned by her father. He, however, denied that she was really his daughter, claiming instead that she was a foundling, abandoned on his doorstep while he was living in Portugal. See *CJ* xiii. 748, 799–800; Wilfred S. Samuel, 'The First London Synagogue of the Resettlement', *Transactions of the Jewish Historical Society of England*, 10 (1921–3), 116; Lionel D. Barnett (ed.), *Bevis Marks Records . . .* (2 pts.; London, 1940–9), pt. 1, p. 35; Albert M. Hyamson, *The Sephardim of England . . .* (London, 1951), 124.

were the papist more avers to our religion then the Jews: that the Jews in
portugall and other parts pretended themselves papists there and When they
came hither they owned themselves Jews and then wee went into the committee of supply: nota on friday [*13 Mar. 1702*] Sir John Bolles Came to see me
and told me he was pleased with my Motion[376] and shewed me the journalls
how they gave the king but from year to year and that this was to[o] much[377]
and that he would oppose it all I said was you will Change your mind I beleive
and so it proved for [*16 Mar. 1702*] he after a flourish in Commendation of the
Queen proposed to continue the 50000 shee had and to give her for life what
the king had Lowns said the prince had a right to 30000 li. per an: that tho
nobody could be joynt tenant with the Queen that this was vested in trustees
and that he must be at some more Expence and after he seconded Bollesses his
question which was put without one negative given:[378] Nota the last sessions
we took an 100000 from the kings civill list and then it was said if the princes
was Queen that we should take 50000 from her:[379] but nobody stirred at this I
did all I could to animate them I tryed Sir Ri[*chard*] Onslow he was Cold I
could not make him stirr he told me that if ever we lost our liberties it must be
upon an accession to the crown: that indeed I saw for now were all men busie
in making bargains musgrove and Seymour they say sold us and I beleive it
was true I went to my Lord Hartington and begged him I told him our all was
at stake his honour his great estate he told [m]e that we were represented as
enemies and that this would make her beleive so: I said my lord there is not
[?a] man off us can expect favour we shall all be turned out if we make
opposition we shall keep our

[*fo. 8*]
repute in the country if we do not we shall shew we have no spirit: we shall be
insulted and that deserv[?edly ?so ?without] Pitty or regard my Lord I am
ashamed that I that have a small estate and nothing near your reputation
should th[?ink ?myself ?to] preserve what you think so little worth your care
my Lord said if any body began the debate he would come into it but would
not begin: mr Dormir told me some very good freinds of mine lords and
com[*mone*]rs were against my beginning the debate I answered all his objections but I fancyed that the 4 impeached lords[380] were against our going on

---

[376] On the civil list: see above, pp. 243–4.
[377] i.e. to grant Queen Anne the Civil List for life.
[378] That the vote passed *nem. con.* is confirmed by Luttrell (*Brief Relation*, v. 153), and Henry
St John (BL Trumbull Misc. MSS xlvi, St John to Sir William Trumbull, [16] Mar. 1701[/2]).
[379] See above, p. 108.
[380] Those who had been impeached in the preceding session, i.e. Lords Halifax, Orford,
Portland, and Somers: a shorthand reference to the leaders of the Whig party.

with such a debate least it might be insinuated that they had promoted it: I
thought it very hard to find the last parliament so hard to that great victorious
king th[e] glory of Europe and so tamely submit to a woman but they knew his
ministers they knew his great soule was above rev[?enge] and resentment from
her and hers they feared it and some expected Places Others thought they
should get something or [an]other: mr Bromley of warwickshire said he would
have came into it: but nobody Could I rely on to second me but h[o]nest Sir
Ed[*ward*] Hussey and he and I seeing such a fear aw and ambition in the house
that we should make nothing of it thought it better to be at quiet then to
expose[381] our selves and give our adversaryes an opportunity of making their
Court they were uneasy that they had no occasion to make use of their
Flattering speeches they ha[d] made and the Harleys and Folios[382] would have
voted with us in order to have preserved their interest in the Country and the
Speaker could have given that reason to excuse them at Court: I did intend to
have said as follows m[r] Granville[383] the searcher of hearts knows I speak true I
loved the late king of great and glorious memory at that rate that I would not
only have exposed my all but my life[384] to have prolonged and I will never be
wanting in my duty and my loyalty to the Queen that now sitteth on the
throne but to that King I never made my court by giving up the peoples or
more money then was necessary: I have learned this lesson in this house that if
we give to[o] much we give up we endanger our liberties if ever the throne
should be possessed by an ambitious aspiring prince I have heard the parliament that gave the civill list and setled for life censured and reproached and
our necessityes forced us the last year to breake in upon that very act and take
100000 li. from the civill list Established by act of parliament I heard it then
said there was 50000 li. per an: allowed for king James 30000 li. per an:
allowed for the Duke of Gloucester 20000 li. per an: allowed for to make
the sum even and 50000 li. allowed for the princes[385] and dos any man living
said they then imagine that if the crown should descend to the princes if we
should think fitt to give that to the crown this was said then and our
necessityes forCed[386] us to break thro that act are we less necessitous now
have we not mortgaged again the Generall mortgage[387] have we not given that
ungratefull Duty upon malt have we not been forced to give an ayd out of the
English grants becaus we Cou[ld] find nothin else to rais money on have we

---

[381] 'my' erased.

[382] A common sobriquet for the Foley family: see e.g. BL Loan 29/184, fo. 311.

[383] The chairman of the committee of supply, to whom Cocks's speech would have been
addressed.   [384] 'but my life' interlined.

[385] The Princess Anne, i.e. the present Queen. See above, p. 108.

[386] The letter 'C' begins a new line in the MS.   [387] See above, p. 198, n. 60.

not given four shillings on land have we not ground the face of the poor: I
ha[ve] heard it said that the riches of a prince are the hearts and affections of
the people:[388] I have learned this lesson in this house that if ever we mean to
have good laws we must have them in the reigns of good princes then we must
make good presidents this Queen has told us shee has an heart intirely English
What is that in english but to say I will not oppres my subjects to make my
Courtiers live in plenty and abound I have the misfortune to have no child
living you are my Children I know you will provide for my Crown and dignity
and I will take Care you shall not be oppressed; this is an heart Entirely
English 70000 li. will maintain 40000 men generalls and officers our necessityes require us to good husbandry and providence from the prince that sitteth
on the throne to the Peasant that Laboureth in the feilds: this can be no
reflection upon the Queen beyond sea[389] no but the Contrary they will say
there that we are grown a provident and wise people and if we are a provident
sober and religious people we shall then flourish at home and be a terror to
our enemies abroad the division for taking 100000 li. from the civill list was
for taking it 214 against it 169[390] pray sir lett us be Loyall and wise: we have
need of good laws and good presidents to secure us for the future such as
posterity may lay hold on all governments decline at some times the the [sic]
very great people of Rome their senate was so debased in Tiberiuses time that
he said if then O Homines ad servitutem natos[391] Sir upon these and many
other considerations I would descend to particulars and give what was
necessary and no more and give it *but from time to time* [sic]: I have here
given in what I[392] thought to have said: they said in private disCourses[393] in
the house that this could not inslave us for the Crown must annually depend
upon the parliament, to maintain the guards and garrisons: and it was truly
said that it was not the toryes that made the Queen this Compliment but the
wigs when they setled it upon King william

March 17th [1702]

this day nothing materiall but the report of East Redford Election the first
question was whether the yonger sons of freemen had a right to be free for it
173 against it 175 next question was whether Thornagh was duly Elected for
him 177 against him 175 the next was Whether White was duly Elected that he
was 179 that he was not 177:[394] then we balloted for Commissioners and there

---

[388] See above, p. 45.
[389] i.e. it would not be seen by those overseas as a reflection on the Queen.
[390] The division of 5 May 1701. See above, p. 111, and n. 335.   [391] *Recte* 'paratos'.
[392] 'said' erased.   [393] The letter 'C' begins a new line in the MS.
[394] Although the numbers in the first of these three divisions are confirmed in *CJ*, the second is
given there as 176:174, and the third as 177:175: xiii. 805.

Mr Scobell Carried first for he was a man of no great fortune[395] nor repu[te] and we found they had setled their list which we could not oppose having never considered of it, having never had an[y] thought about it and so we thought we would blemish their Com[*mi*]s[*sione*]rs by naming the least of theirs and by putting hi[m] in our list make him first of the Commission:[396] March 18th [1702]

This day we had a report relating to the viCtualling office: in which it was proved that the Queens Brewer had taken the top of the[397] Guile and stole 26 barrells out of one or two Guiles that was not certain which spoyled the seamens drink: this it seemed they claimed as their perquisite but we could not allow of that so we Censured the thing and voted no perquisites and ordered the privy councill to lay the vote before the queen it was aggreed by all that if it was not censured it was established and Sir Ed[*ward*] Seymour said it was like a quiet fellow that was gasing about and had an arrow struck thro his nose and said if the arrow came ther again he would break it: then mr Smith moved to consider of our taking the Abjuration oath for that the time was expiring[398] and moved to Looke in the Lords Journalls Sir Jo[*hn*] Bolles talked like a foole: Sir Xto[*pher*] musgrove would have this oath set right by a new law explained altered they all agreed it could not be this sessions by the orders of parliament I said there needed no explanation we might take it as it was only alter the words of the King for the Queen and leave out what was necessary upon the death of the King and succession of the princes Sir Xto[*pher*] musgrove asked by what law that could be done he would desire that Gent[*leman*] to tell him I answered by the same law that we left out Q[*ueen*][399] Mary without an act when shee dyed: then stood up Sir Ed[*ward*] Seymour and said we were beholding to the gent[*leman*][400] for putting us in mind of it that tho he was not very fond of it before yet now it was an act he was for our taking it and

---

[395] 'and' erased.

[396] The Country party/Tory slate for the ballot for accounts commissioners comprised six Tory Members, all of whom were elected behind Scobell: William Bromley (MP Oxford Univ.), Thomas Coke, Henry St John, Robert Byerley, Sir Godfrey Copley, and James Brydges. Huntington Lib., Stowe MS 26(2), James Brydges' diary, 4 Mar. 1702. Scobell himself was a grandson of the Clerk of the Parliaments in 1642.

[397] 'new' erased. The report of the committee (which had included Cocks) appointed to inquire into the abuses committed in the 'Queen's Brewhouse', a naval brewery at St Katherine's Wharf in London, one of those administered directly by the Victualling Office: *CJ* xiii. 767, 809–10; P. Mathias, *The Brewing Industry in England 1700–1830* (Cambridge, 1959), 201. The 'head brewer', William Marshal (*CJ* xiii. 809–10), was accused of skimming from the gyle, the amount of drink brewed at any one time.

[398] By the terms of the act for the further security of His Majesty's person and the succession of the Crown in the Protestant line, no MP was to be permitted to sit after 25 Mar. 1702 unless he had taken the abjuration oath (13 & 14 Gul. III, c. 6, s. ix).   [399] 'Q[*ueen*]' interlined.

[400] Originally 'Smith'.

that wee did not want any act to explain it but that we might take it after wee had made the necessary amendments to make it sence that we all ought to stand on the same bottom and that we might make an explanatory Clause for those without doors and this was agreed to:[401] Nota before my Lord Cheif Justice Hales came into the house they[402] were of an opinion that when any act passed that the sessions was determined:[403] they were used to be passed all together heretofore

[fo. 8^v

March 19th 1702] reading private bills and things on cours: at last the bill for the com[mi]s[sione]rs for taking and stating the publick accounts was read the last time to which Sir Ed[ward] Hussey offered a rider which made the Com[mi]s[sione]rs uncapable for one year viz so long as their Commission lasted to accept of any other place: this passed without any difficulty: Sir Godfery Copley seconded it tho most thought Bridges and St Johns were not well pleased with it: then we came upon the union recommended to us from the late k[ing] and the now Queen:[404] Sir Ed[ward] Seymour musgrove and all that party whether it was out of kindnes to the Church of which they are incomparable members or out of some nobler principle I cant tell, told us of the many difficulties the many times it had been attempted and that we did not Know that the Scotch were willing and that to be too forward would make our bargain the wors:[405] that this had been aymed at ever since K[ing] J[ames] 1st viz 100 [years] Coll[onel][406] Stanhop spoke warmly but very well and said what would we do with the Scotch would we conquer them that he did not question but we might but then what would we do with them, would we keep them in subjection by a standing army, that would be very dangerous for that army might do as much for us and that he never desired to see slavery uppon any part of this Continent that it was ketching as contagious as any thing again and he moved that we should come to a vote declaring that it was the

---

[401] A committee was appointed, including Cocks, to consider what amendments it was necessary to make to the abjuration oath as a consequence of the death of King William: *CJ* xiii. 808.

[402] 'they' interlined. Sir Matthew Hale (1609–76), lord chief justice of King's Bench 1671–6, had first been returned to Parliament (for Gloucestershire) in 1654.

[403] 'The passing of any bill or bills with the Royal Assent doth not make a session, nor the giving of any judgment, but the session continueth until the session be prorogued or dissolved': *The Original Constitution, Power, and Jurisdiction of Parliaments . . . Being a Manuscript of the Late Judge Hales* (London, 1707), 37.

[404] For King William's message recommending an Anglo-Scottish union, see above, p. 229; for Queen Anne's comment, in her speech from the throne, above, p. 243.

[405] James Lowther reported that Seymour and Musgrave had been the leading speakers in this debate, against the idea of union: Cumbria RO (Carlisle), D/Lons/W, James to Sir John Lowther, 19 Mar. 1701[/2]. [406] 'Coll[onel]' interlined.

opinion of this hous that it was our interest to unite: this was thought too much[407] [?but] Sir Rowland Gwinn moved to bring in a bill to enable the Queen to appoynt Com[*mi*]s[*sione*]rs Sombody said the danger of our religion would be in[?creased] by it and how our vote would alter things in parliament to this I said I looked upon the act of union with wales[408] and that was to prevent Robberys thefts and murders I beleived the same were as much used on the borders of Scotland that I did not know what religion they were of before but I was sure they had done very well in our senate their princes were proud of being our senators and sō[*me*] of them had deservedly been princes of our senate and that I would not repeat any thing that was said but that if we did not conquer Scotland we must keep an army to defend us[409] and that I thought would not very well agree with the sence of this house I therefore seconded Sir Row[*land*] Gwin: and it was urged that we and they were to be dissolved and that We did not know what opinion the next house would be of here or there and that Scotland being the inferiour kingdome ought to Truckle: after we had debated this sufficiently the question was putting and musgrove and Bierly moved and seconded it that the previous question should be put and that was put and for putting of the questions viz the nos that it be not now put 96 they went out that it be now put 131 Nota it was remarkable that all that were for the new Court were [a]gainst this[410] that was part of the Queens Speech recommended to us and all of the late court were for it: it may be the new Court knew the Queen did not intend it but put it in only to oblige Scotland becaus it was in the kings Speech and they might have been offended had shee shown no Concern for them: and it may be a sowr principle guided by Church narrow notions governed them and other party that have Large principles and are acted by their countryes interest perswaded them: it was not said in the debate but so it was that the thing that obstructed the union in K[*ing*] J[*ames*] the first time was the relation and regard he had for that nation had they been made english they had had all the places of Profitt and trust in the kingdom and had been a dead weight to serve his will and pleasure in the house which was not so now: and if the Queen should have dyed before the next sessions of Parliament as princes are mòrtall as well as others the slight

---

[407] James Vernon informed Stanhope's father that 'none who spoke in the debate contributed to it so remarkably as your son; it was the first time of his speaking and he is highly approved of by all that were of his opinion': Centre for Kentish Studies, Maidstone, U1590/O53/10, Vernon to Alexander Stanhope, 19 Mar. 1701[/2].

[408] The act of 1536 for the administration of justice in Wales (the first Act of Union): 27 Hen. VIII, c. 26. [409] 'us' interlined.

[410] Bonet (DZA, Rep. XI Eng. 25c, fo. 79), and the French diplomat de Vaudoncourt (PRO 31/3/190/40), both observed that the Tories had opposed the motion. Sir Rowland Gwynne was one of the tellers in favour; Robert Byerley against.

we had put upon them would have inraged them to that degree that they would have set up for themselves: and I am of opinion that were they united they would rather strengthen and Confirm our liberties and priviledges in the house then Lessen them for suppose they were mercenary and the crown bought them that they were poor and would sell if they all sold there would be the less to give the english who are as mercenary I beleive as the Scotch and then[411] the english would be disobliged: and suppose the lesser number of the Scotch were bribed the ballance would then be of our side in short I beleive they would be a Bulwark to our liberties and a great good to England and so would the uniting of Ireland

March 20th [1702]

after the reading of private bills we ordered the civill list bill to be[412] read but that was not [to] be found the Speaker told us we ought not to take any bill off the table during the sitting of the house that it was against order that there had been formerly a bill lost: and that it occasioned a Call if the house [sic] and the attendance of every member to clear himself by solemn protestations in his place[413] Sir Edward Seymour said that when the house was possessed of the bill it was the houses and no member ought to touch it of the table I sat by mr Sollicitor Holles[414] and he told me that in king Charles the first time there was a Committee appoynted to manage matters against my Lord Straffords tryall and that there were some minutes taken by Sir H Fane who was Secretary of State formerly to king C[harles] the first which mentioned a letter of advice from my Lord Strafford to that King advising him to bring over his Irish army to subdue his[415] English subjects these minutes were before the Committee and were the principall evidence against that Lord and those minutes could not be found upon which the Committee were every one ordered to attend in their places and obliged to purge themselves solemnly which they all did and my Lord Digby Changed his side and was afterwards Secretary to that King and in some defeat they tooke his papers and amongst other things these very minutes he had so solemnly disowned the knowledge of:[416] the Bill was found I beleive it was left in the Clerks Desk: as for the bill that the Speaker

---

[411] 'good' erased.   [412] 'ordered the civil list bill to be' interlined.

[413] Presumably Harley is referring to the Clandestine Marriages Bill, which had been taken out of the House on 14 Feb. 1678. Nine days afterwards all Members had been required, by an order, to subscribe a protestation disclaiming responsibility. *CJ* ix. 441, 445.

[414] Sir John Hawles.   [415] 'Irish' erased.

[416] The trial of Thomas Wentworth (1593–1641), Earl of Strafford. The minutes, which had originally been made by Sir Henry Vane (1589–1655), Secretary of State 1640–1, were of a discussion at the Privy Council on 5 May 1640. Vane's son had discovered them and made them over to John Pym to be used against Strafford. HMC, *3rd Report*, 1, 3; Rushworth, *Hist. Colls.*, viii. 45. George Digby (1612–77), 2nd Lord Digby of Sherborne and 2nd Earl of Bristol,

mentioned it was found and the Gent[*leman*] upon whom it was found was feighn to ask pardon on his knees at the barr:[417] there were severall instructions moved for as that a duty collected in the plantations might be appropriated for the repair of their forts harbours and Guns etc.[418] this was said was irregular for to have any thing appropriated to another use in this bill but that wee might move in the Committee to leave out any duty but by the orders we could add none and that then it would belong to the Queen by the laws of the assembly and then by petition or address the Queen might be moved to appropiate for those necessary services of the Islands the plantations: then Sir Edward Hussey moved that it might be an instruction to provide that we What we [*sic*] had given might not be begged by lords and ladys that such a proviso would be of great service to the Queen and hinder her from importunityes and sollicitations: mr Lownds answered and said there was no need of such a Clause in this reign and flattered the Queen for her providence and manage of the revenew tho small when shee was princes Sir Ed[*ward*] Hussey tooke him down to order and said he had as great a regard for the Queen as any body but to say What the Queen would do was not fitting to be said here for it would spoyle all debate: this was true and lownds said if he could not talk after that manner he Could say nothing Sir Ed[*ward*] Seymour commended the motion and seconded it mr Boyle spoke to it and approved of it and said the Queen would pay the Kings servants and so we read the bill the second time and went into the Committee of the land tax[419] nota Coniers was abroad after the death of his wife and some Cryed Mr Boyle but mr Coniers tooke the Chaire:[420] and there was a little debate about the mending of misnomas[421] and lowns spoke to have leave to add a few names Where the old ones were dead but that was not allowed

Nota this motion to hinder the Queen from making grants would be of little signification her revenew being only for life but that the duty upon the excise was part of the haereditary revenew: this day Sir Ed[*ward*] Seymour moved for a call of the house in order to put of[*f*] the Scotch union[422]

then MP for Dorset, had been the chief suspect in the hue and cry over the missing document. A manager of Strafford's impeachment, he changed sides and voted against the bill of attainder, becoming in due course Secretary of State to Charles I 1643–5. The minutes were eventually discovered in King Charles's chest, captured at Naseby. See *CSP Dom.*, 1640–1, pp. 559–60; *DNB* (*sub* Sir Henry Vane).

[417] The *Journals* record no such incident in 1678. That the Clandestine Marriages Bill was retrieved is indicated by the fact that it was read on 8 Mar. of that year: *CJ* ix. 451.

[418] In response to a petition from the agents, planters, and merchants of Barbados: *CJ* xiii. 813.

[419] On the Land Tax Bill. [420] See above, pp. 235, 241.

[421] i.e. misnomers in the list of commissioners in the bill.

[422] According to Thomas Johnson, the motion was John Granville's, though he agreed with Cocks as to its tactical purpose: Liverpool RO, 920 NOR 2/222, Johnson to Richard Norris, 21 Mar. 1701[/2]. The House appointed a call for 2 Apr.: *CJ* xiii. 813.

March 21 [*1702*]

Things of cours, and at last Sir Rowland Gwin reported from the Committee that were to consider of the abjuration oath that they had made nothing more then litterall amendments: Sir Xto[*pher*] musgrove said he beleived there never was such a thing done before no president of it: Sir Ed[*ward*] Seymour said there never was such an accident before: and that we were tyed down so by the law that if we did not take it, by the 25th of this month we were no Parliament and that it was now to[*o*] short a time before that to do any thing and that therefore we must take it and that he was for taking it[423] as it was, tho against it at first: then it was ordered to bring in a bill to declare the explanation of the bill for that was lawfull the same sessions tho we could not alter or repeale any law the same sessions[424] this was in favour of the Justices and the [i]nferiour courts to whom it was not convenient to allow such a power nor leave to make a president to alter any

[*fo.* 9]

thing this was agreed to and power allso to repeale part of two act[*s*] relating to the association:[425] the reason of the [?association ?was] from the time of the design to assasinate the king and that being now out of doors upon his death, and the substance of the [a]ssoc[iation] bill being in the abjuration oath which was stronger then the association that being only subscibed and this sworn to and sub[scr]ibed so this was ordered[426] and then we read some Irish bill and adjourned to

23d [*Mar. 1702*] nothing worth observing: Sir Ed[*ward*] Hussey brought in a clause to prevent the Queens granting pensions out of her Civill list (Nota that word is not relished as new and unparliamentary)[427] for her own life or for years: shee was hindered from alienating her revenue Even of the hered[*it*]ary part by a clause lowndes brought in: this claus was read the first time but not permitted a 2d reading for they said it would put unusuall hards[*hi*]ps upon the Queen: that there was no reason for that shee was a good manager and that shee would be uncapable Of rewarding services done for her and the crown: and that it would signify nothing for that shee might give annually What shee pleased that pensions when given were not Well paid if the princes favour did not Continue and that wee did not intend to make her accountable

---

[423] 'it' interlined.

[424] For this rule, and a similar exception, see [Hatsell,] *Precedents*, 83, 85.

[425] The 1696 act for the better security of His Majesty's person and government (7 & 8 Gul. III, c. 27, ss. iii–xxi); see above, p. 7.

[426] The instruction was for an amendment to declare the Association to be 'determined', 'what is contained therein being provided by the said oath': *CJ* xiii. 816.

[427] Presumably the very term 'civil list', which did not appear in the official title of the Civil List Bill, which the House was discussing in committee.

how and for what shee laid out the money that it would signifye nothing but repro[?ach] on the other side it was said that princes were ministers intrusted by the publick that vast pensions had been granted to the impoverishing of the publick that this would hinder Flatterers and beggers and that if the princes disposed of their revenues the people must suppor[t] the honour and dignity out of their own pockets that it was in a manner giving away the peoples land and property: Hussey is very honest but has no great judgment and a great opinion of his own abilityes that he thinks nobody able to advise him[428] there was nothing in this Clause but an air of popularity and tho we had no appearance of a voyce for us in comparison of what was against us nor were our arguments better then our neighbours yet he would divide the house I mean the committee there were for the Clause 50 against it 80 or thereabout 24th [*Mar. 1702*] was spent in taking the abjuration oath and in reporting the civill list bill Lord Sherwood brought in a Clause to enable the Queen to Confirm those grants that were made by King william and had a privy seal[e] to pass them and were granted upon valuable Considerations[429] the question was put whether it should be read a second time it passed in the negative 25th [*Mar. 1702*]

Things of cours till they went into the examination of a paper laid before the house relating to the tardy payme[nts] of the Receivours Generall and the slow payments of the Custome house bonds: this was particularly inquired into upon the account of Sir J manwaring of Cheshire Who had always disobliged these angry Gent[*lemen*] by voting contrary to their minds the Receivour was one whitlee now in Newgate for the Kings debt: it seems the king has power to put his debtors in what prisonne he pleases and it was wispered about that whitlee should say that the reason why he did not pay the money was becaus it was in Sir John Manwerings hands Sir Michaell Bidolph another member was the other security[430] this was not said in the house but every one knew the meaning of the motion to appoynt a Committee to

---

[428] 'him' interlined.

[429] Lord Sherard, who in Apr. 1697 had himself received a grant, of Windmill Fields, in St James's: *Cal. Treas. Bks.*, xii. 146. In *CJ* xiii. 818, the clause runs simply, 'that contracts may be perfected'.

[430] Morgan Whitley, former receiver-general for Cheshire and N. Wales. On 20 Mar. the agents for taxes were ordered by the Treasury to pursue the recovery of Whitley's debt (given as £4,600) from Mainwaring, as one of the securities, Biddulph being the other: *Cal. Treas. Bks.*, xvii. 17, 171, 317. Mainwaring had married into the Whitley family; Biddulph was 'a poor, weak, man, of a very mean understanding, and so consequently easily led away by the nose of his friends, of whom Sir John Mainwaring . . . has the most predominant power over him': Centre for Kentish Studies, Maidstone, U1590/C9/0, Lord Stanhope to James Stanhope, 26 Apr. 1702. Before his election Biddulph had promised to vote with the Tories in the Commons, but had evidently broken his word: HMC, *Cowper MSS*, iii. 419, 451.

Examine Whitlee why he was so negligent and refused payment: it was said that the Committee could not send for him out of newgate for if he was taken out of Custody that would be an escape in the Goaler, and that Whitlee had offered the sherriffe 1000 to take him before a judge upon some account: the Committee was named[431] and empowered to send for persons papers and records but it seemed to be the sense of the house that the Committee must go to Newgate: they also appoynted a committee to inspect Gree[n]wich Hospitall severall abuses in relation to the misapplying the money appoynted to build there being complained of by the Commieee that were appoynted by the house to consider of matters relating to the said hospitall:[432] and as to the Receivours they came to these generall resolutions that the Receivours keeping the publick money so long in their hands was a damage to the publick: and that they should pay interest for it: and so for the Customhouse [*sic*] debts that it was a damage to the publick: and that there was a neglect in not calling on them for their money:[433] Nota the design of inquiring into the mismanagement of the Receivours was not only in particular to reflect on Sir John manwaring and Sir Michaell Bidolph but also to Censure the Lord Hallifax mr Smith[434] and that set of the Treasury

26th [*Mar.*]

1702 this day there was Nothing worth observing but a division relating to the Irish petitions in the case of Sir Daniell Arther now a Banker in paris and his case was this he formerly had a great hand in the popish plot and w[hen] he found he was discovered he left this Kingdom and to escape justice he went into France and setled at paris: he has since been Knighted by King James at St jermans and followed that Court he was attainted of Treason in Ireland he is above or about 80 year old and has an estate of 300 li. per an: for life in Ireland:[435] he Petitioned to have his Estate and to bring in a bill to revers his outlawry it was said for him that he had not been in Ireland for 20 years that

---

[431] Including Cocks: *CJ* xiii. 819.

[432] In fact, the task of investigation was handed over to the committee originally appointed on 4 Mar. (including Cocks) to receive proposals 'for the encouraging' the Royal Hospital at Greenwich: ibid. 775, 819.   [433] The three resolutions are given in full ibid. 819.

[434] John Smith, MP Andover, a Lord of the Treasury 1694–9, and Chancellor of the Exchequer 1699–1701.

[435] Sir Daniel Arthur had forfeited a mortgage interest on property at Whitefriars, 'in the suburbs of Dublin', arising from an advance of £4,300 made to the owner, Lord Longford, in 1684: HMC, *House of Lords MSS*, NS iv. 39; PRO T.1/62/267–79 (calendared in *Cal. Treas. Pprs.* 1697–1702, p. 317); HMC, *Ormonde MSS*, NS vii. 200, 296. For his activity as a Jacobite banker in Paris, see HMC, *Downshire MSS*, i. 681; John Ainsworth (ed.), *The Inchiquin Manuscripts* (Irish Manuscripts Commission; Dublin, 1961), 268. One English MP engaged in business dealings with Arthur, and called upon in return to back 'his case in Ireland', was Sir Godfrey Copley: Sheffield Archives, Copley MSS, CD 473, Copley's 'letter register', fos. 7, 9.

in france he had done severall services to the English Merchants that he had
done severall kindnesses to Gent[*lemen*] that travailed there and returned
money for their service Mr Granville divided the house those that were for
releiving him according to his petition were 16 those that were against
releiving him 148

27th [*Mar. 1702*] There was a petition offered relating to a bill that was
ordered to be reported and it was agreed that it was to ly on the table till
the report was Made for the bill could not be recommitted after the report
was ordered, till the report was taken and then the bill relating to the SCotch
union was read: and when a 2d reading was[436] moved for they would have had
it put of[*f*] till after the call of the house a long debate but Nothing worth the
mentioning at last the question was put for munday for it 166 against it 119[437]

28th [*Mar. 1702*] after private bills and motions Mrs [*sic*] Bridges moved
that the house should take in to considerati[on] a matter of consequence in
relation to a Breach of Priviledge com[*mit*]ted by Ed[*ward*] Owen[438] an
Alderman of Coventry upon an assistant to the Serjeants officer one Ed[*ward*]
Bosworth:[439] the case was this the Serjeants officer was sent down to take the
sherriffes of that place into custody he tooke this fellow a Barber to assist him
and they searched severall places and amongst the rest this Aldermans for his
son that was sherriffe: and after that the alderman comitted Bosworths[440]
sister for some misdeameanour and this fellow acquainted the house that he
went to baile his sister and offered himself and another sufficient person to be
his security that the Alderman refused him to baile his sister and told him that
he had assisted the house of com[*mo*]ns officer and that for so doing he was a
Rascall and that he would ruine him for so doing or to that purpose upon this
followed a pretty warm Debate one side were for taking the alderman into
custody the other side were for appoynting him

[*fo. 9ᵛ*

a day to ap]pear before the Committee of priviledges to vindicate himself and
that then if he did not Clear himself that then he should be committed and
that this was according to the orders of the house that none should be
committed before the Cause was Examined by the Committee and reported:
all agreed this to be the orders but others said here was the man that viva voce

---

[436] 'order[*ed*]' erased.
[437] *CJ* xiii. 823, gives the figures as 165 : 119. The call was scheduled for 2 Apr.
[438] 'Ed[*ward*] Owen' interlined.
[439] 'one Ed[*ward*] Bosworth' interlined. For this episode, which arose from the election hearing
on 24 Feb., see *CJ* xiii. 825–6; T. W. Whitley, *The Parliamentary Representation of the City of
Coventry* . . . (Coventry, 1894), 130–1. For Alderman Edward Owen (d. 1705), a capper and
feltmaker, and a Dissenter, who had been mayor in 1680 and 1696, see Hurwich, ' "Fanatick
Town" ', 38; Fox (ed.), *Coventry Constables' Presentments*, 32.   [440] Originally 'his'.

proved that he was an assistant to the officer of the house of Commons, and that he was abused and threatned for so doing that the house was ingaged in honour to vindicate their servants and that if they tooke that long way of summoning him and referring the examination to a Committee the house would rise and the Criminall escape punishment and that tho the orders of the house was to reffer the examinations of such things to the committee of priviledges yet the practiCe had been often otherwise: the Speaker said the orders of the house required us first to vote a crime and then the punishment: but that was not regarded and they proceeded on with the debate: in which mr Hoppkins one of the members of Coventry told the house that they searched severall persons of good qualityes houses some resented that way of proceeding:[441] but it was agreed that tho it was not a very easy practice yet it was necessary and Could not be restrained for that Criminalls woud seldom meet them in the streets and that it was necessary to search for them: at last the Speaker was[442] obliged by the orders to put the question that was first moved and seconded which was a Complicated question: that Edward owen was guilty of a Breach of priviledge of the house and contempt against the same by using threatning language against the person that assisted the Serjeant at arms that attended this house[443] the house divided and the ays carryed it by 8[444] and then owen was uppon another division orderd to be taken into Custody the ays went out: this was a very hard case for most of those that were against the question beleived that Bosworth Complained only against Owen to be revenged of him for Committing his sister: and these frequent and too Easy Commitments occasion a detestation of the house of Com[*mon*]s and make them odious to the people and too frequent an use of such power may make the people weary of that part of the legislative power and throw themselves into the protection of a Tyrant: Then there was a report made by mr Dormir[445] in relation to John Holder a merchant the case was thus John Holder had laden the Cloudesley Galley with rich merchandise of severall merchants of severall Countryes and some of his own and had ensured the same very high at great rates and then john Holder Contrived some way to take out the goods and burn the ship: this was proved before my Lord Cheif justice Holt by the Captain who was hired by the said Holder to burn the ship

---

[441] In his 'memoirs' Edward Hopkins gave an account of this speech, in favour of 'one of my best friends, a principal alderman of Coventry, being thro' party malice ordered into custody'. He went on to claim that 'old Sir Edward Seymour . . . showed much venom upon this occasion, and on others a particular aversion to me, even descending to discant upon what I offered in debate'. Mary Dormer Harris, 'Memoirs of the Right Hon. Edward Hopkins, M.P. for Coventry', *English Historical Review*, 34 (1919), 498–9.   [442] 'forced' erased.

[443] *Recte* 'the serjeant at arms in execution of the orders of this House': *CJ* xiii. 825–6.

[444] In fact the division was 112 : 90: ibid. 826.   [445] 'that' erased.

Holder and the captain had fell out about the reward and the merchants concerned had some suspicion of the matter and offered 1500 to any one that would make discoverys of the matter upon which the Captain came in and this was proved before my Lord Cheif justice who committed Holder to the Keeper of the[446] Fleet William Weeden Ford Esqr this Ford let this Holder go at large Mr Dormir reported this matter and the House resolved that the petitioners had fully proved their allegations and that Holder was Guilty of a villanous practice and Highly dishonourable to the [sic] and prejudiciall to the trade thereof: and that Ford in letting Holder Escape was guilty of a notorious breach of his duty: and mr Dormir was ordered to bring in a bill for summoning John Holder to render himself to justice in a certain time under a penalty:[447] Nota this was done in the Case of Sir [*Thomas*] Sandys that cut Sir John Coventrys nose in K[*ing*] C[*harles*] 2d time:[448] nota Mr Colepeper was gone to Holland and the sherriffes of Coventry absconded and the Serjeant declared he had sent after them and Could hear nothing of them: and it was ordered that[449] an addres be presented to the Queen to issue out her proclamation for the apprehending of them[450]

30 [*Mar. 1702*] this day the bill for the enabling the Queen to treat with Scots etc. was read a 2d time and Committed without any opposition the Queen sent the usher of the black rod[451] to the house to Command the Honourable house to attend her in the house of Lords Where shee passed many bills private and publick amongst the rest that for the Maintenance of the household and

---

[446] 'Keeper of the' interlined.

[447] Probably the John Holder (b. 1662), of St Giles-in-the-Fields, Middx., who was son to Richard Holder, a merchant and shipowner of Rood Lane, Fenchurch St., London: *Allegations for Marriage Licences Issued by the Vicar-General of the Archbishop of Canterbury, July 1679 to June 1687* (Harleian Soc., 30; London, 1890), 285; Mrs E. P. Hart (ed.), *Merchant Taylors' School Register* (2 vols.; London, 1936), no pagination; Woodhead, *Rulers of London*, 91; *Cal. Treas. Bks.*, ix. 281. For this episode, see *CJ* xiii. 826–8; and *CSP Dom.* 1702–3, p. 416. The voyage had taken place in 1699, and it had been on the second leg, from Cadiz to Genoa, that the fire had been started, by the captain, John Snapes. According to the evidence, the cargo had been insured for £16,000 in London, and a further 12,000 dollars at Cadiz. The warden of the Fleet was William Weedon Ford.

[448] Sandys was a lieutenant under Monmouth in the King's Troop of Horse Guards: Dalton, *Eng. Army Lists*, i. 99; Basil Duke Henning (ed.), *The Parliamentary Diary of Sir Edward Dering 1670–1673* (Yale Historical Publns., xvi; New Haven, 1940), 44–5. Sir John Coventry (*c.*1636–85), of Mere, Wilts., and Suffolk Street, Westminster, was MP Weymouth and Melcombe Regis 1667–81: *HC 1660–90*, ii. 154–6. On 10 Jan. 1671 the Commons ordered a bill to set a day for Sandys and the other perpetrators of the attack on Coventry to give themselves up or face banishment: *CJ* ix. 188–9. [449] 'it was ordered that' interlined.

[450] The serjeant had reported the abscondment not only of the two sheriffs sought for their conduct in the Coventry election, John Collins and Abraham Owen, but also of the Kentish Petitioner, Thomas Colepeper: *CJ* xiii. 826; Whitley, *Parlty. Rep. of Coventry*, 130–2.

[451] Sir David Mitchell: see above, p. 62, n. 10.

honour and dignity of the crown[452] and shee made a gracious speech and gave
them this year 100000 li. back out of the money they gave her considering the
great necessityes of the nation:[453] affter the Speaker had read this speech
amongst many nawseous and Flattering expressions of thanks some of them
would have had this of the giving back this money to be particularly Mentioned others thinking it too little to be mentioned were for thanks in generall
Sir Thomas powis said it ought to be expressed infinite goodnes: Mr Anderton
was for giving her two Hundred thousand pound more to return the compliment: Sir Edward Seymour said wee might see by this What it was to have a
queen that was intirely English and spoke so that every one thought he
reflected upon the king Mr Smith said the king was intirely English and he
should be glad to see king or Queen do more for england[454] my Lord Spencer
said that those that reflected upon that king for not being English had french
hearts St Johns said Qui Capit ille facit:[455] the Gallery was stuffed with
dutchesses Countesses and ladys at last the heat was over and we ordered
an address and a Committee to draw it etc.[456] and we then went upon the land
tax Nota[457] this 100000 li. Which is given back will cost us not only much
flattery but more money in the end and we shall be told of it. 100000 times
March ult [*i.e. 31st 1702*]

this day nothing done or said worth the writing the report of Bishops Castle
Election was made the Committee came to this resolution that neyther mason
nor the petitioner Walcut were duly Elected mason had a good cause enough
of it but his freinds did not appear for him because he was a scandalous
scoundrill Fellow and the very Committee that voted mason not duly Elected
could not vote walKut Elected for it was proved that he was guilty of notorious
bribery and had not the majority but mr Bruges and Sir Thomas powis[458]
spoke for him and they divided the house in his favour for walkut 100 against

---

[452] The Civil List Bill.   [453] The text of this speech is printed in *CJ* xiii. 830.

[454] In reporting this exchange between Seymour and Smith, Bonet paraphrased the latter's
speech as follows: 'le Sr. Smith, du party Whig, voyant qu'il [Seymour] réflechissoit sur le feu Roy,
ajouta qu'à la verité la nation pouvoit se féliciter a juste titre d'avoir une Reine si tendre pour son
Peuple, mais qu'on ne devoit pas par cela oublier sitôt les grandes obligations qu'on avoit à un Roy
aussi jaloux des avantages de l'Angleterre qu'a été le dernier'. DZA, Rep. XI Eng. 25c, fo. 108.
Another account has Seymour seconding Sir John Bolles in the motion for thanks, and Smith
commenting that only 'one whose heart was truly French would make a reflection on His Majesty':
Strathmore MSS, box 75, bdle 1, newsletter, 31 Mar. 1702.

[455] From the Latin proverb, equivalent to, 'if the cap fits, wear it'. The Strathmore MSS
newsletter (box 74, bdle. 1, 31 Mar. 1702) confirms St John's comment, though with Smith as
the target; Bonet's account also has St John replying to Smith, with praise for the Queen and
reflections on King William (DZA, Rep. XI Eng. 25c, fo. 108).   [456] 'etc.' underlined.

[457] The committee of the whole on the Land Tax Bill.   [458] 'said' erased.

him 120:[459] Sir Ed[*ward*] Seymour divided against Walkut and Sir Xto[*pher*] musgrove for him there was also a bill for Erecting of 4 courts of Consciens in Southwark[460] that was refused to be committed for the exorbitant powers and the inconveniencyes that would thereon ensue all that was said for it that it did good in london and other places and that the charge of law and the proceedings ruined the poor: there was a petition of the lady Falklands relating to the Irish Claims desiring a longer time to put in her Claim debated shee had a time given her the last sessions of Parliament which shee neglected to use and this was the same petition Bolles spoke against her[461] and said he could not be for her but upon the Division divided for her and the house ordered him to bring in the Bill to expose him:[462] nota Sir Thomas powis reported the addres of thanks and as to the word unparall[*ell*]ed goodnes he sais it reflected upon the late king and that without reason for that he had given us up the Chimney money: the addres to king william upon that subject was unpresidented goodnes:[463] there are to[*o*] many provocations given and taken some times before they are given I really beleive many would rather destroy the opposite party then the French:[464]

Aprill 1st [*1702*][465] no debate nor anything worth observing in the land tax bill Lownds brought in a Long[466] Clause that in those places where by reason of the papists and non jurors taking the oaths severall parishes etc. paid above 4s per Lib[467] that in those cases there should be a generall meeting in June to rais this money as the com[*mi*]s[*sione*]rs should think fit this was reckoned unpracticable unconvenient and that the remedy was wors then the disease so we rejected the clause

Aprill 2d [*1702*] Nothing worth observing: this day Sir Edward Seymour after an orang complaining of the disorders of the house and speaking to order gave it down for a rule and for orders that there ought not to be more then one

---

[459] See above, pp. 123–4, and, for Mason's disreputable character, n. 420. The report of the 1702 case is to be found at *CJ* xiii. 831–3, where the figures for the division are given as 100:126. For Brydges' later involvement in this constituency, see VCH, *Shropshire*, iii. 300.

[460] In fact, for the divisions of Tower Hamlets, Southwark, Holborn, and Islington: *CJ* xiii. 831.   [461] Originally 'for her'.

[462] Rebecca (1662–1709), née Lytton, whose late husband, Anthony Cary, 5th Viscount Falkland [S], had acquired in 1689 a mortgage interest of £400 in the Co. Kildare estate of the Jacobite Patrick Sarsfield, subsequently forfeited: PRO Northern Ireland, D.1854/2/18, fos. 162–3. An earlier petition of hers had been referred by the Commons to the Irish forfeitures trustees on 19 May 1701 (*CJ* xiii. 554), but no report is recorded in the *Journals*. Bolles was ordered to prepare the bill together with John Hayes, one of the tellers in Lady Falkland's favour: *CJ* xiii. 833.

[463] In the address agreed on 1 Mar. 1689, King William's promise to regulate or remove entirely the hearth tax was described as a 'most gracious and unprecedented offer': ibid. x. 39. The phrase in this address was 'unparallelled grace and goodness': ibid. xiii. 830–1.

[464] 'par' erased.   [465] '[?Dn]' interlined.   [466] 'Long' interlined.

[467] In the committee on the bill. See above, p. 20.

unCovered[468] in the house at one time[469] and said that Gent[*lemen*] were come
to such a beauishnes in their perukes that they were affraid to put on their hats
for fear of disturbing their perriwigs and that that[470] Beau had not had his hat
on this fortnight poynting to somebody this made him cover his head and the
house laugh Just after came in mr vice chamberlain Bertie[471] and he knew
nothing of What had past and he sat without his hat and they Called to order
and he did not Know what had passed but at last he was told and was forced
to make an im

[*fo. 10*]

pression upon his fine perriwig by putting on his hat: that was no sooner over
but he cryed to order becaus some [?one ?else's ?hat] was off: and after these
fooleryes were over wee went upon the adjourned report relating to Whitbee
Harbour in Yorkshire[472] Sir Edward Hussey offered an amendment to the bill
before the blanks and amendments made by the Committee were agreed to by
the ho[use] When that was done Sir[473] Xto[*pher*] musgrove said there was a
word in the bill for ever viz the ColleCting of such dut[ies] to repair the peers
should Continue for ever;[474] he said the bill ought to have been brought with a
blank and for that fault i[t] ought to be rejected but he moved to have those
words left out Sir Ed[*ward*] Seymour seconded the motion and the house
agreed [?tha]t What was said was true: so that question was putting and Mr
Nichols[*on*] offered a clause and it was then said and agr[e]ed to by the house
that if any amendment was Made in the bill after that no Clause should be
offered: the meaning of the Clause was to excuse yarmouth from paying any
duty at Whitbee because they repaired their own peers and maintained their
harbour at their own expence without any assistance from the publick:[475]
there were two divisions the one for a recommitment for it 114 against 136 for
the Claus 93 against it 64 or thereabouts: then it was past 3 half an houre and
we were to go to St Jameses at 4[476] so they were for adjourning Toppam[477]
moved that Committees might sit in the recess I seconded him but Seymour

---

[468] The letter 'C' begins a new line in the MS.

[469] Henry Scobell, *Memorials of the Method and Manner of Proceedings in Parliament* . . .
(London, 1670), 6: 'When the Speaker is set in his chair, every Member is to sit in his place with his
head covered.'   [470] 'Gent[*leman*]' erased.

[471] Peregrine Bertie, MP Truro, Vice-Chamberlain of the Household.

[472] The report from the committee on the bill for rebuilding the pier at Whitby.

[473] 'Edward Seym[*our*]' erased.

[474] As enacted, the duties were to be paid to trustees for the term of nine years: 1 Ann., c. xiii, s. 1.

[475] Nicholson, one of the Members for Gt. Yarmouth, was a teller in favour of this clause (*CJ*
xiii. 836), the effect of which was to exempt the inhabitants of Gt. Yarmouth from the duty of $\frac{1}{2}d$.
per chaldron of coal landed at Whitby. It was incorporated into the resultant act as s. 11.

[476] To present the address in reply to the Queen's speech of 30 Mar.: *CJ* xiii. 838.

[477] 'said' erased.

and musgrove Cryed no and said it was not to be endured to have business done in hugg[e]rmugger so: that motion fell and we adjourned to wednesday: Nota this of the Committees sitting in the recess was practiced last year When the house adjourned for the Speakers illnes[478] Nota this report of Witbee[479] was adjourned nine times:[480] Nota the Election of Bishops Castle being made voyd for bribery the house would not grant out a new writ for the Election there this sessions[481]

Aprill 8th [1702] nothing woth [sic] observing private bills were read and a report of an Irish bill relating to a great estate of my lord Bophins in Ireland: we divided about reCommitting it the estate that was forfeited was worth 80000 li. and we divided for the compounding with my Lord for 30000 li. at last it was after we lost that division agreed for 25000 li. and there was a dispute relating to the warwickshire land tax to be heard at the barr of the house but that was referred to my Lord Cheifjustice [sic] when they found they were put of[f] to another day: they referred it by consent being weary of attending: Nota my Lord Bophin was a papist some part of his estate viz 1300 li. was intailed and only forfeitable for my Lords life and the pretence of giving him that was becaus his children were bred protestants and the reasons for compounding with him were many idle storys put together but the truth was his great estate had made him great freinds[482]

Ap 9th [1702] after the reading of private bills Edgworths bill for giving him the estate of Sir Peter Terrill (his wifes father) whose only daughter Edgworth had married) [sic][483] was by order of the day read in this debate

---

[478] See above, p. 104.   [479] 'of Witbee' interlined.

[480] From 18 Mar. to 2 Apr.: *CJ* xiii. 808, 813, 817, 819, 824, 828, 830, 834–5.

[481] Ibid. 835, confirms that on 2 Apr. a motion for the issue of the writ was negatived.

[482] John Bourke (1642–1722), heir to the 8th Earl of Clanricarde [I], and himself created by James II in 1689 Baron Bourke of Bophin[I], had been attainted after his capture by Williamite forces in 1691, but had taken the oaths six years later, and in 1698 had conformed to the Church of Ireland. King William had sought to establish Bourke's entitlement to inclusion within the Articles of Galway, but the precise legal position had proved unclear. The bill, to reverse the outlawry, placed Bourke's estate in the hands of trustees for the benefit of his children, who were to be brought up as Protestants. He was also ordered to pay £25,000 into the public purse. See Simms, *Williamite Confiscation*, 70–1; HMC, *House of Lords MSS*, NS iv. 45; PRO Northern Ireland, T.2812/9/13 (O'Hara MSS), Toby Caulfield to Kean O'Hara, 1 Nov. 1698; and the various printed cases concerning this and related legislation in BL Dept. of Printed Books, 816.m.17, and 1888.c.11; and Bath MSS, Thynne papers, box 52, fos. 239, 242. The Irish forfeitures trustee, Francis Annesley, spoke of soliciting 'several of our friends in the House of Commons' on Bourke's behalf: Nat. Archs. Ireland, Wyche MSS 1/250, Annesley to Sir Cyril Wyche, 9 Apr. 1702.

[483] Robert Edgeworth (aft. 1659–1730), of Kilshruley, Co. Longford, who during the Jacobite war in Ireland raised an independent company to fight for King William, had married in 1692 the daughter and heiress of the deceased Jacobite Sir Edward Tyrrell, 1st Bt. (d. 1691), of Lynn, Co. Westmeath. He persuaded his wife to convert to Protestantism in order to facilitate a claim to her father's forfeited estate, in several counties, on the grounds that Tyrrell had not been outlawed in

mr Smith gave the history of the forfeitures as follows that the parliament had Laid Claim to the forfeitures pretty early and that the king had promised not to dispose of them but by Consent of parliament that the parliament had brought in bills for that purpose[484] one of which had passed this house and that he had the honour of carrying it up to the Lords which after the proviso and savings that were in it were considered it was hardly worth the carrying that there were no grants nor any disposall made of them for many years and then When the King saw that no claim was made of them and that there seemed no intent to dispose of them the king disposed of them[485] and it may be some of the grants Could not be so Well justifyed and then that we were so eager of resuming them that in hast we resumed them and would allow of no petitions so then we resumed all the estates and after that we considered[486] that we had done an hardship in refusing the petitions and then we allowed of all the petitions that we confirmed all the outlawryes that were reversed which was of the same nature as a grant that by this manage we had confirmed all the popish estates in Ireland and all the hardships lay upon the poor protestant purchasers and the protestants in Generall that we had disturbed the quiet of the whole Kingdom and that by what we gave away and what the com[mi]s[sione]rs spent and the charge that attended them there would be but very little left to the publick that he would not say that it was just to releive Edgmorth [sic] as his case was but that he had observed those who had not more right or pretence for releive then Edgworth and that therefore he would not speake against Edgworth: Edgworth had behaved himself bravely for the reducing of Ireland and many things wer[e] said relating to the justice of his petition as well as to the Compassionate part of it so we divided for the committing it and carryed it by a great majority then Came on the Scotch union bill[487] in the Committee of the Whole house some Called Sir Rowland

his own lifetime. See Simms, *Williamite Confiscation*, 132; Harriet J. Butler and Harold E. Butler (edd.), *The Black Book of Edgeworthstown* ... (London, 1927), 54–5; PRO Northern Ireland, D.1854/2/19, fos. 174–5; *The Case of R[obert] E[dgeworth] and Katherine His Wife, Daughter and Heir of Sir Edward Tyrrell, Bar. Deceased* (n.d.); BL Add. MS 28885, fo. 66; Add. MS 28941, fo. 406. Cocks's mistake over Tyrrell's name is probably due to the fact that, besides Sir Edward, there was also a forfeiting proprietor called Peter 'Tirrell': HMC, *House of Lords MSS*, NS v. 140.

[484] 'some' erased.

[485] As early as 30 Apr. 1689 the Convention had adopted a resolution from ways and means to appoint a committee to receive proposals for raising money on the forfeited estates in Ireland. The first bill for the sale of such property was ordered on 10 Dec. following, but failed to make its way into law. After the rejection of a second bill, the King's Speech of 5 Jan. 1691 promised that there would be no grant of forfeited estates in England or Ireland until Parliament had another opportunity to settle the matter. *CJ* x. 113, 304, 536. On the history of forfeitures legislation, see Simms, *Williamite Confiscation*, 82 ff. Neither of the two bills to go to the Lords (in Dec. 1690 and Feb. 1692) was carried up by John Smith: *CJ* x. 523, 662.   [486] 'of' erased.

[487] The bill to enable the Queen to appoint commissioners to treat for a union.

Gwin some mr Boyle to the Chair and and so the Speaker was forced to take the Chaire to put the Questio[n] My Lord Wil[*liam*] pawlett moved for Gwin mitford seconded him Granville moved for Boyle St Johns seconded him and mr Boyle moved that Sir Rowland Gwin should take the Chaire then the Speaker said there was no need of a qustion and after some more little discourses he Left the Chaire, and then both names were called upon in the Committee and the Speaker resumed the Chaire and put the question upon Boyle they that were for Guinne said they moved and seconded Gwinn but the Speaker said their motions were insignificant being made before the mace was laid upon the table and that was allowed of to be true so the Question was put upon Boyle and he carried we expected a debate but there was none nor any alteration but as to the words that empowered the Queen to appoynt Com[*mi*]s[*sione*]rs to treat with those Com[*mi*]s[*sione*]rs that were or should be appoynted by the Scotch parliament and those words were or[488] were left out for many reasons first becaus they said the com[*mi*]s[*sione*]rs appoynted were dead most of them:[489] those to be appoynted ought to be new made, to shew the ScotCh were still of the same mind and then they altered the preamble and added the recitall of the Scoth [*sic*] act which shewed that they first desired it[490] this was done to preserve the honour of the nation as they said: nota the Scotch act was in the house but could not be read publicikly the Committee having no such instruction from the house: then there was the bill for setling the abjuration oath without doors and after the preamble was read and put[491] Sir Ed[*ward*] Hussey would have offered a Clause but that was not Consented to, it being Contrary to orders to receive a clause after the preamble was read and agreed to by the Committee[492]

Ap 10th [*1702*] after common busines was over we went into the Committee of ways and means upon the land tax bill[493] and nota there was a clause not

[488] 'were or' boxed in MS.

[489] The commissioners appointed by the Scottish act of 1689, for which see *The Acts of the Parliament of Scotland* (12 vols.; Edinburgh, 1844–75), ix. 60. Of the twenty-five named, nine had died by Apr. 1702: the 3rd Duke of Hamilton (president), 18th Earl of Crawford, 1st Marquess of Tweeddale, William Blair, Thomas Drummond, Sir Charles Halkett, 1st Bt., Sir John Hall, Sir James Montgomerie, 3rd Bt., and Sir Archibald Murray, 3rd Bt.

[490] Confirmed by Bonet (DZA, Rep. XI Eng. 25c, fo. 118). The Whigs' intention, in demonstrating that the English Parliament was only responding to a Scottish initiative, was to forestall the argument for the calling of another Parliament in Scotland. This demand for a new Parliament was in turn being pressed by Tories, who believed that their Scottish allies, the cavaliers, would be likely to make gains in any new elections. See Riley, *Union*, 25–6.

[491] 'was read and put' interlined. The bill to declare the alterations in the oath made necessary by the accession of Queen Anne.

[492] Consideration of the preamble was always the last task of a 2nd-reading committee, for the simple reason that amendments to the 'body' of a bill might well necessitate alterations to the preamble: Scobell, *Memorials*, 49–50.

[493] The committee of the whole on the Land Tax Bill.

brought in by ins[t]ruction from the house and nothing relating to the land tax offered and received relating to Hungary wines to declare hungary to be part of Germany and to enact that the hungary wines should pay such duty as the Rhenish dos and other wines of the growth of Germany and that the wines should be imported from Hamburg: it was said in the debate that this would make and open a trade with France and that there was a wine called Buda wines that were brought over from Hamburg: and that there was a tryall in which the king was cast against the evidence: others said it would open a tra[de] that was beneficiall to the kingdom and that it was a fair tryall and that they would take off our Cloth and after a tedious debate we divided and those that were against the Clause lost by six viz 88 and 94[494]

Ap 11th [1702]

Nothing but the reading of the Irish bills not read before[495] and the debates wheth[er] they should be read a 2 time there was one great Estate concerned viz Sir Patrick Tran[t's] and when that was over off went a great squadron allmost half the house there was a ver[y] Mercifull disposition in the house this Sir Patrick trant was originally a footman and a great [?Jacobite][496]

[fo. 10ʳ]

Ap [13]th [1702] private bills were and at last Publick bills one of which viz the bill for explaining the oath of abjuration was read and the quakers thought themselves in great danger by that bill for swear they could not and no room was there left for their affirmation so that the best councill advised them to get a liberty to affirm the same words we swore to otherwise they were subject to all the penaltys mentioned in the act of abjuration there was no question made of it all agreed there was no teaching schoole without such a proviso and most were of opinion that they Could not teach in their meetings without such a clause: I advised to prepare such a clause and in their affirmation that they should alter as few words as possibly they Could from our oath they had a mind to have a shorter way I could not satisfye them but they would in a great measure have their own way at last we agreed that they should prepare two

---

[494] By the Tunnage and Poundage Act of 1660 (12 Car. II, c. 4, s. I), subsequently renewed, imported 'Rhenish' wine was to pay a duty of 20s. per 'awne'. Robert Yard's account of this debate noted the objection that the clause would 'give an opportunity to bring in French wines, which might be carried to Hamburg, and from thence brought thither under the name of Buda wine'. He confirms that the clause was carried. BL Add. MS 7074, fos. 206–7.

[495] De Vaudoncourt summarized the day's proceedings in the same way: PRO 31/3/190/50.

[496] Sir Patrick Trant, formerly of Portarlington, Queen's Co., had died in France as a Jacobite exile in 1696. His origins were obscure, and little is known of him before his appointment as a revenue commissioner in Ireland in 1684. The petition came from his son John, on behalf of himself, his mother, and sisters, and concerned the huge Portarlington estate, which had been granted by King William to the Earl of Galway. See S. T. McCarthy *The Trant Family* (Folkestone, 1924), 7–8; HMC, *Downshire MSS*, i. 651; Simms, *Williamite Confiscation*, 88–9.

clauses one as I directed and one that they liked themselves: but they were so long consulting so long preparing that the bill was read before they brought eyther and at last the short one so in I went into the house and opened it as if it had been the long clause and there was a debate and a question put whether I should bring it up that was carryed and when it was read and it differed a pretty deale from what I had opened it: it began her majestys protestant subjects called Quakers: mr Harcourt denied them to be protestants and said the Quakers had eyther abused me or I[497] the house: I told the truth which was the hast and when I saw the house would not receive and that some were for rejecting I asked leave to withdraw it:[498] Nota I advised them to get it by way of amendment in the Lords house which with vast labour and difficulty they obtained and when they had got what they so much desired they used all their interest in the house of Commons to have them disagree to the amendments which they also compassed[499]

then we went into the Committee of ways and means[500] and there was an instruction from the house to the Committee to receive a clause to prevent the officers of the ExChequer from receiving any poundage out[501] of the money given this year: in this debate it was said that nothing in reason ought to be paid out of the taxes that in reason we ought not to charge the people to encrease their salaryes on the other side it was said that the trouble was very great and the office more painfull and laborious and that consequently their salaryes ought to encreas: it was said in this debate that in the year 93 the tellers places were worth 4000 li.[502] at last it was moved and seconded to abate the poundage to one penny per pound this was opposed as being Contrary to the instruction which was to take away all poundage except for the civill list and that we had no power to exceed or deviate from the instruction: the

---

[497] 'me or I' interlined.

[498] *CJ* xiii. 843, records only that a clause was offered to the bill as a rider, but rejected. The minutes of the Quakers' Meeting for Sufferings, whose members organized lobbying on the issue, record no meeting with Cocks, though on 27 Mar. two Friends reported having spoken with 'some Members of Parliament' on this subject. On 12 Apr. the Meeting agreed to solicit a 'short clause', proposed by one of their number to be added to the bill; later it was recorded that this clause had been unsuccessfully presented as a rider. Society of Friends Library, London, Minutes of the Meeting for Sufferings, xv. 309, 318, 320.

[499] The Meeting for Sufferings did indeed object to the 'long clause' added by the Lords (printed in HMC, *House of Lords MSS*, NS v. 27–8), as not 'safe', and pressed for a replacement: Soc. of Friends Lib., Mins. of Meeting for Sufferings, xv. 24, 326–31, 336.

[500] The committee of the whole on the Land Tax Bill: *CJ* xiii. 843.

[501] 'out' interlined. On 3 Mar. the committee had been ordered to receive a clause to prevent Exchequer officers from taking fees for aids given in this session: ibid. 774.

[502] A serious underestimate: see Baxter, *Development of the Treasury*, 141–2, 152–64; HMC, *13th Report*, v. 417, 422–3 (the report of the accounts commissioners in 1691, which estimated the income of the then teller, Sir Robert Howard, at over £7,500 p.a.).

answer to that was that it was not an instruction to[503] bring in a clause but leave to the Committee to receive on[e] and that the committee had power to mend alter or riject the clause and the question was put and the committee divided for reducing the Poundage to a penny in the pound 58 against it 54 and then the Speaker resumed the Chair and the house adjourned etc. Nota in the morning a petition from one Owen an Alderman of Coventry committed before for a breach of priviledge was delivered it shewed that he was committed upon fals suggestions and desired to be heard to it at the barr of the house it was ordered to be referred to the committee of priviledges and that they should sit upon it that night which they did accordingly and they appoynted Wednesday next[504] for the hearing of it

Ap[ri]ll 14 [1702] it was moved that the day appoynted by the Committee for the hearing of the Aldermans owens[505] caus was to[o] short and that a longer day should be given by the house some said that nothing Could be more done in it it being examined upon evidence and Owen upon the hearing of that evidence ordered to be taken into Custody and that we could not undo what was once done in the house and that it was to no purpose to reexamine the matter others said there was a standing order of the house that no one should be taken into Custody upon any Complaint of breach of priviledge relating to a member till the matter was examined and reported to the house from the Committee[506] and that this was a standing order made and to be preferred before an order made upon a motion; The answer was that this case differed from What was put inasmuch as this was not a breach of priviledge relating to a member but to the house and then it was urged that When owen was ordered to be taken into custody that he should be heard and the case examined if he desired it So they directed the Committee to proceed upon this matter on munday and then after that and some other busines of No great concern we went into the Committee of the whole house upon the privateer act:[507] and there were debates relating to the taking of the great duties from the prizes taken and the making the conditions the methods of adjudication easier for they said they were so hard that nobody thought it worth time to set out privateers: and on the contrary they said that the abating the duties would open a trade with France but at last it was agreed that that would be very difficult and that we ought to encourage the privateers that being a great and certain good and the other not so considerable an evill

Ap[ri]ll 16th [1702][508] This day was spent in private busines nothing worth

---

503 'to' interlined.   504 i.e. the 15th.   505 'owens' interlined.
506 See above, pp. 257–8.   507 The bill for the encouragement of privateers.
508 Cocks omits the day's proceedings on 15 Apr.

the observing only a division in Which there were 30 of one side and 30 of the other so the Speaker was forced to determine the matter and he gave it against the petition becaus he said if the petition was allowed it would repeale t[w]o acts of Parliament[509]

Ap[ri]ll 17th [1702]

There was common busines Irish bills after one was read mr Smith said there was not the due care taken that ought to be in intailing the estates on protestants Sir Jo[hn] Bolles brought in the bill and he thought himself concerned[510] and said he defyed mr Smith and that it was fals they Cryed to the barr and at last he was ordered and advised by his freinds to ask pardonne of Mr Smith and the house which he did very awkwardly in his place for he said if he had done any thing to offend eyther the house or that Gent[leman] was was sorry for it he was forced to say so thrice the house was not satisfyed with the first Collonell Warton[511] did not hear the second as he said and then they went upon the land tax[512] and debated the Clause for giving one penny in the pound to the exchequer officers and the house divided for the Claus 24 more then were against it[513] and they threw out the Claus for the rectifying the misnomas of the Com[mi]s[sione]rs names and adjourned: nota those that expected places in the exchecquer helped those that had places and so that claus was kept in I thought more in relation to private ends then publick good

[*fo. 11*]

Ap[ri]ll 18th [1702]

There was nothing but common business and discourses about Keeping of[f] the Mobb at the coronation[514] [it was] ordered that the guard or souldiers should attend Seymour Sir Ed[ward] made an oration for which he seemed to va[?lu]e himself that the constables should Keep orders: but the contrary was

---

[509] [Hatsell,] *Precedents*, 162–3, notes the Speaker's casting vote in divisions where the numbers on each side were equal, and the custom that he should then give 'the reasons which induce him to it'. In *CJ* xiii. 847, the figures for the division, on a motion for leave for a bill for the relief of Sir John Dillon, appear as 31:31.

[510] There is no record in the *Journals* of Bolles bringing in a bill on the 17th. Cocks may have been confusing the day with 11 Apr., when a bill was introduced on behalf of Lady Falkland, which Bolles and John Hayes had been ordered to prepare (see above, p. 261): *CJ* xiii. 841.

[511] Goodwin Wharton.

[512] 'in the Committee of the whole house' erased. The report from the committee of the whole on the Land Tax Bill.

[513] The division was over an amendment to the clause, which would effectively have removed the allowance of a penny in the pound; it was defeated 79:34 (*CJ* xiii. 850).

[514] In response to a message from the Queen, giving the day appointed for her coronation (23 Apr.), and detailing the arrangements that were to be made for the accommodation of the Commons.

ordered before he began to speak I suppose he i[nten]ded it but as a Flourish
and then it was ordered that none should come into the places reserved for the
members u[?pon ?pain] of being taken into custody and a committee was
appoynted to inspect the Conveniency and the safety of the places rese[rved]
for the members and that on munday the members should come to the Speaker
for tickets[515] and then after some reports m[ade] and laid upon the table we
went into the order of the day which was Irish petitions and it hapned in some
debates rela[ting] to the Irish busines some said that there ought to be more
regard to those that were protestants: and it seems [?my ?Lord Su]nderland
had been trying with my Lord Marlborrow about that time[516] to put a stop to
some hot proceedings wh[?ich ?did] anger Mr St Johns and he thought by his
youthfull heat to awe that Cunning old minister Sir sais [he] I am for [taki]ng
great care of the protestants and I abominate those men that have forsaken
their religion and thought that [the]y Could dissemble with god that it was a
scandall to that government that employed such men:[517] Sir John Bo[lle]s Who
allways loved in his foolish mad way to reflect upon my Lord Sunderland[518]
seconded St John and said what a bad thing it was to change ones religion and
that he would name the man it was my Lord Sunderland and that he was a
state b[aw]d and a pymp: he was stopped in his career by severall members
and the Speaker stood up and rebuked Bolles af[ter] which my Lord Spencer
stood up and said that that Gent[*leman*] had often reflected upon his father
but that he never thought any body minded what he said and that therefore he
was not worth the answering but now since he had named him he thought
himself obliged to say something in his vindication he said he must own that
his father When he was minister of state had committed some faults and so
had all before and since him that he knew Of that had been in those great
stations but this he could say for him that he allways Loved england valued his
native Country and never betrayed its interest to France: and that he beleived
the worst[519] fault his father had was that he could not go into and comply
with the councills of those men that had for forty years Last past been selling

---

[515] Confirmed by L'Hermitage (BL Add. MS 17677 XX, fo. 286), and de Vaudoncourt (PRO 31/3/190/53).

[516] Marlborough had only returned to London from the Continent on 7 Apr.: Snyder (ed.), *Marlborough–Godolphin Corresp.*, i. 56.

[517] According to Richard West, St John's words were, 'a man that had denied his God in another reign was trying to insinuate himself': Lambeth Palace Lib., MS 2564, p. 408. Again, I owe this reference to Stephen Taylor.

[518] Robert Spencer (1641–1702), 2nd Earl of Sunderland, for whom see J. P. Kenyon, *Robert Spencer, Earl of Sunderland* (London, 1958).　　　　　[519] Originally 'first'.

us to France:[520] after that Sir Row[*land*] Gwin moved to have Bolleses words set down in order to have him censured Sir Xto[*pher*] musgrove said there was no need no occasion for the censuring of Bolles and desired to know Wh[o] that Lord meant by those[521] that had sold us to France and desired that we might give over our heats and go on with ou[r] busines (Nota Sir Xto[*pher*] musgrove was for 30000 standing forces in King Jameses time and none in King W[*illia*m's]time)[522] and then the question that was moved and seconded and laid a sleep a little by these warmths was put viz to releive those protestant purchasers that had bought of my Lord Athlone for releiving them 125 against releiving them 64 and then the releive we gave them was that they should buie their estates at 13 years purchase and that the third part of their purchase money given them by the act of resumption should be allowed as part of the purchase money[523] and after some more Irish reports some of which were approved of and some not Sir R: Gwin reported[524] the inspection of the conveniencyes provided for the members at the Coronation Ap[*ri*]ll 20th [*1702*]

The bill for setling Sir Thomas Cookes Charity on Gloucester Hall and making of it Worcester Colledge[525] was read the first time and ordered a 2d

---

[520] Richard West's version of Spencer's reply has him saying that 'his father had owned the fault; and was included in the second Act of Indemnity without disapprobation of any Parliament; and never was for levying money without Parliament, nor in a French interest, nor would ever desire to be in the ministry, while some were at the helm, who had been in that interest more than forty years. He aimed at Lord Rochester. The House applauded him extremely.' Lambeth Palace Lib., MS 2564, p. 408. Another account recorded him as saying 'that they need not fear his [Sunderland] coming into the ministry, for that that noble lord would never join with those, who had for 40 years past been betraying their country to Fr[ance]': Strathmore MSS, box 70, folder 1, bdle. 3, newsletter, 21 Apr. 1702.   [521] 'by those' interlined.

[522] For Musgrave's speech in the 1685 Parliament on the supply, which was in effect an acceptance of King James's standing army, see Cobbett, *Parl. Hist.*, iv. 1382; and for his more recent endorsement of the Disbanding Bill of 1698–9, Horwitz, *Parliament, Policy and Politics*, 251.

[523] For Athlone and his Irish grant, see above, pp. 46, 216. The debate followed a report from the forfeitures trustees on a petition from Edmund Francis Stafford, of Brownstown, Co. Meath, and Staffordstown, Co. Antrim, and Samuel Dopping, of Dopping Court, Dublin, on behalf of themselves, and other purchasers, for which see Simms, *Williamite Confiscation*, 101–2, 140–1; and *The Case of the Purchasers under the Earl of Athlone* [?1702]. By the terms of the Forfeitures Resumption Act of 1700 (11 Gul. III, c. 22, ss. xxxi–xxxii), the sum of £21,000 was to be divided among the purchasers, in proportion to their expenses, by way of compensation for losses incurred prior to 10 Aug. 1701. For purchasers from Athlone's estate this amounted in total to £6,170. 16s. 4½d.: HMC, *House of Lords MSS*, NS iv. 212.

[524] From the committee appointed to inspect arrangements for the accommodation of Members of the House of Commons in Westminster Hall and Westminster Abbey during the coronation.

[525] Sir Thomas Cookes, 2nd Bt. (1667–1701), of Norgrove, and Bentley Pauncefote, Worcs. On the controversy surrounding the bill, see Lucy Sutherland, 'The Foundation of Worcester College, Oxford', in id., *Politics and Finance in the Eighteenth Century*, ed. Aubrey Newman (London, 1984), 531–49.

reading we then went into a committee of the whole house upon the bill for making good the deficiencye[526] at which Committee Mr Lownds offered a claus to transfer the securityes that were incumbent on the impropriations in Ireland to other lands charged secured or mortgaged with the impropriations for the same debts (nota by the act of resumption these lands were given I mean the impropriations to build Churches [)][527] there was a short debate whether the Clause should be brought up or not and when it was opened it was not read becaus it was forreign to the bill and there was no instructions to receive such a clause and so it was withdrawn: and when they had refused some considerations refered[528] to them by the house: they setled the manner of their proceedings at the Coronation and it was ordered that they should go two and two according to the manner of the Calling the house Alphabeticall[y] and that no member should presume to take his place in eyther the hall or abbey before the Speak[er] and the house went thither and then we adjourned till the Coronation day

Ap[ri]ll 23d [1702] the house met and the names of the Countyes were Called A[l]phabetically over[529] and the house set out very orderly but no orders were observed after the first setting out: there was one man killed Dead by one of[530] the guard that was to Keep the mobb off severall hurt[531] and nobody there that though[t] the sight[532] worth the trouble and as for the entertainment it Cost the Queen as much as would have made a noble feast for all that were invited I mean that were to be treated that expected it[533] as the Lords and Commons: but all that was saved in the pockets of the managers and undertakers the meat was not extraordinary some hot some Cold some good wine most bad and as for the sweetmeats the lords was well enough ours was shewish but very indifferent

Ap[ri]ll 24th [1702]

publick and private bills were read and finished no debate worth the mentioning[534]

Ap[ri]ll 25 [1702] the same nothing worth observing

---

[526] 'For making good the deficiencies, and preserving the public credit.'

[527] By s. xlvii of the Resumption Act, rectories and tithes impropriated to forfeiting laymen were to be conveyed to trustees; to be used at first for the repair and rebuilding of parish churches in Ireland, and later to augment small livings there. Bishop Ashe and other interested parties had been soliciting 'earnestly' a saving clause for 'our forfeited tithes': Trinity Coll., Dublin, MS 2001/901, Ashe to Bishop King, 2 Apr. 1702.   [528] Originally 'offered'.

[529] 'That the Members of each county might sit together, to the end they might go in the better order . . . to . . . Her Majesty's coronation': *CJ* xiii. 858.   [530] 'one of' interlined.

[531] The *English Post*, 22–4 Apr. 1702, reported the collapse of some jerry-built scaffolds, as a result of which 'several people' were injured.   [532] 'hardly' erased.   [533] 'it' interlined.

[534] *CJ* xiii. 858–9, record two divisions on the Whitby Harbour Bill, and a number of amendments proposed at the report of the bill to preserve the public credit.

Ap[ri]ll 27th [1702]

Nothing worth the mentioning[535]

Ap[ri]ll 28 [1702]

this day was ordered for the reading of the Irish bills and they were read accordingly and Mr Manl[y] stood at the barr with a report relating to some of the Irish bills he complained of the Speakers ill usage in letting him stand so long there and never giving him an opportunity to report he went from the barr up to the Chaire and gave the Speaker some hard words Sir R Gwin observed what he said and Sir Ro[wland] Gwinn said the Speaker behaved himself well in the Chaire and that it was neyther for the honour of the Speaker or the house to have the Chaire bullyed mr St John moved that Manly should withdraw Sir Xto[pher] musgrove agg[r]avated the fault and affront Mr Manly in his place excused himselfe in his place and said he only told th[e] Speaker that he thought it hard that the bill he had in his hand should suffer for no other reason but beca[use] he was the reporter and that he was [sorry] that he had said anything that had offended the house Sir Ed[ward] Seymour excused the matter and so did the Sp[eake]r and then we proceeded (nota Manly was sent to the Tower for[?merly] for some such little boble:[536] for what never another member had been in the least censure

[fo. 11ᵛ]

Ap[ril]l [29]th [1702]

this day we read private bills and after one or two were read the Speaker without any motion called for the [bill] for making of Gloucester hall worcester Colledge: Nota it was very difficult to get a bill read with a motion and many seconds to support the motion: but Sir Xto[pher] musgrove and mr Harcourt and their freinds were there and no freind nor anyone acquainted with the bill for it so that the generous spirit of the Speaker prompted him to call for this bill when his freinds Hartcourt and musgrove were there with their freinds in order to destroy the bill[537] and so it hapned for after the bill was read the 2d time I moved to have it committed and my motion was seconded and Sir Xto[pher] musgrove opposed the Commitment of it saying that it altered Sir Tho[mas] Cookes will and that we ought not to make

---

[535] *CJ* xiii, 860–1, record, *inter alia*, various riders proposed at the 3rd reading of the Land Tax Bill.

[536] On 9 Nov. 1696, for remarks made in the debate on the Fenwick Attainder Bill: *CJ* xi. 581; Cobbett, *Parl. Hist.*, v. 1001–2.

[537] Both Harcourt and Musgrave had close ties with Oxford University, the latter having represented the university constituency in the 1698 Parliament. See Sutherland, 'Foundation of Worcester College', 536, for the university's objections to the bill: the day before the debate Harcourt had complained to Arthur Charlett, the master of University College, that he had received no instructions from Oxford, though he was anxious to oppose the bill.

presidents of such dangerous consequence: I answered that Sir Tho[*mas*]Cookes heir[538] was satisfyed with this settlement of it and that it ought to be Committed and then the truth of this matter would appear to the house and at the report the house would hear the truth mr Hartcourt moved that it might not be committed and said that it altered the [te]stators will and that the heir might indeed be well pleased for that he had a power given him by the act that the will never designed him the question was then put for the Commitment of the bill for it 26 against 47[539] then Sir Xto[*pher*] musgrove Moved to have it rejected and the Speaked [*sic*] said the ays had it I said the noes had it I insisted on it and would have divided the house upon it they said to me why do you spend our time about things of so little moment I said why do you then insist and put such triviall questions: and then we went upon other busines and Sir Ro[*wland*] Gwin moved for a clause to incourage the refiners of sugar[540] and it was then said that it was very inconvenient to bring Clauses into bills that had no relation to the clause and that by such means acts were hard to be found and things passed without due consideration that a rider had the Effect of an act and yet it was dispatched all at one time 3 readings one after another, and then we went into the Committee upon the privateer bill in a committee of the whole house

Ap[*ri*]ll ult [*i.e.* 30th 1702]

this day was spent in the Irish busines wholly my Lord Athlone viz General Gingle Conquered Ireland in one year and the English parliament thanked him for it by their own members and recommended him to the kings favour the king upon it gave him two or 3 thousand pound per an: out of the lands he had Conquered in Ireland this grant was Confirmed to him by the Irish parliament and was resumed by our act of resumption[541] and my Lord pet[*it*]ioned for these reasons to have the grant made to him Confirmed upon the reasons before mentioned: the reasons urged against his petition was [*sic*] that others had Deserved as well as he that were natives and that there was no regard had of their grants and that it would wrong the souldiers at last after a long warm debate we divided 26 and 26 so the Speaker was to decide the matter he gave it

[538] Sir Thomas Winford, 2nd Bt. (*c.*1674–1744), of Glasshampton, Worcs., who, after succeeding Cookes in June 1701, had changed his name to Cookes Winford.

[539] According to *CJ* xiii. 863, the commitment was defeated 43 : 27.

[540] Presumably in the bill for the encouragement of the Greenland trade, to whose committee Cocks had been appointed (*CJ* xiii. 840), the only measure concerned with trade to receive a 3rd reading on this day.

[541] See above, pp. 46, 216. Athlone's estate, totalling over 26,000 Irish acres, was estimated by the purchasers to be worth nearly £4,000 p.a. (*Case of the Purchasers* . . .), and by Athlone's agent, Bartholomew Vanhomrigh, at between £4,000 and £4,200 (Troost (ed.), 'Letters from Van Homrigh to Ginkel', 65–7).

against my Lord Athlone for these reasons first that it overthrow the bill of resumption that was so solemnly made and that it would be too great a destruction to resume some grants of our own natives and to confirm forreigners, nota what my Lord had left was but little and the reason they gave cheifly against Confirming his grant was that he had sold as much as cam to 17000 li.[542] which was reward sufficient there was also a petition prayed[543] from the B[*isho*]ps and Clerg[*y*] that there might be some consideration had of the impropriations of the forfeited Estates that were given to build and repair Churches which wer incumbred with the debts of the forfeiting persons that they Could not be sold to perform the use they were designed for[544] and the design of the petition was to free the impropriations of these debts and put all the Charge upon the other land ingaged for the same debt this was Complyed with and I went to Sir Ed[*ward*] Seymour to desire him to assist me in making a motion to Oblige the Irish Clergy to a residence he moved it and I seconded it I gave my reason which was a very true one that if there was not above 3 or 4 protestants in a parish the parsons usually gave them somthing hired them to remove into some other parish and when the parish was all papist then by the Irish Custom they made sinecures of their livings the bill was ordered to be brought in upon the debate and mr Hartcourt and Gwin[545] were ordered to bring in the bill but for what private ends I know not this Clause was omitted[546] but they promised me to added I [*sic*] by a Claus I know not if they did or not

May 1st [1702]

Irish bills etc.: and then there was a report made relating to Albermale buildings which by articles and agrement could not be set without an act of parliament under under [*sic*] 2 li. 10s the foot there were many debts and incumbrances they laboured under if it remained as it was nobody could make anything of it if the act passed there might something be made of it: it was intimated that if it was builded some lord would build a better house then Sir Ed[*ward*] Seymour had or some house that would hinder his prospect:[547] after

---

[542] Given as £17,684. 12s., in the report of the commissioners of inquiry into the forfeited estates, in 1699: HMC, *House of Lords MSS*, NS iv. 52.   [543] Originally 'considered'.

[544] The petition, from 'the archbishops and bishops of the Church of Ireland', had originally been received and read on 9 Feb., but no further action was then taken. On this day the petition was read again, and the opinion of the forfeitures trustees given. *CJ* xiii. 737, 865.

[545] Sir Rowland Gwynne: ibid. 865.

[546] No record of this motion is to be found in the *Journals* (ibid. 866).

[547] The bill to facilitate the sale of property in the parish of St Martin-in-the-Fields, for payment of the debts of the late John Hinde, goldsmith. Cocks had been included in the committee on the bill, named on 2 Mar.: *CJ* xiii. 771. Albemarle Buildings was situated in what became Bond Street: *London and Its Environs Described . . .* (6 vols.; London, 1761), i. 144. The site of Seymour's London residence has not been identified.

Manly had reported it Sir Ed[*ward*] Seymour moved to have it recommitted for that the Committee had not obeyed the instructions the house gave them and amongst other things Seymour exclaiming against the bill[548] said it was so villanous a busines that there was no sollicitour at liberty rogue enough to manage so foule a matter and at last they were[549] forced to search the prisons for one and in newgate they found one Huson that there was no need of giving him a character for every one knew him now they heard his name Sir Jo[*hn*] Bolles said at first he was against the bill a little afterwards reconciled to it and now he had examined it he was very much for it and as to that part that the Honourable Gent[*leman*] near the barr had said in relation to the sollicitor he must answer that he had known many an honest man Kept in newgate when those that deserved to go thither Went at large this Occasioned a violent laughter and Sir Ed[*ward*] Seymour justly tho foolishly tooke it to himself and said in answer to What that Gent[*leman*] had said of honest mens being kept in newgate and rogues being at liberty I have Known men less mad in bedlam then those that are out up stood Bolles the second time and the house would have him speake and then he said out of the Proverbs[550] unjustice and oppression makes a wise man mad[551] then the report was ordered to ly upon the table but not with an intention to be medled wit[*h*] any more this sessions tuesday was the day for it in the morning I presented a petition from the Gloucestershire Clothiers against the patentees for Embossing of Cloth having their patent inlarged and continued by act of Parliament the Committee had gone thro the bill and the report was ready so I was forced to move to have [*it*] ly upon the table till the report was made[552] and to be then Considered of then there was a foolish heat between Lowns and Sir Jeffery Jefferys and we went into a committee of the Whole house upon the salt[553]

May 2d [*1702*]

Nota before the house sat Captain Huson gave these notes in print[554] in the Speakers Chamber

---

[548] 'exclaiming against the bill' interlined.   [549] 'were' interlined.

[550] 'out of the Proverbs' interlined.

[551] Ecclesiastes 7: 7: 'Surely oppression maketh a wise man mad?' For the precarious state of Bolles's mental health, see above, p. 155, n. 641.

[552] A petition from 'divers clothiers' in Gloucestershire, against a proposed bill to confirm and extend the patent granted in 1695 to Thomas Ferrers and Thomas Matthews, inventors of a process for damasking stuffs. The patentees had petitioned the Commons in February for leave for a bill, and Cocks had been named to the committee to whom the bill was referred. Various objections had been heard by the House on 17 Apr., when the committee was ordered to proceed with drafting a bill. *CJ* xiii. 756, 778, 780, 821, 848–9, 867; *CSP Dom.* 1695, p. 114.

[553] The bill to regulate frauds and abuses in the collection of the salt duties: *CJ* xiii. 868.

[554] 'in print' interlined. Presumably the naval captain Thomas Hewetson, who, having found himself in the Caribbean in 1689 with his ship the *Lion*, continued to act there by virtue of King

Whoever shall presume to say I was a prisonner in newgate upon any pretence whatever is a lyar a villain a corrupted coward witness my hand Thomas Hewetson

Sir Ed[*ward*] Seymour after some Irish bills were read said that he had orders from the Queen to acquaint the house that it was agreed at the convention that the emperour Holland and england should in two

[*fo. 12*]

months declare war unles that in that time the french king and his grandson gave them satisfactio[n ?and ?made] reparation to the emperour for injurye done him by invading the kingdom of Spain and its territoryes and annexing them to france[555] he said this from himself that the last year he was not for runni[*n*]g sillily and hastily into the war and by so doing become principalls that the emperour was now principall and that we had now an opportunity and a necessity to make war to preserve our selves that he did not Know if he should survive it but as long as he lived he would pu[t] his helping hand toward it to promote and carry it on that he had a coppy of the articles in his hand in French and Engli[sh] that the originall was in the lords house that it could not be in two places at the same time but that there they migh[t] have recours to it and then he asked leave to bring it up it was delivered in at the table and read twice and then Sir Ed[*ward*] Seymour moved that we should address the Queen and thank her for communicating this to the house and assure her that we would sufficiently enable her to carry on the warr St Johns stood up to second this motion[556] but the Speaker sai[d] my Lord Conningsbee first then the words and manner presenting it were debated first if it should be presente[d] by the privy Councill that were of the house only they said in answer to that that it would appear better to have it presented by the whole house so that was agreed to as to the words it was debated first if we should say to Carry on the war against france and Spain or against the French king and his grandson untill all the Confederates were satisfyed and so to name them they said France and Spain were the words in the proclamation some of

James's commission and was employed for a time as a quasi-freelance agent by the governments of Bermuda, and the Leeward Islands, before returning to Lisbon in 1692, where he was arrested on suspicion of being about to hand his vessel over to the French. Three years later, he petitioned the Treasury for financial recompense for his losses in the West Indies, and for a recommendation to the Admiralty. *CSP Colonial* 1689–92, pp. 50, 138–9, 154–5, 183, 195, 208, 219, 221, 226–7, 246, 332; Luttrell, *Brief Relation*, ii. 318, 430; *CSP Dom.* 1695, p. 40.

[555] The agreement made at The Hague on 18 Apr. 1702, by representatives of Queen Anne, the Emperor, and the States-General, concerning the declaration of war against France, which is given in detail in *CJ* xiii. 869–70.

[556] Seymour was named first to the resultant committee, to prepare the address, to which St John was also appointed: ibid. 870.

the privy cou[n]cill said so it was agreed to stick to the words in the articles
and not to enumerate particulars least it might crea[te] misunderstandings
hereafter and then we named a small committee to draw up the address and
then the house had an inclination to have the address presented this day that it
might be out on munday with the proclamation for warr and that was
impossible if it was presented aswell as drawn this day so the committee
were ordered to withdraw to prepare the addres and then they expected that
Sir Ed[*ward*] Seymour should go to St Jameses to know the Queens pleasure[557]
and that it might be presented to her this night whilest we were expecting the
addres from the Committee that was withdrawn mr Cooke of Darbyshire
moved to address the [*Queen*] that there should be no officers in the army but
those that were born of English parents[558] he enforced this by saying it was a
shame to have our own want employments and forreigners advanced over their
heads I said I hoped that We should have no such question for it would be very
hard to turn those out of employment that had exposed their lifes for our
service in the last warr and to deny those brave men that have chose rather to
part with their native country their relations and their alls then to part with
their libertyes and religion an opportunity of cutting the throat of that tirant
that had just injured them that I thought that god had not preserved us only
for our sakes but to be a comfort to those poor disconsolate wretches[559] then
they explained it and said it was only intended for the new raised forces: my
Lord Renelagh said this vote would exclude the prince of Denmark from
commanding o[ur] forces[560] and so it would but they made a jest of that,
and not answered it: it was said by others that this would disoblige our allies
and could signify nothing that there was no occasion for such a vote: mr Cook
said there was occas[i]on for such a vote for that one Captain Oldish was an
half pay officer and a forreigner was advanced over his head[561] Nota they

[557] In fact, the House resolved that this duty should be undertaken by all Members who were
Privy Councillors: ibid.
[558] Coke's identity is confirmed by Bonet (DZA, Rep. XI Eng. 25c, fo. 140). He was subsequently a teller in favour of the motion: *CJ* xiii. 870. The wording was 'that no person be an
officer, in England or Ireland, in Her Majesty's new-raised forces, but such as were born in
England, Scotland, or Ireland, or the Dominions thereunto belonging, or of English parents,
unless they were before in half-pay': ibid.
[559] L'Hermitage reports a speech made in these terms, but without naming the Member
responsible; BL Add. MS 17677 XX, fo. 300.
[560] Prince George (1653–1708), Queen Anne's consort, who on 17 Apr. had been appointed
'generalissimo' of all her forces, nominally above the Duke of Marlborough's rank as captain-
general: see *DNB*. Tindal, *Continuation*, i. 545–5, reports this speech without identifying the
speaker. Ranelagh was paymaster-general.
[561] Alexander Oldys, originally commissioned in the 14th Foot in 1689, and raised to a
captaincy by 1696, who had served at the Battle of Landen, and the siege of Namur, where he
was wounded, and who had been placed on half-pay in 1697: Dalton, *Eng. Army Lists*, iii. 53–4.
He was still on half-pay in July 1702: *CSP Dom.* 1702–3, p. 160.

whispered it in the house that Oldish had sold his place and that he had a mind to have it again: Mr Blat[h]weight answered mr Cooke very plainly for he said oldish was no half pay officer and that the forreigner was other [s] said that the forreigners Could not raise men the people did not understand Gibberish and that the question was no more but to prevent forreigners not born of English parents from having command of our forces in England and that they could not think england safe under the command of forreign[562] officers viz if forreigners did command our forces others sa[id] this addres would contradict the other addresses formerly made viz to prefer all the half pay officers[563] and then Cooke said there was an honourable Gent[*leman*] near him that must say if he would speak that allmost all his officers were French: Coll[*onel*] Mordant said that of late he had been disbanded from london and if this vote passed he should be disbanded from his officers his were all half pay officers forreigners civill Gent[*lemen*] and tho he loved his own countrymen very well he could not but own that these French men had behaved themselves very well nay better then the english[564] the debate then languished and they Called for the report nay sais Sir Xto[*pher*] musgrove I will not be against reporting but I promise you wee will have the question afterwards[565] then the Lord Conningsbee moved to add these words to the question except the half pay officers and then the question was put for the adding of this addition to the question and carryed[566] and then the Debate languished of our side and mr king who just came in was against the question for all those additionall words Mr Smith said it was invading the prerogative and that we should grow by degrees and tell the Queen whom shee should employ as well as whom shee should not Mr Cooper said wee should take it unkindly if we should hear that the Dutch had made such an order in relation to the english and that we had reason to expect the same from the Dutch if wee made such an addres he very finely exposed the question mr Boyle spoke well to the same purpose Sir Ed[*ward*] Seymour said

---

[562] 'forces' erased.

[563] A point also noted in Bonet's report of the debate (DZA, Rep. XI Eng. 25c, fo. 141). For the address of 7 Feb. on the half-pay officers, see above, p. 202. William Blathwayt was Secretary at War.

[564] Harry Mordaunt's regiment of marines, which had been disbanded in 1699 (its officers placed on half-pay), was re-formed in Feb. 1702, and by May had been sent to the Channel Islands, where in the following month Mordaunt himself would be given command of all the forces: Dalton, *Eng. Army Lists*, iv. 10, 32; v. 128, 155; *CSP Dom.* 1699–1700, p. 164; 1702–3, p. 61. For the officer-list of this regiment, substantially, but not entirely, composed of Huguenots, see *Cal. Treas. Bks.*, xv. 453; Dalton, *Eng. Army Lists*, v. 128. Tindal, *Continuation*, i. 545, reports Mordaunt as observing, 'that he had some French officers in his regiment, upon whose fidelity and courage he entirely depended, and who kept their companies in as good order, and as complete, as any native'.

[565] Bonet reported Musgrave as speaking in favour of the motion: DZA, Rep. XI Eng. 25c, fo. 140.   [566] A division unrecorded in *CJ* xiii. 870.

the Dutch would not trouble themselves with what we did here he and mr
Smith answered one the Other severall times Sir w[*illia*]m Stricland said he
had rather trust forreigners in the places of state and the army then those
englishmen Who had betrayed their country and were for standing armys in
King Jameses time I sai[d] I said [*sic*] nobody had shewed any reason for the
vote nor did it appear there was like to be occasion that it Could Do no good
but it might do harm and that it would be safer to lett it alone then to put it
that it was very hard to deprive men by a vote of those priviledges we gave
them by act of parliament when we naturalised them that I would put them in
mind of the parable of the jew that fell amongst theives that the levite came by
and shooke his head and that the Samaritan came by and bound up his
wounds and tooke care of him the question was there asked Which was his
neighbour and easily resolved the Samaritan the kingdom of England was the
Jew that fell amongst theives the levite that shooke his head were our levites
and english that instead of binding up our[567] wounds conspired with the
theives to rob and ruine us and would have given up their libertyes and
religion to arbitrary government and to the french power the Samaritan are
those brave out landish forreigners that came over with the prince of orange to
rescue us from those evills and miserys that threatned us[568] I had rather trust
them then such natives and I cannot but think those better men better English
men that worship god after the same manner and wish the good to england
and to the liberties of Europe then those who have no other pretence to be
englishmen then that they have been been [*sic*][569] born of English parents and
have devoured the fat of the land and have wished ill and would destro[y] their
native country Sir John luson[570] desired that we would name them for he
Knew none such: and a little after the question was put for it 91 against it 94
then Mr Wallpoole moved to addres the queen that no officer in the army
should pay anything for renewing their Commissions the Lord Spencer and I
seconded it Sir Xto[*pher*] musgrove said it was reasonable as to the half pay
officers but not for the other I gave the reason for it the Charge of their
Equipage the question was put and carryed and then we read Irish bills till 4 of
the Clock and adjourned to

May the 4th [*1702*]

this day we read the deficiency bill the last time and Mr Hobling offered a
rider to mak[e] good the deficiencyes of the arrears due upon debentures to the
souldiers and Clothiers and transpo[rts][571] it was debated Whether it should

---

[567] 'our' interlined.

[568] Cocks repeats here the analogy he employed in the debate of 5 Jan. 1699: see above, p. 15.

[569] The second 'been' begins a new line in the MS.   [570] Sir John Leveson Gower.

[571] The bill 'for making good several deficiencies and preserving the public credit'. *CJ* xiii. 871,
merely notes a clause 'relating to the transport service, and officers'.

be brought up and then it was ordered to be brought u[p] and then it was debated whether it should be read and it was read the second tim[e

fo. 12ᵛ]

Then [–] the great debate was whether it should be read the third time[572] the reasons against it were that it was giving of money from the Chaire and that was contrary to all rules and dangerous to our Constitution[573] but if they could come at it any other way that was more regular they that spoke most against it declared they would be for it others said it was not so irregular for we had formerly voted to make good all deficiencyes in the Committee to this it was added that the last year we had made one dangerous president in giving 120000 li. for the gaurds and garrisons from the Chair[574] and they offered that if they would withdraw this rider they would annex it to another bill that was before the Committee there were many reflections passed between Sir Edward Seymour and Mr Smith: Seymour and others reflected on the last ministry Mr Smith said he hoped this would be better but it did really not looke very well to have at the beginning when they were resolved to declare war in a day or two to have the Dutch ships taken under the noses of our men of war and [the]y to give no assistance[575] Seymour said when the reasons of it were Known it would not be so lyable to censure I said I hope sir you will not let us spend our time so in unnecessary reflections we are ingaged in a warr with France and I hope we shall reserve all our malice and envy for France and not spend it upon one another I know the hopes and desire to get places has been the only thing that has so long supported party amongst us and I hope that those that have had the places so long will be satisfyed with their so long enjoyment of them and that those that have them now will be satisfyed with the possession of them and that we that never had nor expected any places shall all of us joyne to support our common Country I am sure for my part tho my estate is not a great one yet it serves my turn and I dont spend it all every year if other Gent[*lemen*] would do so too there would not be such hunting after places: All agree that they would be for this Clause were it not

---

[572] The clause.

[573] By an order of 1667, any motion for supply had to be discussed in, and reported from, a committee of the whole House: Erskine May, *Treatise*, 326.

[574] Speaker Arthur Onslow's notes on precedents, 1690–1722, in Surrey RO (Guildford), Onslow MSS, 173/226, confirm that 'the precedent cited last session in the clause about guards and garrisons, that it was brought into the House as a clause, when as neither of them were voted in the comm[*itt*]ee of the whole House'.

[575] At the end of April there had been various reports of French privateers seizing Dutch merchant-men near the English coast: *CSP Dom.* 1702–3, p. 38; Luttrell, *Brief Relation*, v. 167; *Flying Post*, 28–30 Apr. 1702; *English Post*, 29 Apr.–1 May 1702; G. M. Trevelyan, *England under Queen Anne* (3 vols., London, 1930–4), i. 257–8.

dangerous to our constitution to annex it in this way I am of opinion that it will be more dangerous to our Constitution not to reward those that have served us faithfully and much more not to pay those that have shed their blood for us in a former warr now we are forced to use them in this we are now entring upon I will therefore preserve that part of the constitution and venture the other as the less dangerous they still insisted to have Hobling withdraw his rider then littleton Sir Thomas said a Committee of Children if they had a bird in their hands would hardly lose it in hopes to Catch it again mr paget in answer to musgrove said truly he he [sic][576] thought this was not very regular but Gent[lemen] opposed the petition when it was lodged here and when it was to be considered of in the Committee of ways and means they said it would be best when we went upon the deficiencye and now they oppose it there were sure more reasons other reasons then the forms barely this debate lasted about 3 hours and the division for the third reading of it 131 against 66[577] and then they passed the bill and went to St Jameses as the Queen had appoynted and adjourned to

May the 5th [1702]

Irish bills were read and the privateer bill passed with some debate upon [a] rider which would have obliged the master of the ship that ransomed himself to pay double the ransom in a fine this was rejected and Sir R Gwin reported from the committee appoynted to examine Mr Hoogesses petition complaining of the hardships he met with in delaying of justice which proceeded from the neglect of the Lord Grey governour of Barbadoes he complained allso of the undue representations of matters from the com[mi]s[sione]rs of trade[578] the report was laid upon the table and adjourned till to morrow and then upon a debate[579] there was an instruction to the committee to receive a claus to allow the purchasers of my Lord Athlone another third: this was opposed but there was great reason for it for the purchasers bought an Estate granted at the request of an english parliament confirmed by an Irish parliament and the reason given in the debate Why they would not releive my Lord Athlone

---

[576] The second 'he' begins a new line in the MS.

[577] *CJ* xiii. 871, gives 130 : 66.

[578] Thomas Hodges, a counsellor-at-law in Barbados, had originally petitioned the Crown in December 1700 over delays he had suffered in his efforts to obtain a legacy secured on an island plantation: see *Acts of the Privy Council: Colonial Series*, ii. 510; *CSP Colonial* 1700, pp. 754–5; 1702, pp. 51, 106, 295; [Thomas Hodges,] *Plantation Justice* . . . (London, 1702). Ralph Grey (*c*.1661–1706), 4th Baron Grey of Wark, MP Berwick-on-Tweed 1679–81, 1695–8, 1701, had been governor of Barbados, 1698–1701.

[579] On the 2nd reading of the bill for the relief of Protestant purchasers of forfeited estates in Ireland.

according to his petition was becaus he had got 170000 li. from the purchasers now it would have been very hard not to have allowed his grant because he had been sufficiently rewarded by what he had sold to the protestant purchasers and at the same time not to have consideration of those purchasers who Could not recover a farthing of the 2 thirds allowed them by the act of resumption he having no concern in the English dominions: this day in the morning the lord Hartington moved to addres [*the Queen*] to thank her for demonstrating her Zeale for the protestant line in ordering the Princess Sophya to be prayed for[580]

may the 6th [*1702*]

The Queen was to Come to the house of Lords so they read publick and private bills that were ready to pas and the amendments made to the bills by the lords in order to have them pass the Royall assent, there was an amendment to the bill for abjuring the pretended prince of wales which explained and setled the words of the abjuration oath[581] which was to be taken without doors at the Courts of westminster hall and the sessions in the country one amendment was a clause[582] that no one should pay more then one shilling for the taking of the oaths this I said was an invasion of our right of giving of money I recited a president which I had heard often cited in the house of Commons which was that the lords had punished or fined a churchwarden only one halve crown and by that they had prescribed a right of giving money the lawyers favoured the Clause it being for the advantage of the Clerks in westminster hall: So I desired they would only bear me testimony that I had acquainted the house with the matter: then came on the Quakers clause which the Lords had sent down by way of amendment[583] the Quakers had sollicited it much in the house of Commons to have liberty to affirm the oath of abjuration and to leave out only the swearing part and to put the swearing part in as strong words as possibly they Could without an oath they desired me to bring a Claus to this bill by way of a rider and they only failed of having added by not getting it ready time enough and they brought me a short claus which was not full enough so I withdrew it and with great labour and sollicitation they got this clause added to the bill in the lords house by way of amendment and now they had longer and wors Considered of it many of

---

[580] Hartington's responsibility for the motion is confirmed by Bonet: DZA, Rep. XI Eng. 25c, fo. 146. It was duly adopted by the House: *CJ* xiii. 872. By an Order in Council, the Queen had directed that the Electress Sophia be specifically named in the prayers for the Royal Family contained in the Book of Common Prayer, and a newspaper reported that she had indeed been prayed for by name in churches on 3 May: Gregg, *Queen Anne*, 158; *Post Man*, 2–5 May 1702.

[581] The bill to 'declare the alteration in' the Abjuration Oath necessitated by the Queen's accession. [582] 'a clause' interlined.

[583] Clause B in the schedule given in *CJ* xiii. 873.

them sollicited us not to agree with the lords amendment: there are two partys
of them the Pennists and Meadists the Pennists are Jacobites and they were
absolutely against the clause the Meadists are Williamites and they were
inclined for the amendment[584] to stand some sollicited underhand for us to
agree with the lords amendment above board all opposed it, Conyers, King
and I debated for the Clause we said without this they Could not teach Schole
positively[585] nor teach in their conventicles if th[?e] matter was questioned
swear they could not by their religion and if this clause this amendment was
not agreed to there was no other way to preserve them from ruine and that it
was but just [t]o have us all upon the same bottom under the same government
those that argued against agreeing said [o]nly that there was no occasion for
the Clause: and that the Quakers did not desire it: the

[*fo. 13*]

question was put for agreeing with the lords the Speaker said the ays had it the
Noes divided for it a[f]ter [?the question] pu[t] and indeed the ays had it by
the sound a bundantly [*sic*] the Lord Cheney divided the house and the noes
carried it by above 20[586] and then they sent a message to the Lords that they
could not agree with the amendment[587] and then private and publick bills were
read till the Queen came to the Lords house the usher of the black rod[588]
commanded us to attend in the lords hou[se] the Queen said nothing but
passed all the bills that were ready abundance of private bills and then Sir R
Gwin insisted upon it to proceed upon mr Hodgeses report relating to the
Lord Grey and the Com[*mi*]s[*sione*]rs of trade[589] which was adjourned there
were some Gent[*lemen*] that would have had us go into the salt committee[590]

[584] The differences between Quakers on this issue are described in William C. Braithwaite, *The
Second Period of Quakerism* (2nd edn.; Cambridge, 1961), ch. 7, and esp. pp. 207–8. For William
Penn, see above, p. 116; for William Meade (1628–1713), see *DNB*, and Richard L. Greaves and
Robert Zaller (edd.), *Biographical Dictionary of British Radicals in the Seventeenth Century* (3
vols.; Brighton, 1982–4), ii. 234–5.   [585] 'positively' interlined.

[586] The *Journals* give the figures as 53 : 44. Cheyne was not a teller in the division, but was
subsequently named to, and reported from, the committee to prepare reasons for disagreeing with
the Lords. *CJ* xiii. 873–4. On 4 May the Quakers' Meeting for Sufferings had ordered those
Friends appointed 'to solicit Parliament' to seek the rejection of the Lords' clause, and the
subsition of one of the Meeting's own devising, the means of doing so to be left to Lord
Cheyne's discretion: Soc. of Friends Lib., Mins. Meeting for Sufferings, xv. 337–8.

[587] According to *CJ* xiii. 873–4, the House first appointed a committee to prepare reasons for
disagreeing, these to be presented to the Lords at a conference. When the committee reported,
Cheyne was ordered to go to the Lords to desire a conference.

[588] Sir David Mitchell: see above, p. 62, n. 10.

[589] Gwynne had reported on the 5th from the committee examining the petition of Thomas
Hodges.

[590] The committee on the bill for regulating frauds and abuses in the collection of the salt
duties.

and moved and 2d it that the Speaker should leave the Chaire this was debated and a division carried against the Speakers leaving the Chaire[591] then we proceeded on the report and voted first that mr Hodges had not proved any of his allegations next that the allegations in the[592] petition were groundles and scandalous:[593] there was no debate for there was nothing in it Sir Alexand[er] Rigbee in a long set foolish speech commended the Com[mi]s[sione]rs of trade and the Lord Grey[594] the governour Coll[onel] Wheeler complained of the unjust proceedings used in plantations commended by Lord Grey and arraignd all the other governours[595] I moved in Jest that mr Hodges had mistooke the governour upon What Coll[onel] Wheeler said

may 7th [1702]

we proceeded on the Irish bills severall motions were made for instructions to the severall Committees and Sir Tho[mas] littleton moved for a clause to allow the protestant purchasers under my lords Rumney and Aulbermale one third more as we did to my Lord Athlones protestant purchasers this was pretty strongly debated and at last a division those that were for it 89 against it 80 or thereabouts:[596] then those that were against the question said as before that this was not to advantage the purchasers but to save the lords and now they would see whether those Gent[lemen] that had spoke and divided for the protestants had spoke and divided for the Lords or the protestants so they moved that it should be an instruction to the Committee to receive a claus to make trustees and to enable them to [?seue] the lords for two thirds for the use of the publick: the other side said there were only two lords concerned that had been favourites of king will[iam]; that they were very poor insolvent and that this would tear them in peice[s] and whilest We were debating this matter:

---

[591] By 52:49: *CJ* xiii. 876. [592] 'allegations in the' interlined.

[593] 'Vexatious and scandalous': *CJ* xiii. 884.

[594] Rigby had begun his political career as a protégé of the Earl of Macclesfield, an old associate of the Greys. Furthermore, at this time his business ventures, centred upon trade to Leghorn, were in some difficulty, and he may have hoped to curry favour with the Board of Trade for himself and his partners. Draft biography, History of Parliament Trust.

[595] Wheeler was a West Indian planter who had been a member of the Barbados assembly 1695–1700, serving on one occasion as its Speaker. In 1699 Grey had recommended him strongly, but unsuccessfully, to the Board of Trade for appointment to the island's council, and had indeed taken it upon himself to have Wheeler sworn in before the Board's refusal was made known. 'Some Records of the House of Assembly at Barbados', *Journal of the Barbados Museum and Historical Society*, 11 (1943–4), 171–4; *CSP Colonial* 1699, pp. 86–7, 381, 454; 1700, pp. 35–6, 44–5, 189.

[596] Given as 82:79 in *CJ* xiii. 885. A motion for an instruction to the committee on the bill for the relief of Protestant purchasers of Irish forfeited estates, to allow a third more of the purchase money to 'the residue of the purchasers'. For the provision already made for purchasers from Lord Athlone, see above, p. 282. For the cases of purchasers from Lords Albemarle (Arnold Joost van Keppel (1669–1718), 1st Earl) and Romney, see Simms, *Williamite Confiscation*, 125.

Sir R Gwin interrupted the debate and said sir the time is Come that the Lords appoynted for the conference about the amendments: Somebody said the conference was ov[er] up stands Sir John Mordant and said sir the conference is over We have been at it[597] this made the yong members laugh the old members that Keep to order were surprised: for before the members go to the Conference the Speaker from the Chair puts the house in mind of it or some member moves it and th[?en] they read over the names of the Committee that were to draw up the reasons and generally the same ar[e] appoynted to be managers at the Conference and till they re turn [*sic*] the house sits still:[598] the Speaker Who is very exact and able at orders was much surprised himself and told the house the methods and manner of proceeding as to these things and complained of the Gent[*lemen*] that had made this breach The Lord Cheney was ready at the barr to report the conference and then he begged pardon for his ignorance and forgetfulnes and was out of countenance at last Sir R Gwin said sir What will you do you will not send to the lords to tell them that these Gent[*lemen*] had no orders for What they did and that you will not stand to it: if you will not do that you must take no notice of the breach of our order but let the lord report and others take more care for the future to which the house agreed and then we went on with the last debate the question was put and seconded for two thirds only I speaking against that said I could come up to one third: but not for two: Some artificially said this was giving of money from the Chaire[599] I said this Could not be said to be giving of money for it only transferred the right the purchasors had upon a Consideration to the publick and that we must not Consider persons but What is fit for us to Do: I Could have observed that we ought not to have any regard to the luxury and prodigality of these lords from Whence their pove[r]ty Came and at last we came to the question and tho nobody moved nor spoke to one third but me yet the Cunning Speaker said that the question was moved and seconded for two th[irds] but the debate ran for one so he put the question for one third thinking that the more likely to go for the[600] instruction 84 against 89 then it was moved that it should be an instru[c]tion to the Committee to receive a clause to enable the trustees to pay the purchasers all the purchase money and to sell the land to the best bidder there was a vote before passed that the purchasers should repurchase[601] at 13 years value and they said this vote would contradict that Which Would not agree with the orders of the house but they might alter the bill as they pleased at the Committee so that motion

---

[597] The conference concerning the Abjuration Bill. Gwynne was one of the managers: Mordaunt was not: *CJ* xiii. 873, 885.

[598] A procedure described in [Hatsell,] *Precedents* (2nd edn., 4 vols.; London, 1796), iv. 47.

[599] See above, p. 281.   [600] 'question' erased.   [601] 're' interlined.

fell and it being past one they were forced to ask leave to make a motion which must be seconded and agreed to by the house before any new motion Can be made after one[602] this was done in relation to some Irish bill[603] on Which we proceeded till we adjourned

May 8th [*1702*]

this day the Jews bill was reported[604] the same provision for their children as turn protestants as is for the papists children that change their religion it was moved to leave out words that made the determination of my Lord Chancelour finall and hindered their appeales to the Lords upon these words the house divided for[605] leaving the words out 57[606] against 44[607] Mr Boyle reported the Queens answer to our addres of thanks for having the princes SoPhya[608] prayed for the answer was that shee would omit nothing that would promote the protestant interest[609] and then we went into the salt Committee

May 9th [*1702*]

Irish bills and a pretty long debate about mr nugents bill[610] but no division

may 11th [*1702*]

finishing of bills and the salt Committee

May 12th [*1702*]

Irish bills Were reported and those that had purchased my Lady Orkeneys grant viz the private estate of King James were ordered to be reimbursed their purchase mon[ey][611] but this did reach those Who increased their rent presently to inlarge the term [?–

*fo. 13*ᵛ

?of ?upon es]t[at]es they were possessed of before: and this increas of rent commenced before their new t[e]rm comnmenced mr paget brough[t] in a claus for their releive viz that they should be repaid their increase of rent I [2de]d paget Sir Ed[*ward*] Seymour and Sir Xto[*pher*] musgrove opposed we

[602] See above, p. 109, n. 318.

[603] Probably the bill for the relief of Robert Edgeworth (see above, pp. 263–4), to which a rider was offered at the 3rd reading: *CJ* xiii. 885.

[604] The bill 'for obliging the Jews to maintain and provide for their Protestant children' (see above, pp. 245–6).   [605] 'keeping' erased.   [606] 'for' erased.

[607] *CJ* xiii. 886, record that the division, on the question to retain the words, 'which order shall be final', was lost by 54 : 30.

[608] The letter 'P' begins a new line in the MS.

[609] That 'she will omit no occasion of supporting the Protestant religion and maintaining the true interest of England': *CJ* xiii. 886.

[610] Edward Nugent (d. 1733), of Donore, Co. Westmeath: see Lodge, *Peerage of Ireland*, i. 125. His case is discussed in Simms, *Williamite Confiscation*, 92–5.

[611] A further amendment to the bill for the relief of Protestant purchasers of Irish forfeited estates: *CJ* xiii. 890; see above, p. 271. For Lady Orkney, and her grant (from King James II's private estate in Ireland), see above, p. 157, n. 653; p. 214, n. 173.

had the right of our side in the Debate Mr paget told Sir Ed[*ward*] Seymour
the great honour and esteem he had for him made him concerned and mistrust
himself when he differed from[612] that Honourable Gent[*leman*] viz Sir
Ed[*ward*] Sey[*mour*]: Sir Ed[*ward*] Sey[*mour*] answered he and that honourable gent[*leman*] often differed and that he had as little regard for his
judgment as he had for his, mr pagett admired the occasion that
Gent[*leman*] had for such a reflection for he spoke in earnest he said he
hoped that he had so behaved himself in that house that he had never given
occasion for Gent[*lemen*] to think that he said one thing and thought another
he must say that he beleived that Honourable Gent[*lemen*] judged of him by
himself the debate ended in a division and those for the Claus carryed it Bolles
offered a petition from Counter and Bernardi to have them banished and not
imprisonned Anderton seconded Bolles but nobody minded eyther so the bill
was put and agreed to by the house[613]
may 13th [*1702*]

the lords sent word that they did not insist on the amendments (relating to
the quakers) in the abjuration bill: Some Irish bills Were read and we went
upon the report of the Salt act[614] and there was one divi[si]on of 12 against
52[615] Nota upon the report you Can offer no amendment to the body of the
bill till the amendments are reported and agreed or disagred unto by the
house[616]

14 [*May 1702*] nothing worth mention[*i*]ng
may the[617] 15 [*1702*]

a Debate being rose in relation to the inquiry into the abilityes and Conditions
of some to be naturalised the house would not agree to the motion for it was
to have it reported to the house so that it would have been impossible to have
had the bill pas there was a little division[618] and then there was a Committee
of the Whole hous to consider of the bill for laying a duty upon buying selling
or bargaining for shares in any Joint stock of corporations[619] the Committee
were divided 92 two [*sic*] for the Duty 64 against it the reasons for the bill was

---

[612] 'Sir Edward' erased.
[613] The bill to continue the act of 1698 (9 Gul. III, c. 4), for the imprisonment, without benefit
of habeas corpus, of 'Captain' John Counter alias Romsey, John Bernardi, *et al.*, implicated in the
Assassination Plot of 1696 but saved from prosecution for treason by the fact that only one witness
was available to testify against them: see HMC, *Downshire MSS*, i. 658; *CSP Dom.* 1696, pp. 206–
7.   [614] The bill to regulate frauds and abuses in the collection of the salt duties.
[615] The clause for a drawback on salt exported to Scotland was defeated 50 : 14: *CJ* xiii. 892.
[616] As set out in McKay (ed.), *Observations* . . . 72.   [617] '14', then '15', erased.
[618] The motion, on the 2nd reading of the bill to naturalize Stephen Benovad, John Girard, *et
al.*, was for an instruction to the committee to inquire into the 'ability and condition of the
persons named in the said bill'. It was lost 46 : 30. *CJ* xiii. 894.
[619] 'Joint stocks of corporations'.

to rais money to prevent Cheats and frauds the reasons against it Were that it laid a Charge and duty upon that money that was lent to the publick and by act of Parliament excused from taxes there was also a long Debate relating to Sir w[*illia*]m Ashurst bill for giving him leave to get an Irish debt out of the Irish forfeitures the bill was sillily drawn and the Lords made amendments to the preamble of [*it*] and when the amendmends were Considered they said this was giving of money and they could not Consent to agree with the lords but this was more party then reason and the question was put and carryed for Sir w[*illia*]m 21[620]

may 16[621] [*1702*]

intirely Irish

May[622] 18 [*1702*]

a petition of the lady fitsgerrald in relation to the Bill that was to provide for the family of the Trants[623] an order to the Com[*mi*]s[*sione*]rs of accounts to lay before the house the names of those that neglect or refuse to bring in their accounts before the Com[*mi*]s[*sione*]rs[624] a message from the lords of their having agreed to severall bills

May 19 [*1702*]

Iris[*h*] bills and Sir R Gwin reported the reasons for disagreeing with the lords in the amendments to the privateer bill a message from the Lords that they had agreed to severall bills ordered[625] that a conference be desired with the lords upon the subject matter of the last Conference relating to the addres to the Queen:[626] and that the Com[*mi*]s[*sione*]rs for taking and stating the publick acCounts lay before the next parliament the names of the agents and

---

[620] Ashurst, one of the MPs for London, sought relief from the effects of the Irish Forfeitures Resumption Act on his own grant, which had been made in order to satisfy a debt of over £1,200, owed by two Dublin merchants, Andrew and Richard Dalton, both of whom had been outlawed after the Revolution. For the bill, and the Lords' proceedings on it, see HMC, *House of Lords MSS*, NS v. 33. The division, carried 98 : 77, was on agreeing with the first of the six amendments, the remainder being then carried without a further vote: *CJ* xiii. 894.

[621] '16th', then '15', erased.   [622] '17', then '16', erased.

[623] See above, p. 266. The petition had been presented on 16 May, when it was ordered to lie on the table until the bill was reported. The report occurred on the 18th, but the *Journals* make no further mention of the petition: *CJ* xiii. 895, 898. 'Lady Fitzgerald' has not been positively identified, though she may have been Ellen, wife of the exiled Irish Jacobite Sir John Fitzgerald, 2nd Bt., of 'Gortnatubrid', Co. Limerick.

[624] Two days earlier the commissioners for stating the accounts of the army and the prizes had been ordered to lay before the House on the 18th a list of those agents or officers who had failed to bring in their accounts. This they now did. *CJ* xiii. 895, 897.

[625] 'ordered' interlined.

[626] The Lords' address for a prohibition on commerce with France and Spain: *CJ* xiii. 898.

officers that neglect or refuse to bring in their accounts[627] all the rest Irish: the reason of the addres was becaus reported that my Lord nottingam[628] should intend to have a pacquet go all the War from dover to calais: they were jealous of my Lord nottingam and therefore addressed the Queen to engage the emperour and States Generall and the other allies to joyn with the Queen in prohibiting all intercours between us and the subjects of france and Spain

May 20 [1702]

Sir R Gwin reported the Conference with the Lords and so did the lord Hartingdon:[629] a message from the Lords that they have agreed with the Commons in the amendments to the addres and to severall bills all the rest Irish

May 21 [1702] was spent in finishing Irish bills and [a] bill of naturalisation and both houses[630] went upon notice from by [sic] a message that both houses were to attend her majesty at five of the clock at St jameses with the addres and that the lords intend to attend at that time

May 22d [1702]

the Speaker reported the Queens answer[631] which was my Lords and Gent[lemen]

I shall propose to the allies to joyne with me in prohibiting all intercours and correspondence with France and Spain accord I am too much concerned for the publick welfare to omit any necessary precautions for the protection of our trade all the rest Irish only a message of the lords of their agreeing to severall bills

May 23d [1702] a message to the Lords relating to their agreement to some Irish bills

resolved that an Humble address be presented to her Majesty that shee would be Graciously pleased to bestow some dignity in the Church of windsor upon Francis Gastrell dr. of divinity Chaplain to the house[632]

resolved that an humble addres be presented to her Majesty etc. that to give all necessary encouragement for Making Captures on the enemye and particularly that shee will grant Commissions and charters to such of her subjects

---

[627] Agents and officers concerned were now ordered to bring in their accounts ot the commissioners by 24 June: *CJ* xiii. 901.

[628] Daniel Finch (1647–1730), 2nd Earl of Nottingham, and later 7th Earl of Winchilsea. A Tory, he had been reappointed on 2 May 1702 as Secretary of State for the Southern Department.

[629] Gwynne reported from the conference on the Privateers Bill; Hartington from the conference on the address: *CJ* xiii. 903.

[630] 'both houses' was originally 'they'.   [631] Given in full in *CJ* xiii. 905.

[632] Francis Gastrell (1662–1725), Speaker's chaplain, and later Bishop of Chester.

as shall endeavour to make acquisitions in the East and west Indies with such directions instructions and limitations as her Majesty shall think best in her great wisdom:[633] both the addresses to be presented by the Members of the house that were privy Councellours

May 24th [*recte 25th 1702*]

mr Boyle[634] acquainted the house that her majesty will take care the Addres shall be complyed with so far as is in her power viz relating to the Captures and acquisition in the Indies

Mr Secretary Hedges[635] acquainted the house that her majesty[636] having[637] allways a regard to the recommen[da]tion of this house will bestow on Dr Gastrell some considerable dignity in the Church

[*fo. 14*]

a message from the lords relating to the agreement of Irish bills

Sir David mitchell Gent[*leman*] usher of the black rod[638] delivered this message from her majesty viz

Mr Speaker the Queen commands this Honourable house to attend her majesty in the house of peers the hous went and severall Publick and private acts passed and the Queen made this following speech to them[639]

My lords and Gent[*lemen*]

I cannot conclude this session without repeating my hearty thanks to you for all your great care of the publick and the many marks you have given of your duty and Affection to me

And I must thank you Gent[*lemen*] of the House of Commons in particular both for the supplyes you have given[640] to support me in this necessary war and the provisions you have made for the debts contracted in the former your great justice in making good these deficiencyes will be a lasting honour and credit to the nation: [I] wish the difficulties they have brought upon us may be a warning to prevent such inconveniencie[s] for the future I must recommend to you all in your severall Countryes the preservation of the publick peace and due execution of the laws

I shall allways wish that no difference of opinion among those that are Equally affected to my service may be the occasion of heats and animosities among themselves: I shall be very Carefull to preserve and maintain the act of

---

[633] This address is given in full in *CJ* xiii. 907.

[634] 'repor[*ted*]' erased. Boyle spoke in his capacity as Chancellor of the Exchequer. The text of the message is given in *CJ* xiii. 907.

[635] Sir Charles Hedges, appointed on 2 May as Secretary of State for the Northern Department. Text given in *CJ* xiii. 907.

[636] 'will' erased.

[637] 'having' interlined.

[638] See above, p. 62, n. 10.

[639] The text of the speech is given in *LJ* xvii. 150.

[640] 'me' erased.

toleration and to set the minds of all my people at quiet my own principles must allways keep me intirely Firm to the interest and religion of the Church of Englang [*sic*] and will incline me to Countenance those who have the trust Zeale to support it) [*sic*] and afterwards the lord Keeper of the Great Seale by her majestys command prorogued the parliament untill tuesday the 7th of July [*1702*] and must by the demise of the King be determined in six months after his demise[641]

[641] There follows an entry 'taken out of the Lords journalls' for 24 Feb. 1702, recording the passage of the Abjuration Act and the ensuing protest, given in full, by Lord Winchelsea, and nine other peers: omitted here.

Abbrevs. Used in Appendices

Adm., adm.	Admiralty, admiral
brig.-gen.	brigadier-general
bro.	brother
Bt.	Baronet
c.-in-c.	commander-in-chief
col.	colonel
col.of ft.	colonel of foot
com.	commissioner
cos.	cousin
cr.	created
custos rot.	custos rotulorum
dep.	deputy
Drag. Gds.	Dragoon Guards
e.	elder
fa.	father
Ft. Gds.	Foot Guards
gov.	governor
Horse Gds.	Horse Guards
jt.	joint
jun.	junior
kntd.	knighted
lt.-gen.	lieutenant-general
maj.-gen.	major-general
R. Drags.	Royal Dragoons
regt.	regiment
ret.	retired
s.	succeeded
sec.	secretary
sen.	senior
surv.	surviving
yr.	younger

APPENDIX 1

Brief Biographical Notices of MPs Mentioned in the Text

Information given is as follows: name; dates of birth and death if known; principal address(es); dates of parliamentary service; date(s) of any creation or succession to peerage, or significant acquisition of baronetcy or knighthood; Crown office(s) held during the period covered by the diary, Speakership of House of Commons, and/or any major offices held at other times; where a biographical notice or further details may be found.

ANDERTON, JAMES (b. *c.*1661), of I. Temple, and Wigan, Lancs. MP Ilchester 1701(Feb.)–5. Dep. custos rot., Lancs. July 1698. See Sir R. Somerville, *Office-Holders in the Duchy and County Palatine of Lancaster from 1603* (London, 1972), 101.

ASHURST, Sir HENRY, 1st Bt. (1645–1711), of St John's St., Clerkenwell, Middx. and Waterstock, Oxon. MP Truro 1681, 1689–95, Wilton 1698–1700, 1701(Dec.)–1702. See Woodhead, *Rulers of London*, 19; *HC 1660–90*, i. 558–9.

ASHURST, Sir WILLIAM (1647–1720), of Watling St., London, and Highgate, Middx. MP London 1689–1710. Com. of excise July 1698–June 1700. See Woodhead, *Rulers of London*, 19; *HC 1660–90*, i. 559–60.

AYLMER, MATTHEW (*c.*1658–1720), of Westcliffe, nr. Dover, Kent. MP Dover 1697–1713, 1715–d. Vice-adm. 1693 (ret. from active service Nov. 1699), Adm. of the Fleet 1708, c.-in-c. 1709–11, 1714–18; com. of the navy 1694–July 1702; gov., Deal Castle 1701. See *DNB*; Charnock, *Biog. Nav.*, ii. 35–40; *HC 1715–54*, i. 425–6.

BACON, Sir EDMUND, 4th Bt. (1672–1721), of Gillingham, Norf. MP Orford 10 Feb. 1700–8. See *Complete Baronetage*, ii. 32.

BERTIE, CHARLES (*c.*1640–1711), of Uffington, nr. Stamford, Lincs. MP Stamford 1678–9, 1685–d. Sec. to Treasury 1673–9; treasurer of Ordnance 1681–June 1699, June 1702–5. See *HC 1660–90*, i. 639–43.

BERTIE, PEREGRINE (*c.*1663–1711), of Great Marlborough St., Westminster. 2nd son of 3rd Earl of Lindsey. MP Boston 1685–7, 1690–8, 1708–d., Truro Dec. 1701–1705. Vice-Chamberlain of Household 1692–1706; PC 1695–d. See *HC 1660–90*, i. 645.

BIDDULPH, Sir MICHAEL, 2nd Bt. (*c.*1654–1718), of Elmhurst, Staffs., and Westcombe, Kent. MP Lichfield 1679–81, 1689–90, 1695–1700, Dec. 1701–5, 1708–10. See *HC 1660–90*, i. 650.

BIRCH, JOHN (*c.*1666–1735), of Garnstone, nr. Weobley, Herefs. MP Weobley Feb. 1701–2, 1705–15, 1715–32, 1734–d. Attorney-Gen., Brec., Glam., and Rad. 1695–1712; Queen's serjt. 1712; cursitor baron of Exchequer 1729–d. See Foss, *Judges of Eng.*, viii. 102–4; *HC 1715–54*, i. 462.

BLAAKE, HENRY (*c.*1659–1731), of Pinnells, nr. Calne, Wilts., and Bristol. MP Calne 1695–1700, Dec. 1701–2.

BLACKETT, Sir WILLIAM, 1st Bt. (*c.*1657–1705), of Greyfriars House, Newcastle-upon-

Tyne, and Wallington Hall, Northumb. MP Newcastle-upon-Tyne 1685–90, 1695–1700, 1705–d. See R. Welford, *Men of Mark 'Twixt Tyne and Tweed* (3 vols.; London, 1895), i. 301–5; *HC 1660–90*, i. 663–4.

BLAKE, Sir FRANCIS (1638–1718), of Ford Castle, Northumb. MP Berwick-upon-Tweed 1689–95, 1698–1700, Northumb. Dec. 1701–5. See *HC 1660–90*, i. 664–5.

BLATHWAYT, WILLIAM (*c*.1649–1717), of Scotland Yard, Whitehall, and Dyrham Park, Glos. MP Newtown, I.o.W. 1685–7, Bath 1693–1710. Clerk of PC 1678–d.; sec of trade and plantations 1679–96; auditor-gen. of plantations 1680–d.; Sec. at War 1683–9, 1689–1704; ld. of trade 1696–1707. See *DNB*; R. A. Preston, 'The Life and Career of William Blathwayt', MA thesis (Leeds, 1932); Gertrude A. Jacobsen, *William Blathwayt: A Late Seventeenth-Century English Administrator* (New Haven, 1932); *HC 1660–90*, i. 667–8.

BLISS, THOMAS (*c*.1647–1721), of Maidstone, Kent. MP Maidstone 1698–1702, 1704–8. See J. M. Russell, *The History of Maidstone* (Maidstone, 1881), 202–3, 351–2.

BOLLES, Sir JOHN, 4th Bt. (1669–1714), of Scampton, Lincs. MP Lincoln 1690–1702. See *Complete Baronetage*, ii. 48; C. Illingworth, *A Topographical Account of the Parish of Scampton . . . Together with Anecdotes of the Family of Bolle* (1810), 50–1.

BOYLE, CHARLES (1674–1731), of Marston Bigot, Som. Bro. of Lionel Boyle, 3rd Earl of Orrery [I]. MP Huntingdon Feb. 1701–5. *s*. as 4th Earl of Orrery 1703; cr. Baron Boyle 1711. Receiver-gen. in alienation office Oct. 1699–aft. 1715; ld. of bedchamber 1714–16. See E. Budgell, *Memoirs of the Life and Character of the Late Earl of Orrery*, (London, 1732), 155–255; *DNB*; *CP* x. 179–80.

BOYLE, HENRY (d. 1725), of Pall Mall, Westminster. 2nd son of Ld. Clifford. MP Tamworth 1689–90, Camb. Univ. 1692–1705, Westminster 1705–10. cr. Baron Carleton 1714. Ld. of Treasury June 1699–May 1702; Chancellor of Exchequer Dec. 1701–8; PC 1701; Sec. of State 1708–10; Ld. President 1721–d. See *CP* iii. 26–7; *HC 1660–90*, i. 701.

BOYLE, LIONEL, 3rd Earl of Orrery [I] (1670–1703), of Withyham, Sussex. MP E. Grinstead 1695, 1698–1700, Dec. 1701–2. See *CP* x. 178–9.

BRERETON, EDWARD (*c*.1642–1725), of Borras, Denb. MP Denbigh boroughs 1689–1705. See *HC 1660–90*, i. 714.

BREWER, JOHN (*c*.1654–1724), of New Romney, Kent, and Gray's Inn. MP New Romney 1689–1710. Receiver-gen. of prizes June 1702–7. See *HC 1660–90*, i. 717.

BRIDGES, WILLIAM (d. 1714), of the Tower of London, and Wallington, Surr. MP Liskeard 1695–d. Surveyor-gen. of Ordnance June 1702–d.

BROMLEY, WILLIAM (1663–1732), of Baginton, Warws. MP Warws. 1690–8, Oxf. Univ. 21 Mar. 1701–d. Speaker, House of Commons 1710–13; Sec. of State 1713–14. See *DNB*; *HC 1715–54*, i. 493–4.

BROMLEY, WILLIAM (1656–1707), of Holt Castle, Worcs. MP Worcester 1685–1700, Worcs. Dec. 1701–2, 1705–d. See *HC 1660–90*, i. 725–6.

BROTHERTON, THOMAS (*c*.1657–1702), of Chancery Lane, Middx., and the Hey, Newton, Lancs. MP Liverpool 1694–5, Newton 1695–Nov. 1701. See W. D. Pink and A. B. Beavan, *The Parliamentary Representation of Lancashire . . .* (London, 1889), 285.

BROWNLOW, Sir WILLIAM, 4th Bt. (1665–1701), of Humby, Lincs. MP Peterborough 1689–98, Bishop's Castle 1698–3 Feb. 1700. See *HC 1660–90*, i. 736.

BRYDGES, GEORGE RODNEY (d. 1714), of Avington, nr. Winchester, Hants. MP Haslemere 1690–8, Whitchurch Feb. 1701–d. In receipt of a pension of £1,200 on the Irish civil list since 1697 (*Cal. Treas. Bks.*, xii. 123; xvi. 433).

BRYDGES, JAMES (1674–1744), of Canons, Little Stanmore, Middx. 1st son of 5th Baron Chandos. MP Hereford 1698–1714. s. fa. 1714; cr. Earl of Carnarvon 1714, Duke of Chandos 1719. Paymaster-gen. of forces abroad 1705–13; PC 1721. See *DNB*; *CP* iii. 130; C. H. C. Baker and Muriel I. Baker, *The Life and Circumstances of James Brydges, First Duke of Chandos . . .* (Oxford, 1949).

BUCKNALL, RALPH (d. 1710), of Mapledurham, Hants, and St Giles-in-the-Fields, Middx. MP Petersfield 1701.

BURNABY, ANTHONY (d. 1708), of Middle Temple. MP Stockbridge Dec. 1701–5.

BYERLEY, ROBERT (1660–1714), of Middridge Grange, Heighington, Co. Durham, and Goldsborough, Yorks. MP Co. Durham 1685–90, Knaresborough 1695–d. Commr. for Privy Seal 1711–13. See *HC 1660–90*, i. 759.

CALTHORPE, REYNOLDS (1655–1720), of Elvetham, Hants. MP Hindon 1698–13 May 1701, Dec. 1701–2, 1705–8, 1709–10, 1715–d. See *HC 1715–54*, i. 518.

CAVENDISH, WILLIAM, Marquess of Hartington (*c.*1673–1729), of Chatsworth, Derbys., and Devonshire House, Piccadilly. 1st surv. son of 1st Duke of Devonshire. MP Derbys. 1695–1701, Castle Rising 2 Feb.–2 July 1702, Yorks. 1702–7. s. fa. 1707. PC 1707; Ld. Steward 1707–10, 1714–16. See J. Grove, *The Lives of All the Earls and Dukes of Devonshire* (London 1764), separate pagination; *CP* iv. 344.

CHASE, JAMES (*c.*1649–1721), of Westhorpe House, Marlow, Bucks. MP Great Marlow 1690–1710. Apothecary to William and Mary, Anne, and George I 1690–d.

CHEYNE, WILLIAM, 2nd Viscount Newhaven [S] (1657–1728), of Chesham Bois, Bucks., and Chelsea, Middx. Known as Ld. Cheyne. MP Amersham 1681–7, Dec. 1701–2, 1705–7, Appleby 1689–95, Bucks. 1696–1701, 1702–5. Com. for privy seal 1690–2; clerk of the pipe 1703–6, 1711–d. See *CP* ix. 539–40; *HC 1660–90*, ii. 52–3.

CHILD, Sir FRANCIS (1642–1712), of East End House, Fulham, and the Marygold by Temple Bar, London. MP Devizes 1698–1702, 1705–8, 1710–13, London 1702–5. Ld. mayor, London 1698–9. See F. G. Hilton Price, *A Handbook of London Bankers . . .* (2nd edn.; London 1890–1), 31–2; id., *The Marygold by Temple Bar* (London, 1902), 79–85; Woodhead, *Rulers of London*, 46.

CHURCHILL, GEORGE (1654–1710), of St James's, Westminster. Bro. of 1st Duke of Marlborough. MP St Albans 1685–1708, Portsmouth 1708–d. Capt., RN 1678–93; groom of bedchamber to Prince George of Denmark 1689–1708; major, 3rd Life Gds. 1691–2; Ld. of Adm. Oct. 1699–Jan. 1702; member of Adm. Council May 1702–8. See *DNB*; A. L. Rowse, *The Early Churchills . . .* (London, 1956), 352–64; *HC 1660–90*, ii. 68.

CLARKE, EDWARD (d. *c.*1723), of Norwich. MP Norwich Dec. 1701–2.

CLARKE, EDWARD (*c.*1651–1710), of Chipley, Som. MP Taunton 1690–1710. Com. of excise 1694–June 1700. See B. Rand (ed.), *The Correspondence of John Locke and Edward Clarke* (Oxford, 1927).

CLAYTON, Sir ROBERT (1629–1707), of Old Jewry, London, and Marden Park, Godstone, Surr. MP London 1679–Mar. 1681, 1689–90, 1695–8, Feb. 1701–2, 1705–d., Bletch-ingley 1690–5, 1698–1700, 1702–5. Com. of customs 1689–97. See *DNB*; Woodhead, *Rulers of London*, 48; *HC 1660–90*, ii. 84–7; F. T. Melton, *Sir Robert Clayton and the Origins of English Deposit Banking 1658–1685* (Cambridge, 1986).

COCKS, CHARLES (*c.*1642–1727), of Worcester. MP Worcester 1694–5, Droitwich 1695–1708. Clerk of the patents in Chancery May 1699–*c.*1708. See W. R. Williams, *The Parliamentary History of the County of Worcester . . .* (Hereford, 1897), 129.

COKE, THOMAS (1675–1727), of Melbourne, Derbys. MP Derbys. 1698–1700, Dec. 1701–10, Grampound 1710–15. Teller of Exchequer 1704–6; Vice-Chamberlain of Household 1706–27. See J. J. Briggs, *The History of Melbourne . . .* (2nd edn.; London, n.d.), 109–11. .

COLCHESTER, MAYNARD (1665–1715), of Westbury Court, Westbury-on-Severn, and the Wilderness, Abbinghall, Glos. MP Glos. Dec. 1701–8. See J. Stratford, *Good and Great Men of Gloucestershire . . .* (1867), 404–6.

COLT, JOHN DUTTON (1643–1722), of Stafferton House, Leominster, Herefs. MP Leominster 1679–Mar. 1681, 1689–98, 8 Jan.–3 Apr. 1701. Collector of customs, Bristol, 1689–Feb. 1700. See *HC 1660–90*, ii. 110–12.

COMYNS, JOHN (*c.*1667–1740), of Highlands, nr. Maldon, Essex. MP Maldon Dec. 1701–8, 1710–15, 1722–6. Baron of Exchequer 1726–36, chief baron 1738–d.; justice of Common Pleas 1736–8. See Foss, *Judges of Eng.*, viii. 112–14; *HC 1715–54*, i. 569.

CONINGSBY, THOMAS, 1st Baron Coningsby [I] (1657–1729), of Hampton Court, Herefs. MP Leominster 1680–1710, 1715–16. cr. Baron Coningsby 1716, Earl of Coningsby 1719. Ld. justice [I] 1690–2; vice-treasurer [I] Oct. 1698–1710; PC 1693–1724. See *DNB*; *CP* iii. 395–6; *HC 1660–90*, ii. 115–17; *HC 1715–54*, i. 570–1.

CONWAY, FRANCIS SEYMOUR: see SEYMOUR.

CONYERS, JOHN (1650–1725), of Hoe St., Walthamstow, Essex. MP East Grinstead 1695–1708, 1710–d., West Looe 1708–10. High steward of Havering, Essex 1688–1715. See *HC 1715–54*, i. 572.

COOKE, JOHN (*c.*1648–1726), of Petworth, Suss. MP Midhurst 1681, Arundel 1694–5, 1698–1702. See *HC 1660–90*, ii. 119–20.

COPLEY, Sir GODFREY, 2nd Bt. (*c.*1653–1709), of Sprotborough, Yorks. MP Aldborough 1679–Mar. 1681, Thirsk 1695–d. See *HC 1660–90*, ii. 127.

CORNBURY, Viscount: see HYDE, EDWARD.

COTESWORTH, WILLIAM (1665–1730), of St James Clerkenwell, Middx. MP Great Grimsby 10 Jan.–6 Mar. 1701, Dec. 1701–2, 1705–10, 1713–15, Boston 1711–12, 1712–13. See J. C. Hodgson, 'Observations on the Pedigree of Cotesworth of the Hermitage', *Proceedings of the Society of Antiquaries of Newcastle-upon-Tyne* (4th ser.), i (1923–4), 264–5.

COTTON, Sir ROBERT, 1st Bt. (*c.*1635–1712), of Combermere, Chesh. MP Chesh. 1680–Mar. 1681, 1689–1702. Steward, lordship of Denbigh 1689–1702; custos rot., Denbighs. 1699–1702. See *HC 1660–90*, ii. 142–3.

COULSON, THOMAS (*c.*1645–1713), of Friday St., London. MP Totnes 1692–5, 1698–1708, 1710–13.

COWPER, WILLIAM (*c.*1665–1723), of Colne Green, Hertingfordbury, Herts. MP Hertford 1695–1700, Bere Alston 7 Mar. 1701–5. cr. Baron Cowper 1706, Earl Cowper 1718. KC 1689; Ld. Keeper 1705–7; PC 1705; Ld. Chancellor 1707–10, 1714–18; ld. justice 1714; Ld. High Steward 1716. See *DNB*; *CP* iii. 483–4; Lord Campbell, *Lives of Ld. Chancellors*, iv. 257–429.

COX, CHARLES (d. 1729), of Southwark, Surrey. MP Southwark 1695–10 Nov. 1702, 25 Nov. 1702–13.

COXE, CHARLES (*c.*1661–1728), of Lower Lypiatt, Glos. MP Cirencester 1698–1705, 1708–9, 1709–13, Gloucester 1713–22. Serjt.-at-law Oct. 1700; King's serjt. Feb. 1701; puisne judge, Brec., Glam., and Rad., June 1702–4, chief justice 1704–14. See *HC 1715–54*, i. 590–1.

CUTTS, JOHN, 1st Baron Cutts [I] (*c.*1661–1707), of Childerley, Cambs. MP Cambs. 1693–1702, Newport, I.o.W. 1702–d. Brig.-gen. 1693, maj.-gen. 1696, lt.-gen. 1703; gov., I.o.W. 1693–d.; col., 2nd Ft. Gds. 1694–d.; lt.-gen. of forces [I] 1705–d.; ld. justice [I] 1705. See *DNB*; *CP* iii. 583–5; S. S. Swartley, *The Life and Poetry of John Cutts* . . . (Philadelphia, 1917).

DAVALL, Sir THOMAS (1644–1712), of London, and Dovercourt, Harwich, Essex. MP Harwich 1695–1708.

DAVENANT, CHARLES (1656–1714), of Red Lion Sq., Middx. MP St Ives 1685–7, Great Bedwyn 1698–Nov. 1701. Com. of excise 1678–89; inspector-gen. of imports and exports 1703–d. See D. A. G. Waddell, 'The Career and Writings of Charles Davenant', D.Phil. thesis (Oxford, 1954); id., 'Charles Davenant (1656–1714): A Biographical Sketch', *Economic History Review* (2nd ser.), 11 (1958–9), 279–88; *HC 1660–90*, ii. 196.

DAVERS, Sir ROBERT, 2nd Bt. (*c.*1653–1722), of Rougham, and Rushbrooke, Suff. MP Bury St Edmunds 1689–1701, 1703–5, Suffolk 1705–d. See *HC 1660–90*, ii. 196–7; *HC 1715–54*, i. 606.

DORMER, ROBERT (1650–1726), of Lee Grange, Bucks. MP Aylesbury 22 Feb. 1699–1700, Bucks. Dec. 1701–2, 1705–6, Northallerton 1702–5. Serjt.-at-law 1706; justice, Common Pleas 1706–d. See Foss, *Judges of Eng.*, viii. 29–30.

DRAKE, Sir WILLIAM, 4th Bt. (*c.*1659–1716), of Mount Drake, Devon, and Ashe House, Dorset. MP Honiton 1690–1713, Honiton and Dartmouth 1713–15. Ld. of Admiralty 1710–14. See W. H. Wilkin, 'Notes on the Members for Honiton, 1640–1688', *Transactions of the Devonshire Association* . . . , 66 (1934), 263.

DUNCOMBE, (Sir) CHARLES (1648–1711), of Teddington, Middx., and Barford, Wilts. MP Hedon 1685–7, Yarmouth, I.o.W. 1690–5, Downton 1695–1 Feb. 1698, 1702–d., Ipswich 1701. Kntd. 20 Oct. 1699. See *DNB*; Hilton Price, *Handbk. of London Bankers*, 108–10; Woodhead, *Rulers of London*, 63; *HC 1660–90*, ii. 242–3.

DYOTT, RICHARD (1667–1719), of Freford, Staffs. MP Lichfield 1690–5, 1698–1708, 1710–15. See J. C. Wedgwood, *Staffordshire Parliamentary History* . . . (3 vols., Staffs. Historical Colls., William Salt Soc.; Stafford, 1917–33), ii. 176.

ETTRICK, WILLIAM (1651–1716), of Holt Lodge, Dorset, and Middle Temple. MP Poole 1685–7, Christchurch 1689–d. Attorney to Prince George of Denmark by 1692–1708. See *HC 1660–90*, ii. 277–8; *HC 1715–54*, ii. 17–18.

EYRE, ROBERT (*c.*1667–1735), of New House, Whiteparish, Wilts. MP Salisbury 1698–1710. Solicitor-Gen. 1708–10; justice, Queen's Bench 1710–23; ld. chief baron of Exchequer 1723–5; ld. chief justice, Common Pleas 1725–d. See Foss, *Judges of Eng.*, viii. 121–3.

FAIRFAX, THOMAS, 5th Lord Fairfax [S] (1657–1710), of Denton, and Cookbridge Hall, Yorks. MP Malton 1685–7, Yorks. 1689–1702, 1707. Col., 3rd Drag. Gds. 1694; brig.-gen. 1696. See *CP* v. 231–2; *HC 1660–90*, ii. 293–4.

FELTON, Sir THOMAS, 4th Bt. (1649–1709), of Whitehall, Westminster, and Playford, Suff. MP Orford 1690–10 Feb. 1700, Bury St Edmunds 1701 (Dec.)–d. Master of the hawks 1675–1703; master of the Household 1689–1708, comptroller 1708–d. See *Complete Baronetage*, i. 155.

FINCH, HENEAGE (*c.*1649–1719), of Albury, Surrey. MP Oxf. Univ. 1679, 1689–98, Feb. 1701–3, Guildford 1685–7. cr. Baron Guernsey 1703, Earl of Aylesford 1714. Solicitor-Gen. 1679–86; PC 1703–8, 1711–d.; chancellor, Duchy of Lancaster 1714–16. See *CP* i. 364–5; *HC 1660–90*, ii. 322–4.

FOLEY, EDWARD (1676–1747). 2nd son of Thomas Foley, sen., of Witley Court, Worcs. (q.v.); yr. bro. of Thomas Foley, jun., of Witley Court (q.v.) MP Droitwich Dec. 1701–11, 1732–41. See *HC 1715–54*, ii. 40.

FOLEY, PAUL (*c.*1645–99), of Stoke Edith, Herefs. Yr. bro. of Thomas Foley, sen., of Witley Court (q.v.) MP Hereford 1679 (Mar.)–1681 (Mar.), 1689–d. Speaker, House of Commons 1695–8. See *DNB*; *HC 1660–90*, ii. 336–8.

FOLEY, PHILIP (1648–by 1716), of Prestwood, Kingswinford, Staffs. Yr. bro. of Thomas Foley, sen., of Witley Court (q.v.) and Paul Foley (q.v.) MP Bewdley Mar. 1679–Mar. 1681, Stafford 1689–90, 1695–1700, Droitwich 1690–5, 1701. See *HC 1660–90*, ii. 338–9.

FOLEY, THOMAS (*c.*1670–1737), of Stoke Edith, Herefs. 1st son of Paul Foley (q.v.) MP Weobley 1691–8, 12 Dec. 1698–1700, Hereford Feb. 1701–22, Stafford 1722–7, 1734–d. Ld. of trade 1712–13; jt. auditor of imprest 1713–d. See *HC 1715–54*, ii. 41.

FOLEY, THOMAS, sen. (*c.*1641–1701), of Witley Court, Worcs. MP Worcs. Mar. 1679–1698, Droitwich 14 Jan. 1699–1700, 13 Jan.–1 Feb. 1701. See *HC 1660–90*, ii. 340.

FOLEY, THOMAS, jun. (1673–1733), of Witley Court, Worcs. 1st son of Thomas Foley, sen. of Witley Court (q.v.) MP Stafford 1694–1712. cr. Baron Foley 1712. See *CP* v. 535.

FOX, Sir STEPHEN (1627–1716), of Farley, Wilts. and Whitehall. MP Salisbury 1661–Jan. 1679, 1685–7, 1714–15, Westminster 1679, 1691–8, Cricklade 26 Jan. 1699–1700, Feb. 1701–2. Paymaster of forces 1661–76, 1679; Ld. of Treasury 1679–85, 1687–9, 1690–May 1702, First Ld. 1696–7. See *DNB*; C. Clay, *Public Finance and Private Wealth: The Career of Sir Stephen Fox, 1627–1716* (Oxford, 1978); *HC 1660–90*, ii. 356–9.

FREKE, THOMAS (1660–1721), of Hannington, Wilts. MP Cricklade 1685, 1689–90, Weymouth and Melcombe Regis 1691–1700, Lyme Regis 1705–10. See *HC 1660–90*, ii. 366–7.

FREMAN, RALPH (*c.*1665–1742), of Aspenden Hall, Herts. MP Herts. 1697–1727. See *HC 1715–54*, ii. 54.

FURNESE, Sir HENRY (*c.*1658–1712), of London, and Waldershare, Kent. MP Bramber 1698–14 Feb. 1699, Sandwich 3 Jan.–19 Feb. 1701, 1701 (Dec.)–d. cr. Bt. 1707. See *Complete Baronetage*, v. 1.

GODFREY, CHARLES (*c.*1648–1715), of Windmill St., Westminster. MP Malmesbury 1689–90, Chipping Wycombe 1691–1713. Dep. constable of the Tower 1694–?1698; master of the jewel office May 1698–1704. See Rowse, *Early Churchills*, 132–4; *HC 1660–90*, ii. 402–3.

GORGES, HENRY (*c.*1665–1718), of Eye, nr. Leominster, and the Mynde, Herefs. MP Herefs. 1698–1708, Weobley 1708–10, Leominster 1713–15. See W. R. Williams, *The Parliamentary History of the County of Hereford . . .* (Brecknock, 1896), 58.

GRANVILLE, JOHN (1665–1707), of Stowe, Corn. 2nd son of 1st Earl of Bath. MP Launceston 1685–7, Plymouth 1689–90, Newport 1698–1700, Fowey 1701, Corn. Dec. 1701–3. cr. Baron Granville 1703. Lt.-gen. of the Ordnance June 1702–5; PC June 1702–d. See *CP* vi. 88; *HC 1660–90*, ii. 434–5.

GULSTON, WILLIAM (1652–1737), of M. Temple. MP Bridport 1701 (Feb.)–1702.

GWYN, FRANCIS (*c.*1648–1734), of Llansannor, Glam., and Forde Abbey, Devon. MP Chippenham 1673, 1673–9, Cardiff boroughs 1685–7, Christchurch 1689–95, 1701 (Dec.)–1710, 1717–22, Callington 1695–8, Totnes 11 Jan. 1699–1701, 1710–15, Wells 1722–7. Clerk of PC 1679–85; Under-Sec. of State 1681–3; jt.-sec. to Treasury 1685–7; chief sec. [I] Dec. 1700–3; PC [I] June 1701; ld. of trade 1711–13; Sec. at War 1713–14.

See *HC 1660–90*, ii. 455–7; *HC 1715–54*, ii. 92; P. Jenkins, 'Francis Gwyn and the Birth of the Tory Party', *Welsh History Review*, 11 (1982–3), 283–301.

GWYNNE, Sir ROWLAND (*c.*1658–1726), of Llanelwedd, Rad. MP Rad. 1679–Mar. 1681, 1689–90, Brec. 1690–5, 1698–1702, Bere Alston 1695–8. Treasurer of the chamber 1689–92; custos rot., Rad. 1689–1702. See *HC 1660–90*, ii. 458–9; *DNB (Missing Persons)*.

HALES, Sir CHRISTOPHER, 2nd Bt. (*c.*1670–1717), of Whitefriars, Coventry, Warws. MP Coventry 1698–1701, 24 Feb. 1702–7, 1711–15. See *Complete Baronetage*, iii. 116; Whitley, *The Parliamentary Representation of . . . Coventry . . .* , 124.

HAMMOND, ANTHONY (1668–1739), of Somersham, Hunts. MP Hunts. 1695–8, Camb. Univ. 1698–1701, Huntingdon 1702–5, New Shoreham 1708. Com. of navy May 1702–8. See *DNB*.

HARCOURT, SIMON (1661–1727), of Stanton Harcourt, Oxon. MP Abingdon 1690–1705, 1708–9, 1710, Bossiney 1705–8, Cardigan Boroughs 1710. cr. Baron Harcourt 1711, Viscount Harcourt 1721. Solicitor-Gen. June 1702–7; PC 1710–14, 1722–d.; Ld. Keeper 1710–13; Ld. Chancellor 1713–14; ld. justice 1714, 1723, 1725, 1727. See *DNB*; *CP* vi. 298–300; Campbell, *Lives of Ld. Chancellors*, iv. 430–500.

HARLEY, EDWARD (1664–1735), of Eywood, Herefs. Yr. bro. of Robert Harley (q.v.) MP Droitwich 1695–8, Leominster 1698–1700, 3 Apr. 1701–22. Jt. auditor of imprest 1703–d. See *HC 1715–54*, ii. 110.

HARLEY, ROBERT (1661–1724), of Brampton Bryan, Herefs. MP Tregony 1689–90, New Radnor 1690–1711. cr. Earl of Oxford 1711. Steward of Crown manors, Rad. 1691–1714; Speaker, House of Commons, 1701–5; Sec. of State 1704–8; PC 1704–8, 1710–14; Chancellor of Exchequer 1710–11; Ld. Treasurer 1711–14. See *DNB*; *CP* x. 263–6; R. B. Ballinger, 'Robert Harley: His Early Life and Connexions', M.Litt. thesis (Cambridge, 1955); B. W. Hill, 'The Career of Robert Harley, Earl of Oxford, from 1702 to 1714', Ph.D. thesis (Cambridge, 1961); A. McInnes, *Robert Harley, Puritan Politician* (London, 1970); *HC 1660–90*, ii. 498–9.

HARLEY, THOMAS (*c.*1667–1738), of Kinsham Court, Herefs. Yr. bro. of Robert Harley (q.v.) and Edward Harley (q.v.) MP Rad. 1698–1715. Jt. sec. of Treasury 1710–14. See W. R. Williams, *The Parliamentary History of the Principality of Wales . . .* (Brecknock, 1895), 174–5.

HARTINGTON, Marquess of: see CAVENDISH, WILLIAM.

HARVEY, MICHAEL (*c.*1635–1712), of Clifton Maybank, Dorset. MP Weymouth and Melcombe Regis 1679–Mar. 1681, 1689–1701. See *HC 1660–90*, ii. 509–10.

HARVEY, STEPHEN (1655–1707), of Betchworth, Reigate, Surrey. MP Reigate 1698–d. Puisne judge, Anglesey, Caern., and Merion. 1706–d. See W. R. Williams, *The History of the Great Sessions in Wales . . .* (Brecknock, 1899), 112–13.

HARVEY, WILLIAM (1663–1731), of Hempstead, Essex. MP Old Sarum 1689–1705, 1708–10, Appleby 1705–8, Weymouth and Melcombe Regis 1711–13, 1714–15, Essex 1715–16, 1722–7. See *HC 1660–90*, ii. 510–11; *HC 1715–54*, ii. 116.

HAWLES, Sir JOHN (*c.*1645–1716), of Lincoln's Inn. MP Old Sarum 1689–90, Wilton 1695–8, 1702–5, Mitchell and Bere Alston 1698–1700, Truro 4 Mar.–11 Nov. 1701, St Ives Dec. 1701–2. KC 1694; Solicitor-Gen. 1695–June 1702. See *DNB*; *HC 1660–90*, ii. 514.

HEATHCOTE, Sir GILBERT (1652–1733), of Forest House, Low Leyton, Essex. MP London 1–22 Feb. 1701, Dec. 1701–10, Helston 1715–22, Lymington 1722–7, St Germans 1727–d. See *DNB*; Evelyn D. Heathcote, *An Account of Some of the Families Bearing the Name of Heathcote . . .* (Winchester, 1899), 79–86; *HC 1715–54*, ii. 123.

HEDGES, Sir CHARLES (*c.*1650–1714), of Richmond, Surrey, and Compton Bassett, Wilts. MP Orford 1698–10 Feb. 1700, Dover 1701, Malmesbury Dec. 1701–2, Calne 1702–5, W. Looe 1705–13, E. Looe 1713–d. Judge of Adm. court 1689–Dec. 1701; Sec. of State Nov. 1700–6; PC Nov. 1700. See *DNB*.

HERNE, FREDERICK (1667–1714), of St Stephen, Colman St., London. Neph. of Sir Joseph Herne (q.v.) MP Dartmouth 1698–d.

HERNE, Sir JOSEPH (1639–99), of King's Arms Yard, Colman St., London. MP Dartmouth 1689–d. See Woodhead, *Rulers of London*, 88–9; *HC 1660–90*, ii. 537–8.

HERNE, NATHANIEL (1668–1722), of St Michael Bassishaw, London. Yr. bro. of Frederick Herne (q.v.) MP Dartmouth Jan. 1701–13.

HERVEY, JOHN (1665–1751), of Aswarby, Lincs., St James's Sq., Westminster and Ickworth, Suff. MP Bury St Edmunds 1694–1703. cr. Baron Hervey 1703, Earl of Bristol 1714. See *DNB*; *CP* ii. 322–3; *Hervey Letterbks.*; S. H. A. Hervey (ed.), *The Diary of John Hervey, First Earl of Bristol . . . 1688 to 1742* (Suff. Green Bks. 2; Wells, 1894).

HICKMAN, Sir WILLOUGHBY, 3rd Bt. (1659–1720), of Gainsborough, Lincs. MP Kingston-upon-Hull 1685–7, E. Retford 1698–1700, 15 Apr.–11 Nov. 1701, 28 Nov. 1702–6, Lincs. 1713–d. See *HC 1660–90*, ii. 546; *HC 1715–54*, ii. 137.

HOBLYN, JOHN (*c.*1660–1706), of Middle Temple and Bradridge, Corn. MP Bodmin 1695–d.

HOLLAND, Sir JOHN, 2nd Bt. (*c.*1669–*c.*1724), of Quidenham Hall, Norf. MP Norf. Dec. 1701–10. Comptroller of Household 1709–11; PC 1709. See *Complete Baronetage*, ii. 74.

HOOPER, NICHOLAS (1654–1731), of Inner Temple, Barnstaple, and Fulbrook, Devon. MP Barnstaple 1695–1715. Serjt.-at-law 1700; Queen's serjt. 1702–8. See Daphne Drake, 'Members of Parliament for Barnstaple, 1689–1832', *Trans. Devon. Assoc.*, 73 (1941), 182.

HOPKINS, EDWARD (*c.*1675–1736), of Coventry, Warws. MP Coventry Dec. 1701–2, 1707–10, Eye 1713–27. Com. of rev. [I] 1716–22; chief sec. [I] 1721–4; PC [I] 1721. See Mary D. Harris, 'Memoirs of the Right Hon. Edward Hopkins, M.P. for Coventry', *EHR* 34 (1919), 491–504; *HC 1715–54*, ii. 148–9.

HOTHAM, Sir CHARLES, 4th Bt. (1663–1723), of Scorborough, nr. Beverley, Yorks. MP Scarborough 1695–1702, Beverley, 1702–d. Col. of ft. 1705; brig.-gen. 1710. See *HC 1715–54*, ii. 151–2.

HOWARD, WILLIAM (*c.*1674–1701). 2nd surv. son of 2nd Earl of Carlisle. MP Carlisle 1695–1700, Northumb. 24 Jan. 1701–d. See R. S. Ferguson, *Cumberland and Westmorland M.P.'s from the Restoration to the Reform Bill of 1867 . . .* (1871), 383.

HOWE, EMANUEL SCROPE (d. 1709). MP Morpeth 1701–5, Wigan 1705–8. Col. of ft. 1695–9. See *DNB*.

HOWE, JOHN GROBHAM ('Jack') (*c.*1657–1722), of Stowell, Glos. MP Cirencester 1689–90, 1690–8, Glos. 1698–Nov. 1701, 1702–5. Vice-Chamberlain of Household 1689–92; PC Apr. 1702–14; jt. paymaster-gen. Dec. 1702–14. See *DNB*; *HC 1660–90*; ii. 608–10.

HOWE, RICHARD GROBHAM (*c.*1652–1730), of Chedworth, Glos. MP Hindon 1679–Jan. 1681, Tamworth 1685–7, Cirencester 1690–8, Wilts. 1701, 1702–27. s. fa. as 3rd Bt. 1703. See *HC 1660–90*, ii. 610; *HC 1715–54*, ii. 156.

HUNGERFORD, Sir GEORGE (*c.*1637–1712), of Cadenham, Bremhill, Wilts. MP Cricklade 1661–Jan. 1679, Calne Oct. 1679–81 (Mar.), Wilts. 1695–Nov. 1701. See *HC 1660–90*, ii. 614–16.

HUSSEY, Sir EDWARD, 3rd Bt. (*c*.1661–1725), of Caythorpe, and Welbourne, Lincs. MP Lincoln 1689–95, 1698–1700, Dec. 1701–5. See *HC 1660–90*, ii. 622.

HUSTLER, Sir WILLIAM (*c*.1658–1730), of Ackham, Cleveland, and Little Hatfield, Holderness, Yorks. MP Northallerton 1695–1702, 1705–10, Ripon 1702–5. See W. W. Bean, *The Parliamentary Representation of the Six Northern Counties of England* (Hull, 1890), 958.

HYDE, EDWARD, Viscount Cornbury (1661–1723). Only son of 2nd Earl of Clarendon. MP Wilts. 1685–95, Christchurch 1695–Nov. 1701. s. fa. 1709. Col., R. Drags. 1685–9; gov., New York June 1701–3, New York and New Jersey 1703–8; PC 1711. See *CP* iii. 267–8; A. D. Pierce, 'A Governor in Skirts', *Proceedings of the New Jersey Historical Society*, 83 (1965), 1–9; *HC 1660–90*, ii. 624–5; P. A. Stellhorn and M. J. Birkner (edd.), *The Governors of New Jersey* (New Jersey Historical Commission; Trenton, NJ, 1982), 36–8.

HYDE, HENRY, Lord Hyde (1672–1753). Only son of 1st Earl of Rochester. MP Launceston 1692–1711. s. fa. 1711, cos. Edward Hyde (q.v.) as 4th Earl of Clarendon 1723. Major, Horse Gds. 1691–3; jt. vice-treasurer and paymaster-gen. [I] 1710–16; PC 1710–14. See *CP* iii. 268.

JACOB, THOMAS (*c*.1653–*c*.1730), of Norton, Wilts. MP Wootton Bassett 1695–8, Dec. 1701–2.

JEFFREYS, Sir JEFFREY (*c*.1652–1709), of St Mary Axe, London, and the Priory, Brecon. MP Brecon 1690–8, Feb. 1701–d. See Williams, *Parl. Hist. Wales*, 24–5.

JEKYLL, Sir JOSEPH (1663–1738), of Brookmans, N. Mimms, Herts. MP Eye 1697–1713, Lymington 1713–22, Reigate 1722–d. Serjt.-at-law Oct. 1700, King's serjt. Oct. 1700; chief justice, Chester 1697–1717; PC 1717; commr. of Great Seal 1725; Master of Rolls 1717–d. See *DNB*; Foss, *Judges of Eng.*, viii. 127–31.

JERVOISE, THOMAS (1667–1743), of Herriard, Hants. MP Stockbridge 1691–5; Hants 1698–1702, 1705–8, 1709–10, Plympton Erle 1702–3, Hindon 1704–5. See F. H. T. Jervoise, 'The Jervoises of Herriard and Britford', *The Ancestor*, 3 (1902), 7–8.

JOHNSON, WILLIAM (*c*.1660–1718), of London. MP Aldeburgh 1689–d., Orford 10 Feb.-19 Dec. 1700. Gent. of privy chamber 1690–1702. See *HC 1660–90*, ii. 656–7.

JONES, RICHARD, 1st Earl of Ranelagh [I] (1641–1712), of Chelsea, Middx. MP Plymouth 1685–7, Newtown, I.o.W. 1689–95, Chichester 1695–8, Marlborough 1698–Nov. 1701, W. Looe Dec. 1701–3. Chancellor of Exchequer [I] 1668–74; PC [I] 1668; com. of Treasury [I] 1670–5; vice-treasurer [I] 1674–82; gent. of bedchamber 1679–85; paymaster-gen. 1685–Dec. 1702; PC 1692–d. See *DNB*; *CP* x. 732–5; *HC 1660–90*, ii. 661–3.

KING, PETER (1669–1734), of Ockham, Surrey. MP Bere Alston Feb. 1701–15. Kntd. 1708; cr. Baron King 1725. ld. chief justice, Common Pleas 1714–25; PC 1715; Ld. Chancellor 1725–33; ld. justice 1725, 1727. See *DNB*; *CP* vii. 275–6; Campbell, *Lives of Ld. Chancellors*, iv. 567–647.

KING, THOMAS (?bef. 1660–1725), of St Margaret's Westminster, and Sheerness, Kent. MP Queenborough 1696–1708, 1710–22. Lt.-col., 1st Ft. Gds. 1689; lt.-gov., Sheerness 1690–d. See *HC 1715–54*, ii. 190.

LAWSON, GILFRID (*c*.1657–1749), of Brayton, Cumb. MP Cumberland 1701, 1702–5, 1708–34. See *HC 1715–54*, ii. 200.

LEVESON, GOWER, Sir JOHN, 5th Bt. (1675–1709), of Trentham, Staffs. MP Newcastle-under-Lyme 1692–1703. cr. Baron Gower 1703. Chancellor, Duchy of Lancaster May 1702–6; PC 1702–7. See *DNB*; *CP* vi. 36–7.

LITTLETON, Sir THOMAS, 3rd Bt. (1647–1710), of N. Ockendon, Essex, and Stoke St Milborough, Salop. MP New Woodstock 1689–1702, Castle Rising 1702–5, Chichester 1705–8, Portsmouth 1708–d. Ld. of Treasury 1696–June 1699; Speaker, House of Commons 1698–1700; treasurer of navy June 1699–d. See *DNB*; *HC 1660–90*, ii. 751–3.

LOWNDES, WILLIAM (1652–1724), of Chesham, Bucks. MP Seaford 1695–1715, St Mawes 1715–22, E. Looe 1722–d. Clerk of Treasury *c.*1675–95, sec. 1695–d. See *DNB*; *HC 1715–54*, ii. 225–6.

MACKWORTH, Sir HUMPHREY (1657–1727), of Gnoll Castle, Neath, Glam. MP Card. 1701, 1702–5, 1710–13, Totnes 1705–8. See *DNB*; Mary Ransome, 'The Parliamentary Career of Sir Humphry Mackworth, 1701–1713', *University of Birmingham Historical Journal*, 1 (1947–8), 232–54; S. Evans, 'An Examination of Sir Humphrey Mackworth's Industrial Activities . . . ', MA thesis (Wales, 1953).

MAINWARING, Sir JOHN, 2nd Bt. (1656–1702), of Baddiley, Chesh. MP Chesh. 1689–1702. See *HC 1660–90*, iii. 4.

MANLEY, JOHN (*c.*1655–1713), of Truro, Corn. MP Bossiney 1695–8, Dec. 1701–1708, 1710–d., Camelford 1708–10. Sub-com. of prizes at Plymouth June 1702–5.

MANNERS, JOHN, Lord Roos (1676–1721). 1st surv. son of 1st Duke of Rutland. MP Derbys. 1701, Leics. Dec. 1701–2, 1710–11, Grantham 1705–10. s. fa. 1711. See *CP* xi. 266–7.

MARSHAM, Sir ROBERT, 4th Bt. (1650–1703), of Whorn's Place, Cuxton, and The Mote, nr. Maidstone, Kent, and Bushey Hall, Herts. MP Maidstone 1698–8 Dec. 1702. One of the six clerks in Chancery 1680. See *Complete Baronetage*, iii. 284.

MARTIN, JOSEPH (*c.*1649–1729), of London, and Wanstead, Essex. MP Ipswich 1701, Hastings 1710–15. Kntd. 1712. Consul in Moscow 1702–5.

MASON, CHARLES (aft. 1656–1739), of Rockley Hall, nr. Bishop's Castle, Salop. MP Bishop's Castle 1695–13 May 1701, Dec. 1701–31 Mar. 1702, 1702–5, 1708–10, 1715–22, 1726–7, Montgomery boroughs 1705–8. Jt. comptroller of the Mint 1696–May 1701. See *HC 1715–54*, ii. 245.

MEREDITH, THOMAS (*c.*1665–1701). MP Kent 1701(Feb.)–d.

MERES, Sir THOMAS (1634–1715), of The Close, Lincoln, and Southampton Sq., Bloomsbury, Middx. MP Lincoln 1659, 1660–87, 1701, 1702–10. Ld. of Adm. 1679–84. See *HC 1660–90*, iii. 48–59.

MITFORD, MICHAEL (*c.*1655–1707), of London, and Clapham, Surrey. MP Gt. Bedwyn Dec. 1701–2.

MOMPESSON, CHARLES (1670–1714), of Mompesson House, The Close, Salisbury, and Little Bathampton, Wyley, Wilts. MP Old Sarum 1698–1705, 1705–8, Wilton 1708–13.

MOMPESSON, ROGER (*c.*1661–1715), of Lincoln's Inn, and Dunford, Dorset. MP Southampton 27 Dec. 1699–1701. Chief justice, New York 1704–d., New Jersey 1705–9, 1709–11, Pennsylvania 1706. See J. G. Wilson and J. Fiske (edd.), *Appleton's Cyclopedia of American Biography* (6 vols.; New York, 1894) iv. 354.

MONCKTON, ROBERT (*c.*1659–1722), of S. Newbald, Yorks. MP Pontefract 1695–8, Feb. 1701–13. Ld. of trade 1704–14. See Bean, *Parl. Rep. Six N. Cos.*, 994.

MONTAGU, CHARLES (*c.*1658–1721), of Belford, Northumb. 5th son of 1st Earl of Sandwich. MP Durham 1685–7, 1695–1702. See *HC 1660–90*, iii. 82.

MONTAGU, CHARLES (1661–1715), of Jermyn St., Westminster. MP Maldon 1689–95, Westminster 1695–13 Dec. 1700. cr. Baron Halifax 1700, Earl of Halifax 1714. Clerk to PC 1689–92; Ld. of Treasury 1692–4, First Ld. 1694–Nov. 1699, 1714–d. PC 1694–

Mar. 1702, 1714–d.; Chancellor of Exchequer 1694–May 1699, auditor Nov. 1699–1714; ld. justice, 1698, 1699, 1714. See *DNB*; *CP* vi. 245–6; M. J. H. Henderson, 'Charles Montague, Earl of Halifax, 1661–1715: A Study of Patronage', M. Litt. thesis (Bristol, 1971); *HC 1660–90*, iii. 80–2.

MONTAGU, CHRISTOPHER (*c.*1655–1735), of St Anne's, Westminster, and Middle Temple. E. bro. of Charles Montagu of Jermyn St. (q.v.) MP Northampton 1695–1702. Com. for stamp duty May 1694–Aug. 1698; com. of excise Aug. 1698–June 1700, 1706–d.; auditor of Exchequer Sept. 1698–Nov. 1699.

MONTAGU, EDWARD (*c.*1672–1710), of Lackham, Wilts. MP Chippenham 1698–1700.

MONTAGU, IRBY (*c.*1666–1704). E. bro. of Charles Montagu of Jermyn St. (q.v.) and of Christopher Montagu (q.v.) MP Maldon 1695–1701. Capt. and lt.-col., 1st Ft. Gds. 1694–d.

MONTAGU, SIDNEY WORTLEY: see WORTLEY.

MOORE, ARTHUR (*c.*1666–1730), of Fetcham Park, Surrey. MP Gt. Grimsby 1695–1700, Dec. 1701–15, 1721–2. Ld. of trade 1710–14. See *HC 1715–54*, ii. 270–1.

MORDAUNT, HARRY (1663–1720). Bro. of 3rd Earl of Peterborough. MP Brackley 1692–8, Feb 1701–2, 1705–8, Richmond 1708–d. Col. of ft. 1694–Aug. 1708, 1703–13, of marines Aug. 1698–May 1699, Apr. 1702–3; treasurer of Ordnance June 1699–June 1702, 1705–12. See *HC 1715–54*, ii. 272.

MORDAUNT, Sir JOHN, 5th Bt. (*c.*1650–1721), of Walton D'Eiville, Warws. MP Warws. 1698–1715. See *Complete Baronetage*, i. 62.

MORDAUNT, JOHN, Lord Mordaunt (*c.*1681–1710). 1st son of 3rd Earl of Peterborough. MP Chippenham Feb. 1701–5, 1705–8. Col., 21st Ft. 1704–6, 1709–d., 28th Ft. 1706–9; brig.-gen. 1710. See *CP* x. 503–4.

MORGAN, THOMAS (1664–1700), of Tredegar, Mon. MP Brecon 1689–90, Mon. 1690–8, Mon. and Brecon 1698–d. Steward of Monmouth, Duchy of Lancaster 1697–d. See *HC 1660–90*, ii. 98–9.

MORLEY, GEORGE (*c.*1664–1711), of Inner Temple. MP Hindon 13 May 1701–27 Nov. 1702, 1705–8, 1710–d. Master in Chancery in alienations office 1687–93, 1696–June 1702; sewer, Household 1692–1704; com. of prizes June 1702–6.

MUSGRAVE, Sir CHRISTOPHER, 4th Bt. (*c.*1631–1704), of Edenhall, Cumb. MP Carlisle 1661–90, Westmld. 1690–5, 1701, 1702–d., Appleby 1695–8, Oxf. Univ. 1698–1700, Totnes Dec. 1701–2. Com. of Ordnance 1679–81, lt.-gen. 1681–7; teller of Exchequer June 1702–d. See *HC 1660–90*, iii. 116–20.

MYDDELTON, Sir RICHARD, 3rd Bt. (1655–1716), of Chirk Castle, Denb., and Soho Sq., Westminster. MP Denb. 1685–d. Steward, lordship of Denbigh, June 1702–d. See *HC 1660–90*, iii. 122–4; *HC 1715–54*, ii. 288.

NAPIER, Sir ROBERT, 1st Bt. (*c.*1640–1700), of Puncknowle, Dorset. MP Weymouth and Melcombe Regis 1689–90, Dorchester 1690, 1698–d. See *HC 1660–90*, iii. 128–9.

NEVILLE, RICHARD (1655–1717), of Billingbear, Berks. MP Berks. 1695–1710.

NEWHAVEN, 2nd Viscount: see CHEYNE, WILLIAM.

NEWPORT, THOMAS (*c.*1655–1719), of Brigstock, Northants. 5th son of 1st Earl of Bradford. MP Ludlow 1695–8, 1 Mar. 1699–1700, Winchelsea, 7 Jan.–27 Feb. 1701, Much Wenlock 1715–16. cr. Baron Torrington 1716. Com. of customs Nov. 1699–1712; Ld. of Treasury 1715–18; PC 1717; teller of Exchequer 1718–d. See *CP* xii. 787–8; *HC 1715–54*, ii. 294.

NEWTON, ISAAC (1642–1727), of Woolsthorpe, Colsterworth, Lincs., and Trinity Coll., Cambridge. MP Camb. Univ. 1689–90, Dec. 1701–2. Kntd. 1705. Warden of Mint

1696–Jan. 1700, master Jan. 1700–d. See *DNB*; D. Brewster, *Memoirs of the Life, Writings and Discoveries of Sir Isaac Newton* (2 vols.; Edinburgh, 1855); H. W. Turnbull *et al.* (edd.), *The Correspondence of Isaac Newton . . .* (7 vols.; Cambridge, 1958–77); *HC 1660–90*, iii. 138–9.

NICHOLSON, JOHN (*c*.1662–*c*.1711), of Bury St., London, and Woodford, Essex. MP Gt. Yarmouth 1698–1700, Dec. 1701–8.

OGLETHORPE, Sir THEOPHILUS (1650–1702), of Westbroke, Godalming, Surrey. MP Morpeth 1685–7, Haslemere 1698–1701. Com. of the stables 1682–5, equerry 1685–8; col. of ft. 1685–8. See *HC 1660–90*, iii. 170–1.

ONSLOW, Sir RICHARD, 3rd Bt. (1654–1717), of West Clandon, Surrey. MP Guildford 1679–87, Surrey 1689–1710, 1713–15, St Mawes 1710–13. cr. Baron Onslow 1716. Ld. of Adm. 1690–3; Speaker, House of Commons 1708–10; PC 1710–d.; Chancellor of Exchequer 1714–15, teller 1715–d. See *DNB*; *CP* x. 66–8; C. E. Vulliamy, *The Onslow Family . . .* (London, 1955), 25–30; *HC 1660–90*, iii. 177–8; *HC 1715–54*, ii. 310–11.

ORRERY, 3rd Earl of [I]: see BOYLE, LIONEL.

PAGET, HENRY (*c*.1663–1743), of W. Drayton, Middx. 1st surv. son of 7th Lord Paget. MP Staffs. 1695–1712. cr. Baron Burton 1712, Earl of Uxbridge 1714; s. fa. 1713. Ld. of Treasury 1710–11; PC 1711–15. See *CP* x. 286–7.

PAKINGTON, Sir JOHN, 4th Bt. (1671–1727), of Westwood, nr. Droitwich, Worcs. MP Worcs. 1690–5, 1698–1727. See *HC 1715–54*, ii. 321.

PALMER, NATHANIEL (*c*.1661–1717), of Fairfield, Stogursey, Som. MP Minehead 1685–90, Som. 1690–5, 10 May 1699–1700, Dec. 1701–8, Bridgwater 1695–8, 1710–15. See *HC 1660–90*, iii. 198.

PALMES, WILLIAM (b. *c*.1638), of Lindley, Yorks., and Ashwell, Rutland. MP Malton 1668–Mar. 1681, 1689–1708, 1708–13. See *HC 1660–90*, iii. 201–2.

PAPILLON, THOMAS (1623–1702), of Fenchurch St., London, and Acrise Place, Kent. MP Dover 1674–Mar. 1681, 1689–95, London 1695–1700. Com. for trade 1668–72; com. for victualling 1690–d. See *DNB*; A. F. W. Papillon, *Memoirs of Thomas Papillon . . .* (Reading, 1887); Irene Scouloudi, 'Thomas Papillon, Merchant and Whig, 1623–1702', *Proceedings of the Huguenot Society of London*, 18 (1947–52), 49–72; *HC 1660–90*, iii. 202–5; D. Ormrod, 'Puritanism and Patriarchy: The Career and Spiritual Writings of Thomas Papillon 1623–1702', in A. Detsicas and N. Yates (edd.), *Studies in Modern Kentish History* (Kent Archaeological Society; Maidstone, 1983), 123–37.

PARKER, HUGH (*c*.1674–1712), of Honington, Warws. MP Evesham Dec. 1701–8. See Williams, *Parl. Hist. Worcs.*, 149.

PARKHURST, JOHN (*c*.1643–1731), of Catesby, Northants. MP Durham 1678–9, Northants. 1679–Mar. 1681, 1690–5, 1698–1701, Brackley 1689–90. Com. for prize appeals 1689–May 1699, jt. collector of arrears June 1699–aft. 1705. See *HC 1660–90*, iii. 208.

PAUNCEFORT, EDWARD (aft. 1652–1726), of Pall Mall, St James's, Westminster. MP Malmesbury 1698–1705. Dep. to receiver-gen. and paymaster-gen. [I] 1690–July 1698; yeoman of the jewel house 1696–1725, dep. master 1698; cashier to paymaster of forces abroad 1699–*c*.1700, dep. paymaster *c*.1700–5; comptroller of excise 1710, receiver-gen. 1710–14, jt. receiver-gen. 1715–d.

PELHAM, HENRY (*c*.1661–1721), of Stanmer, Sussex. MP Seaford 1690–5, Lewes 1695–1700, Dec. 1701–2. Clerk of the pells Jan. 1698–d.

PELHAM, THOMAS (*c.*1653–1712), of Halland, Laughton, Sussex. E. bro. of Henry Pelham (q.v.) MP E. Grinstead 1678–July 1679, Lewes 1680–1702, Sussex 1702–5. Com. for customs 1689–90; Ld. of Treasury 1690–2, 1697–June 1699, Mar. 1701–May 1702. See *HC 1660–90*, iii. 220–1.

PITFIELD, ALEXANDER (1659–1728), of St Helen's Bishopsgate, London. MP Bridport 1698–1708. Cursitor, Kent and Devon by 1700–bef. 1707.

POPE, ROGER (1668–1706), of Wolstaston, and Diamond Hall, Bridgnorth, Salop. MP Bridgnorth 4 May 1699–1702. See Henry T. Weyman, 'The Members of Parliament for Bridgnorth', *Transactions of the Shropshire Archaeological Society* (4th ser.), 5 (1915), 64; R. C. Purton, 'The Popes of Wolstaston', ibid. 50 (1939–40), 47.

POWLETT, LORD WILLIAM (*c.*1667–1729), of Chilbolton, Hants, and Marrick Priory, Yorks. 2nd son of 1st Duke of Bolton. MP Winchester 1689–1710, 1715–d., Lymington 1710–15. Farmer of green-wax fines 1690–1706; teller of Exchequer 1714–d. See *HC 1660–90*, iii. 280–1.

POWYS, Sir THOMAS (*c.*1649–1719), of Henley, nr. Ludlow, Salop, and Lilford cum Wigsthorpe, Northants. MP Ludlow Feb. 1701–13. Solicitor-Gen. 1686–7; Attorney-Gen. 1687–8; Prime Serjt. June 1702–13; judge, Queen's Bench 1713–14. See *DNB*; Foss, *Judges of Eng.*, viii. 55–7.

PULTENEY, JOHN (*c.*1661–1726), of London. MP Hastings 1695–1710. Under-Sec. of State 1689–90, 1690–2; chief clerk to master-gen. of Ordnance 1693–June 1702, clerk of deliveries Feb. 1701–3; ld. of trade 1707–11.

RANELAGH, 1st Earl of [I]: see JONES, RICHARD.

RICH, Sir ROBERT, 2nd Bt. (*c.*1648–99), of Roos Hall, Beccles, Suff. MP Dunwich 1689–d. Ld. of Adm. 1691–d. See *HC 1660–90*, iii. 328–9.

RIGBY, Sir ALEXANDER (*c.*1663–1717), of Layton, nr. Liverpool, Lancs. MP Wigan Dec. 1701–2. Clerk of Crown at Lancaster 1697–Aug. 1702; com. of customs [S] 1706–10. See W. D. Pink and A. B. Beavan, *The Parliamentary Representation of Lancashire* . . . (London, 1889), 231.

ROOKE, Sir GEORGE (1650–1709), of St Lawrence, nr. Canterbury, Kent. MP Portsmouth 1698–1708. Ld. of Adm. 1694–Jan. 1702; adm. of the White 1695; member, Adm. Council May 1702–5; PC 1702–5. See *DNB*; Charnock, *Biog. Nav.*, i. 402–31.

ST JOHN, HENRY (1678–1751), of Lydiard Tregoze, Wilts., and Bucklebury, Berks. MP Wootton Bassett Feb. 1701–8, Berks. 1710–12. cr. Viscount Bolingbroke 1712. Sec. at War 1704–8; PC 1710–14; Sec. of State 1710–14. See *DNB*; *CP* ii. 205–7; H. T. Dickinson, *Bolingbroke* (London, 1970).

ST QUINTIN, Sir WILLIAM, 3rd Bt. (*c.*1662–1723), of Harpham, Yorks. MP Kingston-upon-Hull 1695–d. Com. of customs July 1698–Nov. 1701; com. of rev. [I] 1706–13; Ld. of Treasury 1714–17; jt. vice-treasurer [I] 1720–d. See *HC 1715–54*, ii. 405.

SCOBELL, FRANCIS (1664–1740), of Menaguins, and Tregonan, Corn. MP Mitchell 1690–5, Grampound 16 Jan. 1699–1708, St Germans 1708–10, Launceston 1710–13, St Mawes 1713–15.

SEDLEY, Sir CHARLES, 5th Bt. (1639–1701), of Southfleet, Kent and Bloomsbury, Middx. MP New Romney 1668–Mar. 1681, 1690–5, 1696–d. See *DNB*; V. De Sola Pinto, *Sir Charles Sedley* . . . (1927); *HC 1660–90*, iii. 409–10.

SEYMOUR, Sir EDWARD, 4th Bt. (1633–1708), of Maiden Bradley, Wilts., and Berry Pomeroy, Devon. MP Hindon 1661–79, Devon 1679, Totnes 1680–1, 1695–8, Exeter 1685–95, 1698–d. PC 1673–89, 1692–6; Speaker, House of Commons 1673–9; Ld. of Treasury 1691–4; comptroller of Household Apr. 1702–4. See *DNB*; R. W. Clayton,

'The Political Career of Sir Edward Seymour, Bart., 1633–1708', D.Phil. thesis (York, 1976); *HC 1660–90*, iii. 411–20.

SEYMOUR CONWAY, FRANCIS (1679–1732), of Lisburn, Co. Antrim. MP Bramber 1701–3. cr. Baron Conway 1703. Yr. son of Sir Edward Seymour, 4th Bt. (q.v.) See *CP* iii. 402–3.

SHEPHEARD, FRANCIS (aft. 1673–1739), of London, and Exning, Suff. 1st son of Samuel Shepheard, sen. (q.v.) MP Andover 8 Jan.–19 Mar. 1701, 1701 (Dec.)–1708.

SHEPHEARD, SAMUEL, sen. (1648–1719), of St Magnus the Martyr, and Bishopsgate, London. MP Newport, I.o.W. 8 Jan.–16 Apr. 1701, London 1705–8. See J. Carswell, *The South Sea Bubble* (London, 1961), 283; Woodhead, *Rulers of London*, 147.

SHEPHEARD, SAMUEL, jun. (aft. 1674–1748), of London, and Exning, Suff. 2nd son of Samuel Shepheard, sen. (q.v.) and yr. bro. of Francis Shepheard (q.v.) MP Malmesbury 8 Jan.–17 Mar. 1701, Cambridge 1708–10, 1710–15, 1715–22, 1747–d., Cambs. 1724–47. See *HC 1715–54*, ii. 420–1.

SHERARD, BENNET, 3rd Baron Sherard [I] (1677–1732), of Stapleford, Leics. MP Leics. Dec. 1701–2, Rutland 1713–14. cr. Baron Harborough 1714, Visc. Sherard 1718, Earl of Harborough 1719. See *CP* vi. 295–6.

SHOWER, Sir BARTHOLOMEW (1658–1701), of Temple Lane, London, and Pinner Hill, Middx. MP Exeter 1698–d. See *DNB*.

SLOANE, JAMES (1655–1704), of Boswell Court, Little Lincoln's Inn Fields, London. MP Thetford 1696–26 Jan. 1700, 8 Feb.–19 Dec. 1700. Sec. to chief justice in eyre, s. of Trent 1697–1702. See E. St John Brooks, *Sir Hans Sloane: The Great Collector and His Circle* (London, 1954), 25, 29, 35, 77, 214–15.

SMITH, JOHN (*c.*1651–1718), of Beaufort Buildings, The Strand, Westminster. MP Southampton 1698–1700. Com. of excise July 1698–June 1702. See W. Marston Acres, 'Directors of the Bank of England', *Notes and Queries*, 179 (1940), 40.

SMITH, JOHN (*c.*1656–1723), of S. Tidworth, Hants. MP Ludgershall 1679, 1689–90, Bere Alston 1691–5, Andover 1695–1713, E. Looe 1715–d. Ld. of Treasury 1694–Dec. 1701; PC 1695–d., Chancellor of Exchequer June 1699–Mar. 1701, 1708–10, teller 1710–12, 1715–d.; Speaker, House of Commons 1705–8. See *DNB*; *HC 1660–90*, iii. 442–3; *HC 1715–54*, ii. 427.

SOAME, EDMUND (*c.*1669–1706), of Dereham Grange, W. Dereham, Norf. MP Thetford 1701, 1702–5. Capt., 2nd Queen's Regt. Ft. Feb. 1702–3; lt.-col., Elliott's Ft. 1703–5; col. of ft. 1705–d.

SPENCER, CHARLES, Lord Spencer (*c.*1674–1722), of Althorp, Northants, and Sunderland House, Piccadilly. Only surv. son of 2nd Earl of Sunderland. MP Tiverton 1695–28 Sept. 1702. s. fa. 28 Sept. 1702. Sec. of State 1706–10, 1717–18; PC 1706; Ld. Lt. [I] 1714–15; Ld. Privy Seal 1715–16; jt. vice-treasurer [I] 1716–17; Ld. President 1717–19; First Ld. of Treasury 1717–21; ld. justice 1719, 1720. See *DNB*; *CP* xi, pt. 1, pp. 487–9; H. L. Snyder, 'Charles Spencer, 3rd Earl of Sunderland, as Secretary of State, 1706–10 . . . ', Ph.D. thesis (Berkeley, 1963); G. M. Townend, 'The Political Career of Charles Spencer, 3rd Earl of Sunderland, 1695–1722', Ph.D. thesis (Edinburgh, 1985).

STANHOPE, JAMES (1673–1721), of Whitehall, and Chevening, Kent. MP Newport, I.o.W. 7 Mar.–2 July 1702, 1717, Cockermouth 1702–11, 1711–13, 1715–17, Wendover 1714–15. cr. Viscount Stanhope 1717, Earl Stanhope 1718. Lt.-col., 1st Ft. Gds. 1695; sec. to embassy in Paris, 1698, in The Hague 1700–1; col., 11th Ft. Feb. 1702–5, of drags. 1710–12; brig.-gen. 1704, maj.-gen. 1707, lt.-gen. 1709; c.-in-c., forces in Spain 1708–10; ambassador to Vienna 1714, to Paris and Madrid 1718, to

Paris 1720, to Berlin 1720; Sec. of State 1714–17, 1718–d.; PC 1714–d.; First Ld. of Treasury and Chancellor of Exchequer 1717–18. See *DNB*; *CP* x. pt. 1, pp. 229–33; B. Williams, *Stanhope: A Study in Eighteenth-Century War and Diplomacy* (Oxford, 1932); A. Newman, *The Stanhopes of Chevening* (London, 1969), 15–101; *HC 1715–54*, ii. 435–6.

STRICKLAND, Sir WILLIAM, 3rd Bt. (1665–1724), of Boynton, Yorks. MP Malton 1689–98, Feb. 1701–8, 1722–d., Yorks. 1708–10, Old Sarum 1716–22. Muster-master gen. 1720–d. See *HC 1660–90*, iii. 506–7; *HC 1715–54*, ii. 453.

STRINGER, THOMAS (*c.*1660–1706), of Clitheroe, Lancs. MP Clitheroe 1698–d. Capt., Sir Richard Atkins's Ft. 1694–6, maj. 1696–Aug. 1699, Sir Mathew Brydges' Ft. Aug. 1699–Apr. 1700; capt. and lt.-col. 1st Ft. Gds. Apr. 1700–Feb. 1702; col. of ft. Feb. 1702–d. See Pink and Beavan, *Parl. Rep. Lancs.*, 258.

THOMPSON, EDWARD (*c.*1639–1701), of York. MP York 1689–90, 1695–8, Feb. 1701–d. Registrar of indentured servants going to the plantations, 1691–*c.*Mar. 1699. See *HC 1660–90*, iii. 551.

THOMPSON, MAURICE (1675–1745), of Haversham, Bucks. 1st son of 1st Baron Haversham. MP Bletchingley 1695–8, Gatton 1698–1705. s. fa. 1710. Capt., 1st Ft. Gds. 1695–7, Coldstream Gds. 1697–Jan. 1702; treasurer of excise 1717–18. See *CP* vi. 410–11.

THORNHAUGH, JOHN (1648–1723), of Fenton, Notts. MP E. Retford 1689–28 Nov. 1702, Notts. 1704–10. See *HC 1660–90*, iii. 556–7.

THURSBY, WILLIAM (1629–1701), of Abington, Northants. MP Northampton 1698–d.

TOLLEMACHE, LIONEL, 3rd Earl of Dysart (1649–1727), of Helmingham, Suff. MP Orford 1679–Mar.1681, 1685–7, Suffolk 1698–1707. See *DNB*.

TOPHAM, RICHARD (*c.*1671–1730), of St Andrew's, Holborn. MP New Windsor 1698–1713.

TREDENHAM, JOHN (1668–1710), of Tregonan, Corn. 1st son of Sir Joseph Tredenham (q.v.) MP St Mawes 1690–1705, 1701–d. See *DNB*.

TREDENHAM, Sir JOSEPH (*c.*1643–1707), of Tregonan, Corn. MP St Mawes 1666–Jan. 1679, 1680–Mar. 1681, 1689–95, 1698–d., Grampound 1679, 1685–7. Gent. of privy chamber 1664–85; jt. comptroller of army accts. 1703–d. See *HC 1660–90*, iii. 583–6.

TREVOR, Sir THOMAS (1658–1730), of Bromham, Beds. MP Plympton Erle 1692–8, Lewes 1701. cr. Baron Trevor 1712. KC 1689; Solicitor-Gen. 1692–5; Attorney-Gen. 1695–June 1701; chief justice, Common Pleas June 1701–14; PC June 1702–14, 1726–d.; First Com. of Great Seal 1710; Ld. Privy Seal 1726–30; ld. justice 1727; Ld. President 1730–d. See *DNB*; *CP* xii. pt. 2, pp. 30–1; Foss, *Judges of Eng.*, viii. 71–6.

VERNON, JAMES (1646–1727), of Frith St., Westminster. MP Camb. Univ. 1679, Penryn 1695–8, 1705–10, Westminster 1698–1702. Dep. Sec.-at-War 1678–9; Under-Sec. of State 1689–90, 1693–7; Sec. of State 1697–May 1702; PC 1697–d.; teller of Exchequer June 1702–10; com. for Privy Seal 1716. See *DNB*; Elizabeth O. Keller, 'The Career of James Vernon in Relation to Politics and Administration in the Reign of William III', MA thesis (Manchester, 1977); *HC 1660–90*, iii. 639–40.

WALCOT, GEORGE (1667–1743), of London. MP Bishop's Castle 1701. See H. T. Weyman, 'The Members of Parliament for Bishop's Castle', *Trans. Shropshire Arch. Nat. Hist. Soc.* (ser. 2), 10 (1898), 54; J. R. Burton, *Some Collections towards the History of the Family of Walcot . . .* (Shrewsbury, 1930), 77–8.

WALMESLEY, WILLIAM (d. 1713), of Lichfield. MP Lichfield 1701. See Wedgwood, *Staffs. Parl. Hist.*, ii. 187–8.

WALPOLE, ROBERT (1676–1745), of Houghton, Norf. MP Castle Rising Feb. 1701–2, King's Lynn 1702–12, 1712, 1713–42. KB 1725; cr. Earl of Orford 1742. Member of Adm. Council 1705–8; Sec.-at-War 1708–10; treasurer of navy 1710–11; PC 1714; paymaster of forces 1714–15, 1720–1; First Ld. of Treasury and Chancellor of Exchequer 1715–17, 1721–42. See *DNB*; CP x. 81–4; J. H. Plumb, *Sir Robert Walpole* (2 vols.; London, 1956–60); *HC 1715–54*, ii. 513–17.

WARD, JOHN (d. 1755), of Hackney, Middx. MP Bletchingley Feb. 1701–8, Reigate 1710–13, Ludgershall 1714–15, Weymouth and Melcombe Regis 1722–6. See *HC 1715–54*, ii. 519–20.

WEBB, JOHN RICHMOND (1667–1724), of Biddesden House, Ludgershall, Wilts. MP Ludgershall 1695–8, 11 Feb. 1699–1705, 1706–13, 1715–d., Newport, I.o.W. 1713–15. Col., 8th Ft. 1695–1715; brig.-gen. 1704, maj.-gen. 1706, lt.-gen. 1709; gov., I.o.W. 1710–15; c.-in-c. land forces in GB 1713. See *DNB*; *HC 1715–54*, ii. 526–7.

WHARTON, GOODWIN (1653–1704), of Soho Sq., Westminster, and Waddesdon, Bucks. MP E. Grinstead 1680–Jan. 1681, Westmld. 1689–90, Malmesbury 1690–5, Cockermouth 1695–8, Bucks. 1698–d. Capt., Macclesfield's Horse 1694–1704; Ld. of Adm. 1697–May 1699. See *HC 1660–90*, iii. 695–6; J. K. Clark, *Goodwin Wharton* (Oxford, 1984).

WHEELER, WILLIAM (d. 1708), of St Michael's, Barbados. MP Haverfordwest Feb. 1701–2.

WHITE, THOMAS (1667–1732), of Wallingwells, Notts. MP E. Retford 11 Jan.–15 Apr. 1701, 2 Dec. 1701–28 Nov. 1702, 1708–11, 1715–d. Clerk of Ordnance 1718–d. See *HC 1715–54*, ii. 534–5.

WILLIAMSON, Sir JOSEPH (1633–1701), of Whitehall, and Cobham, Kent. MP Thetford 1669–87, Rochester 1690–d. Under-Sec. of State 1660–74; clerk of PC 1672–4; plenipotentiary, congress of Cologne 1673–4, of Nijmegen 1676; Sec. of State 1674–9; Ld. of Adm. 1674–9; PC 1674–9, 1696–d.; ambassador to United Provinces 1696–Mar. 1699. See *DNB*; *HC 1660–90*, iii. 736–40.

WINNINGTON, SALWEY (d. 1736), of Stanford Court, Stanford-on-Teme, Worcs., and St James's, Westminster. MP Bewdley 1694–1708, 1710–15. See Williams, *Parl. Rep. Worcs.*, 169.

WORTLEY MONTAGU, SIDNEY (1650–1727), of Wortley, Yorks. 2nd son of 1st Earl of Sandwich. MP Huntingdon 1679–Mar. 1681, 1689–95, 1713–22, Camelford 1696–8, Peterborough 1698–1710, 1722–d. See F. R. Harris, *The Life of Edward Mountagu, K. G. First Earl of Sandwich* . . . (2 vols.; London, 1912), i. 232–8; ii. 160, 235, 288–90; *HC 1660–90*, iii. 759–60; *HC 1715–54*, ii. 557.

YATE, ROBERT (d. 1737), of The Red Lodge, Wine St., Bristol. MP Bristol 1695–1710.

YONGE, Sir WALTER, 3rd Bt. (1653–1731), of Colyton, and Escott, Devon. MP Honiton 1679–Mar. 1681, 1690–1710, Ashburton 1689–90. Com. of customs 1694–Nov. 1701, 1714–d. See *HC 1660–90*, iii. 789–90.

APPENDIX 2

The Politics of MPs Mentioned in the Text:
The Evidence of Parliamentary Lists

Key

Column 1: A comparative analysis of the old and new Houses of Commons, *c.* Aug. 1698, derived from Robert Harley's papers (BL Loan 29/35/12) and printed in part in H. Horwitz, 'Parties, Connections, and Parliamentary Politics, 1698–1714: Review and Revision', *Journal of British Studies*, 6 (1966–7), 62–9. (*a*) MPs marked therein with a √ to indicate 'Country party' or opposition) are here given 'Cy', those with + or x (to indicate 'Court') are here given 'Ct'; a dash indicates those marked in the original list with 'q' (query?) or 'D' (doubtful?); (*b*) a further attempt to classify some of those MPs who had been identified as Court, or marked 'q', or left unmarked, using the further symbols Q (query?), abs (absent), and/or O (opposition?).

Column 2: A list of the new House of Commons, *c.*Aug. 1698, with 110 pl[acemen] marked: *A Compleat List of the Knights, Citizens and Burgesses of the New Parliament* (BL Add. MS 40772, fo. 8; BL Dept. of Printed Bks., 1850.c.6 (16)).

Column 3: A list of the C[ountr]y party in the new House of Commons *c.*Sept. 1698, in the papers of the Duke of Leeds (BL, Eg. MS 3359, fos. 35–6), and printed in D. Hayton, 'The Country Party in the House of Commons 1698–1699: A Forecast of the Opposition to a Standing Army?', *Parliamentary History,* 6 (1987), 145–60.

Column 4: The black list of those C[our]t supporters who voted against the 3rd reading of the Disbanding Bill, 18 Jan. 1699, and thus for the maintenance of a standing army, four versions of which have hitherto been discovered: BL Add. MS 28091, fo. 167 (printed in A. Browning, *Thomas Osborne Earl of Danby and Duke of Leeds 1632–1712* (3 vols.; Glasgow, 1951), iii. 213–17); *A List of the Members of the Last House of Commons . . . Who Voted for a Standing Army* ([1701]: Newberry Library, Chicago, Case 6a 160, no. 70); Nat. Lib. Wales, Carreg-Lwyd MSS, ii. 74; Magdalene College, Cambridge, Pepys Library, PL 2179, pp. 71–4.

Column 5: An analysis of the House, *c.*Jan.–May 1700, in Robert Harley's papers (BL Loan 29/35/12), assigning MPs to various interests, including: 'D[uke of] Bedf[ord] & E[arl of] Orf[or]d' (B/O); 'L[or]d Tank[erville]' (T); 'E[?arl of] S[?underland]' (ES); 'Mr. H[enry] B[oyle]' (HB); 'D[uke of] Leeds' (Leeds); 'O[ld] E[ast India] C[ompany]' (OEICo.); 'Sir E. Seymour' (Sey.); 'Auditor [Charles] Montagu' (Mont.); 'L[or]d Som[ers] etc.' (Junto); 'L[or]d Warrington' (Warr.); 'L[or]d Stamford' (Stam.); 'E[arl of] Bradford' (Brad.); and 'Places' (pl.), the remaining names being grouped under 'Q[?uery i.e. opposition?]'.

Column 6: A list of MPs (BL Add. MS 28091, fos. 179–80), datable to 22 Feb. 1701, and probably a forecast of those who would support the C[our]t on the question of agreeing with the committee of supply to make good the principal and interest due on parliamentary funds granted since the accession of King William.

Column 7: The black list of those T[ories] in the House in the 1701 Parliament who were opposed to making preparations for war with France, two versions of which have hitherto been discovered: [T. Savage,] *A List of One Unanimous Club of Members of the Late Parliament . . . that Met at the Vine Tavern in Long Acre; Who Ought to Be Opposed in the Ensuing Elections, by All that Intend to Save Their Native Country from Being Made a Province of France; by Reason of Their Constant Voting with Davenant, Hamond, and Tredenham, Who Were Caught with Monsieur Poussin the French Agent* (1701); and a MS in the possession of Dr Eveline Cruickshanks.

Column 8: A list of election returns, c.Dec. 1701, annotated by Charles, Lord Spencer, in terms of 'g[ains]' and 'l[osses]' to the Whig side, in Blenheim MSS (the Duke of Marlborough, Blenheim Palace, Woodstock, Oxon.), printed in H. L. Snyder, 'Party Configurations in the Early Eighteenth-Century House of Commons', *Bulletin of the Institute of Historical Research*, 45 (1972), 54–8.

Column 9: An analysis of the new House of Commons, c.Dec. 1701, annotated by Robert Harley (BL Harl. MS 7556, fos. 96–100), in which MPs are classified as A (T[ory]), B (W[hig]) or C.

Column 10: The 'white list' of T[ory] MPs who voted on 26 Feb. 1702 that 'the House of Commons had not right done them in the matter of the impeachments in the last Parliament': [J. Drake,] *Some Necessary Considerations Relating to All Future Elections of Members to Serve in Parliament, Humbly Offer'd to All Electors* (1702), reprinted in *Somers's Tracts*, xii. 215–18.

	1	2	3	4	5	6	7	8	9	10
	a/b									
Anderton, James							T			T
Ashurst, Sir Henry	Ct/—				Junto					
Ashurst, Sir William	Ct/Q	pl	Cy	Ct	[?Junto]	Ct				
Aylmer, Matthew	Ct/abs	pl			B/O	Ct			W	
Bacon, Sir Edmund						Ct	T		T	T
Bertie, Charles	Ct/—	pl	Cy		Leeds	Ct	T			T
Bertie, Peregrine	Ct/—							g		
Biddulph, Sir Michael	Ct/—				Q^a				C	
Birch, John							T		T	
Blaake, Henry	Ct/—			Ct	Junto				W	
Blackett, Sir William	Ct/Q			Ct	Warr.					
Blake, Sir Francis	Ct/Q			Ct	Warr.					
Blathwayt, William	Ct/—	pl		Ct	—^{b}	Ct				
Bliss, Thomas	Cy/—		Cy			Ct	T			T
Bolles, Sir John	Cy/—		Cy			Ct	T			T
Boyle, Charles									T	T
Boyle, Henry	Ct/—		Cy	Ct	—^{b}				W	
Boyle, Lionel, E. of Orrery	Cy/—	pl			Junto			g	W	
Brereton, Edward	Cy/—		Cy			Ct			T	T
Brewer, John	Ct/—		Cy	Q		Ct			[?T]	T
Bridges, William	Ct/Q		Cy	Q		Ct			T	T
Bromley, William (of Baginton)	Cy/—						T			T
Bromley, William (of Holt Castle)	Ct/Q		Cy		Junto				W	
Brotherton, Thomas	Cy/—		Cy			Ct	T			
Brownlow, Sir William	Ct/Q		Cy	Ct						
Brydges, George Rodney									W	
Brydges, James	Ct/Q		Cy		OEICo.	Ct	T		T	T
Bucknall, Ralph										
Burnaby, Anthony									T	T

	1 a/b	2	3	4	5	6	7	8	9	10
Byerley, Robert	Cy/—		Cy			Ct			T	T
Calthorpe, Reynolds	—/O		Cy		OEICo.				T	T
Cavendish, William, Mq. of Hartington	Ct/Q				Q					
Chase, James	Ct/—		Cy	Ct	pl	Ct			W	
Cheyne, William, Visc. Newhaven	C/—		Cy			Ct	T		T	T
Child, Sir Francis	Ct/Q		Cy		OEICo.	Ct	T		T	T
Churchill, George	Ct/—	pl	Cy		pl	Ct			T	T
Clarke, Edward (of Norwich)								g		
Clarke, Edward (of Chipley)	Ct/—	pl		Ct	[?Junto]					
Clayton, Sir Robert	Cy/—		Cy		OEICo.	Ct				
Cocks, Charles	Ct/—				Junto				W	
Cocks, Sir Richard^c	Ct/Q	pl			Mont.				W	
Coke, Thomas	Cy/—		Cy		Q			l	T	T
Colchester, Maynard								g	W	
Colt, John Dutton										
Comyns, John								l	T	T
Coningsby, Thomas, B. Coningsby	Ct/—	pl		Ct	pl				C	
Conyers, John	Cy/—	pl	Cy				T		T	T
Cooke, John	Ct/Q				Junto				W	
Copley, Sir Godfrey	Cy/—		Cy		Leeds	Ct	T		T	T
Cotesworth, William										
Cotton, Sir Robert	Cy/—		Cy		Q	Ct			W	
Coulson, Thomas	Cy/—		Cy		Sey.	Ct	T		T	T
Cowper, William	Ct/—	pl			Mont.				W	
Cox, Charles	Ct/Q			Ct	Junto				W	
Coxe, Charles	Cy/—		Cy				T		T	T
Cutts, John, B. Cutts	Ct/—	pl		Ct	pl	Ct			W	
Davall, Sir Thomas	Cy/—		Cy		OEICo.	Ct	T		T	T
Davenant, Charles	Cy/—		Cy		OEICo.	Ct	T			

	1	2	3	4	5	6	7	8	9	10
	a/b									
Davers, Sir Robert	Cy/—	Cy				Ct	T			
Dormer, Robert					Q			g	W	
Drake, Sir William	Ct/—	Cy							T	T
Duncombe, (Sir) Charles						Ct	T			
Dyott, Richard	Ct/Q					Ct			T	T
Ettrick, William	Ct/Q	Cy				Ct	T		T	T
Eyre, Robert	Cy/—	Cy			Junto				W	
Fairfax, Thomas, Ld. Fairfax	Ct/— pl				pl					
Felton, Sir Thomas	Ct/— pl		Ct					g	W	
Finch, Heneage	Cy/—					Ct	T			T
Foley, Edward									T	T
Foley, Paul		Cy								
Foley, Philip	Cy/—	Cy					T		T	T
Foley, Thomas (of Stoke Edith)	Cy/—	Cy					T		T	T
Foley, Thomas sen. (of Witley Court)	Ct/—									
Foley, Thomas jun. (of Witley Court)	Cy/—	Cy				Ct	T		T	T
Fox, Sir Stephen	Ct/—					Ct			W	
Freke, Thomas	Ct/—				Mont.					
Freman, Ralph	Cy/—	Cy				Ct	T		T	T
Furnese, Sir Henry	Ct/— pl		Ct						W	
Godfrey, Charles	Ct/— pl		Ct	pl					W	
Gorges, Henry	Cy/—	Cy							T	T
Granville, John	Cy/—	Cy				Ct	T	l	l	T
Gulston, William									W	
Gwyn, Francis	Cy/—					Ct	T	l	T	T
Gwynne, Sir Rowland	Ct/—		Ct		Stam.				W	
Hales, Sir Christopher	Cy/—	Cy					T		T	T
Hales, Sir Thomas									T	T
Hammond, Anthony	Cy/—	Cy			Q	Ct	T			

	1	2	3	4	5	6	7	8	9	10
	a/b									
Harcourt, Simon	Cy/—		Cy			Ct	T		T	T
Harley, Edward	Cy/—		Cy				T	l	T	T
Harley, Robert	Cy/—		Cy			Ct	T		T	T
Harley, Thomas	Cy/—		Cy				T		T	T
Harvey, Michael	Cy/—		Cy				T			
Harvey, Stephen	Ct/—			Ct	Junto				W	
Harvey, William	Cy/—		Cy						T	
Hawles, Sir John	Ct/—	pl		Ct	Mont.				W	
Heathcote, Sir Gilbert						Ct				
Hedges, Sir Charles	Ct/—	pl		Ct		Ct			T	T
Herne, Frederick	Cy/—		Cy		OEICo.	Ct	T		T	T
Herne, Sir Joseph	—/Q		Cy							
Herne, Nathaniel						Ct	T		T	T
Hervey, John				Ct	[?Junto]				W	
Hickman, Sir Willoughby	Cy/—		Cy				T			
Hoblyn, John	Cy/—		Cy		Bath	Ct	T		T	T
Holland, Sir John								g		
Hooper, Nicholas	Cy/—		Cy		Q		T		T	T
Hopkins, Edward									W	
Hotham, Sir Charles	Ct/Q				Junto					
Howard, William	Ct/abs					Ct				
Howe, Emanuel Scrope										
Howe, John Grobham	Cy/—		Cy		Q	Ct	T			
Howe, Richard Grobham	Cy/—					Ct				
Hungerford, Sir George	Cy/—		Cy		Q		T			
Hussey, Sir Edward	Cy/—		Cy		Q					
Hustler, Sir William	Cy/—			Ct	Junto	Ct			W	
Hyde, Edward, Visc. Cornbury	Ct/—			Ct						
Hyde, Henry, Ld. Hyde	Cy		Cy			Ct	T		T	

	1 a/b	2	3	4	5	6	7	8	9	10
Jacob, Thomas	Cy/—								C	
Jeffreys, Sir Jeffrey	Cy/—					Ct	T		T	T
Jekyll, Sir Joseph	Ct/—	pl		Ct	[?Junto]				W	
Jervoise, Thomas	—/Q				Q		T		W	
Johnson, William	Cy/—		Cy						T	T
Jones, Richard, E. of Ranelagh	Ct/—	pl		Ct				g	W	
King, Peter						Ct			W	
King, Thomas	Ct/—	pl	Cy	Ct	OEICo.					T
Lawson, Gilfrid						Ct				
Leveson Gower, Sir John	Cy/—		Cy			Ct	T		T	T
Littleton, Sir Thomas	Ct/–	pl			Junto	Ct				
Lowndes, William	Ct/–	pl		Ct	pl	Ct			C	
Mackworth, Sir Humphrey						Ct	T			
Mainwaring, Sir John	Ct/—			Ct	Q^d				W	
Manley, John	Cy/—						T		T	
Manners, John, Ld. Roos						Ct		g		
Marsham, Sir Robert	Cy/—			Ct	Q					
Martin, Joseph										
Mason, Charles	Ct/—	pl		Ct	[?Junto]					
Meredith, Thomas										
Meres, Sir Thomas						Ct				
Mitford, Michael								g	W	
Mompesson, Charles	Cy/—				Junto				W	
Mompesson, Roger					Q		T			
Monckton, Robert	Cy/—					Ct			C	
Montagu, Charles (of Belford)	Ct/—			Ct	Mont.				W	
Montagu, Charles (of Westminster)	Ct/—	pl		Ct	—[b]					

	1	2	3	4	5	6	7	8	9	10
	a/b									
Montagu, Christopher	Ct/—	pl		Ct	[?Junto]					
Montagu, Edward	—/QO				Junto					
Montagu, Irby	Ct/—	pl		Ct	Mont.					
Moore, Arthur	Cy/—		Cy		OEICo.					T
Mordaunt, Harry	Ct/—									
Mordaunt, Sir John	Cy/—		Cy			Ct	T		T	T
Mordaunt, John, Ld. Mordaunt							T		T	
Morgan, Thomas	Ct/—				[?Junto]					
Morley, George									T	T
Musgrave, Sir Christopher	Cy/—		Cy				T		T	T
Myddelton, Sir Richard	Cy/—		Cy		Q^b	Ct			T	T
Napier, Sir Robert	Cy/—	pl	Cy		Q					
Neville, Richard	Ct/Q	pl		Ct	Tank.	Ct			W	
Newport, Thomas	Ct/—				Brad.					
Newton, Isaac								g	W	
Nicholson, John	—/QO		Cy					l		T
Oglethorpe, Sir Theophilus			Cy			Ct	T			
Onslow, Sir Richard	—/Q				Q				W	
Paget, Henry			Cy			Ct			T	
Pakington, Sir John	Cy/—		Cy			Ct	T		T	T
Palmer, Nathaniel	Cy/—									T
Palmes, William	Cy/—			Ct	Junto				W	
Papillon, Thomas	Ct/—	pl			pl					
Parker, Hugh								l	T	T
Parkhurst, John	Ct/—	pl		Ct	[?Junto]					
Pauncefort, Edward	Ct/—	pl		Ct	Q				T	T
Pelham, Henry	Ct/—	pl		Ct	pl			g		
Pelham, Thomas	Ct/—	pl			Q				W	
Pitfield, Alexander	Cy/—		Cy		Q				W	
Pope, Roger										

	1	2	3	4	5	6	7	8	9	10
	a/b									
Powlett, Ld. William	Ct/—			Ct	[?Junto]				W	
Powys, Sir Thomas						Ct	T			T
Pulteney, John	Ct/—	pl		Ct	pl				W	
Rich, Sir Robert	Ct/—	pl		Ct						
Rigby, Sir Alexander								g		
Rooke, Sir George	Ct/—	pl			pl	Ct			T	T
St John, Henry						Ct	T		T	T
St Quintin, Sir William	Ct/—	pl		Ct	Junto					
Scobell, Francis						Ct	T		T	T
Sedley, Sir Charles	Ct/—			Ct	HB					
Seymour, Sir Edward	Cy/—		Cy		—[b]		T		T	T
Seymour Conway, Francis							T		T	
Shepheard, Francis									W	
Shepheard, Samuel, sen.										
Shepheard, Samuel, jun.										
Sherard, Bennet, B. Sherard								g		
Shower, Sir Bartholomew	Cy/—		Cy		Q	Ct	T		T	
Sloane, James	Ct/—	pl	Cy	Ct						
Smith, John (of Beaufort Bldgs.)	Ct/—	pl		Ct	Q					
Smith, John (of S. Tidworth)	Ct/—	pl		Ct	pl				W	
Soame, Edmund							T			
Spencer, Charles, Ld. Spencer	Ct/—			Ct	Q				W	
Stanhope, James										
Strickland, Sir William	Ct/—								W	
Stringer, Thomas	Ct/—		Cy	Ct	HB					
Thompson, Edward	Ct/—									

	1	2	3	4	5	6	7	8	9	10
	a/b									
Thompson, Maurice	Ct/—	pl		Ct	pl	Ct			W	
Thornhaugh, John	Ct/Q			Ct	Warr.	Ct				
Thursby, William	Cy/—		Cy							
Tollemache, Lionel, E. of Dysart	Cy/—		Cy			Ct	T		T	T
Topham, Richard	Cy/—				Q	Ct			W	
Tredenham, John	Cy/—		Cy		Sey.	Ct	T		T	T
Tredenham, Sir Joseph	Cy/—		Cy		Sey.	Ct	T		T	T
Trevor, Sir Thomas	Ct/—					Ct				
Vernon, James	Ct/—	pl		Ct						
Walcot, George										
Walmesley, William										
Walpole, Robert						Ct				
Ward, John									W	
Webb, John Richmond	Ct/—					Ct			T	
Wharton, Goodwin	Ct/—	pl		Ct	ES				W	
Wheeler, William									T	
White, Thomas										
Williamson, Sir Joseph	Ct/—	pl			pl					
Winnington, Salwey	Cy/—		Cy			Ct	T		T	T
Wortley Montagu, Sidney	Ct/—				[?Junto]					
Yate, Robert	Ct/Q									
Yonge, Sir Walter	Ct/—	pl		Ct	Mont.				W	

[a] Additional note: 'Sir J. Mainwaring' (q.v.)
[b] Name given as a heading.
[c] No entry in Appendix 1.
[d] See Sir Michael Biddulph.

APPENDIX 3

Schedule of Contents of the Cocks Manuscripts

MS Eng. hist. b. 209

Front to back:

fos. 1–4v: 'Of Confideing in god of Contentednes: to prove by reason there is [?–] benefit of Confiding'.[1]

fos. 4v–6r: 'Postscript': 'a discours pertinent to the foregoing with some arguments fit to be inserted in this discours'.

fos. 6r–6v: 'A dialogue between a Hugonote and a papist made 1687 for those times'.

fo. 6v: 'An Argument' (an essay on the virtues of argument).

fo. 7r: 'Of Good Breeding' (the necessity of a polite education).

fos. 7v–9v: 'Of Wills entailes and Setlements 17 June [16]94'.

fo. 9v: 'A true Church'; 'Honour'; 'Of Feare, and rashnes'.

fo. 10r: 'Of Wit'; 'Why do silly men put in places defend themselves with notions that whatever reflec[ts] on them reflects on the government it self that employs them'; 'How may a wise man live quietly and securely all his life'; 'A good subject'; 'of Celibacy'.

fo. 10v: 'of marriage'; 'Of the sap of trees'.

fo. 11r: What appears to be the conclusion of a discourse on tyranny and its inevitable failure, with special reference to the reign of James II.

fos. 11r–11v: 'That we ought not to fear censure'.

fo. 11v: 'Religion'.

fos. 11v–12: 'Love'.[2]

fo. 12r: 'Of Lust Called Love'

fos. 12r–12v: 'Drunkennes'.

fos. 12v–13r: 'Of Death'.

fo. 13r: 'Sin mimicks virtue and the reaons'.

fo. 13v: 'Of Thanksgiving'.

fos. 14r–14v: 'Of Wisdom'.

fos. 15r–15v: 'Of Virtue and the beauty thereof'.

fos. 15v–16v: 'Of Mercy'.

fos. 16v–17r: 'Justice'.

fos. 17r–17v: 'Against Xmas'.

---

[1] Between fos. 3 and 4 is the residue of two sheets which have been torn out, evidently before or during the writing up of this essay.

[2] Between fos. 11 and 12 is the residue of two sheets torn out, again without impairing the flow of the prose.

fos. 17ᵛ–18ʳ: 'That the greatest favourites are not allways the best subjects made 1683'.

fos. 18ʳ–19ᵛ: 'A periphrase on the 12th Chapter of the first book of kings made 1682' (in verse).

fo. 20ʳ: 'My thoughts on the talk of the repealing the test and penall laws in King James the seconds time' (in verse).

fos. 20ʳ–20ᵛ: 'Hos sequentes versas feci accademicus De Conjugio Regis et Reginae Gulielmi et Mariae' (Latin verses on the marriage of William and Mary aft. *c.*1677.)

fo. 21ᵛ³: 'a prayer against vain glory and pride'; 'a prayer after the Sacrament the 17th day of March 1694–5'; 'May the 12th [16]95 after the Sacrament' (prayer).

fo. 22ʳ: 'A prayer for all times made upon the thoughts of my discours of Xmas'.

fos. 22ʳ–22ᵛ: 'A prayer of Confession'.

fos. 22ᵛ–23ʳ: 'A prayer for a sick wife'.

fo. 23ʳ: 'A prayer of Thancksgiving'; 'A prayer for all times'.

fo. 23ᵛ: 'On Whitsunday' (prayer); 'A prayer for wisdom to Salvation'; 'A prayer made for faith upon the cure of the french maid'.

fo. 24ʳ: 'A prayer on the fast commanded by authority Sep[tem]b[e]r 18th 1694'.

fo. 24ᵛ: 'A prayer for the King Queen and people'.

fos. 24ᵛ–25ʳ: 'a prayer for a penitent' (himself).

fo. 25ʳ: 'A prayer for Easter day after the Sacrament'; 'A prayer for a man in law and particularly for myself'.

fo. 25ᵛ: 'A prayer for fair wheather in harvest'; 'a prayer for all conditions'; 'a Collect for –⁴ protection'.

fos. 25ᵛ–26ʳ: 'On Mich[aelmas] day [?1695]' (prayer).

fo. 26ʳ: '. . . after the Sacrament' (prayer), 6 Oct. 1695; 'Easter day [16]96' (prayer); 'after the Sacrament Easter day [16]96' (prayer); 'before the Sacrament [?23 Oct. 16]96' (prayer); 'After the Sacrament [?23 Oct. 1696]' (prayer).

fo. 26ᵛ: Address to King William from the high sheriff, grand jury, deputy lieutenants, justices of the peace, gentlemen etc. of Gloucestershire, drawn up at the assizes at Gloucester, 7 Mar. 1695[/6], signed by Cocks as foreman of the grand jury.

fos. 27ʳ–28ʳ: 'An Extempore Charg deliverd Easter Sessions 1694 partly to answer a speech calld of a [–] made by Sir J. K[nigh]t in Parliament the last Sessions'.⁵

fos. 28ʳ–29ʳ: 'My Charg spoken Midsummer sessions 1694'.

fos. 29ʳ–30ᵛ: 'A Charg', *temp.* William III.

fo. 30ᵛ: a brief draft of a charge to a grand jury, Midsummer sessions 1695; 'A preparation for Witsunday Sacrament 1696'; 'after the Sacrament Witsunday 1696' (prayer).

fos. 31ʳ–32ʳ: 'A preparatory for the Sacrament on Mich[aelmas Day] 1694'.

fo. 32ʳ: 'A prayer after the Sacrament'; two brief penitential prayers, the second dated 24 May 1696.

fos. 32ᵛ–37ʳ: 'Of Oaths in generall and particularly concerning publick oaths that relate to government', *temp.* William III.

fo. 37ᵛ: copy of a covering letter sent with the disquisition 'Of Oaths . . . ' and addressed to 'my Lord [?Somers]'.

fos. 37ᵛ–38ʳ: 'My letter to Mr Bulstrode upon his denying of a message sent me by Mr

---

³ Roughly the topmost third of this folio has been cut out. ⁴ 'grace' erased.

⁵ The Tory MP Sir John Knight's speech in Jan. 1694 on the General Naturalization Bill. See above, p. xxxv.

Collet viz that I should take care for the papists had a design against me and would entrap me', 1688.

fo. 38^r: 'My letter . . . to Mr [?Staigler] of Teuxbury', Sept. 1695 (concerning the Tewkesbury election and the competition to obtain a new borough charter).

fos. 38^r–38^v: copy of a letter to Lord Keeper Somers, [12 Oct. 1695], to prevent the passage of a new charter for Tewkesbury promoted by Sir Francis Winnington.[6]

fo. 38^v: another draft of a letter to Somers about the Tewkesbury charter [1695].

fos. 39^r–39^v: A charge to a grand jury, Easter sessions 1696, 'not approved of by M Lane and Mr Stafford and Mr Shepperd'.

fos. 39^v–40^r: 'Of Magistracy and Magistrates', 30 May 1696.

fos. 40^r–40^v: 'Of Faith', June 1696; 'of Hope', 2 Aug. 1696.

fos. 40^v–41^r: 'Of the World Orbis', 9 Aug. 1696.

fo. 41^v: 'Of heaven', 6 Sept. 1696.

fo. 42^r: 'Of Hell', 13 Sept. [?1696].

fos. 42^v–43^r: 'Of life', [?20–]21 Sept. [?1696].

fo. 43^v: 'Of Idlenes'.

fos. 44^r–44^v: 'Mr Spons answer to father Le Chaise perswading him to change his religion and Conform wit[h the] Church of Rome'.[7]

fos. 44^v–46^v: 'my Comments on despond'.

fos. 47^r–63^v: a history 'of the transactions of the whole world', in fact the diplomacy early sixteenth-century Europe; evidently written by a Frenchman and presumably translated by Cocks. Peters out in 1547 (with the '4th book').[8]

Back to front:

fo. 104^v: four prayers: of penitence; 'after Sacrament witsunday [16]98'; 'upon my bei Elected for the County Aug 3d [16]98'; 'upon the finishing and building my hous 22 Oct. 1699.

fo. 104^r: two prayers: 'upon my being Elected the 17 of Jan[ua]ry 1700 for the Count 'upon my being Elected the 4th of Dec[em]b[e]r 1701 for the County'.

fos. 103^v–103^r: blank.

fos. 102^v–101^v: sermon on Ecclesiastes 5: 11.

fos. 101^v–100^r: sermon on Ecclesiastes 5: 2.

fos. 100^r–99^r: sermon on 2 Maccabees 3: 1.

fos. 98^v–98^r: sermon on Ecclesiastes 4: 2.

fos. 98^r–96^v: sermon on Acts 15: 28.

fo. 96^r: blank.

fo. 95^v: 'an Extempore Charg Xmas [16]96'; 'An Address to W[illia]m 3d from Xn Sessions [16]97'.

fos. 95^v–94^v: 'My Charge Xmas sessions [16]97'.

fos. 94^v–94^r: charge 'spoke midsummer sessions 1699'.

fos. 93^v–64^v: parliamentary diary and speeches etc. 1698–1701.

---

[6] The original of this letter was in Surrey RO (Kingston), Somers MSS 371/14/E5.

[7] J. Spon, *Lettre au Père La Chaise du Projet pour Réunion des Deux Religions* (1682).

[8] fo. 63^v begins 'The 4th book 1547'.

Ms Eng. hist. b. 210

fos. 1^r–14^r: parliamentary diary, etc. 27 Jan.–24 May 1702.

fo. 14^v: table of 'Taxes and Revenues of the Crown from 1688 to Mich[*ael*]mas 1697', calculated on an annual basis.

fos. 15^r–22^v: folios cut or torn out;[9] on what remains of fos. 17^r–17^v, Cocks has entered a fuller account of the origin of the occasional conformity bill, 1701, than that found at MS Eng. hist. b. 209, fo. 77.[10]

fo. 23: 'Postscript' to a political essay, *c.*1705, against High Church; 'A prescription for the gout wrote at Bath May 1726', in verse (urging the sufferer to have patience and trust in God).

fos. 23^v–27^v: accounts, *c.*1663–5, crossed through by Cocks.

fos. 28^r–29^v: folios cut or torn out.[11]

fos. 30^r–30^v: 'March 1705:6 my letter to Sir Rowland Gwinne at Hannover in answer to printe[d Lett]er of his'[12] (opposes notion of inviting over the Hanoverian heir presumptive).

fos. 31^r–31^v: accounts 1661–2.

fo. 32^r: 'The Preamble of my Charge given mich[*aelmas*] sessions 1706 at Glouc[*este*]r'.

fo. 32^v: Verses addressed to the Duke of Marlborough, 1 Feb. 1707, conveying praise and warning, in the form of an imaginary letter from Scipio Africanus from the Elysian Fields.

fos. 33^r–33^v: a prose version of the above, same date.

fos. 34^r–39^r: draft of an essay against religious persecution (recommending comprehension), n.d.

fos. 39^v–43^r: draft of an account of 'Utopia', intended to be published (covering *inter alia*, the politics, laws, and character of the people, and their manner of 'electing their representatives'), n.d.

fo. 43^r: 'A dialogue Between the French king and the Pretender upon the Idle discours of a design to murder the Queen Augt. 1708 at Windsor to the tune of Old Chiron' (in verse).

fo. 43^v: 'A translation of the 11th Epod of Horace' [1708] (in verse, with contemporary allusions).

fos. 43^v–44^r: 'A Banter on the Banterer or a poem to cure insincerity Cyder to Harley' [1708] (in verse).

fos. 44^r–45^r: 'An excellent new farce as it was acted at Kinsington by her majestys and the pr[*ince*] of Wa[*les's*] sworn servants' (satirical playlet, in verse, directed against the Harleyites, and the Tories in general).

fo. 45^v: 'the vote of the house of Commons of the 23d of 9:br [*i.e.* November] 1708' (verse satire, from the viewpoint of an 'old Whig', on the 'new Whig' indulgence to placemen and electoral corruption).

---

[9] Nine folios in all have been torn out, the last not being numbered.

[10] See above, pp. 81–2.

[11] Four folios in all have been torn out, the first and last not being numbered.

[12] *A Letter from H.R.H. the Princess Sophia . . . to . . . the Archbishop of Canterbury, with Another from Hannover, Written by Sir Rowland Gwynne to the . . . Earl of Stamford* (London, 1706), the letter from Gwynne having been condemned by the Commons in Mar. 1706. (In fact it had been written by Leibniz and only translated by Gwynne.) See Cobbett, *Parl. Hist.*, vi. 519–33; R. M. Hatton, *George I: Elector and King* (London, 1978), 78.

fos. 46^r–46^v: 'A translation of the 34th Chap[*ter*] of Genesis from the Caldee'.

fo. 46^v: 'the preamble of my Charge at Mid[*summer*] sessions 1709'.

fos. 47^r–48^v, 49^r–52^r: an 'Answer' to Lord Shaftesbury's *Sensus Communis: An Essay on the Freedom of Wit and Humour* (1709), apparently unpublished.

fos. 52^r–60^v: a set of essays, written for publication, on the 'more profitable better more beneficiall management of the poor',[13] the 'corruptions of juryes' and the 'ill practices in the law'.

fos. 60^v–61^r: a mock 'letter from S[*ir*] Xto[*pher*] musgrove to Robert Harley Esqr . . . No[*vem*]b[*e*]r ult 1709'.

fos. 61^r–62^v: 'A speech not spoke' [*c.*1709] (against electoral corruption).

fos. 63^r–63^v: 'An imaginary spech for the bringing over the house of Hannover not spoke'.

fos. 63^v–64^r: 'A speech and answer against invitting over the Hannoverians B[*y*] a Courtier' – ends, '(letter to Sir Rowland Gwin to finish this speeck)'.[14]

fo. 64^r: 'To the Queens most excellent majesty the humble Address of: not signed' [*c.*1714] (in favour of inviting over the Hanoverian heir presumptive).

fo. 64^v: commentary on Tacitus, *Annals*, 15. 67 (Subrius Flavus' defiance of Nero).

fos. 65^r–65^v: further commentary on same text.

MS Eng. misc. b. 433[15]

fo. 30^r: conclusion of an attack upon 'priestcraft' [aft. *c.*1720].

fos. 30^r–31^v: a second copy of 'Mr Sponds answer to Father Le Chais . . . '[16]

fo. 32^r: conclusion of a letter to Prince Frederick [aft. *c.*1717].

fos. 32^r–33^r: 'The rule to examine and try the veracity and excellency of our religion . . .' [aft. *c.*1720].

fos. 33^r–33^v: letter to an unnamed recipient, to lay before the lords justices his *Perfect Discovery of the Longitude* (London, 1721); draft of an essay, or part of an essay, justifying parliamentary control over the Church [*c.*1721]; satirical attack on the High Church followers of Bishop Atterbury, in form of a letter [*c.*1721–2].

fos. 34^r–35^r: essay on the function and duties of bishops, in the form of a visitation sermon on 1 Timothy, 3: 1.

---

[13] See above, p. xxxii. [14] See above, p. 323, n. 12.

[15] Photostats of these separates, purchased by the Bodleian in 1964 from Richard Gilbertson, and now MS Facs. b. 18, fos. 119–30, show the documents before the loss of several words from the corners of some leaves. [16] See above, p. 322, n. 7.

Index

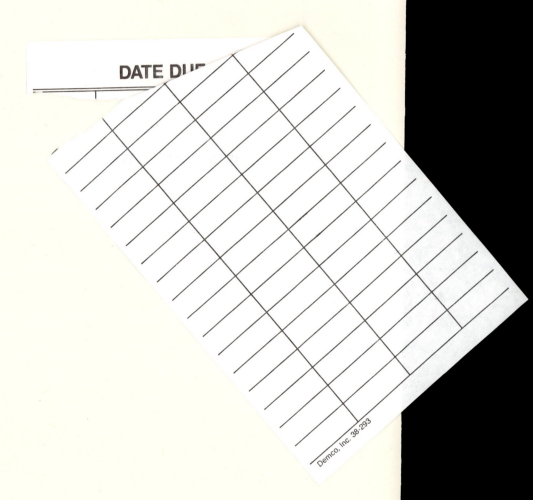

DATE DUE

Demco, Inc. 38-293